LAW IN A CYNICAL SOCIETY? OPINION AND LAW IN THE 1980's

Edited by

DALE GIBSON

JANET K. BALDWIN

1985

CARSWELL LEGAL PUBLICATIONS
WESTERN DIVISION

Calgary Vancouver

Canadian Cataloguing in Publication Data

Main entry under title:

Law in a cynical society?

Papers presented at the conference, Law in a Cynical Society?: an International Conference on Law and Public Opinion, held Nov. 18-20, 1982 at the University of Manitoba.

Includes index.

Bibliography: p. 429

ISBN 0-459-37260-2

1. Law — Canada — Public opinion — Congresses. 2. Justice, Administration of — Canada — Public opinion — Congresses. 3. Public opinion — Canada — Congresses. I. Gibson, Dale. II. Baldwin, Janet K., 1943- III. Law in a Cynical Society?: an International Conference on Law and Public Opinion (1982: University of Manitoba)

KE436.L38 1982 349.71 C85-091144-3

BIOGRAPHICAL NOTES

ALBINI, Joseph, B.A., M.A., Ph.D., Professor of Sociology, Wayne State University.

BALDWIN, Janet, LL.B., LL.M., Professor and Associate Dean, Faculty of Law, University of Manitoba

BATTEN, Jack, B.A., LL.B., journalist

BOROVOY, Alan, Q.C., B.A., LL.B., LL.D., General Counsel, Canadian Civil Liberties Association

BRICKEY, Stephen, M.A., Ph.D., Professor of Sociology, University of Manitoba

BRILLON, Yves, B.A., Ph.D., Principal Investigator, Research Group on Attitudes to Criminality, International Centre for Comparative Criminology, University of Montreal

BURBIDGE, Scott, B.A., M.S.W., M.A., Senior Research Officer, Police Research Section, Research Division, Solicitor General of Canada

CRISPO, John, B.Comm., Ph.D., Professor of Political Economy, Faculty of Management Studies, University of Toronto, formerly Professor of Business Administration, Simon Fraser University

CURRAN, Barbara A., B.A., LL.B., LL.M., Associate Executive Director of the American Bar Foundation

DEBECK, E. Paula, Associate Professor of Sociology, University of Victoria, British Columbia

DEBICKI, Marek, LL.B., LL.M., Ph.D., Associate Professor of Political Studies, University of Manitoba

ESAU, Alvin, B.A., LL.B., LL.M., Associate Professor, Faculty of Law, University of Manitoba

FORTIER, Yves, Q.C., B.A., B.C.L., B.Litt., Montreal lawyer, and then President of the Canadian Bar Association

FRASER, Murray, Q.C., B.A., LL.B., LL.M., N.S., Vice-President Academic and Professor of Law and formerly Dean, University of Victoria

FRIEDENBERG, Edgar, Z., B.S., M.A., Ph.D., Professor of Education, Dalhousie University

GIBSON, R. Dale, B.A., LL.B., LL.M., Professor of Law, University of Manitoba

GLASBEEK, Harry, LL.B., J.D., Professor of Law, Osgoode Hall Law School, York University

GRANT, Alan, LL.B., Professor of Law, Osgoode Hall Law School, York University, and previously of the London Metropolitan Police (U.K.)

GREENAWAY, Bill, Ph.D., LL.B., Winnipeg lawyer, formerly Associate Professor of Sociology, University of Winnipeg

HANSEN, Inger, Q.C., LL.B., first Canadian Correctional Investigator, Canada's first Privacy Commissioner, and presently Information Commissioner

HEXHAM, Irving, B.A., M.A., Ph.D., Associate Professor, Department of Religion, University of Manitoba

HNATYSHYN, Ray, P.C., Q.C., M.P., then Conservative Justice Critic

HOGARTH, John, LL.B., Ph.D., Professor of Law, University of British Columbia

HYLTON, John, B.A., M.S.W., D.S.W., Director, Policy, Planning and Evaluation, Saskatchewan Department of Justice, formerly senior policy advisor with the Saskatchewan Department of Social Sciences and Professor, School of Human Justice, University of Regina

JEWETT, Pauline, B.A., M.A., Ph.D., M.P., then N.D.P. critic on external affairs and post-secondary education

KAPLAN, Robert, P.C., Q.C., B.A., LL.B., M.P., then Solicitor General of Canada

KELLOUGH, Gail, B.A., M.A., Professor of Sociology, University of Toronto, formerly of the John Howard and Elizabeth Fry Society of Manitoba

KENT, Tom, M.A., O.C., Editor *Policy Options Politiques* for the Institute of Research on Public Policy, formerly Chairperson, Kent Royal Commission, and Dean, Faculty of Administrative Studies, Dalhousie University

KITTRIE, Nicholas, M.A., LL.B., LL.M., S.J.D., Professor of Criminal and Comparative Law at the American University Law School

KOENIG, Dan, A.B., M.S., Ph.D., Professor of Sociology, University of Victoria, British Columbia

KOPSTEIN, Judge Robert, B.A., LL.B., Provincial Court of Manitoba (Criminal Division)

LAFONTAINE, Yves, LL.B., Chief Executive Officer of Quebec Legal Services Commission; previously Professor of Law, University of Sherbrooke

LARSEN, Norman, B.A., LL.B., LL.M., Assistant Deputy-Attorney-General of Manitoba, formerly Professor of Law, University of Manitoba

LINDEN, Rick, B.A., M.A., Ph.D., Associate Professor of Sociology, University of Manitoba

LOCKWOOD, Mr. Justice George H., M.A., Manitoba Court of Queen's Bench

MACNAMARA, Sister Geraldine, B.A., B.Ed., LL.B. (deceased), former Director of Rossbrook House, Winnipeg, Manitoba

MANDEL, Michael, B.C.L., LL.B., Associate Professor, Osgoode Hall Law School, York University

MARTIN, Dick, Executive Vice-President of the Canadian Labour Congress, previously President of the Manitoba Federation of Labour

MCDONALD, Mr. Justice David C., B.A., M.A., B.C.L., Alberta Court of Queen's Bench

MEISEL, John, B.A., M.A., Ph.D. (Econ.), Sir Edward Peacock Professor of Political Science, Queen's University, formerly Chairperson, C.R.T.C.

MOORE, Robert J., B.A., Ph.D., Associate Professor of Psychology, Campion College, University of Regina

MORRISON, Terry, B.Ed., M.A., Ph.D., Assistant Deputy Minister of Post-Secondary Adult and Continuing Education, Manitoba Department of Education, previously Dean of the Continuing Education Division, University of Manitoba

MULDOON, Mr. Justice Francis, Q.C., B.A., LL.B., Justice of the Federal Court of Canada (Trial Division), formerly President, Law Reform Commission of Canada

PODGORECKI, Adam, Ph.D., Professor of Sociology and Anthropology, Carleton University

PENNER, Roland, Q.C., B.A., LL.B., M.L.A., Attorney-General, Province of Manitoba, previously Professor of Law, University of Manitoba

PRÉFONTAINE, Dan, Q.C., B.A., LL.B., LL.M., Assistant Deputy-Minister, Policy Programmes and Research Branch, Department of Justice

RAZ, Joseph, M.Jr., D.Phil., Fellow of Balliol College, Oxford

REASONS, Charles E., A.A., B.A., M.A., Ph.D., Professor, Department of Sociology, Faculty of Social Sciences, University of Calgary

SAWATSKY, Terry, B.A., M.A., Director of Preventive Security, Correctional Services, Ottawa, formerly Warden, Stony Mountain Institute, Manitoba

SCHAFER, Arthur, B.A., B.(Litt.), Professor, Department of Philosophy, University of Manitoba and Lecturer in Bio-medical Ethics, Faculty of Medicine, University of Manitoba

SCHNEIDER, Hans, Commissioner under the *Law Enforcement Review Act*, Province of Manitoba, formerly Commissioner of Corrections, Province of Manitoba

SCHWARTZ, Bryan P., LL.B., LL.M., Associate Professor, Faculty of Law, University of Manitoba

TAPP, June, B.A., M.S., Ph.D., Professor of Child Psychology and Criminal Justice Studies, University of Minnesota

TOMASIC, Roman, B.A., LL.B., M.A., Ph.D., Senior Lecturer in Law, Department of Legal Studies, Kuring-gai College of Advanced Education, Australia

TRAKMAN, Leon E., B.Comm., LL.B., LL.M., S.J.D., Professor, Dalhousie Law School

WACHTEL, Andy, B.A., M.A., Ph.D., Research Associate, United Way of the Lower Mainland, Vancouver, British Columbia

WATTS, A. McKibbin, B.A., B.D., Ph.D., Dean of Theology, University of Winnipeg

WILSON, D. K., Assistant Commissioner, R.C.M.P., Vancouver, British Columbia

TABLE OF CONTENTS

Part III: The Dynamics

PREFACE

"Every opinion," said Holmes J., "tends to become a law."[1] Many other observers have also found linkages between public opinion and the legal system. If these alleged linkages are real and important, we must understand them before we can fully understand the legal system. This collection of essays examines the nature, the extent, and the significance of the relationship between law and public opinion in the 1980's.

The book began with a conference, and the conference began with a cri de coeur by a noted Quebec judge in a controversial labour-relations dispute.

The subway workers of Montreal were illegally on strike. The Quebec Superior Court had issued an injunction ordering them back to work, but they had refused to obey the order. Their employer, the Transport Commission, now petitioned the court to punish the union and certain of its members for contempt of court. Chief Justice Jules Deschênes (as he then was) refused to do so, pointing to the futility of such a sanction in an era when public respect for authority in general, and for the courts in particular, has deteriorated. After explaining an alternative, jurisdictional, reason for denying the application, he continued:

Indépendamment de cette question de juridiction, il existe un second motif, de nature sociale celui-là, pour lequel la Cour ne croit pas devoir accueillir les requêtes	Independently of this jurisdictional question there is a second reason, social in nature, for which the court does not believe it should grant these petitions . . . .
[D]ans le domaine privé, d'une part, on assiste depuis peu à une sorte d'explosion du recours à l'injonction	[I]n the private sector . . . there has been, in the last little while, a sort of explosion of recourse to the injunction . . . .
[O]n ne saurait nier aux citoyens l'accès aux tribunaux non plus que l'exercice du droit à l'injonction dans les cas appropriés. S'il survient ensuite une violation de l'ordonnance de la Cour, celle-ci possède les moyens de se faire respecter . . . . Les remèdes et pénalités prévus par le Code de procédure sont . . . propres à assurer avec efficacité l'observance de la loi et la soumission à l'ordonnance judiciaire. Le règne nécessaire de la loi entre parties privées n'est pas encore menacé.	[C]itizens will not be denied access to the courts or . . . the right to injunctions in appropriate cases. If there is a violation of an order of the Court, it possesses the means to command respect . . . . The remedies and penalties provided by the Code of Procedure are . . . sufficient to ensure observance of the law and submission to judicial orders. The necessary authority of the law as between private parties is not yet threatened.
Il en fut longtemps de même dans le domaine public; mais la situation s'est détériorée au cours des récentes années.	It was long the same in the public sector; but the situation has deteriorated in the course of recent years.

1 *Lochner v. New York* (1905), 198 U.S. 45 at 76 (U.S.S.C.).

Alors que les conflits sociaux se font de plus en plus virulents et que le monde des travailleurs, tant intellectuels que manuels, se forge une unité et se découvre une solidarité nouvelles, trois phénomènes parallèles se manifestent dans la société contemporaine, en particulier au Québec: le rejet de l'autorité, qu'elle soit religieuse ou politique ou judiciaire, l'installation progressive d'un amoralisme généralisé et, enfin, la politisation des masses.

De là, compte tenu également de la conjoncture économique difficile, naissent chez nous des conflits socio-économiques de plus en plus nombreux, de plus en plus ramifiés et de plus en plus politisés . . . .

[Q]uand . . ., un groupe de salariés décide, comme en l'espèce, de prendre la loi entre ses propres mains et de violer son contrat collectif de travail, la scène est alors prête pour le déroulement d'un scénario bien connu: l'employeur demande à notre Cour, qui ne peut pas la refuser dans le cours normal des choses, l'émission d'une injonction défendant la grève et ordonnant le retour au travail.

À date, c'est le seul remède que le législateur a pu imaginer pour amorcer une tentative de règlement de ce genre de conflit.

Or l'esprit frondeur qui s'est emparé de notre société a émoussé le tranchant de cette arme qu'autrefois l'on respectait. On a appris, en effet, que le défi d'une injonction de retour au travail pouvait entraîner une condamnation à l'amende et à la prison pour outrage au tribunal. Or des hommes se sont levés qui se sont déclarés prêts à encourir ces peines plutôt que d'obéir à la loi du pays et aux tribunaux qui l'appliquent en leur âme et conscience.

Puis des groupes entiers ont compris qu'ils pourraient, par une simple résistance passive, enrayer le mécanisme judiciaire et rendre impossible le gouvernement politique. Nous sommes ainsi entrés, au Québec, dans l'ère de la désobéissance civile . . . .

Prise dans cet engrenage, la C.T.C.U.M. recourt au seul remède que la loi prévoit maintenant et elle cite ses employés devant la Cour pour obtenir des condamnations pour outrage au tribunal. Qu'un premier effort se fasse en ce sens, passe encore. Mais espère-t-on régler le conflit de cette façon à longue échéance?

As social conflicts grow more and more virulent, and as workers, both intellectual and manual, forge a unity and discover a new solidarity, three parallel phenomena manifest themselves in contemporary society, particularly in Quebec: the rejection of authority, whether religious, political or judicial; the gradual emergence of a general amorality; and, finally, the politicization of the masses.

Those developments, combined with difficult economic circumstances, have given birth in our land to socio-economic conflicts that are more and more numerous, more and more ramified, and more and more politicized.

When . . . a group of employees decides, as in this instance, to take the law into its own hands and to violate its collective agreement, the scene is set for the unfolding of a familiar scenario: the employer asks our Court, which cannot normally refuse, to issue an injunction prohibiting the strike and ordering a return to work.

To date, this is the sole remedy that legislators have been able to think of in attempting to control this type of dispute.

But the recalcitrant mood that has taken hold of our society has dulled the edge of this previously respected weapon. It is known that defiance of an injunction to return to work can result in fine or imprisonment for contempt of court. But some came forward who declared themselves ready in conscience to pay these penalties rather than to obey the law of the land or the courts which apply it.

Entire groups then realized that they could, by simple passive resistance, jam the judicial mechanism and make political government impossible. We have thus entered in Quebec the era of civil disobedience . . . .

Caught in this bind, the Commission resorts to the only remedy the law now provides, and brings its employees before the Court to obtain convictions for contempt of court. This might still be acceptable as a first step. But does one hope to control the conflict this way in the long run?

La Commission a déjà obtenu contre le syndicat une condamnation à une amende de $50,000 . . . . [T]héoriquement, elle pourrait demander une semblable condamnation pour chaque jour où la grève se prolonge. Mais quand même elle ruinerait financièrement le syndicat, contribuerait-elle pour autant au règlement du conflit?

Et que dire maintenant des syndiqués eux-mêmes? Aujourd'hui la Commission en assigne devant la Cour une centaine; demain elle pourra en assigner le double et, finalement, elle pourra demander contre tous ses employés en grève une condamnation à l'amende et à la prison. Devra-t-on bâtir des installations spéciales pour ces quelques 1,600 prisonniers et, surtout, pense-t-on remettre le métro et les autobus en service par ce moyen draconien?

Non, ce n'est pas de cette façon que se règle ce genre de conflit socio-économique, même s'il se traduit au départ par une violation de la loi. Le recours à l'outrage au tribunal consécutif à l'injonction, même s'il demeure adapté à la solution des conflits privés, ne répond plus, en thèse générale et sauf exceptions, aux impératifs de notre époque dans le domaine des conflits collectifs. On peut, on doit même, regretter le temps où le respect de la loi imprégnait les moeurs et l'autorité des tribunaux recueillait l'assentiment populaire. Mais les regrets sont stériles.

C'est vers l'avenir qu'il faut porter nos regards et notre effort de réflexion afin d'inventer des moyens nouveaux pour régler des situations de conflit nouvelles que nos pères n'auraient même pas osé imaginer.

Mais cet effort d'imagination, cette adaptation nécessaire aux réalités de notre temps, c'est d'abord le pouvoir politique qui doit s'y astreindre. Il n'a pas le droit de laisser le pouvoir judiciaire être saisi de ces conflits sociaux dans le cadre insatisfaisant des lois actuelles. Il n'a pas le droit de se décharger sur le pouvoir judiciaire de son obligation politique et d'abandonner la solution de ces conflits à la seule arme extrême de l'outrage au tribunal. Il n'a pas le droit de jouer délibérément avec le risque, présent en Cour ce jour, d'un usage abusif de seul instrument de sanction que la Cour possède.

Ce n'est pas par de semblables recours massifs à l'outrage au tribunal que l'on rapprochera les parties et que l'on ramènera dans les esprits un sentiment de soumission à la loi et de respect pour les décisions judiciaires.

The Commission has already obtained a judgment against the union imposing a fine of $50,000 . . . . [T]heoretically, it could demand a similar judgment for each day the strike lasts. But even when it had ruined the union financially, would it have contributed to the settlement of the dispute?

And what about the union members themselves? Today the Commission brings about 100 before the Court; tomorrow it could bring double, and finally it could demand fines and imprisonment for all its striking employees. Should one construct special buildings for these 1600 or so prisoners, and, above all, is it thought that the subway and the buses would be returned to service by this draconian method?

No, that is not the way to control this type of socio-economic dispute, even if it involves a violation of the law. Although it may be still suitable for the resolution of private conflicts, recourse to contempt of court in support of an injunction no longer (generally speaking, and subject to exceptions) answers the needs of our times in the area of collective conflicts. One can, and should, regret the passing of a time when respect for the law was deeply engrained and the authority of the courts had popular acceptance. But regrets are unproductive.

We must look to the future, in order to devise new methods to control new situations of conflict that our ancestors would not even have dared to imagine.

But it is the political authorities who should in the first instance undertake this exercise of the imagination — this necessary adaptation to the realities of our time. They do not have the right to leave these social conflicts to the judiciary within the unsatisfactory framework of existing laws. They do not have the right to delegate their political responsibilities to the judiciary, and leave the resolution of these disputes to the single extreme weapon of contempt of court. They do not have the right to run the deliberate risk, which arises in court today, of abusing the sole sanction the Court possesses.

It is not by such massive recourse to contempt of court that the parties will be reconciled, and that an attitude of submission to the law and respect for judicial decisions will be restored.

D'ici à ce que l'autorité politique trouve des remèdes appropriés à la solution de ces conflits sociaux, je suis d'opinion que la Cour Supérieure ne doit pas prêter son autorité à l'écrasement d'une masse de citoyens par l'amende et la prison. Dans les circonstances qui prévalent actuellement, la Cour, qui doit toujours user de son pouvoir répressif avec circonspection, ne doit pas collaborer à un geste voué d'avance à l'échec et impropre à résoudre un conflit qui relève maintenant, depuis un certain temps, de l'autorité politique.

Nous sommes prompts à nous vanter du progrès technique de notre civilisation: il me répugne de croire que les élus du peuple seraient incapables d'affronter la difficulté avec laquelle notre société est aux prises et de lui trouver la juste solution qu'un effort commun de réflexion devrait permettre d'enfanter.

Les requêtes de la C.T.C.U.M. sont socialement, politiquement et judicairement inopportunes dans leur conception et dangereuses dans leurs conséquences. Pour ce second motif, la Cour se doit de les refuser.[2]

Until political authorities find appropriate solutions for these social conflicts, I am of the opinion that the Superior Court should not lend its authority to the crushing of a mass of citizens by fines and imprisonment. In the circumstances that now prevail, the Court, which must always use its repressive powers with circumspection, should not collaborate in an action doomed to failure, and ill-suited to resolving a dispute which has for some time now moved to the political arena.

We are quick to boast about the technical progress of our civilization: I am loath to believe that the people's elected representatives are incapable of facing the difficulty with which our society is grappling, and of finding the just solution that concerted study should produce.

The petitions of the Commission are socially, politically, and juridically inopportune in conception, and dangerous in consequence. For this second reason, the Court must refuse them.[2]

Chief Justice Deschênes is not alone in his belief that the public has lost respect for the law, among other institutions of authority, nor in his concern about the consequences of popular disillusionment with the legal system. Professor Harold Berman asserts, in a recent book, that growing public cynicism about the law portends the collapse of the western legal tradition:

> Almost all the nations of the West are threatened today by a cynicism about law, leading to a contempt for law on the part of all classes of the population . . . .[3]
>
> [T]he legal systems of all the nations that are heirs to the Western legal tradition have been rooted in certain beliefs or postulates: that is, the legal systems themselves have presupposed the validity of those beliefs. Today those beliefs or postulates — such as the structural integrity of law, its ongoingness, its religious roots, its transcendent qualities — are rapidly disappearing, not only from the minds of philosophers, not only from the minds of lawmakers, judges, lawyers, law teachers, and other members of the legal profession, but from the consciousness of the vast majority of citizens, the people as a whole . . . . Thus the historical soil of the Western legal tradition is being washed away in the twentieth century, and the tradition itself is threatened with collapse.[4]

One does not have to accept either the apocalyptic view of Professor Berman or the more restrained pessimism of Chief Justice Deschênes to

2 *Comm. de Tpt. de la Communauté Urbaine de Montréal v. Syndicat du Tpt. de Montréal,* [1974] Rec. de J. (C.S.) 227. The decision was reversed by (1977), 77 C.L.L.C. 14,098 (C.A.). The English version of the extracts quoted is an unofficial, and rather loose, translation.

3 Harold J. Berman, *Law and Revolution: The Formation of the Western Legal Tradition* (1983), p. 39.

4 *Ibid.*

recognize that there are important links between law and public opinion, such that variations in the climate of opinion may cause or necessitate changes in the legal system. Some aspects of the relationship that seem worthy of consideration are:

Can an unpopular law be effective?

What do people think about the courts? About sentencing and prisons?

Do laws really affect public attitudes and behaviour?

Does public opinion influence law-making? How?

Do police have public support? Do they need it? How do they win it?

Are we more or less cynical about legal institutions than in the past? Does it make any difference?

How much do people know about the law and legal services?

How do courts and law-makers learn about public opinion?

Is the public's image of lawyers accurate? Does it matter?

What is the impact of the media? Of education? Of religion?

Are there significant regional and international differences on these questions?

The interaction of law and public opinion have been addressed before. A. V. Dicey's pioneering study, *Law and Public Opinion in England During the Nineteenth Century*,[5] was published shortly after the turn of the century. But Dicey's work, though elegant, was flawed, and neither it nor the surprisingly few studies that followed it provided, or even attempted to provide, satisfactory answers to many of the questions posed above.[6] And the answers that were offered were based more often on speculation than on empirical data; the work of public opinion surveyors, which has assumed great significance in many other spheres, is still largely ignored by those who administer and study the legal system.

It was decided, therefore, that the Legal Research Institute of the University of Manitoba could make a useful contribution to legal scholarship by sponsoring a symposium about law and public opinion in the 1980's. As the subject involves aspects of many disciplines other than law, it was clear that, besides lawyers, judges, and law professors, the participation of a wide array of others would be needed: sociologists, political scientists, psychologists, as well as representatives of government, religion, education, the news media, and the users of legal services. Plans were laid for a multi-disciplinary conference, tentatively to be called: "Law in a Cynical Society".

If the symposium were to move beyond the speculative sphere to which

5 1905. The second edition, 1914, is still in print.
6 *Infra*, c. 1.

most previous studies had been restricted, it would be necessary to provide participants with some empirical data about the state of contemporary public attitudes concerning law and legal institutions. The Legal Research Institute was able, with generous financial assistance from the Donner Canadian Foundation, to conduct an opinion survey in three Canadian cities: Montreal, Toronto, and Winnipeg.[7] Dr. R. J. Moore, then a professor at the University of Manitoba, undertook the principal responsibility for designing and administering the survey and evaluating the data. The results, which were made available to all participants in advance of the conference, were illuminating. For one thing, public opinion appeared to be less cynical than had been supposed. This revelation led to the addition of a question mark to the conference title: "Law in a Cynical Society?". It did not persuade everyone, however; several participants nevertheless based their presentations on the subjective assumption that the public is very cynical about legal institutions.

The conference took place 18th-20th November 1982, at the Faculty of Law, University of Manitoba. The topic was examined from so many varied points of view that the experience was, for some participants, kaleidoscopic, if not vertiginous. Cynicism was defined and dissected. It was condemned and it was celebrated. Some thought cynicism about the legal system to be rampant; others found it to be in regrettably short supply.

The Deschênes thesis, that respect for authority, legal and otherwise, is declining, found both support and rejection. Among the supporters of the thesis were some who regretted the decline, and others who extolled it. Some saw the process as a continuation of the gradual movement from status to contract in economic, social and legal arrangements. This process, which might also be seen as a shift from reliance on social stereotypes to individualism, was identified by Sir Henry Maine in his classic study of ancient law.[8] Those who invoked the Maine thesis suggested that disrespect for authority may be at least partly rooted in alienation stemming from the competitiveness and insecurity that accompany the abandonment of pre-ordained status relationships, in favour of decision-making on an individualized basis in an unequal world. Others saw the cynicism arising from a return to status, based on increasing intervention by the state — the Orwellian Big Brother of 1984.

For those who regarded declining respect for authority as a product of a shift from status and stereotypes toward increased freedom and individualism, it seemed ironic that the principal modern instrument by which shifting attitudes are studied and documented is the public opinion poll, which is itself a stereotyping device. Opinion polls and pollsters were the targets of considerable cynicism at the conference. For the most part, however, the attention directed to opinion polls was realistic: both their usefulness and their shortcomings for assessing the law-opinion syntax were thoughtfully discussed. Among the shortcomings identified were the frequent failure of polls to

7 *Infra*, c. 2.

8 *Ancient Law*, World Classics ed. (1931), p. 141.

distinguish between mere "armchair" opinions and those which are so firmly held as to influence a person's conduct; or between long-range attitudinal "tides" and more transitory opinion fads or "waves".

Attitudes about various legal institutions were examined: police, lawyers, judges, and prisons. The role of public opinion in sentencing and in industrial relations was discussed. Opinion surveys conducted in various countries were reviewed. Law-abidingness was considered. The influences of religion, education, the communications media, and the law itself, on public attitudes to the legal system, were debated. Politicians and other representatives of government were invited to explain the role of public opinion in the legislative and political processes. And there was more — much more than could be comfortably digested at a 2½-day conference. At the conclusion one participant noted a parallel to *La Grande Bouffe*, a movie about a group of people who set about, as earnestly and intently as those who took part in this conference, and in a comparable time span, to eat themselves to death at a gargantuan feast.

Only a book could do full justice to the intellectual feast served at the conference. This volume makes available in written and edited form, and to a larger audience, the gist of the material presented at the Cynical Society (?) conference. Books demand a more disciplined form of presentation than conferences, and that characteristic, coupled with the complex nature of the topic and severe space limitations, has necessitated heavier-handed editing than the editors would have preferred under other circumstances. We have been forced to truncate some contributions, to summarize others, and to delete a few items altogether. While we regret some of these deletions and reductions, we believe that the book represents the essence of the conference more faithfully than would an unexpurgated transcript. In any event, books and conferences involve different modes of communication, and we hope that the book will constitute, in its own right, a significant new contribution to the literature about law and public opinion.

We are grateful for:

the tenacity of Joe Hershfield and Alvin Esau, former Director and member, respectively, of the Legal Research Institute of the University of Manitoba who nursed our opinion survey in its infancy;

the advice and financial support of the Donner Canadian Foundation, Department of Justice, the Ministry of the Solicitor General, the Attorney General of Manitoba, the Social Sciences and Humanities Research Council of Canada, the Saskatchewan Law Foundation, The British Council, The Law Society of Manitoba, the Law Reform Commission of Manitoba, the Canadian Association of Law Teachers, the University of Manitoba, and particularly President Arnold Naimark, the Research Grants Committee of the Research Board for the Samuel Weiner Distinguished Visitor Award, the Office of Research Administration, and particularly Henry Jacobs, the Continuing Education

Division, the Faculty of Law, and particularly Dean Jack London (as he then was), Mr. Joseph Telgarsky, and Mr. David G. Newman and Mrs. Jean Newman;

the practical help of innumerable students, staff and faculty colleagues from many departments;

the intense involvement of all the speakers and participants in the conference;

the research assistance of Alison Diduck and Kris Lercher;

the rapid word-processing of Sue Frenette;

and, above all, the administrative and editorial efficiency of Joanne Burke and Cheryl Hapko, and their overall dedication to the project.

Janet K. Baldwin
Dale Gibson
July 1984

PART I

OVERVIEW

1

PUBLIC OPINION AND LAW: DICEY TO TODAY

Dale Gibson

THE DICEY LEGACY

A. V. Dicey was not the first scholar to take an interest in the relationship between law and public opinion. He drew consciously on the work of David Hume,[1] for example, and perhaps unconsciously on that of F. K. Savigny, the father of sociological jurisprudence.[2] In fact, the theme of Dicey's great book, *Law and Public Opinion in England During the Nineteenth Century*[3], was not originally his own idea; it was suggested to him by Charles Eliot, then President of Harvard University, as a suitable topic for a series of lectures at Harvard, upon which the book was eventually based.[4] Yet the book, published in 1905 and still in print, treated the subject so extensively, so elegantly and so provocatively that it became an instant classic, deserving, even now, first attention in any survey of writing about law and public opinion.

The Thesis

Dicey informed his readers at the outset that his aim would be

> to exhibit the close dependence of legislation, and even the absence of legislation, in England during the nineteenth century upon the varying currents of public opinion.[5]

The major steps of the argument by which he attempted to prove this hypothesis were as follows:

1. England experienced a dramatic legal revolution during the nineteenth

---

1 A. V. Dicey, *Law and Public Opinion in England During the Nineteenth Century,* 2nd ed. (1914), pp. 2, 14. The Introduction at pp. lxxii, xci, xcii, also refers to the work of A. L. Lowell.

2 No doubt Savigny's "Volksgeist" involved more than "public opinion". It is probable that Dicey was also familiar with the even more relevant work of Savigny's successor, Eugen Ehrlich, although the latter's most influential work, *Fundamental Principles of the Sociology of Law,* was not first published until 1912.

3 *Supra,* note 1. All subsequent references are to this edition.

4 R. A. Cosgrove, *The Rule of Law: Albert Venn Dicey, Victorian Jurist* (1980), pp. 170-71.

5 A. V. Dicey, *Law and Public Opinion in England During the Nineteenth Century,* 2nd ed. (1914), p. 1.

century, with almost every important area of law undergoing significant legislative reform.[6]

2. The legislative revolution cannot be attributed solely to the growing democratization of the British system of government, because a similar revolution did not occur in other countries, such as the United States, France, Switzerland, Australia or Canada, where democratization had been even more extensive.[7]

3. The true explanation can be found in the uniquely

> close and immediate connection . . . which in modern England exists between public opinion and legislation[8] . . . . Nowhere have changes in popular convictions or wishes found anything like such rapid and immediate expression in alterations of the law as they have in Great Britain during the nineteenth century, and more especially during the last half thereof.[9]

The British Parliament, he thought, responded more adequately "to the sentiment of the age"[10] than any other legislative body.[11]

4. The opinions that influenced legislation were those of particular groups or classes that happened to be predominant at the time. Although he often referred loosely to the views of "Englishmen"[12], "the English people"[13] or "the mass of the people"[14], Dicey left no doubt that it was a much more select group whose attitudes constituted "legislative opinion"[15] at any point in time:

> [T]he beliefs or sentiments which, during the nineteenth century, have governed the development of the law have in strictness been public opinion, for they have been the wishes and ideas as to legislation held by the people of England, or, to speak with more precision, by the majority of those citizens who have at a given moment taken an effective part in public life.[16]

5. This phenomenon can be demonstrated, he claimed, by observing how British legislation during the nineteenth century tended to reflect the views of those who were politically dominant at various times. He divided the century into three periods:[17]

   (i) *Tory optimism* (1800-1830) — marked by legislative quiescence;

   (ii) *Benthamite individualism* (1825-1870) — marked by legislative activism designed to strengthen individual rights, laissez-faire

6 *Ibid.*, p. 7.
7 *Ibid.*, pp. 7-9, 53, 60, 219.
8 *Ibid.*, p. 7.
9 *Ibid.*
10 *Ibid.*, p. 5.
11 *Ibid.*, p. 7.
12 *Ibid.*, p. 139.
13 *Ibid.*, p. 111.
14 *Ibid.*, p. 3.
15 *Ibid.*, p. 17.
16 *Ibid.*, pp. 9-10.
17 *Ibid.*, p. 62, *ff.*

economics, and other matters highly regarded by the middle class; and

(iii) *Collectivism* (1865-1914) — marked by increasing legislative support for socialistic or otherwise collective measures such as trade unions, government health insurance, and public education.

6. The factors contributing to the formulation of the views that found favour during each of those periods were thought by Dicey to be multifarious and complexly interrelated.[18] He placed what may have been unwarranted emphasis on ideology, as expressed in the writings of key figures like Jeremy Bentham, John Stuart Mill, and Charles Dickens. This could have been due, in part, to the fact that he was a writer himself, but it also reflected an elitist view of the social and political structure. He stressed the importance of "some single thinker or school of thinkers",[19] and often used such phrases as "men of common sense and of public spirit"[20] to describe those whose opinions mattered. The effect of self-interest on opinion was under-emphasized, though Dicey acknowledged its existence,[21] and referred at several points to the possibility that a fear of revolution or other social disorder might stimulate legislative reforms.[22] He also referred occasionally to the effect of "circumstances"[23], which he may have intended to include self-interest and economic determiners. Religion,[24] foreign developments,[25] and the manipulation of public emotions in the name of patriotism and other causes[26] were thought to be significant. Increasing freedom of speech, which encouraged the challenging of old ideas, played an important role in Dicey's view.[27] Last, but by no means least in his estimation, was the symbiotic effect of the laws themselves in helping to shape opinion: "[N]o facts play a more important part in the creation of opinion than laws themselves."[28]

7. The influence exerted on law by majority public opinion was not thought to be always decisive, however. Dicey observed: "The reigning legislative opinion of the day has never . . . exerted absolute or despotic authority. Its power has always been diminished by the existence of counter-currents or cross-currents of opinion which were not in harmony with the prevalent opinion of the time."[29] These restraining influences

18 *Ibid.*, p. 10.
19 *Ibid.*, p. 22. See also pp. 414-15.
20 *Ibid.*, p. 168.
21 *Ibid.*, p. 12, *ff.*
22 *Ibid.*, pp. 83, 100, 123-24, 172, 427.
23 *Ibid.*, pp. 26, 301-302.
24 *Ibid.*, pp. 332, 353, 339, *ff.*
25 *Ibid.*, p. lxv, *ff.*
26 *Ibid.*, p. 448, *ff.*
27 *Ibid.*, p. 433, *ff.*, 443-44. Dicey regarded it as ironical that the utilitarians, and especially Mill, by stressing freedom of thought, contributed to the eventual downfall of their own ideas.
28 *Ibid.*, p. 465. See also pp. 41, *ff.*, 238, 309.
29 *Ibid.*, pp. 36-37. See also Lecture X.

resulted in frequent legislative compromises,[30] and in gradual rather than precipitous legal reform.[31]

Dicey identified two major institutional sources of these conservative counter-currents. The first was the age and attitude of political leaders. "Law-making in England," he pointed out, "is the work of men well advanced in life . . .",[32] so "[t]he opinion which changes the law . . . has been as often as not in reality the opinion not of to-day but of yesterday."[33]

Dicey left no doubt, by the way, that he generally preferred the opinions of yesterday. He described the compromises necessitated by "conflict between the ideas of the government and the feelings or habits of the governed"[34] as "compromise . . . . between enlightenment and prejudice";[35] and he commented condescendingly on the "deference which statesmen instinctively, and on the whole wisely, paid to the dullness or stupidity of Englishmen . . . ."[36]

The other chief source of institutional conservatism discussed by Dicey was the bench. Although a few judges, such as Mansfield, had occasionally been ideologically ahead of their time,[37] and had sometimes reflected the opinions of the society they served,[38] they were generally more heavily influenced by "professional habits and feeling than by the popular sentiment of the hour",[39] and usually aimed "rather at securing the certainty than at amending the deficiencies of the law".[40] Since judges were often older than politicians, and were always more secure from outside influence, he concluded that "judge-made law occasionally represents the opinion of the day before yesterday".[41]

Criticisms

Dicey's study has been frequently criticized,[42] but not all the criticisms are relevant to the present context. For example, many commentators have taken issue with his concern that the trend he noted toward collectivism was undesirable. While this was certainly one of his principal theses — and probably his real reason for writing the book — it did not affect his observa-

30 *Ibid.*, pp. 10-11.
31 *Ibid.*, pp. 27-33.
32 *Ibid.*, p. 34.
33 *Ibid.*, p. 33.
34 *Ibid.*, p. 10.
35 *Ibid.*
36 *Ibid.*, p. 11.
37 *Ibid.*, pp. 81, 166-67, 368.
38 *Ibid.*, p. 363.
39 *Ibid.*, p. 364.
40 *Ibid.*, p. 366.
41 *Ibid.*, p. 369.
42 See, for example: Julius Stone, *Social Dimensions of Law and Justice* (1966), pp. 153-54. An early review of Dicey's First Edition by an American, Arthur Bentley, complained that "[h]e owed us a social dissection, and not a rhapsody." (Quoted by A. Briggs in "Seventeen Reasonable Men", *New Statesman,* 11th July 1959, p. 52.)

tions about the interrelationship of law and public opinion. Similarly, although one may deplore the condescension that led him to assure his readers of the sympathy felt by "the best men and women in England with the wants of the poorer classes"[43], his elitism had only limited salience to the theme of the study.

Many salient criticisms can be made, however. When discussing the influence of John Stuart Mill, Dicey complained that "(t)he lucidity of his style . . . may sometimes surpass the clearness of his thought,"[44] and that his "matchless skill in the arrangement of arguments . . . occasionally disguises both from himself and from his readers a weakness in the links of his reasoning."[45] His own book is open to similar objections. One commentator has referred to Dicey's "sleight of mind",[46] and another has remarked that "[i]t is always an intellectual treat to see a consummate advocate defending an untenable proposition . . . ."[47]

The major flaw, which undermines much of the study for present purposes, is that Dicey never proved (and never even attempted to prove) the causal relationship he postulated between public opinion and legal reform.[48] He simply assumed its existence. This crucial lapse can be explained in part by the circumstances in which the lectures upon which his book was based were written, and also by Dicey's well documented disdain for the historical method and the techniques of social science. His biographer tells us that he prepared the lectures in a very short period of time, without preliminary research: "The conclusions came first, then came the research."[49] Dicey himself acknowledged that "[i]t cannot claim to be a work of research; it is rather a work of inference or reflection."[50] A lawyer, he thought, "ought not to trespass . . . upon the province of historians, moralists or philosophers"[51], and it is probable that his support for the converse of that statement was even stronger. Many of the lawyers who have written on the subject since then have shown a similar reluctance to consider the data that social science could and has made available.

Perhaps the most surprising omission from Dicey's book, considering its concern with "collectivism" and "socialism", is any reference to Marxist analysis.[52] While this oversight was consistent with the limited role he tended

43 A. V. Dicey, *Law and Public Opinion in England During the Nineteenth Century*, 2nd ed. (1914), p. xciii.

44 *Ibid.*, p. 431.

45 *Ibid.*

46 A. Briggs, "Seventeen Reasonable Men" in *New Statesman*, 11th July 1959, p. 52.

47 H. R. W. Wade, "Law, Opinion and Administration" (1962), 78 L.Q.R. 188 at 191.

48 *Supra*, note 46.

49 R. A. Cosgrove, *The Rule of Law: Alberta Venn Dicey, Victorian Jurist* (1980), p. 171.

50 A. V. Dicey, *Law and Public Opinion in England During the Nineteenth Century*, 2nd ed. (1914), p. viii (from Preface to the First Edition).

51 *Ibid.*, p. 465.

52 See L. M. Friedman and S. Macaulay, *Law and the Behavioural Sciences*, 2nd ed. (1977), p. 624, *ff*.

to attribute to self-interest in the formulation of laws, it was nevertheless strange to disregard altogether a supremely important alternative explanation of the phenomena he was examining. The reason may be linked to Dicey's narrow conception of "the public". He acknowledged that "classes exert a . . . potent control over the making of laws . . ."[53], but he pointed out that even the ruling class's view of its own best interests is influenced by opinion.[54] It may be, therefore, that Dicey regarded Marxism as beside the point in this context. His interest was merely in the factors that moulded the attitudes of the elite who controlled (and should in his view continue to control) the machinery of government.

Even if the views Dicey expressed about law and public opinion had been unchallengeable, so far as they went, they constituted a far from complete study of the subject. Attention was concentrated on the legislative process; relatively little was said about the law-making powers of the courts and the impact of public opinion upon them.[55] The mechanics by which public attitudes are translated into legislative action were largely ignored. The influence, if any, of public opinion upon "law abidingness" was not touched upon. The role of the press in shaping public opinion was not dealt with.

In short, the legacy which this splendid pioneering book bequeathed to the future was a flawed hypothesis and a large assortment of unanswered questions.

DEVELOPMENTS SINCE DICEY: GENERAL

Some of Dicey's legatees have put the bequest to excellent use, improving it by careful re-assessment of the hypothesis and by the exploration of unanswered questions. Others have treated it as a sacred testament, to be preserved intact and recited reverently on ceremonial occasions. Still others have ignored it or attacked it. On the whole, although there have been many important developments, our understanding of the relationship between law and public opinion is much less advanced than it ought to be more than eight decades after Dicey's brilliant beginning.

Historians

The historical dimension remains blurred.

Historians have certainly written about public opinion. Attempts have been made to assess the impact of opinion on events of both the 18th century[56]

53 *Supra*, note 50 at 12.

54 *Ibid.*, p. 13.

55 He did deal briefly with the subject of "judicial legislation" (Lecture XI), but his concern was chiefly for the courts' role in restraining the operation of public opinion.

56 W. T. Laprade, *Public Opinion and Politics in the 18th Century* (1936).

and the first half of the present century.[57] A few specific legal developments have been examined from an attitudinal perspective, as in T. W. Perry's study of the public controversy leading to the repeal of the Jewish Naturalization Bill in England in 1753,[58] and J. M. Beattie's excellent monograph, *Attitudes Towards Crime and Punishment in Upper Canada 1830-1850*.[59] One might even include in the list such speculative essays as A. W. B. Simpson's hypothesis that England's first legal code, the Laws of Ethelbert, was prepared — and written in English — with a view to changing public attitudes about blood feud, and encouraging the population to view compensation as an honourable alternative.[60] Anthropologists have also sometimes concerned themselves with public opinion,[61] and some useful work has been done on techniques for assessing the public opinion of the past.[62]

Yet reliable studies of the interaction of public opinion and historical events are still relatively few and far between, especially with respect to the legal system. Lee Benson's observation that "[h]istorians have not yet scientifically studied past public opinion, not because it is impossible to do, but because they have not yet tried to do so,"[63] is particularly applicable to legal historians.

Opinion surveys

Historians unquestionably face difficult obstacles when attempting to gather data about public attitudes in times gone by. Lawyers and social scientists dealing with contemporary phenomena no longer have that excuse. The major breakthrough in public opinion scholarship since Dicey's time has been the development of empirical methods of determining and evaluating attitudes. Since about the middle of the 1930's, large-scale research activities into virtually all aspects of public opinion, employing progressively more refined techniques, have been carried on in the United States, Canada, and many other jurisdictions.

---

57 M. Ginsberg (ed.), *Law and Opinion in England in the 20th Century* (1959). See review by A. Briggs, "Seventeen Reasonable Men" in *New Statesman*, 11th July 1959, p. 52. Is it reasonable to speculate that the elimination of the word "Public" from a title that otherwise paralleled Dicey's signified rather different *a priori* assumptions by the editor and authors of these essays?

58 *Public Opinion, Propaganda and Politics in 18th Century England* (1962).

59 1977. See also L. Tepperman, "The Ebb and Flow of Punitiveness in Canadian Society", *Proceedings*, Canadian Society for Legal History (1977), p. 41; and J. V. Orth, "The British Trade Union Acts of 1824 and 1825: Dicey and the Relation Between Law and Opinion" (1976), 5 Anglo-Am. L.R. 131.

60 A. W. B. Simpson, "The Laws of Ethelbert" in M.S. Arnold (ed.), *On the Laws and Customs of England* (1981), p. 3.

61 Margaret Mead, "Public Opinion Mechanisms Among Primitive Peoples" in R. O. Carlson (ed.), *Communications and Public Opinion* (1975), p. 529 (originally published in 1937).

62 Lee Benson, "An Approach to the Scientific Study of Past Public Opinion" in Carlson, *ibid.*, p. 541 (originally published 1967).

63 *Ibid.*, p. 586. However, some progress has doubtless been made since that statement was first published in 1967.

Many of these studies are, or ought to be, of interest to students of the legal system. Major surveys have been conducted,[64] some of which include: the principal institutions of the legal system (the courts, the legal profession, the police, *etc.*); serious social-legal problems such as crime, gun control, abortion, and invasion of privacy; and various types of punishment for crime. Smaller-scale opinion polls, conducted on a regular basis by organizations like the Gallup Poll, often deal with aspects of the legal system. Annual summary compilations of Gallup Poll results have been published since 1935 in the United States and since 1967 in Canada,[65] and other similar compilations are also available.[66] *Public Opinion Quarterly,* published under the auspices of Princeton University, has provided a scholarly forum for those engaged in this type of research since 1937.[67]

Social Scientists

Sociology of law, which was an infant discipline when serious public opinion research was getting under way, has made generally good use of the growing body of empirical data about attitudes to law-related subjects. Theories have been formulated and tested about the part that attitudes play in compliance or non-compliance with law, the impact of news media and other influences on the formulation of opinions about law, the role of personal, cultural and geographic factors in such matters, correlations between public opinion and legal developments, and about many other aspects of the law-opinion interface.[68] Yet although a substantial amount of illuminating work has been done, it seems, to an outsider at least, that this branch of legal sociology has not yet reached maturity. Themes are sporadic, and methods are sometimes faulty. Results are often incomplete, inconclusive, or contradictory.

Lawyers

But if sociologists of law have not yet explored the territory fully, lawyers are, for the most part, entirely unaware of its existence. When Sir J. W. Morris, then a member of the English Court of Appeal, and later of the House of Lords, addressed the Holdsworth Club in 1958[69], on the topic of "Law and Public Opinion", he seemed to treat as axiomatic most of the assumptions about the law-opinion nexus that Dicey had made 60 years previously, and included not a single reference to subsequent scholarship on the subject. Professor H. R. W. Wade's 1962 Oxford inaugural lecture, entitled "Law, Opinion and Administration"[70], was similarly deficient. A

64 *Infra.*, notes 151 to 160.

65 G. H. Gallup, *The Gallup Poll: Public Opinion 1935-1971,* and annual volumes for subsequent years; *Gallup Report* (Canada), annual volumes since 1967.

66 See, for example: H. Cantril and M. Strunk, *Public Opinion, 1935-1946* (1951).

67 R. O. Carlson (ed.), *Communications and Public Opinion* (1975), contains an excellent selection of articles from this periodical during its first 35 years of publication.

68 *Infra,* notes 84, *ff.*

69 Presidential Address, Holdsworth Club (1958).

70 H. R. W. Wade, "Law, Opinion and Administration" (1962), 78 L.Q.R. 188 at 191.

symposium on "Law and Authority in an Age of Protest", sponsored by the new Law Faculty of the University of New South Wales in 1970,[71] was surprisingly almost totally silent on the relation of law to public opinion. O. R. McGregor's 1981 Hamlyn Lecture, "Social History and Law Reform",[72] contains not a word about the role of public opinion. While lamenting that "there is very little social research upon which a law reform body can draw"[73], the latter author makes no reference to that which does exist. He then adds insult to injury by asserting that a desire for "collaboration between lawyers and other social scientists" has "unhappily . . . been much more in evidence among lawyers than among social scientists"![74]

Even the relatively more sophisticated discussions of law and opinion by legal scholars tend to overlook or downplay the contributions of social science. Sir C. K. Allen's classic, *Law in the Making,*[75] acknowledged in passing that "there are experts who profess to be able, by various technical devices of 'polls', 'questionnaires', and 'cross-sections', to ascertain the trend of public opinion at any given moment on any given question", but he declined to discuss the "the value of these expedients".[76] Wolfgang Friedman provided, in *Law in a Changing Society*,[77] a thoughtful commentary on the complex dynamics of public opinion on legal matters,[78] but failed to take account of empirical data. Julius Stone's monumental work, *Social Dimensions of Law and Justice*[79], contains much of value on the subject of opinion, including a lucid critique of Dicey and an acknowledgment of the work of the leading legal sociologists, but even it tends to relegate empirical studies to footnote status. In 1957-58, the London School of Economics sponsored an excellent series of 17 lectures by prominent British academics on the subject *Law and Opinion in England in the 20th Century*,[80] but not one of the lectures relied on opinion poll data.

If these were random samples of oversights by legal scholars they might not seem too significant. The fact is, however, that they constitute the bulk of the material on the subject written by lawyers and available in a good Canadian law library. The *Index to Legal Periodicals,* which is the major guide to periodical literature about law in the English language, contains in its subject headings no reference to "public opinion", "opinion",[81] "attitudes", or "polls". As the reviewer of a recent book on legal sociology has said,

71 University of New South Wales, 1970.
72 Hamlyn Lecture, 1981.
73 *Ibid.*, p. 9.
74 *Ibid.*, p. 3.
75 7th ed. (1974).
76 *Ibid.*, p. 431.
77 Pelican Edition (1964).
78 *Ibid.*, pp. 21-37.
79 Stone, *supra,* note 42. Page 40 is especially good.
80 M. Ginsberg (ed.), *Law and Opinion in England in the 20th Century* (1959).
81 It does include the heading "Opinions," but it refers to judicial opinions (reasons for judgment).

"[t]o many lawyers, the sociology of law is an arcane and alien discipline."[82] For most lawyers, Dicey's views on the relation of law and public opinion remain the last word on the subject. And, like Dicey, lawyers who invoke public opinion usually do so without taking the trouble to verify their assumptions. Dr. H. Mannheim has observed that "there is a very strong temptation in our field to base action, or more often still, inaction, on the alleged state of public opinion, without knowing exactly what public opinion really wants and whether it wants anything at all."[83]

It was stated earlier that Dicey left a legacy of unanswered questions about the interaction of law and public opinion. The remaining sections of this essay will attempt to frame some of those questions, and to outline some of the more important work that has been done to answer them since Dicey laid down his pen.

DETERMINING PUBLIC OPINION

What is Public Opinion?

It is important to begin with a common understanding of the notion being discussed. No small proportion of the controversy in the scholarly writing about this subject can be traced to the protagonists' differing conceptions of public opinion. One writer has gone so far as to assert that "there is no such thing as public opinion"[84], and although most others agree that it exists, they appear to entertain widely varied views as to what it means. Definitions range from Sir Robert Peel's cynical "great compound of folly, weakness, prejudice, wrong feeling, right feeling, obstinacy, and newspaper paragraphs"[85], to highly sophisticated modern analyses of the varied meanings the term bears in different contexts. One of the best of the latter type warns that "[t]o speak with precision of public opinion is a task not unlike coming to grips with the Holy Ghost."[86]

One thing about which most of the modern writers seem to agree is the need to recognize that there are many different "publics", some of which are or should be relevant for certain legal purposes, and others relevant for other legal purposes.[87] For example, a commentary on the influences that shaped

82 A. C. Hutchinson, reviewing W. M. Evan (ed.), *The Sociology of Law* (1980), in (1981), 97 L.Q.R. 506.

83 M. Ginsberg, *supra,* note 80 at 283.

84 E. Jordan, *Theory of Legislation: An Essay on the Dynamics of the Public Mind,* 2nd ed. (1974), pp. 339-41. His point seems to be that what wins out in the struggle for legislative attention is the will of the strongest elite, a view that is shared by many who nevertheless believe that public opinion is a real phenomenon.

85 Quoted by A. V. Dicey, *Law and Public Opinion in England During the Nineteenth Century,* 2nd ed. (1914), p. 20

86 J. J. Best, *Public Opinion: Micro and Macro* (1973), p. 1.

87 See A. Podgorecki, *Law and Society* (1974), c. 5, and L. M. Friedman and S. Macaulay, *Law and the Behavioral Sciences,* 2nd ed. (1977), c. 4(c)(2).

British restrictive trade practice law after World War II distinguishes among "legal opinion", "industrial opinion", the opinion of "the general public", and the "informed opinion" that eventually prevailed.[88]

Dicey was under no illusion that public opinion is monolithic. He would have been comfortable with the notion that "informed opinion" (or what Sir J. W. Morris referred to as "reasoned and settled public opinion", and that of "right thinking citizens"[89]) should hold sway. It was this elitist point of view that caused him to identify the body of opinion that was — and should be — relevant to the shape of legislative reforms as "the wishes and ideas . . . held by . . . the majority of those citizens who have at a given moment taken an effective part in public life."[90]

But there is much more than a recognition of elitism in an understanding of the pluralistic nature of public opinion. Many groups other than the governing elite have collective opinions that do or should receive special consideration in relation to particular legal developments. It has been pointed out, for example, that the body of opinion which led to the passage of Britain's first old-age pension legislation in 1908 was that of several groups — friendly societies, insurance companies and trade unions — whose coinciding vested interests made them allies in an effective campaign of political pressure, and that the revolutionary social insurance scheme of 1911 was similarly influenced:

> The vested interests are busily at work mobilizing both public support with disingenuous propaganda and private support with veiled political threats. Once again the politicians are weighing the cost of alternative courses of action. And in the fullness of time, the legislators will act, compromising with those forces they dare not vanquish, subscribing to those dogmas they dare not challenge, but swept onward by the major currents of public opinion.[91]

While some may regard the influence of governing elites or of special interest groups as the antithesis of "public opinion" at work, it seems realistic to treat it as an element of public opinion, and then to enquire as to the appropriate emphasis to be given to that element in particular circumstances, as well as to the nature and weight of other elements that may or should also be involved. If, for example, Parliament is considering a change in juvenile delinquency legislation intended to deter young people from certain conduct, or to rehabilitate young offenders, it would be important to pay special attention to the attitudes of the young concerning the proposed changes. If the changes contemplated would be costly for the public purse, or would involve a possible increased risk to public safety or convenience, it would be appropri-

---

88 Sir David Cairns in M. Ginsberg (ed.), *Law and Opinion in England in the 20th Century* (1959), pp. 190-91.

89 J. W. Morris, Presidential Address, Holdsworth Club, 1958, pp. 1, 22.

90 A. V. Dicey, *supra*, note 85, pp. 9-10.

91 Dr. B. Abel-Smith in M. Ginsberg, *supra*, note 88 at 354-55. Professor R. M. Titmuss in *ibid.*, p. 306, says that the opinion of the medical profession was very influential in bringing about the health insurance scheme of 1911.

ate to consider the views of the general public as to whether the anticipated benefits of the change would justify the cost or the risk. A very different type of situation would arise if a court were asked to decide, under the *Trade Marks Act*[92] or the common law relating to the tort of "passing off", whether an intended trademark or the appearance of a certain product resembled the plaintiff's trademark or product so closely as to confuse the public. If the product or service were offered to the public generally, the court would properly seek information as to the reaction of the general public, but if it were a specialized item, such as particular type of surgical instrument or farm equipment, it would be more suitable to consult the opinion of persons who would be potential purchasers of the product or service, rather than of a wider, less sophisticated group.

Even after the appropriate segment of the "public" has been identified, it is essential to bear in mind that "opinion" is a phenomenon of variable dimensions. There appear to be at least three distinct dimensions affecting the significance of a particular expression of public opinion to a given legal question: breadth, depth (intensity), and longevity. While these variables have all been mentioned in the literature, they have not always been given the emphasis they deserve.

The first dimension — breadth — is closely related to the question of choosing the appropriate segment of public opinion. Opinion on social and legal issues often exhibits regional differences. When the results of an American study on attitudes concerning laws about parental authority are compared with those of a similar Polish study, marked differences are evident.[93] When similar questions about attitudes concerning certain laws and punishments were put to randomly chosen respondents in Belgium, the Netherlands, West Germany and Poland, significant discrepancies were revealed.[94] And even within a single country varied responses on some issues can be expected from region to region, and from urban to rural areas. In selecting the section or sections of the public whose opinion ought to be relevant to a given question, therefore, it is important to consider whether the group selected should be representative of national opinion, or of some more suitable regional point of view.

Some matters clearly call for a localized approach. If, for example, a court were consulting public opinion to decide whether, for the purpose of a change of venue application in a criminal proceeding, public opinion was too hostile to the accused person to permit a fair trial, it would obviously be local rather than national opinion that counted.[95] The same would seem to be true of

92 Trade Marks Act, R.S.C. 1970, c. T-10.

93 A. Podgorecki, "Public Opinion on Law" in A. Podgorecki (ed.), *Knowledge, Opinion and Law* (1973), p. 68, *ff.*

94 J. Van Houtte and P. Vinke, "Attitudes Governing the Acceptance of Legislation Among Various Social Groups", and W. Kaupen, "Public Opinion of the Law in a Democratic Society", in Podgorecki, *Knowledge, Opinion and Law* (1973), p. 13, *ff.*, and p. 43, *ff.*

95 See S. J. Arnold and A. D. Gold, "The Use of a Public Opinion Poll on a Change of Venue Application" (1979), 21 Cr. L.Q. 445.

contempt of court proceedings arising from a pre-trial publication of evidence alleged to prejudice the possibility of fair trial, or from a derogatory comment about the courts which is alleged to "scandalize" the judiciary.[96]

Other matters, such as whether a publication or show would so offend "community standards" as to be obscene within the meaning of the Criminal Code of Canada appear to call for the application of national standards[97] (although there seems also to be room for the use of regional standards under provincial laws relating to censorship or decency[98]). National opinion would obviously be germane to the question of whether national legislation should be enacted about matters affecting all Canadians.

On some matters it is not yet clear whether national or local opinion is more significant. One of the more noteworthy of these unsettled questions is the standard to be applied in deciding, under the Canadian Charter of Rights and Freedoms, whether the use of evidence obtained in violation of the Charter would "bring the administration of justice into disrepute".[99] One high-ranking judge has suggested that this provision refers to practices that would "shock the public", but whether he meant the local public or the national public is not clear.[100]

The importance of the second variable dimension — depth or intensity — is equally great, but less widely appreciated. Most of us hold opinions we are willing to express, over cocktails or in a questionnaire, on thousands of topics. Only a relatively small percentage of those opinions are so deeply held that we are willing to support them with action, especially if the action will or might have unpleasant consequences. Of the rest, we are open to persuasion on some, and others, though firmly held, are just not worth fighting about. Opinion surveys often fail to take account of the varying degrees of intensity with which expressed attitudes are held.

Even those which employ intensity scales (such as "Agree Strongly, Agree, Non-Committal, Disagree, Disagree Strongly") cannot easily distinguish opinions which will influence a person's behaviour from those which will not. Berl Kutchinsky has reported that some surveys of attitudes toward violation of the law indicate that the opinions of convicted criminals do not

96 See *R. v. Murphy; Ex parte A.G.N.B.*, 1 N.B.R. (2d) 297, [1969] 4 C.C.C. 147, 4 D.L.R. (3d) 289, 6 C.R.N.S. 353 (C.A.), and comment in D. Gibson, "Determining Disrepute: Opinion Polls and the Charter of Rights" (1983), 61 Can. Bar Rev. 377.

97 See J. M. H. Lamont, "Public Opinion Polls and Survey Evidence in Obscenity Cases" (1973), 15 Cr. L.Q. 135.

98 See *McNeil v. N.S. Bd. of Censors*, [1978] 2 S.C.R. 662, 44 C.C.C. (2d) 316, 84 D.L.R. (3d) 1, (*sub nom. Re N.S. Bd. of Censors and McNeil*), 25 N.S.R. (2d) 128, 36 A.P.R. 128, 19 N.R. 570.

99 Constitution Act, 1982, Pt. 1, s. 24(2).

100 *Rothman v. R.*, [1981] 1 S.C.R. 640, 20 C.R. (3d) 97, 59 C.C.C. (2d) 30, 121 D. L. R. (3d) 578, 35 N.R. 485 and see D. Gibson, "Enforcement of the Canadian Charter of Rights and Freedoms" in W. Tarnopolsky and G. Beaudoin (eds.), *Canadian Charter of Rights and Freedoms: Commentary* (1982), p. 489.

differ from those of the general population.[101] Although more than one explanation of that phenomenon is possible, Kutchinsky suggests that it may simply reflect that in the case of both the criminal and general populations, legal attitudes are "a matter of very superficial veneer — a set of conventional opinions which everybody can make a show of".[102] A similar conclusion is suggested by the results of a U.S. national survey of attitudes toward communism conducted in 1954, when "McCarthyism" was at its peak.[103] The study indicated, to no one's surprise, that well over 80 per cent of the population opposed the employment by schools or universities of teachers having past or present communist connections. But it also reported that when asked to indicate what they regarded as serious threats to the nation only 1 per cent listed communism. Moreover, while there was considerable evidence that anti-communist sentiments had led to both public and private activity against suspected communists in the educational system, there was no evidence of similar activity directed against atheists or socialist teachers, even though the questionnaire had revealed as much opposition to atheists and socialists in the schools as to communists.[104]

The importance of the intensity factor will vary with the circumstances. While legislators who are trying to decide whether to introduce some change in the law about which they are personally neutral may well want to know both the breadth and the depth of popular support for the measure, those who are already favourably disposed to it may only be interested in breadth of support (and, perhaps, the intensity of opposition). Those attempting to assess the extent of public compliance a new law might encounter will be as concerned with the intensity of attitudes as with their distribution.

The third dimension — time — is of crucial importance. In some respects this is obvious. Attitudes change over time, and law which responds to public opinion will reflect such changes. Attitudes from the Victorian era have no place in a modern assessment of community standards regarding obscenity.

Another aspect of the phenomenon of change — equally important, but not so well understood — is that long-term shifts in attitude are the product of many shorter range fluctuations which in themselves are indicative of very little. The influence on public opinion of current events and the momentary passions they arouse is often intense but temporary. A survey conducted this

---

101 A. Podgorecki, "Public Opinion on Law" in A. Podgorecki (ed.), in *Knowledge, Opinion and Law* (1973), p. 112, *ff*.

102 *Ibid*., p. 119. A Podgorecki, *Law and Society* (1974), pp. 264-65; discusses this phenomenon in terms of "cognitive dissonance".

103 Samuel A. Stouffer, *Communism, Conformity, and Civil Liberty: A Cross-Section of the Nation Speaks its Mind* (1955). See the exhaustive reviews, from a legal perspective, by W. J. Blum and Harry Kalven Jr., "The Art of Opinion Research: A Lawyer's Appraisal of an Emerging Science" (1956), 24 U. Chic. L.R. 1, and by R. D. Schwartz in (1956), 65 Yale L.J. 572.

104 W. J. Blum and H. Kalven Jr., note 103, pp. 57-60.

month might indicate a growing public demand for capital punishment, in response to some unusually horrifying recent crime, and one taken next month, when passions have cooled, might show the opposite. Neither would disclose whether popular support for capital punishment is generally increasing or declining.

Dicey appreciated this problem, and described it by means of an oceanic metaphor: long-range shifts in opinion were likened to rising and falling tides, and short-range flucutations to waves.[105] Some subsequent writers have noted the distinction as well. A review of the communism survey mentioned earlier pointed to the irony that liberals who had previously deplored the lag between law and opinion were now exhorting courts to stand firm on traditional libertarian principles, and not be carried away by popular antipathy to communism. The author of the review shared the conviction that courts should base their decisions on "overriding values of the society", rather than on temporary fluctuations of opinion.[106] A more recent study noted an apparent anomaly in statistics concerning the death penalty in the United States: there has been a declining use of capital punishment by the courts at the same time that public opinion polls show increasing public support for its use. The author rejects the thesis that this is an instance of the judicial elite foisting its will on the majority, and explains it instead in terms reminiscent of Dicey's

---

105 I confess that I have made more of the metaphor than Dicey did, and, indeed, that I have added the "waves". Dicey, *Law and Public Opinion in England During the Nineteenth Century*, 2nd ed. (1914), referred frequently to the "currents of opinion" that were of significance as "permanent" (p. ix), "predominant" (p. 20), or "large" (p. 20) currents, and described their gradual developments as follows (p. 21):

> [A]ny fundamental change of convictions which inevitably affects legislation in all directions has, in England at least, always gone on slowly and gradually, and has been in this respect like the gradual rising of the tide.

The short-range shifts of opinion that I have called "waves", Dicey referred to as "transitory" fluctuations (p. 357), "the popular sentiment of the hour" (p. 364), or "the immediate opinion of the moment" (p. 397). He saw grave danger in the "popular tyranny" (p. 309) which these temporary fluctuations often represented, criticized the "appeal to emotion or to moral rhetoric" (p. 428) and "apotheosis of instinct" (p. 448) which stirred them up. He labeled legislators who allowed themselves to be influenced by these rapid fluctuations as "deficient" (p. 398). The entire book can be seen as an anthem of praise for those aspects of the British legal system which, in Dicey's view, tended to restrain the impact of the "waves", while responding slowly to the "tides". In countries like France and the United States, where events had been more responsive to popular passions, pious declarations of human rights had not been effective in the short-run, though he expressed the belief that they would have a long-range influence on the "tidal" sentiments that he thought ought to prevail (p. 309):

> [T]he Declaration of the Rights of Man did not save from death one among the thousands of innocent citizens dragged before the Revolutionary Tribunal; the American Declaration of Independence, with its proclamation of the inalienable rights of man, did not deliver a single negro from slavery. But these celebrated documents were after all a formal acknowledgement that sovereign power cannot convert might into right. They have assuredly affected public opinion.

106 R. D. Schwartz, *supra*, note 103.

distinction between tides and waves: the courts are merely responding to an inexorable longer-range trend to reduce reliance on capital punishment, and are ignoring current waves of public punitiveness.[107]

It will be recalled that Dicey attempted to explain the temporal dynamics involved in terms of the respective ages of legislators and judges, and their tendency to retain attitudes and values acquired in their early years.[108] Whereas legislators were the voice of yesterday, judges spoke for the day before yesterday. Although that explanation may seem somewhat facile, no one yet seems to have produced a better one. If it is correct, recent trends in the appointment of judges could have serious consequences, for the average age of the Canadian judiciary seems to be dropping. If judges are drawn from the same age group as law makers they will, if Dicey was correct, share their attitudes and be less willing than in the past to frustrate the legislative will. That, for a country which has just adopted a Charter of Rights and Freedoms designed to restrain legislative excesses by judicial review based on long-range values, could be a very significant consequence.

The time dimension also has important implications for the use of public opinion polls in legal proceedings.[109] In some cases, such as change of venue applications or trademark disputes, it is the immediate state of public opinion — the "wave" — that matters, and the direct use of opinion surveys would seem appropriate. In others, such as whether an allegedly obscene publication offends community standards, or whether the use by a court of evidence obtained in violation of constitutional rights would bring the administration of justice into disrepute, it would be better to use opinion polls cumulatively, so

---

107 H. A. Bedau, "The Death Penalty in the United States: Imposed Law and the Role of Moral Elites" in S. B. Burman and B. E. Harrell-Bond (eds.) *The Imposition of Law* (1979), p. 45. It is not always easy to distinguish the tides from the waves, however. The Canadian Gallup Poll reports that 43 per cent of Canadians thought that courts were too easy on criminals in 1966, that this rose to 75 per cent in 1973, and fell back to 60 per cent in 1980: "Waves or Tides?" in *Winnipeg Free Press*, 20th November 1980, p. 14.

108 Dicey, *supra*, note 105, pp. 33, 369; and text associated with notes 161 to 164, *infra*.

109 Much of that type of legislative change is initiated by law reform commissions and similar bodies, which are even less in touch with the public pulse. For a discussion of the difficulties faced by such bodies, see J. M. Farrar, *Law Reform and the Law Commission* (1974), c. 6. Farrar suggests that despite their obvious differences, law reformers and legislators are in much the same position with respect to public opinion (p. 71):

> Burke said of a Member of Parliament that he owed his constituents 'not his industry only, but his judgement; and he betrays, instead of serving you, if he sacrifices it to your opinion.' Obviously there are great differences between Law Commissioners and Members of Parliament but it is submitted that ultimately on this particular matter Burke's principle holds true. The Law Commission should and does consult public opinion.' In the past it has largely done this by circulating the appropriate pressure groups. The family property survey shows perhaps the beginning of a wider consultation. But ultimately they owe us their judgement.

Nevertheless, he welcomes the increased use of opinion poll data by the Commission (p. 78):

> For too long law reform has been carried out on the basis of *a priori* assertions or intuitive assessments of social facts and social consequences by lawyers. In the words of Lord Wilberforce law reform is too serious a matter to be entrusted to the lawyers.

as to allow the court to observe the "tidal" action of opinion over time.

Interpreters of Public Opinion

Assuming that public opinion should have an influence on elements of the legal system, by what means can it be most effectively assessed?

The present design of the legal system seems to contemplate that to the extent public opinion is relevant it should chiefly be determined by the personal experience and observations of the legislators, judges, juries, police, civil servants, and others who supervise and operate the system. This approach has much to recommend it in the case of democratically chosen legislators, who must remain in touch with popular sentiment if they wish to remain in office. But even they have little reason to be aware of public opinion respecting many of the routine law-reform measures — occupier's liability legislation, for example, or changes in the remedial powers of the courts — with which they often have to deal.[110]

Judges, who are chosen from society's elite, and who are deliberately insulated from the political process, are not so well equipped as legislators to act as conduits of general public opinion. Some writers have cautioned against exaggerating this lack of sensitivity. One, a judge himself, asserts that "judges were perhaps never so conservative in their views as Dicey thought them; it may equally be that the change in our social habits marked by two world wars has made our judges less conservative than they were."[111] Professor J. A. G. Griffith points out that although British judges "could not be called social progressives", they did not attempt to frustrate the implementation of the massive legislative reforms that preceded World War I and followed World War II. Indeed, he says of the latter period:

> Sometimes they seemed to be leaning over backwards almost to the point of falling off the Bench, to avoid the appearance of hostility; but also, I believe, it is possible to detect an unconscious attitude that if these were the sort of measures which presumably the electorate had asked for, then the courts would show them just what they had got.[112]

Professor Griffith attributes this attitude to more than bloodymindedness:

> [T]he legal mind is, contrary to popular belief, not a rigid, insensitive or blind instrument. It has a fair measure of flexibility and has, after all, been trained to see what can be said on the other side. To the social needs of the time, I do not think that judges were less sensitive than Cabinet Ministers.[113]

He concedes, however, that "this is not saying much",[114] and he does not deny that judges are to a large extent products of their upbringing and their

110 See D. Gibson, "Determining Disrepute: Opinion Polls and the Charter of Rights" (1983), 61 Can. Bar. Rev. 377.

111 Sir Seymour Karminski, in Ginsberg (ed.), *Law and Opinion in England in the 20th Century* (1959), p. 291.

112 In M. Ginsberg, *ibid.*, p. 120.

113 *Ibid.*

114 *Ibid.*

professional environment. A survey of opinions about the role of courts conducted on a national basis in the United States in 1978 concluded that "there is a profound difference in view — between the general public/community leaders on the one hand, and judges/lawyers on the other hand."[115] It is unlikely that Professor Griffith or anyone else familiar with the British or Canadian legal systems would be surprised if similar findings were made about those jurisdictions.

The jury has long been regarded as a means of injecting "street values" into the judicial process.[116] It is often observed that the lenient attitudes of juries played a large role in the gradual humanizing of British criminal law over the centuries.[117] The use of juries has diminished in modern times, however. In Canada only a very small percentage of criminal cases are tried by juries, and in some provinces, juries are almost never used in civil litigation. While proposals are occasionally advanced to make more extensive use of juries,[118] sometimes for the explicit purpose of bringing law into closer contact with public opinion,[119] there is little empirical information available as to the consequences such a change might have. It is, in any event, unlikely that reliance on juries (or, as some have suggested, lay magistrates[120]), is likely to increase sufficiently in the foreseeable future to seriously alter the reflectiveness of the overall legal system.

Administrative officials, police, boards and commissions, and others who carry out operational functions within the legal system could also act as channels of public opinion, but there is little reason to believe that they are inherently better suited to that task than courts. One distinguished legal scholar has, however, expressed the view that there has been a growing "pluralism" in the staffing of such positions in recent years, with the result that, by being more representative of the various major interest groups in society, they permit a closer link between public opinion and the legal and governmental systems:

> The line between "State" and "Society" has been blurred very deliberately, or to put it differently, the "pressure" of the pressure groups has been so organised as to work inside the legislative, administrative, judicial and policy making processes.[121]

It would be interesting to explore the accuracy of that observation so far as Canadian experience is concerned, and to enquire how pluralism has affected legal policy and practice in this country.

---

115 National Center for State Courts, Williamsburg, Virginia, *The Public Image of Courts* (1978).

116 See H. Kalven and H. Zeisel, *The American Jury* (1966); Patrick Devlin, *Trial by Jury* (1956).

117 *E.g.*, J. W. Morris, Presidential Address, Holdsworth Club (1958), p. 8.

118 *E.g.*, Manitoba Law Reform Commission, *A Review of the Jury System* (1975).

119 J. W. Morris, *supra*, note 117, p. 21 (with respect to the assessment of civil damages).

120 Mannheim in M. Ginsberg (ed.), *Law and Opinion in England in the 20th Century* (1959), pp. 281-82 (with respect to sentencing).

121 Kahn-Freund in M. Ginsberg, *supra*, note 120, p. 226.

If personal experience and observation are inadequate guides to public attitudes, what better indicia are available?

The news media are supposed to monitor the public pulse. Historians who attempt to assess public opinion in times past have few other satisfactory guides, and some studies of early legislative developments have made effective use of the press as a source of attitudinal data.[122] One cannot be entirely confident about press impressions, however. The survey of attitudes about communism in the United States, to which reference was made earlier, indicated that the media had seriously distorted the intensity of popular concern about the "threat" of communism.[123] Impressions of public attitudes drawn from the news media should not be relied on without taking careful account of both the risk of inaccuracy inherent in the hurried assessment techniques that are often used, and the fact that the media are not infrequently engaged in deliberate attempts to shape the opinion they purport to interpret.[124]

It is not uncommon for political leaders faced with a volatile situation about which public sentiments are either unclear or dangerously polarized to refer the problem to a Royal Commission or other public inquiry. In addition to taking the immediate pressure off the politicians, this technique also offers them another way to gauge public opinion. It is not at all certain, however, that these high-profile inquiries always reflect the true street view. It has been pointed out, for example, that two of the most prestigious British Royal Commissions on the reform of criminal law, the Wolfenden inquiry into *Homosexual Offences and Prostitution,* and the *Royal Commission on Capital Punishment,* both of which invoked public opinion in support of their recommendations, did not attempt to determine public opinion scientifically during the several years in which they conducted extensive research of other kinds.[125] The same observation can be made about many important Canadian public inquiries, including the Berger Inquiry into the proposed MacKenzie Valley Pipeline,[126] the Le Dain *Inquiry into The Non-Medical Use of Drugs,*[127] and the McDonald *Inquiry Concerning Certain Activities of the Royal Canadian Mounted Police.*[128] It should not be forgotten, either, that public inquiries, like the news media, can have a profound influence on the very trends of opinion they report.[129]

The referendum is a political tool that can be used to obtain a fairly

---

122 *E.g.*, J. M. Beattie, *Attitudes Towards Crime and Punishment in Upper Canada 1830-1850* (1977), and P. B. Waite, *The Life and Times of Confederation: 1864-1867* (1962).

123 W. J. Blum and H. Kalven Jr., "The Art of Opinion Research: A Lawyer's Appraisal of an Emerging Science" (1956), 24 U. Chic. L.R. 1, p. 63.

124 See *infra*, text associated with note 194, *ff.*

125 Mannheim in M. Ginsberg, *supra*, note 120, pp. 275, 277.

126 *Northern Frontier and Northern Homeland*, Minister of Supply and Services, Canada (1977).

127 Minister of Supply and Services, Canada (1973).

128 Minister of Supply and Services, Canada (1980).

129 See *infra*, text associated with note 204, *ff.*

accurate reading of public opinion about legal or other matters. The best known use of a referendum in Canada in recent years was that in which Quebec voters rejected "sovereignty-association" for their province. Referenda have been rare in this country, however, especially in legal matters. This may, in part, have been the result of a judicial ruling in 1919 that it is not constitutionally permissible to substitute direct legislation by referendum for the normal law-making machinery established by the Constitution.[130] The constitutional obstacle is easy to overcome, however,[131] and referenda about proposed legislative changes or other aspects of the legal system remain rare. Politicians generally prefer to retain for themselves the task of interpreting the public will. Perhaps their reluctance to surrender this role to the more direct and accurate device of the referendum reflects an awareness that the referendum measures "waves" rather than "tides". More cynical explanations are also possible.

The most sophisticated tool for assessing collective attitudes is the public opinion poll. Although an extensive body of expertise has been developed in the almost half-century since such polls have been in widespread use, and an enormous literature exists, lawyers, judges, legislators, and others who staff the legal system have made only minimal reference to this data and expertise when dealing with legal matters that are generally supposed to be influenced by public opinion.

The reluctance of legislators to make extensive use of public opinion polls no doubt stems from some of the same factors that cause them to shy away from referenda. Perhaps they also doubt the accuracy of poll results. In the electoral process, where opinion polls are now a part of every politician's experience, they have seen pollsters' predictions confounded by election results. And most of them are probably also aware that the findings of opinion surveys, like all statistics, are open to varied interpretations. For example, a critical analysis of recent polls concerning the attitudes of Canadians toward criminal law suggests that although the polls seem at first glance to indicate that "Canadians worry about crime, believe it is on the increase and would like the courts to be more severe with criminals as they would be themselves", a closer scrutiny of the results reveals that only 3 per cent of Canadians polled spontaneously mentioned crime as a problem that concerned them, only 20 per cent expressed willingness to pay higher taxes to reduce crime, and when given the facts of specific crimes and asked to indicate appropriate sentences, most respondents were slightly more lenient than judges have been in the

130 *Re Initiative and Referendum Act*, [1919] A.C. 935, (*sub nom. Re Manitoba Initiative and Referendum Act*), 35 T.L.R. 630 (P.C.).

131 The constitutional problem arose because the particular scheme in question, created by a Manitoba statute, called for the legislation to come into automatic effect if approved by the referendum, thus circumventing Royal Assent and interfering with the "office of the Lieutenant-Governor", whose powers were beyond the constitutional reach of provincial legislatures. A referendum scheme which merely called for the approved legislation to be transmitted to the Lieutenant-Governor or Governor-General for Royal Assent would escape the difficulty.

same situations.[132] While these considerations certainly call for care and caution in the use of opinion polls, it is difficult to see how they justify the total disregard of survey data that often marks legislative actions.

The unwillingness of courts to take account of empirical opinion evidence, which is even more pronounced than that of the legislators, appears to be based (apart from simple ignorance) on three grounds. One is a concern that poll results would be inadmissible "hearsay" evidence. The second is a fear that even if the evidence were otherwise admissible, it might not be reliable. And finally, the relevance of the data is doubted in some cases.

None of these concerns justifies the extent of the courts' present failure to consult empirical opinion data. Although survey results may constitute "hearsay" evidence in some circumstances, it seems to be widely agreed that it would nevertheless fall within one of the exceptions to the hearsay rule, and would therefore be admissible.[133] Reliability is an important factor, of course, but the pollster's art has reached a sufficient stage of sophistication to warrant considerable confidence in the work of competent practitioners, and the literature offers plenty of information to equip sceptical lawyers to conduct effective cross-examination as to the reliability of particular surveys.[134] Relevance is crucial, and because opinion polls usually measure "waves" rather than "tides", individual polls may not often be directly relevant in themselves. But the cumulative results of several polls on the same points over a period of time could offer highly relevant evidence about the tidal dynamics. Dickson J. (as he then was) summed up the situation, so far as the courts are concerned, in the following comment, made shortly before he assumed his present duties on the Supreme Court of Canada:

> [W]hen it becomes necessary to determine the true nature of community opinion and to find a single normative standard, the Court should not be denied the benefit of evidence, scientifically obtained in accordance with accepted sampling procedure, by those who are expert in the field of opinion research. Such evidence can properly be accorded the status of

---

132 F. Bertrand, "Public Opinions About Criminal Justice Issues: Some Cautions About Poll Data" in Solicitor General, Canada, *Impact*, #1 (1982), p. 11.

133 See D. Gibson, "Determining Disrepute: Opinion Polls and the Charter of Rights" (1983), 61 Can. Bar. Rev. 377; S. J. Arnold and A. D. Gold, "The Use of a Public Opinion Poll on a Change of Venue Application" (1979), 21 Cr. L.Q. 445; J. M. H. Lamont, "Public Opinion Polls and the Charter of Rights" (1983), 61 Can. Bar. Rev. 377; S. A. Schiff, *Evidence in the Litigation Process* (1978), p. 285, *ff.;* R. C. Sorensen and T. C. Sorensen, "The Admissibility and Use of Opinion Research Evidence" (1953), 28 N.Y.U.L.R. 1213; F. R. Kennedy, "Law and the Courts", in N. C. Meier and H. W. Saunders (eds.), *The Polls and Public Opinion* (1949), p. 92; H. Zeisel, "The Uniqueness of Survey Evidence" (1960), 45 Cornell L.Q. 322; H. C. Barksdale, *The Use of Survey Research Findings as Legal Evidence* (1957); B. W. Roper, "Public Opinion Surveys" (1965), 51 A.B.A.J. 44; "Public Opinion Surveys as Evidence: The Pollsters Go to Court" (1953), 66 Harv. L. Rev. 498; "Opinion Polls and the Law of Evidence" (1976), 62 Virginia L.R. 1101; W. J. Blum and H. Kalven Jr., "The Art of Opinion Research: A Lawyer's Appraisal of an Emerging Science" (1956), 24 U. Chic. L.R. 1.

134 See D. Gibson, *supra*, note 133. For a discussion of some factors affecting reliability, see *supra*, note 96.

> expert testimony. The state of mind or attitude of a community is as much a fact as the state of one's health. . . .[135]

What is now necessary is to make lawyers and judges better aware of the large body of information about opinion polls that can assist them to make effective use of Dickson J.'s advice.

IMPACT OF PUBLIC OPINION ON LAW

Legislation

A large proportion of the writing about the influence of opinion on law deals with the legislative process.[136] Most of it falls into one of two categories: (a) descriptions of the role that public opinion has played in the enactment of particular legislation in the past; or (b) assessment of current attitudes on matters that might be the subject of future legislative change.

A surprisingly high percentage of the commentaries in the first category express a common conclusion: that public opinion did not exert a decisive influence on the legislation in question. While the public's interest was often engaged, and attempts to manipulate public attitudes were frequently made, the key factors appear to have been self-interest and effective lobbying by pressure groups. This was found to have been the case in the United Kingdom with respect to the first old-age pensions in 1908,[137] the institution of national health insurance in 1911,[138] reforms in business legislation following World War II,[139] and more recent changes in labour law.[140] Adam Podgorecki has speculated that the reason law generally provides less autonomy to children than public opinion seems to regard as suitable may be the absence of effective pressure groups in the area of family law.[141] Similar conclusions have been expressed by writers in the United States[142] and Australia.[143]

J. A. G. Griffith has suggested that public opinion may operate (in the elitist manner described by Dicey, but with modifications) with respect to certain relatively uncontroversial matters, such as planning law:

135 *R. v. Prairie Schooner News Ltd.* (1970), 75 W.W.R. (2d) 585, 1 C.C.C. (2d) 251 at 266, 12 Cr. L.Q. 462 (Man. C.A.).

136 For a good introduction to the subject, see R. Tomasic, "Sociology of Legislation" in R. Tomasic (ed.), *Legislation and Society in Australia* (1980), p. 19.

137 B. Abel-Smith in M. Ginsberg (ed.), *Law and Opinion in England in the 20th Century* (1959), pp. 354-55.

138 R. M. Titmuss in M. Ginsberg, *ibid.*, p. 306.

139 L. C. B. Gower in M. Ginsberg, *ibid.*, pp. 146, 151.

140 O. Kahn-Freund in M. Ginsberg, *ibid.*, pp. 222-23. See also A. Allott, *The Limits of Law* (1980), p. 82, *ff.* Allott claims (p. 230) that the British Race Relations Act was "smuggled through Parliament" to avoid the opposition of public opinion.

141 A. Podgorecki, "Public Opinion on Law" in A. Podgorecki (ed.), *Knowledge, Opinion and Law* (1973), p. 69.

142 L. M. Friedman and S. Macaulay, *Law and the Behavioural Sciences*, 2nd ed. (1977), c. 4C2.

143 R. Tomasic (ed.), *Legislation and Society in Australia* (1980).

> [I]n these fields . . . economic, social, and political facts change and . . . a few people in each generation see the implications and likely consequences more quickly than others. And the proposals put forward, in writings and all other kinds of propaganda, have the effect of attracting attention if they appear novel and relevant. The next stage is often the formation of groups and associations to develop these ideas, to emphasise the nature of the changes that are taking place, and to gather support. These *ad hoc* and specialist bodies then may persuade the permanent economic and political groups that there is something in it for them. Finally, there may be the establishment of Departmental Committees or Royal Commissions and ultimately legislation in some form — probably far removed from the ideals and aspirations of the original and primary movers — may be passed. Administration follows, the real effects (if any) are seen, the force of practical application pushes the statutory provisions into different and unlikely shapes, alterations become necessary, and, on the passing of the first piece of amending legislation, the real roots are struck.[144]

It will be noted that even in those situations, Professor Griffith has stressed the importance of political organizations finding "something in it for them". In more controversial areas, such as rent controls, he contends that this process does not operate at all: "We must look for opinion in these fields in the heart of politics and in the powerful general interests which uphold the parties."[145] Even where the broader consultative process does play a role, he warns, one should not pretend that it pays much heed to scientifically determined attitudes: "Opinion and knowledge are imperfect manifestations of human prejudices and passions and so remain but partial determinants of the struggle for power."[146]

A variant of the view that public opinion is seldom decisive in legislative matters is the thesis that it operates in a chiefly negative fashion. Dicey pointed out that "opinion may bear a merely negative character, and operate not by making laws but by forbidding their enactment".[147] A modern commentator has alleged that this is the normal way public opinion functions: "There is a difference . . . between public opinion wanting a certain change and public opinion opposing one . . . By and large, the impact of public opinion on law-making bodies has been stronger in a negative than in a positive direction."[148] If this conclusion is accurate, the explanation may lie in the observation of another writer that the motivating force in these matters is often discontent: "[A] prime source of social change is discontent, especially discontent sharpened by a feeling of injustice."[149]

If one could safely assume that it is usually a concern for self-interest that nourishes discontent and creates opposition to legislative change, it would be possible to connect almost all of the above observations by the common

---

144 J. A. G. Griffith in M. Ginsberg (ed.), *Law and Opinion in England in the 20th Century* (1959), p. 122.

145 *Ibid.*, p. 132.

146 *Ibid.*, p. 142.

147 Dicey, *Law and Public Opinion in England During the Nineteenth Century*, 2nd ed. (1914), p. 18.

148 Mannheim in M. Ginsberg, *supra*, note 144, p. 276.

149 M. Ginsberg in M. Ginsberg, *supra*, note 144, p. 3. Note the similarity to the thesis of Edmond Cohn in *The Sense of Injustice* (1949). See also the remarks of Lord Devlin, *infra*, note 164.

thread of self-interest. That speculative assumption may not be justified, of course, and most of the "conclusions" mentioned above suffer from the same weakness. While the breadth of consensus among the writers about the respective and interacting roles of self-interest and public opinion is striking, it should be borne in mind that their views, like those of Dicey before them, are based chiefly on speculation or, at best, on impressionistic data.[150]

When we turn to the other major category of post-Diceyan scholarship about opinion and legislation — surveys of attitudes about current laws and possible changes — empirical data is abundant. Intensive opinion polls have been conducted in Canada and elsewhere on crime and punishment in general,[151] capital punishment in particular,[152] police,[153] gun control,[154] abortion,[155] and many other subjects of actual or potential legislative regulation. Less thorough glimpses of public attitudes about a wide array of legal topics over many years are available in compilations of Gallup Poll[156] and other[157] surveys.

This information is of considerable interest, and deserves greater attention by our law-makers. It has shortcomings, however. For one thing, most of the major studies relate to a relatively narrow range of legal problems, almost exclusively in the area of criminal law. Opinion polls about topics which affect civil law, such as the recent American study of privacy,[158] are rare. Another weakness is the lack of adequate correlation between studies of

150 It should not be forgotten, either, that many of these opinions were expressed in the course of a single seminar: M. Ginsberg, *supra*, note 144.

151 Some examples: Canada: C. L. Boydell and C. F. Grindstaff, "The Criminal Law: An Empirical Test of Public Attitudes Towards Legal Sanctions" in Boydell, Grindstaff and Whitehead (eds.), *Deviant Behaviour and Societal Reaction* (1972); I. Waller and N. Okihiro, *Burglary: The Victim and the Public* (1978). United States: L. Harris and Associates, *The Public Looks at Crime and Corrections* (1968); A. D. Biderman, *et al*, *An Inventory of Surveys of the Public on Crime, Justice and Related Topics* (1972); H. Erskine, "The Polls" (1974), 38 Pub. Opinion Quarterly, pp. 131, 288, 490. Other: Van Houtte and Vinke in Podgorecki, *Knowledge, Opinion and Law* (1973), p. 13; Kaupen in Podgorecki, *supra*, p. 43.

152 Some examples: Canada: D. B. Chandler, *Capital Punishment in Canada* (1976); E. Fattah, *The Canadian Public and the Death Penalty: A Study of a Social Attitude* (unpublished report, Solicitor General, Canada, 1976). United States: H. A. Bedau, "The Death Penalty in the United States: Imposed Law and the Role of Moral Elites" in S. B. Burman and B. E. Harrell-Bond (eds.), *The Imposition of Law* (1979), p. 45.

153 Some examples: M. C. Courtis, *Attitudes to Crime and Police in Toronto: A Report on Some Survey Findings* (1970); Alberta Bureau of Statistics, *Residents' Attitudes Towards the Police* (unpublished, 1976); D. Chappell and P. Wilson, *The Police and the Public in Australia and New Zealand* (1969); P. Wilson and J. Western, *The Policeman's Position, Today and Tomorrow* (1972).

154 Goldfarb Consultants Ltd., *National Attitudes Towards Crime and Gun Control* (unpublished report, Solicitor General, Canada, 1977); Canadian Facts Co. Ltd., *National Survey of Awareness to the Gun Control Legislation-Highlights Report* (unpublished report, Solicitor General, Canada, 1978).

155 W. A. P. Facer, *Attitudes to Abortion in New Zealand* (1973).

156 G. H. Gallup, *The Gallup Poll: Public Opinion 1935-1971*, and annual volumes for subsequent years; *Gallup Report* (Canada), annual volumes since 1967.

157 See, for example: H. Cantril and M. Strunk, *Public Opinion*, 1935-1946, (1951).

158 L. Harris & Associates and A. F. Westin, *The Dimensions of Privacy* (1981).

similar matters conducted at different times and in different locations. The attempts at correlation which have been made[159] suggest that more extensive comparative data might shed valuable light on conditions that influence opinion, as well as on the validity and significance of Dicey's wave/tide hypothesis. Finally, it must never be forgotten that opinion survey results are often open to differing interpretations. They should, as a previously quoted critic advised, be "used with caution".[160] And perhaps a pinch of scepticism.

Judicial Decisions

The extent to which the decisions of courts and other adjudicators are and should be shaped by public opinion is one of several questions which, despite its great importance, has received no more sophisticated consideration in the past eighty years than it did from Dicey. While Dicey gave the matter comparatively scant attention, his thesis was striking: that judges, like legislators, respond to the tides of opinion that were running in their social seas at the time of their youth, and that whereas legislators speak for yesterday, judges, who tend to be older than politicians, represent the day before yesterday.[161]

The few modern writers who have addressed the question seem to disagree with this view. For example, Professor L.C.B. Gower, who was able to find little correlation between public opinion and *legislative* changes, claims that *judicial* responsiveness to public opinion has resulted in modern decisions that pay less heed to traditional notions of contract, and much more to fairness for the consumer than was once the case.[162] Dr. H. Mannheim has said that in sentencing criminals, the courts tend to be less lenient in small communities than in cities, where they are less likely to feel the brunt of public displeasure.[163] Lord Devlin has suggested that courts are responsive to community opinion to the extent of understanding and dealing with its "sense of injustice . . . The social service which the judge renders to the community is the removal of a sense of injustice."[164] These observations were not based on empirical data, however, and therefore have no more (or less) to recommend them than Dicey's speculations.

There can be no doubt that most fields of law are replete with opportunities for reference to community attitudes where a court chooses to consult them. Juries are almost entirely unhampered in this regard, of course,[165] but

159 *E.g.*, A. Podgorecki, "Public Opinion on Law" in A. Podgorecki (ed.), *Knowledge, Opinion and Law* (1973).

160 F. Bertrand, "Public Opinions About Criminal Justice Issues: Some Cautions About Poll Data" in Solicitor General, Canada, *Impact*, #1 (1982), p. 11.

161 A. V. Dicey, *Law and Public Opinion in England During the Nineteenth Century*, 2nd ed. (1914), pp. 33, 369.

162 L. C. B. Gower in M. Ginsberg (ed.), *Law and Opinion in England in the Twentieth Century* (1959), p. 163.

163 H. Mannheim in M. Ginsberg, *ibid.*, p. 280.

164 "Judges and Lawmakers" (1976), 39 M.L.R. 1. And recall the suggestions of M. Ginsberg and E. Cohn that it is "discontent" or "a sense of injustice" that operates most powerfully: *supra*, note 149.

165 H. Kalven and H. Zeisel, *The American Jury* (1966); Patrick Devlin, *Trial by Jury* (1956).

even judges sitting without juries have ample occasion to reflect street values in their application of flexible standards such as "reasonable care", "indecency", and that which "would bring the administration of justice into disrepute". However, the extent to which judges actually employ these opportunities to incorporate community opinions, as opposed to their own personal values, has never been scientifically investigated on a large scale.[166] Some observers doubt that it is possible for a judge to escape subjective influences. Cardozo J. once said: "We cannot transcend the limitations of the ego and see anything as it really is. . . . The perception of objective right takes on the colour of the subjective mind."[167]

Even if judges are capable of acting as objective interpreters of community opinion, compelling arguments can be made against their doing so in certain situations. Automatic responsiveness to every wave of public sentiment would nullify protections, based on more fundamental community values, that courts have traditionally provided to those who are temporarily unpopular. It is perhaps significant that one of the few formal attempts ever made to require judges to consult the "sound sense of justice of the people" when applying legislation was made in Nazi Germany.[168]

Other Legal Decision-Making

Courts and legislatures are not the only bodies that make decisions affecting the character of the legal system. Governments are called upon, on an almost daily basis, to determine the amount of public money to be spent on the administration of justice (which affects numbers and types of courts, numbers and salaries of judges, size and quality of police forces, penal institutions, and so on), whether and how to exert influence over judicial decision-making, how to discipline erring judges, and many other practical matters that are at least as crucial to the quality of justice as anything in the statute books. Every legal system now entrusts key legal tasks to specialized boards and tribunals, which sometimes deviate widely from standard judicial techniques. Administrative officers, prison officials and police responsible for making the system work at ground level have considerable discretionary powers on many matters. The legal profession plays an important role in determining how the system functions. Even legal academics may occasionally be influential.

If one wants a true picture of the impact of public opinion on the law, these important components of the legal system should not be overlooked. Yet they have been almost completely disregarded so far. There are studies of

166 The survey mentioned in *supra*, note 115 (National Center for State Courts, Williamsburg, Virginia, *The Public Image of Courts* (1978) did, however, note a sharp difference between the attitudes of American judges and the general public.

167 *The Nature of the Judicial Process* (1921), p. 110.

168 Mannheim in M. Ginsberg, *supra*, note 163, p. 281.

public opinion about police,[169] lawyers,[170] and some other legal functionaries, but very little has been written about the effects, if any, that these public attitudes have on the manner in which the functionaries do their work. A survey conducted by the Canada Mortgage and Housing Corporation in 1978 indicated that only 20 per cent of Canadians would be willing to pay higher taxes to reduce the crime rate.[171] While that particular statistic may be suspect because of the hypothetical nature of the question, much more information of that down-to-earth kind (about the public's expectations of the legal system, the practical steps it is willing to take to realize those expectations, the perception of those expectations and the willingness by those who administer the system to listen and act upon those expectations) will be needed before anyone can plausibly claim to understand the full impact of public opinion on law.

Public Compliance, Cooperation and Reliance

The most direct way in which members of the public can demonstrate their attitudes about the legal system is by their actions: obeying or disobeying the law; assisting police and other legal officials with their work, or declining to do so; resorting to legal mechanisms to resolve their problems, or avoiding them. Public opinion is not the sole determiner of any of these issues, of course, but it is thought by many to be influential, and studies of its role in this area have been comparatively plentiful. However, few generally accepted conclusions emerge from the work.

The respective contributions of opinion and other factors to "law abidingness" is a subject that has received an especially large amount of scholarly attention.[172] The pioneering experiments of American psychologist Stanley Milgram,[173] and the theoretical writing of Swedish jurist Karl Olivecrona[174] have stimulated considerable bodies of both supportive and critical scholarship, and much other work has also been done.[175] Yet the

169 Some examples: M. C. Courtis, *Attitudes to Crime and Police in Toronto: A Report on Some Survey Findings* (1970); Alberta Bureau of Statistics, *Residents' Attitudes Towards the Police* (unpublished, 1976); D. Chappell and P. Wilson, *The Police and the Public in Australia and New Zealand* (1969); P. Wilson and J. Western, *The Policeman's Position, Today and Tomorrow* (1972).

170 See, for example, the survey cited in *supra*, note 115, and supra, note 166.

171 Canada Mortgage and Housing Corporation, *Public Priorities in Urban Canada: A Survey of Community Concerns* (1978).

172 For a good introductory sampler, see L. M. Friedman and S. Macaulay, *Law and Behavioural Sciences*, 2nd ed. (1977), c. 3B. A recent, but traditionally intuitive lawyer's view will be found in A. Allott, *The Limits of Law* (1980), p. 81, *ff.*

173 *Obedience to Authority: An Experimental View* (1974).

174 See J. G. Merrills, "Law, Morals and the Psychological Nexus" (1969), 19 U.T.L.J. 46.

175 *Eg:* S. M. A. Lloyd-Bostock, "Explaining Compliance With Imposed Law" in S. B. Burman and B. E. Harrell-Bond (eds.), *The Imposition of Law* (1979), p. 9. The subject of civil disobedience has attracted considerable attention; see E. V. Rostow, *The Ideal in Law* (1978), c. 4, and the useful bibliography at p. 80, note 2.

lawyer who consults this voluminous literature comes away with the impression that it contains more questions than answers.

Several years ago, Chief Justice Jules Deschênes of the Quebec Superior Court declined to punish for contempt of court certain workers who had refused to obey an injunction ordering them back to work. His refusal was based on his belief that it would be futile to use traditional enforcement techniques in the face of determined wide-spread resistance. In recent years, he observed, there has been a "rejection of authority, whether religious, political or judicial", and the time has passed "when respect for the law was deeply ingrained and the authority of the courts had popular acceptance".[176] Neither the validity of Chief Justice Deschênes' observations, nor their implications for the legal system, can be easily determined from existing scholarship.

Most legal systems count on the cooperation of ordinary citizens in reporting crimes, in coming forward as witnesses, and in a variety of other ways. Even the desirability of making full disclosure to one's own lawyer, so as to enable the lawyer to serve one most effectively, may be seen as an illustration of law's dependence on the cooperation of the public. It is often said that people are more reluctant to cooperate with authorities, or to "become involved" in legal matters today than they once were. The evidence advanced in support of this conclusion is usually episodic in nature, however, such as news media accounts of crimes taking place in full view of bystanders, with no effort made to prevent the act or to apprehend the criminal. Little empirical evidence of increasing reluctance to cooperate with the legal system seems to exist.

Assuming that this is an historically accurate generalization, however, a number of tantalizing subsidiary questions arise. Is the reluctance rooted in growing public distrust of legal authorities or institutions? If so, what is the cause of the distrust? Can it be reversed? How?

It would not be quite accurate to say that no scholarly work is being done to find answers to these questions, but the small amount that is being done seems unlikely to yield much helpful information. For example, a newspaper reported not long ago that a New York professor had completed a three year study in 19 American and Canadian cities of citizens' willingness to intrude in an apparent crime in progress.[177] He claimed that only 3 per cent of New Yorkers and 8 per cent of Canadians were prepared to intervene. But the significance of the statistic is put in doubt by the fact that the experiment — having a professional actor enter a locked car by means of a coat-hanger in the presence of witnesses — involved an ambiguous fact situation rather than a

176 *Commission de Tpt. de la Communauté Urbaine de Montréal v. Syndicat du Tpt. de Montréal, CSN et autres,* [1974] Rec. de. J. (C.S.) 227. The decision was reversed by the Quebec Court of Appeal (1977), 77 C.L.L.C. 14,098 (C.A.). For a fuller extract from the decision, see Preface, *supra*, p. 1.

177 "Public Blinks at Crime" in *Winnipeg Free Press,* 5th August 1980, p. 23.

clearly criminal act. Much more work is needed before any confident conclusions can be drawn about the relation between public opinion and cooperation with the law.

A related question is the extent to which citizens choose to take their problems to law for resolution. In many cases they have no alternative. Neither the accused murderer nor the victim's survivors are permitted to resort to private means to "settle" an alleged murder. Yet there are many other situations — especially in the realms of business, politics, labour relations and family matters — where a choice is available between legal and informal techniques of dispute resolution.[178] If we assume that a choice of legal or non-legal approaches in such situations reflects confidence or lack of confidence in the legal system, it would be useful to know whether there has been comparatively greater or lesser resort to law in recent years, and why.

Unfortunately, the small amount of evidence available is equivocal. On the one hand, there appears in certain fields to be a pronounced trend toward arbitration, conciliation, and other non-judicial solutions. The commercial and labour-relations worlds provide many illustrations.[179] On the other, there is unmistakable evidence of increased litigiousness in many other fields. "Why Is Everybody Suing Everybody?," asked a feature article in *U.S. News and World Report* a few years ago, without providing a convincing answer.[180]

This trend is particularly noticeable in constitutional disputes. For Dicey, public opinion provided an alternative to reliance on the courts in most constitutional matters in Great Britain,[181] but modern developments, even in that bastion of unwritten "conventions" and "understandings" have been marked by increasing resort to the courts to determine constitutional questions. In Canada, where constitutional litigation has been even more frequent (and is likely to become more so with the advent of the Canadian Charter of Rights and Freedoms), the Supreme Court has recently agreed to act as interpreter of even the constitutional conventions which, in Dicey's day, were thought to be entirely beyond the reach of courts.[182]

178 It is not always a question of choice. A person may rely on *both* self-help methods such as elaborate burglar alarms, fire-arms, insurance, *etc.*, and legal resources when the older methods fail.

179 L. C. B. Gower (p. 166) and O. Kahn-Freund (pp. 225, 232) in M. Ginsberg (ed.), *Law and Opinion in England in the 20th Century* (1959).

180 4th December 1978.

181 Law of the Constitution, 10th ed. (1939), pp. 439, 444. H. R. W. Wade, in "Law, Opinion and Administration" (1962), 78 L.Q.R. 188 at 190, commented: "The stability of our Constitution in this country is, I think, closely connected with the fact that we make public opinion do much of the work that law has to do in other countries." However, Dicey stressed that opinion wasn't the only sanction for conventions: law stood in the background as an indirect enforcement agency, in the sense that if someone disregarded the conventions restricting their use of legal power A, they might find themselves the target of a refusal by someone else to recognize conventional limits of legal power B.

182 A.G. Man. v. A.G. Can.; A.G. Can. v. A.G. Nfld.; A.G. Que. v. A.G. Can.; A.G. Can. v. A.G. Que., [1981] 1 S.C.R. 753, [1981] 6 W.W.R. 1, 125 D.L.R. (3d) 1 (*sub nom.* Ref. Re Admt. of Constitution of Can. (Nos. 1, 2, 3), 34 Nfld. & P.E.I.R. 1, 11 Man. R. (2d) 1, 95 A.P.R. 1, 39 N.R. 1.

Again, these impressionistic conclusions may be mistaken; reliable statistics are hard to come by. But if the impression of mounting litigiousness is correct, one would like to know why it seems to contradict the widespread belief that people cooperate less with legal authorities than previously. Why would they cooperate less with the system, but rely on it more heavily? What role, if any, does public opinion play? Modern literature does not provide many more answers than Dicey did.

IMPACT OF LAW ON PUBLIC OPINION

It would be appropriate at this point to examine the other side of the coin: the influence that law may have in shaping public attitudes and consequential behaviour by members of the public. I am unable to do so, however.

So far as law's impact on opinions about law is concerned, it will be discussed, together with various other influences, below.[183] The intriguing question of whether and how the legal system contributes to the formation of public attitudes about other matters — moral issues, business ethics, family relationships, or the way baseball and hockey should be played — does not appear to have yet received significant scholarly attention.

INFLUENCING OPINION

A good deal of attention has been paid to the question of how public opinion is shaped. It seems clear that the influences are numerous, but there is as yet little agreement about the respective strengths or interrelationships of these influences.

The Law Itself

It is not unusual for law to "lead" public opinion, and to help shape public attitudes as to what the law should be. I have already mentioned, for example, that England's very first written code of laws, the Laws of Ethelbert, appears to have been primarily intended to influence public attitudes, by persuading wronged individuals that monetary compensation was an honourable and otherwise satisfactory alternative to blood feud as a means of settling disputes.[184]

Dicey noted the sometimes symbiotic nature of the law-opinion relationship,[185] and most other writers on the subject seem to agree that law can influence opinion. Kutchinsky states that public opinion about pornogra-

183 A. W. B. Simpson, "The Laws of Ethelbert" in M. S. Arnold (ed.), *On the Laws and Customs of England* (1981), p. 3.

184 *Ibid.*

185 Dicey, *Law and Public Opinion in England During the Nineteenth Century*, 2nd ed. (1914), p. 465. See also pp. 41, *ff.*, 238, 309.

phy in Denmark appears to have been altered by the repeal of the ban on such material in that country in the late 1960's.[186] Kahn-Freund points out that an important factor in breaking the British General Strike of 1926 was the loss of public support for the strike which apparently resulted from the public statements of a well-known lawyer, and of a Chancery judge, that the strike was illegal.[187] Mannheim claims that the British public was much more tolerant of lesbianism than of male homosexuality for many years because the latter was legally prohibited and the former was not.[188]

Although this factor should not be overlooked, its importance should not be exaggerated. Podgorecki reports that in Poland in 1963, only 45 per cent of the population expressed the opinion that unjust laws should be obeyed,[189] and recent events in that troubled land further demonstrate that there are limits beyond which public opinion refuses to be "led", even under a totalitarian regime.

Personal Characteristics, Knowledge and Peer Pressure

One's attitudes are not determined solely by external stimuli; a wide range of personal factors may also be involved, and a number of studies have examined their influence. Podgorecki, for example, found certain characteristics to correlate highly with "punitiveness" of attitudes about legal subjects, and others with "tolerance":

> The following factors were associated with punitiveness: lower education, manual occupations, feeling of lack of security, social isolation, a severe upbringing, dogmatic attitudes, poor social adjustment, and feelings of frustration. On the other hand, the following factors made for greater tolerance: high school or university level education, non-manual occupation, involvement in voluntary social service, a lack of insecurity, multiple social contacts, an appreciation of one's childhood as lenient, rational attitudes towards problems, good social adjustment, and a lack of feelings of frustration. It is remarkable that only two of these factors (education and occupation) are objective determinants; the others are subjective in character.[190]

Inasmuch as one's attitudes about law will also be affected by one's experience with, and information or misinformation about, the legal system, these factors have also been the subject of several useful studies.[191] One

---

186 Kutchinsky in A. Podgorecki, *Knowledge, Opinion and Law* (1973), p. 131. S. Ozdowski found no such change in attitudes following the enactment of Australian legislation on family law: R. Tomasic (ed.), *Legislation and Society in Australia* (1980), p. 250. Perhaps Australians are more stubborn.

187 O. Kahn-Freund in M. Ginsberg (ed.), *Law and Opinion in England in the 20th Century* (1959), p. 226.

188 Mannheim in M. Ginsberg, *ibid.*, p. 268. One wonders, however, whether factors other than legality were not involved.

189 Podgorecki in A. Podgorecki, *supra*, note 186, p. 80.

190 *Ibid.*, p. 77. See also Kutchinsky in A. Podgorecki, *ibid.*, pp, 122-28, and L. Tepperman, "The Ebb and Flow of Punitiveness in Canadian Society", *Proceedings*, Canadian Society for Legal History (1977), p. 41.

191 *E.g.*, Kutchinsky in A. Podgorecki, *supra*, note 186, pp. 106-108, and Kaupen in A. Podgorecki, *ibid.*, p. 43, *ff.*

distressing finding of a 1978 national American survey was that knowledge about the legal system seems to correlate negatively with respect for it:

> The general public's knowledge of and direct experience with courts is low. But, a very sobering fact is that those having knowledge and experience with courts voice greatest dissatisfaction and criticism. This contrasts sharply with research we have conducted on other institutions and organizations.[192]

Peer pressure and "role models" have been found to be influential of opinion in a number of studies.[193] Other than to provide some possible support for Dicey's "elitism", this finding does not take us much further, however. We must still find what influences the attitudes of the role models.

The Press and Broadcast Media

The power of the media to shape public attitudes is widely perceived to be awesome.[194] "Copy cat crimes" are blamed on publicity given to certain types of offense. Apparent eroding respect for legal institutions is traced to negative images conveyed by the media. Exaggerated views of the seriousness of the "crime problem" are said to originate in sensational reporting and undue emphasis on criminal matters, real and fictional.[195] Special concern is often expressed about the sensitivity of young people to this type of influence. The prevalence of this perception probably accounts for the mountain of papers and monographs that have been written on the subject.[196]

These studies are often inconclusive or mutually inconsistent. One conclusion is persistent, however: that the influence of the media is far from overwhelming, and is difficult to separate from other contributing factors. One recent book reports, for example, that views of crime held by persons subjected to the influence of certain news media over an extended period differed substantially from the picture presented by the media. For example, the respondent's impression of criminals involved a much higher proportion of non-whites and of lower class persons than the media described. Their impression of the victims of crime also overestimated those two groups, as well as the number of women and older people involved.[197] The same group of respondents attributed the cause of crime to personal factors more frequently than did the media reports.[198] The author concluded that

---

192 National Center for State Courts, Williamsburg, Virginia, *The Public Image of Courts* (1978), p. 1.

193 *E.g.*, Kutchinsky in A. Podgorecki, *supra*, note 186; A. Podgorecki, *Law and Society*, c. 15; and N. W. Chamberlain, *Social Responsibility and Strikes* (1953), p. 30.

194 Even in the 18th Century: W. T. Laprade, *Public Opinion and Politics in the 18th Century* (1936).

195 A survey of Chicago television shows in 1976 found that there were 20 prime time dramas in which crime and law enforcement were the main themes, and that such programmes took up a total of 63 hours a week, fully 1/3 of the total programme time: D. A. Graber, *Crime News and the Public* (1980), p. 26.

196 No attempt has been made to review this vast literature. For an interesting recent study, see D. A. Graber, *ibid*.

197 *Ibid.*, pp. 54-55, 67-68.

198 *Ibid.*, pp. 71-72.

> it is well-nigh impossible to assign effects to particular sources when people have been exposed to a variety of sources which carried similar information. We were able to establish that people mention media more often than interpersonal contacts as their best sources of crime and justice news, except for local crime where neighbours are generally ranked first. Among media, television gets first place. Given the general vulnerability of global self-judgments, when compared to actual behaviour, this finding remains tentative. At best, media influence was moderate, judging from limited conformance of audience images to media images.[199]
>
> For many topics, crime among them, people have a backlog of stored knowledge because these problems recur over the years. Stories about these topics therefore are not genuinely 'news' in the sense of something that has not happened before. They are episodes in a continuing story that simply reinforce whatever has been previously perceived as the main story theme. This main theme is modified only occasionally when new episodes clash markedly with established stereotypes and the clash becomes apparent to the audience. This study therefore indicates that audiences select mass media crime and justice information to reinforce existing attitudes. . . . The study also provides evidence of more gradual incremental reshaping that occurs through the combined impact of media and other stimuli over extended time periods.[200]

An interesting explanation for the fact that the public interest in sensational topics that the media reflect does not necessarily indicate public opinion was offered by the authors of a penetrating review of the previously mentioned study of attitudes about communism in the United States during the McCarthy era. After pointing out that the American public did not feel strongly about the alleged threat of communism, and that journalists and editors personally were even less concerned than the general public, they observed:

> In Spring of 1954, if there was any aspect of American life which was conspicuous, it was the preoccupation of the mass media with the Communist question. Domestic Communism was in the headlines day after day after day. How does this fact fit together with the data that the issue had a very low saliency for the public generally and that the newspaper publishers in the sample of community leaders were the most permissive of all the subgroups and were vastly more permissive than the general public? . . . [I]n our view . . . the dominant factor was the pull of McCarthy and others as a spectacle, rather than any pull of the issues themselves. We now tend to feel that what caught the public's fancy, and therefore the publishers' space, was the colourful personalized drama which had developed around McCarthy. The interest of the public was like the annual interest of the public in the World's Series — and perhaps no more political.[201]

If this analysis is correct, it may be that those who concern themselves with the effect of public opinion on law must be able to distinguish not only between attitudinal tides and waves, but also between both of those phenomena and the mere shimmering reflection of the media spotlight on the tranquil or slightly rippled surface of public opinion.

It is also necessary, if the thesis is correct, to turn to the "other stimuli" that may play a role in shaping genuine public opinion.

---

199 *Ibid.*, p.118.

200 *Ibid.*, pp. 121-22.

201 W. J. Blum and H. Kalven Jr., "The Art of Opinion Research: A Lawyer's Appraisal of an Emerging Science" (1956), 24 U. Chic. L.R. 1 at 61.

Pressure Groups, Public Inquiries and Propaganda

Reference has already been made to the fact that major legislative changes are often attributed more to the influence of pressure groups than to the operation of public opinion.[202] Pressure groups usually operate more effectively behind the scenes than in public, of course, but there are occasions when they choose to exercise their influence by attempting to shape public opinion. There is a useful doctoral thesis available about attempts by the American Bar Association to shape public opinion concerning constitutional and legal issues in the 1930's, which concludes that the campaign was successful, among other things, in causing 42 states to teach constitutional rights in the public schools.[203] Such studies are unusual. However, very little information appears to have been published about the prevalence or efficacy of public relations campaigns in relation to legal subjects.

Although they are seldom thought of as "pressure groups", an analogous role is sometimes played by Royal Commissions and other public inquiries into controversial matters, legal and otherwise. The Berger Commission of Inquiry concerning the proposed Mackenzie Valley Pipeline,[204] completed in 1977, spent almost three years holding highly publicized hearings in northern Canada on the subject of aboriginal rights and related matters. The result was not just to gather information and points of view, but to stimulate discussion and to influence opinions about these difficult legal and social questions. A recent commentator has criticized the Berger Commission for playing too activist a role.[205] But the same author praised the work of the Le Dain Commission of *Inquiry Into the Non-Medical Use of Drugs,* which also attempted deliberately, if somewhat less heavy-handedly, to stimulate public opinion on the questions under investigation. Mr. Justice G. E. Le Dain, who chaired the latter inquiry, has, in fact, published a commentary on this aspect of the work of his inquiry, and of others in the past. He stated that "[t]he decision to institute an inquiry of this kind is a decision not only to release an investigative technique but a form of social influence as well".[206]

Professor John Willis, in a comment on Mr. Justice Le Dain's remarks, offered the following sardonic and acute description of the process:

> [W]hat can a royal commission . . . do that cannot be done just as well by civil servants with the help of consultants, the pressure groups and the politicians? . . . [N]othing, with the exception of two incidental side effects, both psychological, which are nevertheless of such overwhelming importance that they justify the whole exercise. The first psychological

202 *Supra,* notes 137-43.

203 M. L. Rutherford, *The Influence of the American Bar Association on Public Opinion and Legislation* (1937).

204 *Northern Frontier and Northern Homeland,* Minister of Supply and Services, Canada (1977).

205 *The Non-Medical Use of Drugs,* Minister of Supply and Services, Canada (1973); and L. Salter, "The Role of the Public in Scientific Determinations of Policy: The Canadian Inquiry Process" (1981), 31 U.T.L.J. 343.

206 G. E. Le Dain, "The Role of the Public Inquiry in Our Constitutional System" in J. S. Ziegel (ed.), *Law and Social Change* (1973), p. 85.

> side effect of a royal commission's public hearings, public statements and publications is that it cools the emotions. Like water dripping onto a stone, these public hearings, statements and publications gradually get across to the "silent majority" the idea that there really is "a problem" about which there can be discussion and on which there can be compromise; they wear away the originally held prejudices. . . . The second psychological side effect is that after months or sometimes years of reading all about the exercise in the newspapers, the average man is so sick of the whole thing that he is ready in the end to accept almost any solution, including the one that the civil servants and their political masters had hoped for in the first place.[207]

Education, Religion and Literature

It would seem reasonable that the two major formal institutions to which society has entrusted the task of indoctrination — the school and the church — would have considerable impact on what people think about law. Perhaps they do, but very little scholarly effort has so far been devoted to the subject.[208]

I have had the same difficulty trying to locate material examining the linkage between opinion about law and the ideas of great writers and thinkers of the past and present. While Dicey has been criticized for making too much of their significance,[209] it seems improbable that the major intellectual currents of the past century did not exert some influence on the tides of public opinion concerning law. Yet substantial studies of that influence do not seem to exist. Edward White's trailblazing book, *Tort Law in America: An Intellectual History*[210] comes close, but his concern is for the effect of general thought trends on the work of legal scholars, and the eventual impact of that work on the reform of tort law. If public opinion, shaped by the same intellectual forces, played a role in either inducing the legal scholars to take account of the new ideas in the first place, or in creating an atmosphere receptive to the reforms on the part of judges or legislators, White gives it no credit; his study eliminates the middleman. Perhaps there was no middleman. If not, the criticisms of Dicey's "elitism" would seem to be misplaced. But if public opinion did perform an intermediary function, the academic world has yet to explain the precise mechanics involved.

Moral relativism has been identified by many writers as one of the central ideas of the twentieth century. White traces some of its apparent ramifications for the law of torts, and many other modern legal developments

207 *Ibid.*, p. 99.

208 Some of the findings as to personal characteristics that influence opinion are very useful in this regard, however, see A. Podgorecki (ed.), *Knowledge, Opinion and Law* (1973), p. 77. Also in Podgorecki, see Kutchinsky, pp. 122-28; L. Tepperman, "The Ebb and Flow of Punitiveness in Canadian Society", *Proceedings,* Canadian Society for Legal History (1977), p. 41.

209 See, for example: Julius Stone, *Social Dimensions of Law and Justice* (1966), pp. 153-54. An early review of Dicey's First Edition by an American, Arthur Bentley, complained that "[h]e owed us a social dissection, and not a rhapsody." (Quoted by A. Briggs in "Seventeen Reasonable Men", *New Statesman,* 11th July 1959, p. 52.)

210 1980.

are commonly thought to be rooted in the notion, from the law's increasing permissiveness in sexual matters to greater flexibility in the provisions of family law and humanitarian reforms in punishment and penology.

Another concept that has played a dominant role in political and legal affairs during the past century is that which Dicey dreaded — economic collectivism. Collectivism seems to be reflected in legal trends such as: the increased regulation of business practices; "risk spreading" in tort law by techniques that range from pro-victim principles like *"res ipsa loquitur"* and strict liability, through contributory negligence legislation, to "no-fault" compensation schemes; publicly funded legal aid programs; and enhanced rights and responsibilities for trade unions. What are the sources of these hugely prolific ideas? If, as seems likely, collectivism is traceable to Marx and the early socialist writers, and moral relativism to the iconoclasm of Darwin, Freud, and perhaps even Einstein, why did it take so long — until after World War II — for the legal system to respond on a massive scale? Was the delay merely a consequence of the generational lag that Dicey postulated, or are there other explanations?

And how do we account for the apparent inconsistency of simultaneous trends toward individualism in the moral realm and toward paternalism in the economic realm?[211] As the legal system tip-toed out of the bedroom, it strode into the board room, and those who deplored or approved the move generally did so with respect to both aspects. Those who denounced the presence of law in the bedroom tended to applaud it in the board room, and vice versa. Therefore, although both groups have often directed their attacks toward "authoritarianism", that does not seem to have been the real issue.

What is the issue? Some have said it is equality of opportunity. Underlying both moral relativism and economic collectivism may be a desire to maximize the opportunities of all humans to share in the pleasures of life.[212] But if an urge for hedonistic equality has provided the fuel for legal change, why have the changes been so unusually rapid in the past 30 or 40 years? The pleasure principle and the notion of human equality have been with us much longer than that. Other factors must be involved.

---

211 Karl Marx himself is said to have been torn between the paternalism that the implementation of many of his ideas seemed to require and his "distaste for any principal or arrangement that could make one man serve the ends of another.": L. L. Fuller, *The Morality of Law* (1964), p. 26.

212 This thought was first suggested to me by Scott Gibson. When I turned back to Dicey, I discovered that he had been willing to grant, for the sake of argument ("though the concession is one which, if we have regard to the facts, must be accompanied by a large number of reservations") that (on p. 51):

> [T]he history of English, as of European civilisation generally, is the record of the continuous, though unconscious progress of mankind towards a condition of equality and similarity . . .

Social, Economic and Technological Factors

Social and economic conditions have a lot to do with the circulation of ideas. As one writer has pointed out:

> It would be fair to say that the England which Dicey surveyed in his *Law and Opinion* was an England at peace, economically prosperous, with a stable currency . . . . Dicey's England was one in which ideas could come slowly to their fruition . . . .[213]

That writer and others[214] have stressed the significance of the periods of war and economic upheaval that have punctuated the years since Dicey wrote. Morris Ginsberg has suggested that war-time conditions stimulated the expectations of society's have-nots, thereby feeding the fires of discontent that he and others believe underlie public pressure for social and legal change:[215]

> [D]uring the war appeal had to be made to the good will of the working classes, and this made them more conscious than ever before of their power and importance to society. . . . The glimpse which the working classes had during the war to something like economic equality had a profound effect on their minds and everywhere fired their imagination.[216]

Ginsberg was speaking of World War I in that passage, but the same point could be made, with at least equal justification, of World War II. The "class" that may have been most affected in that case was women, whose indispensability to the war effort, in both civilian and military capacities, was demonstrated more convincingly than ever before. If the idea of equal opportunity really has exercised a pervasive influence over recent legal developments, the gods of war may be entitled to a fair share of the credit.

But not all of it. Technological advances during the same period have been equally dramatic, and perhaps even more influential. In the realm of ideas, the most important developments have involved communications. The striking coincidence between the burgeoning of television in the mid 1950's and the star-burst of legal reforms that followed a short while later is unlikely to have been accidental. It is tempting to speculate that sparks struck by 19th century writers like Marx and Freud, which merely smouldered for decades, were fanned to substantial flames by the winds of two World Wars, and whipped to a fire storm by the communications revolution. I am not speaking now of the particularized impact of the media on public attitudes about such things as crime or the police, but of their possible influence on more general attitudes, such as contentment with one's lot in life, the desire for social and legal change, and so on.

The possible impact of technology on ideology is not restricted to the field of communications. The fires of opinion that I hypothesize may well have been augmented by incendiary devices like the birth-control pill (without

---

213 W. L. Burn in M. Ginsberg, *Law and Opinion in England in the 20th Century* (1959), pp. 44-45.

214 R. B. McCallum in M. Ginsberg, *ibid.*, pp. 74-75.

215 Ginsberg in Ginsberg, *ibid.*, p. 3. Note the similarity to the thesis of Edmond Cohn in *The Sense of Injustice* (1949). See also the remarks of Lord Devlin, *supra*, note 164.

216 Ginsberg, *ibid.*, p. 20.

which "women's lib" and the "new morality" would be difficult to imagine).

But this is idle speculation, of the type for which we have all criticized Dicey. Where are the solid scholarly excurses? There is so much to wonder about, and so few convincing answers, either from A. V. Dicey or from his scholarly successors.

Professor Leon Trakman, in commenting on Professor Gibson's paper, suggested that the tendency of Dicey, Gibson and others to deplore reliance by the legal system on short-range "waves" of public opinion may be rooted in a conservatism that seeks to obtain "an aloof juridical science, above and superior to man". In his view, even short-term shifts of public opinion should be taken into account, albeit cautiously, by a democratically responsive legal system:

> Spontaneous and intuitive reactions of the public may — although they need not — acquire a lesser level of authority in law than manifestations of public opinion that have developed more gradually, have been better articulated, and are more reflective of the mores of the community at large. Yet, spontaneous public opinion, popularized by such economist-philosophers as Hayek,[217] does have a very real role to play in the evolution of a legal system. For spontaneity serves as the beacon of potential innovation and change. Instant public approval or disapproval, sometimes more intuitive than reasoned, yet still valid in Aristotelian terms,[218] remains an important source of measuring legal development and retardation. To discount the instantaneous reactions of the public to law, which Professor Gibson refers to as the "wave" effect, is to distrust the inevitable interaction between the legal system and the society in which that system must necessarily function. It is to perpetuate an undue reliance upon well established institutions of law in society, in disregard of the fact that formalization in law, as in society, begets harmful rigidity. Isolated from society, law ultimately suffers from a narrowness of vision and an unwillingness or incapacity to change. While instant public opinion is readily produced, is not tried and tested, and is often rudimentary in character, it is an important ingredient in the constantly changing interface between law and community. Undoubtedly, the opinions of the public are only as reliable as the people who hold them. Public views and aspirations are not carved in stone; they are not automatically valid measures in the socio-legal barometer. However, spontaneous in nature, they are open-ended and flexible instruments of progress. Their freshness is often a far greater source of legal growth when compared to sterile legal rules and rigid legal concepts.

Professor Trakman's observations introduced a theme that recurred throughout the conference: that legal institutions functioning within a democratic

217 F. A. Hayek, *Law, Legislation and Liberty,* Vol. I, "Rules and Order" (1973), pp. 8-11; Vol. III, *The Political Order of a Free People* (1979), p. xii; F. A. Hayek, *The Results of Human Action, but Not of Human Design* in *Studies in Philosophy: Politics and Economics* (1967).

218 Aristotle postulated that, in order to attain a just *telos* or end, man employed two instrumentalities: Firstly, the purposeful exercise of deliberative reasoning and secondly, an innate sense of intuition. See Aristotle, *Nicomachean Ethics* (J. L. Ackrill ed., 1973); Aristotle, *Politics* (B. Jowett (ed.), 1905).

political system must be simultaneously sensitive to both the rights of individuals and minority groups, and the often inconsistent wishes of the majority. Although he did not deny the usefulness of the wave/tide distinction to those who must fashion practical compromises between these competing demands, his comments underlined the difficulty of locating the line between "waves" and "tides" of public opinion, and the importance of its placement in determining the character of a particular legal system.

2

REFLECTIONS OF CANADIANS ON THE LAW AND THE LEGAL SYSTEM: LEGAL RESEARCH INSTITUTE SURVEY OF RESPONDENTS IN MONTREAL, TORONTO AND WINNIPEG

Robert J. Moore

INTRODUCTION

While the legal system constitutes an important context within which the members of any society function, little is known about how Canadians view the institutions, procedures and officials responsible for legislating, administering and enforcing the law. A review of the Canadian literature reveals that most research investigating the public's perception and evaluations of the legal system has tended to be limited to public opinion polls on specific issues (*e.g.*, death penalty) or narrowly defined projects reflecting the immediate concerns and theoretical predilections of the researchers involved. This latter research[1] has included such varied topics as knowledge of the law; the general public's views with respect to charges, penalties, and the implementation of penal measures; the fear of crime and of becoming a victim; the public's opinion on the effectiveness of legislation, judicial rules and regulations, and preventative measures; the seriousness of offences and the appropriateness of the institutional response; public satisfaction with the organization and workings of the legal system and its various agencies and officers; the public's view of justice and its expectations in that regard; and the degree of legitimacy attributed to the criminal justice system, its mechanisms and its means of operation.

The major exception to this trend has been the research initiative of the Ministry of the Solicitor General respecting the attitudes of Canadians toward criminal justice policies that is being carried out by the Groupe de Recherche

1 R. J. Moore, "The Attitudes of Canadians Toward the Law and the Legal System", paper presented to the Annual Meeting of the Law and Society Association, Madison, Wisconsin, June, 1980.

sur les Attitudes Envers la Criminalité (G.R.A.C.) of the Centre International de Criminologie Comparée, Université de Montréal.[2] While the present project was developed quite independently, it parallels the G.R.A.C. research in its emphasis on the importance of psychological processes mediating the influence of contextual variables on respondents' perceptions and evaluations, and in recognizing the value of a step-by-step, qualitative-quantitative, research strategy.

THE PRESENT RESEARCH

The impetus of the present project grew out of the refusal by Chief Justice Deschênes of the Quebec Superior Court (as he then was) to employ the contempt of court law to punish Montreal subway workers for failing to obey an injunction of the court. His judgment drew attention to what he saw as public rejection of authority, whether religious, political or judicial, and to the passing of a time when law was deeply respected and the authority of the courts had popular acceptance.[3]

The remarks of Chief Justice Deschênes give rise to a number of questions. At one level is the empirical issue of discovering what the perceptions and evaluations of Canadians are regarding authority in general and the law in particular. Have people really lost respect for authority and the legal system that represents it? Is this a uniform phenomenon or does it affect only certain aspects of the legal system?

A second order of questions might be directed at exploring the context of such views by examining how they are related to traditional demographic variables (*e.g.*, age, education, income), the perceived quality of life (*e.g.*, life satisfaction, interpersonal trust), social-political-economic beliefs and opinions (*e.g.*, social welfare, strike breaking, interest in politics, inequality between the rich and the poor), and specific personality characteristics (*e.g.*, authoritarianism).

Finally, how is reported behaviour (*e.g.*, lawabidingness, litigiousness) in relationship to the legal system affected by such attitudes?

The intention of the present research[4] was to begin the systematic investigation of these questions. While retaining traditional theoretical interests, the research is firmly grounded in the practical concern that failing to accom-

---

2 Y. Brillon, C. Louis-Guerin and M-C. Lamarche, *Les Attitudes du Publique Canadienne envers les Politiques Criminelles: Rapport Final* (unpublished, 1982).

3 See Preface, *supra*, note 2 and accompanying text.

4 This research was generously supported by a grant from the Donner Foundation of Canada to the Legal Research Institute, Faculty of Law, University of Manitoba, and by grants to the author from the Social Sciences and Humanities Research Council, and Campion College, University of Regina.

modate public opinion in the formulation and administration of legal policy may create a risk of indifference and disobedience.

METHOD

Discovering how the public regards a particular issue, however, involves considerably more than the setting up of a stall to which those who wish to may come and express their views. Such a process demands a method, for the representativeness of the opinions obtained cannot be separated from the manner of their acquisition. Thus, it was to the issue of "asking the right questions" that the research initially directed itself. The aim was to ask only those questions which would be meaningful to the respondents; to find out what people think and feel about the law without imposing *a priori* an arbitrary and restrictive framework upon them by "putting words into their mouths". This was an overtly inductive strategy for question development, in contrast to a more "rational" approach in which the questions assembled are representative of the substantive domain delineated by the theoretical concerns of the researchers involved.

To accomplish this goal a "feedback" approach was employed that integrated extensive qualitative explorations with quantitative research in an unusual multi-stage, multi-step format. This format had proven successful in investigating the public's perceptions and experiences concerning a wide variety of social issues ranging from the use of contraceptive pills to the use of automobile safety belts.[5] The underlying rationale of this sequential strategy was to employ initially unstructured, free response, open-ended, clinical approaches involving small representative samples of respondents so as to define and delimit the issue in terms of the salient aspects of each individual's experience. The intention here was to provide a variety of channels through which respondents could express in their own words, not only the commonplace truisms so frequently elicited, but also the unanticipated, more subtle fears and prejudices that form a vital component in the understanding of behaviour. These findings were then integrated with the theoretical concerns of the researchers and employed in the development of a number of question modules which formed the major part of the more highly structured questionnaire used in the survey stage of the research. Thus, the qualitative research prepared the quantitative research by providing a questionnaire that reflected

5 (a) S. L. Ghan, *Women's Attitudes toward Oral Contraceptives* (unpublished master's thesis, University of Regina, 1974); (b) C. K. Knapper, A. J. Cropley, R. J. Moore, *A Quasi-Clinical Strategy for Safety Research* (1973); (c) C. K. Knapper and A. J. Cropley, *Social and Interpersonal Factors in Driving* (1975); (d) C. K. Knapper and A. J. Cropley, *Property Insurance: A Study of Public Opinion* (1975); (e) R. J. Moore and J. Newton, "Attitudes toward Aging, Hospitalization, Serious Illness and Death among the Life Threatened Elderly" (1977); (f) R. J. Moore and H. Mullens, "Love, Sexuality, and Growing Old in Special-care homes and Public Housing in Saskatchewan" (1981); (g) R. J. Moore and D. V. Chalmers, "Traffic Accidents and the Role of Driver Characteristics" (1982).

not only the interests of the researcher, but also those concerns about the law and the legal system that were most relevant to the population to be surveyed. Furthermore, this approach facilitated the analysis and interpretation of the quantitative data by allowing the researcher to turn for guidance to the more open and intimate data obtained during the qualitative investigations.

An outline of this research strategy appears in Table 1.[6] Apart from the initial literature review, each of the principal stages involved a variety of subsidiary steps which are briefly listed to the left of the table. At the end of each stage provision was made for an evaluation and consolidation of the material collected prior to embarking upon the following stage. Columns to the right of the table explain the function of each of the procedures employed.[7]

---

6 Adapted from C. K. Knapper and A. J. Cropley, "A Quasi-Clinical Strategy for Investigating Attitudes in the Transportation Domain", (P. Stringer and H. Enzel, (eds.) (1976), p. 349).

7 See R. J. Moore, "The Public's Perception of the Law and the Legal System: A Strategy for Research" (1981), 1 Windsor Yearbook of Access to Justice 214, for a detailed discussion of the research strategy as it applies to the particular problem of assessing the public's perceptions and evaluations of the law and legal institutions.

TABLE 1
CHRONOLOGICAL OUTLINE OF THE RESEARCH STRATEGY

Stage	Step	Source	Material	Analysis
PrePilot: Preliminary Research	Literature Review	Computer search of relevant data bases	Books, articles commentary	Identification of issues and variables
	Informed Opinion	Experts and opinion leaders	Unstructured Interviews	Content analysis
	Evaluation and consolidation			
Pilot: Qualitative Research	Group Sessions	Members of the public selected on the basis of the anticipated variety views they might represent in terms of socio-demographic variables	In-depth group sessions employing semi-structural interviews	Content analysis
	Individual Interviews	Members of the public randomly selected	Structured face-to-face interviews employing a schedule	Content analysis and simple statistical analysis
	Evaluation and consolidation			
Survey: Quantitative Research	Pretest	Members of the public randomly selected	Highly-structured face-to-face interviews employing a pre-test questionnaire	Complex statistical analysis including multivariate procedures
	Survey	Members of the public randomly selected	Highly-structured face-to-face interviews employing the survey questionnaire	Complex statistical analysis including multivariate procedures

SAMPLE

The population for the study consisted of all non-institutionalized individuals eighteen years of age and over, resident in three Canadian metropolitan areas in May and June of 1980.[8] The cities of Montreal, Toronto, and Winnipeg were selected in order to reflect cultural, linguistic, geographic, and political variability as well as reported differences in the perception of crime.[9] The sample was based on the stratified multi-stage sampling frame developed by the Survey Research Centre, York University, for urban surveys.[10]

8 D. Bates, *Attitudes Toward the Law: Sample Design Report* (1980).
9 T. Atkinson, *A Study of Urban Concerns: Final Report* (1979).
10 D. Bates and B. Patel, *Urban Concerns Survey: Sample Design Report* (1979).

On the basis of sampling and budgetary considerations, it was decided that an obtained sample of approximately 200 face-to-face interviews in each city would provide an acceptable level of precision. Demographic characteristics of the sample are reflected in Table 2.

TABLE 2
DEMOGRAPHIC CHARACTERISTICS

		TOTAL SAMPLE	MONTREAL	TORONTO	WINNIPEG
Sex		(%)	(%)	(%)	(%)
	Male	48.42	46.09	50.80	46.55
	Female	51.58	53.91	49.20	53.45
Age					
	19	6.03	4.32	7.92	3.97
	20-29	27.22	19.46	32.36	33.49
	30-39	21.97	24.04	19.85	23.70
	40-49	13.92	14.01	13.88	13.83
	50-59	13.99	17.36	12.61	7.76
	60-69	11.46	14.40	9.04	11.29
	70-79	4.79	6.42	3.75	3.38
	80+	0.62	0.00	0.69	2.58
	Mean	40.55	43.40	38.48	39.20
	Median	37.24	40.61	34.09	35.24
	Mode	26.00	31.00	26.00	25.00
Relation					
	Head of Household	54.55	57.32	52.01	56.36
	Spouse	23.35	25.13	20.04	30.27
	Son	9.50	6.73	12.78	5.39
	Daughter	8.41	8.73	9.40	2.95
	Other Relative	2.01	1.76	2.35	1.42
	Other	2.19	0.33	3.42	3.60

ANALYSIS

Given the paucity of Canadian research in this area, an exploratory strategy was adopted initially in confronting the analysis of individual differences in respondents' views concerning law and the legal system. Following the item-by-item analysis of each question, the multivariate procedure factor analysis was employed to develop a number of dimensions around which opinions of the legal system varied. These measures were then regressed against four groups of variables: indices of the respondents' subjective quality of life, measures of social-political-economic attitudes, items assessing contact with the legal system, and demographic variables. In selecting these variables, every effort was made to include only those measures whose validity and reliability had been established from previous research.[11]

11 R. J. Moore, *supra*, note 5.

The quality of life variables comprised measures of each respondent's happiness with life and the respondent's satisfaction with "life as a whole", and that person's "financial situation". An additional item looked at the respondent's sense of community. Consistent with the view of Ornstein *et al*[12] that individual differences in the perception of the quality of life are conditioned in part by the "belief that personal misfortunes are not entirely due to one's own inability to carry through his or her plans and some level of trust in other people", measures of personal efficacy and interpersonal trust were also added.

Among the variables assessing political attitudes were those measuring a number of "left-right" issues: the extent of support for social welfare, minority rights, and a more redistributive taxation system, and the extent of agreement with the views that management should be prohibited by law from hiring workers to take the place of strikers, that union leaders and workers who fail to obey back-to-work legislation should be fined or jailed, and that there is too great a difference between the rich and the poor. Questions dealing with "government-related" issues included measures of the extent of disagreement with government priorities, political efficacy, the legitimacy of protest, political activity and involvement, attention to the news media, and authoritarianism.

A number of variables attempted to assess the extent of the respondent's involvement with the legal system. Included were measures of victimization, contact with the police, involvement in "non-normative" behaviour, the use of and satisfaction with lawyers, and courtroom experience.

Demographic variables included indices of gender, age, marital status, level of educational attainment, family income, city of residence, perceived social class, religious preference, and frequency of church attendance.

FINDINGS

The following comments summarize the perceptions of the law and the legal system as expressed by the 640 respondents sampled in the three cities of Montreal, Toronto, and Winnipeg.

Perceptions of the Law and the Legal System in General

Respondents generally defined the "law and the legal system" in terms of personnel and institutions (*e.g.*, police, courts, lawyers, prisons) and rules and regulations.

Virtually all respondents believed that laws were necessary to avoid chaos, to act as guides for living in society, to check impulse, and to prevent

12 M. Ornstein, T. Atkinson and H. M. Stevenson, *Political Attitudes and the Quality of Life in Canada* (1979).

people from simply "doing what they wanted to do". The majority indicated that the law did not have too much control over their personal lives and that a certain amount of regulation and restriction was inevitable and necessary in society.

When questioned regarding the need for government to put more effort into law enforcement and reform of our laws and prisons, such priorities, not surprisingly, received less respondent support than economic issues like inflation and unemployment, but higher endorsement than social issues like helping the poor and health care. Crime prevention ranked second behind controlling inflation as a priority for government action. While there was consensus among respondents that the laws in this country generally stand for what the people want and that people obey the law because they believe it to be right, many were critical of the way in which justice was currently being dispensed: a majority of respondents indicated that something needs to be done to improve the way the legal system operates and the laws it produces; that the legal system favours the rich and powerful, and that it takes too long to get anything done through the legal process. Changes should and could be accomplished within the current political and legislative framework.

This critical attitude was also reflected in respondents' evaluation of the general public's support of the legal system: most estimated that there was less respect for the law today than there was five years ago and only slightly more than half felt that most people were lawabiding.

In response to a number of examples of newspaper stories describing alleged abuses of the law by authorities (*e.g.*, the opening of the mail, raids on residences without a warrant, the restriction of the right to protest), most respondents described such actions as only "mildly serious" to "serious". The one exception to this pattern was illegal wire taps by the police; these were viewed more often as very serious abuses of authority.

However, in spite of these rather cynical views and in spite of the fact that nearly half of the respondents acknowledged that there were "situations" when it was right in their opinion not to obey the law (*e.g.*, emergencies, abortion), the vast majority of people indicated that they would obey the law, even in instances where they might strongly disagree with a specific law.

Answers to a number of items dealing with knowledge of the law on everyday concerns (*e.g.*, property, marriage), revealed that respondents were reasonably well informed. A number of misconceptions centred around differences between American and Canadian law (*e.g.*, "pleading the Fifth Amendment", "being informed of your rights").

When these findings were then viewed in terms of various demographic variables the following patterns emerged:

— Women, when compared to men, were less satisfied with the current operation of the legal system and did not see the law as representing a consensus; they tended to advocate law reform and tougher laws.

— Older respondents indicated that they were willing to comply with the law, saw the law as right and representing a consensus, and advocated law enforcement as a priority. Younger people tended not to view abuses of authority by government agencies as serious.

— Single individuals were less inclined to see law enforcement as a priority; yet they tended to view abuses of authority by government agencies as serious. Respondents who were separated, divorced, or widowed, were less satisfied with the current operation of the legal system and advocated tougher laws.

— Higher levels of education and income were positively associated with satisfaction with the current operation of the legal system, the view that the law represents a consensus, a lack of support for law enforcement and law reform as priorities, and the belief that the law gives too much protection to criminals. Higher levels of education were also associated with less willingness to comply always with the law, and the tendency to see government abuses of authority as serious.

The effects of the demographic variables were then controlled and the findings reviewed in terms of the quality of life variables, social-political-economic attitudes, and experience with the legal system. In terms of the quality of life measures, respondents' views were most affected by the extent of satisfaction they expressed with their financial situation, and their view of human nature. Higher levels of financial satisfaction were positively related to satisfaction with the current operation of the legal system, willingness to comply with the law, and the view that the law is right and represents a consensus. It was negatively related to the need for reform in our legal system and the view that abuses of authority by government agencies were serious.

Individuals who believed that most people can be trusted, are fair and will try to be helpful (interpersonal trust), were satisfied with the current operation of the legal system, saw the law as right and representing a consensus, and did not see law enforcement as a priority.

Finally, respondents who felt a sense of "community" tended to express a need for stronger enforcement of the law.

Conservative opinions on social-political-economic issues such as social welfare, minority rights, distribution of wealth, labour, legitimacy of protest, and government legislative priorities, tended to be associated with satisfaction with the current operation of the legal system — the view that the law is right, represents a consensus, is not in need of reform, and that abuses of authority by government agencies need not be taken seriously.

Law enforcement as a priority was positively related to disagreement with government legislative priorities and support for social welfare; it was negatively related to acknowledging the legitimacy of protest and the fining or jailing of union leaders who disobey back-to-work legislation.

Respondents who tended to view government actions as responsible and understandable (political efficacy) tended to be satisfied with the current operation of the legal system, and to view the law as right and representing a consensus. They did not see either law enforcement or law reform as a priority.

Interest in politics and involvement in political activities were strongly related to the need for legal reform. Avowed New Democratic Party supporters saw law reform as a priority, not law enforcement, and viewed abuses of authority by government agencies as serious. Liberals tended to be more satisfied with the current operation of the legal system. Progressive Conservatives saw the law as representing a consensus, were pro-law enforcement, and did not view abuses of power by the authorities as serious.

The belief that a few strong leaders would make this country better (authoritarianism) was related to dissatisfaction with the current operation of the legal system and, not surprisingly, to support for law enforcement as a priority and to the need for tougher laws.

The most consistent relationship exhibited in the set of variables indexing contact with the legal system was by those questions assessing "non-normative" behaviour. Respondents who admitted to committing fewer of these "socially acceptable" offences (*e.g.*, illegal consumption of drugs or alcohol, theft from work) tended to be lawabiding, satisfied with the current operation of the legal system, saw the law as representing a consensus, supported law enforcement and tougher laws, and viewed abuses of authority by government agencies as not serious.

Recent contact with the police and satisfaction with the job the police are doing were positively related to support for law enforcement as a priority.

The frequency and regularity with which respondents consulted lawyers correlated positively with support for tougher laws, the lack of enthusiasm for law reform, the belief that respect for the law had increased in the last five years, and the tendency to view abuses of authority by government agencies as not serious.

Respondents not satisfied with the services rendered by lawyers, especially with respect to the fees for those services, indicated dissatisfaction with the current operation of the legal system and with failure of the law to represent a consensus. They also supported the need for law reform and the belief that our laws give too much protection to criminals.

More frequent contact with the courts tended to be associated with lack of enthusiasm for law enforcement and law reform as priorities, and with the opinion that the law gives too much protection to the offender.

Being a victim of crime did not appear to affect attitudes toward the legal system in any strong or consistent manner.

Finally, when responses were compared between the cities surveyed a number of noteworthy differences emerged. Respondents in Montreal, compared to residents of Toronto and Winnipeg, endorsed a much stronger position on law enforcement and the need for tougher laws, indicated more of a need for government to give legal issues a higher priority, and expressed a greater desire for reform. They also tended to be more critical, asserting strongly that the system is inefficient, that laws are passed for the benefit of a few people, and that people are constantly breaking the law. Violations of the law by the authorities tended to be regarded as less serious in Winnipeg than in Toronto or Montreal.

Perceptions of the Police

The vast majority of respondents reported they were more than satisfied with the job their local police were doing and that their feelings about their most recent encounter with the police had been favourable. Despite this personal experience, many felt that relations between the police and the public had either remained the same or had become worse in the last five years and that the police deserved more respect. The police were seen in part as responsible for this situation by virtue of the poor job they were doing in informing the public about police roles and objectives. The police were viewed by many as doing a good job of investigating and correcting internal problems.

While many thought that more police were needed, only a minority of respondents would allocate money that could be spent on economic or social programs to improve the resources of the police in their efforts to crack down on crime. Consistent with their reluctance to give police more money was the lack of enthusiasm respondents exhibited for expanding the power of the police. Most felt that the capability of police forces to require persons to answer questions about what they were doing, to search persons or their property, to tap telephones, to open the mail, to deny groups permission to protest, and to use physical force, must continue to be carefully regulated and monitored, and implemented only under limited and clearly defined conditions.

The inclination to increase the powers of the police was more pronounced in respondents with a higher level of income, who were satisfied with that income, who supported conservative social-political-economic views, who supported the Progressive Conservative political party, and employed a lawyer more frequently.

Although indicating that they felt that the police treat suspects about "right", *i.e.*, not too easily but not too harshly, respondents pointed out that in their opinion certain groups do appear to receive more favourable treatment (*e.g.*, the wealthy, the powerful, Caucasians), while other groups are treated less favourably (*e.g.*, blacks, the poor, the young).

Criticism of the job that the police are doing centred on the view that the police are not as concerned about crimes against the ordinary person as about those against business. Opinion was split on whether the police spend too much time on duties not directly concerned with law enforcement and whether they are more interested in making arrests than in preventing crime.

The majority of respondents expressed the belief that the police rarely take bribes, or twist or make up evidence to convict suspects. However, more concern was shown about the unnecessary use of physical force, the use of illegal methods in getting information, the keeping of suspects in jail for excessive periods of time, and, to a lesser extent, the covering up of illegal police activity.

Evaluations of the police tended to be less favourable in Montreal than in Toronto and Winnipeg. Residents of Montreal tended to be more critical of, and less satisfied with, the work of the police. They tended to be less willing to increase the size of the police force, allocate more funds to strengthen the police, or increase the powers of the police. They also tended to a greater extent to believe that the police engage in illegal activities. Relations between the public and the police were seen in Toronto as having deteriorated dramatically in the last five years. Nevertheless, the police were seen as deserving more respect from the public in Toronto and Winnipeg. In Montreal, relations between the public and the police were seen as having remained the same or improved, with the police deserving about the same respect they had at present.

While the claim that certain groups of individuals received either more favourable or less favourable treatment than others by the police did not differ dramatically from city to city (it was slightly lower in Toronto), the issue of racial prejudice surfaced in Toronto and Winnipeg. Whites were seen as being treated preferentially in Toronto, while blacks and native Indians received less favourable treatment in Toronto and Winnipeg, respectively.

Perceptions of Lawyers

The majority of respondents had at some point employed a lawyer, recommended by an acquaintance or by a member of the family, usually to facilitate a real estate transaction or to draw up a will. Most did not use a lawyer on a regular basis, had retained a lawyer's services less than five times, and had never changed lawyers because of dissatisfaction with the services they received.

Based on their most recent personal experiences, respondents generally gave lawyers high marks on the quality of their work. They saw their lawyers as being prompt in taking care of matters, showing interest and concern, being honest, explaining matters fully, keeping them informed of progress, and paying attention to their concerns.

While opinion was split as to whether or not the legal profession was doing its best to make legal services available to all who need them, the majority of respondents thought that lawyers were not doing enough to inform the public of how the legal process works, and of the types of legal services available. Subject to there being regulation, respondents thought that lawyers should be allowed to advertise their services and the fees they charge.

When asked to comment on the remarks about the profession gathered from interviews in the pilot work, respondents agreed with the following litany of complaints: that higher paid lawyers get better results for their clients; that lawyers are always finding loop-holes to get around the law; that lawyers get too many guilty people off; that people have to use lawyers more often than is really necessary; that lawyers do not work as hard for poor clients as for clients who are rich; that lawyers are more interested in making money than in helping their clients; and that lawyers charge too much for their services. Opinion was split as to whether or not lawyers are concerned about doing anything about the "crooks" in their profession.

This negative view of the legal profession was most strongly associated with those variables indexing dissatisfaction with the services received from a lawyer, having a cynical attitude about human nature, holding liberal social-political-economic views, and engaging in "non-normative" behaviour. Individuals with higher levels of education and income, who were satisfied with this income and the way government worked, and who employed lawyers on a regular basis, tended to evaluate the legal profession more positively.

Respondents in Winnipeg and Toronto appeared to engage the services of lawyers more often than did residents of Montreal. Real estate transactions played a particularly prominent role in Winnipeg. The ratings of the quality of work received from lawyers and respondents' evaluations of the profession in general did not differ dramatically from city to city. Residents of Montreal disagreed more frequently with the comment that people have to use lawyers too often, while the sample in Winnipeg was more likely to acknowledge that lawyers are not doing anything about the "crooks" in their profession. Montrealers felt the legal profession could do more to inform the public of how the legal process works and of the types of legal services available. Support for allowing lawyers to advertise their services and fees was much stronger in Winnipeg.

Perceptions of the Courts

The vast majority of respondents indicated they had a very limited experience of courts and court procedures. Those who had been in court had attended either as a spectator or a witness, or because they had been charged with a traffic offence.

In sympathy with their view of the lack of uniformity in the treatment of the public by the police, many respondents were of the opinion that the courts deal with some groups of people more favourably than others (*e.g.*, the wealthy), while certain other groups receive less favourable treatment (*e.g.*, the poor).

Dissatisfaction with the courts was most explicitly indicated by respondents in their agreement with comments that taking someone to court is too expensive for most people, and that the courts take far too long to deal with cases. Although many respondents indicated no opinion, approximately half the sample agreed with the following comments gathered in the pilot interviews: that the individual does not have a chance in court against business; that if a person has enough money, almost anything can be arranged in court; that judges are appointed on the basis of their ability to administer the law and not because of their political support; and that court proceedings might be more effective if the courtroom, the dress of judges and lawyers, and the proceedings, were less formal.

Respondents were split as to whether it is a common occurrence for a guilty person not to be convicted in Canadian courts, and whether court decisions are often influenced by political considerations.

Evaluations of the efficacy of the courts and their susceptibility to influence were generally more critical in Montreal than in Toronto or Winnipeg. Respondents in Montreal were more likely to agree that the guilty are not convicted, that court decisions are influenced by political considerations, and that trials would be more effective if they were less formal. People from Winnipeg were less inclined to agree that money could influence court decisions.

Perceptions of Sentencing

A majority of respondents indicated that in their view, judges should not have to assign the same sentence for a particular offence, but should have discretionary power to make sentences "tougher" or "lighter" depending upon the circumstances of the case. Most specified a preference for the dispensing of tougher sentences (*i.e.*, longer terms, more physical punishment), reflecting the belief that such punitive measures might deter criminal behaviour.

Two thirds of the sample were in favour of capital punishment for the killing of a prison guard or on-duty police officer, and overwhelmingly supported the extension of the mandate to include premeditated murder and sex offences resulting in the death of the victim.

A majority of the respondents felt that imprisonment should only be resorted to after every other alternative had been tried, especially in the instance of young offenders. The most frequent rationale to justify such a course of action was to protect society from criminals and to rehabilitate the offender. The threat of imprisonment was viewed as doing little to deter criminal behaviour in our society.

A factor indexing a punitive attitude regarding sentencing and the treatment of offenders was developed and correlated with a considerable number of variables. Those respondents who were older, those satisfied with the quality of their life, those cynical about human nature, those with a strong sense of community, those in disagreement with government priorities, and those who supported the Progressive Conservative party, tended to reflect a more punitive attitude. On the other hand, if you were single, well-educated (the single best predictor), a holder of liberal political views, critical of government, involved in politics, and a supporter of the N.D.P., you tended to advocate a less punitive attitude in sentencing and in the treatment of inmates.

Comparison of the three cities indicated that most respondents in Montreal felt that judges should have more discretionary power in making sentences tougher or lighter. The call for tougher sentences and punitive measures was strongest in Winnipeg. Support for capital punishment, although given by the majority, was slightly less enthusiastic in Montreal.

Perceptions of Prisons

While respondents viewed prisons as doing only a fair to good job of protecting society from criminals and punishing the offenders for their misdeeds, many more indicated that prisons are doing a poor job of discouraging others from crime and rehabilitating the criminal, the latter being viewed as one of the major functions of imprisonment.

Satisfaction with the job prisons are doing was negatively related to level of education and income, political involvement, and a number of variables indexing experience with lawyers and the courts.

Respondents were split as to whether prisons are too luxurious and pleasant. Although a large number indicated that they did not know, a majority of the remaining respondents disagreed with the claim that a basic problem in rehabilitating prisoners successfully is the brutality and violence of the prison guards. While approximately half of the sample did not subscribe to the increased use of solitary confinement and corporal punishment, well over a third agreed with such measures.

Respondents in Winnipeg and Toronto were more inclined to agree that prisons are too luxurious. There was less support in Toronto for not sending young offenders to prison. Support for prison reform was strongest in Montreal and weakest in Winnipeg.

Perceptions of Crime and Violence

While slightly over half of the respondents indicated that they were not particularly worried that they might become a victim of a crime, over one quarter of the sample indicated that they were very concerned. Those most concerned about becoming victims tended not to have been victims already, to agree with government legislative priorities, and to have engaged more often in "non-normative" behaviour involving drugs and/or alcohol. Respondents were most anxious about crimes against their property, *e.g.*, breaking and entering, theft, vandalism. Crimes against the person centred on safety in the street with particular concern being expressed about rape and assault.

The majority of respondents indicated that they had not done anything to protect themselves, their family or their property against crime. Those who had taken some action reported installing more or better locks and obtaining or increasing their insurance coverage.

Most respondents reported that they avoided certain areas of their city because of the possibility of crime or violence, but felt that the probability of being a victim in their city was no different from that in any other city in Canada.

Violence and crime were attributed to causes reflecting a breakdown in respect for authority or reflecting social inequity. Examples of the former included the use of drugs, the lack of discipline in the home and school, and the increase in organized crime, and of the latter, the breakdown of the family, the high cost of living, and the unequal distribution of wealth. While respondents as a rule tended to attribute more importance to reasons reflecting a general lack of respect for authority, a number of interesting individual differences emerged.

People characterized as being older, married, having less formal education, satisfied with life, experiencing a sense of community, voting Progressive Conservative, and engaging in less "non-normative" behaviour, reflected a tendency to attribute the cause of crime and violence to a general breakdown in respect for authority. Inequities in the social system were more likely to be viewed as precipitating factors in crime in responses given by women, by respondents who earned less money and who were dissatisfied with their financial situation, by persons who experienced less control over their lives, by those who subscribed to liberal positions on various social-political-economic issues, and by those who voted N.D.P.

Fear of victimization was much stronger in Toronto and Winnipeg, especially the latter. Concern over crimes against property was highest in Winnipeg, while respondents in Montreal showed the least worry about crimes against the person. Concern over crimes involving the automobile (*e.g.*, auto theft, reckless driving, hit and run), was, perhaps not surprisingly, highest in Montreal.

While residents of all three cities tended to recognize equally the role that a general breakdown in respect for authority has in breeding crime and violence, respondents in Montreal were more inclined to acknowledge the role of factors indexing social inequities.

SUMMARY

What can be said, by way of review and conclusion, in response to the questions we began with? What is the gestalt that emerges regarding the respondents' perceptions and evaluations of the law and the legal system? What is the nature of the demographic, attitudinal and experiential context in which they are embedded?

Despite their criticisms of the current operation of the legal system, their cynicism regarding the public's lack of respect for the law and its contribution to criminal activity, and their concerns about abuse of power by those in authority, respondents demonstrated support for the legal system. They believe that laws reflect majority opinion, and obey them because they are perceived to be right, not because of fear of retribution. They are willing to comply with the laws of the land even in instances where they might disagree with them.

When these views are examined in the light of the various demographic characteristics of the sample, not a great deal of variability is accounted for. Women are more dissatisfied than men with the current operation of the legal system, and do not view it as representing a consensus. Respondents who report lower levels of education strongly support law enforcement as a priority, display a punitive attitude in sentencing and the treatment of offenders, believe that crime is largely a function of the breakdown of respect for authority, see the need for a few strong leaders, and tend to view abuses of authority by government officials as less serious than others do.

The variables indexing the respondents' perceived quality of life did not appear to influence perceptions and evaluations of the law and the legal system substantially. There is some support, however, for the picture that if you are reasonably satisfied with your life and believe in people and in your ability to run your own life, you are content with the status quo: the legal system and its representatives work efficiently enough for you, and the law is right, represents majority opinion, and is not in need of immediate or drastic reform. Further, you will likely tend to show some support for tougher laws and for increasing the power of the police, and you will not likely be very upset if the authorities bend the rules a little in carrying out their responsibilities.

Respondents' opinions on a number of social-political-economic issues had strong and consistent effects. Liberal opinions on such concerns tended to be associated with dissatisfaction concerning the operation of the legal system, and with the views that the law does not reflect a consensus of opinion, that it is in need of reform, and that the root causes of crime and violence lie in social inequities.

While the majority of respondents were generally satisfied with the job the police are doing, and were sympathetic to increasing the number of police, they were reluctant to see more money spent on law enforcement or on expanding the powers of the police. Traditional complaints about biased treatment of certain segments of society by the police, the failure to give equal attention to crimes against the ordinary person, and police corruption and illegal behaviour, continued to be supported by the present sample.

Respondents were equally facile at damning lawyers as they were in praising them. On the basis of the services provided for a client, respondents gave lawyers high marks. When rating the profession in general, however, the rather negative stereotype of the lawyer as a manipulator of the system, who favours the rich over the poor, who gets too many guilty people off, and who is interested only in making money, surfaced strongly. This stereotype is mitigated to a degree by increased contact with lawyers. It would appear that in addition to public education regarding the legal process and services available, lawyers might well consider their image in the public's eye.

Respondents had serious questions about the efficacy of the courts. They believed that expense and time rule out access to the system for a large number of individuals, and although believing that the courts are administered by competent people, many viewed them as dispensing a questionable brand of justice, one seemingly influenced by money and power.

Judges should have more discretionary power to make sentences "tougher" or "lighter" in the opinion of most. Respondents indicated a preference for tougher sentences. Two thirds of the sample were in favour of capital punishment for the killing of on-duty police officers or prison guards, and voiced support for the extension of the penalty to include premeditated murder and sex offences resulting in the death of the victim. While imprisonment should be resorted to only after other alternatives have been explored, it is justified in order to protect society from criminals and to rehabilitate the offender. A more punitive attitude tended to be associated with lower education, satisfaction with the quality of life, law enforcement as a priority, and a stronger tendency to believe that the root causes of crime lie in the breakdown of respect for authority.

Respondents, especially those who were politically involved, did not see prisons as fulfilling any of their functions very adequately, particularly in the area of rehabilitation and deterrence. It is not difficult to understand the reluctance of a large majority of the sample to support the sentencing of young offenders to these "schools for crime".

For a sizeable portion of the sample, the issue of crime and violence was not immediate. More were concerned about crimes against their property (*e.g.*, breaking and entering, theft, vandalism) than against their person (*e.g.*, rape, assault). The majority of respondents had not done anything to protect themselves or their property, and although most indicated that they avoided certain areas of their city because of the possibility of crime or violence, they estimated the probability of being a victim in their city as no different from that in any other city in Canada. Violence and crime were attributed to causes reflecting either a breakdown in respect for authority or conditions in society which lead to inequities, with respondents tending to give more importance to the former.

Having made these comments, I must sound a note of caution regarding their interpretation.

First, most of the specific relations discussed are based upon coefficients of association of 0.30 or less. While statistically significant and of a magnitude that is typical in this type of research, we must in our discussions of their import never lose sight of the fact that they account for less than 10 per cent of the variance involved in the relationships.

Second, such relationships tend to present a fragmented and over-simplified picture of the nature of the respondents' perceptions and evaluations of the law and the legal system. The analysis presented is useful in that it gives us a picture of what the views of the public are and how they are distributed in society. We have gone beyond the traditional question-by-question analysis in terms of various demographic variables (*e.g.*, age, sex, level of education) because their value in elucidating opinion is limited. We have recognized that the respondents' reflections upon the law and the legal system are embedded within the context of their conceptions of the overall social system. Accordingly, we have reported on the nature of the relationships between respondents' perceptions and evaluations of the law and the legal system and their subjective quality of life, their social-political-economic attitudes, and their experience with the legal system. Such comments are problematic, however, since they tend to promote the misconception that there is a uniformity in viewpoint, a consensus. Obviously to an extent there is: that is why we have discussed the findings in terms like "many", "most", and "majority". However, to a degree such comments are illusionary and negligent of the reality that groups of individuals may maintain clusters of opinions which are qualitatively different and perhaps in some instances incompatible. It is essential that we recognize this, for these diverse points of view influence to a large extent how people interact with the legal system, in terms of both their willingness to comply with the law and their recourse to legal institutions. More work needs to be done to characterize these bodies of opinion, these "ideas" about the law and the legal system that collections of people have, and to identify the psychological dimensions that underlie them.

APPENDIX: QUESTIONNAIRE AND OVERALL FINDINGS

PERCEPTION OF THE LAW AND THE LEGAL SYSTEM

The following report represents the percentage of respondents acknowledging a particular alternative for each item in the survey questionnaire. In the instance of questions where a scale was employed, the median and the mode are reported. (These statistics are indicated by an asterisk).

	Total Sample	Montreal	Toronto	Winnipeg
First, we would like to ask you some questions about the neighbourhood you live in.				
1. Some people think of themselves as being a part of a particular neighbourhood in the community, while others don't consider themselves part of such areas. Do you feel that you are . . .				
. . . a part of this neighbourhood or	70.28	80.31	63.28	64.07
. . . not a part of this neighbourhood	27.85	18.27	34.35	34.60
. . . don't know	1.87	1.42	2.37	1.33
2. How concerned are you that you, your family or your property could fall victim to a criminal act in this neighbourhood? Would you say . . .				
. . . very concerned	28.45	19.67	33.93	36.67
. . . somewhat concerned	17.65	15.86	18.29	21.41
. . . slightly concerned, or	26.19	28.31	25.60	21.05
. . . not at all concerned? (GO TO Q.4a)	27.24	36.16	21.21	20.88
. . . don't know (GO TO Q.4a)	0.47	0.00	0.97	0.00
3. What kinds of crimes are you concerned about happening in your neighbourhood? (CODE ALL MENTIONED)				
a. Arson	7.10	11.31	3.72	6.42
b. Assault	13.25	9.90	16.16	12.84
c. Auto theft	6.34	7.66	5.40	5.67
d. Breaking and entering	40.97	30.79	47.07	51.59
e. Fraud/forgery	1.04	2.52	0.00	0.16
f. Hit and run	2.62	4.36	1.16	2.64
g. Indecent acts	4.70	5.57	4.11	4.04
h. Murder or attempted murder	6.00	7.44	4.87	5.67
i. Purse snatching	7.85	11.27	5.71	4.63
j. Rape	17.73	7.87	24.12	25.98
k. Reckless driving	7.58	13.99	2.78	4.99
l. Thefts	32.01	35.29	30.62	26.15
m. Threats	1.41	3.14	0.00	1.22
n. Trespassing	3.14	6.11	0.40	4.20
o. Vandalism	24.22	20.26	22.93	44.19
p. Other (Specify) Drugs	0.99	0.81	0.89	2.07
Child Molesting	3.37	0.31	6.41	1.36

	Total Sample	Montreal	Toronto	Winnipeg
4a. Have you done anything in the past year to protect yourself, your family, and your property against crime?				
Yes	39.38	39.86	39.76	35.95
No (GO TO Q.5a)	59.71	60.14	58.46	63.56
No Answer	0.91	0.00	1.78	0.48
4b. What have you done? (CODE ALL MENTIONED)				
a. Acquired guard dog	1.88	0.98	2.17	3.88
b. Acquired a weapon	0.00	0.00	0.00	0.00
c. Identified property	2.46	3.89	0.94	3.78
d. Installed alarm	4.31	8.55	1.66	0.32
e. Increased/obtained insurance	11.15	17.43	6.58	8.07
f. Installed lighting-timer devices	2.92	3.94	2.36	1.57
g. Installed more/better locks	18.34	17.07	20.83	14.36
h. Reinforced windows/doors	8.94	7.58	10.99	5.00
i. Other (Specify) Locking doors	1.34	0.24	1.71	3.73
5a. During the past year have you or any person in your household been the victim of a crime?				
Yes	15.53	15.63	14.55	19.41
No (GO TO Q.8)	84.47	84.37	85.45	80.59
5b. How many times?				
1	8.65	10.27	7.37	8.27
2	3.42	2.78	3.13	7.07
3	0.38	0.47	0.31	0.33
Don't know	0.23	0.60	0.48	0.00
6. What kind(s) of crime was/were involved? (CODE ALL MENTIONED)				
a. Arson	0.10	0.24	0.00	0.00
b. Assault	0.45	0.93	0.00	0.62
c. Auto theft	0.39	0.16	0.00	2.89
d. Breaking and entering	4.72	5.09	4.89	2.67
e. Fraud/forgery	0.00	0.00	0.00	0.00
f. Hit and run	0.83	0.00	1.72	0.00
g. Indecent acts	0.31	0.00	0.31	1.47
h. Murder or attempted murder	0.00	0.00	0.00	0.00
i. Purse snatching	1.63	3.57	0.37	0.00
j. Rape	0.02	0.00	0.00	0.00
k. Reckless driving	0.00	0.00	0.00	0.00
l. Thefts	7.07	7.23	6.99	6.86
m. Threats	0.22	0.00	0.30	0.64
n. Trespassing	0.92	1.39	0.56	0.73
o. Vandalism	2.45	1.55	2.45	5.74
p. Other (Specify)				
7. Were the police contacted?				
. . . in all instances	80.18	80.51	82.26	72.49
. . . in some instances, or	3.70	5.39	0.00	10.77
. . . never?	16.00	14.10	17.74	15.91
. . . don't know	0.12	0.00	0.00	0.83

	Total Sample	Montreal	Toronto	Winnipeg
8. Do you avoid certain places and areas of the city because of the possibility of crimes or violence?				
Yes	47.32	44.75	45.04	66.48
No	51.72	53.97	54.14	33.10
Don't know	0.96	1.29	0.81	0.42
9. Compared to other cities in Canada, do you think the danger of becoming a victim of a crime or violence in (name of city) is . . .				
. . . lower . . . 1	16.64	9.41	19.42	31.06
. . . higher, or . . . 2	19.31	16.88	24.42	6.22
. . . about the same as other cities in Canada? . . . 3	58.50	67.89	50.89	56.93
. . . don't know . . . 8	5.55	5.82	5.27	5.79

Now I would like to ask you some background questions.

	Total Sample	Montreal	Toronto	Winnipeg
10. In what country were you born?				
Canada	68.22	79.68	57.96	70.92
England and Wales	3.08		3.91	5.95
France				
Germany				3.02
Greece				
Ireland			2.22	
Italy	4.88	2.86	7.69	
Netherlands				2.21
Poland	2.68		4.51	
Portugal			2.02	
Scotland	2.50	2.55	2.46	2.48
United States				
U.S.S.R.				
All Other (Specify) European	5.07		6.96	5.20
All Others	7.86	6.98	8.96	6.31
11. To what ethnic or cultural group did you or your ancestor (on the male side) belong on coming to this continent? (CIRCLE ONE RESPONSE ONLY)				
Austrian				
Chinese				
Czeck				
English	13.71	6.46	18.09	20.14
Finnish				
French	22.96	54.03		10.51
German	2.24			9.45
Hungarian			2.15	
Irish	6.00		9.45	5.51
Italian	12.87	9.26	18.39	
Japanese				
Jewish	3.38	3.43	3.92	
Native Indian				
Negro		2.68		
Netherlands				3.71
Polish	3.06		4.39	3.40

	Total Sample	Montreal	Toronto	Winnipeg
Russian				
Scandinavian				3.79
Scottish	8.69	4.93	11.75	8.65
Slovak				
Ukrainian	3.38		4.37	9.53
Welsh				
West Indian			2.64	
All Other (Specify) Europeans	7.59	5.12	9.62	7.46
Others	4.56	4.56	4.27	5.75
12. What is your religion? (CIRCLE ONE RESPONSE ONLY)				
No religion (GO TO Q. 14)	6.07		9.16	10.99
Anglican	10.36	5.11	13.41	16.27
Baptist			3.38	
Greek Orthodox				
Jewish	6.80	5.24	8.56	
Lutheran	2.93		4.26	6.77
Mennonite				2.40
Pentecostal				
Presbyterian			3.18	2.47
Roman Catholic	52.48	77.62	36.49	29.96
Salvation Army				
Ukrainian Catholic				2.32
United Church	9.62	5.41	11.55	16.64
All Other (Specify) Protestant	2.42		2.41	5.10
13. In the past year how often have you attended church services? Would you say . . .				
. . . more than once a week	6.77	6.46	6.59	8.78
. . . once a week	17.15	23.37	12.11	14.21
. . . two or three times a month	8.73	8.70	8.25	10.88
. . . once a month	9.45	9.33	9.54	9.54
. . . less than once a month, or	32.08	30.22	32.35	38.29
. . . not at all?	25.81	21.93	31.16	18.30
14. One hears a lot about different social classes. Do you ever think of yourself as belonging to a social class?				
Yes (GO TO Q. 16)	45.62	59.96	36.54	32.71
No	50.00	36.82	57.20	66.88
Don't know	4.38	3.22	6.26	0.41
15. If you had to make a choice, would you say you were in the . . .				
. . . upper class	0.30	0.00	0.48	0.25
. . . upper-middle class	7.63	14.66	8.51	3.51
. . . middle class	49.59	54.26	49.68	39.33
. . . working class, or	28.39	20.89	27.30	48.63
. . . lower class?	3.55	3.10	3.68	4.00
. . . won't say	2.62	1.99	2.93	2.73
. . . don't know	5.92	5.10	7.44	1.54

GO TO Q. 17

	Total Sample	Montreal	Toronto	Winnipeg
16. Which of the following five social classes would you say you were in . . .				
. . . upper class	1.87	2.45	0.79	3.28
. . . upper-middle class	16.39	17.10	16.57	10.65
. . . middle class	64.89	67.80	61.55	61.09
. . . working class, or	14.42	10.78	17.73	22.77
. . . lower class?	1.41	1.23	1.50	2.21
. . . won't say	0.19	0.35	0.00	0.00
. . . don't know	0.84	0.29	1.75	0.00

17. We would like to know how much effort you think government should put into a number of activities. Please choose the answer on the card which comes closest to your opinion about the effort that should be made in each of the areas I am going to mention. Remember that putting more effort into one of these areas would require a shift of money from other areas or an increase in taxes . . .

CODES: *

MUCH LESS EFFORT	LESS EFFORT	ABOUT THE SAME EFFORT	MORE EFFORT	MUCH MORE EFFORT	DON'T KNOW
1	2	3	4	5	8

	Total Sample	Montreal	Toronto	Winnipeg
. . . a. first of all, how much effort should be put into controlling inflation?	4.19, 4*	4.24, 4	4.13, 4	4.24, 4
. . . b. reform of our laws?	3.89, 4	3.98, 4	3.83, 4	3.87, 4
. . . c. dealing with unemployment?	4.10, 4	4.27, 5	4.00, 4	4.01, 4
. . . d. law enforcement?	3.81, 4	4.12, 4	3.46, 3	3.84, 4
. . . e. helping the poor?	3.84, 4	4.06, 5	3.66, 4	3.83, 4
. . . f. eliminating pornography?	3.50, 5	3.73, 5	3.34, 3	3.43, 3
. . . g. eliminating discrimination against women?	3.90, 4	3.98, 4	3.86, 4	3.80, 4
. . . h. crime prevention?	4.14, 4	4.39, 5	3.96, 4	4.01, 4
. . . i. health and medical care?	3.40, 3	3.73, 3	3.28, 3	3.27, 3
. . . j. supporting the business community?	3.11, 3	3.18, 3	3.06, 3	3.09, 3
. . . k. prison reform?	3.92, 4	4.17, 5	3.80, 4	3.49, 3

18. Now, I would like to talk to you about some opinions that you hear different people giving. As I read each one, I would like you to tell me whether you strongly disagree, disagree, agree or strongly agree with the statement . . .

CODES: *

STRONGLY DISAGREE	DIS-AGREE	AGREE	STRONGLY AGREE	NO OPINION
1	2	3	4	8

	Total Sample	Montreal	Toronto	Winnipeg
. . . a. generally, those elected to Parliament soon lose touch with the people	2.88, 3*	2.93, 3	2.83, 3	2.90, 3
. . . b. I don't think that the government cares much what people like me think	2.69, 3	2.87, 3	2.48, 2	2.75. 3
. . . c. sometimes politics and government seem so complicated that a person like me can't really understand what's going on	2.80, 3	2.73, 3	2.83, 3	2.86, 3

	Total Sample	Montreal	Toronto	Winnipeg
. . . d. people like me don't have any say about what the government does	2.60, 2	2.61, 3	2.57, 2	2.69, 3
. . . e. a few strong leaders would make this country better than all the laws and talk	2.64, 3	2.60, 3	2.65, 3	2.77, 3
19. Now some questions about you. Generally speaking, how happy would you say you are. Would you say . . .				
. . . not too happy	4.73	5.63	4.18	3.83
. . . fairly happy, or	50.20	51.97	49.50	46.79
. . . very happy?	44.64	42.40	45.63	48.54
. . . don't know	0.43	0.00	0.69	0.84
20. Generally speaking, would you say that most people can be trusted or that you can't be too careful in dealing with people?				
People can be trusted	47.59	37.23	54.91	53.81
One can't be too careful	51.05	62.62	42.82	44.39
Don't know	1.36	0.15	2.27	1.81
21. Would you say that most of the time people try to be helpful or that they are mostly just looking out for themselves?				
Try to be helpful	42.97	26.32	55.50	50.68
Look out for themselves	55.50	73.51	42.96	42.91
Don't know	1.52	0.17	1.54	6.40
22. Do you feel that most people would try to take advantage of you if they had the chance or would they try to be fair?				
Take advantage	39.75	44.61	37.07	33.48
Be fair	57.16	52.55	60.31	60.55
Don't know	3.09	2.84	2.62	5.97
23. Some people feel they can run their lives pretty much the way they want to, others feel the problems of life are sometimes too big for them. Which are you most like?				
Can run own life	84.61	84.87	83.47	88.61
Problems of life too big	12.68	13.16	13.05	9.33
Don't know	2.71	1.97	3.47	2.06

24. HAND R. CARD C

Here is a card that I want you to use to tell me how satisfied or dissatisfied you are with your life as a whole. If you are completely satisfied with it you would say "eleven" and if you are completely disatisfied with it you would say "one." If you are neither *completely* satisfied nor *completely* dissatisfied with your life as a whole you would put yourself somewhere from "two" to "ten." The higher the number, the more satisfied you are . . .

	Total Sample	Montreal	Toronto	Winnipeg
All things considered, how satisfied or dissatisfied are you with your life as a whole? Which number comes the closest to how you feel?				
Number	8.76, 9*	8.83, 10	8.78, 8	8,38, 8
25. I would now like to ask you some questions about your schooling. What is the highest level of education that you have completed?				
No schooling				
Did not complete grade school	8.00	12.71	4.42	6.28
Primary school (with Graduation/Certificate)	9.60	9.99	9.17	10.08
High School (no Graduation/Certificate)	19.16	15.19	21.37	24.09
High School (with Graduation/Certificate)	21.25	18.33	23.06	23.99
Technical training beyond secondary school	2.81	3.95		4.69
Some community college	5.09	6.62	4.98	
Community college (with diploma)	6.74	6.45	7.53	4.40
Some university	8.47	6.30	9.54	11.77
Bachelor's degree	11.09	13.60	9.61	8.37
Master's degree	2.37	2.40	2.76	
Professional degree or doctorate	5.42	4.46	6.14	5.78
Don't know				
26. What about your father — what is the highest level of education that he completed?				
No schooling	4.03	4.83	3.55	3.14
Did not complete grade school	20.72	27.45	14.61	22.75
Primary school (with Graduation/Certificate)	20.74	17.03	23.95	20.35
High School (no Graduation/Certificate)	9.52	9.32	9.55	10.13
High School (with Graduation/Certificate)	11.59	9.98	11.80	16.54
Technical training beyond secondary school	2.29	3.84		2.06
Some community college		2.03	2.03	
Community college (with diploma)	3.13	7.04		
Some university	2.59		3.94	3.25
Bachelor's degree	3.73	2.61	4.94	2.48
Master's degree			2.06	
Professional degree or doctorate	4.54	5.60	4.08	2.68
Don't know	13.62	7.93	17.87	15.95
27a. What was the main occupation of your father when you were growing up? (If father was deceased then ask, "What *was* your father's main lifetime occupation?")				
27b. In what sort of business or industry did he work?				
27c. Did he work . . .				
. . . in his own business . . . 1	31.66	34.87	27.05	39.73
. . . for the government, or . . . 2	15.98	16.55	13.56	24.22
. . . in a business he did not own? . . . 3	49.40	46.62	55.40	33.87
. . . don't know . . . 8	2.96		3.99	2.18

	Total Sample	Montreal	Toronto	Winnipeg
28. What about your mother — what is the highest level of education that she completed?				
No schooling	4.44	5.57	2.98	6.26
Did not complete grade school	19.66	23.93	16.12	19.45
Primary school (with Graduation/Certificate)	23.22	21.95	24.82	20.92
High School (no Graduation/Certificate)	-13.80	11.85	15.08	15.36
High School (with Graduation/Certificate)	14.41	11.39	17.55	11.78
Technical training beyond secondary school	3.65	3.61	3.55	4.20
Some community college				
Community college (with diploma)	4.10	8.81		2.82
Some university		2.28		2.47
Bachelor's degree	3.21	2.38	4.07	2.51
Master's degree				
Professional degree or doctorate				
Don't know	10.64	6.41	13.45	13.87

We would now like to ask you a few questions about your family situation.

	Total Sample	Montreal	Toronto	Winnipeg
29. Are you single, married, widowed, separated, divorced or living with someone?				
Single (GO TO Q. 32)	28.27	26.67	31.72	19.08
Married	53.93	53.24	52.06	64.54
Living with someone	4.46	3.33	5.53	3.95
Widowed	6.44	7.49	6.02	4.47
Separated	3.82	5.53	2.18	4.66
Divorced	3.08	3.74	2.48	3.29
30. What is (was) the highest level of education completed by your wife/husband/friend?				
No schooling				
Did not complete grade school	5.61	8.74	2.92	5.82
Primary school (with Graduation/Certificate)	8.29	9.81	6.88	8.92
High School (no Graduation/Certificate)	15.53	12.69	16.50	21.70
High School (with Graduation/Certificate)	18.48	17.16	18.87	21.60
Technical training beyond secondary school	3.03	3.99	1.49	6.24
Some community college			2.13	
Community college (with diploma)	2.46	3.46		2.66
Some university	3.82	4.79	3.16	3.16
Bachelor's degree	6.87	5.33	8.72	4.43
Master's degree				
Professional degree or doctorate	3.62	3.40	3.50	4.89
Don't know				
31a. What is (was) her (his) occupation?				
31b. In what sort of business does (did) she (he) work?				
31c. Does (did) she (he) work . . .				
. . . in her (his) own business	16.69	16.20	18.57	11.48
. . . for the government, or	19.93	22.26	15.15	24.21
. . . in a business she (he) did not own?	63.95	61.54	66.27	64.07
. . . don't know	0.03	0.00	0.00	0.24

	Total Sample	Montreal	Toronto	Winnipeg
Now I would like to ask you some questions about the work you do.				
32. Are you working at the present time, full time or part-time, self-employed, a student, retired, homemaker or something else?				
Self-employed	4.60	3.23	6.21	2.59
Employed full-time	55.87	51.04	60.09	55.22
Employed part-time	5.96	4.74	6.51	8.02
Laid-off temporarily				
Unemployed	1.49	1.42	1.56	1.39
Retired or permanently disabled	8.95	9.46	7.79	12.07
Student (GO TO Q. 35)	8.24	6.85	10.26	4.53
Homemaker (GO TO Q. 35)	14.90	23.26	7.57	16.81
33a. What is (was) your main occupation. What kind of work do (did) you do? (PROBE FOR EXACT JOB DESCRIPTION)				
33b. In what kind of organization, business or industry do (did) you work?				
33c. Do (did) you work . . .				
. . . in your own business	11.85	10.91	13.44	7.66
. . . for the government, or	19.50	22.64	15.65	26.81
. . . in a business you did not own?	68.65	66.44	70.91	65.52
. . . don't know				
34. Overall, how satisfied or dissatisfied are you with the job you have(had)? Give me a number from this card which best describes how you feel.				
Number	8.89, 10*	9.43, 10	8.70, 10	8.33, 10
35. What was *your* total income before taxes in 1979? Include your income from your job, family allowance, investment profits, interest on savings or mortgages, Canada Pension Plan, unemployment, and any other sources. Just give me the letter from this card.				
CODES:				
a. Nothing	6.43	6.60	6.27	6.50
b. $1 - $1,999	6.40	6.12	5.22	12.54
c. $2,000 - $3,999	9.31	13.33	6.01	9.09
d. $4,000 - $5,999	9.75	10.45	9.25	9.34
e. $6,000 - $7,999	3.44	2.83	3.60	4.91
f. $8,000 - $9,999	6.42	7.57	4.56	10.36
g. $10,000 - $11,999	8.00	8.05	8.05	7.58
h. $12,000 - $13,999	6.08	5.38	6.96	4.80
i. $14,000 - $15,999	10.04	8.64	11.27	9.78
j. $16,000 - $17,999	5.53	4.36	6.25	6.62
k. $18,000 - $19,999	4.53	2.62	5.99	5.17
l. $20,000 - $24,999	7.22	5.34	9.34	4.85
m. $25,000 - $29,999	5.41	7.08	4.88	

	Total Sample	Montreal	Toronto	Winnipeg
n. $30,000 - $39,999	4.41	5.19	3.97	3.46
o. $40,000 - $49,999	2.75		3.65	2.39
p. $50,000 - $74,999			2.11	
q. $75,000 - $99,999				
r. $100,000 and over				
Refused				

36. What was your total *family* income, including your own income, before taxes in 1979? Just give me a letter from the card.

	Total Sample	Montreal	Toronto	Winnipeg
a. Nothing				
b. $1 - $1,999				
c. $2,000 - $3,999	2.31	3.69		4.38
d. $4,000 - $5,999	3.55	4.14	3.07	3.48
e. $6,000 - $7,999	3.11	4.79		5.05
f. $8,000 - $9,999	4.14	5.56	2.48	6.19
g. $10,000 - $11,999	3.79	5.08	2.77	3.55
h. $12,000 - $13,999	4.85	6.81	3.27	4.53
i. $14,000 - $15,999	5.84	5.02	6.08	7.83
j. $16,000 - $17,999	5.50	6.01	4.20	9.24
k. $18,000 - $19,999	5.55	5.04	5.57	7.30
l. $20,000 - $24,999	13.89	11.18	15.41	17.19
m. $25,000 - $29,999	10.64	6.76	14.63	7.47
n. $30,000 - $39,999	14.11	14.61	14.80	9.29
o. $40,000 - $49,999	5.83	6.32	6.16	2.68
p. $50,000 - $74,999	5.75	4.36	7.23	4.46
q. $75,000 - $99,999	2.68	2.69	2.92	
r. $100,000 and over	7.23	7.42	7.56	5.14
. . . Don't know				

37. All things considered, how satisfied or dissatisfied are you with your present financial situation — your income, standard of living, debts, savings and so on?

	Total Sample	Montreal	Toronto	Winnipeg
Number	7.83, 9*	8.09, 9	7.56, 9	7.75, 8

38. Here is a series of statements about the way our economy works. Please choose the answer on this card which comes closest to your opinion about each one. If you have mixed feelings about a statement you should use the "neither agree nor disagree" answer. Use the "no opinion" answer if you really have no views on the statement at all . . .

CODES:
*

STRONGLY DISAGREE	DISAGREE	NEITHER AGREE NOR DISAGREE	AGREE	STRONGLY AGREE	DEPENDS	NO OPINION
1	2	3	4	5	6	8

	Total Sample	Montreal	Toronto	Winnipeg
. . . a. there is too much of a difference between rich and poor in this country	3.85, 4*	3.92, 4	3.75, 4	3.94, 4
. . . b. unemployment is high these days because it is too easy to get welfare assistance	3.84, 4	3.89, 4	3.76, 4	3.93, 4

	Total Sample	Montreal	Toronto	Winnipeg
. . . c. the government should provide jobs for Canadians who want to work but cannot find a job . . .	3.89, 4	4.07, 4	3.75, 4	3.84, 4
. . . d. people with high incomes should pay a greater share of the total taxes than they do now	3.45, 4	3.41, 4	3.51, 4	3.25, 4
. . . e. during a strike, management should be prohibited by law from hiring workers to take the place of strikers	3.59,4	3.65, 4	3.59, 4	2.76, 2
. . . f. union leaders and workers who fail to obey back-to-work legislation should be fined or jailed . . .	3.97, 4	4.13,4	3.85, 4	3.91, 4

39. Now I would like to ask you some questions about the law.

	Total Sample	Montreal	Toronto	Winnipeg
a. First of all, can a landlord *legally* seize the property of a tenant when the rent has not been paid?				
Yes	44.59	46.49	43.72	41.41
No	42.87	42.59	42.76	44.34
Don't know	12.54	10.39	13.52	14.25
b. Is it *against the law* to pay women less than men for similar work?				
Yes	67.66	64.59	74.10	50.99
No	27.00	29.16	22.65	38.01
Don't know	5.34	6.25	3.26	11.01
c. Can a husband *legally* disinherit his wife?				
Yes	32.31	48.32	20.89	23.54
No	54.28	42.00	63.06	60.85
Don't know	13.41	9.67	16.05	15.61
d. Before a policeman questions you, must he inform you that you have the right to remain silent?				
Yes	71.63	79.44	62.94	80.69
No	21.44	15.83	27.36	16.27
Don't know	6.93	4.73	9.69	3.04
e. Do the police need a warrant to search your house if they believe you possess illegal material?				
Yes	85.90	90.88	81.60	86.35
No	12.52	8.51	16.31	10.69
Don't know	1.58	0.61	2.09	2.96
f. Can you refuse to testify in court on the grounds that the evidence you give might incriminate you?				
Yes	56.02	60.72	52.85	52.55
No	28.64	23.95	31.88	31.74
Don't know	15.34	15.33	15.27	15.70

	Total Sample	Montreal	Toronto	Winnipeg
40. I am going to describe some events which require the actions of the authorities in dealing with suspected crime and violence. I would like you to comment on the seriousness of such actions using the answers on this card . . .				

CODES:
*

NOT SERIOUS AT ALL, SUCH ACTIONS ARE JUSTIFIED BY THE CIRCUMSTANCES	MILDLY SERIOUS	SERIOUS	VERY SERIOUS	EXTREMELY SERIOUS, SUCH ACTIONS ARE UNACCEPTABLE IN A DEMOCRATIC SOCIETY	DON'T KNOW
1	2	3	4	5	8

	Total Sample	Montreal	Toronto	Winnipeg
. . . a. Last summer, newspapers reported a series of controversial drug raids carried out by under-cover agents in Vancouver without first securing search warrants as required by law. The agents claimed they had to move quickly and that there was no time to request a warrant from a judge. How serious an abuse of government power would you say these raids were?				
Number	2.47, 1*	2.60, 1	2.43, 1	2.18, 1
. . . b. A recent newspaper article reported that a large group of persons who had travelled to Ottawa to protest the government's economic policies were denied permission by officials to parade and assemble in the area of the parliament buildings because of the possibility of violence. How serious do you think is the authority's denial of the group's right to protest?				
Number	2.53, 2	2.48, 3	2.65, 2	2.26, 2
. . . c. It has been reported in the press that custom officials have, for the past two years, been systematically censoring incoming material for certain political groups. Several groups have complained that it is almost impossible to obtain literature and pamphlets from outside the country. How serious a matter is the government's censorship in your opinion?				
Number	2.56, 2	2.51, 3	2.64, 2	2.53, 3
. . . d. It has been stated by the press that the RCMP has maintained illegal wiretaps on the telephones of about 60 persons in Quebec since the FLQ crisis of 1970. The police reportedly never sought court approval of the wiretaps and have denied their existence.				

	Total Sample	Montreal	Toronto	Winnipeg
How serious a matter would you say the illegal wiretaps are?				
Number	3.55, 4	3.51, 4	3.62, 4	3.41, 4

41. We have put into pairs a number of comments people have made about the law and the legal system. We would like you to tell us which one of the pair you agree with or think best represents the law as you see it. Here are the questions.

PLEASE CIRCLE THE NUMBER (1 or 2) BESIDE THE STATEMENT WHICH BEST REPRESENTS YOUR OPINION. THERE ARE NO RIGHT OR WRONG ANSWERS.

	Total Sample	Montreal	Toronto	Winnipeg
. . . a. Our laws give too much protection to criminals	41.63	32.66	48.59	44.44
We would have fewer problems if our laws were tougher	56.91	65.38	50.03	55.56
Don't know	1.46	1.96	1.38	0.00
. . . b. The law as a whole is fundamentally sound	54.90	54.14	58.15	43.25
Laws are frequently unjust	44.85	45.86	41.32	56.75
Don't know	0.25	0.00	0.53	0.00
. . . c. The legal system favours the rich and powerful	62.25	60.44	62.71	66.96
All people are equal before the law	37.21	39.56	36.19	33.04
Don't know	0.53	0.00	1.10	0.00
. . . d. Our system of laws is in touch with modern conditions	21.02	19.53	23.37	16.30
Something needs to be done to improve the way the legal system operates and the laws it produces	77.90	80.47	74.52	83.08
Don't know	1.08	0.00	2.10	0.62
. . . e. A person should obey only those laws which seem reasonable	13.21	13.47	13.49	11.00
Even though one might strongly disagree with a law, after it has become law, one ought to obey it	86.54	86.53	85.98	89.00
Don't know	0.25	0.00	0.53	0.00
. . . f. The law works as efficiently as possible to deal with people's problems	38.56	43.83	34.92	34.81
It takes too long to get anything done through the process of law	60.53	56.17	63.18	65.19
Don't know	0.90	0.00	1.89	0.00
. . . g. Laws are passed for the benefit of those few people who make and enforce them	27.32	33.44	23.21	22.57
The laws in this country generally stand for what the majority of people want	71.71	66.12	75.15	77.43
Don't know	0.97	0.45	1.64	0.00

	Total Sample	Montreal	Toronto	Winnipeg
. . . h. It is all right to break the law as long as you don't get caught	6.79	7.29	6.30	7.11
I must always obey the law	93.21	92.71	93.70	92.89
Don't know	0.00	0.00	0.00	0.00
. . . i. Laws are obeyed to avoid punishment	36.42	41.20	34.13	28.60
People obey the law because they believe it to be right	63.23	58.80	65.15	71.40
Don't know	0.34	0.00	0.72	0.00
. . . j. Most people obey the law	54.71	44.81	63.09	55.07
I see people breaking the law every day	45.16	54.88	36.91	44.93
Don't know	0.13	0.31	0.00	0.00
. . . k. There are situations when it is right not to obey the law	46.86	38.57	52.89	51.79
Disobedience of the law can never be tolerated	52.20	59.77	46.57	48.21
Don't know	0.94	1.66	0.54	0.00
. . . l. People have more respect for the law today than ever before	15.5	16.5	14.8	15.0
There is less respect for the law today than there was five years ago	82.7	81.3	82.5	84.5
Don't know	1.8	2.2	2.6	0.5

Now, we would like to ask you some questions concerning the police.

2. Do you think more money should be spent on strengthening police forces to crack down on crime or should more money be spent on trying to improve the economic and social conditions underlying social problems?

	Total Sample	Montreal	Toronto	Winnipeg
More money to strengthen police	23.34	8.54	36.81	18.72
More money to improve economic and social conditions	53.87	55.38	52.82	52.94
Both	21.02	33.03	9.77	26.08
Don't know	1.77	3.04	0.60	2.26

3. Do you think that the police are generally too easy, too harsh, or about right in dealing with people who are suspected of breaking the law?

	Total Sample	Montreal	Toronto	Winnipeg
Too easy	14.16	14.12	12.53	21.21
Too harsh	14.79	13.31	15.83	15.78
About right	65.03	65.28	67.00	55.77
Don't know	6.02	7.29	4.64	7.25

4a. Do you think there are any groups in Canada who receive more *favourable* treatment from the police, who are treated *better* than the rest of society?

	Total Sample	Montreal	Toronto	Winnipeg
Yes	54.04	55.31	52.56	55.82
No (GO TO Q.45a)	38.22	37.51	39.50	35.18
Don't know (GO TO Q.45a)	7.74	7.18	7.93	9.00

	Total Sample	Montreal	Toronto	Winnipeg
44b. Which groups are these?				
1) Rich, Wealthy	43.49	46.18	38.07	55.97
2) Influential People	9.30	7.80	11.92	3.99
3) Upper Class	5.83	3.57	6.74	10.27
4) Whites	6.66	1.91	11.82	2.68
5) Politicians	6.07	6.59	5.97	4.62
45a. Do you think there are any groups in Canada who receive more *unfavourable* treatment from the police, who are treated *worse* than the rest of society?				
Yes	51.39	55.96	45.70	59.36
No (GO TO Q.46)	40.76	35.15	47.19	28.84
Don't know (GO TO Q.46)	8.36	8.89	7.11	11.80
45b. Which groups are these?				
1) Blacks	18.51	10.13	32.26	1.89
2) Poor, Underprivileged	16.51	24.16	8.19	17.78
3) Young	9.22	10.36	8.99	6.12
4) Criminals	8.48	15.65	2.68	3.11
5) Native Indians	6.99	0.55	3.28	41.16

46. Here are a number of comments people have made about the police in (name of city). Please choose the answer on this card which comes closest to your opinion about each one. If you have mixed feelings about a statement you should use the "neither agree nor disagree" answer. Use the "no opinion" answer if you really have no views on the statement at all.

CODES:
*

STRONGLY DISAGREE	DISAGREE	NEITHER AGREE NOR DISAGREE	AGREE	STRONGLY AGREE	DEPENDS	NO OPINION
1	2	3	4	5	7	8

	Total Sample	Montreal	Toronto	Winnipeg
. . . a. the police spend too much time on duties not directly concerned with law enforcement	3.26, 4*	3.72, 4	2.56, 2	2.99,2
. . . b. the police are more interested in making arrests than in preventing crime	3.30, 4	3.77, 4	2.45, 2	2.48, 2
. . . c. the police are as concerned about crimes against the ordinary person as those against business	3.70, 4	3.41, 4	3.82, 4	3.77, 4
. . . d. when the police do something wrong they do a good job of investigating and correcting the problem themselves	3.51, 4	3.28, 4	3.62, 4	3.01, 4
. . . e. we need more police	3.73, 4	3.68, 4	3.73, 4	3.92, 4
. . . f. the police don't do a very good job of informing the public about police roles and objectives	3.75, 4	3.81, 4	3.70, 4	3.71, 4

	Total Sample	Montreal	Toronto	Winnipeg
47. Do you think the police should have the right . . .				

CODES:
*

NEVER	UNDER VERY FEW CIRCUMSTANCES	UNDER MOST CIRCUMSTANCES	UNDER ANY CIRCUMSTANCES	DON'T KNOW
1	2	3	4	8

	Total Sample	Montreal	Toronto	Winnipeg
. . . a. to require a person to answer questions about what they are doing, where they have been or where they are going? Would you say never, under very few circumstances, under most circumstances or under any circumstances?	2.15, 2*	2.04, 2	2.18, 2	2.42, 2
. . . b. to search a person and his property?	1.90, 2	1.73, 2	1.99, 2	2.02, 2
. . . c. to tap telephones?	1.65, 2	1.49, 1	1.77, 2	1.65, 2
. . . d. to open the mail?	1.37, 1	1.27, 1	1.49, 1	1.33, 1
. . . e. to deny groups permission to protest?	1.81, 2	1.82, 2	1.79, 2	1.87, 2
. . . f. to use physical force?	1.81, 2	1.66, 2	1.94, 2	1.74, 2

48. Various accusations have been made about the behaviour of the police. Using this card I'd like you to tell me whether you think some of these accusations are true or untrue of the police in (name of city) . . .

CODES:
*

ALMOST NEVER	OCCASIONALLY	FREQUENTLY	VERY FREQUENTLY	DON'T KNOW
1	2	3	4	5

	Total Sample	Montreal	Toronto	Winnipeg
. . . a. do you think the police take bribes almost never, occasionally, frequently or very frequently?	1.80, 2*	2.05, 2	1.57, 1	1.67, 2
. . . b. use more physical force than is necessary?	2.05, 2	2.23, 2	1.87, 2	2.03, 2
. . . c. employ illegal methods in getting information?	2.14, 2	2.24, 2	2.07, 2	2.09, 2
. . . d. keep suspects in jail for excessive periods?	2.04, 2	2.17, 2	1.93, 2	2.15, 2
. . . e. twist or make up evidence to convict suspects?	1.70, 1	1.73, 1	1.69, 2	1.61, 1
. . . f. cover up illegal police activity?	2.07, 2	2.07, 2	2.05, 2	2.15, 2

I would now like to ask you some questions about your experiences with the police.

49a. Has there been any occasion in the past year when you, or a member of your household had contact with the police?

	Total Sample	Montreal	Toronto	Winnipeg
Yes	47.54	38.33	53.85	53.71
No (GO TO Q.50)	52.46	61.67	46.15	46.29

49b. On the most recent occasion, what was the nature of the contact?

	Total Sample	Montreal	Toronto	Winnipeg
Traffic Offences	20.83	12.72	24.62	25.10
Auto Accidents	12.26	9.65	15.35	5.53
Theft from homes	9.49	11.66	8.61	7.76

	Total Sample	Montreal	Toronto	Winnipeg
Other Thefts	8.93	17.49	4.56	6.07
Physical Assault	3.68	4.09	3.04	5.42
50. Generally speaking, how did you feel about your *most recent* experience with the police? Was your reaction favourable or unfavourable?				
Favourable	65.30	51.17	76.83	63.25
Neither favourable nor unfavourable	9.24	18.30	2.02	9.84
Unfavourable	18.12	17.58	17.88	20.99
Don't know	7.34	12.96	3.27	5.92
51. Over the last 5 years do you think that relations between the public and the police have . . .				
. . . become worse	36.65	19.84	51.76	32.46
. . . remained the same, or	36.77	46.82	27.33	41.07
. . . become better?	18.74	24.86	14.39	15.26
. . . don't know	7.84	8.48	6.53	11.21
52. Do you believe the police deserve more respect from the public, about the same as they have now or do they deserve less respect?				
Less respect . . . 1	4.75	5.22	4.47	4.26
About the same as they have now . . . 2	45.11	56.75	37.53	35.56
More respect . . . 3	48.42	36.23	56.75	56.73
Don't know . . . 8	1.73	1.80	1.26	3.45
53. All things considered, how satisfied or dissatisfied are you with the job the (name of city) police are doing?				
Number	7.77, 8*	6.97, 6	8.33, 8	7.53, 8
54. Here are some questions we would like you to answer on your own. Please read the questions and circle the number of your answer to each. When you finish, please fold the paper and place it in this envelope. Your answers will be kept completely confidential so please answer freely. The information will be compiled as group answers. No individual responses will ever be used for any purpose.				
54a. During the past year have you been charged with any offence(s) against the law? Do *NOT* include speeding, going through a light or other minor traffic offences. *DO* include impaired driving and driving without a license.				
Yes	3.29	3.48	3.07	3.54
No (GO TO Q. 56)	96.71	96.52	96.93	76.46
54b. In one or two words, what was the nature of the offence(s)?				
55. As the result of any charge against you, have you been on probation?				
Never	78.67	64.98	100.00	46.92
Once or twice	18.54	35.02	0.00	25.87
Between three and five times	1.05	0.00	0.00	10.24
Six to ten times	1.74	0.00	0.00	16.97
More often				

56. Have you ever had to pay a fine? (excluding parking tickets and minor offences)?

	Total Sample	Montreal	Toronto	Winnipeg
Never	85.54	88.23	85.39	76.24
Once or twice	11.70	7.84	13.47	18.29
Between three and five times	2.19	3.28	1.14	2.75
Six to ten times	0.23	0.00	0.00	2.07
More often	0.34	0.66	0.00	0.65

57. How often have you been sentenced to a term of imprisonment of some form?

	Total Sample	Montreal	Toronto	Winnipeg
Never	97.19	98.67	96.20	96.07
Once or twice	2.70	1.33	3.80	2.91
Between three and five times	0.00	0.00	0.00	0.00
Six to ten times	0.00	0.00	0.00	0.00
More often	0.11	0.00	0.00	1.02

*

NEVER	ONCE OR TWICE	BETWEEN 3-5 TIMES	6-10 TIMES	MORE THAN 10 TIMES
1	2	3	4	5

						Total Sample	Montreal	Toronto	Winnipeg
58a. Have you ever consumed alcohol in violation of the law?	1	2	3	4	5	1.21,1*	1.08, 1	1.33, 1	1.42, 1
b. Have you ever used illegal drugs?	1	2	3	4	5	1.15, 1	1.08, 1	1.22, 1	1.18, 1
c. Have you ever omitted or reported items incorrectly on your income tax to lower your taxes?	1	2	3	4	5	1.04, 1	1.04, 1	1.04, 1	1.04, 1
d. Have you ever given false information when applying for work, any kind of license, bonus, relief, etc.?	1	2	3	4	5	1.04, 1	1,04, 1	1.05, 1	1.05, 1
e. Have you ever taken anything from a store without paying for it?	1	2	3	4	5	1.14, 1	1,10, 1	1.17, 1	1.21, 1
f. Have you ever taken anything from your place of employment without paying for it?	1	2	3	4	5	1.17, 1	1.11, 1	1.23, 1	1.17, 1

Now I would like to ask you some questions about lawyers.

59. About how much do you think a lawyer would charge the average person to advise and represent them, if they were buying a house?

$ ______________________________

60a. Have you ever used a lawyer?

	Total Sample	Montreal	Toronto	Winnipeg
Yes	67.37	69.82	63.16	76.71
No (GO TO Q. 68)	32.63	30.18	36.84	23.29

	Total Sample	Montreal	Toronto	Winnipeg
60b. Please think about the first time you consulted with a lawyer. How did you find that particular lawyer?				
Advertisement	10.19	15.30	6.36	6.89
Business acquaintance	21.89	20.05	20.53	28.88
Family recommended	39.00	30.60	48.48	33.03
Friend recommended				
Lawyer's directory				
Legal aid/assistance				
Real estate agent/bank manager recommended	11.48	13.53	8.28	16.10
Reputation				
Service club/organization member				
Sign at lawyer's office				
Telephone book				
Other (Specify)				
Don't know				
61. Do you have a lawyer whom you use on a regular basis?				
Yes	38.57	33.29	43.58	38.25
No	61.43	66.71	56.42	61.75
Don't know	0.00	0.00	0.00	0.00
62. How many times have you used a lawyer's services?				
Once or twice	50.69	52.62	49.67	47.90
Between three and five times	28.43	27.31	30.41	25.12
Six to ten times	10.25	11.47	7.49	16.05
More than ten times	10.63	8.60	12.43	10.93
63. For what reasons did you require those services? (CODE ALL MENTIONED)				
a. To purchase or sell a house	39.60	36.22	37.91	59.30
b. To deal with a problem concerning my business, or employment	11.90	10.64	13.54	9.39
c. To deal with an accident or incident involving injury or damage to property	10.38	13.72	7.73	9.69
d. To act on my behalf when I was charged with a criminal offence	2.78	3.13	1.73	6.04
e. To deal with a family matter (separation, divorce, child custody and support, juvenile delinquency)	8.25	7.52	8.66	9.13
f. To draw up a will or set up a trust	21.62	25.44	18.42	21.56
g. To settle an estate	8.61	12.29	5.70	7.85
h. Other (Specify)				
Marriage contract	22.36	43.76	0.00	0.00
Property	6.64	2.90	8.85	22.44
Tenant-Landlord	5.84	5.23	7.39	0.00
Inheritance	3.34	1.61	5.89	0.00
Purchase of goods	3.60	4.56	1.49	10.32
Traffic offence	7.25	0.00	15.13	12.67
64. Have you ever changed lawyers because you were dissatisfied with the services you were getting?				
Yes	18.80	16.54	23.11	11.03
No	81.20	83.46	76.89	88.97

	Total Sample	Montreal	Toronto	Winnipeg
65. Based on your most recent experience, I want to rate your lawyer on each of the following characteristics. Make your rating on the basis of your own personal experience with him (her) and the services he (she) provided for you . . .				

CODES:
*

POOR	FAIR	GOOD	VERY GOOD	EXCELLENT	DON'T KNOW
1	2	3	4	5	8

	Total Sample	Montreal	Toronto	Winnipeg
. . . a. what about promptness in taking care of matters? Would you rate your lawyer poor, fair, good, very good or excellent?	3.62, 4*	3.79, 4	3.49, 4	3.56, 4
. . . b. what about interest and concern about your problem?	3.56, 4	3.62, 4	3.55, 4	3.41, 3
. . . c. honesty in dealing with you?	3.95, 5	4.05, 4	3.90, 4	3.86, 4
. . . d. explaining matters fully to you?	3.87, 4	3.86, 4	3.91, 4	3.76, 4
. . . e. keeping you informed of progress?	3.56, 4	3.65, 4	3.56, 4	3.30, 3
. . . f. paying attention to what you had to say?	3.81, 4	3.96, 5	3.74, 4	3.62, 3
66. Did you feel the fee was reasonable in relation to the amount of work he(she) had to do in connection with this matter, or do you think it should have been lower or higher?				
Should have been lower	26.31	28.09	25.87	22.06
Was reasonable	66.10	66.24	63.73	74.20
Should have been higher	5.44	3.13	8.86	0.61
Don't know	2.15	2.53	1.54	3.12
67. All things considered, how satisfied or dissatisfied are you with the lawyer(s) you have had contact with?				
Number	8.89,11*	8.66,11	9.08, 11	8.79, 10
68. Do you think the legal profession in the community is doing its best towards making legal services available to all who may need them regardless of their economic status, race, religion, or position in life?				
Yes	55.63	62.18	51.20	51.20
No	34.57	31.31	37.67	32.81
Don't know	9.81	6.51	11.13	15.99
69. Do you think lawyers and the legal profession in general do enough to inform the public of how the legal process works and the legal services available?				
Yes	29.41	32.22	28.47	23.33
No	63.83	62.12	65.70	61.96
Don't know	6.76	5.67	5.83	14.71

	Total Sample	Montreal	Toronto	Winnipeg
70. Would you be in favour of allowing lawyers to advertise their services and the fees they charge? Would you favour . . .				
. . . unrestricted advertising	33.06	30.18	31.07	52.13
. . . limited advertising, or	50.46	50.42	52.32	42.54
. . . no advertising?	12.73	16.75	11.78	2.18
. . . don't know	3.75	2.65	4.82	3.15

71. The statements below are comments people have made about lawyers. Please choose the answer on this card which comes closest to your opinion about each one. If you have mixed feelings about a statement you should use the "neither agree nor disagree" answer. Use the "no opinion" answer if you really have no views on the statement of all . . .

CODES:
*

STRONGLY DISAGREE	DISAGREE	NEITHER AGREE NOR DISAGREE	AGREE	STRONGLY AGREE	DEPENDS	NO OPINION
1	2	3	4	5	7	8

	Total Sample	Montreal	Toronto	Winnipeg
. . . a. higher paid lawyers get better results for their clients	3.61, 4*	3.51, 4	3.71, 4	3.50, 4
. . . b. lawyers are always finding loop-holes to get around the law	3.84, 4	3.71, 4	3.93, 4	3.92, 4
. . . c. lawyers get too many guilty people off	3.72, 4	3.79, 4	3.68, 4	3.65, 4
. . . d. we have to use lawyers more often than is really necessary	3.54, 4	2.88, 2	3.69, 4	3.53, 4
. . . e. lawyers will use only honest methods to help their clients	2.44, 2	2.63, 2	2.34, 2	2.40, 2
. . . f. lawyers are not concerned about doing anything about the "crooks" in the legal profession	3.24, 4	3.42, 4	3.16, 4	2.21, 2
. . . g. lawyers will work as hard for poor clients as for clients who are rich	2.25, 2	2.20, 2	2.29, 2	2.34, 2
. . . h. lawyers charge too much for their services	3.78, 4	3.78, 4	3.81, 4	3.54, 4

The following questions concern the courts.

	Total Sample	Montreal	Toronto	Winnipeg
72. How often have you been in a courtroom?				
Never (GO TO Q.74)	38.17	38.15	37.48	41.26
Once or twice	39.00	38.14	40.08	37.44
Between three and five times	13.13	12.96	14.47	7.92
Six to ten times	4.32	4.91	3.25	6.75
More than ten times	5.39	5.84	4.72	6.63
73. On those occasions, why were you in court? (CODE ALL MENTIONED)				
a. As an accused person in a civil case	5.86	8.01	4.23	5.07
b. As an accused person in a criminal case	3.32	1.75	3.66	7.56
c. As a juror	1.98	2.61	1.31	2.59
d. As a lawyer or judge	1.24	1.54	1.07	0.88

	Total Sample	Montreal	Toronto	Winnipeg
e. As a spectator/on a tour	19.99	17.22	21.70	22.59
f. As a witness	21.64	25.90	17.93	22.16
g. To sue someone	7.12	9.82	5.66	3.55
h. Other (Specify)				
Traffic offence	51.31	16.60	69.83	32.65
Divorce/Separation	19.82	37.42	10.19	31.32
Pay a fine	1.47	0.00	1.16	9.72
Work related	5.70	13.77	1.08	12.64
Citizenship	2.73	5.44	1.03	6.23

HAND R. CARD E

74. I am going to read some statements that people have made about the courts and judges. Please choose the answer on this card which comes closest to your opinion about each one. If you have mixed feelings about a statement you should use the "neither agree nor disagree" answer. Use the "no opinion" answer if you really have no views on the subject at all . . .

CODES:
*

STRONGLY DISAGREE	DISAGREE	NEITHER AGREE NOR DISAGREE	AGREE	STRONGLY AGREE	DEPENDS	NO OPINION
1	2	3	4	5	7	8

	Total Sample	Montreal	Toronto	Winnipeg
. . . a. if a person has enough money, almost anything can be arranged in court	3.57, 4*	3.68, 4	3.50, 4	3.10, 2
. . . b. the courts take too long to deal with cases	4.14, 4	4.12, 4	4.18, 4	4.08, 4
. . . c. the individual does not have a chance in court against big business	3.64, 4	3.64, 4	3.64, 4	3.61, 4
. . . d. it is a common occurrence for a guilty person not to be convicted in Canadian courts	3.15, 4	3.68, 4	2.44, 2	2.77, 2
. . . e. judges are appointed on the basis of their ability to administer the law, not because they support the political party in power	3.67, 4	3.44, 4	3.80, 4	3.67, 4
. . . f. trials would be more effective if the courtroom, the dress of judges and lawyers, and the proceedings were less formal	2.69, 2	3.51, 4	2.39, 2	2.37, 2
. . . g. taking someone to court is too expensive for most people	4.04, 4	4.04, 4	4.04, 4	4.05, 4
. . . h. court decisions are often influenced by political considerations	3.20, 4	3.56, 4	2.85, 2	3.15, 4

75. In general, do you feel that judges should . . .

	Total Sample	Montreal	Toronto	Winnipeg
. . . be required to give the same sentence for a particular crime, regardless of the circumstances of the case	11.17	9.48	13.44	7.63
. . . have *limited power* to make sentences "tougher" or "lighter" depending on the circumstances of the case, or	43.87	39.17	47.13	47.09
. . . have a *great deal of power* to make sentences "tougher" or "lighter" depending on the circumstances of the case?	38.92	43.78	35.10	37.51
. . . don't know	6.04	7.57	4.34	7.76

	Total Sample	Montreal	Toronto	Winnipeg
76. In general, do you think sentences *should* be "tougher," "lighter," or stay about the same as they are now?				
Tougher	56.84	54.70	55.97	68.29
Stay the same as now	30.68	30.98	31.73	25.15
Lighter	3.69	3.07	4.69	1.74
Don't know	8.79	11.25	7.62	4.83
77a. Do you think that the courts treat some groups of people better than others				
Yes	53.44	50.90	55.11	55.41
No (GO TO Q.78a)	34.92	35.45	35.95	28.57
Don't know (GO TO Q.78a)	11.64	13.65	8.94	16.02
77b. Which groups of people do you think are treated better?				
Rich wealthy	48.12	59.78	37.00	57.26
Influential people	9.81	9.30	11.12	5.78
Upper class	8.00	2.94	11.65	9.26
78a. Do you think that the courts treat some groups of people worse than others?				
Yes	47.73	48.91	46.88	47.12
No (GO TO Q.79)	41.52	40.27	44.56	32.85
Don't know (GO TO Q.79)	10.75	10.81	8.56	20.04
78b. Which groups of people do you think are treated worse?				
Poor underprivileged	41.05	53.79	33.16	26.47
Lower class	6.73	2.98	8.65	12.76
Criminals	5.07	7.69	3.39	2.26

79. Here are some comments people have made about sentencing. Please choose the answer on this card which comes closest to your opinion about each one. If you have mixed feelings about a statement you should use the "neither agree nor disagree" answer. Use the "no opinion" answer if you really have no views on the statement at all . . .

*

STRONGLY DISAGREE	DISAGREE	NEITHER AGREE NOR DISAGREE	AGREE	STRONGLY AGREE	DEPENDS	NO OPINION
1	2	3	4	5	7	8

	Total Sample	Montreal	Toronto	Winnipeg
. . . a. people should be sent to prison *only* after every other alternative has been tried	3.71, 4*	3.81, 4	3.66, 4	3.10, 4
. . . b. if judges would give longer sentences, fewer convicted criminals would break the law again	3.61, 4	3.64, 4	3.61, 4	3.53, 4
. . . c. if people knew they would be physically punished, there would be far less crime	3.74, 4	3.78, 4	3.69, 4	3.81, 4
. . . d. the threat of punishment does little to prevent crime in our society	3.74, 4	3.79, 4	3.69, 4	3.77, 4

	Total Sample	Montreal	Toronto	Winnipeg
80. Do you favour or oppose capital punishment for the killing of a prison guard or an on-duty policeman?				
Favour (GO TO Q.82)	68.14	63.66	71.32	70.54
Oppose	28.12	31.53	25.95	25.16
Don't know	3.74	4.80	2.73	4.30
81. Are there *any* crimes for which you would be in favour of bringing back the death penalty?				
Yes	27.81	30.89	26.49	19.52
No (GO TO Q. 83a)	66.75	63.03	69.87	70.35
Don't know (GO TO Q. 83a)	5.44	6.08	3.64	10.12

82. Would you favour capital punishment for the crime of . . .

*	Favour	Oppose	No Opinion	Total Sample	Montreal	Toronto	Winnipeg
	1	2	8				
. . . a. pre-planned murder?	1	2	8	1.04, 1*	1.02, 1	1.07, 1	1.02, 1
. . . b. murder in the course of a crime such as robbery or arson?	1	2	8	1.22, 1	1.14, 1	1.29, 1	1.27, 1
. . . c. murder resulting from sex offenses?	1	2	8	1.11, 1	1.08, 1	1.15, 1	1.07, 1
. . . d. murder resulting from an argument?	1	2	8	1.86, 2	1.87, 2	1.87, 2	1.76, 2
. . . e. anything else? (Specify)	1	2	8				

Now I'd like to ask you a few questions about prisons.

83a. HAND R. CARD J

First, here is a card listing four of the things that prisons do. Which of these four do you think should be the most important job of the prison system . . .

	Total Sample	Montreal	Toronto	Winnipeg
. . . to protect society from criminals	36.65	39.18	33.30	41.59
. . . to discourage others from crime	9.06	11.07	7.87	6.78
. . . to rehabilitate the criminal, or	37.79	32.28	42.30	38.81
. . . to punish the criminal?	15.72	17.47	14.94	12.66
. . . don't know	0.78	0.00	1.59	0.16

83b. Which should be the second most important job . . .

	Total Sample	Montreal	Toronto	Winnipeg
. . . to protect society from criminals	28.57	29.94	27.26	29.18
. . . to discourage others from crime	29.03	24.11	33.54	27.76
. . . to rehabilitate the criminal, or	22.01	25.83	18.24	24.10
. . . to punish the criminal?	19.62	20.13	19.37	18.80
. . . don't know	0.78	0.00	1.59	0.16

	Total Sample	Montreal	Toronto	Winnipeg
83c. Which should be the *least* important job . . .				
. . . to protect society from criminals	10.35	11.91	8.72	11.50
. . . to discourage others from crime	31.45	33.83	29.53	30.81
. . . to rehabilitate the criminal, or	16.62	17.03	16.08	17.40
. . . to punish the criminal?	38.58	37.23	39.67	38.96
. . . don't know	3.00	0.00	6.01	1.34
84a. Are there other things you think prisons should be doing?				
Yes	31.41	12.71	47.63	30.38
No (GO TO Q.85)	67.40	86.83	50.40	69.10
Don't know	1.19	0.46	1.97	0.52
84b. What kinds of things?				
Prisoners should work to repay society	31.17	12.43	36.73	22.15
Teach skills, educate	17.05	10.26	18.27	19.11
Improve conditions	11.00	5.18	12.95	6.77
Should be harsher, too much freedom	10.24	7.17	8.49	26.38
Help adjust when they leave	10.17	10.75	10.72	5.63

85. Using this card would you tell me how good a job the prisons are doing? First of all, how good a job are they doing . . .

* CODES:

POOR	FAIR	GOOD	VERY GOOD	EXCELLENT	DON'T KNOW
1	2	3	4	5	8

	Total Sample	Montreal	Toronto	Winnipeg
. . . a. in protecting society from criminals? Would you say a poor job, fair, good, very good or excellent?	2.27, 2*	2.35, 2	2.18, 2	2.47, 2
. . . b. how good a job are they doing in discouraging others from crime?	1.78, 1	1.88, 1	1.72, 2	1.77, 2
. . . c. how about rehabilitating the criminal?	1.77, 2	1.81, 1	1.72, 2	1.84, 2
. . . d. and how about in punishing the criminal?	2.23, 2	2.48, 2	2.10, 2	1.94, 2
86. Some people say that prisons are too luxurious, that too much is done to make them pleasant places for people who don't deserve it. Do you . . .				
. . . agree, or	45.91	40.21	49.64	50.65
. . . disagree?	41.67	45.01	40.89	32.94
. . . don't know	12.42	14.78	9.48	16.41
87. Some people also say that prison guards are brutal and violent and this makes it difficult for prisons to successfully rehabilitate criminals. Do you . . .				
. . . agree, or	34.28	36.61	35.09	22.42
. . . disagree?	42.87	40.28	44.33	46.07
. . . don't know	22.84	23.11	20.58	31.51

	Total Sample	Montreal	Toronto	Winnipeg
88. Some people say that young offenders should only be sent to prison as a last resort because the prison experience makes them more likely to commit more crimes. Do you . . .				
. . . agree, or	70.71	77.56	64.00	74.60
. . . disagree?	24.20	18.70	29.97	19.43
. . . don't know	5.09	3.74	6.03	5.97
89. Some people say that corporal punishment and solitary confinement should be used more frequently. Do you . . .				
. . . agree, or	36.61	35.50	35.80	44.10
. . . disagree?	53.71	58.14	54.59	33.85
. . . don't know	9.68	6.37	9.61	22.05

90a. A lot of different reasons have been given for crime and violence. We would like your opinion on how important some of these are. Using the seven point scale on the card, please tell me how important or unimportant you think each reason is, as a cause of crime and violence. If you think it is very important you would say "seven" and if you think it is not important at all you would say "one." If you think it is neither very important or very unimportant you would put yourself somewhere from "two" to "six" . . .

CODES:
*

NOT IMPORTANT AT ALL						VERY IMPORTANT	NOT SURE
1	2	3	4	5	6	7	8

	Total Sample	Montreal	Toronto	Winnipeg
. . . a. where would you place general breakdown in respect for law and order?	5.11, 4*	5.18, 7	5.05, 5	5.14, 4
. . . b. increase in organized crime?	5.85, 7	6.23, 7	5.46, 7	5.67, 7
. . . c. use of alcohol, drugs, dope?	6.33, 7	6.49, 7	6.11, 7	6.45, 7
. . . d. the courts are too lenient?	4.77, 4	4.76, 4	4.64, 4	5.27, 7
. . . e. general lack of religious training?	3.73, 4	3.83, 4	3.65, 4	3.77, 4
. . . f. unequal distribution of wealth?	4.30, 4	4.57, 4	4.10, 4	4.41, 5
. . . g. high prices, cost of living, inflation, unemployment?	5.49, 7	5.74, 7	5.28, 7	5.35, 7
. . . h. lack of meaningful work, boring, dead-end jobs?	4.62, 5	5.03, 7	4.18, 3	5.50, 6
. . . i. desire for excitement, kicks, rebellion?	4.52, 4	4.56, 5	4.41, 4	4.87, 4
. . . j. breakdown of family?	5.43, 7	5.48, 7	5.42, 7	5.29, 7
. . . k. lack of discipline in school and home?	5.78, 7	5.76, 7	5.79, 7	5.84, 7
. . . l. lack of tough law enforcement by police?	4.59, 4	4.88, 4	4.32, 5	4.74, 4
. . . m. violence on TV and in films, in the news coverage of crime, riots, terrorism?	5.37, 7	6.12, 7	4.77, 7	4.55, 4

	Total Sample	Montreal	Toronto	Winnipeg
91. We would like to know how involved you have been in politics and in your community. Could you tell me how often you have done each of the following things *in the past five years:* never, once or twice, three to five times, or more than five times. How often have you . . .				

* CODES:

NEVER	ONCE OR TWICE	BETWEEN 3-5 TIMES	MORE THAN 5 TIMES
1	2	3	4

	Total Sample	Montreal	Toronto	Winnipeg
. . . a. been a volunteer worker during a political campaign?	1.12, 1*	1.13, 1	1.11, 1	1.12, 1
. . . b. worked with others in your community to try to solve some community problem?	1.23, 1	1.29, 1	1.18, 1	1.27, 1
. . . c. attended a protest meeting or demonstration supporting something you believe in?	1.19, 1	1.22, 1	1.19, 1	1.11, 1

92. We would like to know how you feel about different kinds of actions which might be used to get the government to change its policies.

* CODES:

OFTEN	SOMETIMES	NEVER	DON'T KNOW
1	2	3	8

	Total Sample	Montreal	Toronto	Winnipeg
. . . a. what about strikes, do you think they can often be justified, that they can sometimes be justified, or that strikes are never justified to change government policy?	2.09, 2*	2.05, 2	2.13, 2	2.07, 2
. . . b. what about boycotts?	2.02, 2	2.05, 2	2.01, 2	1.97, 2
. . . c. what about legal and *peaceful* demonstrations like marches, rallies and picketing?	1.80, 2	1.81, 2	1.75, 2	1.95, 2
. . . d. and what about illegal but peaceful demonstrations, like sit-ins?	2.42, 3	2.62, 3	2.29, 2	2.27, 2

The following questions concern politics and political events.

93. How interested are you in politics and political events? Would you say . . .

	Total Sample	Montreal	Toronto	Winnipeg
. . . very interested	24.69	29.22	22.06	19.67
. . . fairly interested	45.88	40.89	47.59	56.58
. . . not very interested, or	18.50	19.58	17.96	16.95
. . . not at all interested?	10.93	10.31	12.40	6.81

94. Thinking of *federal* politics, do you usually think of yourself as a Liberal, Progressive Conservative, N.D.P., Social Credit, or what?

	Total Sample	Montreal	Toronto	Winnipeg
. . . Liberal	53.10	69.06	44.32	32.86
. . . Progressive Conservative	15.20	4.45	21.33	27.86

	Total Sample	Montreal	Toronto	Winnipeg
. . . N.D.P.	12.38	5.90	14.87	25.26
. . . Social Credit	0.43	1.00	0.00	0.21
. . . Other (Specify)	3.35	5.59	1.75	2.14
. . . Independent or none	7.96	12.68	4.30	6.55
. . . don't know	7.58	1.32	13.43	5.12

95. Thinking of *provincial* politics, do you usually think of yourself as a Liberal, Progressive Conservative, N.D.P., Social Credit, P.Q. (in Quebec only) or what?

	Total Sample	Montreal	Toronto	Winnipeg
Liberal	38.83	60.29	24.93	21.28
Progressive Conservative	20.72	0.36	36.50	26.35
N.D.P.	11.82	0.00	16.10	35.90
Social Credit				
P.Q. (in Quebec only)	—	26.50	—	—
Other (Specify)	2.00	2.59	1.39	2.44
Independent or none	6.68	7.21	5.92	8.02
Don't know	8.81	2.03	15.15	6.01

Finally we would like to get an idea about *how people get their news information?*

96. First, do you read the newspaper? . . .

	Total Sample	Montreal	Toronto	Winnipeg
. . . every day	56.12	53.42	57.17	61.40
. . . several times a week	24.16	24.67	24.59	20.45
. . . about once a week, or	15.07	18.72	12.91	11.19
. . . never?	4.65	3.19	5.33	6.97

97. Do you read the newspaper editorials . . .

	Total Sample	Montreal	Toronto	Winnipeg
. . . every day . . . 1	24.48	25.95	22.94	25.77
. . . several times a week . . . 2	26.34	24.69	28.97	20.86
. . . about once a week, or . . . 3	24.93	22.93	24.70	33.33
. . . never? . . . 4	24.25	26.43	23.38	20.04

98. Do you watch the news on the television . . .

	Total Sample	Montreal	Toronto	Winnipeg
. . . every day . . . 1	58.18	69.51	49.89	52.96
. . . several times a week . . . 2	26.68	21.62	29.52	32.73
. . . about once a week, or . . . 3	10.87	7.33	13.88	10.68
. . . never? . . . 4	4.27	1.53	6.71	3.63

99. Finally, do you listen to the news on the radio . . .

	Total Sample	Montreal	Toronto	Winnipeg
. . . every day . . . 1	64.78	64.27	63.47	72.33
. . . several times a week . . . 2	18.83	17.07	21.79	12.38
. . . about once a week, or . . . 3	7.97	7.51	7.50	11.62
. . . never? . . . 4	8.42	11.14	7.24	3.67

3

OTHER SURVEYS

As Professor Gibson's paper pointed out, it is important that both the geographic and temporal dimensions of public attitudes be borne in mind when considering the significance of opinion poll data. To provide some comparative information against which to assess the results of the Legal Research Institute survey, scholars responsible for related polls, in other places and at other times, were asked to describe their findings.

CYNICISM AND AMBIVALENCE TOWARDS LAW AND LEGAL INSTITUTIONS IN AUSTRALIA

Roman Tomasic

INTRODUCTION

At a time when the ideologies of informalism and delegalization are being widely advocated, and attacks upon legal professional conduct are occurring throughout the world, it is not surprising to note that there has been increasing cynicism and ambivalence concerning the value and uses of legal ideals and legal institutions. Such cynical, or at best ambivalent, attitudes are by no means entirely new. Public criticism of legal ideals, lawyers and the legal process has long been common, although it has tended to wax and wane. To a large degree, this can be related to transformations occurring in the wider society at any particular point in time. It can be shown, for example, that attacks upon lawyers and legalism in societies such as Jacksonian America in the early nineteenth century, modern day China, and perhaps even contemporary Japan, reflect the rapidly changing nature of those societies, as well as their need to avoid the potentially stultifying effects of legalism. In our own contemporary western societies such as Australia, Britain, Canada, and the United States, the reaction against legalism and legal institutions is quite complex, although it can be related to a reaction against the rule of law in post-liberal capitalist societies. What is noteworthy is that broadly similar features appear in different societies. This paper will seek to focus on the Australian case.

AUSTRALIAN LEGAL ATTITUDINAL DATA

The 1970's saw a number of attitudinal surveys in regard to law, lawyers, and legal institutions conducted in Australia. These included the 1973 legal needs survey of the Australian Government Commission into poverty,[1] victimization data collected by the Australian Bureau of Statistics in 1975,[2] and surveys of public attitudes to crime.[3] There have also been a number of surveys of the attitudes of lawyers and judges to various aspects of law and the legal system.[4] On the whole, however, there is considerable reason for further survey research into legal consciousness, a field that has barely begun to be explored in Australia.[5]

This paper is based upon two surveys undertaken in 1975 and 1978. The first of these was a survey of public attitudes of a sample of respondents drawn from New South Wales (NSW) and the Australian Capital Territory (ACT). New South Wales is Australia's most populous state, while the ACT is located within the geographical boundaries of NSW. A total of 927 persons responded to this survey, that being a 40 per cent response rate. The questionnaire was left with respondents to complete and mail back to the researchers upon completion. Fuller reports of this study and a more detailed exposition of its methodology were published in the preliminary and final reports on the survey.[6] The second data base drawn upon in this paper is the 1977 NSW survey of the attitudes of a sample of over 600 lawyers. The preliminary report on this survey was published in 1978[7] although the final report has yet to appear.[8] Both of these surveys were supported by the Law Foundation of New South Wales, and provided previously unavailable broadly based attitudinal information regarding law and legal institutions.

In the next section, data drawn from the 1975 NSW survey of public

1 M. Cass and R. Sackville, *Legal Needs of the Poor* (1975).

2 Australian Bureau of Statistics, *Social Indicators No. 3, 1980*.

3 P. Wilson and J. W. Brown, *Crime and the Community* (1973); A. A. Congalton and J. Najman, *Safety in the Suburbs* (1974).

4 J. Fitzgerald, *Poverty and the Legal Profession in Victoria* (1977); M. Hetherton, *Victoria's Lawyers: A First Report* (1978); M. Hetherton, *Victoria's Lawyers: A Second Report* (1981); Australian Law Reform Commission, *Sentencing of Federal Offenders* (1980).

5 See, however, S. Ozdowski, "The Family Law Act 1975 and the Family" in R. Tomasic (ed)., *Legislation and Society in Australia* (1979), p. 259.

6 R. Tomasic, *Law, Lawyers and the Community* (1976); R. Tomasic, *Lawyers and the Community* (1978).

7 R. Tomasic and C. Bullard, *Lawyers and their Work in New South Wales: Preliminary Report* (1978).

8 See, however, R. Tomasic and C. Bullard, "Lawyers and Legal Culture in Australia" (1979), 7 Int. Journal of the Sociology of Law 417; R. Tomasic, "Typifying Lawyers: A Sociological Study of the Legal Profession in New South Wales" (unpublished Ph.D. dissertation, 1979); R. Tomasic, "Criminal Lawyers and their Clients" (1981), 14 Australian and New Zealand Journal of Criminology 147; R. Tomasic, "Social Organization Amongst Australian Lawyers" (1983), 19 Australian and New Zealand Journal of Sociology 447; R. Tomasic, "Lawyers and Social Control — a preliminary inquiry" (1983), 3 Windsor Yearbook of Access to Justice (forthcoming).

attitudes are compared with those of the recent survey by Professor Moore for the Legal Research Institute of the University of Manitoba. This is followed by a comparison of data drawn from the author's two surveys with a view to exploring the issue of cynicism regarding aspects of law on the part both of lawyers and the community.

AN AUSTRALIAN-CANADIAN COMPARATIVE PERSPECTIVE

The data collected in the author's NSW survey[9] have many parallels with the findings recently available from the University of Manitoba Legal Research Institute survey.[10] A brief attempt to contrast these findings might be useful, although it should be obvious that it is always difficult to compare findings collected by surveys constructed in different ways and using different questions. Interpreting survey evidence is often problematic at best, and this difficulty is accentuated in any attempt to compare different surveys. Having said this, it does seem to be possible to discern the existence of broad tendencies in comparable survey findings, which can be contrasted with each other.

At the outset, it seems that Canadians are somewhat more critical of legal institutions and of law than are Australians. This may in part be attributable to the more extensive range of legal experiences and contacts enjoyed by the former when compared with the latter. While there are a number of clear similarities between these two sets of responses, there are also some quite vivid differences, both of which are worth exploring further. Australians, for example, tend to be a little more optimistic about the operations and effectiveness of their legal system than are Canadians. This is perhaps surprising, given the fact that Canada is often seen in Australia as a country most like itself in terms of historical background, federal structure, and size. Yet, while 69.2 per cent of the Australian respondents felt that "on the whole our legal system does a good job in protecting the public"[11], only 38.6 per cent of the Canadian sample agreed that "the law works as effectively as possible to deal with people's problems",[12] although 54.9 per cent of the latter group felt that "the law as a whole is fundamentally sound"[13].

While Canadians seem to be more convinced of the need for improvement in their legal system than are Australians, the former seem to be more liberal with respect to the imposition of harsher penalties, as well as somewhat more aware of the existence of discrimination in their legal system than are Australians. For example, while 59.7 per cent of the Australian sample

9 R. Tomasic, *Lawyers and the Community* (1978).

10 R. Moore, *Perceptions of the Law and the Legal System: A Preliminary Report of the Findings* (1981).

11 R. Tomasic, *Lawyers and the Community* (1978), Appendix C, c. 11.

12 R. Moore, *Perceptions of the Law and the Legal System: A Preliminary Report of the Findings* (1981), Q. 41F.

13 *Ibid.*, Q. 41B.

felt that they "need new laws to protect the community's rights"[14], 77.9 per cent of the Canadian sample felt that "something needs to be done to improve the way the legal system operates and the laws it produces"[15]. Yet, only 36.6 per cent of the Canadians sampled agreed that "corporal punishment and solitary confinement should be used more frequently"[16], while 64.8 per cent of the Australians sampled felt that "the threat of severe punishment is the best way to prevent further crime"[17]. On the issue of discrimination, while 51.4 per cent of the Canadian sample agreed that there are "groups in Canada who receive unfavourable treatment from the police, and who are treated worse than the rest of society"[18], 27.9 per cent of the Australians sampled felt that "the law is unfairly used against young people"[19], and 47.3 per cent agreed that "when it comes to legal rights, aborigines are generally discriminated against"[20]. Unfortunately, these last sets of statistics are not exactly comparable. A similarly inconclusive contrast is evidenced by the fact that while 71.7 per cent of Canadians sampled felt that their laws "generally stand for what the majority of people want"[21], 65.1 per cent of Australians sampled felt that "the law is basically fair to everyone in the community"[22]. Both of these sets of responses left considerable room for cynicism about the treatment of minorities in both societies. On the whole, the legal systems of both countries were seen to be somewhat removed from the needs of society. Thus, while only 21 per cent of Canadians sampled agreed that their legal system was "in touch with modern conditions"[23], 68.3 per cent of Australians agreed, and 18.9 per cent disagreed with the proposition that many of their laws "don't make sense for our modern society"[24]. This high level of disenchantment with the legal system was also evident in the finding that 79.1 per cent of Australians and 60.5 per cent of Canadians felt that "it takes too long to get anything done through the process of law"[25]. The question of legal delay seems to be of slightly greater concern to Australians. This may be a function of contacts with lawyers.

Since the 1963 Missouri Bar survey, if not earlier, it has been known that contact with lawyers tends to diminish the level of respect that clients have for them. However, clients who have regular contacts with their lawyers seem to have less critical attitudes towards lawyers and the legal system, suggesting either that lawyers serve to moderate or defuse critical attitudes, or that clients may obtain insights from such contact which lead them to change or moderate

14 R. Tomasic, *supra*, note 11, c. 20.
15 R. Moore, *supra*, note 12, Q. 41D.
16 *Ibid.*, Q. 89.
17 R. Tomasic, *supra*, note 11, c. 15.
18 R. Moore, *supra*, note 12, Q. 45a.
19 R. Tomasic, *supra*, note 11, c. 7
20 *Ibid.*, c. 5.
21 R. Moore, *supra*, note 12, Q. 41G.
22 R. Tomasic, *supra*, note 11, c. 3.
23 R. Moore, *supra*, note 12, Q. 41d.
24 R. Tomasic, *supra*, note 11, c. 19.
25 *Ibid.*, c. 17; R. Moore, *supra*, note 12, Q. 41F.

their attitudes[26]. Having regular contacts with a lawyer, therefore, may well moderate cynical attitudes. This phenomenon merits further scrutiny. While about 58 per cent of the Australian respondents stated that they had a "regular solicitor"[27], about 39 per cent of Canadian respondents claimed to have a lawyer whom they used "on a regular basis"[28]. This difference seems to be attributable to the apparently greater use made of lawyer services in Australia for conveyancing or land transfer transactions. While about 57 per cent of the Australians sampled attributed the reason for their last contact with a lawyer to a conveyancing problem[29], only about 40 per cent of Canadians sought lawyer services for this reason[30]. It is evident from the work of Mayhew and Reiss,[31] as well as from Australian research,[32] that contacts with lawyers in respect to property-related transactions play an important part in facilitating access to legal services, and in developing regular contacts between lawyers and their clients. However, it seems that Australians may not use lawyers as frequently as do Canadians, once they have initiated contact with them, although Australians may use the same lawyers more frequently. Of the 78 per cent or so of those in the Australian sample who had experienced contact with lawyers, 75 per cent had consulted one or two lawyers "over the years"[33]. Of the 67.4 per cent of Canadians who had ever used lawyers[34], a little over 50 per cent had used lawyers only once or twice, the remainder having used lawyers more frequently.

While Australians seem to be more likely than Canadians to have established regular contacts with a lawyer, other parts of the legal system seem to be less familiar to them. For example, while over 50 per cent of Australians seem never to have set foot into a courtroom[35], only about 38 per cent of Canadians fell into this category[36]. Court experience seems to be a major factor contributing to cynicism concerning the legal system; those who are more exposed to the court process seem to be more likely to be critical of the legal system. This may help to explain why Canadians seem to be more cynical of their legal systems than are Australians. The fact that 51.3 per cent of the Canadian sample had been to court for a traffic offence seems to be an important difference. In contrast, 68.9 per cent of the Australian sample reported never having been apprehended on a driving offence, and of those that had been very few had gone to court. However, certain kinds of legal

26 R. Tomasic, *supra,* note 11, pp. 30-31, 63.

27 *Ibid.,* Appendix C., c. 40.

28 R. Moore, *supra,* note 12, Q. 61.

29 R. Tomasic, *supra,* note 11, c. 110.

30 R. Moore, *supra,* note 12, Q. 63.

31 L. Mayhew and A. J. Reiss, "The Social Organization of Legal Contacts" (1969), 34 Amer. Sociological Rev. 309.

32 R. Tomasic, *Lawyers and the Community,* pp. 59-65.

33. *Ibid.,* Appendix C, c. 60.

34 R. Moore, *Perceptions of the Law and the Legal System: A Preliminary Report of the Findings* (1981), Q. 60a.

35 R. Tomasic, *supra,* note 32, c. 120.

36 R. Moore, *supra,* note 34, Q. 72.

experiences seem to inculcate cynical attitudes towards the legal system and its personnel. For example, while 29 per cent of those in the Australian sample who had received a driving infringement notice felt they had been unfairly treated by the police at some time, only 6.5 per cent of those who had never received an infringement notice felt that they had been unfairly treated by the police at some time[37]. This difference may well explain why 65 per cent of the Canadian respondents had a "favourable"[38] attitude towards the police while 79 per cent of Australian respondents reported that they had never been unfairly treated by the police[39]. Contact with the police, especially where this leads to a court appearance, may be an important factor in explaining cynical attitudes towards the legal system. This can also be said of litigation generally, especially in relation to divorce matters. For example, while 7 per cent of the whole Australian sample felt that they had been unfairly treated by the courts, 25.8 per cent of the divorced and the separated felt unfairly treated. However, as noted earlier, having regular contacts with a lawyer does greatly moderate attitudes regarding the discriminatory nature of the legal system. For example, while 22.6 per cent of the Australian respondents having regular contacts with lawyers felt that "the law is used unfairly against young people", 34.7 per cent of those without such contacts felt this way. Similarly, while 66.4 per cent of persons in the Australian sample who reported regularly seeing a lawyer felt that they were sure they would get a fair trail if they were accused of a crime, only 56.8 per cent of those who did not have such lawyer contacts felt this way.[40] A better impression of the effects of different kinds of legal experiences can be gained from Table 1.

37 R. Tomasic, *supra*, note 32, c. 125.
38 R. Moore, *supra*, note 34, Q. 50.
39 R. Tomasic, *supra*, note 37.
40 *Ibid.*, pp. 30-31.

TABLE 1
ATTITUDES, CONTACTS AND EXPERIENCE
PERCENTAGE WHO AGREE AND WHO:

	Have regular solicitor contacts	Don't have regular solicitor contacts	Have been called for jury service	Have been charged with a criminal offence	Reported that unfairly treated by the police	Reported that unfairly treated by the Courts	Total sample
STATEMENT	(N=531)	(N=396)	N=64)	(N=51)	(N=61)	(N=12)	(N=927
Q.57 "There is one law for the poor and one for the rich."	43.0	48.0	53.5	55.3	68.7	63.2	45.3
Q.10 "Our present legal system favours the rich and powerful."	54.6	55.1	57.9	71.2	71.4	73.7	54.8
Q.60 "The law is basically fair to everyone in the community"	68.5	61.0	75.7	59.1	46.0	49.8	65.1

	Have regular solicitor contacts	Don't have regular solicitor contacts	Have been called for jury service	Have been charged with a criminal offence	Reported that unfairly treated by the police	Reported that unfairly treated by the Courts	Total sample
Q.59 "If I was accused of a crime, I'm sure I would get a fair trial."	66.4	56.8	74.0	55.9	43.5	44.5	62.1
Q.58 "When it comes to legal rights, aborigines are generally discriminated against."	43.2	52.5	39.5	58.9	62.7	60.6	47.3
Q.4 "The law should be the guardian of community standards."	82.2	76.2	95.6	61.4	75.0	71.9	89.5
Q.16 "The law is unfairly used against young people."	22.6	34.7	14.9	49.8	44.8	48.0	27.9
Q.18 "Our legal system is too corrupt for my liking."	25.4	29.2	21.9	43.5	53.4	48.4	27.0
Q.11 "On the whole, our legal system does a good job in protecting the public."	55.9	60.8	68.1	47.8	49.6	52.3	69.2
Q.13 "Too many activities in life are restricted by rules and regulations."	36.6	40.6	40.7	56.1	52.1	56.6	38.4
Q.5 "The law should only be changed slowly and carefully."	71.2	63.0	72.0	53.1	71.8	62.0	67.5
Q.8 "The way court proceedings are run are as well as can be expected."	31.4	27.5	27.5	33.2	13.1	28.8	29.6
Q.6 "It takes too long to get anything done through the process of law."	81.7	75.8	85.8	80.6	93.5	87.2	79.1
Q.79 "Legal people use language that is hard to understand."	61.7	59.3	63.0	66.4	75.2	68.4	60.6

CYNICISM AMONG LAWYERS AND THE PUBLIC

Up to this point only rather limited allusions have been made with regard to the existence of cynical attitudes towards law in Australia. In this section I want to examine and compare more fully the attitudes towards law and legal ideals held both by lawyers and the public. This task is made considerably easier than might otherwise be the case by the fact that it was possible to ask many of the same questions of respondents to both the lawyer and the general community surveys. The method relied upon is a factor analysis of both groups of responses. As lawyers play key roles in shaping and administering legal ideals and legal institutions, this analysis will focus on the respective perceptions of both lawyers and the public of the manner in which these officials of justice are motivated. A useful point of departure is the traditionally held official view that lawyers and legal institutions exist to serve the community or to provide a service, rather than merely to support the life styles of legal officials such as lawyers. In effect, an attempt will be made to examine the hypothesis that lawyers are motivated by the ideal of service. What will soon be obvious is that both lawyers and the public are sceptical of the reality of this ideal, and that the ethics of profit and self-interest are seen to be uppermost in the minds both of lawyers and the public.

The Community Survey

In the factor analysis of responses from the community survey, three main factors were extracted, based upon 57 questions used in the survey. These questions provided the variables upon which the three factors reported in Tables 2, 3, and 4 are based. These three factors accounted for 27.3 per cent of the variance in the total eigenvalue. Factor 1, the "lawyers are self-interested" factor, accounted for 64.9 per cent of the variance for these three factors, and as such was clearly the single most important community attitude regarding lawyers. This factor (Table 2) indicates that the general public has little confidence in the professed service ethic of lawyers, and instead seems to suggest that the wider community perceives business or profit motives as being dominant in the minds of lawyers. This view is remarkably similar to the findings of a narrower earlier survey of poorer respondents undertaken by the Australian Commission of Inquiry into Poverty. This earlier study also undertook a factor analysis of respondent attitudes, and revealed that the dominated respondent value orientation (Factor 1) was described as "lawyers are mainly interested in money and [are] devious where necessary."[41]

The second factor extracted from the community attitudinal survey accounts for 20.7 per cent of the variance for the three factors and is reported in Table 3. This factor has been dubbed the "avoid solicitors if possible" factor, and reflects an apparent reluctance by members of the public to seek

41 M. Cass and R. Sackville, *Legal Needs of the Poor* (1975), p. 85.

legal assistance in dealing with their problems. This attitude can be linked to a wide-ranging scepticism regarding the efficacy of law and legal institutions. On the whole, this "avoid lawyers if possible" factor suggests self-help, self-reliance, and an attempt to delegalize problem solving. Once again, behind this factor set, there seems to rest a deeper cynicism, or at least an ambivalence regarding the resort to legal officials or experts such as lawyers. The second factor is complemented by the third or "the law is too complex" factor, reported in Table 4. This factor accounted for 14.4 per cent of the total variance for the three factors. Law and lawyers were seen as being distant and unresponsive. There also seems to be a desire for simpler means of dealing with legal problems; legal culture is seen as mystifying law and legal relations. At the same time, however, there is also an ambivalent acceptance of lawyers as best able to understand law.

If one thing stands out from the three community attitudinal sets or factors, it is the extent to which there seems to be a deep-seated distrust and cynicism regarding the motivations of lawyers when these are seen in the context of the idealized expectations of service which are frequently held out as epitomizing the values of lawyers. This is largely the result of the first factor, which is a general factor loading significantly on a wide range of variables. The apparent gap or mismatch between the legal ideal and actual community perception could perhaps be dismissed as merely attributable to a lack of information or faulty or distorted perceptions of law and lawyers on the part of the community. However, if we go on to compare these community attitudes with the attitudes or perceptions that lawyers have of themselves, we find that this explanation is largely misguided. Curiously, lawyers themselves are as cynical about the professed ideal of service as is the general public. Like the public, lawyers also point to the predominance of the ideals of profit or commerce in the values of lawyers. All this suggests that attitudes of cynicism in fact have structural roots, and are not based merely upon distorted or inaccurate perceptions of reality. It is appropriate, therefore, to look more closely at these lawyer attitudes.

TABLE 2
FACTOR LOADINGS OF PRINCIPAL VARIABLES FOR FACTOR 1 — "LAWYERS ARE SELF INTERESTED" BEFORE AND AFTER ROTATION OF FACTOR AXES

			Factor Loadings		
Variable	Response	Attitude	Before Rotation	Oblique	Rotation*
			Factor Matrix	Pattern Matrix	Structure Matrix
Q.114	Agree	Most solicitors are more interested in making money than in helping their clients	.69	.43	.55
Q.70	Agree	Solicitors do not care whether their clients fully understand what needs to be done and why	.61	.39	.49
Q.113	Agree	Solicitors needlessly complicate clients' problems	.60	.38	.49
Q.74	Agree	Solicitors don't really try to understand what their clients want	.59	.35	.46
Q.112	Disagree	Solicitors try hard to solve their clients' problems	–.59	–.56	–.60
Q.56	Agree	As soon as you get in the hands of the legal profession you are bound to lose in some way	.58	.20	.36
Q.176	Disagree	Solicitors' ethical standards are generally very high	–.57	–.64	–.66
Q.175	Disagree	Solicitors' fees are usually fair to the client	–.55	–.58	–.60
Q.57	Agree	There is one law for the rich and another for the poor	.52	.30	.39
Q.174	Disagree	Most solicitors can be trusted to look after clients' money if necessary	–.51	–.54	–.56
Q.60	Disagree	The law is basically fair to everyone in the community	–.48	–.56	–.56
Q.173	Disagree	Most solicitors can be trusted to keep clients' personal matters to themselves	–.50	–.54	–.57
Q.75	Disagree	In general a solicitor tries to explain to a client just what he or she plans to do for the client in a particular matter	–.49	–.54	–.55
Q.80	Disagree	Most solicitors will work just as hard for a client who can't afford to pay as one who can	–.49	–.51	–.53
Q.59	Disagree	If I was accused of a crime, I'm sure I would get a fair trial	–.47	–.51	–.52
Q.73	Disagree	Solicitors are prompt about getting things done	–.45	–.49	–.48

*DELTA EQUALS 0.500. THIS ALLOWS AN EXTREMELY OBLIQUE SOLUTION.

TABLE 3
FACTOR LOADINGS OF PRINCIPAL VARIABLES FOR FACTOR 2 — "AVOID SOLICITORS IF POSSIBLE" BEFORE AND AFTER ROTATION OF FACTOR AXES

Variable	Response	Attitude	Factor Loadings: Before Rotation — Factor Matrix	Oblique Rotation* — Pattern Matrix	Oblique Rotation* — Structure Matrix
Q.109	Agree	I would only need a solicitor's services if something bad happened	.41	.59	.57
Q.52	Agree	People should only go to a solicitor if they can afford to pay	.40	.54	.47
Q.106	Agree	People should not take their problems to a solicitor before they have tried every way they themselves can to solve them	.38	.49	.49
Q.110	Agree	If I can help it I don't get involved with solicitors at all	.34	.48	.51
Q.55	Agree	People are better off not taking a problem to a solicitor until they have exhausted every other possible way of solving it	.34	.46	.47
Q.51	Agree	People who use solicitors so they can take you to court about something are just troublemakers	.32	.46	.44
Q.49	Agree	People are generally better off it they look after their own problems instead of involving a solicitor	.23	.49	.51
Q.56	Agree	As soon as you get in the hands of the legal profession you are bound to lose in some way	.26	.44	.55
Q.108	Agree	I'd probably feel uncomfortable if I had to talk to a solicitor about some legal matters	.22	.42	.40
Q.179	Agree	If you are badly treated by your solicitor there's really nothing you can do about it	.11	.41	.47
Q.114	Agree	Most solicitors are more interested in making money than in helping their clients	.08	.33	.50
Q.113	Agree	Solicitors needlessly complicate clients' problems	.05	.30	.44
Q.182	Agree	Most people who complain to the Law Society about a solicitor are not likely to get much help	.06	.37	.43
Q.74	Agree	Solicitors don't really try to understand what their clients want	.08	.28	.43

*DELTA EQUALS 0.500. THIS ALLOWS AN EXTREMELY OBLIQUE SOLUTION.

TABLE 4
FACTOR LOADINGS OF PRINCIPAL VARIABLES FOR FACTOR 3 — "LAW IS TOO COMPLEX" BEFORE AND AFTER ROTATION OF FACTOR AXES

Variable	Response	Attitude	Factor Loadings		
			Before Rotation	Oblique	Rotation*
			Factor Matrix	Pattern Matrix	Structure Matrix
Q.181	Agree	Most people don't know enough about what the Law Society does	.43	.44	.39
Q.180	Agree	You can always take a problem with solicitors' charges or service to the Law Society of N.S.W.	.32	.29	.23
Q.73	Disagree	Solicitors are prompt about getting things done	−.30	−.31	−.34
Q.6	Agree	It takes too long to get anything done through the processes of law	.28	.33	.35
Q.76	Agree	Most solicitors charge more than their services are worth	.28	.39	.45
Q.78	Disagree	Solicitors keep their clients informed of progress when things take more than a few days	−.27	−.25	−.27
Q.61	Agree	Lawyers deal best with legal problems	.25	.23	.17
Q.79	Agree	Legal people use language that is hard to understand	.25	.37	.41
Q.81	Agree	Legal people could put things in simple language if they wanted to	.32	.41	.41
Q.72	Agree	Solicitors are generally not very good at keeping clients informed of how things are going with their problems	.25	.37	.44
Q.57	Agree	There is one law for the rich and another law for the poor	.23	.36	.42
Q.171	Agree	There are many things that solicitors handle — for example tax matters or estate planning — that can be done as well, and less expensively by other professionals — like accountants and insurance agents	.22	.31	.32
Q.54	Agree	A lot of people do not go to solicitors because they have no way of knowing which solicitor is best able to handle their particular affairs	.19	.26	.28
Q.70	Agree	Solicitors do not care whether their clients fully understand what needs to be done and why	.08	.23	.32
Q.74	Agree	Solicitors don't really try to understand what their clients want	.08	.22	.31

*DELTA EQUALS 0.500. THIS ALLOWS AN EXTREMELY OBLIQUE SOLUTION.

The Lawyer Survey

Once again three main factors were extracted from the attitudinal responses of the approximately 600 NSW lawyers answering the mail questionnaire. The first factor accounted for over 61 per cent of the variance attributable to these factors, while the remaining two factors accounted for 22.3 per cent and 16.5 per cent of the variance, respectively. These three factors are outlined in Tables 5, 6, and 7. By far the most important factor for our purposes is the first, which is also a general factor. This has been described as "the cynical realism" factor. Table 5 is based upon the ten attitudinal variables which characterize "cynical realism". It shows us that lawyer respondents tend to believe that monetary or commercial considerations are most important to lawyers as a group. At the same time, lawyer respondents are sceptical as to whether the ideal of achieving social justice in fact ranks very high in the view of lawyers. Lawyers are not seen as being very interested in promoting law reform, and instead are seen to be mainly concerned with preserving the status quo. Lawyers seem to realize and accept that clients are relatively powerless in the face of breaches of duty to them by lawyers. As a consequence, legal professional associations are seen to be primarily concerned with protecting their members, rather than with thoroughly investigating client complaints. Consequently, the client is seen to be in a very weak position in relation to the lawyer, and this position is further weakened by the predominant monetary values and objectives to which lawyers subscribe. Lawyers are themselves, therefore, well aware of the limitations of the service ideal, and are quite sceptical of the possibilities of elevating it further in the consciousness and practice of most lawyers.

Professional bodies tend to be seen as largely symbolic organizations which serve to undercut or downplay client demands for accountability on the part of lawyers. This cynical business-oriented attitude is further enhanced by the fact that the Law Society (i.e., as in Table 5) is seen to be more interested in protecting lawyers who are employers than those who are employees. Employers will be far more interested in the business of the practice of law, while employees may be expected to show more concern for the ideal of service. Overall, this attitude, which I have characterized as cynical realism, seems to be the dominant perspective of Australian lawyers. It is no wonder that members of the community take a similarly cynical attitude towards law and lawyers in relation to the attainment of legal ideals.

Two other factors are also evident in the attitudinal sets of lawyers. These have been respectively characterized as the "laissez-faire" factor (Table 6) and the "gemeinschaft" factor (Table 7.)

The second or "laissez-faire" factor once again stresses a business orientation. The view is taken that the practice of law should not be restrained by excessive regulation, such as that respecting the advertising of lawyer services. Here, lawyers are reacting against the constraints imposed upon the marketing of their services by the existence of ethical rules. As to legal fees, two variables in this factor suggest that lawyers should be free to make their own arrangements with their clients with regard to charges for their legal work. In effect, this probably means allowing lawyers to charge what they think the market will bear. This factor also reflects a significant degree of cynical self-interest on the part of lawyers.

The laissez-faire factor should be compared with the third or "gemeinschaft" factor, which seems to reflect the importance attached to a professional community orientation. While this factor also illustrates a desire on the part of lawyers for freedom from regulation, it tends to represent the particular viewpoint of small firms and sole practitioners. There is a strong concern here for the role of legal professional associations and their relationship to the smaller practitioner, a group seen as being somewhat removed from the rest of the legal profession. However, an interest in legal fees is still a fundamental issue here, even though this third factor is by far the weakest of the three factors based upon lawyer attitudes. The "gemeinschaft" value orientation therefore seems to be that of the lawyers who feel unduly hampered by ethical rules, insufficiently protected by their professional association, and concerned about their economic situation.

While "cynical realism" is by far the most important single value orientation held by lawyers, there are nevertheless features of all three factors which seem to stress the importance of a commercial orientation on the part of lawyers. It is notable that each of these three value orientations becomes more deeply entrenched as lawyers become older. The cynical realist orientation seems, however, to be most strongly held by property or conveyancing lawyers, who comprise the largest single group within the profession. This "cynical realism" factor is remarkably similar to the main factor extracted from the survey of community attitudes — the "lawyers are self interested" factor. The fact that the bulk of community contacts with lawyers arise out of property transactions may well provide an opportunity for the public to confirm or reinforce the widespread cynicism which already exists regarding legal ideals and legal institutions.

TABLE 5
FACTOR LOADINGS OF PRINCIPAL VARIABLES FOR FACTOR 1 — (THE CYNICAL REALISM FACTOR) AFTER THE ROTATION OF FACTOR AXES BY ORTHOGONAL AND OBLIQUE METHODS

Variable	Response	Attitude	Factor Loadings: Orthogonal Rotation — Factor Matrix	Factor Loadings: Oblique Rotation* — Pattern Matrix	Factor Loadings: Oblique Rotation* — Structure Matrix
SERVE6	Agree	Most solicitors are more interested in making money than in helping their clients	.69	.71	.69
SITLAW13	Disagree	Most lawyers are genuinely interested in achieving social justice	–.58	–.59	–.58
SERVE4	Agree	If a client is badly treated by a solicitor there is very little he can do about it	.57	.57	.57
SITLAW11	Agree	Lawyers are mainly interested in preserving the status quo	.54	.55	.54
ROLASS1	Agree	The Law Society is more concerned with protecting its members than with investigating complaints thoroughly	.54	.54	.55
SITLAW12	Agree	Most lawyers are not concerned with promoting law reform	.51	.54	.53
SITLAW9	Disagree	The main motivation of lawyers is the provision of an adequate service for their clients	–.52	–.53	–.52
SERVE5	Disagree	Clients who complain to the Law Society about a solicitor are likely to obtain a reasonable amount of assistance	–.49	–.49	–.50
ROLASS11	Agree	The Law Society is more concerned with lawyers who are employers than with lawyers who are employees	.48	.47	.49
ROLASS2	Agree	The Bar Association is more concerned with protecting its members than with investigating complaints thoroughly	.46	.45	.49

*DELTA EQUALS 0.500. THIS ALLOWS AN EXTREMELY OBLIQUE SOLUTION.

TABLE 6
FACTOR LOADINGS OF PRINCIPAL VARIABLES FOR FACTOR 2 — (THE LAISSEZ-FAIRE FACTOR) AFTER THE ROTATION OF FACTOR AXES BY ORTHOGONAL AND OBLIQUE METHODS

Variable	Response	Attitude	Factor Loadings: Orthogonal Rotation — Factor Matrix	Factor Loadings: Oblique Rotation* — Pattern Matrix	Factor Loadings: Oblique Rotation* — Structure Matrix
SERVE9	Disagree	It is unnecessary and unbecoming for a professional group to advertise	–.76	–.75	–.76
SERVE10	Agree	The advertising of appropriately registered specialties ought to be permitted	.68	.68	.69
SERVE11	Agree	Lawyers should have an unfettered right to advertise their services	.56	.55	.57
ATFEES8	Agree	A lawyer ought to be able to undertake cases on the understanding that he will receive a percentage of the proceeds if the case is successful	.39	.38	.41
ROLASS5	Agree	Lawyers who act unethically should be judged by the community as a whole and not by their professional colleagues	.28	.23	.31
SERVE7	Agree	Lawyers have to tout in some way or other to survive	.26	.21	.30
SITLAW5	Agree	The growth of large firms is increasing the quality of legal services	.26	.28	.24
ROLASS3	Disagree	Lay people should not be represented at all on lawyers' disciplinary bodies	–.26	–.23	–.27
SITLAW5	Disagree	The legal departments of governmental agencies are taking away too much of the work of private practitioners	–.26	–.26	–.26
ATFEES3	Disagree	A lawyer should not be able to do work on the understanding that he will only get paid if the case is successful	–.25	–.24	–.25

*DELTA EQUALS 0.500. THIS ALLOWS AN EXTREMELY OBLIQUE SOLUTION.

TABLE 7
FACTOR LOADINGS OF PRINCIPAL VARIABLES FOR FACTOR 3 — (THE GEMEINSCHAFT FACTOR) AFTER THE ROTATION OF AXES BY ORTHOGONAL AND OBLIQUE METHODS

Variable	Response	Attitude	Factor Loadings: Orthogonal Rotation — Factor Matrix	Oblique Rotation* — Pattern Matrix	Oblique Rotation* — Structure Matrix
ROLASS6	Agree	The Council of the Law Society is not really in touch with the needs of its members	.51	.47	.54
ATFEES7	Agree	Too many areas of legal work are covered by out-of-date fee scales which do not reflect current costs of overheads	.47	.49	.46
ROLASS8	Disagree	The Law Society concerns itself sufficiently with the problems of the smaller practitioner	–.45	–.45	–.46
ROLASS9	Agree	Ethical rules at present tend to restrict the smaller practitioner more than they do the larger firms	.43	.41	.46
ATFEES6	Agree	At present, too many areas of legal work are covered by fee scales	.42	.43	.42
ATFEES4	Agree	The legal profession should not be hampered in setting fees by restrictions imposed by courts, the Law Society or government	.39	.41	.38
ERVE7	Agree	Lawyers have to tout in some way or other to survive...........................	.35	.31	.39
ROLASS7	Agree	The Bar Council is not really in touch with the needs of the members	.34	.30	.38
ERVE8	Agree	The practice of touting is more widespread than most lawyers are prepared to admit ...	.32	.28	.36
ATFEES8	Agree	A lawyer ought to be able to undertake cases on the understanding that he will receive a percentage of the proceeds if the case is successful	.30	.29	.33

DELTA EQUALS 0.500. THIS ALLOWS AN EXTREMELY OBLIQUE SOLUTION.

CONCLUSIONS

This paper has sought to explore aspects of cynicism in Australian society. Specifically, attitudes to law, lawyers, and legal institutions have been singled out for analysis both from the point of view of the general public and from the perspective of lawyers. It is clear that we are witnessing a contemporary crisis in legal ideals among both professionals and the public. The values which lawyers have historically seen as justifying the high esteem attached to legal officials and legal ideals have begun to be seriously eroded by a deep undercurrent of cynicism or, at best, ambivalence.

This process can be seen to have structural roots in the nature of capitalist society, and in the phenomenon of the commodification of justice. A transformation in the nature of legal ideals and experiences has taken place. The willingness of lawyers to acknowledge the current state of cynicism pervading their legal culture is evidence of this. It is evident that lawyers have become increasingly uneasy with the ideal of service, and have openly turned to the ideal of profit. Given the nature of capitalist society, it is probably naive to expect anything else. However, this ready acceptance of cynical attitudes towards legal practice may well signal a wider transformation of the ideology of liberal legalism, with the effect of limiting the rule of law. If this is the case, current changes in the legal consciousness of both lawyers and the public may well be seen as serving to legitimize this transformation.

While the kinds of conclusions reached in this paper have attracted interest at an academic and journalistic level in Australia, there has been a reluctance upon the part of Australian policy-makers to explore their full implications. At best, the raw attitudinal data has been used in minor instrumental ways by policy-makers. It would be difficult to imagine how mainstream political actors could do more than this. This is especially so in Australia, due to the low level of theoretical development in the socio-legal studies field, and the limited application of this kind of research to public policy purposes.[42]

42 See generally: R. Tomasic, "From Empiricism to the Quest for Theory: Towards a Synthesis in the Sociology of Law" (1983), 1 (2) Australian Journal of Law and Society 149; "The Quest for an Adequate Theory of Criminal Justice" (1981), 14 Australian and New Zealand Journal of Criminology 170.

SURVEYING THE LEGAL NEEDS OF THE PUBLIC: WHAT THE PUBLIC WANTS AND EXPECTS IN THE LAWYER-CLIENT RELATIONSHIP

Barbara A. Curran

There are commonalities between Professor Moore's survey of the public's perception of law and the legal system and that which I directed for the American Bar Association in the mid-1970's, but the overall research objectives of the two studies differ substantially.[43] The central concern in the Canadian study is public attitudes and expectations with respect to the law and legal system as instrumentalities of social control and regulation. To this end, the inquiry (1) explores respondents' notions of what the role of law ought to be in shaping the quality of the social environment and regulating social exchange; and (2) examines respondents' assessments as to the efficacy of the legal system in serving this function. On the other hand, the objective of the U.S. study was (1) to measure the extent to which, and the ways in which, the public use the legal system and, in particular, lawyers' services in dealing with individual, personal problems encountered in the social exchange; and (2) to explore determinants of problem-solving behaviour, including attitudes and expectations about the law and the legal system, and particularly about lawyers as purveyors of legal services.

Because of fundamental differences in objective, the two studies vary substantially in depth of coverage of various matters. One illustration of this is the detailed examination made in the U.S. study of the kinds of legal problems respondents encountered, how they proceeded to deal with these problems, and the nature of the lawyer-client exchange when the advice of a lawyer was sought. The Canadian study's exploration of these matters is far more limited. On the other hand, the Canadian study explores in considerable detail respondents' views of what constitutes anti-social/criminal behaviour, and when the law may be expected to effectively regulate, deter, or punish such behaviour.

Both surveys include questions that elicit respondents' attitudes about the law, the legal system and lawyers, and in several instances, similar or

43 The U.S. survey was conducted in the mid-1970's by the American Bar Foundation. This national survey is described and the results are reported in Barbara A. Curran, *The Legal Needs of the Public: The Final Report of a National Survey* (1977). The discussion of the nature and scope of the Canadian survey is derived from Robert J. Moore, *Perceptions of the Law and the Legal System: A Preliminary Report of the Findings* (Legal Research Institute, University of Manitoba, 1981).

identical attitudinal questions are used.[44] In spite of these similarities, the overall orientations of the attitudinal inquiries differ. The U.S. survey emphasizes matters that might logically relate to individual use of legal services in resolving certain kinds of problems, while the Canadian study emphasizes respondents' views of the legal system generally, and gives particular attention to criminal justice. Consequently, analyses of attitudinal data from the two studies are likely to proceed from different theoretical perspectives. In sum, the studies should be viewed as complementing each other in various respects, but not as replicating each other.

This paper illustrates one of the ways in which responses to questions in the U.S. survey are used to identify and analyze factors that may underlie the decision to use legal services. It deals with but one aspect of an overall analysis now underway and presents the results of preliminary work. Nevertheless, it exemplifies the orientation of the U.S. study, and in so doing makes use of a number of questions involving respondents' perceptions of lawyers and evaluations of lawyers' work, some of which are common to both surveys, and some of which are included only in the U.S. survey.[45]

FACTORS INFLUENCING USE OF LEGAL SERVICES

Various factors influence the decision to seek the advice or help of a lawyer in dealing with a problem. Some relate to the individual's personality and particular problem-solving style. Others relate to the nature of the problem, its seriousness and urgency as perceived by the individual, and to the individuals' ability or inclination to define a problem as legal, that is, as one about which a lawyer could or should be consulted. Still others involve the individual's

44 Both the Canadian and U.S. surveys inquire into respondents' prior use of lawyers, how lawyers are selected, the reasons for the consultations, evaluation of services received and satisfaction with lawyers. Both studies explore attitudes and perceptions about lawyers. The Canadian study includes many more questions on attitudes towards the police, the courts, and the legal system than the U.S. study and the U.S. study covers attitudes and perceptions about lawyers and their work in more detail than the Canadian survey.

45 In comparing results from the two studies, differences between the studies in the populations surveyed should be taken into account. The Canadian study surveyed a sample of adults in each of three cities; the U.S. study was based on a national sample of adults. Thus, the Canadian study reflects the attitudes of urban populations while the U.S. study includes both urban and rural respondents. Other demographic differences exist between the populations covered by the two studies which, if controlled for, might show greater differences between the two populations than preliminary comparison of marginal results suggest. For example, the overall proportion of respondents in the three-city Canadian survey who reported ever having consulted a lawyer was 65 per cent, remarkably close to the 66 per cent for the U.S. national sample. However, in addition to the essentially urban character of the Canadian samples, data set forth in the preliminary findings from the Canadian survey also suggest other differences in the demographic characteristics of the populations covered by the two surveys with respect to matters such as age and sex composition that are highly related in the U.S. study to prior use of a lawyer. Thus, one cannot conclude without further investigation of these data that lawyer use in the Canadian and U.S. populations is essentially the same.

judgment as to the potential cost and effectiveness of legal assistance as compared with other possible ways of dealing with the problem: using other types of assistance, handling the problem by oneself, ignoring the problem, or letting the passage of time resolve matters.

The decision to seek a lawyer's help, however, involves not only the determination that a lawyer's help is appropriate, desirable, or necessary for the particular problem at hand. It also involves the individual's confidence that he or she is likely to select a lawyer who can, and will, perform the job the individual wants done at a reasonable and affordable price. The perception of how lawyers behave or are likely to behave towards the client, coupled with the individual's own priorities as to what is important in the lawyer-client relationship, undoubtedly colour the judgment as to whether seeking a lawyer's help is an appropriate course of action for solving various kinds of problems. This paper will examine these perceptions and priorities.

QUALITIES SOUGHT BY CLIENT IN THE LAWYER-CLIENT EXCHANGE

When asked what qualities they would look for in selecting a lawyer, respondents focused primarily on the attitude and behaviour of the lawyer towards the client as a person.[46] The four most frequently mentioned qualities that people say they look for in selecting a lawyer are commitment, integrity, competence, and fairness and reasonableness of fee.

Over 52 per cent of respondents seek commitment from a lawyer, that is, they want a lawyer who will be concerned about them individually and interested in their particular problems. They seek a personalized lawyer-client relationship in which they can feel confident that the lawyer will make it his business to understand the individual client's needs and objectives, as defined by that client, and to conscientiously serve the client's interests. And, as evidence of commitment (or lack of it), they look to the level and extent of the lawyer's responsiveness to them as individuals: attentiveness, capacity and willingness to communicate, and respect for the client's intelligence and judgment.[47]

46 Two questions concerning the qualities or attributes desired in a lawyer were asked of all survey respondents:

''In choosing a lawyer, what kinds of things about a particular lawyer would make you decide you wanted to use him?''

''What kinds of things about a particular lawyer would make you decide not to use him?''

For each question, the respondent was free to say nothing at all, or to mention any number of attributes. Responses to these two questions were coded on the basis of the coding scheme set forth in Barbara A. Curran and Katherine J. Rosich, *Data Manual for the Survey of the Legal Needs of the Public* (1980), pp. 170-72.

47 The following are illustrative of the statements from which the quality of ''Commitment'' is derived:

I would want a lawyer who . . . would look out for my best interests; was concerned about my

The second most frequently mentioned quality that is considered important in the lawyer-client exchange is the lawyer's integrity (identified by 46 per cent of respondents). This quality embraces honesty, trustworthiness, candidness, moral and/or ethical standards, and behaviour. Although some respondents express concern about a lawyer's professional behaviour towards others (''I wouldn't want a lawyer if I heard he did dirty tricks for his clients''), emphasis tends to be on the lawyer's integrity in relation to the client (''I want a lawyer who would be truthful with me, who would keep my secret, who was above-board with me'').[48]

While commitment and integrity deal with the lawyer's behaviour towards and communication with the client, competence focuses on the lawyer's professional skills and qualifications. The 42 per cent of respondents who express concern about competence emphasize the importance of selecting a lawyer with knowledge and experience in handling the particular kind of problem with which the client is confronted.[49]

The fourth most frequently mentioned concern relates to lawyers' fees. Thirty per cent of the population say they want a lawyer whose fee is fair and/or reasonable. In many cases, it is clear that they seek a lawyer who will act fairly and responsibly in arriving at the charge for his or her service. For this group, the question is whether the particular lawyer's fee is likely to be out-of-line, either in relation to what other lawyers charge for similar work, or in relation to the service provided or work performed. For others, it is equally

---

problems; showed his concern in handling my case; would care about my understanding what he was going to do; showed a willingness to listen to me; explains matters to me; would openly discuss all the facets of the case with me; would talk easily with me; was interested in my case; would care about me and my problem.

I would not want a lawyer who . . . acted like he didn't care; had a bad reputation for not really caring; seemed indifferent or cold about matters that pertained to my case; didn't really care if he won our case; talked down to me; acted as if I were dumb; was real curt to me; just looking for the almighty dollar; was just in it for the money; seemed only interested in his fee; is uninterested or indifferent.

48 In addition to the examples cited in the text, the following are illustrative of the statements from which the quality of ''integrity'' is derived:

I would want a lawyer who . . . is open and forthright; keeps his word; will be honest with me on what's going on; is trustworthy; is ethical; has integrity.

I would not want a lawyer . . . if I heard he had been involved in any crooked dealings; if he's been dishonest; if he had been involved in tax evasion of his own; who would do anything for a dollar; if I heard he had done things I didn't feel are right; if he had shady ideas; if he would sell you out to the highest bidder; if he seems more interested in winning the case than the legalities; if he used undesirable methods.

49 The following are illustrative of the statements from which the quality of ''competence'' is derived:

I would want a lawyer who . . . is competent, knowledgeable; strikes me as capable; is well versed in the law; has background as far as types of cases he handled; who knew a lot about what I wanted him for; had handled similar cases in the past; was specialized in the field.

I would not want a lawyer . . . if he were incompetent; if I heard he took a case and didn't do a good job on it; if he didn't have enough experience in the area in which I need service; if he was an old fogey who doesn't keep up with the law; if he was not confident in the area of the law my problem was concerned with.

clear that the central issue is whether they will be able to afford the fee that the particular lawyer will charge. Some respondents, however, simply refer to the "reasonableness" or "fairness" of the fee. In such cases, the central concern may be the affordability of the fee; it may be the lawyer's fairness in setting the fee; or it may be a combination of both.[50]

RELATIONSHIP OF QUALITIES SPECIFIED TO PRECONCEPTIONS ABOUT LAWYERS, PRIOR USE OF LAWYERS' SERVICES, AND SEX

Is there an association between the qualities an individual identifies as important in the lawyer-client exchange, on the one hand, and his or her preconceptions about the way that most lawyers are likely to behave, on the other? Is there a relationship between prior experience with lawyers, and qualities identified as important in that exchange? Do men and women emphasize different qualities when selecting a lawyer?

Commitment of the lawyer is the quality about which there is the least variation based on prior experience with a lawyer. As shown by Table 1, however, women are somewhat more likely than men to express concern about a lawyer's commitment. And this sex difference persists among those who have previously consulted a lawyer and those who have not. In response to attitudinal statements dealing with lawyers' commitment to clients, women are more positive than men. However, women who believe that most lawyers will be attentive and concerned are as likely to identify commitment as an important quality as are women who hold a less optimistic view of lawyers. On the other hand, men who are sceptical about the commitment of lawyers generally are least likely to express concern about this quality when selecting a lawyer.[51]

---

50 The following are illustrative of the statements from which the quality of "fairness and reasonableness of fee" is derived:

I would want a lawyer . . . whose fees should be in keeping with the general trend; whose fees I was able to afford; whose fees are fair; whose fees are reasonable.

I wouldn't want a lawyer . . . if I thought he'd charge too much; if his fees were way out; if his fees were overly high or overly low; if I don't have enough money to pay him; if his fees are excessive; if he is someone who is really going to soak me; if he's not fair as to price; if I thought he'd gouge me; if he should be out of range — it's a question of finances.

51 Respondents were asked to specify whether they strongly agreed, slightly agreed, slightly disagreed, or strongly disagreed with each of 28 statements covering lawyers, courts, and the legal system. For a full discussion of all 28 statements presented to respondents, see B. Curran, *The Legal Needs of the Public: The Final Report of a National Survey* (1977), pp. 227-58.

The following attitude statements relate to commitment:

Lawyers don't really try to understand what their clients want.

Lawyers do not care whether their clients fully understand what needs to be done and why.

Lawyers work harder at getting clients than in serving them.

The following table shows the relationship between responses to the above statements and the mention of commitment as a quality sought. For purposes of this table, any respondent who

TABLE 1
COMMITMENT

		Males N = 817	Females N = 1018	Total N = 1835
% of N who mentioned commitment		49%	55%	52%
		Male Non-users N = 260	Female Non-users N = 379	All Non-users N = 639
% of N who mentioned commitment		48%	56%	53%
		Male Users	Female Users	All Users
% of N who mentioned commitment		49%	54%	52%
A.	Total population	Males N = 817	Females N = 1018	Both Sexes N = 1835
1.	% of N who responded positively to related attitude statements	71%	77%	74%
2.	% of N who responded negatively to related attitude statements	29%	23%	26%
3.	% of those responding positively to related attitude statements who mentioned commitment (N = 1 above)	50%	55%	53%
4.	% of those responding negatively to related attitude statements who mentioned commitment (N = 2 above)	44%	55%	50%
B.	Persons who had not used a lawyer	Male Non-Users N = 260	Female Non-Users N = 379	All Non-Users N = 639
1.	% of Non-users who responded positively to related attitude statements	70%	75%	73%
2.	% of Non-users who responded negatively to related attitude statements	30%	25%	27%
3.	% of those responding positively to related attitude statements who mentioned commitment (N = 2 above)	51%	56%	54%
4.	% of those responding negatively to related attitude statements who mentioned commitment (N = 2 above)	39%	55%	48%
C.	Persons who had used a lawyer	Male Users N = 557	Female Users N = 639	All Users N = 1196
1.	% of Users who responded positively to related attitude statements	72%	78%	75%
2.	% of Users who responded negatively to related attitude statements	28%	22%	25%
3.	% of those responding positively to related attitude statements who mentioned commitment (N = 1 above)	50%	54%	52%
4.	% of those responding negatively to related attitude statements who mentioned commitment (N = 2 above)	47%	54%	51%

Women are even more likely than men to identify integrity as an important quality (see Table 2). This distinction between men and women persisted when their responses were controlled for prior experience with lawyers. Among women, however, those who have previously consulted lawyers are somewhat more likely to mention integrity than non-users. Preconceptions about lawyers' honesty do not seem to affect identification of integrity as an important quality in lawyer selection. The one exception was found among women with prior lawyer experience — those with a negative view of lawyers' integrity are more likely to mention integrity than any other group.[52]

Men are substantially more likely than women to identify competence as an important consideration. The difference between the two groups is most striking among persons with no prior experience with lawyers. As shown by Table 3, the likelihood of women focusing on competence increases with prior experience. When users are classified into those who have only used a lawyer on one occasion and those who have had multiple experiences with lawyers, no difference emerges among the two groups of male users. In the case of women, however, one-time users, although more likely to mention competence than non-users, are less likely to do so than women with multiple experience (see Table 2, Pt. c). Men and women with prior experience, who think that lawyers will accept a case even when not qualified to do so, are more likely to mention competence as an important consideration in lawyer selection than non-users who share an equally pessimistic view of lawyers.[53]

---

strongly or slightly disagreed with two or three of the above statements was treated as having a positive attitude on the matters covered by these statements. A respondent who strongly or slightly agreed with two or three of the above statements was treated as having a negative attitude on matters covered by these statements. In the underlying analysis, a four-way breakdown of responses was used: All positive, two positive and one negative; two negative and one positive; all negative. The two-way breakdown is used in the table for simplicity and economy of space; no different pattern emerges with the four-way breakdown.

52 The following attitude statements relate to integrity:
Lawyers usually try to be frank and open with their clients.
Lawyers can be trusted to keep their clients' secrets.
Most lawyers would engage in unethical or illegal activities to help a client in an important case.
The following table shows the relationship between responses to the above attitude statements and the mention of integrity as a quality. For purposes of this table, any respondent who strongly or slightly agreed with two or three of the above statements was treated as having a positive attitude on the matters covered by these statements. A respondent who strongly or slightly disagreed with two or three of the above statements was treated as having a negative attitude on matters covered by these statements. Responses on the third statement shown above were first reversed to be consistent with the first two statements. The discussion on the four-way breakdown in note 51 also applies here.

53 The following attitude statement relates to competence:
Lawyers will take a case only if they feel sure they know enough about that area of the law to handle the cases well.
Table 3 shows the relationship between responses to the above attitude statement and the mention of competence as a quality. For purposes of this table, any respondent who strongly or slightly agreed with the above statement was treated as having a positive attitude on matters covered by the statement. A respondent who strongly or slightly disagreed with the statement was treated as having a negative attitude on matters covered by the statement.

Overall, women are just about as likely as men to express concern about fees in selecting a lawyer. However, while there are substantial differences between men who have previously consulted a lawyer and men who have not, approximately the same proportion of women without prior experience identify fees as do women with previous lawyer contacts. As shown by Table 4, men without prior contact with lawyers are more likely to mention fees than men who have consulted a lawyer on some occasion in the past.

TABLE 2
INTEGRITY

	Males N = 839	Females N = 1048	Total N = 1887
% of N who mentioned integrity	40%	50%	46%
	Male Non-users N = 266	Female Non-users N = 396	All Non-users N = 662
% of N who mentioned integrity	38%	45%	42%
	Male Users N = 573	Female Users N = 652	All Users N = 1225
% of N who mentioned integrity	41%	52%	47%

		Males N = 839	Females N = 1048	Both Sexes N = 1887
A.	Total population			
1.	% of N who responded positively to related attitude statements	83%	86%	85%
2.	% of N who responded negatively to related attitude statements	17%	14%	15%
3.	% of those responding positively to related attitude statements who mentioned integrity (N = 1 above)	40%	49%	45%
4.	% of those responding negatively to related attitude statements who mentioned integrity (N = 2 above)	41%	52%	46%

		Male Non-Users N = 266	Female Non-Users N = 396	All Non-Users N = 662
B.	Persons who had not used a lawyer			
1.	% of Non-users who responded positively to related attitude statements	83%	86%	85%
2.	% of Non-users who responded negatively to related attitude statements	17%	14%	15%
3.	% of those responding positively to related attitude statements who mentioned integrity (N = 1 above)	38%	46%	43%
4.	% of those responding negatively to related attitude statements who mentioned integrity (N = 2 above)	39%	42%	40%

C.	Persons who had used a lawyer	Male Users N = 573	Female Users N = 652	All Users N = 1225
1.	% of Users who responded positively to related attitude statements	82%	87%	84%
2.	% of Users who responded negatively to related attitude statements	18%	13%	16%
3.	% of those responding positively to related attitude statements who mentioned integrity (N = 1 above)	41%	51%	47%
4.	% of those responding negatively to related attitude statements who mentioned integrity (N = 2 above)	42%	59%	50%

	Mentioned Competence
Males who used lawyer once only (N = 222)	49%
Males who used lawyer more than once (N = 344)	49%
Females who used lawyer once only (N = 311)	49%
Females who used lawyer more than once (N = 341)	42%

TABLE 3
COMPETENCE

	Males N = 829	Females N = 1050	Total N = 1879
% of N who mentioned competence	51%	36%	41%
	Male Non-users N = 263	**Female Non-users N = 399**	**All Non-users N = 662**
% of N who mentioned competence	54%	32%	41%
	Male Users N = 566	**Female Users N = 651**	**All Users N = 1217**
% of N who mentioned competence	49%	38%	43%

A.	Total population	Males N = 829	Females N = 1050	Both Sexes N = 1879
1.	% of N who responded positively to related attitude statement	56%	65%	61%
2.	% of N who responded negatively to related attitude statement	44%	35%	39%
3.	% of those responding positively to related attitude statement who mentioned competence (N = 1 above)	52%	37%	43%
4.	% of those responding negatively to related attitude statement who mentioned competence (N = 2 above)	49%	35%	42%

B.	Persons who had not used a lawyer	Male Non-Users N = 263	Female Non-Users N = 399	Both Sexes Non-Users N = 662
1.	% of Non-users who responded positively to related attitude statement	65%	66%	66%
2.	% of Non-users who responded negatively to related attitude statement	35%	34%	34%
3.	% of those responding positively to related attitude statement who mentioned competence (N = 1 above)	57%	36%	45%
4.	% of those responding negatively to related attitude statement who mentioned competence (N = 2 above)	47%	24%	33%

C.	Persons who had used a lawyer	Male Users N = 566	Female Users N = 651	All Users N = 1217
1.	% of Users who responded positively to related attitude statement	52%	64%	59%
2.	% of Users who responded negatively to related attitude statement	48%	36%	41%
3.	% of those responding positively to related attitude statement who mentioned competence (N = 1 above)	48%	37%	41%
4.	% of those responding negatively to related attitude statement who mentioned competence (N = 2 above)	50%	41%	46%

TABLE 4
FEES

	Males N = 783	Females N = 950	Total N = 1733
% of N who mentioned fees	29%	32%	30%
	Male Non-users N = 244	Female Non-users N = 359	All Non-users N = 603
% of N who mentioned fees	35%	32%	33%
	Male Users N = 539	Female Users N = 591	All Users N = 1130
% of N who mentioned fees	26%	32%	29%

A.	Total population	Male N = 783	Female N = 950	Both Sexes N = 1733
1.	% of N who responded positively to related attitude statements	22%	27%	21%
2.	% of N who responded negatively to related attitude statements	45%	41%	43%
3.	% of N who gave a mixed response to related attitude statements	33%	32%	33%
4.	% of those responding positively to related attitude statements who mentioned fees (N = 1 above)	21%	24%	23%

A.	Total population	Male N = 783	Female N = 950	Both Sexes N = 1733
5.	% of those responding negatively to related attitude statements who mentioned fees (N = 2 above)	33%	36%	35%
6.	% of N who gave a mixed response to related attitude statements who mentioned fees (N = 3 above)	28%	32%	30%

B.	Persons who had not used a lawyer	Male Non-Users N = 244	Female Non-Users N = 359	All Non-Users N = 603
1.	% of Non-users who responded positively to related attitude statements	19%	19%	19%
2.	% of Non-users who responded negatively to related attitude statements	45%	46%	46%
3.	% of N who gave a mixed response to related attitude statements	36%	35%	35%
4.	% of those responding positively to related attitude statements who mentioned fees (N = 1 above)	22%	28%	25%
5.	% of those responding negatively to related attitude statements who mentioned fees (N = 2 above)	44%	37%	40%
6.	% of N who gave a mixed response to related attitude statements who mentioned fees (N = 3 above)	29%	28%	29%

C.	Persons who had used a lawyer	Male Users N = 539	Female Users N = 591	All Users N = 1130
1.	% of Users who responded positively to related attitude statements	23%	31%	27%
2.	% of Users who responded negatively to related attitude statements	45%	38%	42%
3.	% of N who gave a mixed response to related attitude statements	32%	31%	31%
4.	% of those responding positively to related attitude statements who mentioned fees (N = 1 above)	21%	23%	22%
5.	% of those responding negatively to related attitude statements who mentioned fees (N = 2 above)	28%	36%	32%
6.	% of N who gave a mixed response to related attitude statements who mentioned fees (N = 3 above)	27%	35%	31%

The mention of fees in connection with the selection of a lawyer is related to preconceptions about lawyers' fees. Respondents were asked to respond to two attitudinal questions relating to cost of lawyers' services. One question dealt with lawyers' fairness in setting fees and the other dealt with the value of lawyers' services in relation to cost. While only 23 per cent of those who responded positively to both questions identified fees as a concern in lawyer selection, 30 per cent of those who responded negatively to one of the questions mentioned fees, and 35 per cent of those responded negatively to both questions mentioned fees. This pattern held among users and non-users, as well as among men and women.[54]

CONCLUSIONS AND OBSERVATIONS

The results reported in the preceding sections are preliminary. Further analyses of these data are still underway and will determine whether these initial observations are in fact substantiated. In particular, we are exploring patterns that emerge when the various qualities specified by each respondent are taken into consideration. Multivariate analysis employing all 28 attitude statements is being used to determine whether it is possible to identify linkages with respect to various subgroups between qualities mentioned and overall responses to the attitude questions.

However, even the descriptive statistics presented here raise intriguing questions. For example, are there fundamental differences among men and women in their assumptions, expectations, and concerns about the nature of the lawyer-client relationship? It is conceivable that apparent differences may simply reflect idiosyncratic ways of verbalizing what are basically similar concerns about and conceptions of the lawyer-client relationship. For example,

54 The following attitude statements relate to fees:

Lawyers' fees are usually fair to their clients, regardless of how they figured the fee.

Most lawyers charge more for their services than they are worth.

Table 4 shows the relationship between responses to the above attitude statements and the mention of fees as a quality. For purposes of this table, any respondent who strongly or slightly disagreed with the second of the above statements and agreed strongly or slightly with the first statement was treated as having a positive attitude on the matters covered by these statements; a respondent who strongly or slightly agreed with the second of the two statements and disagreed strongly or slightly with the first statement was treated as having a negative attitude on matters covered by these statements; a respondent who was positive in his response on one of the above statements but negative on the other was treated as mixed in his attitude on matters covered by these statements.

the quality of fairness of fees may be subsumed under the quality of integrity. It would seem that a person who identifies integrity as an important quality would expect that a lawyer possessing that attribute will be fair and responsible in arriving at the charge for services. On the other hand, it is also possible that the data reflect culturally based differences between men and women, either in their notions of what the nature of the lawyer-client relationship should be or in the level of concern about various aspects of that relationship.

The relationship of qualities mentioned to prior use of lawyers also raises interesting questions. Why is it more likely that non-users raise the issue of fees and users mention competence? It seems reasonable to conclude that it is prior legal experience that moderates concern about fees and enhances concern about competence. On the other hand, it may be equally valid to conclude that persons who mention concern about competence are predisposed by nature, general experience, and situation to use lawyers' services while non-users who mention fees are predisposed not to avail themselves of lawyers' help.

Certainly the differences between men and women as well as users and non-users deserve further examination, and perhaps, with refinements of the analysis, the nature of these distinctions may be better understood. The existence of these differences, intriguing as they may be, should not overshadow the fact that a substantial proportion of men and women, both users and non-users, identify commitment and integrity as important considerations. What this may suggest is that there is a commonly shared view of what is basically important to the client (or prospective client) in the lawyer-client relationship, namely, the personal and individuated character of that relationship. And, indeed, the apparent lack of substantial variability between those who responded positively and those who responded negatively to related attitude questions would seem to underline the possible validity of this hypothesis.

PUBLIC OPINION ABOUT THE PENAL SYSTEM: A CYNICAL VIEW OF CRIMINAL JUSTICE

Yves Brillon
(Translated by D. R. Crelinsten)

WHY STUDY THE OPINIONS OF CITIZENS ABOUT CRIME AND JUSTICE?

In most industrialized countries today, the number of surveys on crime and criminal justice is increasing at a tremendous rate, to the point where, as Mary-Lou Kegels[55] says, crime is now appearing at the top of the hit parade of opinion surveys. Why?

To Find Out the Population's Perception of Crime

One of the reasons for the numerous surveys in the field of justice is that crime seems to have become uncontrolled and uncontrollable. In the United States, between 1946 and 1973, the statistics show an increase of 370 per cent in the rate of murders, the most rapid occurring after 1965. The rate of serious thefts is similar: during the same period, it soared by 300 per cent. In 1978, the figures showed a crime of personal violence every 30 seconds and an attack against property every three seconds.[56] By comparison, in Canada, the crime situation is less frightening but nonetheless disturbing. The Canadian statistics, which give an account of the evolution of crime between 1977 and 1981, show a rise, in four years, of 29 per cent in the rate of crimes against property. Incidentally, the solution rate for these crimes in 1981 was only 25.2 per cent. Furthermore, at the present moment, a crime of violence is committed every four minutes and a theft every 15 seconds. These facts show the need to find out how the population perceives the extent and evolution of crime and to ascertain the public's attitude toward the system of criminal justice. These two undertakings are very necessary if we are to improve the safety of the citizen and design more adequate crime policies.

To Ascertain the Image People Have of Criminal Justice

A second important reason for research on public attitudes is that the people's image of justice and how it works is often very negative. Based on opinion surveys, this is how, according to Alain Peyreffite,[57] the French judge their criminal justice system:

55 M. L. Kegels, "Actualitiés Bibliographiques: Le crime, puisqui'il faut l'appeller par son nom . . . la 'peur du crime' " (1982), VI:2 Déviance et Société 209.
56 H. E. Figgie, *America Afraid: The Figgie Report on Fear and Crime, Part I* (1980), p. 8.
57 A. Peyrefitte, *Les Chevaux du Lac Lagoda* (1981), p. 23.

As a guide, let us note the epithets the French themselves use when asked to describe justice: justice is *lenient* to the point of showing criminals an indulgence that encourages crime; *inequitable* to the point of becoming a lottery; *inaccessible* because it is expensive, complicated, antiquated, esoteric, intimidating, to the point that no one knows how or wants to resort to it; *congested* because it is so slow; *stifling* because it opposes power against liberty. In short, for all these reasons, profoundly unjust.

This picture of justice that Peyreffite draws, based on the opinions expressed by the French, is almost identical to that of Canadians. In a study done at the International Centre for Comparative Criminology by the Research Group on Attitudes Toward Crime, the findings were similar. The Canadian sample[58] shows:

— that 72 per cent of the respondents think the sentences passed by the court are not severe enough;

— that 67 per cent feel that justice today favours the rich over the poor;

— that 75 per cent feel that justice is so complicated it's impossible to understand it;

— that 64 per cent of the persons questioned find the present laws well behind the times;

— that 81 per cent agree that justice is so slow that the citizens are reluctant to resort to it; and

— that 74 per cent of the respondents are of the opinion that those guilty of a crime can always get away with it if they have a good lawyer.

Research undertaken by Professor Moore for the Legal Research Institute of the University of Manitoba[59] arrives at similar results with a sample of people from Montreal, Toronto, and Winnipeg. Among the persons questioned, 42 per cent believe that our laws give too much protection to criminals; 57 per cent think we would have fewer problems if our laws were tougher; 62 per cent are of the opinion that the legal system favours the rich and the powerful; 61 per cent find that it takes too long to get anything done through the process of law; and 78 per cent say that something needs to be done to improve the way the legal system operates and the laws it produces.

The fact is, the opinion that citizens have of the criminal justice system can have a decided effect on the administration of justice. A negative image of

---

58 This research was on attitudes of the Canadian public toward crime policies. For more details, see the final report of the pilot enquiry: Y. Brillon, C. Louis-Guerin and M-C Lamarche, *Les Attitudes du Publique Canadienne envers les Politiques Criminelles: Rapport Final* (1982), p. 302. It was done at the request of the Department of the Solicitor General of Canada, which financed it. The ''theoretical'' sample was made up of a highly urbanized population from Montreal, Toronto and Winnipeg: N = 614, and by a rural population from the provinces of Quebec, Ontario and Manitoba: N = 203. The total sample comprised 817 subjects. The ideas expressed here are solely those of the author.

59 R. J. Moore, *Perceptions of the Law and the Legal System: A Preliminary Report of the Findings* (1981).

the penal agencies, and a lack of confidence in the police, the judiciary and the correctional institutions, can prompt certain social groups to set up, if not their own system of justice, at least their own methods of control. This is far from being a guarantee of better justice and a greater respect for people's rights and liberties. When the chiefs of police of Los Angeles and Miami say to their constituents: "Arm yourselves, we can no longer protect you",[60] it is not very reassuring.

It seems essential, then, to analyze the state of public opinion concerning the system of criminal justice in order to be able to discover its faults and weaknesses, and to try to adapt the institutions to the needs and values of society. If, in any community, justice is seen by its members as "unjust", it is because it is not fulfilling its role, and has become dysfunctional. This is extremely serious, and can be considered a real crisis in the matter of justice. And if there is a crisis, there must be radical changes and profound reform to resolve it.

To Measure the Impact of Crime on the Lives of Citizens

Finally, a third reason which prompted the tremendous increase of "criminological" research on the public's attitudes, is that victimization has proved to be much more widespread than the official statistics show. The surveys undertaken in the United States by the President's Commission on Law Enforcement and Administration,[61] as well as those done since 1972 by the American Bureau of Statistics on behalf of the Law Enforcement Assistance Administration, have furnished frightening evidence of the amount of victimization, and as a consequence, the fear it engenders in the population. In addition, a great many opinion surveys have shown that in every industrialized country crime has become one of the main concerns of the citizens, and for a considerable proportion of them, a source of anxiety and fear.

In the United States, the fear of crime has been so great that it has upset the way of life of most Americans. According to David A. Ward,[62] the sharp increases in crime, particularly in those crimes that are personally threatening — assault, robbery, rape and residential burglary — have made fear of crime such a serious problem that it has changed the daily living habits of most Americans. Furthermore, this fear is amplified by the fact that people are becoming more and more aware that the police cannot protect them against crimes of violence. But it is primarily the courts that are being held responsible for both the increase in crime and the resulting fear of victimization:

> When asked in the *Newsweek* survey how much confidence they had in the courts to sentence and convict criminals, 59 per cent of the respondents replied, "not very much", and 11 percent responded, "none at all". The courts are faulted for granting probation instead of prison terms, for giving short rather than long sentences, for making sentences

60 D. A. Ward, "How Fear of Crime has Changed the Daily Living Habits of Most Americans" (1982), The 1982 Wilson Lecture in American Penology.

61 N. de B. Katzenbach *et al.*, *The Challenge of Crime in a Free Society* (1967).

62 See *supra*, note 60.

concurrent rather than consecutive, for permitting ''technical'' flaws in arrests and in trial procedures to result in defendants being freed, and for allowing defendants out on bail pending their trial.[63]

Along the same lines, in the report of research sponsored by Harry E. Figgie Jr. on fear of crime, he concludes that there is a link between the fear of crime and the negative view that citizens have of criminal justice: ''However, given the high levels of fear of crime which pervade American life, it is not surprising that public attitudes toward the criminal justice system are cynical and attitudes toward the treatment of criminals themselves highly punitive.''[64] However, there is no link between the fear of crime and punitiveness. Thus, surveys on the fear of crime sometimes give rise to misuse and this can result in the justification, for example, of either more vigorous intervention on the part of the police or more repressive measures on the part of the courts.

There may be some question, then, whether by talking in emotional and alarmist terms about the threat of violence to the community, we may be contributing to, or even increasing, the population's fear of crime. Weis and Milakovich point this out when they declare that the ''fear has become a problem as serious as crime itself''.[65] It is necessary to be aware that opinion surveys can easily become instruments of manipulation and vehicles of ideology.

Nor must we forget that the fear of crime is frequently exacerbated by the mass media, and exploited for partisan reasons by certain groups, including the police forces. It might be in the latter's interest, by juggling the figures and percentages, to see the volume of crime increase, for their power and prestige depend on it.[66] Crime engenders profound feelings of fear in people, and so promises to reestablish law and order and to make the streets safe are profitable ways of being assured of popular support.[67] Nor is it unusual, as Christie[68] says, for the authorities to use the pretext of an apparent renewal of violence to demand more police, firearms, and technological gadgets, as well as much more severe punishment for delinquents and criminals.

WHY DO PEOPLE HAVE A NEGATIVE OPINION OF CRIMINAL JUSTICE

The research done by the Montreal team[69] shows that in the Canadian

63 See *supra,* note 60, pp. 6-7.

64 See H. E. Figgie, *America Afraid: The Figgie Report on Fear and Crime, Part I* (1980), p. 135.

65 K. Weis and M. E. Milakovich, ''Political Misuses of Crime Rates'' (1974), 11:5 Society 27.

66 D. Brown, ''Canada and the Noose'', interview with H. Mohr, *Quest* (1976).

67 J. E. Conklin, *The Impact of Crime* (1975).

68 N. Christie, ''Definition of Violent Behaviour'', XXIII Int. Course in Criminology (1974).

69 See *supra,* note 58, p. 189.

sample, 86 per cent of the respondents say they are satisfied with the work of the police. This is similar to the results obtained by Figgie in the United States, according to which 84 per cent of Americans show a high level of satisfaction with the police forces.[70] In general, the greater people's satisfaction with the police, the less they find that there are "too many" police (gamma = .38), and the more they believe that police are necessary to life in society (gamma = .50). In Canada, a person's satisfaction with the police is connected with feelings of security, social integration, victimization, age, and contacts with the system of criminal justice. For example, we find that 66 per cent of the people have a feeling of truly belonging to their neighbourhood, that 90 per cent feel very (30 per cent) or fairly (60 per cent) safe where they live, and that 89 per cent have great respect for the police in their district.

In the United States, according to the Figgie report, there is a predominantly positive attitude held by Americans toward the police. But this positive attitude, unfortunately, is not echoed in the way Americans feel about the criminal justice system. As the following facts show:

> Eight out of every ten Americans feel that the American judicial system is not effective in rehabilitating criminals or in helping them return to society as law-abiding citizens. In addition, more than half of all Americans feel that present prison sentencing does not serve as a deterrent to crime. Overwhelming majorities believe that we can neither help those who commit crimes nor control criminal activity through our present judiciary structure. By contrast, a clear majority of Americans (66%) do feel that the death penalty would be an effective deterrent to the crime of murder.[71]

Our research shows the same contrast between the attitudes of the public toward the police and those toward the courts and correctional institutions. The courts are even seen as being obstacles to police action: for 57 per cent of the respondents, "the judges' decisions prevent the police from being effective". How? Because the judges, according to 72 per cent of the persons interviewed, do not hand down severe enough sentences; because a criminal, according to 74 per cent of those questioned, can always go free if he or she has a good lawyer; and because, according to 77 per cent, the fact that the sentences are not harsh enough encourages people to commit crimes.

Because the Courts Are Not Severe Enough

People's negative image of the courts is largely due to the fact that sentences handed down by the judges do not have the deterrent power the public desires and expects. On the whole, what the surveys indicate is a disparity between the severity of the punishment the citizens want and the courts' sentencing of criminals. But this analysis of the results of the surveys where the punitive attitude of the population is concerned seems to us superficial and even excessive.

Stinchcombe *et al*[72] think that the question about harsher courts encour-

70 H. E. Figgie, *America Afraid: The Figgie Report on Fear and Crime, Part I* (1980).

71 *Ibid.*, p. 125.

72 L. A. Stinchcombe *et al.*, *Crime and Punishment: Changing Attitudes in America* (1980), p. 143.

ages people to consider the average crime, the average criminal, and perhaps the average victim, and to make an overall judgment. However, this hypothesis doesn't seem to be true — quite the contrary. When citizens are asked whether they would say, in general, that the sentences handed down by the courts are too severe, just severe enough, or not severe enough, most of them answer, not in terms of the average criminal, but of the most dangerous criminals. At least, this is what emerged from the C.R.O.P. survey[73] and our own study.[74]

In both cases, the people questioned were asked to specify the type of criminal they had in mind when giving their opinions on the severity of the sentences. In the C.R.O.P. sample, 41 per cent of the people had murderers in mind, 5 per cent had rapists, and 14 per cent dangerous criminals (*e.g.*, those involved in kidnapping, grievous assault and armed robbery). Thus, 60 per cent of the respondents thought of a criminality of violence, whereas 70 per cent said that the courts were not harsh enough. Our own data lead to the same conclusion: 32 per cent of the people were thinking of various forms of assassination and murder, 10 per cent of rape, and 22 per cent of grave criminality. Thus, of the 72 per cent who felt that the courts were too lenient with criminals, 64 per cent were thinking of "major" crimes and violent criminals. It seems evident, then, that for the general population, it is the dangerous criminal, the recidivist and the unrelenting criminal, who serve as the gauge by which they judge the severity of the courts and judges.

Most of the people interviewed blame the judges and the courts for not being severe enough, not with all criminals, but with the most dangerous ones, those who are a serious threat to the safety of the citizens. As they see it, it is mostly the habitual criminals who manage to pay the best lawyers and thus slip more easily through the hands of justice. Three out of four respondents think that a guilty person can always get off if he has a good lawyer. And added to this belief in the relative impunity of the most dangerous criminals is that of the inequality of justice.

Because Justice is Unequal and Discriminatory

A second reason why the public is cynical about criminal justice is that to many people it seems unequal and discriminatory.

Among those we questioned, two out of three people believed that the justice system today favours the rich over the poor. The study done by Moore for the Legal Research Institute records similar results. About half the population analyzed think that the courts treat some groups of people better than others (rich, wealthy, influential people, upper class, *etc.*) and some other groups worse than others (the poor, underprivileged, lower class, and criminals, *etc.*).

73 C.R.O.P., *5:3 Omnibus* (1980).

74 Y. Brillon, C. Louis-Guerin and M-C Lamarche, *Les Attitudes du Publique Canadienne envers les Politiques Criminelles: Rapport Final* (1982), p. 207.

The same view of justice is found in most countries. In France, to cite only one example, during a survey of the I.F.O.P., in March 1977, 66 per cent of the French agreed that French justice does not defend the poor as well as it does the rich. In February of the same year, 71 per cent of the French citizens who were questioned during a survey by SOFRES, agreed in saying that justice is not the same for people of modest means as it is for others.[75]

Our research data shows that it is the youngest and poorest people who most believe in the discriminatory nature of justice. This is probably because they live in areas where there are the greatest numbers of criminals and victims, and they belong to groups that are socially far removed from those to which the members of the courts belong. The result is that, due to the procedures, the legal language, and method of functioning, the justice system is considered by three out of four persons as so complicated that it's impossible to understand. And we must say that very little effort is made by the courts to simplify the functioning of the criminal justice system, and make it more accessible and comprehensible to the majority of the population.

Because the Criminal Justice System is Incapable of Neutralizing Criminals and Ensuring the Safety of Citizens

A third reason that seems to explain the public's negative attitude to the criminal justice system is that it has shown itself unable to make criminals ineffective and protect the citizens. The latter don't understand the mechanisms of sentencing and some of the prosecutorial decisions. And among these, the practice most disapproved of is that of plea bargaining. People seem to feel that if they can bargain with justice, it is not real justice. This type of procedure, in our opinion, is certainly bound to make people cynical about criminal justice.

Furthermore, as the public sees it, the fact that criminals, once convicted, can be released on parole removes the deterrent influence that punishments could have on potential delinquents. Besides, the indeterminate aspect of the sentences that parole introduces seems to make the population feel insecure. In our sample,[76] 56 per cent of the people think that, in general, prisoners are released too soon. Incidentally, we observed that there was a correlation between the fear of crime and the fact of being opposed to parole (gamma = .20; p = .002). A similar correlation also exists with regard to the fear of victimization (gamma = .17; p = .003).

This does not mean that the most concerned or the most fearful people are the most punitive. Our data clearly prove the contrary, that there is no connection between the fear of crime and punitiveness. In this, our results coincide with most of the research done on the fear of crime, as well as with the Figgie report, which confirms the absence of any correlation:

75 A. Peyrefitte, *Les Chevaux du Lac Lagoda* (1981), p. 5.

76 See *supra*, note 74, p. 309.

> With regard to *both* types of fear (concrete and formless), almost equal numbers of the fearful and non-fearful favor the death penalty and long prison sentences. The fearless are no more likely than the fearful to believe that long prison sentences discourage crime.[77]

Our figures, too, show a total absence of correlation between punitiveness and any of the following: victimization (gamma = .09), feelings of security (gamma = .02), the fear of going out alone at night because of crime (gamma = .03), gender (gamma = .01), the fear of being robbed (gamma = .09), or the fear of being attacked at home (gamma = .05). In spite of the fact that, since 1965, in the United States and elsewhere, there has been a constantly growing percentage of persons who say they are afraid of crime and of people who would like the courts' sentencing of criminals to be harsher, there is no direct relationship between the two phenomena.

People have become more punitive these last fews years than they were before because, it seems, the increase in crimes of violence has made them see almost all delinquents as dangerous criminals. Whether afraid or not, people have the same image of the offender, and it is this image, not fear, that determines their punitive attitudes. In other words, a large majority of the people questioned, 64 per cent as we saw, have murderers, rapists, and violent criminals in mind when they say that sentences are not severe enough.

The punitiveness of the population, then, reflects the gravity of the crimes used as scales to evaluate the severity of sanctions, and not the fact that these grave crimes create in some people more than in others a fear of crime or of victimization. If fear is an emotional reaction, then punitive or non-punitive attitudes seem to stem more from a person's lifestyle or world view. Our research has established a connection between punitiveness and conservatism or resistance to change. Thus, among the most punitive people we find those who are culturally the most deeply rooted in the past, in ancestral values and institutions, and those who are most in favour of maintaining the established order and acquired rights, namely, property owners, persons with high incomes, elderly persons, and rural residents.

Let us come back to the relationship mentioned earlier between the fear of crime and victimization and the strong opposition to parole. It shows that the public is not very happy about the fact that people condemned to prison can fairly quickly be released and start their criminal activities over again. The people feel that the criminal justice system is too flexible, and that it much too readily releases individuals who are a menace to society. They would like the correctional institutions to respect the judges' decisions and immobilize dangerous criminals by keeping them in prison.

CONCLUSION

By using the title "Public Opinion About the Penal System: A Cynical

77 H. E. Figgie, *America Afraid: The Figgie Report on Fear and Crime, Part I* (1980), p. 127.

View of Criminal Justice'', we wanted to show that the population's view of the penal system is far from positive. Justice has always been the subject of lively criticism, and has never ceased being regarded by most people in a cynical way. This is because justice is an ideal concept, a basic value which, since it is administered by human beings, is destined to be scoffed at, manipulated, and disdained. This is inevitable, since between the ideal and the reality, there will always be a certain amount of distortion. As far as the public today is concerned, this distortion seems to be assuming alarming proportions, to the point where many people are losing confidence in criminal justice. This is a serious matter. And it is up to the public authorities to make the reforms necessary to ensure equality before the law, to eliminate discrimination, and to ensure that justice is rendered to both the accused and the population. People have the right to live with the knowledge that the law ensures peace and public safety.

ASPECTS OF PUBLIC OPINION ABOUT LAW IN POLAND[78]

Adam Podgorecki

PRESTIGE OF THE LAW

It is possible to discuss the prestige of labour law, of criminal law, of administrative law, *etc.*, and it is also possible to discuss the prestige of the law as a whole. Respect for labour law, criminal law, administrative law, and even more of constitutional law depends greatly on the legitimacy of the legal system as a whole. This legitimacy depends on attitudes which have both political and economic dimensions, but are predominantly of a socio-psychological nature.

The Polish example is striking in this respect.[79] It is well known that in Poland the existing version of socialism does not enjoy the support of the population. One may venture that in a free democratic election the present political system would be abolished by an overwhelming majority. Nevertheless, even in this situation, almost half of the population expresses respect for the law (45%).[80]

78 This paper consists of extracts from a longer paper presented at the conference entitled ''Homo Juris.'' Other material from the longer presentation is included in *infra,* c. 9.

79 The material upon which this paper is based has been drawn from data previously published by the author. See A. Podgorecki, *Law and Society* (1974), esp. pp. 83-124; A. Podgorecki and M. Los, *Multidimensional Sociology,* (1979), pp. 160-66.

80 See A. Podgorecki, *ibid,* p. 95. This research showed the general respect for law in Poland was directed predominantly to civil and family law, and to the part of criminal law that deals with conventional crimes. Constitutional norms and the part of criminal law dealing with political matters were regarded as belonging to the political rather than the legal realm.

Polish socio-legal studies present a clear socio-psychological picture of the law-oriented and obedient personality. The following social categories are associated with a relatively higher respect for the law; people between the ages of 35-49 and those over 60; persons with higher education; white-collar workers; those whose families belong to the intelligentsia; people who feel secure;[81] people having limited affiliations;[82] the rationally disposed (not dogmatic);[83] and those engaged in social service work. These people tend, more than others, to respect the law even when it is considered wrong.

Correspondingly, the categories which more often than others declare a disposition to circumvent, ignore or violate legal regulations include: the 25-34 year age group; those either having no education or only elementary schooling; the offspring of strata other than the intelligentsia; unskilled workers (violation); skilled workers (circumvention); the inhibited (violation); the frustrated; those whose value systems are not dogmatic;[84] and, finally, people who are not engaged in social service work.

Additional data taken from Holland and West Germany give a possibility of some cross-national comparisons:

ATTITUDES TOWARDS THE LAW IN POLAND, HOLLAND AND WEST GERMANY[85]

Question (Statement)	Poland	Holland	West Germany
The law should always be obeyed even if, in your opinion, it is wrong. Agree	45%		
Do you think a law should be obeyed, even when you feel this law is unjust? Agree		47%	
You should obey the laws, even if you do not think that they are just. Agree			66%

These findings in general give a fairly consistent picture. This general

81 One of the main indicators: "Do you think that people should be trusted?"

82 Indications as to whether or not a person belonged to small primary groups was given, for example, by a response which read: "Apart from your family, do you know many people whose friendship and warm feelings you do not doubt? 1. No one, 2. Only a few, 3. A large number, 4. Don't know."

83 The indicator of mental inhibition was, for example, a question which read: "If you are in a large company and someone who is very sure of himself argues for a view that is the opposite of your own view, what would be your reaction? Would you 1. Give way, or withdraw your own view? 2. Show that he is wrong? 3. Carry on the conversation and find out during the discussion who was right? 4. Don't know."

84 Dogmatism is indicated by response to the question: "There are people who find it easy to judge the behaviour of others as good or bad, while other people have doubts about such judgments. Do you ever have such doubts? 1. On the whole I have no such doubts, 2. Sometimes I do have doubts, 3. I often have doubts, 4. I very often have such doubts, 5. Don't know, 6. I never think about such things."

85 See A. Podgorecki, *Law and Society* (1974), p. 95. (The Polish study, conducted in 1964, initiated similar research not only in Holland and West Germany but also in Bulgaria, Japan and some other countries.)

picture is that the law on the whole is accepted, and, additionally, that "those at the top", more than "underdogs", express a tendency to support the law.

Public opinion polls usually reveal only the *declaratory level* of manifested attitudes. This declaratory level is superficial, and may conceal inconsistent attitudes at deeper levels. The subject gives answers which are convenient in the circumstances. If somebody in a totalitarian regime casts a vote against his or her conscience, that person is declaring something contradictory to his or her real values.

It seems to be useful, therefore, to develop a device, which might be called a "commitment probe", that would make it possible to assess deeper attitudinal levels.

The first of these deeper strata that such a probe might reach below the declaratory level would be the *level of acceptance,* at which the subject gives answers corresponding to his or her real values. There is an even deeper level of commitment, however: the *level of dormant behaviour*. This is the level at which the subject is willing to act on his or her beliefs. In a totalitarian regime, this level is reached by the person who spoils his or her ballot, or, with even deeper commitment, refuses to sign a "loyalty oath", or refuses, perhaps under torture, to denounce co-workers.

Commitment probing would be very difficult to conduct in a totalitarian society. In democratic societies, it may easily be used at the declaratory and acceptual levels, but its use at the behavioural level might generate ethical objections.

PRINCIPLED AND INSTRUMENTAL ATTITUDES

One may analyze social and legal systems in terms of principled and instrumental attitudes. The "principled" attitude can be defined as a direct, spontaneous acceptance or rejection of some rule of behaviour. The "instrumental" attitude is one which makes the acceptance or rejection of behaviour dependent upon a calculation of possible alternative behaviour and an evaluation of their respective consequences. A principled attitude has reference to general and binding principles. An individual with a tendency to adopt a principled attitude will, in an unexpected situation for which there are no direct standards, patterns, or solutions, look for some general rule among those known to him. An individual with instrumental attitudes, when faced with a new, difficult and unexpected situation, will be inclined to consider it upon the basis of his or her own individual store of knowledge, and to choose the course of action that appears most profitable.[86]

This sort of distinction between attitudes concerning legal and moral behaviour may prove especially fertile. One is bound to assume that in stabilized political systems, principled attitudes will prevail, reflecting order

86 See A. Podgorecki and M. Los, *Multidimensional Sociology* (1979).

in the social structure. In changing systems, on the other hand, instrumental attitudes will prevail, as being more adequate to continually shifting circumstances. An overwhelming predominance of principled attitudes may be symptomatic of stagnation in a given social system. On the other hand, an overwhelming preponderance of instrumental attitudes may be a pathological situation as well, depriving the system of the core of elementary social values and ties that are indispensable to any society.

The Polish population was tested for instrumental and principled attitudes toward legal and moral questions in studies conducted in 1966 and 1970. Below is one of the more basic questions upon which this study was built:

''Some people have firm moral principles, and they are true to them regardless of the result — others strive above all to attain their goal. What is your opinion on the subject?''

		Per cent	
		Urban	Rural
1.	One should always be true to one's principles in behaviour regardless of the result (principled attitude)	22.5	22.3
2.	If conformity to principles were to bring undesirable results, it would be better to think over one's principles and adapt them to the situation (mixed attitude)	39.3	32.8
3.	Rigid principles are altogether superfluous; one should behave so as to obtain the desired effect (instrumental attitude)	31.2	31.6
4.	I am unable to decide	6.7	13.0
	(in research of 1966, N = 3,178) . . . . (repeated in research of 1970, N = 2,197)	99.7	99.7

A summary of the major findings is as follows:

1. Principled attitudes increase with age.

2. An increase in the level of education basically increases instrumental attitudes. However, a college education produces a mixed attitude which is a compromise between the principled and instrumental.

3. Leadership positions are linked with either principled or mixed attitudes.

4. Skilled workers and craftsmen are predominantly instrumentally oriented; white-collar workers are oriented toward mixed attitudes.

5. Insecurity and lack of good life-adjustment are related to instrumental

attitudes, while principled attitudes seem to be correlated with security and good life-adjustment. Further analysis also shows that rural inhabitants tend to have principled orientations, while city dwellers are more instrumentally oriented.[87]

SANCTIONS AND PUNITIVENESS

According to the series of Polish studies devoted to this subject, attitudinal severity toward criminals is associated with the following features: lower education, blue collar work, feelings of insecurity, social isolation, severe upbringing, dogmatic life orientation, social maladjustment, and frustration. Tolerance is associated with characteristics such as: relatively high education, white collar work, psychological security, lack of social isolation, "participation in social work" (willingness to perform certain social tasks without reimbursement), tolerant upbringing, social adjustment, and lack of frustration. Generally speaking, two findings were striking: (1) Traditional "objective" sociological variables, such as sex, age, or father's occupation, were less decisive than subjective ones such as frustration, maladjustment, and rationality; (2) "Underdogs" had a tendency towards expressing severity, whereas "topdogs" associated themselves mainly with tolerant attitudes.

Since some of these findings were somewhat contradictory to the main tenor of reliable Scandinavian studies,[88] additional Polish inquiries were designed to analyze this matter in a more detailed way. Four basic areas were singled out for closer attention.[89] The basic results of these tests were:

(i) Infringements of the norms of procedure were more strongly condemned by those with principled attitudes (spontaneous acceptance or rejection of rules of behaviour without regard to possible consequences), those without insecure feelings, and those who regarded themselves as socially well adjusted.

(ii) Breaches of the institution of ownership were tolerated more by those with lower social position (with respect to occupation), younger persons, those with lower education, and those expressing attitudes of insecurity and instrumentality. The following categories were more inclined to support more rigorous legal sanctions for property offenses: those with higher social position (with respect to occupation), those with higher education, older persons, those without insecurity feelings, those with principled attitudes, and those with better social adjustment.

(iii) Condemnation of violations of elementary norms of social coexist-

87 See A. Podgorecki, *supra,* note 85, pp. 99-100.

88 B. Kutschinski, "Law and Education: Some Aspects of Scandinavian Studies into 'The General Sense of Justice' " (1966), 10 Studia Sociologica, Fasc. 1-2 at 21.

89 See A. Podgorecki, *supra,* note 85.

ence (for example: unwillingness to provide help for somebody in danger; bigamy; lies which do not bring profit but cause moral harm; drunkenness, *etc.*) is connected with lower social position (on the occupational scale), older age, widowhood, principled attitudes, good social adjustment, and lack of insecurity feelings. Tolerance in this area is associated with relatively higher social position (in the occupational scale), youth, bachelorhood, instrumental attitudes, social maladjustment, and attitudes of insecurity.

(iv) As far as pure punitiveness (the tendency to choose those punishments which are more severe) is concerned, the findings were different for two different situations. (1) When the infringements of the law were not clearly recognized as such, or when there was wide disagreement about appropriate sanctions for particular infringements, then those in a lower social position, and those who were less educated, insecure, and maladjusted, demanded more punitiveness. (2) When the infringements of the law were clearly recognized as such, or when there was general agreement on sanctions, those who had higher social positions, who had higher education, who were psychologically secure, and who were well socially adjusted, were more punitive.

One of the general conclusions of the Polish studies on tolerance and punitiveness is that: attitudes of tolerance or severity with respect to the legal system reflect much more than one's concern for the system (although lawyers certainly respond to such institutional concerns); they are also rooted in many other social and personal factors. Moreover, there is not just one type of tolerance and severity, but there are various sub-categories of these attitudes applicable to different areas of social life. The second general conclusion is that a relatively higher social position is associated with more tolerant attitudes toward: (1) alien ideas,[90] (2) violation of norms based on generally accepted values, and (3) the use of punishment. At the same time, higher social position correlates with less tolerance towards infringement of the norms of procedure and the abuse of the institution of property ownership. In other words: The "top dogs" more strongly defend adherence to the rules of procedure and those which protect their possessions, whereas the "underdogs" demand harsher than usual punishments when basic inter-human values are violated. In sum, in the case of the selection of appropriate sanctions for a given infringement, an individual may react on the basis of his or her attachment to the ideology, spirit, or practice of the given legal system, or on that of his or her socio-psychological conditioning.

Another Polish study indicates that the Polish legal system is very

90 W. Wisniewski, "Tolerancja a Egalitaryzm" [Tolerance versus Egalitarianism] (1963), 2 *Studia Socjologiczne*, p. 203.

punitive.[91] It is, in fact, one of the most punitive legal systems in Europe.[92] It is possible to explain this severity as a reflection of certain public attitudes. According to the previously quoted studies, members of the "lower" strata of Polish society adopt a more punitive attitude toward punishments. It is generally well known that those people who presently constitute the newer elite in Poland belong to the traditional "lower" classes. If the Polish legal system is punitive, the punitive values held by the new elite may be at least partly responsible.

A concluding commentary by Scott Burbidge, of the Ministry of the Solicitor General of Canada, included a note of caution about the usefulness of public opinion surveys:

> The public attitude research that has been done has purported to show us the major concerns of Canadians vis-à-vis crime and the criminal justice system, but it has also shown us many limitations in this information. These limitations raise very serious questions about the use of such data in law making. We know, for example, that the public endorses the value of rehabilitating prison inmates, but when people are probed further, they can give very few specific descriptions of how we should go about rehabilitating offenders. We know that the public is satisfied with the police, but they don't know very much about what the police do. And we know that the public is concerned about dangerous offenders, but grossly exaggerates the extent of dangerous crime in our society.
>
> We also know from our research that the results of public attitude polls are often a product of the way surveys are conducted, and the way questions are asked. A particularly good illustration of this phenomenon is drawn from research to measure the level of public concern with crime as a social problem in Canada.[93] One approach to this problem in the polls has been to present respondents with a list of social problems including crime, unemployment, inflation, *etc.*, and to ask them to indicate the relative importance that they attach to each. When the public is presented with these predetermined lists of social problems, crime invariably comes out about third. However, when we try to get at the same information by asking a general question, such as: "What do you think are the major social problems facing Canada today?", or some variant of that, crime is very rarely mentioned. It virtually disappears from the list. So the question remains open as to what is the real level of public concern about crime in Canada?

---

91 J. Jasinski, "Punitywnosc Systemow Prawnych" [Punitiveness of Criminal Systems] (1973), 35 *Studia Prawnicze*. In this study punitiveness was measured by several indicators. Among others the following were taken into consideration: the number of prisoners per capita, the judges' tendency to choose prison sentences over fines, the duration of the prison sentence, and special sanctions like the death penalty. Research was focused on the behaviour of the representatives of administration of justice (not on the behaviour of "average citizens"). Although in the modern world there is a tendency to use fines instead of prison sentences (85-92%), in Poland this tendency is much weaker (70%). In 1970-72, 6% of Polish prisoners were sentenced to more than one year, whereas this per cent was 69.1% in Italy, 59.3% in Belgium, 57.6% in France and 55% in German Fed. Republic. In Poland sentences of five years were used more often.

92 J. Waller and J. Chan, "Prison Use: A Canadian and International Comparison" (1974-75), 17 Criminal Law Quarterly 47.

93 Francine Bertrand, "Public Opinion About Criminal Justice Issues: Some Cautions About Poll Data" (1982), *Impact* (No. 1) 14 (Ministry of the Solicitor General of Canada).

> And a second question arises: to what extent is this particular example of variation in poll results a reflection of a systemic inability of the polls to provide valid measures of public concerns about criminal justice?
>
> We also have to keep in mind that the results of these polls are published. Thus the responses of Canadians are likely influenced by having read the published results of previous surveys.
>
> In my more cynical moments I've felt that perhaps it would be useful if we could declare a moratorium, perhaps a five-year moratorium, on taking any further surveys. We could use that period to see how our policy-making proceeds in the absence of such information, to digest the results of the surveys done to date, and to design more innovative approaches to the public for the future. That's my reaction in my more cynical moments. On the other hand, I recognize that polls have become firmly entrenched in our public debate on criminal justice issues, and that we must be prepared to deal with them, and consider their possible implications for criminal justice making. It is very important, however, to ensure that both the public and the policy-makers who use and absorb the results of these polls fully understand the limits of the information with which they are dealing.

Richard Linden, who chaired the conference panel on "other studies", expressed concern about the uses to which the survey results might be put:

> What is to be done with the results of these surveys? What are the policy implications? Now that pollsters have talked to the public, and the public have given their opinions, what is to prevent the data becoming, in Professor Raz' delightful phrase, a mere "haphazard assemblage of curiosities"?

He pointed to the difficulty of translating public opinion into policy in a manner that avoids, on the one hand, automatic reliance on transitory, uninformed or localized opinion, and, on the other, ideologically "filtered" interpretation of public opinion, by which the interests of special groups can be substituted for those of the general public. This is a topic to which we will return in Chapter 11.

PART II

SPECIFICS

4

PUBLIC OPINION AND THE POLICE

William Greenaway pointed out that during the last 30 years, there have been many studies of the police and public attitudes towards the police,[1] though there have been few attempts to analyze the determinants of these attitudes. Public opinion surveys have rather consistently shown positive attitudes towards the police, and the Legal Research Institute Survey in general supported that conclusion.[2]

John Hylton agreed with these Legal Research Institute Survey results, but noted that the public was concerned about some specific issues — in particular, police-community relations and the lack of communication between police and the public,[3] police integrity[4] and the inequities of the justice system as a whole.[5]

PUBLIC ATTITUDES TOWARDS CRIME AND THE POLICE IN A PRAIRIE CITY[6]

John H. Hylton

PREVIOUS STUDIES

While each of the [few major studies[7] of public attitudes towards crime

1 Arthur Niederhoffer, *Behind the Shield: The Police in Urban Society* (1967); Jerome Skolnick, *Justice Without Trial: Law Enforcement in Democratic Society*, 2nd ed. (1975); W. A. Westley, *Violence and the Police: A Sociological Study of Law, Custom and Morality* (1970); R. V. Ericson, *Reproducing Order: A Study of Police Patrol Work* (1982); J. H. Hylton, *A Directory of Justice Services for Persons of Indian Ancestry in Manitoba, Saskatchewan and Alberta* (1980).

2 *Supra*, The Legal Research Institute Survey, c. 2, questions 43, 50.

3 *Ibid.*, question 46(f).

4 *Ibid.*, question 48(a-f).

5 *Ibid.*, question 44(a), (b).

6 This paper appears in full in (1980), 4:4 Can. Police College Journal 243. Permission from the Canadian Police College to include these excerpts in the proceedings is gratefully acknowledged.

7 E. A. Fattah and A. Normandeau, *Sondage D'Opinion Publique Sur La Justice Criminelle au Quebec Montreal* (1969); M. C. Courtis and I. Dussuyer, *Attitudes to Crime and the Police in Toronto: A Report on Some Survey Findings* (1970); M. C. Courtis, "The Police and the Public" in C. L. Boydell, P. C. Whitehead and C. F. Grindstaff (eds.), *The Administration of*

and the police in Canada] contributes to our understanding of the impact of the justice system on the public, when taken together, a number of gaps in knowledge are evident. Firstly, much of the research cited above is now dated. Since the experiences and the attitudes of the public do not remain constant over time, studies conducted five or ten years ago may not accurately reflect current opinions or concerns. Secondly, there have been few studies of a national scope and most of these have dealt with circumscribed issues, such as capital punishment. Attitudinal research from the prairies and the Atlantic provinces is noticeably absent from the literature. Thirdly, there has been little attempt systematically to examine the relationships among attitudes, experiences, knowledge, and behaviour. Fourthly, many studies have suffered from methodological problems. Adequate sampling and poor return rates for mailed questionnaires have been particularly troublesome. Finally, not much emphasis has been placed on the development of reliable and valid measures for assessing public attitudes towards the criminal justice system.

BACKGROUND TO THE PRESENT STUDY

In the summer of 1978 the chief of the Regina Police Department appointed a steering committee to study the feasibility of adopting a system of zone policing in the city of Regina. In collaboration with representatives of the Regina City Policeman's Association, the committee undertook an examination of the philosophical assumptions underlying the zone policing model, discussed implications with various government officials, and visited cities where zone policing was in operation. As a result of its investigation, the committee recommended that a system of zone policing be adopted in Regina.

On March 1st, 1979, two members of the Regina Police Department were appointed to examine the implications of implementing zone policing for research, planning, and training. Because the introduction of zone policing required some significant changes in the organization of policing services, it soon became evident that consideration should be given to the development of a mechanism for monitoring public experiences with and public attitudes towards crime and the police. On the one hand, there were concerns that the proposed changes would disrupt traditional police practices, while on the other hand, zone policing had been widely acclaimed as a method for improving the quality of services provided to the community.

Criminal Justice in Canada (1974); C. L. Boydell and C. F. Grindstaff, "Public Opinion and the Criminal Law" in C. L. Boydell, C. F. Grindstaff and P. C. Whitehead (eds.), *Deviant Behaviour and Societal Reaction* (1972); D. J. Koenig, *British Columbians' Attitudes and Experiences Relevant to the Police, Law and Crime* (1974); M. L. Goetz, *Citizen Attitudes Toward the Police in Vancouver*; E. A. Fattah, *The Canadian Public and the Death Penalty* (1976); C. H. S. Jaywardene, *The Penalty of Death: The Canadian Experiment* (1977); A. Singh, "Attitudes of Canadians Toward Crime and Punishment" (1979), 21 Can. Journal of Criminology.

It was decided that a survey would be conducted prior to the implementation of zone policing, in order to gather baseline information about public experiences and attitudes. By surveying a second time after zone policing had been implemented, it would then be possible to determine whether or not any significant changes had occurred. . . . This paper discusses how the survey was conducted and what the findings of the study were.

METHODOLOGY

The investigation of public attitudes towards crime and the police in Regina entailed the administration of a questionnaire to a sample of Regina citizens. . . .

Method of Drawing the Sample

The sample was drawn from the 1978 city directory for Regina. This directory lists the names of residents, over eighteen years of age, by street and number. Every 76th name was chosen, resulting in a sample of five hundred and seventy-six (576). Some of those whose names were listed in the directory had moved while others had apparently been listed incorrectly. Of the original 576 individuals selected for inclusion in the study, questionnaires were actually dropped off to 552 persons.

Completed questionnaires were received back from 438 of the 552 respondents (this is a return rate of almost 80%). Figure 1 illustrates how the city of Regina has been divided into zones for the purpose of zone policing.

FIGURE 1

The City of Regina illustrating Police Zones

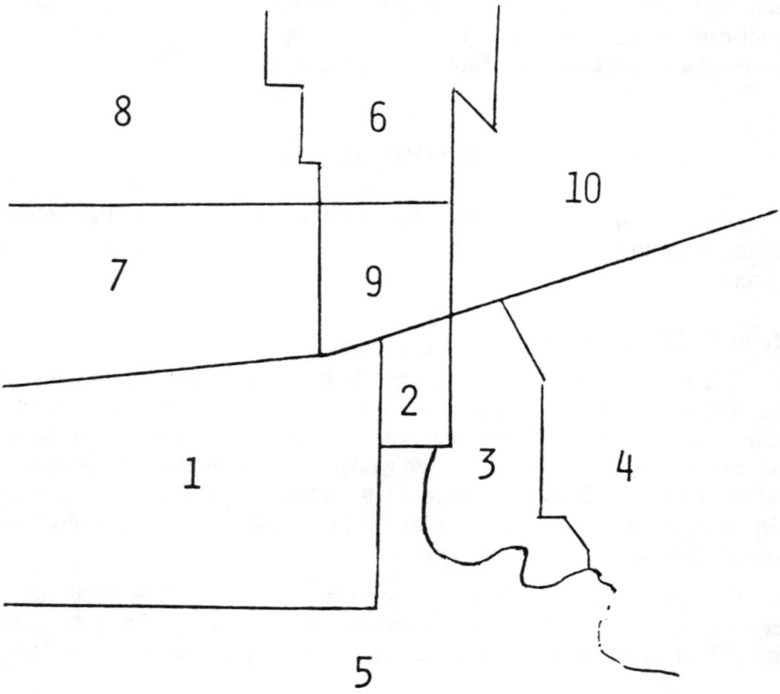

Zone 2 — downtown business core.
Zone 1, 3, 7, 9 — mixed residential and business districts; older housing and some deteriorating conditions are evident close to the downtown business core.
Zone 4, 5, 6, 10 — primarily residential; more modern housing and facilities. Zone 10 contains an industrial area.

The Characteristics of the Sample

Some characteristics of the study sample include:

1. Sex: 44.7% male; 53.7% female;

2. Marital Status: 71.5% married; 15.8% single; 12.7% widowed, separated or divorced;

3. Age: Average age was 42.2 years;

4. Racial and Ethnic Origin: 50% English, Scottish or Irish descent; 20% German descent; 10% Ukrainian descent; less than 1% North American Indian descent;

5. Education: 68% had completed high school education;

6. Income: Average family income was between $20,000 and $30,000 per annum;

7. Employment: 73.3% were employed; 13.5% were homemakers; 7.5% were retired; 2.5% were unemployed; there were 2 students;

8. Transience: On average, respondents had lived in their current neighbourhood for 10 years and in Regina for 20 years;

9 Type of Dwelling: 85% resided in single family dwellings; 15.6% resided in apartments or other multiple family dwellings;

10. Living Arrangements: 80% lived with their immediate family; 11% lived alone.

These characteristics of the sample could, in many instances, be compared with the characteristics of the total Regina population as reported in Statistics Canada census tracts. The comparisons revealed that the sample was generally representative of the larger Regina population. . . . While there are estimated to be between 20,000 and 30,000 persons of Indian ancestry living in Regina (13%-20% of the total population), less than 1% of the respondents indicated an Indian ancestry. Thus, the sample seriously under-represented persons of Indian ancestry, while it somewhat over-represented better educated respondents, those living with their families and those living in single family dwellings.

Problems of representativeness may be attributed to two facts: the city directory was used to draw the sample and not all the respondents selected to participate in the study returned completed questionnaires. Those who can't afford telephones, who move frequently, or who live with more than one family in a single dwelling, are less likely to have their names listed in the city directory. Those who were not literate in English, or who did not want to participate in a study sponsored by the police would have been less likely to return completed questionnaires. These factors may help to explain why the poor (and this includes a very large proportion of the Native community) were less likely to be represented in the sample. These problems of representativeness need to be taken into consideration when interpreting the findings of this study.

CRIME AND CONTACT WITH THE POLICE IN REGINA

The questionnaire administered to the sample contained a number of items to determine whether or not the respondents had been victimized by cirme, as well as to gauge the amount of contact the respondents had had with the police. We felt that this information, while valuable in itself, might help explain attitudes towards crime and the police. This section presents the findings with respect to the victimization questions and the questions about police contacts. In the next section the relationships between these variables and public attitudes are explored.

Crime in Regina

1. The Number of Victims and the Types of Crime

Of the 438 respondents, 74 (16.9%) indicated they had personally been victimized by crime in the previous six months. Most of the offences were property crimes and a large number of these appeared to be relatively minor offences such as theft of goods under $200. Violent crimes, or crimes against the person, were reported much less frequently. Although 8.3% of the offences related to threats, only three assaults were reported and no one reported rape, attempted rape, murder, attempted murder, or indecent acts.

In addition to the 74 respondents who reported they had been victimized, 97 respondents (22.1%) reported a member of their household, relative, neighbour or friend had been victimized in the previous six months. In all, 171 respondents (39.0%) indicated they, or someone they knew personally, had been victimized in the previous six months.

2. Alcohol and Drugs

Respondents who had been victimized were asked to indicate whether alcohol and/or drugs had played some part in the crime. Fourteen per cent of the respondents felt alcohol had been a consideration, while three per cent felt drugs had been a factor. Eighty-three per cent indicated alcohol or drugs were not factors, or that they didn't know whether substance-use was involved.

3. Where the Crimes Were Committed

Forty of the victims (54.1%) reported they had been victimized in their residence or on their property. Twenty-seven respondents (36.5%) reported they had been victimized in a public place, such as a hotel or on the street. Only three respondents reported the crime had been committed in the residence or on the property of a friend, relative or neighbour.

4. Hour of the Day

Respondents were asked to report, to the best of their knowledge, what hour of the day they were victimized. One third of the respondents who answered this question reported they had been victimized between 10:00 p.m. and 1:59 a.m. An additional 20% reported being victimized in the early morning between 2:00 and 5:59 a.m. From 6:00 a.m. to 10:00 p.m. the number of incidents reported was noticeably lower.

5. The Relationship Between Offender and Victim

Respondents were asked if they had any knowledge of the person who had victimized them. About a third of the respondents indicated they did not know who had victimized them. Half the respondents said the offender was a complete stranger. Nearly 20% of the respondents said they did know the offender. With the exception of three cases, these latter respondents indicated they had been victimized by a neighbour.

6. Involvement of the Police

Of the 74 respondents who indicated they had been victimized in the previous six months, 46 (66.7%) reported the crime to the police while 23 (33.3%) did not. Five respondents did not answer this question. The 23 repondents who did not report the crime to the police were asked why. The most common reason, given by 13 respondents, was the feeling that the offence was too minor to bother with. Four of the 23 respondents indicated they did not report the offence because they felt the police would not do anything about it anyway.

The 46 repondents who reported the crime to the police were asked what immediate action the police took. In over half the cases the police provided information or assistance of one form or another. In 20% of the cases no action was needed or taken. In a small number of situations (3.7%) respondents said there was no response to the call. Other actions included making arrests, giving warnings, and referring problems to other agencies.

7. Events Since the Crime Was Reported to Police

Respondents who reported a crime to the police were asked what had happened since they made the report. The vast majority of respondents (33 or 84.6%) indicated they had not been informed of police progress while only a few (6 or 15.4%) said they had been kept informed.

Respondents were asked if they had received any compensation for the crime. Half said they had not. Of those who had received some form of compensation, over 80% had been compensated by their own insurance companies. Only two victims said they had been compensated by persons who had victimized them.

Respondents were also asked if they knew what had happened to the person who had victimized them. Over three quarters of the respondents indicated they did not know. Of those who did know, six reported the offender had not been charged and three said the offender had been tried and convicted.

8. Some Characteristics of the Victims

Those who reported they had been victimized in the last six months were different in important respects from others in the sample. The areas hardest hit by crime would appear to be Areas 1, 7 and 9. These areas border the downtown business district to the north and west. These areas also generally contain the older housing in the city and in some, like the warehouse district, conditions have deteriorated in recent years. On average, one in four respondents in these areas reported being victimized while, in the remainder of the city, the average was one in eight.

On average, just over one in five respondents reported they knew someone who had been victimized. In some areas of the city, however, the figure approached a third of the respondents while in other areas of the city, the figure was one in six or less.

Victims were more likely to be single, widowed or separated while those who did not report being victimized were more likely to be married. This suggests that married persons are less susceptible to crime while persons who live alone are more susceptible.

Victims were, on average, better educated than those who did not report being victimized. Of course, education is only one element in overall occupational status, income and lifestyle. Better educated respondents might be expected to have more material possessions and, in this sense, they would more likely be the victims of theft or vandalism.

Contact With the Police in Regina

Respondents were asked a variety of questions concerning the amount and type of police contact they, and others close to them, had experienced in the previous six months.

1. Police Contacts Related to Charges and Arrests

Respondents were asked if members of their household, relatives, friends or neighbours had had contacts with the police in the previous six months. Respondents were also asked if they had had any experience with the police themselves. Thirty-two respondents (7.6%) indicated a charge had been laid against a member of their household in the previous six months. A similar number indicated charges has been laid against friends. Only 18 respondents (4.2%) said they themselves had been charged. One respondent reported he had been arrested.

2. Other Police Contacts

Contact with the police for reasons other than a charge or an arrest appear to be quite common. Over one third of the respondents (152 or 35.7%) said they themselves had experienced such contacts with the police in the previous six months.

Respondents who indicated they had had some official contact with the Regina City Police in the previous six months, for some reason other than a charge or an arrest, were asked to indicate the reason for the contact and the action taken by the police. The most common reasons given for this type of police contact were related to the operation of motor vehicles. A third of the respondents indicated they had come into contact with the police for a traffic violation or in relation to a traffic accident. Other common reasons included the reporting of a dangerous, suspicious or annoying situation (17.5%); reporting being a witness to a crime (4.9%); and requesting information (11.2%) or assistance (10.5%).

Respondents who indicated they had experienced some official contact with the Regina City Police in the previous six months were asked to report the action taken by the police. Cases where a criminal charge was laid against the respondent or where the respondent was arrested were excluded from this analysis since these cases were dealt with separately.

The most common actions of the police included filling out a report (27.3%), providing information (21.7%), and issuing a traffic ticket (19.3%). Other less frequently reported actions included issuing a traffic warning, referring the problem to another agency, and correcting a dangerous, suspicious or annoying situation. Ten per cent of the respondents indicated no action on the part of the police was needed or taken.

3. Some Characteristics of Those Who Came Into Contact With the Police

As with the victims of crime, those who reported coming into contact with the police were different in important respects from those who reported no police contacts. Contacts with the police, for reasons other than a charge or an arrest, were correlated with whether or not the respondent was employed, the education of the respondent, and his or her occupational status. It should be recalled that the major reasons for this type of contact had to do with [the] reporting of information to the police, requesting the help or assistance of the police, and instances relating to the operation of motor vehicles. The findings suggest that "lower-class" respondents are less likely to report these kinds of contacts with the police than are "middle-class" respondents. It is interesting to note, however, that occupational status is negatively associated with being charged by the police. "Lower-class" respondents were more likely to report being charged than were "middle-class" respondents.

Male respondents and those who reported they did not live alone were also more likely to have contacts with the police not related to a charge or arrest. The greater involvement with the police reported by men may reflect the fact that men have traditionally assumed responsibility for communicating with the police on behalf of their families. In addition, men are more frequently involved in unlawful activity, and thus, are more frequently the subject of police investigations. That those who live alone have less frequent contact with the police may indicate there is a segment of society isolated from some activities in the larger community. This may be particularly true, for example, of elderly persons who live alone.

It is interesting to note that there is a close relationship between being victimized by crime and coming into contact with the police. Moreover, those who were charged or arrested by the police were also more likely to report being victimized in the previous six months. These findings suggest there may be considerable overlap among the "victims" and the "victimizers".

PUBLIC ATTITUDES TOWARDS CRIME

In this section the findings respecting public attitudes towards crime and the police are presented. Respondents were asked to react to some 75 statements about crime and the police by indicating: 'strongly agree'; 'agree'; 'disagree'; or 'strongly disagree'. These individual items needed to be organized in some meaningful way. To do this, factor analysis was used and simple additive scales were created . . . .

Fear of Crime

Eight questionnaire items concerned whether or not respondents feared being victimized by crime. Some of the items concerned the extent to which respondents felt safe living in Regina. Other items referred to behavioural manifestations of fear and the public's conception of the role of the police in reducing fear.

About a third of the sample worried a lot about becoming a victim of crime. Only 6% of the sample reported being afraid to walk alone in their neighbourhood during the day; however, a third reported they were afraid to walk alone at night. Although many respondents reported feeling safe in their own neighbourhood, only 4% of the sample could agree that a person could walk alone anywhere in Regina without fear of crime.

In terms of behavioural manifestations of fear, one in six respondents reported fear of crime had led them to change or limit their normal activities in some way, and 6% of the respondents agreed their neighbourhood was so dangerous they would like to move. Most respondents seemed to feel that the police have a role to play in reducing the fear of crime. Half indicated that more police officers were needed in their neighbourhoods and an equal number said they would feel safer if police walked around in their neighbourhood.

The [statistical] analysis indicates that the fear of crime was associated with a number of socio-demographic variables and also with a number of variables respecting victimization and police contacts. Among the socio-demographic variables, both sex and marital status were significantly correlated with fear of crime. Women were significantly more likely to report they feared crime. Single and married respondents had lower [fear of crime] than widowed, separated or divorced respondents. The living situation of respondents also seemed to be important. [Fear of crime was] lower among those who reported living with their immediate family and higher among those who reported living alone, with relatives or with friends. Fear of crime was significantly lower among respondents who reported living in single family dwellings, when compared with those who reported living in a duplex, apartment or condominium. Moreover, there were significant differences in the fear of crime associated with the area of the city in which respondents lived. By far the greatest fear of crime was reported by respondents in Area 2, that is, the downtown business core area. Somewhat less fear was reported by respondents in Areas 3, 7, 9 and 10. Still less fear was reported by respondents in Areas 1, 4, 6 and 8. The least fear was reported by respondents in Area 5.

The fear of crime was associated with the social class of respondents. Respondents who reported higher incomes, those who were better educated, and those who reported working in jobs with higher occupational status, were less likely to fear crime.

A number of variables associated with victimization and police contacts were related to the fear of crime. If respondents had been victimized by crime, or if they had friends who had been victimized, they were more likely to report fear of crime. Among the victims, those who reported they had a personal relationship with the person who victimized them were more likely to [fear crime] than those who did not know who had victimized them. Interestingly, victims who had been compensated were significantly less likely to be afraid of crime, when compared with victims who had not been compensated.

Police contacts, other than for a charge or arrest, were also important in accounting for fear of crime, but the reason for the contact seemed to determine the nature of the relationship. If the reason for the contact was to report being a victim of crime or to report a dangerous, suspicious or annoying situation, or if it was related to a request for information or assistance, then respondents seemed to be more afraid than if the contact was related to a traffic violation, a traffic accident, or a routine traffic check.

Taken together, these findings suggest that many Regina citizens fear being a victim of crime. Fear appears to be most evident among that segment of the community which is most vulnerable to crime, particularly women, those not living with their immediate families, and those who reside in apartments or multiple unit dwellings close to the downtown business district. Among those who are high in social status, the fear of crime is not as acute. This may reflect perceptions about the hardship that might accompany crime. Since those high in social status would be in the best position to cope with the consequences of some crimes, particularly property crimes, they may not perceive crime to be as great a threat as other respondents. Consistent with this interpretation, compensation appears to reduce the fear of crime. It is also likely, however, that some segments of the community are better able than others to avoid environments where there is a high probability of being victimized.

Among individual respondents, fear of crime was associated with being victimized in the previous six months. Among the victims, fear was heightened if some personal relationship existed between the victim and the victimizer. Because neighbours were most frequently singled out in cases where the offender was known to the victim, the findings suggest the fear of crime is greatest in areas where there is a high probability of being victimized by a neighbour.

The fear of crime is also closely related to the area of the city in which respondents reported residing. Of course, this variable is closely associated with type of housing, social class, and other factors. Yet it is somewhat puzzling that respondents in Area 2, the downtown core area, reported the greatest fear of crime, while the respondents in the zones bordering the downtown core (Areas 1, 7 and 9) reported being victimized the most. This suggests [that] no simple relationship between the fear of crime and the probability of being victimized exists. In the downtown area, the visibility of the police, the visible measures for deterring crime adopted by many businesses, and other factors may heighten the fear of residents who live in that area. In other words, there may well be environmental conditions which heighten or lessen the fear of crime and which are independent of the actual volume of crime in a given area.

The Seriousness of Crime and Measures Required to Cope with Crime

Unlike the items which concentrated on subjective feelings of safety or fear, the eleven items discussed [in this part of the study] concentrate on public opinions about the extent of the crime problem and the appropriate measures for dealing with crime. Some of these items deal with the extent of crime and the nature of criminals. Other items concern perceptions about the appropriate treatment of offenders. The final three items have to do with views about the public's role in coping with crime.

Nearly three quarters of the respondents felt crime in Regina was more serious than portrayed in the media. Nearly half the respondents felt most criminals had criminal personalities and two thirds indicated police had to treat suspects with authority if they were not to be seen as weak. Nearly 90% of respondents felt it was the threat of punishment that kept crime from getting out of control in society.

Many respondents favoured harsher treatment of offenders. Two thirds of the sample said they felt there was too much emphasis on the rights of offenders. Over half said the police were too lenient with juveniles. Eight out of ten respondents felt convicted offenders should receive longer sentences and nearly 80% favoured the reinstatement of capital punishment.

While over 90% of the respondents felt the public should be more involved in crime control programs in their neighbourhoods, less than one in four respondents felt the public should be able to possess any weapon for protection. Eight in ten respondents said they would strongly recommend police work to someone they knew was interested.

The [statistical] analysis indicates that views about the seriousness of crime are associated with respondents' socio-demographic characteristics. Respondents who were high in terms of occupational status, those who had larger incomes, and those who reported more education, were less likely to perceive crime and criminals as a serious problem. Respondents who had lived in Regina longer, and those who reported residing in their present neighbourhoods longer, were more likely to emphasize the seriousness of crime. Respondents who reported owning a business were also more likely to underscore the seriousness of crime.

Views about the seriousness of crime and criminals were also associated with police contacts. The more often friends or neighbours had come into contact with the police, the more respondents were inclined to perceive crime and criminals as a serious problem. Among respondents who had themselves been victimized, those who reported the crime to the police were less likely [to perceive crime as a serious problem than those who did not report the crime]. If the respondents knew who had victimized them, they were more likely to think crime was a serious problem.

Taken together, the findings would seem to indicate many Regina citizens perceive crime to be a serious problem. Most seem to believe [that] the exercise of authority and the use of punishment are needed to deter crime and that offenders, because of their unique personality makeups, are not deterred in the same way as most other people. Given these views, it is probably not surprising that most respondents felt harsher treatment of offenders was appropriate and that the community needed to be more fully involved in measures to cope with crime.

The respondents who believed crime and criminals were a serious problem shared many characteristics in common with those who feared crime. In fact, there was a high correlation between the scores on the two scales. Respondents who scored high in terms of occupational status, for example, were less likely to be alarmed. As with the fear of crime, this is probably related to how respondents viewed their abilities to cope with the consequences of crime. If crime was prevalent in the respondent's community (that is, if friends and neighbours had come into contact with the police, or the respondent had been victimized by a neighbour or had reported a crime to the police), then the crime problem was perceived to be more serious. Once again, however, there was no simple relationship between being victimized by crime and viewing the crime problem as serious. In fact, respondents in areas hardest hit by crime were not those who scored highest on the seriousness scale. Once again, other environmental factors seem to play a part in shaping respondents' perceptions.

PUBLIC ATTITUDES TOWARDS THE POLICE

Communication With The Public

The first two scales concerned public perceptions about crime. Here we turn to an examination of public perceptions about the police. Five questionnaire items focused on the quality of communication between the police and the public, and on the public's desire to improve communication. Three of these items concerned the public's perception of police efforts to communicate, while the remaining two items had to do with the public's interest in improving communication.

Over 50% of the respondents felt the police did not receive adequate training on how to deal with the public. Two thirds felt the police were not doing an adequate job informing the public about police roles and objectives, and an equal number felt the police did not spend enough time educating the public about how to reduce crime.

Most respondents expressed interest in improving communication. Over 80% felt meetings between the police and the public would be beneficial. Two thirds reported they were interested in knowing police officers on a first-name basis.

The [statistical] analysis indicates that the more contacts the respondent reported with the police, the more likely he or she was to feel that communication between the police and the public needed to be improved. Similarly, those respondents who knew others who had been victimized, or others who had had contacts with the police, were more likely to voice the need for better communication.

The need for better communication was also associated with a number of respondent characteristics. Respondents with higher incomes, those with better education, and employed as opposed to unemployed respondents, were more likely to feel better communication was desirable. Respondents who had lived in Regina for a long time and those who had resided in their neighbourhoods for a long time, however, were generally more positive about the state of communication between the police and the public.

The zones in which respondents resided also proved to be important. The need for better communication was most frequently identified by respondents in Area 2. Somewhat less emphasis was placed on the need for better communication by respondents in Areas 3, 7, 9 and 10. Still less emphasis was evident among those from Areas 1, 5, 6 and 8, while those in Area 4 appeared most satisfied with the state of communication.

Taken together, the findings indicate many respondents were concerned about the quality of communication between the police and the public. Most respondents appeared to feel the police needed more training on how to deal with people and a substantial number seemed to feel the police could do much more by way of public education. Most respondents advocated strategies for bringing the public more closely in touch with police work.

Not all respondents expressed the same concerns. Respondents who had been in contact with the police and who knew others who had been in contact with the police were more likely to identify problems in communication. This finding can be interpreted in two ways. It may mean that contact with the police makes respondents more aware of the need for better communication. It may also mean, on the other hand, that contact with the police is associated with experiences with crime and these experiences lead respondents to feel more needs to be done to cope with crime. For these respondents, improved communication may be seen as one way of coping with crime.

Interestingly, the emphasis placed on improving communication was closely associated with the characteristics of respondents. There was no direct relationship between the volume of crime in a particular area and the need expressed by respondents in that area for better communication. However, areas of the city containing many respondents of high social status emphasized the need for better communication, while areas containing many respondents who were long-time residents of Regina and long-time residents of their neighbourhoods placed less emphasis on improving communication. Perceptions about the quality of communication may be very closely tied to respondents' views about the importance of public involvement and good communication.

Police Powers

Eight questionnaire items concerned public perceptions about the extent of police powers. Most of these questions had to do with the latitude given the police in law enforcement and whether . . . this power ought to be increased or decreased. Two related items concerned the right of the police to strike and the public's knowledge about how to bring a complaint against the police.

Over 90% of the respondents could not agree with the statement that the police have too much authority and should have their powers strictly limited. Only one third of the sample felt police should be able to search private property whenever they want. Interestingly, nearly three out of ten respondents would be strongly opposed to this practice. Respondents were about equally divided on the question of whether or not the police should have the power to search those persons they stop. Nearly three quarters of the respondents felt the police should have the right to stop people and ask for identification. Surprisingly, a third of the respondents agreed that when a person was disrespectful or abusive to the police, that person deserved to be knocked around. Nearly half the respondents felt the police should be able to use any method to combat crime, although one in five respondents would be strongly opposed to this practice.

On two related questions, two thirds of the respondents felt the police should not have the right to strike. Less than one in five respondents could agree that procedures for bringing a complaint against the police were well known.

The [statistical] analysis indicates that respondents wishing to place limits on police powers were significantly different from other respondents in several important respects. Respondents wanting to limit police powers were more often single, divorced or separated, while those wishing to see police powers broadened were more often married or widowed. Geographic mobility was also important. Respondents who had lived in Regina for longer periods of time and those who reported residing in their present neighbourhood for longer periods were more likely to endorse a broadening of police powers. Respondents living alone were more prepared than other respondents to see a broadening of police powers. Respondents working in positions with higher occupational status, those with higher incomes, and those with more education were more likely to express concerns about a widening of police powers.

Differences in opinion were also associated with the area in which respondents lived. Those most concerned with the extent of police powers resided in Areas 1, 5, 6 and 8. Somewhat less concern was voiced by respondents in Areas 4, 7 and 9, while the advocates of greater police powers were more likely to be from Areas 2, 3 or 10.

Opinions concerning police powers were also associated with respondents' previous contacts with the police. Those respondents who said that relatives, friends, or neighbours had been victimized in the previous six months, were more likely to want limits on police powers. Similarly, if members of the respondent's household, relatives, friends, or neighbours had had contacts with the police for reasons other than a charge or arrest, the respondent was more likely to feel limits should be placed on the powers of the police.

Taken together, the findings suggest there is a wide diversity of opinion on the question of whether . . . police powers should be broadened. While respondents generally felt the police did not have too much authority at present, they were nonetheless reluctant to give the police blanket powers to search persons or property, or to use any method to combat crime. Two out of three respondents would deny the police the right to strike.

The data also indicate quite clearly that those who are most vulnerable to crime are more prepared to see a broadening of police powers. Not surprisingly, respondents who were afraid of being victimized, and those who underscored the seriousness of crime, were more likely to advocate an expansion of police powers.

Only one in six respondents could agree that procedures for bringing a complaint about the abuse of police powers were well known. This finding is consistent with the earlier findings that showed communication to be a problem insofar as many respondents were concerned. Interestingly, a negative relationship existed between scores on the communication and police powers scales. This indicates that respondents who expressed greatest concern about the quality of communication were least likely to endorse an increase in police powers. It would seem that, in respondents' minds, communication and trust are closely related. When the respondent views communication as being fairly positive, he or she is also more likely to trust the police with greater powers.

The negative relationship between scores on the two scales may also help to explain why respondents who reported they and others close to them had experienced many police contacts were less likely to endorse a broadening of police powers. While those affected by crime want police to have adequate powers, it was shown earlier that police contacts were associated with a more negative view about the quality of police-community communications. Respondents who feel communication is a problem are less likely to advocate an increase in the powers of the police.

Adequacy of Law Enforcement

Five questionnaire items focused on the adequacy of law enforcement. These items concerned whether or not the police were perceived by the public as wasting time on matters not related to law enforcement and whether or not service to the public was affected. The public's perception of how the police use their time and priorize their activities is an element common to all five items.

Only one in five respondents felt the police spent too much time on duties not related to law enforcement. Three in ten respondents, however, felt there was too much emphasis on traffic and traffic enforcement. Over 90% of the respondents could not agree that the police spent too much time on counselling activities. About one in four respondents agreed the police spend too much time riding around in cars. Over 85% of the sample could not agree the police ignored the problems of those who called them for help.

The [statistical] analysis indicates [that] opinions about the emphasis the police place on law enforcement are very much associated with the type of neighbourhood in which respondents lived. Respondents who reported neighbours had been charged by the police in the previous six months were more likely to feel [that] the police were spending too much time on activities not related to law enforcement. The number of charges laid against neighbours was also significant. Similarly, the number of times neighbours were arrested, the number of times neighbours had been in contact with the police for reasons other than a charge or arrest, and the number of times neighbours had been victimized, were all associated with the view that more emphasis should be placed on law enforcement. Among those respondents who had had contact with the police for some reason other than a charge or arrest, the need for greater emphasis on law enforcement was more frequently cited in instances where the police had given a traffic warning or issued a ticket, or had responded by referring a problem to another agency, than in instances where they actually corrected a dangerous situation, made an arrest, or completed a report.

The respondents' opinions about the need for greater emphasis on law enforcement were also associated with a number of personal characteristics. Older respondents were more likely to emphasize the need for law enforcement, as were those respondents who owned a business. Respondents living in single family dwellings were less inclined to think the police were wasting their time if they were not involved in law enforcement than were respondents living in apartments, duplexes or condominiums.

Taken together, the findings suggest there is a good deal of satisfaction with the amount of emphasis the police currently place on law enforcement activities. Most respondents seem to feel the police are quite effective in this area. Some diversity of opinion was evident, however. Respondents residing in neighbourhoods with a crime problem were more likely to emphasize the law enforcement role of the police. In addition, those respondents who perceived themselves as most vulnerable to crime, by virtue of being old, owning a business, or living in an urban rather than a suburban area, tended to place greater emphasis on law enforcement activities. The strong relationship between scores on this scale and scores on the seriousness and fear of crime scales bears out this correlation.

Interestingly, those respondents who had come into contact with the police in relation to the operation of a motor vehicle thought the police were not spending enough time on law enforcement. These respondents, especially those who received a traffic ticket, probably did not view [the] issuing of a ticket as law enforcement. No doubt many of them wished the police had been involved in some activity other than the enforcement of traffic laws.

Scores on the scale respecting the adequacy of law enforcement were correlated with scores on the scales discussed in previous sections. As already noted, respondents who said they were afraid of crime and those who underscored the seriousness of crime were more likely to feel law enforcement services were inadequate. On the other hand, respondents who had positive perceptions about the quality of police-community communications and those who were prepared to see a broadening of police powers also rated the police highly in terms of their law enforcement services.

The Scope of Police Services

Eight questionnaire items concerned the public's perception of the scope of police services. These items asked whether or not the respondent felt satisfied with the range of services offered by the police. Some of the items had to do with "response time" of the police and the level of protection provided to the public. Other items focused on the sensitivity of the police to citizens' problems. The final two items concerned the ability of the police to mobilize support from other agencies, and the quality of services provided by the R.C.M.P. in comparison to the Regina City Police. All these questions reflect the public's view about the scope of services they feel the police are able to provide.

Some concern was expressed about the ability of the police to respond promptly when called. One third of the sample could not agree [that] the police responded promptly. Some 85% of the respondents reported, however, that the police provided an adequate level of protection to the public.

Concerning the sensitivity of the police to public problems, over 90% of the respondents indicated the police were respectful. In a similar vein, nearly 90% of the respondents said the police were concerned about their problems when they came to their homes. Eight in ten respondents agreed [that] the police were willing to help with problems other than solving crime, although over two thirds of the sample agreed [that] the police did not get to know them or their problems.

Over 75% of the respondents agreed [that] the police were able to mobilize the resources of social agencies. Only one in five respondents felt the R.C.M.P. would be able to do a better job than the Regina Police Department.

The [statistical] analysis indicates [that] perceptions about the scope of the police services were very much related to the type and frequency of contacts with the police. Respondents who reported that members of their households, friends, and neighbours had been victimized by crime were more likely to see the police as having limited scope in the delivery of police services. The number of times relatives or neighbours had been victimized, and the number of times members of the respondent's household or neighbours had been charged by the police were also important. Police contacts for purposes other than a charge or an arrest, whether they were with the respondent or with friends of the respondent, also proved to be correlated with perceptions about the scope of police services. Among respondents who had had contacts with the police, attitudes were more positive if the police corrected a dangerous situation, made an arrest or completed a report, than if they issued a traffic warning or a ticket. Respondents who had lived in Regina for a long time, those who had lived in their neighbourhood longer, those who were married, and those who lived with their immediate family, were more likely to view the scope of police services in a positive light. The area in which respondents resided was also important. Respondents from Area 2 had the most critical views, while respondents from Areas 3, 5, 7 and 9 were more positive. Respondents in Area 8 had the most favourable views.

Taken together, the findings indicate [that] the respondents generally held positive views about the range of services provided by the police. Two exceptions may be noted. First, some respondents expressed concern about the amount of time the police took to respond to calls. This question requires further exploration. It is unclear whether respondents experienced unnecessary delays or whether even a quick response to a request for help seems slow in . . . an emergency. Secondly, many respondents agreed the police did not get to know "us or our problems". This appears to be another dimension of the problems with respect to communication that have been discussed previously.

As with some of the other scales, views about the scope of police services appeared to be very much related to the type of neighbourhood in which respondents lived and the personal characteristics of respondents associated with vulnerability to crime. Respondents who indicated they and those in their immediate surroundings had needed to rely on the police were more likely to report some disillusionment with the police. Those respondents who by virtue of their marital status and living situation, were less vulnerable to crime, were more likely to perceive the scope of police services in a positive light.

Scores with respect to the scope of police services were correlated with scores on a number of other scales. Respondents who reported they were afraid of crime were more likely to perceive the scope of police services as being quite limited. Those who viewed communications in a positive light, those who felt law enforcement services were adequate, and those who advocated an expansion of police powers, were more likely to be satisfied with the scope of police services. There was no relationship between opinions about the scope of police services and the perceived seriousness of the crime problem.

Police Competence

Seven questionnaire items focused on the extent to which the police were perceived as competent or incompetent by the public. These items dealt with a variety of subjects from the emphasis police placed on monitoring criminals, to perceptions about the difficulty of police work and the ability of the police to do their job.

A few respondents believed too much emphasis was placed on monitoring criminals. Only one in four respondents felt not enough time was spent on crime prevention. About one in five agreed that if a person has a criminal record the police never leave them alone. Over 90% of the respondents felt the courts' failure to convict offenders was not due to the incompetence of the police.

Eight out of ten respondents indicated [that] the public does not understand what police work is all about. Over 90% could not agree the police drive too fast when responding to calls. Only one in six respondents said they were inclined to treat police officers differently in social situations, and support for the view that all the present police should be replaced by new ones was virtually nonexistent.

The [statistical] analysis indicates respondents' views about the competence of the police are associated with police contacts. The number of times neighbours had been charged or arrested by the police and the number of times neighbours were reported to have been in contact with the police for reasons other than a charge or arrest were associated with a negative view of police competence. Similarly, if the respondent had been arrested, he or she was less likely to view the police as competent. Older respondents, those who were employed, and those who had lived in Regina longer, tended to view the police more positively.

Taken together, the findings indicate respondents generally held positive opinions about the way police exercised their authority. There was some indication, however, that respondents' opinions about the courts might be more critical. In addition, there was some public recognition of the difficulty of police work. Moreover, few respondents acknowledged treating the police differently. This suggests an absence of negative stereotypes on the part of the public.

Generally speaking, the public's respect for the competence of the police was independent of the characteristics of the respondents or the area of the city where respondents lived. While there was some tendency for more established citizens [to perceive the police as competent], these relationships were weak. Thus, respect for police competence appears to be fairly universal. The one exception was among respondents who reported their friends or neighbours, or they themselves, had been charged or arrested by the police.

Scores on the police competence scale were correlated with scores on some of the other scales. Those who viewed the police as competent tended to have positive views concerning the broadening of police powers, the adequacy of law enforcement services, and the scope of police services. Respondents who underscored the seriousness of crime, on the other hand, were more likely to be critical of the competence of the police. There was no relationship between scores on the scale respecting police competence and scores on either the fear of crime or quality of communication scales.

Integrity of the Police

The final dimension of public attitudes towards the police identified in our analysis concerned the public's perception of the integrity of the police. The questionnaire contained ten items in this general area. Some items asked whether the police showed favouritism or whether they provided equal and fair treatment, while other items concerned the public's view about police corruption and unethical police practices.

Nearly 40% of the respondents agreed [that] those who could afford good lawyers had less to worry about from the police than those who could not. Ten per cent of the sample agreed [that] police beat up people they do not like, and over 40% could not agree [that] all people are treated the same by the police. Most respondents (some 75%) believed the police were as concerned with crimes against the ordinary citizen as with those against businesses, and an equal number could not agree [that] the police were more concerned with arrests than they were with justice.

Nearly half the respondents agreed [that] the police cover up their own wrongdoings, but over 75% felt the police do a good job investigating and correcting problems themselves. Only 10% of the sample felt police work had a bad effect on people, while 90% could not agree [that] the police are forced into using unfair methods to obtain information. One in five respondents, however, could not agree that the police seldom engage in brutality towards suspects.

The [statistical] analysis indicates respondents were more likely to be suspect of the integrity of the police if they reported having friends who had been victimized, or if they themselves had come into contact with the police for some reason other than a charge or arrest. A more positive view of the integrity of the police was reported by older respondents and those who had lived in their present neighbourhood longer.

Taken together, the findings indicated a wide diversity of opinion on the question of police integrity. Many respondents, however, felt this was a problem area. Of course, these opinions may or may not be based in reality, but the findings do indicate [that] the public has questions about the integrity of the police.

Interestingly, opinions about the integrity of the police were largely independent of client characteristics and experiences with the police. There were a few weak relationships indicating more established citizens and those with fewer contacts were more positive in their opinions. Generally speaking, however, the findings suggest [that] concern about the integrity of the police is evident in all segments of the community.

Scores on the scale respecting police integrity were correlated with scores on a number of other scales. Those who had positive views respecting the integrity of the police were more likely to endorse a broadening of police powers, to be satisfied with the adequacy of law enforcement services, to be satisfied with the scope of police services, and to view the competence of the police in a positive light. Respondents who were satisfied with the quality of police-community communications were also more likely to view the police as possessing integrity. Respondents who feared crime, on the other hand, were more likely to express concerns about the integrity of the police.

DISCUSSION

It is beyond the scope of this brief section to draw out all the implications of the present study. Therefore, the discussion will be confined to an examination of some key questions and issues raised by the findings.

Our findings show the geographic zones in the city with the highest rates of crime were not the zones where respondents reported the greatest fear of crime or where respondents were most inclined to underscore the seriousness of crime. These findings confirm those of a recent survey by [the] Canada Mortgage & Housing Corporation,[8] wherein it was documented that citizens

8 *Regina Leader Post*, 7th November 1979.

living in the innercity areas of Regina were more concerned about crime than citizens in 22 other Canadian cities. These concerns cannot be accounted for on the basis of the volume of crime in Regina. It appears there is no simple, direct relationship between "amount of fear" and "amount of crime". It also suggests [that] the amount of fear can be disproportionate to the probability of being victimized and that other factors in the environment can serve to heighten or lessen the fear of crime, even while the volume of crime does not change.

The volume of offences and the types of crime reported by our sample has obvious implications both for policing [and] broader criminal justice programming. Most of the crimes reported by the citizens who participated in the study were property offences and many were of a minor variety. In some 20% of the cases the victim actually knew the offender on a personal basis. Taken together, this would seem to suggest the potential of innovative restitution programs that would divert selected offenders from formal processing in the criminal justice system.

Restitution and victim compensation programs seem all the more important when it is remembered that only half the victims in our sample received any form of compensation. Only two victims reported they were compensated by the person who victimized them. The fact that there is some overlap between those who are victimized and those who victimize others also suggests that restitution programs may have widespread applicability. It should also be remembered that the compensation of victims appears to be a way of lessening the fear of crime.

At several points in the discussion of the results we have had occasion to point out the public's desire for better communication with its police force. Sometimes concerns have surfaced as criticisms of the police, while at other times they have been manifested in the public's desire to be more fully informed and involved. While the degree of concern and the desire for greater participation varied somewhat from respondent to respondent and from one zone in the city to another, the need for better communication appeared to be one of the few areas where most citizens felt significant improvement could occur.

Opinions about the quality of police-community communications were not unrelated to other opinions about the police. On the contrary, those who perceived a communication problem were likely to be generally critical of the police, while those who perceived the quality of police-community communications to be quite good were generally positive in their opinions about the police. Opinions about the quality of communication were also related to fear of crime and views about the seriousness of crime.

Quite a few respondents expressed concerns about the ability of the police to provide equal treatment for all citizens. Some felt the police were inclined to cover up their own wrongdoings and were not in the best position to investigate and correct their own problems. These views were closely related to opinions about the quality of communication. When communication was viewed in a positive light, respondents were more likely to see the police as possessing integrity. These findings suggest that improved communication, while an important goal in and of itself, might also have the effect of improving the police image and reducing public concern about crime.

A recent survey, conducted by the Canadian Institute of Public Opinion, suggested that the number of persons approving of the way the police conduct their duties has declined in Western Canada over the last number of years. It is clear from the findings of this study, however, that the vast majority of Regina citizens have positive opinions about the Regina Police Department. While specific concerns were voiced, and while there was some consensus that communication could be improved, the weight of the evidence suggests [that] the police command the respect and admiration of the public. Unfortunately, no comparative data are available [to measure] whether respect for the police is more widespread in Regina than respect for the police in other cities. Until a further survey is conducted, after the implementation of zone policing, it is also impossible to assess whether opinions are [becoming] more positive or more negative over time. These results should provide insights into the impact of a decentralized policing model on the public's experiences and attitudes relevant to crime and the police. At present, however, widespread public support for the police appears to exist.

The present study does not come close to overcoming all the gaps in knowledge discussed in relation to the existing Canadian literature. The findings can only be generalized to the city of Regina. While the technique we employed with mailed questionnaires resulted in the highest rate of return reported in the literature, problems of representativeness were still quite evident in our sample. Although we sought to examine the relationships existing between experiences and attitudes, we did not explore the knowledge or behaviour of our respondents to any significant degree. In addition, while some of the analysis was specifically concerned with identifying dimensions of attitudes towards crime and the police, and while we sought to construct scales to tap these various dimensions, the reliability and validity of these measures has not yet been established.

. . . . .

The present study, while it is limited in a number of important respects, does demonstrate that current, useful information about public attitudes can be generated quite quickly and efficiently.

In contrast to this generally positive public attitude towards the police is perceived cynicism within the police, perhaps because familiarity breeds cynicism.[9]

---

9 See also J. H. Hylton, "The Assessment of Police Job Satisfaction" (1980), 4:3 Can. Police College Journal 189.

CAUSES OF POLICE CYNICISM

Donald K. Wilson

THE PROBLEM

Cynicism within the police is something which should be of concern to all of us, if only because it severely impacts upon the police officer's ability to perform effectively. Cynical police officers are not effective operationally. They do not communicate well with the public they serve and they are not responsive to the authority to which they are accountable, whether that authority is within the police organization, or is that ultimate authority which vests in the political head.

CONTRIBUTING FACTORS TO POLICE CYNICISM

General

There are a number of contributing factors to the development of cynicism within the police. These include legislators who have passed laws which appear not to be in support of the preservation of the peace and the prevention of crime and the apprehension of criminals mandate which has been given to police organizations. Similarly the courts, from time to time, do not appear to reflect the seriousness of crime in their findings and in their sentencing. Finally, there is a vocal and sometimes organized minority within our society, whose primary purpose in life seems to be to undermine public attitudes towards the police at every opportunity. While this practice may be attributed to individuals or groups with an identifiable political orientation from time to time, all too often, it is a function of liberal thought, which chooses either to be ill-informed or to misinterpret.

Stereotyping *re* Native People

There are three factors on which I wish to reflect in order to identify some of the causes of police cynicism. The first is that the police, and in particular the R.C.M.P., are stereotyped. They are stereotyped in terms of responsibilities and actions which occurred decades ago, but which are interpreted in terms of today's standards and values. The stereotype depicts the police as an oppressive agency of government, in a number of areas. One of these areas is in relation to the native people of Canada. We have been reminded by one of the principal speakers at this conference that in establishing control of the western plains in the nineteenth century, the North-West Mounted Police were oppressive to the aboriginal people — the suggestion being that that early oppression continues through until today in our dealings with the native people. Whether the manner in which the West was made ready for settlement constitutes "oppressive" treatment is open to debate, particularly when compared to the experiences of the United States of America during the same era. Be that as it may, present-day critics have chosen to be less than well informed in using their interpretation of nineteenth century events to measure our law enforcement today. The stereotype of the great oppressors fails to consider that at the present time, law enforcement is closer to the Indian and Metis populations, and to their leaders and organizations, than it has ever been in the past. There is presently among police organizations an understanding of native culture and social values which permits them to work effectively with the natives in preserving peace in their communities as well as in the communities of the white population. The perfect relationship has not been achieved, but significant progress has been made and will continue.

Stereotyping *re* Labour

Similarly, police are stereotyped in terms of their relationship with labour. The stereotype comes largely from events of decades ago, such as the Regina Riots and Winnipeg Strike. The police are seen as the agent of the government, working in opposition to labour movements. An informed critic will know that we have built a close working relationship with very senior personnel in all areas of labour, and here I speak particularly with respect to British Columbia, the jurisdiction in which I work. We have reached the point where, if it is anticipated that a strike or other labour unrest is imminent, we participate in planning meetings. We are advised where a strike will be and how pickets will be set up. We know who the picket captains will be. We make a point of understanding the issues and give advice on what the responsibilities of the labour unit are, as well as our responsibilities, and those of management. We work cooperatively in order to ensure that a peaceful labour situation may exist.

Stereotyping *re* Activist Groups

With respect to activist groups, the police are again stereotyped as those who work against the interests of such bodies. Yet, when activist groups wish to hold a parade in order to protest or support some particular issue, we work with the group, determining where the march or protest will take place, establishing traffic control and ensuring that opposition protesters do not interfere with the lawful protest. To a great extent, the peace is maintained.

In these three examples I am suggesting that the stereotype is not an honest reflection of what is transpiring. Still, it serves the purpose of some elements of society to perpetuate the stereotype — to the disadvantage of law enforcement and of the community at large. It is small wonder that cynicism sets in.

Inadequate Communication with the Community

A second cause of cynicism within the police stems from inadequate communication between the police and the community (the community as represented by elected people), as to the needs of the community. Police tend to think in terms of absolutes: good and bad, right and wrong, the permitted and the prohibited. It is the responsibility of the police to identify those who break the law and deal with them according to law. At the same time, however, the legislators circumscribe the action of the police by severely limiting the means by which crime may be identified and solved.[10] So there appears to be a conflict. Criminal law defines the work for the police to undertake. Other law limits the effectiveness of the police. The latter frustrates the attempt to achieve the former. What society has not communicated well to their police is the fact that in order to preserve human rights, it is satisfied to accept a given level of criminal activity in the community. Failing to understand that this is the posture of the community, the police see their efforts to achieve their duty frustrated. They are left with the impression that society no longer cares. If society no longer cares, why should they? The cynicism sets in.

Role Definition

My final point is that the police are presently having difficulty with role definition. It was not too long ago that police in the community were all things to all people. They had a tacit mandate to correct minor aberrant behaviour on sight, whether that behaviour was of a young person or of a more mature trouble-maker. The freedom to act at will on the spot no longer exists. Furthermore, in order to solve crime, the police needed information. Information was where the police could find it. There was freedom to go to members of the medical profession, the local telephone company, government agencies, or businesses, and with the cooperation of the personnel in any of these areas, to receive any information that they might have available. The right of access to various kinds of information is now severely restricted and police are having difficulty coming to terms with that fact. The police officer's traditional freedom of movement, freedom of action, and his general access to information have all been severely limited. Such traditions do not die overnight. Practices are not automatically changed as a result of legislation, obscure or otherwise, which alters the status and the role of law enforcement. Because the role of the police has recently been defined in a radically different way and because a century of tradition still persists in the minds of many, there is confusion in the law enforcement community generally in attempting to determine what its role truly is. Unfortunately, at the same time that the community is telling police what they may not do, there has been a failure to communicate what they may do and what their role is perceived to be. This has led to confusion, conflict, and cynicism.

10 But see A. Borovoy, *infra*, c. 10.

IS THERE A SOLUTION?

The cynicism within the police is pervasive but not so entrenched that it cannot be eradicated. There is, however, a critical need for objective analysis and communication from other segments of our legal system and from the community at large. Only with that communication will the police continue to be the accepted and effective agents of the community it serves.

Alan Grant pointed out that the majority of the respondents to the Legal Research Institute Survey who had positive feelings about the police had had no contact with the police, at least in situations of potential conflict.[11] He suggested that had younger, "street" people[12] been surveyed in such situations, attitudes might have been somewhat different.

He agreed with Donald Wilson that police are cynical but gave an additional reason for this, i.e., that police discretion is rendered largely insignificant by the prior political discretions which have been exercised to organize police forces to deal with overt-predatory crime (crime in the streets) at the expense of clandestine crime and institutional corruption, (crime in the suites). He advocated greater public input into police policy-making and priorities perhaps through local police boards.

> Parliament and the legislatures should make it clear that a Chief of Police, while not subject to direction on how to deal with individual cases, is, nevertheless, subject to policy direction by the appropriate police governing authority to whom should be delegated the right and obligation to publish written policies for the delivery of police services, including law enforcement priorities, applicable to local needs. The legislature would lay down the essential general principles, *e.g.*, that law enforcement should occur across all socio-economic boundaries and without regard for colour, race, class or creed and that police forces shall be organized to ensure they possess [a] minimum capability-factor. . . . Within that general policy, local police governing bodies would make rules outlining the way in which the law would be enforced which would meet particular local needs but not be inconsistent with general law enforcement policy. Such open handling of a subject at present shrouded in mystery would engender public debate on appropriate resource allocation and ensure accountability. For this purpose it would be necessary to ensure that police governing authorities, which should continue to comprise a mixture of elected and appointed members, had the necessary resources to play a policy-making role.[13]

He finally commented cynically on the lack of police training in many municipalities in Canada and the absence of a police college in Manitoba.

In conclusion, Daniel Koenig felt that the Institute survey results generally showed realism rather than cynicism[14] and questioned Deschênes C.J.'s

---

11 See *e.g.*, *supra*, The Legal Research Institute Survey, c. 2; questions 49 and 50.

12 The Legal Research Institute Survey interviewed respondents who were 18 years and older.

13 Alan Grant, *The Police: A Policy Paper* (1980), p. 65.

14 See *e.g.*, *supra*, The Legal Research Institute Survey, c. 2, questions 44(a), 44(b), 71, 74, 77, 78.

assumptions of rejection of authority, and increasing amorality and political awareness.[15] He also, however, questioned whether public opinion surveys provide new or reliable information, suggesting that they are more likely to be used as a basis for manipulation of public opinion. The path to change is through public involvement in policing and, in particular, community-based policing programs.

In the first part of his paper,[16] Daniel Koenig developed a theoretical framework for understanding crime and disorder as an outgrowth of "routine activities" of society as they affect not only the motivation of potential offenders, but also target suitability and effective guardianship over persons and property. He forecast various long-range, "tidal" changes in Canadian society, expected to affect crime patterns to the year 2000. He then examined the role of the police in the larger social control network and the need for proactive police intervention in cooperation with the community.

PROACTIVE POLICE INTERVENTION AND IMMINENT SOCIAL CHANGE[17]

Daniel J. Koenig

and

E. Paula DeBeck

INTERVENTIONIST PROGRAM DEVELOPMENT

. . . . .

Motivated Offenders

. . . . .

The police can . . . initiate or encourage several kinds of programs to minimize an . . . increase [in the potential level of offender motivation]. More specifically, there is some behavioural research evidence that at least certain types of anti-social behaviours are inhibited among individuals who

---

15 *Comm. de Tpt. de la Communauté Urbaine de Montreal v. Syndicat du Tpt. de Montreal et autres*, 77 C.L.L.C. 14,098 reversing [1974] C.S. 227 at 231.

16 D. J. Koenig, "Routine Activities, Impending Social Change and Policing" (1983), 7 Can. Police College Journal.

17 This publication contains a summary of and excerpts from a report on the Future of Canadian Policing commissioned by the Canadian Police College which is being published by the Canadian Police College Journal in two parts. Permission from the Canadian Police College to include these excerpts in the Proceedings is gratefully acknowledged.

have a stronger stake in conformity.[18] A stake in conformity[19] means that an individual is obtaining certain positively valued rewards, which will be jeopardized or lost because of inappropriate behaviours. There are two general classes of such rewards, one external to the individual and the other based upon the individual's self-concept. Examples of the former are possession of or access to tangible rewards such as a job, family life, a home and personal possessions (for example, a stereo system, cars, recreational equipment and facilities), as well as possession or acquisition of more intangible rewards such as prestige, recognition, security, new experience, and favourable social response from others. Rewards related to the individual's self-concept include seeing oneself as possessing personality characteristics one values, such as honesty, cheerfulness, self-discipline, cleverness, or altruism.

It follows that a variety of experimental programs can be implemented to encourage pro-social activities by providing people with a stake in conformity, with valued rewards which will be lost through anti-social behaviours. Such programs may be initiated or directed by the police, by other social service/health care agencies and organizations, or by private interests. For instance, large centralized enterprises can foster a stake in conformity and decrease social alienation by providing their employees, and even the general public, with recreational activities which will foster an identification with the enterprise; by being attentive to basic human needs such as prestige and recognition; and by profit sharing for employees and rebates or other perquisites for clients.

Such programs and practices do already exist, but most are ineffective because they do not derive from any goal-based philosophy and have been implemented with no specific objective. They are merely exercises in public relations and as likely to increase alienation as to develop a stake in conformity through a positive identification with the enterprise. To be perceived as rewarding, such programs must involve recognition of the worth of individuals and provide for meaningful input by those individuals.

A similar criticism is relevant to many service agencies and fraternal organizations which provide facilities for various activities of youth, or others. Participants often do not identify with these facilities or programs, and are as likely to vandalize them as to use them constructively. A positive identification would be fostered by involvement of participants in the planning and decision-making, as well as the related fund-raising and work, which are required to bring such facilities and programs onstream. As a result, participants can come to see the programs as an extension of themselves and have a stake in their continued successful operation, as well as being involved in constructive activities which replace their availability for anti-social activities.

18 J. Short and F. Strodtbeck, *Group Processes and Gang Delinquency* (1965), especially pp. 185-216; R. Cloward and L. Ohlin, *Delinquency and Opportunity* (1960), especially 176-77; D. Glaser, *The Effectiveness of a Prison and Parole System* (1964), especially 469-71.

19 For elaboration on the conceptual meaning of "stake in conformity", See J. Toby, *Contemporary Society: Social Process and Social Structure in Urban Industrial Societies* (1964), pp. 290-91.

Both of these factors can be expected to reduce offender motivation among people who are either unemployed or have a surplus of unfocused leisure time.

Other programs which have the potential of minimizing the probability of offender motivation through enhancing the stake in conformity of target populations would be programs which are oriented toward strengthening inner containments[20] and positive role modelling, like those which have as their objectives the development of "positive peer culture",[21] or programs such as those which have been successfully implemented by the Boys' Club of America.[22]

Programs of this nature cannot automatically be assumed to be effective[23] and they should be evaluated to ascertain their effects, but some *do* work. For example, the nine city juvenile delinquency intervention [programs sponsored] by the Boys' Clubs of America reported a 31 per cent reduction from the expected arrest rate after three years. Some examples of the programs provided by the Boys' Clubs were sponsorship of family night activities, skills development, subsidized work experience, Wilderness Challenge, operation of day care and big brother-type programs by participants, and a variety of related programs involving supervised community service, counselling, and leadership skills training.

Finally, other possibilities for minimizing offender motivation can occur without police involvement. One example would be government policies for income redistribution. Another possibility which merits closer scrutiny and evaluation is outlined in two recent reports which claim that the occurrence of crime is reduced when substantial proportions of people within an area engage in the practice of Transcendental Meditation.[24] Improbable as this claim appears to outsiders such as ourselves, methodologically sound replications by outside researchers, if forthcoming, would suggest value in encouraging widespread application of Transcendental Meditation for purposes of minimizing offender motivation for anti-social behaviours.

---

20 For more extensive discussions of the notion of inner containment see Walter Reckless, "A New Theory of Delinquency and Crime" (1961), 25 Federal Probation 42-46; Walter Reckless, *The Crime Problem*, 4th ed. (1967), especially pp. 444-85.

21 H. H. Vorrath and L. K. Brenthro, *Positive Peer Culture* (1974).

22 John Badger, *National Juvenile Justice Project: Special Report* (1981).

23 Walter Reckless and Simon Dinitz, *The Prevention of Juvenile Delinquency: An Experiment* (1972).

24 M. C. Dillbeck, G. Landrith III and D. W. Orme-Johnson, "The Transcendental Meditation Program and Crime Rate Change in a Sample of Forty-Eight Cities" (1981), IV Crime and Justice 25; A. Aron and E. Aron, "Experimental Intervention of High Coherence Groups into Disorderly Social Systems", a paper presented at the American Psychological Association Annual Convention, 1981.

Effective Guardianship

. . . . .

Both individuals and organizations can do many things to enhance effective guardianship. Individuals may increase effective guardianship both through formal means (greater use of private security personnel and hardware), and informal means (such as arrangements with neighbours for mutual surveillance, locking doors and windows when away, locking cars, and not leaving expensive and portable objects where they are vulnerable to theft).

Tactics available to large, centralized enterprises include target hardening in the form of improved environmental design and enhanced plant security through controlled access to the more common desirable targets of abuse, as well as monitoring target removal by using readily available (and increasingly less expensive) technological guardianship in the form of robotics, lasers, and various sophisticated sensors. Among the latter are those which make it possible to "home-in" on any location to which materials may have been relocated; to monitor physical penetration by detecting variations in levels of noise and vibration or penetration of electronic beams and barriers; and to respond to selected odors, metal strips or other specialized identifiers to prevent illicit removal of goods and equipment. In addition, of course, centralized enterprises can be expected, more than smaller enterprises, to attend to the development of *processes* intended to enhance security, and to have specialized personnel to promote security.

. . . . .

Other police initiatives to enhance effective guardianship through increased surveillance, with minimal or non-existent cost implications, are the development of close working relationships and telecommunication links with private security industry personnel and with persons routinely travelling in public spaces, such as taxi-drivers, bus drivers, delivery or home repair personnel, or emergency personnel. Travelling [salespersons] or members of the public generally can assist in extending effective guardianship by reporting incidents of disorder, suspicious circumstances, or anti-social behaviours which they observe.

Effective guardianship can also be enhanced by more effective implementation of community-based programs, such as property marking, and programs intended to extend watchful eyes over persons and their property. These include block parent programs, letter carriers alert, *genuine* neighbourhood watch programs, counter-attack programs in which motorists are encouraged to report impaired drivers to the police, emergency lines to report suspected or known cases of child abuse to welfare authorities, crime stoppers programs[25] whereby a special phone line is available to receive information anonymously,

25 T. Coleman, "The Public, Media and Police Working Together to Solve Crime" (1983), 2:4 Can. Police Chief Newsletter 2.

and more comprehensive programs such as the "Operation Knockout"[26] program developed in Saanich, B.C.

Another form of community-based policing which can maximize effective guardianship at any given level of resource allocation is active involvement of other social service and health care organizations in team efforts to prevent and contain anti-social behaviour within neighbourhoods and communities.[27]

Other strategies to increase effective guardianship without increasing the resource base include effective management in setting priorities for personnel and equipment allocation, as well as monitoring the efficiency of those allocations and, with the help of a crime analysis unit (really a *problem* analysis unit),[28] pinpointing special problem areas for alternative patrol deployments, particularly the use of foot patrols in selected problem areas.[29] Such foot patrols will also be useful in negotiating a *modus vivendi* in specific neighbourhoods among sub-populations whose consensual view of social order may diverge somewhat from that of the general community. This variation of community-based policing . . . can complement other community resources to provide for order maintenance while recognizing the increasing cultural heterogeneity within our society.

Effective guardianship can also be enhanced, at minimal cost, by maximizing police visibility. Police personnel could, for example, be assigned marked police vehicles for personal use, on the understanding that while using them they will be receptive to civilian-initiated contacts and will respond to more serious legal infractions and specified traffic violations, whether or not they are on duty. This would, of course, require special arrangements for insurance and regulations dealing with the conditions for off-duty use, including whether passengers may or may not be transported.

A similar tactic would be to permit police officers to accept rental accommodations free of charge in large residential buildings whose management feels that the sporadic presence of a police officer will enhance effective guardianship and order maintenance. Such a practice would also reduce the social isolation which is so characteristic of police, and would enhance community contact and community-based policing.

The programs which have been mentioned are not generally new. Many have been around for years and, when tried, have often been dismissed as ineffective. Generally, however, there has been considerable slippage in the implementation of the programs, so that in essence, the program has not really

---

26 R. Goodacre, *Operation Knockout* (1983).

27 For an example of an approach to community-based policing, see J. Hest, *Community Policing: An Alternate Community-Based Policing Model* (1982).

28 H. Goldstein, "Improving Policing: A Problem-Oriented Approach" (1979), 25 Crime and Delinquency 236.

29 G. Kelling, *The Newark Foot Patrol Experiment* (1981).

been implemented at all. A particular example is neighbourhood watch. It should not be surprising that a program which is limited to a group-showing of a crime prevention film, property marking, erection of a billboard, and the distribution of neighbourhood watch decals for display on windows, doors, and cars, is almost totally useless, regardless of its name. In fact, there may be no neighbourhood watch whatsoever involved. It is for reasons such as these that we now turn to the crucial issue of program implementation.

PROGRAM IMPLEMENTATION

Successful implementation of any program requires that the program be supported, clearly understood, and effectively implemented by those affected. Thus, the human side (particularly motivational aspects) of any program must be considered, as well as system design or program development. In particular, managers should consider the advantages a program offers to those from whom cooperation is desired, whether such individuals will have a stake in ensuring the success of any program, and whether such individuals are assured that they will not lose anything if the program is implemented.[30]

These concerns require that attention be given both to the external environment (*e.g.*, the general public, special interests, and civilian masters) and to the internal environment of the police (*e.g.*, the police rank and file, police unions/associations, and the reward structure within the organization).

In the external environment, the police manager is unlikely to find strong support for programs which are perceived to have the potential to increase taxes, decrease public or personal security, decrease police responsiveness and accountability to the public, or permit an erosion of existing levels of public order. Thus, before instituting an innovative program, it would be helpful for the police manager to engage in a marketing and evaluation strategy to ''sell'' the program to the community, to ascertain community desires about perceived needs and to ensure active involvement of the community in the program. This implies, at minimum, a dialogue with the public through the use of the media, through well-advertised public meetings, and through meetings with special interests within the community.

At these meetings, the public can be informed of problems confronting the police, initiatives being considered to address such problems, and how community participation and involvement can assist the police to provide levels of order and security desired by the public without requiring additional resources. Public reaction and input to the proposed program can be solicited at these meetings and by other means, such as opinion surveys of the general

30 Many of these insights have been liberally borrowed from remarks made by Ken Matsune at a Workshop on Community Policing in Parksville, B.C., 23rd-25th March 1982.

public and of community influentials[31] and analyses of incoming calls for service. This input can then be used to revise the program as appropriate and necessary for widespread community involvement and support. Throughout this process, the police manager can continue [the] "advertising" campaign using, in addition to the media, mailings enclosed with property tax notices or, where this can be arranged, utility bills.

An effective marketing program requires more than a one-sided, or one-shot public relations program. It is an ongoing process involving researching community needs and desires, developing, selling, and evaluating the program, re-examining community needs and desires, revising and reselling the program, and so on. Continuing community support also implies continuing input to ensure that the community perceives a payoff to the program and has a stake in its success. This may involve the public in "selling" the program to others, such as youth communicating the program to other youth, as in "Project Pride" and "Positive Peer Culture" programs.

One way to increase community involvement is the development of a specialist unit [responsible for] encouraging community involvement and participation on a proactive basis, as well as involving vested interests both reactively and proactively. On a reactive basis, community groups and vested interests — whether agencies or special interest groups — can be challenged to become involved in bringing problems to the attention of the police, and actively assisting the police to resolve or neutralize them. Proactively, the police can reach out to such groups to seek their cooperation and involvement in resolving or neutralizing problems which directly affect or concern them.

The above comments have been concerned with the external environment of policing, but the police manager must recognize that the internal environment of the police force itself is as important for successful implementation. Brown has identified three major obstacles to the renewal of policing in this country: the paramilitary structure, implementation problems, and police unions and associations.[32] . . .

The police manager who wishes to adapt to changing circumstances will need to engage in a continuing dialogue to explain his objectives, obtain and respond genuinely to feedback, explore the limits of participatory democracy, and be empathetic towards the concerns of both the union and the rank and file. This does not generally happen today in Canada. Following an extensive study of police labour-management relations in Canada, Forcese[33] noted that

31 For example, those conducted in Regina, Selkirk and La Pas, Manitoba and Pitt Meadows and Maple Ridge, B.C.; see, among others, J. H. Hylton *et al.*, *Public Attitudes Towards the Regina Police Force* (1979); R.C.M.P., *Crime Problem Analysis of Selkirk Municipal* (1981); Maple Ridge R.C.M.P. Detachment, *Crime Analysis of Maple Ridge/Pitt Meadows, British Columbia, 1981/82* (1982).

32 William J. Brown, "The Future of Policing in Canada" in W. I. McGrath and M. P. Mitchell (eds.), *The Police Function in Canada* (1981), pp. 243-69.

33 D. Forcese, "Police Unionism: Employee-Management Relations in Canadian Police Forces" (1980), 4 Can. Police College Journal 79.

both management and labour are becoming more aggressive, with unions seeking a greater role in organizational decision-making. But if unions/associations must modify their posture, so also must management.

Such modifications can include greater attention to staff recruitment and development, changes in managerial styles, and improvements in the administrative structure of the department. If successful program implementation is to occur, the police executive must be seen to be committed to, and to be clearly in charge of, any program change. As well, both the police rank and file, and the union or association, must be involved from the outset in the process of program development so that they, too, see the program as being a useful one and see themselves to have a stake in its success.

Such involvement also provides the opportunity for dialogue to assuage doubts on the part of the rank and file that the program threatens their quality of working life or general well-being. An abstract program on paper is probably doomed to failure if abstract goals are emphasized rather than the day-to-day *activities* of the members who are tasked with realizing those goals. While goals are easily changed on paper, routine work activities are more resistant to change. A change in the latter requires the understanding and enthusiastic support of the organizational goals and objectives by those directly affected by any change. As Brown has noted, the paramilitary structure of policing is also an obstacle to the renewal of policing. Consideration can be given to job enhancement through increasing autonomy on the part of highly trained rank and file by reducing the half dozen or so layers of authority which typically are found in police departments.

Finally, the police manager who wishes to change the activities of the rank and file must not only be seen to be committed to such changes, but he must also be attentive to the reward structure within the department. Daily activities are much more likely to be altered by tangible payoffs than by specification of abstract goals and objectives, or even by a well-designed program. Attention can be given to altering working activities by changing the reward structure through resource reallocation ([staffing], budget, and even realignment of the rank structure within various divisions) from lower priority to higher priority activities; job enrichment, increased prestige, autonomy and the provision of some additional perquisites for those involved in the activities desired to be implemented; and tying promotional criteria more closely to demonstrable success in implementation of the altered goals which are seen to be most important.

5

LAWYERS AND LEGAL SERVICES

Jack Batten agreed with Norman Larsen that public opinion, encountered in promoting his books *Lawyers* and *In Court,* is overwhelmingly hostile to lawyers. People complained that lawyers have too much power, that law is a "closed shop", that fees are too high, that lawyers are dishonest, and that they aggravate disputes, particularly in family cases. He felt that this hostility might be partly because the media are quite ignorant of what lawyers and courts do, and report cases inadequately and inaccurately, although lawyers and judges are approachable and anxious to make their work known.

Yves Lafontaine spoke about the public image of lawyers in Quebec.

ARE LAWYERS A VIVID CONTRADICTION?

Yves Lafontaine

PUBLIC OPINION OF LAWYERS: A CONTRADICTION

Between 1968 and 1982, at least six surveys were conducted in Quebec on the public picture of lawyers.[1] These surveys reflect popular old tags and traditions disparaging the legal profession while, at the same time, recognizing its usefulness.

I should like to examine the public opinion of lawyers, the rationale behind this opinion and the way in which it is slowly changing.

General Hostile Attitude

It seems that the legal profession has always been the object of general

1 a) Cadres Professionels Inc., *Les Avocats du Québec* (1968);
b) Govt. of Que., *La société face au crime (The Prevost Report), schedule 4, La justice criminelle* (1969);
c) Centre du recherche en droit public, *Place du juriste dans la société québecoise* (1976);
d) Comm. des services juridiques, *Des avocats de notre bord* (1978);
e) Office des professions, *Le public québecois et les services professionels* (1980);
f) Min. of Justice, *Les justiciables et la justice* (1982).

hostile criticism and old adages (which usually typify popular wisdom) are numerous and commonly endorsed.

Now and then, we hear clichés such as these: "As thievish and dishonest as lawyers"; "Saint Yves was a lawyer but he was honest"; "Unlike a barrow's wheel, lawyers squeak even louder when greased"; "They want your wealth so much that they keep it to themselves"; "If you want to live a long and happy life, try to keep away from doctors and lawyers." In the same vein it was said of Pennsylvania: "They have no lawyers . . . it's a happy country." Lawyers were even banished from some American states.[2]

The low esteem in which lawyers were held is also revealed in numerous caricatures drawn by the famous Honoré Daumier.

This adverse opinion still prevails nowadays among citizens, and even recent surveys show that lawyers are not well regarded. The only differences between today's scientific surveys and the old adages are that surveys are expressed in percentages (40 per cent answer yes, 39 per cent answer no, 20 per cent are reserved and 1 per cent do not know) and in degrees (such as very, fairly, enough, not very, not enough, not at all; much more, more, more or less, less, much less). It looks like a new method, discovered by surveyors, the bigwigs of democracy, of playing, "She loves me, she loves me not". The consequence is that, without altering the final result, the new method is a means of achieving greater scientific exactness, although at the expense of colour.

According to the surveys, 36.9 per cent of lawyers are honest, while 62.4 per cent, *i.e.*, nearly two out of three are rather hypocritical.

In answer to a question of whether fees generally charged by criminal lawyers were "too low, fair, or too high", 59.1 per cent said that fees were too high, while 35.2 per cent found that they were fair and 1.6 per cent answered that they were too low.[3] The scientific exactness of surveys prevents us from determining whether the questioners were really serious about the last item.

According to another survey[4] of laypersons, "Lawyers are there, only because laws are complex", and because "We don't know what to say, how to word our defence". In the course of the same survey, it is said that "Half of the claim goes into the lawyer's pocket", and that "When you discuss your problem with a lawyer, you always have a good case". The public also adds that lawyers can hold conflicting theories, which will vary according to the amount at stake for themselves.

Finally, 52 per cent of respondents stated that lawyers rank first among snobs, while teachers are second with 14 per cent.

---

2 T. Erlich, "Legal Pollution", *The New York Times Magazine* (8th February 1976), p. 17.

3 *Supra*, note 1(b).

4 *Supra*, note 1(f).

Specific Positive Perceptions

This eschatological perception is, however, greatly improved when other questions are asked of the same persons as part of the same surveys.

With respect to the question, ''Do you agree with the following old tag: 'Lawyers are thieves and dishonest persons?' '', 62 per cent of Quebec citizens said that they did not agree, while 34.4 per cent agreed.[5] Moreover, two persons out of three believe that lawyers are competent. One can argue that lawyers cannot be very happy with such figures since, to one third of the population, they still appear dishonest and incompetent. Considering, however, that they were once so maligned, lawyers can pride themselves (which they usually do) on some improvement.

Data from these surveys also indicate that 78.2 per cent of respondents think that criminal lawyers are useful to the community; moreover, according to 81.1 per cent of respondents, lawyers must defend both innocent and guilty persons.

The picture of lawyers is completely different when it comes to the question of satisfaction. In this respect, the popularity of lawyers is at its best, with 74 per cent of the people being very satisfied and 85 per cent being moderately to very satisfied.

These few examples taken from similar surveys conducted over lengthy periods tend to show that lawyers are seen as contradictory persons.

Is the public wrong, or can it be said that the lawyer's function is a controversial one?

I, for one, am inclined to think that the public is right in claiming that lawyers are both honest and dishonest, a calamity but a requisite, whose fees are high but reasonable.

REASONS FOR THIS CONTRADICTION

For most trades, this apparent dichotomy could be solved by arguing that in all activities involving men and women, some are honest while others are not, some are useful while others are not, some demand high prices, whereas others do not. To me, this explanation seems over-simplified and the public takes this into account when assessing professional people as a whole. On this point, respondents admit[6] that their trust in any professional is limited and circumstantial. This leads me to believe that the fluctuating opinions expressed about lawyers can be best explained by the characteristics of their profession.

Unlike doctors, engineers, teachers, dentists and accountants, lawyers act as agents for people who hire their services. They are their spokespersons.

5 *Supra*, note 1(b).
6 *Supra*, note 1(e).

Judgments on lawyers are perhaps judgments on their clients. Does a poor opinion of lawyers show a desire to kill the bearer of bad news?

Lawyers represent persons accused of crimes such as sadistic rapes as well as the community outraged by them. Some rationalization is necessary in order to accept that lawyers marshal all available resources to ensure a full and complete defence for their client in such circumstances.

Victims and their families will not have friendly feelings towards a defence lawyer, especially if he or she subjects them to lengthy cross-examination or if the accused is found not guilty.

In civil matters, where damages are almost invariably claimed for negligence, there is one lawyer for the plaintiff and one for the defendant. According to their client's versions, both of them may be right, even though they studied the same code and cases. Only one party, however, wins the case.

All surveys conducted on "satisfaction" show a clear relationship between the degree of satisfaction and the result obtained by the client. People who win their case are always inclined to find qualities in their own lawyer but maybe not in all lawyers, because that would include the opponent's attorney, who tried to make them lose the case.

It seems to me that this remark is relevant to the fact that citizens hold negative views of lawyers in general, but not of their own lawyers. There is a general consensus on old adages concerning lawyers when no other detail is added. No one, however, will readily agree with the contention that his or her own lawyer, who often acts according to instructions, is dishonest or unskilled.

As lawyers are the ones who know the law, they will be asked how it should be complied with and how it can be evaded to satisfy private interests. Rich people and major corporations pay large amounts of money in order to take advantage of loopholes in income tax legislation. These clients are undoubtedly quite pleased with their lawyers. On the other hand, other taxpayers might question this role of lawyers.

Any lawyer obtaining a "technical verdict of not guilty" will be highly thought of by the client, but will be considered dishonest by the public and accused of pettifogging.

Before the inception of legal aid, and still to a lesser degree nowadays, one segment of public opinion came from people who had lawyers (who could afford to pay one). Lawyers were sometimes considered necessary by rich people, although their services were deemed expensive. Lawyers could collect moneys from unwilling debtors, settle fence or will disputes, *etc*. The other segment of public opinion was, however, deprived of such services. Poor people knew lawyers in general as professionals writing oppressive demand letters, refusing settlements in order to increase their costs or sending bailiffs to seize whatever property or wages they possessed.

The question of fees does not altogether improve the general opinion of lawyers. The profession as a whole is quite secretive in this respect. To me, this aspect is one of the most serious contentions of public criticism.

The public is not easily cheated. The question of fees figures among grounds of dissatisfaction most often invoked by citizens, even against their own lawyers. This question is an ambiguous one and the profession has done so little to clarify it that authorized legal fees are considered to be highly excessive. I admit that the silence of a bar association may lead to such an interpretation. How can we explain the fact that a bar association institutes proceedings against lawyers who attempt to post prices for their services, thereby violating professional ethics? Those who question lawyers' honesty and frankness will always find good support among the population as long as people remain unable to assess, if not the quality, at least the reasonable value, roughly speaking, of a professional service. The fact that client-professional disputes are referred to professional bodies also deters prejudiced clients from submitting any complaint.[7]

This is a vicious circle. Clients, unaware of the meaning of reasonable costs, believe that services are expensive. They are, however, reasonably satisfied, since rumour has it that legal services are expensive. Consequently, they refrain from complaining too much, since they know that the dispute will be arbitrated by professional bodies (the members of which are colleagues).

In the past, professional bodies have been helpful to lawyers (if not to the public), allowing them to charge fees according to each client's purse. As opportunity often makes the thief, some colleagues have claimed and still claim exaggerated costs from their clients. Such attitudes, when not officially and strongly objected to by the profession, give rise to criticism. Moreover, no improvement can be anticipated in this respect.

One does not have to be a prophet to claim that thieves will grow more and more numerous, considering the glut in the profession, the decrease in the number of clients and the narrowing of traditional fields of practice. Several provincial bar associations are assailed with claims from people trying to recover amounts allegedly taken by lawyers.

In short, it seems that lawyers are looked upon in the same way as gods in antiquity. They should be provided with sacrificial offerings, for their involvement is necessary to human beings. The consequences of these offerings, however, are by no means certain.

CHANGES IN PUBLIC OPINION

Is this opinion likely to change in the long run? There are some precursory signs to that effect.

7 *Supra,* note 1(e).

Effect of Legal Aid

People are more educated and want to know more.[8] To meet this demand, the Quebec Commission des services juridiques, part of whose mandate consists of advising people of their rights and obligations, uses various tools: television (a weekly half hour program broadcast throughout Quebec by a commercial television chain), radio (three times each day on most stations), articles in dailies, press conferences, brochures, photo-novels, comic books, public information meetings, and free legal advice. In addition to supplying information, the Commission des services juridiques, which administers legal aid, knows that such popularization of the law contributes towards demystifying the lawyer's function. In time, citizens are aware that laws are enacted for them and that they can understand them. When priests stopped speaking Latin, they were demystified.

The inception of legal aid has already slightly altered the public opinion of lawyers, as is shown by this statement from a recent survey of former legal aid clients: "I now know what is meant by the words 'to have my own lawyer'. It is somebody who is on my side, who speaks for me and can be understood by the judge."[9]

In other words, it means that the lawyer is not always a calamity for poor people but may even help them. Quebec indigent people now have their own professional agents who marshal all available resources to enforce their rights against any other party, including the state.

Legal aid clients no longer wonder if their salaried attorney is confronted with a conflict between the value of the legal opinion and the amount of money that may be derived by arguing such opinion. The salary paid to the lawyer will not change according to his legal opinion of the case.

No longer deprived of legal services for a lack of financial resources, laypeople will perhaps be more prone to seek professional advice before taking any recourse, thus limiting costs for themselves and the community.

The implementation of legal aid has also had an impact on tariffs charged to the community as a whole. In compliance with the provisions of legal aid legislation, the Bar Association negotiated and was even forced to accept, on one occasion, a tariff in criminal matters, with respect to which no tariff had ever been applied. Through these negotiations between the state and the professional bodies, the state as a paying agency for legal aid recipients grew more aware of consequences arising from the increase in the general tariff applying to the community at large.

Development of Law

If the image of lawyers can be improved by legal aid, surely the

8 Comm. des services juridiques, *Les mains de la loi* (1975).
9 *Supra*, note 1(d).

perception of the lawyer's role will be enhanced by the development of law itself. Such development seems to be occurring at a fast pace, although traditionally "speed" and "law" were not even remotely connected.

The law which used to govern relationships between citizens and corporations applies more and more to state-citizen relationships. This is a consequence flowing from the "welfare state" philosophy, according to which the state creates social programs aimed at improving the distribution of resources. State funds are allocated to poor people as well as to multinational corporations.

Emerging new values were followed by laws enacted to protect them, such as laws regarding the environment, the protection of individual life, respect for minorities and consumer protection. These laws and regulations created the so-called "legal pollution"[10] and numerous tribunals and administrative boards. If all citizens were aware of the large number of regulations affecting them today, they would undoubtedly be inclined to take law courses. Consequently, given the same pattern, lawyers will be faced with a tremendous amount of work, on a short term basis. Lawyers would be involved more and more actively in all regulated fields and the number of lawyers working for the state should increase steadily.

On the other hand, law seems to be becoming less absolute as a value, perhaps because it has appeared in so many forms. Some groups of citizens challenge injunctions, while others refuse to abide by laws.

As the courts now have to solve increasing numbers of constitutional issues (between the federal and the provincial governments, between provinces or between state corporations and federal or provincial governments), it is suspected that confusion will arise between the functions of courts, *i.e.*, to enforce laws, and the government's role, *i.e.*, to enact and amend laws, thus leading citizens to believe that judges are legislators.

On the whole, I feel that tomorrow's lawyers will reflect the community of individuals seeking their services.

10 *Supra*, note 2.

ALIENATION AND THE CRIMINAL JUSTICE SYSTEM

Stephen L. Brickey

[Stephen Brickey discussed attitudes to the criminal justice system, disagreeing with Jack Batten that public ignorance is the cause of cynicism.]

The theme of this conference is the issue of public cynicism toward the law. Questions are being raised about the extensiveness of cynicism, its causes, and the possible implications. The focus of this paper is cynicism toward the criminal justice system.

LIMITED INVOLVEMENT OF VICTIM AND ACCUSED IN THE SYSTEM

It is ironic that the system developed to manage law breaking has transformed the two most important players into the role of bit players. These players are the victim and the accused. There is increasing evidence that individuals who find themselves in the position of victim or accused come to the realization that the criminal justice system is one in which they are objects and not subjects; *i.e.*, they are in the system but have little or no control over what takes place in the system. In other words, they are in a condition of alienation where their participation has been reduced to the absolute minimum.

In order to demonstrate the nature of the problem, a brief description will first be given of the limited involvement that the victim and accused have in the current system. Following this description, an explanation will be offered to account for the historical process that has had the result of altering the involvement of the above individuals from the role of participants to the role of spectators. The argument will be made that the major cause of cynicism in the criminal justice system is alienation produced by structural changes in society that have effectively placed the public in the margins of the criminal justice system.

The Role of the Accused

Ever since social scientists began to collect data on the criminal court process, there has been an awareness that a major discrepancy exists between the formal role of the accused in the adversarial system and reality. We have known for some time that the accused is processed through the system in what has been called an assembly line procedure[11] through the use of plea bargaining. Although there is disagreement on the precise percentage of verdicts in Canada that are arrived at through plea bargaining,[12] there is general agreement that plea bargaining is the modal form of settling criminal cases.

In contrast to the adversarial procedure, where legal guilt is determined by an impartial third party after hearing evidence from the defence and the Crown, plea bargaining requires that the defence attorney and the Crown attorney presume guilt and arrive at a mutually acceptable solution to dispose of the case. Even more importantly, for the purposes of this paper, defendants have only minimal involvement in the actual negotiations.[13] Rather, they must rely on their defence lawyer to assess accurately the strength of the Crown's case. The defendant is faced with the decision to accept his lawyer's advice on the advantages of pleading guilty in exchange for specific concessions.

Although some might argue that the defendant is free to make the choice of going to trial, if the defendant's lawyer recommends taking the bargain, the defendant is understandably reluctant to ignore this advice. This reluctance is partially based on the defendant's assumption that the lawyer is acting in the defendant's best interests and partially on the belief that the lawyer's expertise enables him or her to make the best decision. The situation is analogous to the medical patient who is relucant to ignore the advice of the doctor. In our society, we have been socialized to trust the experts.

The accused, then, has been placed in a position where the result is determined by the Crown attorney and the defence lawyer: two individuals who both have something to gain by presuming the defendant to be guilty. The less the defendant is involved with the process, the easier the process becomes for the two lawyers. A recent textbook on criminal justice characterized the position of the defendant in the following way:

> The situation the defendant faces in the period preceding his eventual plea is, in many respects, an extension of his life in the streets. . . . You are to a large extent at the mercy of others and of fate. You try to get what you want, but whether you get it or not often has little to do with your efforts.[14]

The Role of the Victim

A similar case can be made that victims have no viable role in the criminal justice system. Criminology's focus on victims in the past several years has revealed that the police and the courts virtually ignore the needs and concerns of victims. After making a statement to the police, the vast majority

11 H. Packer, *The Limits of the Criminal Sanction* (1968).

12 S. Verdun-Jones and F. Cousineau, "A Critical Analysis of Plea Bargaining in Canada" in Boydell and Connidis (eds.), *The Canadian Criminal Justice System* (1982).

13 D. Sudnow, "Normal Crimes: Sociological Features of the Penal Code in a Public Defender Office" (1965), 12:3 Social Problems 255.

14 J. Kaplan and J. Skolnick, *Criminal Justice: Introductory Cases and Materials*, 3rd ed. (1982).

of victims will receive no other communication from the criminal justice system.

Within the past year, the author conducted a study for the Ministry of the Solicitor General on the experiences of victims and witnesses, and their perception of the criminal justice system.[15] The findings from 300 interviews with victims and witnesses showed a consistent insensitivity to their needs. For example:

— Seventy per cent of the victims interviewed stated that they wanted information on the progress of the police investigation but only 31 per cent received any information, mainly on their own initiative. Interviews with the police revealed that no system existed to keep victims informed of the status of the police investigation.

— Fifty per cent of the victims did not know whether or not someone had been charged with the offence. Since some of the victims inferred that nobody had been charged because there had been no communication from the police, 50 per cent is probably a conservative estimate of uninformed victims.

— Seventy-nine per cent of the witnesses interviewed stated that they had no contact with a Crown attorney prior to their court appearance. Many of these individuals lacked such basic information as the legal meaning of a subpoena, the physical location of the court and the role of a witness in court.

— Forty-one per cent of the witnesses, who arrived at court on the day specified on the subpoena, were told that their testimony was no longer required. This was usually due to a bargain made between the Crown attorney and the defence lawyer immediately prior to the trial. The witnesses were given no information on the nature of the bargain. Surprisingly, only 37 per cent were not satisfied with the way in which the case was handled by the court.

One must conclude from these findings that victims and witnesses occupy the most marginal roles in the criminal justice system. Their participation has been reduced to those situations where the Crown must proceed with a case in the formal, adversarial manner. Even in this situation, the victim is often limited to appearing in court and giving testimony.

TOWARD AN EXPLANATION

How have we come to a system where the accused and the victim play such peripheral roles in the criminal justice system? The popularly accepted explanation argues that the process of handling criminal cases is the direct result of setting organizational efficiency as a priority of the system.

15 S. Brickey, *Winnipeg Victim/Witness Assessment Program: Planning Phase* (unpublished), Department of the Solicitor General (1982).

The essence of this explanation is that determining guilt through the formal, adversarial process is both time consuming and economically prohibitive to the state, given the large volume of cases that must be processed through the system.[16] In order to deal with these problems, it became necessary to develop a more informal method of processing defendants efficiently through the system. This method is plea bargaining. According to adherents of this explanation, the diminished participation of the victim and the accused is an inadvertent consequence of organizational efficiency.

There are two weaknesses in this explanation. First, it assumes that there is an inherent contradiction between bureaucratic efficiency and participation of the accused and the victim in the judicial process. Yet there is no evidence to suggest that any attempts have been made to develop a system that is both organizationally efficient and involves the central actors in the criminal event. In fact, the only demonstrated fact is that the formal, adversarial process is inefficient.

This leads to the second weakness of this explanation. That is the assumption that the elimination of plea bargaining would result in a return to a system where the accused and the victim are major players in the system. Although it is true that a return to the due process model would require more involvement by the victim and the accused than is found at present, if we look closely at the adversarial system, we note that even here the victim and the accused are spectators and not full participants in the system. It is still the Crown attorney, the defence lawyer, and the judge who are the key players in the system.

In order to develop an understanding of how victims and offenders have become objects and not subjects within the judicial system, it is necessary to take an historical look at the system. It is only through historical analysis that we can avoid the myopic weaknesses noted in the organizational efficiency explanation.

Fortunately, a number of anthropologists and sociologists have provided us with insights that allow us to develop a plausible explanation of the historical transformation of the roles of the accused and the victim.

The key to the transformation can be found by comparing preliterate, egalitarian societies to societies that have the elementary components of social stratification and centralization of power. The available evidence indicates that this fundamental societal shift to a hierarchical system brought about a qualitative change in the philosophy and practice of settling disputes. To support this argument, a description will first be given of the features of dispute settlement within egalitarian societies and this will be followed by noting the changes that take place when a society develops a system of structural inequality.

16 A. Blumberg, "Crime and the Social Order" in A. Blumberg (ed.), *Current Perspectives on Criminal Behavior*, 1st ed. (1974).

If one were asked to describe the dispute settling process of egalitarian societies in one word, that word would be compromise. When two individuals in the community encountered a conflict situation that required resolution, the general procedure was to seek a solution that satisfied both parties to the conflict.[17] Whether the compromise was arrived at through direct interaction between the parties or through the use of a mediator, the goal was the same: resolve the dispute in such a way that the parties in conflict perceived that justice had been done.[18] Contrary to the Durkheimian thesis that preliterate societies could be characterized as repressive in their methods of social control, these societies could best be characterized as restitutive in their approach to dispute resolution.[19]

One of the major consequences of emphasizing compromise in dispute resolution is that the enforcement of norms, customs, rules, *etc.*, is of secondary importance. That is, the specific content of the custom or rule must be ignored or changed if priority is given to reaching a solution agreeable to both parties.[20] If emphasis is placed on enforcing the rule and punishing the rule breaker, the potential for reconciliation is diminished.

When we turn our attention to societies referred to as proto-states[21] (states that show the rudimentary forms of social stratification and centralization of power), we can observe two major shifts in dispute settlement. These shifts are a change to giving priority to rule enforcement over compromise and a redefinition of who is the victim.

The shift to rule enforcement as the priority is directly related to the existence of a stratification system:

> Economic stratification always entails control of the surplus by the upper class, and struggle for a more equitable share by the lower class. The upper classes inevitably look for coercive means to maintain their superior position. They must have the norms of property and contract enforced, not compromised. One does not bargain with a thief in order to find a compromise that will enable all of us to live together amicably from here on. The central theme of dispute-settlement becomes not reconciliation but rule enforcement.[22]

Thus, when maintenance of power and privilege requires that the content of the rule takes priority over the relationship between parties in conflict, compromise resolutions become less likely.

A second major change that emerges in proto-states is the reconceptualization of who is the victim when a rule has been broken. Increasingly, the person with power over a subordinate becomes defined as the victim if the

17 W. Chambliss and R. Seidman, *Law, Order and Power,* 2nd ed. (1982).

18 M. Barkun, *Law Without Sanctions: Order in Primitive Societies and the World Community* (1968).

19 R. Schwartz and J. Miller, ''Legal Evolution and Societal Complexity'' (1964), 70 Amer. Journal of Sociology 159.

20 P. Gulliver, *Social Control in an African Society* (1963).

21 S. Diamond, ''The Rule of Law versus the Order of Custom'' in C. Reasons and R. Rich (eds)., *The Sociology of Law* (1978).

22 *Supra,* note 17.

subordinate suffers loss from a criminal event. The rationale for this redefinition is that the subordinate is the property of the person and if one's property is damaged, the property owner is the victim.

There are numerous historical examples of this reconceptualization, where slaves, women, and children are victims of illegal conduct, but the victim recognized in law is the owner of these individuals.[23] Historically, men have been viewed as the legal victims of rape:

> Under Anglo-Saxon law, rape, along with most other offences, was punished by orders to pay compensation and reparation. If a woman was raped, a sum was paid to either her husband or father, depending on who still exercised rights of ownership over her, and the exact amount of compensation depended on the woman's economic position and her desirability as an object of an exclusive sexual relationship. The sum was not paid to the woman herself; it was paid to her father or husband because he was the person who was regarded as having been wronged by the act.[24]

After the emergence of the proto-state, we find that over the centuries the state evolves into the locus of power in society. Corresponding to this centralization of power is the increasing tendency to define the state as the victim in all criminal offences. All citizens have become the property of the state and any criminal act against a citizen is legally viewed as a criminal act against the state. Thus, if an offender is required to pay a fine for his or her criminal transgression, the state is the recipient of the fine. The pervasiveness of the idea of the citizen as the property of the state is noted in a discussion of the definition of attempted suicide as a criminal act: "The individual, it was assumed, had no right to take his own life; that was the sole prerogative, presumably, of the state, whose property he was conceived to be."[25]

These two historical transformations, then, help to explain the present marginality of victims and offenders and the alienation that stems from this marginality. When the emphasis is placed on rule enforcement, the direct involvement of the offender in the process of dispute resolution is no longer necessary. The accused simply becomes an object to which others affix guilt and administer punishment.

Similarly, the victim's involvement is no longer required because he or she is no longer legally viewed as the victim. He or she may be required to give testimony but the major concern is that the legal victim is satisfied that justice has been done.

DISCUSSION

On the assumption that the reader finds some plausibility in these ideas, what are the implications for changing the criminal justice system? Since it is

23 D. Black, *The Behavior of Law* (1976).

24 L. Clark and D. Lewis, *Rape: The Price of Coercive Sexuality* (1977).

25 *Supra*, note 21.

unlikely that society will shortly evolve into an egalitarian system, we should expect the basic structure of the criminal justice system to stay the same. Any changes that are introduced are likely to be in the context of reforms within the structure.

In the past two years, the Ministry of the Solicitor General and the Department of Justice have been involved in the implementation of victim assistance programs in every region of the country. These programs provide emotional support to victims, inform victims of the police investigation, inform victims of relevant social service agencies, describe court procedures, and expedite the return of stolen property.

Although all of the above services offer significant improvement over the current situation of neglect, they do not address the issue of victim involvement in the system. There is, however, one program, implemented under the rubric of victim assistance, that does attend to involvement. This program is usually referred to as victim-offender mediation. The major feature of victim-offender mediation is the direct interaction of the two parties for the purpose of arriving at a mutually agreeable solution to the conflict. Both the victim and the offender must agree to mediation as an alternative to the traditional route of the criminal court.

The major advantage of the victim-offender mediation program to the conflicting parties is that they are allowed to have significantly more control of the dispute-settling process. Their involvement in the process is no longer that of objects but of full participants. The advantage of the program to the state is the savings in time and costs by allowing a proportion of cases to be dealt with outside the criminal justice arena. If one accepts the thesis that direct involvement of the victim and offender in dispute resolution can reduce alienation, this type of program should be strongly encouraged.

The use of victim-offender mediation in a small proportion of criminal cases is obviously not the definitive solution to the public's cynicism toward the law. It is, however, a reform that has the potential of partially ameliorating one condition that produces cynicism. That, in itself, is no minor accomplishment.

LAWYERS AND LEGAL SERVICES: CASE STUDIES IN CYNICISM

F. Murray Fraser

[Murray Fraser studied cynicism about family law, and access to and costs and quality of legal services.]

In this paper I attempt to illustrate that the results of law reform and policy-making in certain legal institutions generate cynicism in the minds of the citizens to whom the reforms and policies are directed.

I have chosen to make the argument by using case studies — three from family law and two from legal institutions, the governing bodies of the legal profession.

I have drawn examples from family law because I suspect that more Canadian citizens come into contact with and are affected by family law than by any other area of the law. Family law has experienced a ''high profile'' in that there has been considerable public debate concerning some major court decisions and legislative changes in recent years. All law reform commissions have engaged in research and study with respect to aspects of family law, and most legislatures have passed statutes which incorporate major policy changes. In addition, case studies in this area are useful because they show the direct impact of law and legal processes upon individuals.

I have chosen two issues in which the governing bodies of the legal profession — the law societies — have been involved. For the most part, law societies and the policies they develop and apply have remained somewhat removed from the public eye, and, until recently, there has been little academic writing about these institutions. At the same time, their decisions have tremendous impact upon the public and these decisions tend to generate strong views and attitudes about the law, legal institutions, and lawyers.

My conclusion is that cynicism with respect to the law, lawyers, and legal institutions may be inevitable, but that we may now be at a point where public concern has surpassed cynicism and reached a degree of anger and frustration which may bring about significant changes in the delivery of legal services.

I agree with those who argue that part of the problem lies in the complexity of law and a failure of the public to understand the responsibilities of the lawyer. However, I suggest that to a large extent the situation has been created by the failure of the law, the legal profession and legal institutions to respond sensitively and positively to social problems.

I shall begin by criticizing that branch of the legal profession from which I come — the academic side of law. Full-time legal education in the university setting in Canada is a relatively modern phenomenon. Although some progress has been achieved in recent years, it is my view that, with few exceptions, university law faculities have as yet been unable to provide students with rich intellectual educational experiences over the three years of the degree program. The curricula are pedestrian; the teaching methodologies are primitive; research and writing are narrowly based. The seeds of cynicism find fertile ground in many programs of legal education. In a sense, the negative position in which the legal profession presently finds itself may be traced, to some extent, to lack of leadership in the academic community.

FAMILY LAW

Divorce

Let me now turn to family law and, in particular, the law relating to divorce. For almost 100 years most Canadians endured a regime of divorce law that was both unreasonable and unrealistic. In most provinces, the sole ground for divorce was adultery. Where that ground could not be proven, individuals remained together in the shell of marriages that had broken down or they moved outside the law and formed common-law unions that caused both legal and psychological stress.

Where adultery could be proven, access to the courts for divorce purposes was limited to those with financial resources and certainly was not available to those who would now qualify for legal aid. In many cases, evidence was fabricated to permit those who could afford it an escape from an unhappy marital situation. Family law was unknown to the curricula of law faculties and was almost unknown to the practising bar — save and except a few practitioners who were known as "divorce lawyers", many of whom were viewed with some suspicion by their colleagues.

Issues short of divorce, such as maintenance and the division of property, were often not the subject of litigation and were usually resolved in favour of the husband. The wife could rarely afford a lawyer and the law militated against her chances of recovery in any event. No legal aid plan existed.

Throughout this period of hypocrisy, less than 20 years ago, the leaders of the legal profession, academic and practising, remained inactive, uninterested, and uncommitted to reform. The real push for change came from social workers and others who worked in the field and saw the dramatic negative effects of laws which worked in harsh measure against many individuals.

It is true that lawyers and lawyers' associations played major roles in the later stages of reform, culminating in 1968 in the Divorce Act.[26] But it is also

26 1967-68 (Can.), c. 24 [now R.S.C. 1970, c. D-8].

fair to state that the lawyers hopped onto and eventually drove a bandwagon constructed by others.

What has happened in the past 15 years? Perhaps the start of another cycle of cynicism. With the passage of the Divorce Act, family law became legitimate. It became respectable within the profession. It was a money-maker. Family law was recognized as a subject worthy of study and research in law faculties. Public pressure gradually pushed family law to the top of the agenda for most law reform commissions. The social and political climate of the time encouraged reform. Legal aid plans permitted previously unrepresented parties the opportunities to pursue their legal remedies.

The Divorce Act of 1968 was a product of compromise and political accommodation. As such, even upon its enactment, it deserved close scrutiny and further reform in a short period of time. Some bodies have acted. The Law Reform Commission of Canada, in a paper published a few years ago, recommended substantial changes, but for the most part these words have gone unheeded. I suggest that now is the time to consider changes in divorce legislation and related matters. Its strengths and weaknesses are known. Reform should be designed this time to focus upon procedures to reduce bitterness, costs and delay, and to permit the parties to be treated sensitively and with respect by the legal process. It would be interesting to consider the development of a statement of social interests whereby changes in proposed legislation might be seen clearly.

Family Property Law

A more startling example of reform that may have created a monster is found in the area of family property law. The late 1960's provided a climate, politically and intellectually, which demanded recognition of the right of each spouse to an equal division of family property upon the breakup of a marriage in all but exceptional circumstances.

This result was attempted by the passage of legislation in all the common law provinces during that short period of time at the end of the last decade.

What has happened as a result of this legislation, at least in some provinces, however, is a commentary upon the failure of reform in substantive matters to anticipate the problems in procedural and human terms.

1. Rather than encouraging spouses to settle their affairs amicably and without resort to the formalities of the court processes, the legislation has resulted in a tremendous increase in litigation. In many circumstances, lawyers advise their clients to take the issues of property division to the courts because the legislation is so ambiguous and the courts have been unable to respond with useful declarations of principle to be applied in particular cases.
2. The courts in some provinces are completely bogged down at the trial

level due to extensive litigation, much of it arising from the family property field.

3. The focus on litigation and the adversary system has increased the strife, added greatly to the costs, and extended the time over which settlements are concluded.

4. In some jurisdictions, individual lawyers have applied contingency fee arrangements to family property settlements, thereby using a device that is, in my view, entirely inappropriate to the resolution of the problems at hand.

A graphic illustration of the discontent of the public is the fact that complaints to the Law Society of British Columbia in the first half of 1982 indicate family law as the second most popular area of discontent. The major concerns relate to fees and the quality of services.

In short, legislative reform, designed to achieve a desirable social purpose, has brought about extremely serious problems.

Family or Child Advocate

My final example from family law is the rise and fall of the family or child advocate. Separate legal representation of the interests of a child in a variety of legal proceedings, including custody and child protection matters, was a natural outcome of many of the reforms in family law in the past 15 years.

In most provinces there is legislative recognition of the right of a child to independent legal representation. As is the case in many circumstances, however, this ''right'' is now in danger of elimination due to economic constraints. In British Columbia, the provincial government has placed severe limitations on the circumstances in which a family advocate or child advocate may be appointed. These restrictions have been dictated entirely by budgetary concerns. One can hardly expect anything other than cynicism (and more) from the reasonable observer of the process. One notes a cycle: the creation of a right, its recognition in legislation, and within a few short years, the elimination of what was seen to be a precious right of a party who normally cannot be heard and has no political lobby. The elimination occurs without debate and without evidence of serious public concern. One might also express the same general concerns with respect to cutbacks in legal aid services which are occurring and may be expected to continue within the next few months.

LAW SOCIETIES

I wish to conclude with two examples of what I would call unfortunate decision-making by the law societies in dealing with issues of considerable public interest.

Advertising

In British Columbia, the issue of advertising by lawyers became a public cause cèlébre. In 1978, Donald Jabour, a practising lawyer, established a legal services clinic, advertised his services and fees, and was cited by the Law Society for conduct unbecoming a member of the profession. Mr. Jabour wanted to provide basic legal services on a high-volume/reasonably low-cost basis. A discipline committee recommended that Mr. Jabour be suspended for six months. To make a very long story short, the case became a major constitutional battleground and proceeded on that basis to the Supreme Court of Canada.[27] The issue of advertising was not directly dealt with in any of the decisions other than to confirm that the power with respect to advertising lay with the governing body. Ironically, as the case proceeded through the courts, the Law Society changed its policies with respect to advertising to permit lawyers to advertise their fees and areas of practice. The case cost the Law Society of British Columbia a substantial sum and the taxpayers of Canada an even greater amount as the constitutional issues were argued.

Regardless of the correctness of the decision of the Law Society with respect to Mr. Jabour's initial conduct, the public perception, generated to a large extent by the manner in which the Law Society handled the case, is probably one of increased scepticism about the ability of the governing body to act in the public interest. The public may well perceive the Jabour case as confirming the reputation of the profession as restrictive, insensitive to public concerns, unresponsive to issues of access and costs of legal services, and self-serving in a rather punitive manner.

To be fair, the law societies carry very heavy responsibilities and have acted positively and extensively to improve competency and proper conduct within the profession. In many instances, the governing bodies have simply failed to communicate to the public the actions which they have taken in the public interest. But there are a number of disturbing instances, the Jabour case being one example, where the public interest may not have been served, and the public perception of lawyers and the legal process has been negative, to put it mildly.

Competence

I shall close with one more illustration. The law societies are charged with the responsiblity of monitoring and enforcing standards of competence. In recent years, there have been a great number of policy changes designed to improve competency and to protect the public in cases of incompetence. In Ontario, however, some leaders of the legal profession have linked the problem of incompetence and criminal activity by lawyers to the growing number of practising lawyers, suggesting as a solution an artificial reduction

27 *A.G. Can. v. Law Soc. of B.C.; Jabour v. Law Soc. of B.C.*, [1982] 2 S.C.R. 307, [1982] 5 W.W.R. 289, 37 B.C.L.R. 145, 19 B.L.R. 234, 66 C.P.R. (2d) 1, 137 D.L.R. (3d) 1, 43 N.R. 451.

in the number of lawyers admitted to the practice of law each year. The answer to the problem, they say, is to reduce the number of new lawyers. This fails to connect the problem and the solution. In effect, it can be argued, and may well be seen by the public, to be an attempt at protectionism — to stifle competition, to emphasize a concern about wealth, power and personal gain, rather than to concentrate upon the improvement of the quality of service and increased access to legal services, two of the most important issues facing both the public and the legal profession.

In conclusion, an optimist may suggest that enlightened leadership and continued dedication to the service of the public will solve the immediate problems. But one must also note that the storm clouds on the horizon may well produce more than cynicism and could indeed result in a public demand for major changes in the way in which legal services are provided and the legal profession is governed.

The illustrations to which I have referred, taken individually, may not have had much impact upon public attitudes and perceptions. The creation of expectations through changes in policy and through law reform measures, however, are often followed by the failure to realize those expectations. Reality crashes down upon the public and confirms its tentative view that law, legal institutions, and lawyers give with one hand and take away with the other.

THE CANADIAN BAR ASSOCIATION — A REPLY

Yves Fortier

[Pursuant to Murray Fraser's latter comments, Yves Fortier stated that lawyers should not be allowed to advertise areas of specialization without mandatory programs of continuing legal education. He spoke generally about the attempts of the Canadian Bar Association to improve the poor image of lawyers.]

PUBLIC PERCEPTION OF LAWYERS

The perception of the lawyer and of the legal profession in this country is appalling.

In 1978, a Gallup Poll was conducted for the Canadian Bar Association on public attitudes to lawyers. When asked to rate various professions, some

16 per cent of those interviewed voted lawyers as having low or very low standards of honesty and ethics. Only 72 per cent of those interviewed felt that lawyers had average, high or very high standards of honesty and ethics. Compare this with 96 per cent for doctors, 92 per cent for police officers, and 85 per cent for university teachers. This is not only a Canadian problem. A 1978 Harris Poll in the United States rated public confidence in 16 institutions. Law firms finished last.

As these earlier surveys showed, our score card is disastrous. We are perceived as tending to overcharge, to be slow, to be uncommunicative and obtuse in our dealings with clients. If, as I believe, every lawyer is an ambassador for the profession, we are not experts in the art of diplomacy. Now, we find, as the Legal Research Institute's important findings demonstrate, it is not only lawyers but the whole system of justice which is viewed poorly by the public.

Over 60 per cent of those responding to the Institute's survey felt that our legal system favoured the rich and the powerful[28] — a damning indictment not only of the administration of justice but also of the liberal democratic system which obtains in this country.

We, as judges, lawyers, academics, or others involved in the legal system, can respond to these alarming perceptions in one of two ways. We can shake our heads and say, "They just don't understand", or we can accept that there are fundamental problems with our legal system and that much of the responsibility for current attitudes towards the law and lawyers rests with all of us. There is no doubt in my mind that the solutions rest with us.

RESPONSE OF CANADIAN BAR ASSOCIATION

Let met take a few of the Legal Research Institute's findings and demonstrate to you what the Canadian Bar Association has already done and intends to do to remedy these perceived and real deficiencies in our legal system.

Delivery of Legal Services

First, many think that it takes far too long to accomplish anything through the process of law.[29] The Canadian Bar Association agrees.

In 1979, we began an in-depth consideration of the delivery of legal services in Canada. We realized that civil courts were faced with a tremendous backlog of cases. This often meant excessive costs for litigants, frustration, and ultimately disrespect for a legal system that was designed in the Victorian age and that cannot cope with the burdens forced upon it today.

28 See the Legal Research Institute survey, question 41(c), *supra*, c. 2.

29 *Ibid.*, question 41(f), *supra*, c. 2.

We responded to the problem. With the support of a $300,000 grant from the Donner Foundation, the Canadian Bar Association in 1981 undertook in Windsor, Ontario, a two-year pilot mediation project as an alternative to the civil court process. The project, known as the Windsor-Essex Mediation Centre, is testing the concepts of mediation and conciliation in the resolution of minor civil disputes. We are monitoring very closely the results of this program. If it is successful, we hope it will provide a model for other dispute resolution centres across the country. It already has in Quebec. The results we are looking for: faster, less costly, and more accessible justice.

Our criminal court system is the object of a similar study by a special committee of the Canadian Bar Association.

Promotion of Legislation and Law Reform

Second, the Institute's survey demonstrates that something drastic needs to be done about the way the legal system operates and how laws are made.[30] We also agree.

Concerned that Parliament had failed to modernize and streamline its primary role as a law-maker, the Canadian Bar Association in 1981 established a committee of distinguished Canadians to examine the role of Parliament. The committee issued a bold and imaginative report, "Parliament as a Lawmaker", which was submitted to all parliamentarians, and early in 1983, the committee appeared before a committee of the House of Commons in Ottawa to explain the proposals.

The Canadian Bar Association is becoming increasingly active at the federal level in programs of legislation and law reform. In 1978, after a year of deliberations, the Canadian Bar Association delivered a massive report on the constitution, "Towards a New Canada". We saw this report take an important place in the process of constitutional revision in Canada.

The Canadian Bar Association also published a model Freedom of Information Act to spur provincial and federal governments to legislate in this area. With legislation now in place, we intend to monitor its application.

In recent years, it is fair to say that not one important federal legislative project was tabled in Parliament upon which we did not comment by way of a brief. As active as we have been in promoting legislation and law reform, I hope that the Canadian Bar Association will become even more active. We have a privileged relationship with the Department of Justice in Ottawa and we are now working far more closely with the Law Reform Commission of Canada. The knowledge and experience of our 30,000 members can greatly assist in the development of sound legislation.

30 *Ibid.*, question 41(d), *supra*, c. 2.

Public Legal Education

But there is another means of coping with a cynical society. It is surely recognized that the poor perception of laws and lawyers often stems from a lack of knowledge. To many people, the law is a costly mystery. It does not seem to protect them from crime. It does not always secure solutions to their problems and it can deal a crippling financial blow to all but the wealthy when it is used to resolve disputes. Above all, citizens of this country do not understand how the legal system operates. Hence, they sometimes blame it and the lawyers who perform in it for faults that the system cannot correct, or rather, that the system cannot correct because the system is aloof, mysterious, and obtuse to all but the lawyers.

The Canadian Bar Association is beginning to act in the field of public legal education. We established a committee on public legal education and information in 1981 to reflect our belief that in order to function effectively in our complex world, average citizens need basic legal information. This information can help them plan their affairs, deal with potential legal problems, ascertain their rights, and know when and how to seek professional assistance. We cannot ignore the fact that better knowledge of the law will lead to less distrust of the legal system in Canada. The committee's report and recommendations urged us to promote, within our sphere of competence, increased legal content in school curricula, the establishment of lawyer referral services, and legal education and information programs for the disabled. By way of "active programs", the committee recommended the establishment of legal information telephone systems in all provinces, the creation of a Canadian Bar Association Speakers' Bureau, and the delivery of direct legal information to the public.

This is an ambitious program for the Canadian Bar Association but public legal education is a crucial element of our collective professional task. By informing the public, lawyers can help to demystify the law. In this way, we can alleviate much of the suspicion of law and lawyers that characterizes current public attitudes. Our goal must be to convince Canadians that the law can be comprehensible and that its presence ensures the smooth operation of a rapidly changing society.

As an element in its program of public legal education, the Canadian Bar Association sponsored for the first time a national "Law Day" in 1983 with the object of educating Canadians about the legal system.

You can see that we are attempting through some innovative measures to improve the poor image of lawyers and of the legal system in Canada. The deficiencies which we acknowledge in the system are being addressed.

Public attitudes do not change easily. Perhaps we shall have to accept that, to a certain degree, the law and lawyers will always be perceived with cynicism. Members of the legal profession, however, are no longer complacent about that cynicism. Cynical attitudes do affect negatively the administration of justice in Canada and we cannot allow that. We believe we can improve the legal system in such a way that it will earn more respect from the public. The whole fibre of our society depends upon respect for the rule of law which we are all committed to uphold.

6

COURTS AND JUDGES

KEEPING PACE WITH CHANGING TIMES

George Lockwood

INTRODUCTION

Shakespeare had something to say about judges. King Lear is sitting on the heath. He is blind and supposedly mad, and he says to the Duke of Gloucester:

> . . . see how yond justice rails upon yond simple thief. Hark, in thine ear: change places, and, handy-dandy, which is the justice, which is the thief?[1]

In part, this observation simply expresses an important truth about judges: judges, like other people, fall into three general categories, good, bad and indifferent. They are ordinary men and women, judging other ordinary men and women, and their claims against each other.

But there is more than that in King Lear's remark: it also conveys an attitude of cynicism about the judiciary — an attitude that one still encounters today.

The purpose of this paper is to question whether Canadian courts are as modern and efficient as they ought to be and are capable of becoming. Unless the law keeps pace with changing conditions and scientific developments, cynicism about its relevance to modern society will surely develop.

THE JURISDICTION OF THE COURTS

One source of negative public perceptions of the courts is the jurisdictional maze, with which litigants must contend.

The public generally does not understand the difference between the various courts. A court is a court, and a judge is a judge. Appearances are deceptive. In Canada, some of the judges are appointed by the provincial governments, some by the federal. In several provinces, in the field of

1 W. Shakespeare, *King Lear*, Act IV, Scene 6.

criminal law, there are three trial courts, one staffed by provincially appointed judges, two by federally appointed judges.

In a field that touches most people, family law, jurisdiction in many provinces is shared by four courts, some provincial and some federal, with varying degrees of jurisdiction. Divorce legislation is solely within the power of the federal government, which has designated the superior courts of the provinces to hear divorce cases, assisted by County Court Judges, in those provinces where they still exist, sitting as local judges of those courts. Other family-related matters are dealt with by provincial legislation.

The situation is, no doubt, puzzling to the layperson. It results, in part, from the unavoidable division of legislative power between the federal and provincial governments. In part, however, it is an aspect of an outmoded court system which, in many provinces, still retains a superior court, the High Court or the Court of Queen's Bench, and an inferior court, the County or District Court. To add to the confusion, the jurisdiction of these inferior courts has over the years become almost identical to that of the superior courts. Fortunately, change is taking place, albeit slowly. A rationalization of the court structure has already taken place in some provinces and is now moving ahead in Manitoba.[2]

THE CEREMONIAL ASPECT OF THE COURTS

Before magistrates became Provincial Judges, they were addressed as "Your Worship". They are now addressed as "Your Honour". County Court and Surrogate Court Judges are addressed as "Your Honour". Court of Queen's Bench Justices, Federal Court Justices, Justices of the Appeal Courts and of the Supreme Court of Canada are addressed as "Your Lordship". One may well question the use of titles of honour, particularly "Your Lordship", in North America in the latter part of the twentieth century. The question was raised by the late Chief Justice of the Supreme Court of Canada, Bora Laskin, when he was a judge of the Court of Appeal of Ontario:

> So far as I have been able to determine, the present-day salutation of "Your Lordship" has no formal basis; it rests on exaggerated courtesy, and perhaps on an assumed enhancement of prestige to mark the superior courts off from the inferior county and district courts whose presiding officers are "Their Honours". I cannot forbear to note that a judge of the High Court of Australia is "His Honour" despite the fact that he may be knighted. A judge of the Supreme Court of the United States is also "His Honour" without the redeeming possibility of a title. It may strike others, as it strikes me, to be pretentious for Canadian society, which rejects titles of honour in the formal gift of the British monarch, that any class of judges should be addressed as "My Lord".[3]

---

2 The amalgamation of the Court of Queen's Bench and the County Courts was effected in Manitoba as of 1st July 1984: see 1982-83-84 (Man.), cc. 81-85 for provisions transferring County Court actions to Court of Queen's Bench and related changes.

3 B. Laskin, *The British Tradition in Canadian Law* (1969), p. 32.

Some 26 years earlier, in 1943, Dennistoun J. of the Court of Queen's Bench of Manitoba made the same point in more pungent terms:

> We judges have no legal right to be so addressed. We are not Lordships, and in a country where real titles have been discarded, it seems inconsistent to perpetuate fictitious ones. They savour of old colonial days when official snobbery was in evidence. We have in Canada no Lord Justices of Appeal, nor Lords of Appeal in Ordinary, nor are we members of the House of Lords. English judges so created are rightly addressed as Your Lordships. We have no such right.[4]

A judge sitting in the Central Criminal Court in London, which used to be known as The Old Bailey, once said that over the years he had been addressed in many different ways. He had been called "Your Worshipful Holiness" on more than one occasion. He had even been addressed as "Your Majesty". But the salutation he liked the best was when an old lag, who had been before him many times, addressed the judge as "Me Old Cock".

Another question worth considering is that of court dress. At the outset in Canada, judges simply wore black gowns, as do their counterparts in the United States of America. A more recent development has been to introduce a more elaborate form of dress. Thus, in the Court of Queen's Bench in Manitoba, the attire is more like a dress proper, zipped all the way up the front and worn with a red sash and mauve cuffs. The other courts too have become more decorative. Thus, in the Provincial Court in Manitoba, the judges' gowns have scarlet facings with a scarlet collar. Similar colour combinations are the mode in the other provinces of Canada.

The legal profession is probably the only profession, apart from the clergy, that continues to dress up in outmoded clothes to do its job. The gown, after all, derives its origin from early clerical dress. One may question its suitability in twentieth century Canada for any purpose other than purely ceremonial occasions. Ironically, in England, where it all started, the Lords of Appeal, the judges of the highest court in the land, the House of Lords, do not wear robes at work.

What effect does the wearing of archaic dress have on litigants and witnesses, and the quality of their testimony? What effect does it have on public perceptions of the judiciary? Although such questions are not easy to answer, it seems reasonable to speculate that the outmoded garb of the courtroom contributes to an image of being preoccupied with the ceremonies of the past, rather than with important issues of the present day. That cannot be beneficial.

There might be a practical advantage in modernizing this aspect of court life by adopting twentieth century dress. Such a change would probably tend to demystify the courts. In a less formal setting, witnesses might well be less awed and thus give more accurate testimony. Nor is it likely that respect for the judicial process would be adversely affected. On the contrary, it could

4 Dale and Lee Gibson, *Substantial Justice* (1972), p. 287.

well be enhanced with the theatrical aspect removed. Thus would judges and counsel alike be seen to be citizens, doing a necessary job of mediating between party and party in a civil trial or between the state and the accused in a criminal trial.

On the symbolic level, the abandonment of pretentious titles, and of ostentatious and outmoded court dress might avert any perception of the courts and judges as being out-of-date and socially irrelevant.

THE COST OF JUSTICE

The subtitle under this heading might well be ''Can the average person afford the luxury of going to court?'' The short answer, in most cases, would be a resounding ''no''.

In a civil case, parties to a dispute have some control over the cost. They may choose not to seek a remedy at all. They may succeed by the mere threat of litigation. They may stop short of a trial with a negotiated settlement. The accused in a criminal case has no such choice. Even the innocent may face ruination before a verdict of not guilty is pronounced. A measure of financial relief could be provided in criminal cases if the court had a discretion to award costs in favour of the successful accused and against the state.

There are, in all parts of Canada, legal aid schemes to assist poor people. The rich, by definition, need no financial assistance. It is those people in the middle-income groups, who earn too much to qualify for legal aid, who are most vulnerable to financial hardship if they become involved in litigation.

In civil cases, too, poorer people can usually expect varying degrees of assistance from legal aid schemes, but many types of claims do not qualify, and the middle-income groups are again without recourse. Litigants in small claims may resort, without legal counsel, to small claims courts, but for larger claims the average person faces the prospect of a bill for legal services, which cannot normally be ascertained at the outset and will usually be substantial. Successful litigants usually receive an award of costs from the other party, but it is seldom sufficient to cover actual expenses.

All this means that courts have a deserved reputation of being easily accessible only to the well-to-do, and that many people with legitimate claims are deterred from recourse to law because of the high cost of litigation. Here again, is an area which merits a serious and urgent attempt to find a solution. In some jurisdictions, less formal and costly modes of dispute resolution have been developed. The adversary system, however, is arguably best suited to ensure that an innocent person is not convicted in a criminal case, and to discover the truth of the matter and provide a reasonably fair resolution of a dispute in a civil case. Thus it would be advisable to look for a solution to the problem of cost within the system as it exists.

The answer may well be a system of insurance in both criminal and civil cases. Insurance schemes to cover the costs of litigation have been developed in the United States, and something similar might be possible in Canada, either in the public or private sectors. In criminal cases, accused persons found not guilty could thus be compensated. In civil cases litigants might receive some reasonable measure of protection in regard to costs.

Apart from the financial burden of defending a criminal case, there is the real danger of permanent loss of reputation, even when the accused is finally acquitted. This, of course, raises another question, namely, whether publication of the names of accused persons should be permitted, unless there is a conviction.

PLANT AND EQUIPMENT

Ensuring a fair trial depends not only on the personnel involved, but also to some extent on the working conditions in the courtroom.

In old court houses across the country, the acoustics are often inadequate. Many such buildings lack efficient heating systems for the winter months and air conditioning for the summer. Courtrooms still exist in which the choice is between a primitive and noisy system of air conditioning and hearing the witnesses. It must be acknowledged, however, that in recent years new buildings have begun to appear in the principal judicial centres throughout Canada.

An equally serious question is the absence of modern equipment in the courtroom. The term ''equipment'' is not here used with reference to chairs and tables, but to such things as telephones, recording equipment, television, and other developing electronic techniques.[5]

Telephones are a rarity in a courtroom.

In the main, court reporters continue to record evidence manually. Why not a modern, electronic recording system? Such a system is in operation in the new court house in Halifax, Nova Scotia. It is centrally operated by remote control. Play-back of the evidence at any given time can be obtained without delay from the central controller.

Television could be used imaginatively in the court process. Some day it may be used to take the evidence of a witness in another province or country. It could also be used as a form of public education. It was so used in Angola in 1976 during the famous trial of the white mercenaries. The court proceedings were televised during the day and broadcast in the evening, so that everyone would have an opportunity of seeing the trial in its entirety. After all, one of the principles of sentencing is said to be deterrence. The question arises as to

5 Address by Le Batonnier P. Vézina, *Ouvrez La Cour à l'Electronique* Assembly of Superior Court Judges, Quebec City, October 1979.

how anyone can be deterred if unaware of the punishment imposed in any particular case or type of case. The media, at present, report only a minute number of cases and, in the main, only the most sensational. Public access to important legal proceedings by means of television might contribute significantly to reducing the ignorance on which at least some cynicism about legal institutions is founded.

Computers could be used for clerical work, preparation of lists, assignment of cases and the computation of judicial statistics. Beyond that, there is such a profusion of statutes, orders in council, regulations, and legal precedents, both reported and unreported, that in order to provide everyone with access to the law, the use of the computer is no longer a luxury but a necessity. More and more legal data are being stored on computer tape, and increasingly effective search systems are being devised. As yet, however, access to this information is usually through a few specialized libraries. How much more satisfactory it would be to have a comprehensive computer service available in the law courts themselves.

Even the telephone, invented almost a century ago, is not used to its full extent. In Canada, litigants and lawyers and courts are often separated by great distances. More use could be made of the conference telephone. It is used in some courts for motions, but this is only a small beginning. More imaginative use of modern techniques should be made as they become available.

The Supreme Court of Canada has conducted one successful experiment using satellite television. The court, sitting in Ottawa, heard motions presented by counsel in Vancouver. It is a hopeful sign that the highest court in the land has begun to set the pace of change in this area.

CONCLUSION

With the pace of change in society accelerating all the time, the entire legal system falls behind at its peril. The legal profession and the public must encourage legislative bodies to implement necessary reform speedily. Judges themselves must be open to rapid and imaginative change of their own procedures where change is warranted. If we are content with outmoded laws and outmoded procedures, we may expect the legal system to be bypassed by a society which will be justified in regarding it with cynicism.

THE THOUGHT OF ONE JUDGE

R. L. Kopstein

[R. L. Kopstein began by describing his own informal survey of public opinion in three areas of law — sentencing of criminals, obscenity and possession of cannabis — as expressed in the daily press and other commonly available publications in Winnipeg over a seven month period. The weight of opinion was that the courts are too lenient in sentencing and that the law is too harsh towards possession of cannabis. Opinion on the issue of obscenity was diverse.]

THE VALUE OF PUBLIC OPINION

Questions relating to the respect which should be accorded public opinion are not novel. Plato, for instance, urged that what is right, honourable, and good should prevail over public opinion. In the dialogue between Socrates and Crito, Socrates having been condemned to death for offending the establishment of the day, Crito attempted to persuade Socrates to escape. Popular opinion, Crito argued, opposed the sentence upon Socrates and would favour his escape. Socrates replied as follows:

> But my dear Crito, why do we care so much for what most people think. . . . Ought we to follow and fear the opinion of the many or that of the one, if there is anyone who knows about men, whom we ought to revere and fear more than all the others? And if we do not follow him, we shall injure and cripple that which we used to say is benefitted by right and is ruined by the wrong.[6]

Upon Crito's affirmation of that proposition, Socrates continued:

> And so you introduced the discussion wrongly in the first place, when you began by saying we ought to consider the opinion of the multitude about the right and the noble and the good and their opposites.[7]

Some twenty-three centuries later, John Stuart Mill wrote:

> At present individuals are lost in the crowd. In politics it is almost a triviality to say that public opinion now rules the world. The only power deserving the name is that of the masses, and of governments while they make themselves the organ of the tendencies and instincts of the masses . . . And what is a still greater novelty, the mass do not now take their opinion from dignitaries in church or state, from ostensible leaders or from books. Their thinking is done for them by men much like themselves, addressing them or speaking in their name on the spur of the moment, through the newspapers. I am not complaining of all this. I do not assert that anything better is compatible, as a general rule, with the present low state of the human mind, But that does not hinder the government of mediocrity from being mediocre government.[8]

6 H. N. Fowler (trans.), Plato, *Crito* (1914), pp. 155, 165, 167.

7 *Ibid.*

8 John Stuart Mill, *On Liberty* (1933), pp. 81, 82.

Espoused by those who can rely on the power of the state to enforce their view of "right", the theory that right should prevail over popular opinion can be an attractive deception. Espoused by those in office whose intentions are honourable but whose view of "right" is so rigid as to render them virtually deaf to competing views, the theory that right must prevail over popular opinion is equally dangerous. "Right" is no more than the opinion of those who assert it. The colour of right has as many different shades as there are people with divergent interests and differing philosophies of life. Nor does wisdom, let alone "right", respecting law-related social issues reside exclusively with judges or legislators any more than with any segment of public opinion. The most that can be said for judges and legislators is that they are likely to have better access to information and expert advice than is generally available.

In the absence of absolutes, "right" respecting law-related social issues must be rooted in public opinion not because of any superior wisdom necessarily associated with that opinion, but because the absence of broad public support for decisions upon those issues will adversely affect public confidence in the law. A twofold problem, however, arises: first, the problem of measuring public opinion to ascertain which opinion, if any, upon a given issue represents a broad public consensus, and second, the problem of ascertaining whether those members of the public who express opinions are sufficiently knowledgeable respecting the issues to formulate a well-founded opinion.

Public consensus may be perceived through the popular press from the volume of letters, articles, and editorials published in support of or in opposition to a given proposition. Those expressions of opinion by themselves, however, may be nothing more than the vocal opinion of a minority and they may or may not be well informed. It is probably true that those who oppose a decision or practice are more likely to write letters than those who have no particular quarrel with it. It is likely, also, that those with a special interest in an issue will be more vocal than those without such an interest. Notwithstanding their frequency in the press, therefore, opinions expressed therein may not be representative of public opinion. Articles and editorials are merely public expressions of private opinions and do not at any time necessarily represent public opinion. Majority opinion cannot be determined with any certainty, therefore, from the expressions of opinion in the popular press.

The most scientific method of ascertaining public opinion appears to be the public opinion poll. The validity of a poll, however, depends upon the integrity of the pollster and also the skill in polling a truly representative segment of the population. Again the value of the poll as an instrument to guide decision-making upon law-related social issues will hinge upon the degree of awareness among those polled of the factors involved in the issue in question.

> The polls have come to have a far reaching and often dangerous impact, largely because the pollsters have intimidated most of their potential critics. The pollsters would have us believe that to criticize their calling is to oppose democracy, but, their claims to the contrary, public opinion and the public opinion polls are two quite different things.[9]

Wheeler also says that it is difficult to assess the honesty of those who respond to opinion polls. After the Watergate scandal broke in the United States, public opinion pollster Pat Caddell asked people whether they had voted for presidential candidate Nixon or McGovern in the 1972 election. Curiously, even in those states where Nixon had actually won in 1972, the majority who responded to Caddell's poll after Watergate claimed to have voted for McGovern. It is further indicated by Caddell that George Wallace's success based upon pre-election polls was always underestimated. Even in post-election polls, people were reluctant to admit that they had voted for him.

Concerning awareness, Gallup reported in 1973 that while 76 per cent of the people believed that President Richard Nixon was involved in Watergate, only 35 per cent believed he should be impeached. Later in 1973, Burns Roper conducted his own poll of those who were opposed to impeachment. He inquired as to the reasons for their opposition. He discovered that more than 50 per cent misunderstood the nature of the impeachment process. They believed that impeachment meant forced removal from office without trial rather than investigation and indictment by a legislative body. Pat Caddell, according to Wheeler, conducted a number of surveys:

> The problem really was semantic. The way Gallup posed the question, it seemed that only 35% said Nixon should be impeached, but when asked "Do you think he should be tried and removed from office if found guilty?", then 57% said he should.[10]

Clearly, without an adequate understanding of the meaning of the terms employed to ask a question and without a wholesome appreciation of the issues to which a question relates, the opinion given and the statistics resulting will be less than useful. In that regard, it is interesting to note some of the responses to the Legal Research Institute Survey.[11] Question 57 indicates that 97 per cent of the respondents had never been sentenced to prison. In response to question 86, however, 88 per cent of them had an opinion about whether prisons were too luxurious and pleasant. Only about 12 per cent said they did not know. Question 48(e) asks: "Do you think the police twist or make up evidence to convict a suspect?" The most frequent response was, "almost never". While that opinion may be of value in assessing the public attitude toward police integrity, question 73 reveals that some 63 per cent of the respondents had never been in court as a witness or a party.

Question 74(f) of the same survey asks respondents if in their opinion trials would be more effective if the courtroom, the dress of the judges and

9 M. Wheeler, *Lies, Damn Lies and Statistics* (1976), p. xvii.
10 *Ibid.*, p. 167.
11 *Supra*, The Legal Research Institute survey, c. 2.

lawyers, and the proceedings were less formal. The majority thought that trials would not be more effective. It is interesting to speculate upon what the word "effective" meant to the respondents in that context. Assuming that it meant something to them, however, more than 38 per cent of the sample, according to question 72, had never been in a courtroom.

It follows that where issues are complex, as most law-related social issues are, knowledgeable public opinion cannot be assumed and, therefore, public opinion is of little value as a factor in determining the course of the law.

OFFICIAL REGARD FOR PUBLIC OPINION

Some judicial protestations to the contrary, courts are influenced by their perceptions of public opinion. Three 1981 decisions of superior courts in this country seem to demonstrate that point.

The Ontario Court of Appeal in a judgment on an appeal from a two-month sentence for indecent assault and gross indecency said, ". . . the sentence of two months' imprisonment does not adequately reflect the gravity of the conduct and . . . *society's abhorrence* of that conduct. . . ."[12]

In a recent decision the British Columbia Court of Appeal dealt with an appeal from a suspended sentence requiring the accused to perform 200 hours of community service work upon conviction for armed robbery. In sentencing the accused to imprisonment for one year, Seaton J.A. said: ". . . I think that a minimum sentence to act as a deterrent and *express society's condemnation* is a sentence of one year. . . ."[13]

In the Alberta Queen's Bench in a 1981 decision, the accused had pleaded guilty to five charges of bank robbery with threats of violence in each. In his reasons for judgment, Decore J. indicated the importance of retribution as an element of sentence, ". . . *not because society seeks to meet out vengeance but rather as an attempt to express its repudiation of the crime committed.*"[14]

Concerning the simple possession of cannibis, the responsibility for the law itself is, of course, in the hands of Parliament. If public opinion is perceived as favouring a change in the law, and no good reason appears forthcoming for failing to change it, one may ask why the law has not been changed. Are there, perhaps, good reasons which have not been publicly articulated? Would public opinion support the status quo if such good reasons

12 *R. v. Bumbacco* (1981), 23 C.R. (3d) 183 at 186 (Ont. C.A.). Emphasis added.

13 *R. v. Campbell*, [1982] 1 W.W.R. 739 at 743, 26 C.R. (3d) 279, 64 C.C.C. (2d) 336 (B.C.C.A.). Emphasis added.

14 *R. v. McWhinnie*, [1982] 1 W.W.R. 389 at 392, 25 C.R. (3d) 342 (Alta. Q.B.). Emphasis added.

were made known? Whatever the case, the government seems, in fact, to have responded to public opinion, indirectly at least. The law has not been changed, but federal prosecutors have for several years recommended discharges to the courts upon first offence simple possession charges involving small amounts of cannibis. Courts also responded to public opinion in that regard, since, even before the Department of Justice Crown attorneys made that recommendation, some courts were granting discharges to first time simple possession offenders.

As well, on the issue of obscenity, judges do respond to public opinion either as established by evidence or on the basis of their own perceptions of community standards.[15]

One may question, however, whether those various responses have been adequate. Notwithstanding the view of the writer that attempted assessments of public opinion are open to many questions and that such assessments of complex social issues are valueless other than to test general attitudes, it is vitally important for judges and legislators to respond to the public expression of opinion, whether in fact it represents the view of the majority or not. Even a view without initial public support and not well-founded, if expressed by the members of a vocal minority frequently enough and eloquently enough, may influence and promote widespread public opinion in support of it. That may particularly be so when those who could inform are reticent.

The passing of the time when respect for the law was ingrained and the authority of the courts had popular acceptance, referred to by Deschênes C.J.S.C. (as he then was),[16] probably coincided, roughly, with higher standards of literacy and improved methods of mass communication. It may be that the time past to which His Lordship was referring was that lengthy period in the history of the western world during which officials of church and state were held in awe by a population which was largely illiterate and had no means or information to question their wisdom. True, the public may have lost some of its respect for the law since the decline of that epoch. True, too, the popular acceptance of the courts may be diminished. It is possible, however, that the conditions which in an earlier age fostered that greater respect and acceptance, were fear and abject ignorance in comparison with the greater general awareness of a world in the late twentieth century. The return of those conditions is no more desirable than it is likely. Public confidence, however, that the law-makers and judges are attuned and responding to the concerns of the population which they serve, is essential to the concept of democracy and ultimately to civil peace within a democracy.

Perhaps, to build and to maintain that confidence, legislators and judges will have to learn and employ better communication skills vis-à-vis the public

15 See, for example, *R. v. Towne Çinema Theatres (1975) Ltd.*, [1982] 1 W.W.R. 512 at 543 (Alta. Q.B.).

16 *Comm. de. Tpt. de la Communauté Urbaine de Montréal v. Syndicat du Tpt. de Montréal*, 77 C.L.L.C. 14,098, reversing [1974] Rec. de J. 227 at 231 (C.A.).

— judges, perhaps even more than legislators, since the public has no opportunity in this country to express its displeasure with judges through the election process.

In regard to legislators, however, question 18 of the Legal Research Institute Survey[17] asked respondents whether they "strongly disagree", "disagree", "agree", "strongly agree", with or have "no opinion" on the following statements: (a) "Generally, those elected to Parliament soon lose touch with the people," and (b) "I don't think that the government cares much what people like me think". To both statements, the most frequent response was "agree". It is hoped that the belief expressed by that answer is unfounded. If unfounded, however, it would appear that there is indeed something amiss in the communication between the legislators and the people.

It would be naive to think that any decision by legislators or by a judge was capable of rallying unqualified public support. Indeed, upon most issues of any substance, there are at least two legitimate points of view, and adverse public reactions are to be expected. That is part of a healthy dialogue within a democracy. An expectation or hope, moreover, that today people will accept, with resignation, the decision of a government official or court official merely out of respect for his or her status is unrealistic. A decision of legislators or of a judge which is blatantly unappealing to the common sense of the public will understandably confound the public. The failure to provide meaningful explanations which reach the public leaves the media with nothing to print or air but critical expressions of opinion, and they may abound. The decisions of legislators and of judges on law-related social issues such as those earlier discussed may often be well-founded and would probably rally the support of many if the foundations were known and understood. The failure to communicate the reasons for decisions effectively and meaningfully to the public in terms that are direct and unpretentious does a disservice to that public as well as to the political and judicial systems. The failure alienates people and promotes disillusionment with those systems.

LAW IN A CYNICAL SOCIETY?

In order to place the topic in perspective, one should assume from the outset that the society to which the title refers is one that conceives of itself as free and democratic. The degree to which the government of such a society may endure as an efficient governing force in the absence of police-state coercion will depend in large measure upon the public perception of that government as one that may be trusted broadly to reflect the values of the society which it governs. By definition, that state abhors the employment of police-state methods, both to sustain itself in power and to foster the observance of law.

In such a state, there should be substantial observance of the law, not

17 See *supra*, The Legal Research Institute Survey, c. 2.

because of its legal authority, but because of its moral authority — that authority which it acquires by virtue of mass public belief that it is "right" and that public officials may be trusted. Beyond the legal authority of the law, it is its moral authority which will foster tolerance to its imposition, substantial obedience to its letter, and acceptance of its administration.

A cynical society which rejects significant elements of the law because it believes that the law fails to reflect its values, or because it lacks trust in those it places in public office, is likely to suffer both the civil disruptions that would be suppressed in a totalitarian state, and the social and financial costs of a growing police presence which is characteristic of the totalitarian state.

Illegal strikes require the deployment of police to suppress them. Large scale disregard of the laws relating to the possession of marijuana encourages large scale importing and trafficking which in turn, create the need for armies of police to ferret out, often by foul means, those who so engage themselves. In essence, law in that free and democratic society acquires the characteristics of law in a totalitarian state.

Public opinion may be an unreliable guide to decision-making. It is, however, a factor within society which, if disregarded by the decision-makers, will promote cynicism, weaken the moral authority of the law, encourage more and larger pockets of hostility to the law, and make necessary larger and stronger police forces to enforce laws which the public does not necessarily support.

The decision-makers cannot escape the responsibility either for creating public opinion or for doing nothing to reverse it. If published reports and letters frequently criticize the courts because it is perceived that the courts are too lenient, judges must be prepared to respond. Silence is likely to be seen as arrogance or indifference to concerns legitimately expressed, and will promote cynicism. Judicial explanation of the practices complained of, communicated to the public clearly and unpretentiously, would at least expose the real issues to the public view and would be likely to generate a current of favourable public opinion. In the result, the public is more likely to understand the complexities of the issue, be more tolerant of the decisions that are made, and be less prone to cynicism.

If published articles and letters are frequently critical of the government for failing to reform the marijuana law, legislators should be prepared to defend the law publicly or to modify it. To do neither is to undermine public confidence and to promote cynical attitudes.

Government inaction in the reform of the marijuana law has been attributed[18] to a strong police lobby. The police empire, it was suggested, owes its existence, in large measure, to the perpetuation of that law. It was also suggested that the law is retained in its present state so that law firms

18 N. Boyd, "Taking a Well-Aimed Potshot", in *MacLean's*, 18th January 1982, p. 10.

friendly to the government in power can be rewarded through lucrative justice department retainers to prosecute offenders. The failure of legislators to provide the public with some other basis for its apparent inaction will give credence to such cynical accusations.

The late Sister McNamara presented the view of the accused, typically young, poor, native and a recidivist, and of courts and judges as forbidding, unpredictable and enormously powerful. She discussed the didactic role of the judge in setting the tone of behaviour in court by treating the accused with respect, discernment and understanding.

COMMENTARY

D. C. McDonald

INTRODUCTION

In my view there are clear limitations on the kinds of opinions judges ought to express publicly, except in open court and when those opinions are related to the issues before them in a case.

This is not to say that judges should be unaware of the currents that sweep around them in society. While their mouths should remain reasonably closed, they should keep their eyes and ears open.

GENERAL

I think members of the public at large realize that the responsibilities that a judge assumes are serious and are taken seriously.

I think members of the public expect a great deal of the judges and are entitled to do so.

I think that members of the public would be even more satisfied if they knew more about the personal and physical hardships frequently faced by judges, and about the extent to which they undertake enhancement of their potential as judges by voluntary participation in programs of judicial training and in learning the other official language.

Judges should be aware of their own limitations, conscious of the likely influence of their own backgrounds, and open-minded in the face of the swell of new ideas. If the judges achieve such a paradigmatic perfection, or even approach it, the public will continue to respect them and the institutional objectives they serve.

I begin by commenting on several matters discussed in Judge Lockwood's paper.

THE CEREMONIAL ASPECT OF THE COURTS

I have found it difficult to detect any causal connection between these issues and the existence of any alleged cynicism in society toward the law.

Modes of address and of dress may seem antiquated but, like table manners, they serve a useful social function. They remind us all that the courts have a role in dispute-resolution and the enforcement of the law, which, imperfect as any human institution may be, is deeply-rooted and not subject to the whims of public fancy, or personal whim or caprice.

In any event, having recently sat as a spectator in a number of courts in another province, where the judges and the bar have relaxed standards of attire, and the lawyers look like members of Fagin's gang, I hope that we maintain our traditions. As a judge, the fewer distractions the more easily I can concentrate on what the lawyers *say*. Yellow trousers and pink shirts are a distraction.

JURISDICTION OF THE COURTS

Simplicity is not necessarily a virtue. Change should be undertaken only as part of a comprehensive program of rationalization, such as the English Royal Commission (Beeching) on the courts. Significant and complex changes resulted. They were for the better but they were not simple.

TELEVISION IN THE COURTS

If television is to be allowed in the courts, great care is needed, lest the monster devour the child. There is a danger of increasing the impossibility of having a fair trial or a fair second trial. The object of a trial is to achieve justice, not to entertain the people. No matter how discreet the cameras, there is a danger of intrusion into the integrity of the process. There is also a risk that the public will gain a cheapened, trivialized notion of what it is all about.

COSTS

Concern has been expressed about the costs faced by an accused who is acquitted. Such concern may well be justified, but in those jurisdictions outside Canada where there is any such system of compensation to acquitted persons, it has been limited to extreme cases where the prosecution ought not to have been launched or ought not to have been continued beyond a certain stage.

Legal aid protects the indigent. Thus it is principally the middle-class accused who suffers. It is questionable that all such persons should, if acquitted, have all or part of their legal costs paid by the state, in the absence of malice or negligence in the decision to prosecute or to continue to prosecute. Certainly any such scheme should not be disproportionate to standards of compensation for persons injured by crimes of violence, or whose property has been damaged or taken by crimes of violence.

Moreover, any scheme of compensation for acquitted persons would be likely to meet with a degree of public outcry if it were not balanced by a statutory scheme, such as exists in England, which would permit the court to require *convicted* persons, if they have the means, to contribute to the state's costs of the prosecution.

Where persons have been convicted as a result of a miscarriage of justice and consequently, upon discovery of the error, are released from custody and perhaps pardoned, the integrity of the system may require that there be a system of compensation by the state not entirely in the discretion of the executive. This may be not only sound in justice but required in the fulfilment of Canada's international obligation, found in Article 15.6 of the International Covenant on Civil and Political Rights.

Let me discuss briefly the question of the cost of litigation in civil cases. This is where the middle class suffers most. Sir John Donaldson M.R., in a recent labour law case, criticized badly drafted statutes:

> At the beginning of this judgment I said that whilst I had reached the conclusion that the law was tolerably clear, the same could not be said of the way in which it was expressed. The efficacy and maintenance of the rule of law, which is the foundation of any parliamentary democracy, has at least two prerequisites. First, people must understand that it is in their interests, as well as in that of the community as a whole, that they should live their lives in accordance with the rules and all the rules. Second, they must know what those rules are. Both are equally important, and it is the second aspect of the rule of law which has caused me concern in the present case, the ITF [International Transport Workers Union] having disallowed any intention to break the law.
>
> In industrial relations it is of vital importance that the worker on the shop floor, the shop steward, the local union official, the district officer and the equivalent levels in management should know what is and what is not "offside". And they must be able to find this out for themselves by reading plain and simple words of guidance. The judges of this court are all skilled lawyers of very considerable experience, yet it has taken us hours to ascertain what is and what is not offside, even with the assistance of highly experienced counsel. This cannot be right.

> . . . My plea is that Parliament, when legislating in respect of circumstances which directly affect the "man or woman in the street" or the "man or woman on the shop floor", should give as high a priority to clarity and simplicity of expression as to refinements of policy. Where possible statutes, or complete parts of statutes, should not be amended but re-enacted in an amended form so that those concerned can read the rules in a single document. When formulating policy, ministers, of whatever political persuasion, should at all times be asking themselves and asking parliamentary counsel: "Is this concept too refined to be capable of expression in basic English? If so, is there some way in which we can modify the policy so that it can be so expressed?" Having to ask such questions would no doubt be frustrating for ministers and the legislature generally, but in my judgment this is part of the price which has to be paid if the rule of law is to be maintained.[19]

If society is cynical about the cost of justice, our legislative bodies have some responsibility for answering to that criticism.

SENTENCING

Among the papers presented at this conference are found some interesting expressions of opinion, not necessarily supported by fact, as to the sentencing process.

There is no doubt that there are frequent expressions, in public form, of views by persons not associated with the judicial system, that sentences are too lenient. Seldom do members of the pubic complain that sentences are too harsh. The compassion that frequently influences judges seldom is expressed by members of the public, but that does not mean that compassion and mercy are not found in our society.

There can be no way in which the judges can satisfy public opinion except by explaining their reasons for a sentence. Regrettably, the media report these reasons only seldom and in selected cases — often selected at random. I wish that the provincial attorneys-general and the federal Department of Justice would develop means of ensuring that sentences and the reasons for sentences could be reported broadly (particularly) in the press, even if the newspapers cannot be expected to have the resources to have reporters sitting in every courtroom.

Without such broad and organized dissemination, one of the principal functions of sentencing — that of general deterrence — has a hollow ring because those who might be deterred are unaware of the consequences of criminal conduct.

THE CANADIAN CHARTER OF RIGHTS AND FREEDOMS[20]

How can it be said that a society which has just vested a significantly

19 *Merkur Island Shipping Corp. v. Laughton; Hoegh Anapa, The* [1983] 1 All E.R. 334 at 351, affirmed [1983] A.C. 570, [1983] 2 All E.R. 189 (C.A.).

20 Canada Act, 1982 (Eng.), c. 11, s. 52.

enhanced degree of power, indeed a new *kind* of power in its judges, is cynical about the quality of the performance of our courts?

Whatever meaning is ultimately assigned to the provisions of the Charter, there can be no doubt that, as it is part of the supreme law of the land, it must be interpreted by the judges. In consequence judges may now hold to be of no force and effect decisions and actions taken by legislatures and members of the executive, where no such power existed before. Judges may now award a remedy where there has been a legislative or executive — perhaps even a private — violation of a right or freedom guaranteed under the Charter, where no such remedy could have been awarded before. A peaceful revolution has taken place in the structure of government in this country, one consented to by the federal Houses of Parliament and by the governments of nine out of ten provinces.

Could the men and women who are elected or appointed to the federal legislative assemblies of this country, and those elected to form the governments in the provinces, be so unrepresentative of public opinion that they were off in left field in consenting to the radical surgery? I ask the question but, as there must be a strong political component in providing the answer to the question, it is best that a judge refrain from providing even a personal answer.

Can there be any doubt that the burden placed upon the judges by the Charter is one which demands qualities of them that have, up to this time, not generally been expected? The public issues hitherto faced by our courts have demanded that judges gravely reflect upon their role in society more rarely than will henceforth be the case.

7

SENTENCING AND PRISONS

Marek Debicki reviewed some of the findings of the Legal Research Institute survey[1] on sentencing and prisons. There was some agreement that money can buy justice and the individual does not have a chance against big business in court;[2] there was support for differential sentencing depending on the circumstances of the case;[3] there was a perception that the courts treat rich people better than the poor and underprivileged;[4] there was significant support for harsher sentences[5] and strong support for the re-introduction of capital punishment though little agreement for what offences.[6]

The respondents indicated that prisons should protect society from criminals, rehabilitate the criminal, and discourage others from crime, rather than punish the criminal;[7] prisoners should work;[8] prisons do at best a fair job;[9] and prisons are too luxurious;[10] but the sample did not support the more frequent use of corporal punishment and solitary confinement.[11]

---

1 *See supra*, c. 2.
2 *Ibid.*, Question 74 a) and c).
3 *Ibid.*, Question 75.
4 *Ibid.*, Questions 77 & 78. See also Yves Brillon, *supra*, c. 3.
5 *See supra*, c. 2, Question 76. See also Kopstein, *supra*, c. 6.
6 *See supra*, c. 2, Questions 80-82.
7 *Ibid.*, Question 83.
8 *Ibid.*, Question 84.
9 *Ibid.*, Question 85.
10 *Ibid.*, Question 86.
11 *Ibid.*, Question 89.

SENTENCING AND SOCIO-ECONOMIC STATUS

Marek Debicki

INTRODUCTION

"The poor are arrested more often, convicted more frequently, sentenced more harshly. . . ."[1] Statements of this nature are frequent.[2] The importance of such charges against the courts cannot be overestimated. If indeed these opinions are correct, then it is a powerful indictment of the judicial decision-making process. Differential sentencing on the grounds of sex, ethnicity, educational background, type of employment, or affluence goes strictly against the normative model of criminal justice. Well-documented evidence of such practices could undermine the stability of the courts, and could clearly provide munition for powerful demands in a democratic society. The political system at large would most likely face, in such a situation, many stressful demands, and have to respond with extraordinary policies. Yet this is precisely what many of the critics of the court system claim to be the case.

OTHER STUDIES

It is surprising that in the light of the gravity of such charges, empirical studies assessing the relationship between the socio-economic status of the accused and the sentence are scarce and far from conclusive. In Canada, there are so far only three studies which shed some light on the problem; these studies, however, are limited in scope. K. B. Jobson provides some evidence that "poor people go to jail for lack of money".[3] He also finds differences in the sentencing practices of various lower criminal courts in Nova Scotia. His findings are, unfortunately, limited to fines, and furthermore, he provides practically no data in support of his above statement. R. Bienvenue and A. H.

1 P. M. Wald, "Poverty and Criminal Justice" in (1971), 2 Crime and Justice 582.

2 John Turner, "Justice for the Poor: The Courts, The Poor and the Administration of Justice", address to the International Conference of the North American Judges Association, 1st December 1969, reprinted in (1970), 12:1 Can. Journal of Corrections 1; E. Ehrlich, "Fundamental Principles of the Sociology of Law" in J. E. Carlin, J. Howard, and S. L. Messinger (eds.), *Civil Justice and the Poor* (1967), p. 13; J. Lambert, *Crime, Police and Race Relations* (1970), p. 283; United States President's Commission of Law Enforcement and Administration of Justice, "The Challenge of Crime in a Free Society" (1967), p. 6; J. H. Tieger, "Police Discretion and Discriminatory Enforcement," [1971] Duke Law Journal, p. 717; J. H. Tieger, "Fining the Indigent" (1971), 71:7 Col. L.Rev. 1281; S. R. Bing and S. Rosenthal, *The Quality of Justice in The Lower Criminal Courts of Metropolitan Boston* (1970), pp. 26-27.

3 K. B. Jobson, "Fines" (1970), 16:4 McGill Law Journal 633 at 665.

Latif conclude that the relationship between socio-economic status and sentence is at best tenuous. They also find no evidence of harsher sentencing of native people.[4] Their lack of analysis of the legal determinants of sentencing limits the value of their findings. D. J. Schmeiser *et al.* find that "native inmates in the Prince Albert Penitentiary obviously have a higher proportion of sentences in the short sentence categories than non-native inmates".[5] They also find that native offenders are less likely to receive probationary sentences than non-natives. As these conclusions are reached on the basis of the records of inmates in the penitentiary without any analysis of the sentencing process leading to the disposition, they provide little information as to the sentencing behaviour of various courts.

The above-mentioned studies do not provide sufficient evidence to sustain sweeping generalizations about the court system in Canada providing different "justice for the poor". The courts and policy-makers will find it easy to criticize these claims, thus reducing the resulting stress.[6]

Most studies of sentencing disparities come from the United States, and Canadian scholars are clearly influenced by the American findings.[7] The debate, however, as to the impact of non-legal variables on sentencing is still unresolved. Some studies emphasize the importance of socio-economic variables:

> [We] have concluded, on the basis of hard statistical data, that in determining guilt or innocence a man's finances are more important than the circumstance surrounding the charge. And ultimately money determines the final disposition.[8]

Others are equally vehement that, in a sample of non-capital cases, however, the relationship between class and disposition was diminished in strength, and reduced below statistical significance.[9]

Typical of those who find a positive relationship between the severity of sentences and socio-economic status are S. R. Bing and S. Rosenthal, who found that 55 per cent of their sample earned $75 a week or less, and that the

4 R. M. Bienvenue and A. H. Latif, "Arrests, Disposition and Recidivism: A Comparison of Indians and Whites" (1971), 16:1 Can. Journal of Criminology and Corrections 105.

5 The Law Reform Comm. of Can., "The Native Offender and the Law" (1974), p. 59. See also, The Canadian Corrections Assoc., "Indians and the Law" (1967), in particular pp. 42-65. This study reports five times the conviction rate for indictable offences for native offenders. It also provides evidence of slightly larger sentences for minor offences received by natives.

6 See *e.g.*, N. Gross, W. S. Mason and A. W. McEachern, *Explorations in Role Analysis* (1958). Also, R. L. Khan, "Some Propositions Towards Researchable Conceptualization of Stress" in J. E. McGrath (ed.), *Social and Psychological Factors in Stress*, p. 97 at 103.

7 Even the literature utilized in the studies provides evidence of that influence, *e.g.*, The Law Reform Commission of Canada, *Discovery in Criminal Cases* (1974).

8 S. R. Bing and S. Rosenthal, *The Quality of Justice in The Lower Criminal Courts of Metropolitan Boston* (1970), p. ix.

9 J. Hagan, "Extra-Legal Attributes and Criminal Sentencing: An Assessment of a Sociological Viewpoint" (1974), 83:3 Law and Soc. Rev. 357 at 378. See also, D. Jaros and R. I. Mendelsohn, "The Judicial Role and Sentencing Behaviour" (1967), 11:4 Midwestern Journal of Political Science 471.

poor person was two to three times more likely to be sentenced to jail than an affluent person.[10] Similar findings emerge from R. Hood's study of four magistrate courts in London, England.[11] He discovered that some of the courts under examination treated defendants with regular jobs and "good" working habits more favourably. Such offenders were more likely to receive probationary sentences, whereas those with unsteady working habits more likely faced imprisonment. Hood finds, however, that the characteristics of the area within which the court is operating contribute more to the variance in sentencing than do individual characteristics.[12] Cressey provides a different, twofold explanation of the higher rate of arrests, convictions, and prison sentences among people on a lower socio-economic plane: First,

> the statistics on ordinary crime so consistently show an over-representation of lower class persons that it is reasonable to assume that there is a real difference between the behaviour of the members of this class and the members of other social classes so far as criminality is concerned.[13]

Furthermore,

> the person's position in the occupational structure determines the opportunity for some kinds of crime and also determines whether or not a person will possess the skills necessary to perpetrate some type of offence.[14]

In Cressey's opinion, members of the lower class have the skills necessary to commit crimes against property. This whole argument is based on a very loose interpretation of crime statistics.[15]

Studies examining selected socio-economic variables are more frequent. The sentencing of black Americans has been most closely scrutinized. The majority of the studies finds no relationship between ethnicity and the severity of the sentence.[16] Some of the authors find different (but not necessarily discriminatory) treatment of black Americans. Thus, M. Mileski found that "the court incarcerates over three times as many white defendants as black

10 S. R. Bing and S. Rosenthal, *supra,* note 8, p. 124. See also, S. Box and J. Ford, "The Facts Don't Fit: On The Relationship Between Social Class and Criminal Behaviour" (1971), 19:1 The Sociological Rev. 31; M. A. Forslund, "Age, Occupation, and Conviction Rates of White and Negro Males: A Case Study" (1969), 6:1 The Rocky Mountain Social Science Journal 141; S. Nagel, *The Legal Process From A Behavioral Perspective,* (1969); the literature in J. Hagan, *supra,* note 9; M. Mileski, "Courtroom Encounters: An Observation Study of a Lower Criminal Court" (1971), 5:1 Law and Soc. Rev. 473; R. Hood and R. Sparks, *Key Issues in Criminology* (1970), c. 5.

11 R. Hood, *Sentencing in Magistrates Court* (1962).

12 *Ibid.* at 59-60. See also L. Phillips and H. L. Votey, "An Economic Analysis of the Effect of Law Enforcement on Criminal Activity" (1972), 63 Journal of Criminal Law, Criminology and Police Science 330.

13 D. Cressey, "The Correlates of Crime" in S. M. Sykes and T. E. Drabeck (eds.), *Law and the Lawless* (1962), p. 192 at 201.

14 *Ibid.* at 202.

15 See also, M. Mandel, *infra,* text to note 40.

16 E. Green, *Judicial Attitudes Toward Sentencing* (1961); J. Skolnick, *Justice Without Trial* (1966); D. J. Black, "Production of Crime Rates" (1970), 35:4 Amer. Sociological Rev. 733; A. S. Trebach, *The Rationing of Justice: Constitutional Rights and the Criminal Process* (1969); see M. Mileski "Courtroom Encounters: An Observation Study of a Lower

defendants . . . for intoxication . . . The treatment is plainly different, but not plainly discriminatory''.[17] She suggests as a partial explanation that the white offender comes from the skid row area while his black counterpart is younger, more often employed and dressed comparatively better. She provides no evidence to support this conjecture. Even if she is correct, one form of discrimination replaces another.[18] There are, however, some studies which do claim discrimination on the grounds of ethnicity.[19] Other studies examine the relationship between age, education and religious affiliation, and sentencing. The usual conclusion is that there is no significant relationship between these variables and the sentence.[20]

J. Hogarth provides us with some socio-economic status correlates of judicial attitudes toward various types of sentences:

> Older magistrates tend to be somewhat more offence oriented than offender oriented. They also appear to be rather more discriminating in assessing offences, considering a large number of factors to be ''essential'' to the proper assessment of a criminal act.[21]

He found magistrates with a professional family background to be more positive toward parole and probation. Conversely, those from a working class background were more punitive.[22] Hogarth also reports variance between urban and rural magistrates:

> Urban magistrates tend to simplify the decision process by operating with a large number of presumptions which guide them in the exercise of discretion. Moreover, these presumptions are more likely to be in the direction of using imprisonment rather than probation or fines.[23]

As the relationships between judicial attitudes, socio-economic status characteristics and sentencing behaviour have never been tested, they remain hypotheses only.

The most authoritative evaluation of the whole area of the relationships

---

Criminal Court'' (1971), 5:1 Law and Soc. Rev. 473; see J. Hagan, ''Extra-Legal Attributes and Criminal Sentencing: An Assessment of a Sociological Viewpoint'' (1974), 83:3 Law and Soc. Rev. 357 at 373; see D. Jaros and R. I. Mendelsohn, ''The Judicial Role and Sentencing Behavior'' (1967), 11:4 Midwestern Journal of Political Science 471.

17 M. Mileski, *supra,* note 16, p. 507.

18 *Ibid.* at 511.

19 See *e.g.*, J. D. Casper, ''Having Their Day in Court: Defendant Evaluations of the Fairness of Their Treatment'' (1979), 13:2 Law and Soc. Rev. 567. He provides evidence of harsher sentences received by black Americans.

20 See *e.g.*, R. Carter and L. Wilkins, ''Some Factors in Sentencing Policy'' (1967), 58:4 Journal of Criminal Law, Criminology and Police Science 503; also, R. Hood, *Sentencing in Magistrates Court* (1962).

21 J. Hogarth, *Sentencing as a Human Process* (1971), p. 211. Albeit in the context of a very different court, one American study found that the differences in the socio-economic status characteristics of the justices explained 70 per cent of the variance in voting in criminal cases. See S. S. Ulmer, ''Social Background as an Indicator to the Votes of Supreme Court Justices in Criminal Cases: 1947-56 Terms'' (1973), 17:3 Amer. Journal of Political Science 622.

22 See J. Hogarth, *supra,* note 21, p. 212.

23 *Ibid.* at 221.

between the socio-economic characteristics of the offenders and sentencing decisions is found in the work of J. Hagan, who evaluated a representative sample of studies claiming a positive relationship between race, socio-economic status, age and sex, and the sentencing process. Ironically, although this is the work of a Canadian scholar, not a single Canadian study is included. Among the studies which Hagan critically analyzed, not one definitively proved a significant relationship with respect to the impact of socio-economic status on sentencing. Some of the studies did, however, show a modest relationship between race and disposition. No relationship was shown to exist between age and sex, and sentencing. Many of the studies under consideration did not examine the necessary legal variables, and in some instances, the characteristics of the populations in question were so skewed as to render statistical tests impossible.[24]

Hood and Sparks point out three future research strategies which should be utilized in order better to understand the determinants of sentencing disparities and the causes thereof:

1) Comparisons should be made between the proportions of offenders receiving various sentences in different courts;

2) Studies of a large number of cases should be undertaken on the assumption that different variables will be distributed at random; and

3) Studies should be undertaken controlling for different offenders appearing before different judges by using matching or predictive techniques.[25]

Since studies of this nature are difficult to conduct, the research will probably continue to confine itself to case studies of one court.

DATA ANALYSIS

The data for this paper were obtained from my earlier study of the Winnipeg Provincial Court,[26] based on direct observation and analysis of all 1,194 cases, decided by the court over a three-month period, from 17th May to 9th August 1973.[27]

First, the data indicate a high rate of conviction. Acquittals account for only 1.4 per cent of over 1,100 cases. This figure is understandable, as 94.9

24 See J. Hagan, "Extra-Legal Attributes and Criminal Sentencing: An Assessment of a Sociological Viewpoint" (1974), 83:3 Law and Soc. Rev. 357 at 378, particularly tables 1, 2, 3, 4 and 9, and p. 378.

25 For a more detailed analysis and criticism of sentencing studies, see R. Hood and R. Sparks *Key Issues in Criminology* (1970).

26 Now Provincial Court; see Provincial Court Act, 1982-83-84 (Man.), c. 52 (also C.C.S.M., c. C275) [repealing and replacing Provincial Judges Act, 1972 (Man.), c. 61 (also C.C.S.M., c. P148)].

27 M. Debicki, *Sentencing in a Lower Criminal Court*, Proceedings of the C.P.S.A. (1976).

per cent of the accused pleaded guilty. These two figures indicate that both the police forces and the Crown perform extremely well in screening cases coming before the court. Since both cases ending in acquittal and those in which a not guilty plea has been entered are more time-consuming, the organs of arrest and prosecution function remarkably well as stress reducers. By assuring that the courts have only a small number of time-consuming cases, they assist the court in coping with the volume of "business". (Plea bargaining, if utilized, occurred as a result of totally informal negotiations between the Crown and the defence counsel. Furthermore, nothing in the courtroom indicated whether such negotiations had taken place.)

Fines compose the largest group of sentences. Of all sentences, 43.4 per cent are fines,[28] with only 24.5 per cent being fines of $100 or more. This also acts as a stress reducer, since "fines have the advantage of requiring less thought"[29] and therefore these decisions take less time to reach. It is also perhaps worth mentioning that fines (in general) provide a relatively large source of income. This fact also has stress reducing properties in times when governments are concerned about expenditures. Jail sentences form 30 per cent of all dispositions, 48.9 per cent being for a period not exceeding six months. Probationary sentences compose 24.1 per cent of all sentences. There is a marked judicial preference for probation without supervision, which composes 61.9 per cent of the total probationary disposition. Such sentences are not only less time-consuming but may also be a reflection on already over-taxed supervisory services.

The data have been analyzed from two perspectives:

1. The total population; and

2. Controlling for charges.

The Total Population

The analysis of the total population shows an interdependence between various socio-economic variables and the type and severity of sentence. The analysis of the relationship between the severity of the sentence for employed as opposed to unemployed defendants shows that there are no marked differences in sentences on the lighter end of the scale (see Table 1-1). The difference manifests itself from the medium to the harsher end of the scale, with the employed receiving a greater proportion of sentences of medium severity while the unemployed receive a greater proportion of harsher sentences. Although the differences are not greater than 6.3 per cent at the harsh end of the scale, they are nevertheless statistically significant.

---

28 K. Jobson, "Fines" (1970), 16:4 McGill Law Journal 633 reports a slightly higher percentage of fines — 48 per cent. This study also provides comparative figures for fines from various jurisdictions.

29 See J. Hogarth, *Sentencing as a Human Process* (1971), p. 211 at 217.

TABLE 1-1
(row percentages)
SEVERITY OF THE SENTENCE BY EMPLOYMENT STATUS
Total Population

EMPLOYMENT STATUS	Low 1	2	3	4	5	6	7	8	9	High 10	11	N
Employed	5.4%	6.4	13.7	13.7	7.6	8.6	10.3	4.2	.7	9.3	20.3	409
Unemployed	4.8%	5.9	12.8	8.9	4.6	3.5	3.5	6.2	6.2	17.0	26.6	564

Chi Square = 77.461
dF = 10 significant at .001

Similar overall results were obtained utilizing the Blishen socio-economic index (see Table 1-2), although the differences become more pronounced — 69.5 per cent of those scoring relatively higher on the scale received sentences in the lower range as opposed to 46.1 per cent of those with lower scores on the socio-economic index. No variance can be found in the severity of the sentences in relationship to the ethnicity of the accused.[30]

TABLE 1-2
(row percentages)
SEVERITY OF THE SENTENCE BY SOCIO-ECONOMIC INDEX (BLISHEN SCORE)
Total Population

S.E.I.	Low 0	1	2	3	4	5	6	7	8	High 9	10	N
High	16.7%	2.8	8.3	25.0	13.9	2.8	8.3	.0	.0	11.1	11.1	36
Medium	4.1%	5.4	12.1	11.7	6.3	8.9	10.2	5.7	2.5	11.7	21.3	315
Low	5.1%	7.3	15.7	8.6	5.7	3.7	4.3	5.7	4.1	14.5	25.1	509

Chi Square = 56.903
dF = 18 significant at .005

Since the above analysis is based on standardized sentences, it will be followed by an analysis of the type of sentence received by various socio-economic groups irrespective of charges. The assumption underlying this type of analysis is that fines and jail sentences are more severe than probationary sentences. (It is of course possible and even probable that an affluent person would rather pay a fine and "forget the whole thing" than be placed on probation; however, the population under consideration is generally so poor that it does not warrant this assumption.) Employment proves to be a good predictor of the type of sentence a person receives (see Table 1-3). The

30 Only in the case of one charge has a modest relationship between severity of the sentence and ethnicity (favouring the natives) been found.

unemployed are more than six times as likely to face jail sentences as those who are employed. The employed are more likely to be sentenced to pay a fine. In probationary sentences, the unemployed are more likely to be sentenced to probation with supervision whereas the employed have a better chance of being placed on probation without supervision. As the number of acquittals is so limited, it is impossible to assess the significance of the socio-economic status of those who are acquitted. The same applies to the small percentage of defendants who receive both time in jail and a fine. Yet another division of the population, into skilled as opposed to unskilled labourers, reveals that those who are in skilled labour positions receive 13.4 per cent of the jail sentences and 18.4 per cent of the probationary sentences, whereas those who are in the unskilled category receive 22.1 per cent of the jail sentences and 12.4 per cent of probationary sentences, showing a marked tendency for harsher sentencing of the unskilled. Furthermore, businesspersons are more likely than any other occupational group to be given a fine (56.3 per cent) and only 12.5 per cent of accused businesspersons receive a jail sentence (see Table 1-4). These findings are supported by many scholars who in other settings observed the importance the magistrates attach to the working habits of the offenders.[31]

TABLE 1-3
(row percentages)

TYPE OF SENTENCE BY EMPLOYMENT STATUS
Total Population

Employment Status	Acquittal (0)	Probation (1)	Probation With Supervision (2)	Probation Plus Fine (3)	Fine (4)	Time (5)	Time Plus Fine (6)	N
Employed	2.3%	14.3	7.3	3.3	66.7	5.6	.5	371
Unemployed	.9%	16.7	13.7	1.8	36.8	29.4	.7	568

Chi Square = 141.352
dF = 5 significant at .005

TABLE 1-4
(row percentages)

OCCUPATION BY TYPE OF SENTENCE

Occupation	Acquittal (0)	Probation (1)	Probation With Supervision (2)	Probation Plus Fine (3)	Fine (4)	Time (5)	Time Plus Fine (6)	N
(1) Military	14.3%	.0	.0	.0	57.1	14.3	14.3	7
(2) Farmer	12.5%	12.5	.0	.0	62.5	12.5	.0	8

31 See *e.g.*, R. Hood and R. Sparks, *Key Issues in Criminology* (1970), note 10.

(3) Business	3.1%	15.6	6.2	6.2	56.3	12.5	.0	32
(4) Domestic	.0%	22.2	5.6	5.6	50.0	16.7	.0	18
(5) Student	.0%	23.4	12.8	6.4	31.9	25.5	.0	47
(6) Pensioner	.0%	16.7	16.7	8.3	41.7	16.7	.0	12
(7) On Welfare	.0%	12.8	20.5	2.6	30.8	33.3	.0	39
(8) Housewife	.0%	57.1	19.0	4.8	14.3	4.8	.0	21
(9) Unemployed	.0%	14.5	12.7	1.8	36.4	34.5	.9	55

Chi Square = 102.232
dF = 48 significant at .005

The explanation for the obvious disparities in sentencing practices is not necessarily simple. In cases where a fine is not paid, the offender has to be "processed" once more by the court in order to convert the fine into a jail term. Thus, perhaps, the judges are not behaving in a consciously discriminatory manner, but rather attempting to save themselves to some extent the trouble of having to deal further with the offender who is less likely to pay the fine.

The relationship between socio-economic status and the type of sentence is again confirmed utilizing the Blishen socio-economic index. As the socio-economic status of the offender increases, so does the probability of his or her receiving a fine (see Table 1-5). A decrease in social status increases the probability of incarceration. The only type of sentence where those with higher status seem to be more penalized is in the case of probationary sentences reinforced by fines. The most severely penalized offender is the single person who is unemployed and on welfare. Thirty per cent of these offenders receive jail sentences (see Table 1-6).

TABLE 1-5
(row percentages)
TYPE OF SENTENCE BY SOCIO-ECONOMIC INDEX
Total Population

S.E.I.	Acquittal	Probation	Probation With Supervision	Probation Plus Fine	Fine	Time	N
1	.0%	8.3	.0	.0	87.5	4.2	24
2	.0%	16.7	16.7	8.3	58.3	.0	12
3	.0%	5.9	11.8	5.9	76.5	.0	17
4	3.7%	15.6	7.5	3.1	53.1	16.8	160
5	1.2%	18.1	10.8	1.2	42.2	26.5	83
6	3.9%	15.0	7.2	3.3	58.8	11.8	153
7	.6%	16.2	13.1	1.7	45.4	23.0	474
8	.0%	20.8	14.6	6.2	35.5	22.9	48
9	.0%	9.8	12.2	4.9	46.3	26.8	41

Chi Square = 66.8
dF = 48 significant at .005

TABLE 1-6
(row percentages)
TYPE OF SENTENCE BY INCOME

Income	Acquittal 0	Probation 1	Probation With Supervision 2	Probation Plus Fine 3	Fine 4	Time 5	Time Plus Fine 6	N
$8-10,000	.0%	23.1	.0	7.7	61.5	7.7	.0	13
$6-8,000	3.4%	8.6	5.2	1.7	79.3	1.7	.0	58
$6,000 or lower	2.6%	13.9	9.4	3.5	62.3	7.7	.6	310
Student	.0%	20.8	16.7	4.2	39.6	18.8	.0	48
Unemployed, single on welfare	.5%	15.5	13.4	1.6	38.3	30.0	.7	426
Married, no children, on welfare	.0%	34.6	3.8	3.8	42.3	15.4	.0	26
Married children, on welfare	5.1%	23.1	25.6	.0	20.5	23.1	2.6	39

Chi Square = 153.359
dF = 36 significant at .005

Keeping in mind the fact that single welfare recipients constitute 44.4 per cent of the total population, this figure becomes even more startling. In other words, this type of offender is more than four times as likely to receive a jail sentence as someone who is employed. These findings are further reinforced when married welfare recipients and married welfare recipients with children are treated as additional separate categories.[32] These two groups also more frequently receive jail sentences than those who are employed. Housewives are more likely than any other group to receive lighter sentences. A housewife has a 57.1 per cent chance of being put on probation without supervision, as opposed to a 4.8 per cent chance of receiving time in jail (see Table 1-4).

Ethnicity as an independent variable does not contribute to the type of sentence a person receives. This conclusion is reinforced by the analysis of sentences for specific types of offences. (Only in the case of one charge has a limited association between sentence and ethnicity been found.)

Analysis By Charge

A series of analyses has been performed dividing the population according to the offences with which the defendants were charged. The general policy of sentencing which can be deduced from the data shows a consistent pattern of treating various offences differently. Conclusions as to the assessment of the gravity of various offences by the judges can also be reached.

The data show that magistrates consistently distinguish between major

32 No distinction is made between common law marriages and other marriages.

and minor theft. Offenders convicted of minor theft have an approximately 25 per cent chance of receiving a jail sentence. Given that the value of stolen property in such cases does not exceed $50, that policy is questionable. As one would expect, as the value of stolen property increases, so does the chance of incarceration. Offenders convicted of theft of property worth over $50, have an approximately 50 per cent chance of serving a jail sentence. For other common offences, the possibility of a jail sentence dramatically decreases. In liquor offences the possibility of a jail sentence is approximately 1:10, for major traffic offences 1:15, and for minor traffic offences 1:33.

a) Theft under $50

The analysis of sentencing controlling for charges confirms the earlier observation about the interdependence of socio-economic status and the severity of the disposition. In cases of theft under $50 the pattern of disposition reveals that all of the jail sentences were imposed on unemployed offenders (see Table 1-7), and that 70.6 per cent of those sentenced to jail were single and on welfare. Furthermore, evidence indicates that when jail sentences and fines are converted into a standard measure, the unemployed offenders are treated more harshly (see Table 1-8). Since 45 per cent of the unemployed offenders had no previous record, this disparity cannot necessarily be explained by the differences in patterns of previous criminal behaviour. The pattern of sentencing further reveals that in the instance of probationary sentences the trade-off is different. The unemployed are more likely to receive probation with supervision, whereas the employed receive a greater share of probationary sentences reinforced by fines or probation with no further stipulation. The unemployed are less likely to be acquitted, although the small number of cases in this category decreases the significance of this finding.

TABLE 1-7

(column percentages)

THEFT UNDER $50

Employment Status by Type of Sentence

EMPLOYMENT STATUS	**Acquittal**	**Probation**	**Probation With Supervision**	**Probation Plus Fine**	**Fine**	**Time**
	%	%	%	%	%	%
Employed	66.7	31.0	73.9	28.6	68.0	.0
Unemployed	33.3	69.0	26.1	71.4	32.0	100.0
N	3	58	23	7	25	34

Chi Square = 37.942
dF = 5 significant at .005

TABLE 1-8
(column percentages)
THEFT UNDER $50
Employment by Time Plus Fine (in days)

	N	%	Mean in Days
Employed	24	33.3	15.958
Unemployed	48	66.7	61.437
Total	72	100.0	46.278

F(1.70) = 9.960
Prob. < 01

b) Theft Over $50

Similar results emerge from the analysis of sentences in cases of theft over $50. Of those who receive jail sentences, 63 per cent are single and on welfare. As the social status of the offender decreases, the probability of incarceration increases. As in cases of minor theft, the imposition of fines seems to be reserved for those of a relatively higher status. The relationships between various types of probationary sentences, however, are not as clearly portrayed as in the data pertaining to minor theft, and no clear-cut pattern can be detected (see Table 1-9). The data pertaining to major theft also reveal harsher sentences in the combined category of time and fine for offenders of lower status (see Table 1-10).

TABLE 1-9
(row percentages)
THEFT OVER $50
Socio-Economic Index By Type of Sentence

S.E.I.	Probation	Probation With Supervision	Probation Plus Fine	Fine	Time	N
4	33.3%	13.3	13.3	6.7	33.3	15
5	.0%	33.3	.0	.0	66.7	6
6	53.8%	.0	.0	.0	46.2	13
7	18.3%	19.7	7.0	4.2	50.7	70
8	14.3%	57.1	.0	.0	28.6	7

Chi Square = 81.51
dF = 16 significant at .005

TABLE 1-10

THEFT OVER $50

Socio-Economic Index By Time Plus Fine (In Days)

	S.E.I.	N	%	Mean
	4	8	13.3	230.625
Medium	5	6	10.0	389.333
	6	46	77.7	266.956
	Total	60	100.0	

F(3,58) = 6.767
Prob. < 01

c) *Offences Against Property*

Additional analysis has been performed grouping together most of the offences against property. This analysis reveals further evidence of the consistent pattern of differential sentencing. Unemployed offenders are again more likely to serve a jail term or to be subjected to probation with supervision. Employed offenders constitute 68 per cent of those fined, and 75 per cent of those receiving both probationary sentences and fines (see Table 1-11). Likewise, unskilled labourers receive harsher sentences than those who are skilled.

TABLE 1-11

(row percentages)

OFFENCES AGAINST PROPERTY

Employment Status by Type of Sentence

EMPLOYMENT STATUS	Acquittal	Probation	Probation With Supervision	Probation With Fine	Fine	Time
Employed	66.7%	32.8%	25.0%	76.7%	68.0%	4.3%
Unemployed	33.3	62.7	75.0	23.3	32.0	93.5
N	3	64	30	8	25	45

Chi Square = 43.864
dF = 5 significant at .005

d) *Minor Traffic Offences*

In minor traffic offences the pattern of fines for the employed and the increased likelihood of jail sentences for the unemployed is repeated, although jail sentences for this type of offence are exceptional (see Table 1-12).

TABLE 1-12
(column percentages)
MINOR TRAFFIC OFFENCES
Employment Status By Type of Sentence

EMPLOYMENT STATUS	Acquittal	Probation	Probation With Supervision	Probation With Fine	Fine	Time	Fine Plus Time
Employed	50.0%	.0%	.0%	.0%	72.2%	25.0%	50.0%
Unemployed	50.0	.0	.0	.0	22.2	75.0	50.0
N	2	0	0	0	102	4	2

Chi Square = 26.321
dF = 6 significant at .005

e) Major Traffic Offences

In major traffic offences the well established pattern of jail sentences for the unemployed (66.7 per cent) and fines for those who are fortunate enough to have jobs (56.9 per cent) is again portrayed.

f) Liquor Related Offences

As is shown by Tables 1-13 and 1-14, liquor related offences show similar results.

TABLE 1-13
(column percentages)
LIQUOR RELATED OFFENCES
Employment status by Type of Sentence

EMPLOYMENT STATUS	Acquittal	Probation	Probation With Supervision	Probation With Fine	Fine	Time
Employed	.0%	22.2%	13.6%	33.3%	36.6%	3.2%
Unemployed	.0	77.8	86.4	.0	63.4	96.8
N	0	18	22	1	41	31

Chi Square = 90.024
dF = 5 significant at .005

TABLE 1-14
(column percentages)

LIQUOR RELATED OFFENCES
Socio-Economic Index By Type of Sentence

S.E.I.	Probation	Probation With Supervision	Fine	Time
4	27.8%	9.1%	28.0%	.0%
5	.0	4.5	13.8	12.9
6	5.6	4.5	.0	.0
7	55.6	77.3	58.2	74.2
8	11.1	.0	.0	3.2
9	.0	4.5	.0	9.7
N	18	22	36	31

Chi Square = 39.6
dF = 15 significant at .001

g) Crimes Against Persons and Sexual Offences

These findings are further confirmed by an analysis of the combined category of crimes against persons and sexual offences. The unemployed constitute 90.4 per cent of those sentenced to jail (Table 1-15), and 67.3 per cent of those sentenced to jail are single and on welfare. The unskilled again tend to receive harsher sentences. The utilization of the Blishen socio-economic index in crimes against persons also indicates that those who score lower are more likely to receive harsher sentences. This category of offences, as expected, carries a higher proportion of longer jail sentences (Table 1-16).

TABLE 1-15
(column percentages)

OFFENCES AGAINST PERSONS
Employment Status by Type of Sentence

EMPLOYMENT STATUS	Acquittal	Probation	Probation With Supervision	Probation With Fine	Fine	Time
Employed	66.7%	28.1%	16.7%	68.4%	50.0%	9.6%
Unemployed	33.3	71.9	50.0	31.6	50.0	90.4
N	3	32	36	4	56	52

Chi Square = 85.747
dF = 5 significant at .005

TABLE 1-16
OFFENCES AGAINST PERSONS
Socio-Economic Index By Time in Jail

	CODES	N	%	Mean in Days
Medium	4	5	10.2	362.000
	6	6	12.2	389.333
Low	7	38	77.6	320.474
Total		49	100.0	

$F(3,47) = 5.398$
Prob. < 01

CONCLUSION

Does, then, the justice system favour the rich over the poor? This cannot be tested by court data, as the rich and well educated do not appear in any significant number as the accused in criminal courts.

The analysis of the relationship between the socio-economic status of the offender and the severity of the sentence, however, does provide evidence of differential treatment. Whether income, social status or type of job is used as a measure, similar results emerge. Those of lower socio-economic status are treated more harshly. The best measure has proved to be employment status. Similar results were obtained when the population was treated as a homogeneous group and when specific charges were analyzed. The pattern is clear. Those who are employed pay for their crime with money, and those who are unemployed with a relatively short loss of freedom. The only socio-economic variable which did not point to differential sentencing is ethnicity. The claims of harsher treatment made by various native organizations are not supported by these data.

It is possible that the underlying reason for sentencing disparities is based on the current life patterns of the offenders. Someone who does not have a job may be considered to suffer less as a result of imprisonment than someone who is employed. In addition, someone who is employed may be considered less likely to commit another offence if not incarcerated and thereby enabled to maintain employment.[33] Another possible explanation lies in the judicial expectation that those who are employed are more likely to pay their fines, thus saving the taxpayers money. This, rather than rehabilitation or crime prevention, is perhaps the underlying rationale for sentencing decisions.

The analysis also indicates a preference for definite sentences (fines or jail terms rather than probation), which constitute 73.4 per cent of the total. Such sentences reduce the potential future involvement of the court with the offender who does not meet the conditions of probation. The data also

33 This hypothesis is not really supported by M. Mandel, *infra,* note 39, pp. 57-58.

indicate a preference for sentencing decisions which take less time to reach.[34] In the case of fines and to some extent even jail sentences, there is no need for interaction between the court and other organizations such as organs of supervision and mental hospitals. This is also revealed in probationary dispositions, since there is a marked preference for probationary sentences without supervision.

The data do not support the hypothesis that the court system is a structure experiencing difficulty in coping with stress. The outputs are consistent, and also indicate that the court acts in a manner which serves to save time and hence assists in coping with the volume of cases. The trend to avoiding involvement with other structures aids in neutralizing potential sources of secondary stressors. The evidence of the reported differential treatment is not highly visible. Several controls must be applied to hundreds of cases before even tentative conclusions as to differential treatment begin to emerge.[35] Perhaps the most important indicator of the lack of stressful demands is the fact that most defendants expect to be punished, as the large majority plead guilty. There is little likelihood and no evidence of stressful demands coming from the victims of discrimination.

The sentencing decisions are neither unduly harsh nor particularly lenient.[36] The one value transgression which meets with more severe treatment is the transgression against property. There is also some evidence that society is not upset about the severe treatment of the offender. If anything, there are articulated demands for more severe treatment.[37]

Although there is evidence that differential treatment on the basis of socio-economic status does exist, there is no congruent evidence that it contributes to the malfunction of the court sytem. If anything, differential treatment on the basis of socio-economic status as currently practised may even enhance the equilibrium of the structure.

There are, however, other areas of law, such as tax, corporate and even labour law, more central to the problem of differential treatment than criminal law. Although criminal law has high visibility and surface intelligibility, its relevance in this respect is marginal. Attempts to achieve equality by focusing on criminal law and tinkering with the criminal justice system are at best futile and at worst cynical.

---

34 See J. Hogarth, *Sentencing as a Human Process* (1971), pp. 215-18. See also, M. Friedland, "Magistrate Court: Functioning and Facilities" (1968), 11:1 Criminal Law Quarterly 52; Canadian Civil Liberties Association, "Due Process Safeguards: Canadian Criminal Justice, A One Month Inquiry" (1971); B. Grossman, *The Prosecutor: An Inquiry Into The Exercise of Discretion* (1969), pp. 51-54.

35 See G. Kellough, *infra, re* the isolation of researchers from the community.

36 See also, Canadian Civil Liberties Association, "Due Process Safeguards: Canadian Criminal Justice, A One Month Inquiry" (1971).

37 See *e.g.*, The Legal Research Institute survey, *supra*, c. 2, question 76.

Question:

> You suggested that analysts perhaps should pay less attention to criminal sentencing variations, because those who appear before the criminal courts are a homogeneous class, and that they should look at tax law. . . . [T]he litigants in those cases have common characteristics as well, *i.e.* money, and I should like to know how you would overcome that problem.

Marek Debicki:

> I was thinking about the basic principles underlying the law rather than litigation. . . .
>
> Public opinion polls are a two-way street. By stressing public attitudes to criminal law, we teach people that criminal law is central to the problem of equality. . . .

Michael Mandel also referred to the public perception that the legal system discriminates on the basis of socio-economic status, despite the legal and democratic principle of equality before and under the law:

> Is the legal system really able to stand apart from the class structure of Canadian society? If [the Institute] survey[38] is representative, Canadians are certainly s[c]eptical about this. Sixty-two percent agreed with the statement "The legal system favours the rich and powerful" while only thirty-seven percent preferred the statement "All people are equal before the law" (Question 41(c)). Most people seem to believe either that the police treat the rich better or that they treat the poor worse (Questions 44 and 45). The same seems to hold for their opinion of the courts (Questions 77 and 78).[39]

He argued that the state and legal institutions, specifically prisons, reflect and protect the social relations of production, rather than equal individuals,

> [that the] prison population is heavily skewed in favour of the economically marginal groups in the social structure, . . . [and that] property offences [are] a bare majority (50.5%) of the grounds for imprisonment of Canada's daily prison population.

This does not, however, necessarily demonstrate discrimination.

> It might be that crime itself varies in amount and seriousness by class and that the social skew in prison is due merely to an impartial law being applied to the same social skew in criminal behaviour.[40]

38 *Supra*, Legal Research Institute survey, c. 2.

39 M. Mandel, "What Prisons are for: An analysis of the role played by imprisonment in contemporary Canadian capitalism", p. 2. This is a brief summary of the above paper, to be published with slight revisions in two parts: M. Mandel "Democracy, Class and Canadian Sentencing Law" (1984), 21/22 Crime and Social Justice (forthcoming); and M. Mandel, "Democracy, Class and the National Parole Board" (available from author). All quotations and references, unless otherwise indicated, are to the original paper.

40 M. Mandel, "Democracy, Class and the National Parole Board", *supra*, note 39, p. 3.

He therefore focused on the prison selection process, in particular sentencing and parole. The Canadian sentencing system gives enormous discretion to the judge.

> [I]n the decision to imprison and if so for how long, the criminal record and the nature of the offence compete with one another for predominance, the former having an apparent edge. An independent contribution is also often made by demographic features, most consistently employment status but occasionally race and sex as well.[41]
>
> [T]he courts consider it a legitimate part of the sentencing function to determine the severity of the sentence on the basis not only of the nature of the offence, but also of the nature of the offender, not as offender but as *social being,* part of which has to do with criminal record, but a good part of which has as [much] to do with the extent to which the offender fulfills his or her role in the productive apparatus.[42]

This approach is justified by the "prescribed purposes" of sentencing: 1) denunciation of the *offence*; 2) reform (or rehabilitation), intimidation, or incapacitation of the *offender*; and 3) general deterrence of *potential offenders*.

Denunciation is supposed to express public abhorrence of an offence against social values, but rather itself influences public opinion:

> [T]he social origin of denunciatory justice, as with the abstract (or divine) origin of retributive justice, turns out to be largely theoretical:
>
> "society, through the courts, must show its abhorrence of particular types of crime, and the only way in which the courts can show this is by the sentences they pass. The courts do not have to reflect public opinion. On the other hand, courts must not disregard it. Perhaps the main duty of the court is to lead public opinion."[43]
>
> This statement, of course, also contains a statement of the social *function* of denunciation, which another court has put as follows:
>
> "The denunciatory sentence plays an important part in maintaining the righteousness of society values. The community demands that certain conduct be heavily punished and when the Courts fail to satisfy this demand to support core values, the public, in my view, can justifiably complain that the Courts have failed in their duty."[44]
>
> The Law Reform Commission of Canada, which has made denunciation the corner stone of its approach to criminal law, has provided a vivid articulation of the notion:
>
> "Criminal law, then, primarily has to do with values. As such — as wrongful acts — they demand response. . . . To be fully human and hold certain values means responding when they are violated. Such violation requires public condemnation, and this is preeminently the job of criminal law.
>
> "This job — condemning crime — is not an end in itself. It is part of the larger aim of producing a society fit to live in. Such a society is less one where people are too frightened to commit crimes than one where people have too much respect for one another to commit them. Fostering this kind of personal respect is a major aim of parents, teachers, churches, and all other socializing agents. One such agent, though far less important than the others, is the criminal law. In its own way the criminal law re[i]nforces lessons about our social values, instills respect for them and expresses disapproval for their violation. This — what some call 'general deterrence' — is the moral, educative role of criminal law. . . ."[45]

---

41 See research discussed in M. Mandel, *supra,* note 39, pp. 10-13.

42 See cases cited in M. Mandel, *supra,* note 39, pp. 14-19.

43 *R. v. Sargeant* (1974), 60 Cr. App. R. 74 at 77 (C.A.), quoted in *R. v. Atkinson* (1978), 5 C.R. (3d) S-30 at S-32, 43 C.C.C. (2d) 342 (Ont. C.A.).

44 *R. v. Wood,* [1976] 1 W.W.R. 135 at 143, 26 C.C.C. (2d) 100 (Alta. C.A.).

45 Law Reform Comm. of Can., *Our Criminal Law* (1976), p. 5.

At first sight, denunciation would seem to be concerned with the offence, but it vindicates social values by punishing the offender, whose adherence to other social values and socio-economic status are therefore assessed.

> [R]eform . . . of the offender is much more obviously connected with . . . social characteristics. . . . [such as] good character . . . which means . . . properly fulfilling a valued role in the productive apparatus,

although recidivism seems "to be quite independent of the sentence".

General deterrence is intended to make not only the offender, but also potential offenders, afraid to offend.

> [G]eneral deterrence has had a rather precarious existence as an official purpose in sentencing [in Canada]. . . . Cases where an attempt is made to verify the general deterrent effect of a given sentence are almost non-existent
>
> [and there is]
>
> some confusion as whether factors relative to the offender as well as to the offence are relevant to the general deterrence question.
>
> [Mandel argued]
>
> that, in the current Canadian sentencing system, general deterrence can only be a *pseudo*-purpose

as penalties are unknown and virtually unpredictable. He advocated the principle of "utilitarian general deterrence": "one must determine what penalty is *warranted* for a given crime" depending on the harm done to its victims; and *necessary* to deter, as established by empirical research. This requires fixed penalties, which can be systematically varied and do not take class into account. Such a system would maximize the prevention of crime through general deterrence, and be more egalitarian in its treatment of both offenders and victims. Legislative penalties are also more within popular control.

> I wish I could say with confidence that this [system based on utilitarian general deterrence] is also more democratic in the sense that it is what Canadians *want*, but the question seems never to be put in these terms. Certainly it was not so put in [the Institute] survey, though it is encouraging to see that the functions of imprisonment concerned with the material prevention of crime ("protection of society", "rehabilitate the criminal", "discourage others") were greatly preferred by respondents to the abstract function "punish the criminal" which presumably stands for denunciation/retribution. (Question 83)
>
> [W]hatever democratic elements remain in sentencing are completely undermined by . . . "the principle of modulation of penalties";[46] in particular the parole system.

The parole authorities have enormous power:

> Only about one third of those eligible for full parole ever receive it, and less than half of those receive it as soon as they are eligible, . . . day parole [is] granted to only about half those again who receive parole [and] "normal eligibility" for parole [is extended] from one third . . . to one sixth of the sentence. . . . Even this can be eclipsed by a . . . broad interpretation of the phoenix-like "parole by exception" provisions.[47]
>
> [A]ll terminations of parole are within the discretion of the Board.

46 M. Foucault, *Discipline and Punish* (1977), p. 269.
47 See sources cited in M. Mandel, *supra*, note 39, p. 48.

"The policy of the board is, as far as possible, to . . . treat the offender rather than the offence"[48] stressing "individual preventive concerns", such as criminal record, socio-economic environment and attitude:

> [T]he proper attitude is one that exhibits an acceptance of one's responsibility for the crime, an acceptance that it was "wrong" and a deferential and co-operative attitude with authority.

Important concrete factors, only partly related to the risk of recidivism, remain criminal record, class, race, sex, age and employment status.[49]

The prison evaluation is perhaps the most important factor, because, Mandel hypothesized, it demonstrates the degree of "willingness to submit to arbitrary personal authority", the role assigned to most people by capitalism. Thus the penitentiary "is like a factory producing proletarians".[50]

Those with longer sentences are more likely to receive parole, which destroys "the seriousness ranking which has been done by the courts both within legal categories of offences and between them". Parole thus

> further removes the penalty in any case and in all cases from popular control. Indeed, its *point*, according to some of its supporters, is precisely to deceive the public about penalties. Waller considers one of the "valuable functions" of parole to be "to placate public opinion with the claim that justice is being done and protection being given, even though criminals are being set free"[51] and Norval Morris considers it an important "latent purpose of the division of power between judge and parole board . . . to give the possibility of some clemency while appearing in the public eye to be imposing a more severe punishment."[52]

Considerable discussion took place in regard to sentencing and particularly the general deterrence theory.

Mr. Justice McDonald:

> Frequently members of the public complain in the media about the leniency of sentences meted out by the judges. Seldom do the members of the public complain that the sentences are too harsh. Frequently judges pass lesser sentences than have been asked for . . . by the Crown and in doing so, . . . the judges are giving effect to . . . the moral authority of the law derived from its commitment to protect as well as to punish those who come before it, and especially those whom public opinion would condemn.
>
> Now, having said that, it is true that . . . our courts of appeal tell trial judges to pass sentences in regard to certain kinds of crimes and in particular crimes of violence, to deter other members of the community apart from the accused. . . . There is, however, a degree of futility in giving emphasis to that principle of sentencing when frequently no one outside

48 T. G. Street, *Handbook on Parole* (1960).

49 See research discussed in M. Mandel, *supra*, note 39, pp. 53-60.

50 D. Melossi and M. Pavarini (G. Cousin (trans.)), *The Prison and the Factory: Origins of the Penitentiary System* (1981), p. 145.

51 I. Waller, *Men Released from Prison* (1974), p. 16.

52 N. Morris, *The Future of Imprisonment* (1974), p. 48.

those in the courtroom and those in the system are aware of the reasons for the sentence. Is there some means by which provincial governments or the federal government, within their respective jurisdictions, could without creating another bureaucracy, assist the media, particularly the printed media, to publicize the reasons? If these were better known it would not only result in the general deterrence theory being carried out, but reduce the degree of misinformation or lack of information on the part of the public, which may in part be the reason for public criticism of sentencing policies.

Marek Debicki:

> The general deterrence theory seems to be discredited. Legal anthropologists point out that what might have worked was justice administered in and by the community. . . . There are some attempts to take the court to the community in which the offence has been committed and some studies which indicate that that kind of publicity has some success. . . . In terms of media information, the federal government is now attempting to create a system of criminal justice statistics. The press generally reports only spectacular cases and contributes to the misinformation of the public. If media were better informed in terms of routine cases, that would be desirable. . . . The probability of us learning from judicial reasoning, given cynical studies of press readership, is, however, low.

Michael Mandel reiterated that general deterrence cannot be effective in our system given the unsystematic variation in penalties, depending among other things, on the judge:[53] "[T]he general deterrence theory, however, is not discredited so much as a philosophical theory as an empirical theory." The severity of our penal system prevents proportionately little crime. "If punishment just deters a little bit, then it is only a little bit legitimate."

Mr. Justice McDonald:

> In large measure, deterrence is greatly overrated but there are some crimes where the people who are perpetrating the crime know full well what the likely penalty is and their likelihood of being caught. When those circumstances arise, with a small minority of offenders, a sentence can have a deterrent effect. For example, lawyers know that if they dip into the trust funds they will end up in the penitentiary for four to five years, and consistency in sentence is real in that area. The same is true of drunken drivers. . . .
>
> In general, I am mystified by the suggestion that sentence should be the same in every instance, given the same crime under the Criminal Code, [as the characteristics of the offence may be enormously different]. If we are not satisfied with giving a judge discretion in this area, we could further codify the law and have different categories: first category of manslaughter, second category of manslaughter, *etc*. There are, however, a lot more things to be considered than the categories. . . . So, I am in favour of giving the judge a wide discretion in terms of sentence. . . . It is not random. We are guided by precedent, by a kind of range, but given the discretion to take into account personal matters. Those personal matters are not distinctions between a rich person and a poor person or a native person and a non-native person, but between a person who is penitent and one who is not. The discretion will not be exercised, at least intentionally or by design, in favour of the wealthy against the poor, but it is a discretion that we ought to exercise in proper circumstances.

Audience:

> How come 95 per cent of the people in prison are poor?

Mr. Justice Huband:

> The trend to harsher punishment as a deterrent is not noticeable. In many cases the appeal

53 See J. Hogarth, *Sentencing as a Human Process* (1971), p. 211.

> court reduces the sentence. Many people are confined because of their financial situation. One of the best deterrents, is plain, hard, manual work. . . .
>
> The news media, especially the print media, are very influenced by the United States' ultra conservative news media and are a destructive influence in our society.

Inger Hansen took up Michael Mandel's point in regard to the discretionary powers involved in "the modulation of penalties",[54] in particular the choice of institution.

USING HUMAN RIGHTS LEGISLATION TO ASSIST WOMEN PRISONERS

Inger Hansen

INTRODUCTION

> Law reflects but in no sense determines the moral worth of a society. The values of a reasonably just society will reflect themselves in a reasonably just law. The better the society, the less law there will be. In Heaven there will be no law, and the lion will lie down with the lamb. The values of an unjust society will reflect themselves in an unjust law. The worse the society, the more law there will be. In Hell there will be nothing but law, and due process will be meticulously observed.[55]

I construe this to mean that in heaven, discretion will be total. In hell, there will be no discretion. In the real world, however, we need some rules in advance to maintain certainty in law and human relations, but there must also be flexibility to allow for special cases, or individualized justice.[56] The quest for an appropriate balance between rule and discretion will carry on throughout history.[57]

To descend to a narrower topic, I should like to look at some laws which apply to prisoners in Canada, to discover how cynical we ought to be.

---

54 *Supra,* text to note 46.

55 A. Gilmore, *The Ages of American Law* (1977), pp. 110-11.

56 See K. Culp Davis, *Discretionary Justice: A Preliminary Enquiry* (1969).

57 I. Hansen, Notes for Presentation, National Conference on Discretion in the Correctional System, 17th-19th November, 1981.

DISCRETION TO TRANSFER INMATES

Under the Penitentiary Act,[58] the Commissioner of Corrections[59] has absolute authority to determine in which institution an inmate serves his or her sentence.[60] He also has and may delegate the authority to transfer an inmate from a given institution to another in Canada. There is no authority to review the commissioner's discretion and there is no right in an inmate to reside in one prison rather than another.

As a matter of general practice, however, a male inmate is usually received first in an institution in his province, although transfers may take place for security reasons, for administrative reasons, and sometimes for no reason at all.

A complaint, however, has been made to the Canadian Human Rights Commission stating that by moving all female inmates in the first instance to the Prison for Women in Ontario, the federal government discriminates against women. Are women only entitled to separate but equal facilities? Are they not equal once they are committed to penitentiary? As there is only one Prison for Women, it houses all three levels of security, and most of the female inmates are moved away from their community ties and do not have as many options for education and services as male inmates.

Now why is there this difference? It is simple. There are so few women in our penitentiaries today. On the average, there are about 200 women compared to about 10,000 men. The women are gathered for the sake of convenience, and anyone who has worked in a large bureaucracy knows that it is next to impossible to create justice, equality or special treatment for a small minority.

Many committees have recommended that the Prison for Women be closed. It has been suggested that the women should be housed in the provincial institutions, but that is even more unfair, because the women serving long-term sentences would be an even smaller minority in the provincial setting. The provision of long-term programs would become impossible or impractical on that scale.

In the complaint to the Canadian Human Rights Commission, it was argued that the Canadian Human Rights Act[61] applied to prisons, as providing goods, services, facilities, and accommodation customarily available to the general public, and should prohibit differential treatment based on gender as well as on race or national origin.

The Human Rights Commission substantiated the complaint in every

58 R.S.C. 1970, c. P-6.

59 Section 2, "Commissioner" [am. 1976-77, c. 53, s. 35(1)] (re-designation of title).

60 Section 13 [am. 1976-77, c. 53, s. 38].

61 1976-77 (Can.), c. 33. See also Canadian Charter of Rights and Freedoms (or Constitution Act, 1982, Pt. I), Canada Act, 1982 (Eng.), c. 11, s. 52.

respect except one — it disagreed that all senior administrators at the institution were male.[62] The conciliation process is continuing.

In these cynical times a new law was used to break new ground for a purpose which, in my view, would meet with public approval; the finding drew attention to an unjust situation. The final effect is not yet known.

There will be resistance in society, among staff and among the inmates, to solutions such as co-educational institutions. But I predict that as society changes, so will attitudes among staff, inmates and policy-makers.

Attitudes to what is just change, and ten years from now, the idea of placing women in one institution may be unthinkable. Because of the changing lifestyles of women, there may be more convicted women. Because of the changing attitudes of judges, prosecutors, and police officers (many of whom will be women), there will probably be less compassion and charity extended to women when they are charged with a crime.

The controls on the system are based not only on law, on review by courts and tribunals, but also on what people consider fair. The ultimate control is public opinion.

THE COMMUNITY, PRISON AND POLITICS

Gail Kellough

[Gail Kellough talked about how to influence policy-makers]

INTRODUCTION

The theme of this conference relates to a cynical community, and the topic of this panel is sentencing and prisons. While I admit to a certain degree of cynicism on the topic of prisons, I must confess to a certain amount of optimism regarding the potential for change within a "cynical society".

At present, there is little contact between the community and the prison. The majority of the community learn about the world of law and prison through media reports at a time of crisis or when community concern over violent crime and personal safety is highlighted. The collective perception of the community is then gauged by opinion polls or studies similar to the one which forms the basis for this conference.[63]

62 Canadian Human Rights Commission press release dated 14th December 1981.

63 The Legal Research Institute Survey, *supra*, c. 2.

A third isolated world also exists — that of the academic and research community. For years social scientists have been conducting studies and compiling information on the criminal justice system. Problems now under investigation are not new. But even where such knowledge is corroborated by individuals working within the system, it is not usually translated into policy decisions. For example, it is generally accepted that prisons do not rehabilitate, nor do they provide any measure of security against crime. Naive students of criminology can never understand why the current system continues to operate in the face of such evidence. What they fail to realize is that prisons continue to exist not because they rehabilitate, not because they protect society, and not even because there are no alternatives. They continue to exist because decisions in favour of change are not in the form of rational choices made on the basis of evidence; rather, these decisions are a matter of *politics*. Politicians make decisions based on their perception of a public mood, which is in turn based on community perceptions of happenings reported in the media. Often public perceptions and factual information are not congruent.

But even in the criminal justice system, a system notoriously resistant to change, progress can be made. Change based on knowledge and experience, however, requires that such knowledge must be translated into policy. It is in this process that I believe a "cynical" society can become the catalyst for change. In many areas of our society, citizens are demanding a greater participation in the affairs which affect their welfare and quality of life. Groups have organized in such diverse areas as civil rights, the labour movement, women's rights, the peace movement, *etc*. In doing so, they have demonstrated, to a greater or lesser extent, their power to effect change or to ensure that changes taking place are considerate of their rights and interests. They have also raised the consciousness of the community as a whole. There is little question that social action is an important ingredient in certain kinds of change.

If such participation and community control were to occur in the criminal justice system, it would have to go further than the type of involvement usually associated with volunteers in the system. From a perspective of democratization of the criminal justice system, planned change could occur at different levels, and each level requires a different degree and type of involvement. Because community members *are* concerned about crime, they are likely to respond to community development efforts around crime prevention.[64] The same assumption regarding community enthusiasm for participation in groups dedicated to legal equality and justice in the courts and prisons may be an oversimplification.[65] Experiences of voluntary agencies operating within the system, however, confirm that there are many individuals who respond to

64 Indeed, the experience of "Project Prevention" in mobilizing diverse sections of the community within Manitoba bears this out.

65 Offenders, victims and other groups affected by the system traditionally have had little access to the political process and have had to rely on community groups to articulate their interests.

opportunities to participate in furthering these goals. That society as a whole is interested in both reform of the system and in justice and equality is not such a far-fetched idea. In reviewing the data from the Legal Research Institute survey, I noted that, in response to how much effort government should put into various activities, crime prevention and prison reform ranked at the top, along with inflation and unemployment.[66] Additionally, when asked which response best represented the law as they saw it, two of the largest response categories indicated that "something needs to be done to improve the way the legal system operates and the laws it produces"[67] and that "the legal system favours the rich and the powerful".[68]

In the first part of this paper, I should like to examine reasons and strategies by which community groups may begin to democratize the system. I will attempt to bring together insights gained by researchers and students of social change. In the second part of the paper, I will examine one particular group of citizens who have set out to promote social reform in one part of the criminal justice system in Manitoba, suggesting some ways in which the literature applies to this particular group.

A COMMUNITY PARTICIPATION MODEL

Having said that changes can be brought about by democratizing the criminal justice system, I hasten to add that we must not be sentimental about what "the people" can accomplish.

> For every citizen's group that changes the course of history, there are thousands, perhaps hundreds of thousands, that never create a ripple.[69]

History has shown that there are other factors necessary before change can be accomplished — even by the most organized and active group. Within the legal system, these factors are usually found during a period of vast discrepancy between practice and legal precept.[70] These anomalies, while necessary for change, are not, however, sufficient in and of themselves for a radical change in law or procedure. The anomalies must first be recognized and brought forward into the political arena before any but short term adjustments can be accomplished. It is in bringing forward these anomalies and participating in the decision-making process that interest groups can affect the form and course a reform will take.

Interest groups are and have been an important component in the political process of determining policy. Some pressure groups, however, have greater access than others. For various reasons, prisoner-interest groups or citizen

66 The Legal Research Institute survey, *supra*, c. 2, question 17.

67 *Ibid.*, question 41D.

68 *Ibid.*, question 41C.

69 J. Gardner, *In Common Cause* (1972).

70 Edwin M. Lemert, *Social Action and Legal Change, Revolution Within the Juvenile Court* (1970). See also M. Mandel, *supra*, text to note 38,*ff*.

groups concerned with ideals of legal equality have not usually had the kind of power or the access required to effect change.[71] Studies of interest group action in Canada have shown political influence achieved mostly by business or professional groups.[72]

While business and professional groups do have advantages of power and influence in the political process, some of this influence has resulted from the decline of the voluntary association as a genuine instrument of the public.[73] While this decline is partly the result of growing professionalization and vast bureaucracies within our society, it is also related to the unwillingness of citizen groups to acquire a grasp of the processes of government and to engage in the inevitable conflict. It is conflict which provides the energy that generates change. Our industrialized large-scale society has served to suppress the necessary conflict by excluding large segments of the community from any measure of control. Without the conflicts within the system being made visible, the necessary processes for change become paralyzed.[74] As one student of interest groups noted:

> Change without conflict is no doubt the dream of every politician and public servant but this is not the way society operates.[75]

If citizen groups are to begin to exert any real influence in the policy process, their actions must first be timely, that is, they must occur when there is no obvious institutional mechanism for correcting anomalies and in a period of growing concern within the system itself. Further, reformers cannot assume that a good idea need only be put forward in order for it to be acted upon. Their actions in promoting alternatives must take the form of informed, organized pressure. As Alan Borovoy has noted, "pressure without reason may be irresponsible but reason without pressure is ineffectual".[76]

Even when a group is prepared to apply pressure at an optimum time, there are other elements to be considered by citizens intent on bringing about various kinds of institutional change. By examining case studies of interest group activity, we can learn something about power and can begin to identify factors which help promote change, as well as those factors which tend to distort reform from the original intentions of the group.

Essential functions of interest group activity in the policy process can be

---

71 M. Ryan, *Radical Alternatives to Prison and the Penal Lobby* (1978).

72 F. Thompson, F. & W. T. Stanbury, *The Political Economy of Interest Groups in the Legislative Process in Canada*, Occasional Paper 9, Institute for Research on Public Policy (May 1979).

73 F. J. Bregha, "Community Development in Canada: Problems and Strategies" in Social Science Research Council of Canada, James A. Draper (ed.), *Citizen Participation: Canada* (1971).

74 Nils Christie, "Conflicts as Property" (1977), 17:4 The British Journal of Criminology 1.

75 R. Alexander Sim, "The Innocence of Community Development" in Social Science Research Council of Canada, James A. Draper, (ed.) *Citizen Participation: Canada* (1971).

76 Alan Borovoy, "Civil Liberties in the Imminent Hereafter" (1973), 51:1 Can. Bar Rev. 93 at 94.

described as agenda setting, decision-making, policy implementation and watchdog operations.[77] If interest groups are to be effective in bringing about change, if the change is to occur in the desired direction, and if the change is to be implemented without changing the intent of the policy, then the community needs to be involved in all four functions. In other words, a process of democratization needs to occur at both the political and procedural level.

The first function, agenda setting, has been described as "the process of moving an issue from the general socio-economic environment into the governmental policy process",[78] and as "the power to determine which issues are to be considered and which options become legitimate alternatives".[79] A problem or an issue can be around for a long time without ever appearing on the agenda of political decision-makers. The issue or anomaly within the system needs to be projected into the political arena in such a way that it can no longer be ignored or normalized, but can be made the focus of discussion.[80] An active interest group can help create this visibility and the social learning, which must take place before a new policy idea can even become an acceptable option. The difficulty for most community reform-oriented groups is in gaining access to the critical stages. They may fail because they do not know to whom to talk, when they should act, or what the relevant anomaly is.[81] Or they may fail because they are "defined out" of the political process for being irrelevant, unpopular, unrepresentative, *etc.*[82] The opportunity to participate is important because it has been shown that groups in Canada have influence only when they have access.[83] Too often the principle of community participation is honoured verbally but denied in practice by denying access to crucial stages of the policy-making process.

Once an issue has been moved onto the political agenda, a community group must still find ways to participate at the next stage — the decision-making process. Just because the group has succeeded in introducing a problem into the realm of political possibility does not mean that there are not obstacles to be faced. For example, even if the decision is made to act upon a particular issue, it does not necessarily follow that the action will be in the direction envisioned by the originating group.

It also follows that participation at the decision-making level is not

77 I have combined the categories found in Erika S. Fairchild, "Interest Groups in the Criminal Justice Process" (1981), 9:2 Journal of Criminal Justice 181 at 191, and Peter H. Solomon, "Policy Process in Canadian Criminal Justice" (1981), 23:1 Can. Journal of Criminology 5 at 8.

78 Erika S. Fairchild, *ibid.*

79 Peter H. Solomon, *supra,* note 77.

80 See Edwin M. Lemert, *Social Action and Legal Change, Revolution Within the Juvenile Court* (1970).

81 See F. Thompson, F. & W. T. Stanbury, *The Political Economy of Interest Groups in the Legislative Process in Canada,* Occasional Paper #9, Institute for Research on Public Policy (May 1979).

82 See M. Ryan, *Radical Alternatives to Prison and the Penal Lobby* (1978).

83 See F. Thompson, *supra,* note 81.

sufficient to bring about a desired reform. The community must also be represented in the implementation of the proposed change and in ''watch-dog'' strategies. At the level of implementation, the conflict will have moved into the bureaucracy. It is generally easier to get the rules changed than it is to get individuals to alter the way they do things. If at the earlier stage of decision-making, the impact of a new policy on different actors in the system has been considered, the conflict may be lessened but it is unlikely that it will be completely eliminated.

If ongoing participation of the community can be effected at all four levels, and if coordination can be effected between community groups operating at each level, the changes which occur will have less chance of being diverted from the original goal. These are, unfortunately, big ''ifs''. On the plus side, however, the experiences of other community action groups can be helpful in organizing and strategizing for participation in the future. This paper will, therefore, elaborate on a few of the important factors which appear to have influenced successful social action.

The first prerequisite of successful social action is to identify the principle or principles which are being violated in practice. Concepts that are presumed to be the basis of our legal system, but which in reality are being violated, need to be articulated and consistently referred to both in the policy process and in the implementation stage.[84] By focusing on particular principles which are violated in practice, the interest group accomplishes several things. First, they gain support for their cause within the overall community[85] and second, they reduce the chance of an alternative being adopted which will have unintended consequences.

A second prerequisite for effective social action involves obtaining information regarding the problem. Gardner has noted that ''all democratic theory assumes that the citizen must first of all be informed''.[86] Interest groups must collect information on how the system currently operates and its consequences as well as on alternative strategies. Unfortunately, gaining access to relevant and detailed information within the bureaucracies of the criminal justice system is no mean feat. This is precisely why ''freedom of information'' is so important in promoting democracy. The world of research is relevant here — critical research can bring anomalies to light and help to identify possible consequences of different patterns of action. Empirical studies have played a major part in promoting change in a variety of contexts while studies of unmet needs help to form the climate of opinion necessary for

84 Where principles themselves appear to be in contradiction, those seeking change must be aware of the consequences of a change which addresses one principle while adversely affecting another. This type of problem will be addressed in the latter part of this paper when the actions of a particular interest group are addressed.

85 D. F. Greenberg, and D. Humphries, ''The Co-optation of Fixed Sentencing Reform'' (1980), 26:2 Crime and Delinquency 206.

86 See J. Gardner, *In Common Cause* (1972).

change.[87] Since information gathering and research play a vital role in the process of converting anomalies into issues, community interest groups must develop the capacity to back up their activities with relevant data.

Research into successful community action projects has shown that members of interest groups need to develop certain qualities, such as commitment, enthusiasm, patience, stamina, and the ability to limit their targets and tasks.

Commitment usually results from having come face-to-face with a particular problem. In the context of this paper, this usually means that individuals have had some opportunity to participate in the criminal justice system. It is, therefore, important that various aspects of the criminal justice system become democratized. "If we are serious about social change, we must multiply the number of experiences in which commitment may occur."[88] This means that professionals have to be encouraged to value community participation despite the resulting inconveniences. It is in the process of becoming committed through participation that marked shifts in attitude can occur: "Public opinion is as much something to be mobilized as to be read".[89]

While nothing is so frustrating to professionals in the field as the undisciplined enthusiasm of citizen volunteers, "the one thing worse than undisciplined ardor is no ardor at all".[90] While it is important for a group to hold their enthusiasm in check and to hold action in abeyance until the parameters of the problem are known, it is equally true that "no-one will accomplish very much if he waits until the conditions are perfect; they rarely are. Most efforts to change involve a calculated risk, and some degree of failure will be experienced by anyone who tries often".[91]

Because a certain amount of failure is inevitable in a system where the community holds little real power, the successful reformer must have stamina. In fact, one of the most important rules is not to accept any reverse as final but to learn to take a long view. Prison reform is "no sport for the shortwinded".[92] Related to the quality of stamina, but not necessarily identical, is the quality of patience. As Kidd has noted, those who yell "we want it now" don't really know anything about the conditions required for effective change.[93] Short of a societal revolution, *real* change is seldom accomplished quickly and citizen

---

87 See Edwin M. Lemert, *Social Action and Legal Change, Revolution Within the Juvenile Court* (1970); Michael Zander, "Promoting Change in the Legal System" (1979), 42:5 M.L.R. 489.

88 J. Roby Kidd, "Adult Education, the Community and the Animateur" in Social Science Research Council of Canada, James A. Draper (ed.), *Citizen Participation: Canada* (1971), p. 156.

89 See Peter H. Solomon, "Policy Process in Canadian Criminal Justice" (1981), 23:1 Can. Journal of Criminology 5 at 12.

90 See J. Gardner, *In Common Cause* (1972), p. 79.

91 *Supra*, note 88, p. 153.

92 *Supra*, note 90, and also M. Zander, *supra*, note 87.

93 *Supra*, note 88.

groups have to learn to develop the appropriate styles and stamina when the anwer is an unacceptable ''no''.

Another common failing among voluntary groups is the diffusion of energy and resources over too many targets. ''The accomplishment of significant change requires clear-cut targets and a massing of energy and resources.''[94] According to the ''experts'' in the field of community action, the most effective strategy is to select a limited number of clearly-defined targets and to stay with the battle until it is won or lost.

Because the above set of characteristics is a lot to ask of community members, who are giving voluntary time to the task of change, it is important that there be some unchanging presence within the group. This usually means professional support or voluntary organizational backing.[95] Analysis has shown that successful community change has most often been initiated and carried out at the organizational level.[96] If, however, an organization does not exist which will support the ''cause'' of the community interest group, it should first consider ways and means of securing professional support to help it cope with problems of morale and momentum.[97] While an on-the-scene staff person may not always be required, if the task requires organization, coordination and information gathering, a staff person may spell the difference between success and failure. In the final analysis, however, it must be the community group who adopt the strategies to be followed and who take responsibility for the actions of the group.

Other strategies that need to be learned by a community interest group include how to use the media, when and where to join forces with allied groups, and the seeking out of allies within the bureaucracy itself.

Effective communication of a group's position is important both in getting an issue into the political arena and in moving it to the next stage. As well, the public needs clear, concise information on any given issue. The media perform this function in their dramatization of issues. Thus, a knowledge of the workings of the mass media is indispensable.[98]

Once a problem has been moved to the public arena, other community groups will often respond. The initiating group should remember that strength lies in numbers at the same time as they ensure their guiding principles are not compromised by joint action. Occasionally another group is better able to

94 *Supra,* note 90.

95 A number of such groups with interest in the criminal justice system currently exist. Two in Manitoba with a reform emphasis are the John Howard and Elizabeth Fry Society and the Manitoba Association of Rights and Liberties.

96 Coolie Verner, ''Community Action and Learning: A Concept Analysis'' in Social Science Research Council of Canada, James A. Draper (ed.), *Citizen Participation: Canada* (1971).

97 Sydney Jacobs, ''Community Action in a Glasgow Clearance Area'' in Peter Leonard (ed.), *The Sociology of Community Action,* (1975), p. 21.

98 See J. Gardner, *In Common Cause* (1972); Peter H. Solomon, ''Policy Process in Canadian Criminal Justice'' (1981), 23:1 Can. Journal of Criminology 5 at 8; M. Zander, ''Promoting Change in the Legal System'' (1979), 42:5 M.L.R. 489.

cope with a particular aspect of the problem. The initiating group needs to welcome such support without jealously guarding "their territory". Successful change often requires other group support or the letting go of some part of the action. Additionally, reformers should understand that the anomalies within the system affect individuals within the bureaucracy itself. Support for the cause can often be depended upon from this quarter, if the citizen group is sensitive to the problems experienced by these individuals. These public officials can often prove to be invaluable advisors and allies.[99]

Any discussion of community groups dedicated to social change and citizen democracy must eventually face the problem of co-optation. Critics of community action have charged that participation and political integration into the established power structure lead inevitably to tokenism and the eventual political neutering of the community activity. This viewpoint sees community participation as increasing the stability of an inadequate or oppressive system rather than increasing the potential for change. While there is evidence to show that such a pessimistic position is warranted, there is also support for the view that when citizen groups fight for real participation with a clear view of their goals, they can avoid the danger of co-optation.

The more optimistic view of citizen participation suggests that reforms *need not be* the conservative force they are sometimes deemed to be.[100] The groups point out the importance of the political education and advancement which can be achieved even where concrete gains are not made towards a paticular goal. The activities of the groups often serve to strengthen their position within the political arena, thus making real achievements easier in the future.[101] Their efforts may also gain valuable publicity for their goal. Additionally, the absence of concrete gains may be compensated for by the hard political lessons learned — lessons which will strengthen organizations and leadership resources for the future.[102]

In concluding this discussion of the promotion of reform and change through community participation, it is important to note that democratization will not lead to more efficient programs. Democracy has always been a messy business. Nevertheless, participation is worthwhile for the simple reason that individuals not employed in the system bring an uncommitted, sceptical (cynical, even?) approach. They are, therefore, usually free of the type of conventional thinking which "normalizes" inequities and injustices. New ways of looking at problems are most likely to come from those who lack commitment to current rules of procedure and methods of operation.

---

99 See J. Gardner, *ibid*.

100 See M. Ryan, *Radical Alternatives to Prison and Penal Lobby* (1978).

101 Norman Dennis, "Community, Quasi-Community and Anti-Community Action" in Peter Leonard (ed.), *The Sociology of Community Action* (1975), p. 21.

102 See Peter Leonard, *ibid;* D. M. Austin, "Resident Participation: Political Mobilization or Organizational Co-optation" (1972), 32 Pub. Admin. Rev. 409.

A CASE STUDY: PRE-TRIAL DETENTION IN MANITOBA

During the early part of the 1970's, extensive problems were occurring in the area of pre-trial detention in Manitoba. At that time the Winnipeg Remand Centre was administered by the Winnipeg Police Department. Individuals within the system felt that most of the problems could be handled if the administration of such detention were transferred to the province. On 1st October 1977, a transfer of responsibility was made, bringing remand detention under the authority of the Adult Corrections Directorate, the unit which also administered the operation of the provincial jails. Prior to the transfer, a government task force had been established to report on the requirements of a new detention facility. The final report of this task force took for granted the need for a new facility and provided projections that clearly indicated that remand populations would be beyond current holding capacities within a very short period of time. Before the report was tabled, however, a new government was elected in Manitoba. Operating under new priorities and a program of protracted restraint, the new government never placed the question of a new detention facility on its political agenda.

In the ensuing four years, reports of overcrowding and deteriorating conditions occasionally surfaced. By the fall of 1981, concern was being expressed in many different parts of the system. Those individuals most affected by the conditions — the remand inmates — had few avenues for expressing their complaints. The John Howard and Elizabeth Fry Society of Manitoba was one organization operating in the system with a mandate to speak for these inmates. A community-based organization, committed to reform through participation of the community, the agency established a "community task force" to enquire into the conditions and the process of pre-trial detention, and to report to the society board.

In a number of different ways, the establishment of this community committee was a timely event. The system itself was proving to have a limited ability to cope with increasing remand admissions. During 1981, admissions to the Remand Centre had increased by 12 per cent over the preceding year and the rate was steadily rising. In September 1981, the number of admissions to the Remand Centre was 20 per cent higher than during the same period of 1980. The effects of this increased population were being felt throughout the system. The staffing component of the centre had not kept pace with the increase in population during the previous four years. When the province took over the centre, the daily population was 45 individuals; at its height in 1981, it was 128 individuals. During the same period, the increase in remand staff was only two to three guards. The remand staff was facing extreme problems in carrying out its assigned duties. The increase also affected the functioning of the provincial jails. Longer-term remands and the overflow from the Remand Centre were transferred to the Headingly and Portage Correctional Centres to await trial. During 1981, the remand inmates at Headingly comprised between 16 and 25 per cent of the total population. At Portage (the women's institution), a 25 per cent increase in admissions was experienced during 1981, entirely due to remand admissions. These increases had effects on the handling of sentenced prisoners as well as remand inmates; several disturbances at Headingly were traced to problems within the remand section. While these conditions created support for change from most levels of the correctional system, actors at the court level were also expressing concern. Both private defence lawyers and legal aid lawyers complained of being unable to contact clients and of the treatment which their clients were receiving. As well, the media had already focused on a number of incidents at the detention centre. Support for change was experienced throughout the system, although there was less agreement on the type of change required or on where the fault lay.[103]

Secondly, the establishment of the community committee was timely on the political scene. A provincial election had been called, and candidates for all parties were informed of the existence of the committee. When the New Democratic Party defeated the reigning Progressive Conservatives, written support for the committee's task was received from the Attorney-General and the Minister of Community and Correctional Services as well as from the premier. As a result of this political support, as well as that emanating from within the bureaucracy itself, the committee was able to gain access to both prisoners and correctional staff as well as to statistical information collected by Adult Corrections.

Thirdly, the release of their report coincided with the proclamation of the new Canadian Charter of Rights and Freedoms.[104] This gave other groups an avenue to pursue the legality of the conditions under which persons were being detained. The description of these conditions in the committee's report acted as a further catalyst for court actions on behalf of remanded inmates.[105] The Charter thus helped to focus attention on the relevant issues in the initial stages of projecting them onto the political agenda. The Charter will probably have additional influences on the direction of reform during future stages.

The committee was given a broad mandate by the John Howard and Elizabeth Fry Society. As its work progressed, two guiding principles emerged and provided a theoretical framework for analyzing information and making recommendations. The right to due process of law and the presumption of innocence until proven guilty became the operating principles of the committee. The articulation of these principles was important in the initial stage of projecting the issues onto the political agenda and is likely to become even

---

103 See report of the John Howard and Elizabeth Fry Society, *Presumed Innocent? A Report on Pre-Trial Detention* (unpublished 1982).

104 Canada Act, 1982 (Eng.), c. 11, s. 52.

105 Based on some of the findings of the committee, court action was initiated against the provincial government by Legal Aid Manitoba on behalf of a remanded inmate. Discussions with a community group in Saskatchewan played some part in a similar action in that province.

more important if reforms are to take the direction of a "justice" model. The potential for reform of this kind is usually only realized when an issue is made of the discrepancy between accepted principles and actual procedures. Public and political support can be gained because "even those who do not particularly value economic equality are likely to believe that at least in court, everyone should be treated equally".[106]

At present, the John Howard and Elizabeth Fry Society has succeeded in putting the issue of pre-trial detention onto the political agenda. Its challenge will be to keep it there and to move it to the next stage. If the society is to ensure that reforms are faithful to the concepts of presumption of innocence and due process, it will have to continue participation at the decision-making stage. It will be important to ensure that its involvement does not lead to tokenism. As community agencies know full well, "governments can so easily destroy effective and meaningful involvement of the people by defining the terms of participation solely in the light of their own objectives".[107] It will be important to remember that many of the recommendations in the report are interdependent. For example, the original committee deliberated over recommending that a new institution be built. It was felt that a new facility would not end overcrowding and could even lead to greater use of unnecessary detention. To offset this unintended consequence, the committee made specific recommendations as to the size of the institution to be built as well as recommending changes in the court process and alternative methods to detention. For various reasons (*e.g.*, support of the bureaucracy, the labour intensive construction policy of the government), it is possible to foresee success in obtaining a new remand centre[108] without attention being given to these other recommendations. While a new facility is necessary in order to implement recommendations in a manner consistent with the principles, a new remand centre would not necessarily ensure that the resulting reform would lead to a greater adherence to such principles. For this reason it is important that the committee not consider the building of a new institution as proof of successful reform. It may not be. It is when theoretical principles are lost sight of that reforms do become a conservative force rather than a force for change.

A proposal for ensuring community input into both the implementation and monitoring functions has been submitted to the federal Department of Justice and the provincial Attorney-General's Department. The need for such participation at these stages is based on the recognition that procedures within a bureaucracy often become values. These values are usually more difficult to change than the substantive policy. As the transition from one type of

106 See D. F. Greenberg, and D. Humphries, "The Co-optation of Fixed Sentencing Reform" (1980), 26:2 Crime and Delinquency 206 at 211.

107 F. J. Bregha, "Community Development in Canada: Problems and Strategies" in Social Science Research Council of Canada, James A. Draper (ed.), *Citizen Participation: Canada* (1971).

108 A new remand centre of 220 beds has just been approved in principle by the provincial government. Though no target date for the beginning of construction has been set, the design phase is proceeding. (Ed. June 1984.)

correctional process to another requires basic changes in these informal values, there is a continuing role for the public. For example, where a bureaucracy is often concerned with efficiency, the community can continue to promote justice.

Follow-up on the proposal for community participation in the whole pre-trial detention process may be timely for several reasons. First, if the community group manages to obtain meaningful input when alternatives are being considered, it will be in a position to put forth community participation alternatives. Secondly, while funding for new projects is at a low ebb, commitments have been made by both the federal and provincial governments to the United Nations regarding pre-trial detention. Additionally, since alterative programs have been shown to decrease the high costs associated with incarceration, this will be an important factor for governments to consider, given their current budgetary restraints.[109]

The preceding discussion is intended to illustrate the importance of community input at all stages of the policy process. The difficulty is in gaining access to these various stages. Certain factors helped the committee to project the issues into the political arena. These factors are likely to remain important during future action. The information base upon which recommendations were made required access to inmates, staff and statistical information. Since it will continue to be necessary to act from an informed base, an ongoing community group will need to establish mechanisms for the collection and analysis of such information.

During its investigation of pre-trial detention, the committee relied on many supporters from within the system. These links will need to be strengthened and maintained to the degree that they do not change the original goals of the group. Other groups will also become increasingly important during future stages, and alliances and liaisons should be established with all those groups which support the operating principles of the proposed reform.

During the five-month period of investigation, the task force had staff support for activities of coordination and information gathering. As both staff and volunteer members were able to focus their activities on a particular target, their efforts were not diluted by trying to operate on too many fronts at once. If proposals for future community participation are followed up, professional staff support will still be necessary for the coordination, liaison and information gathering functions of the group.

The stamina, enthusiasm, and commitment of the seven members of the original committee cannot be overstated. Numerous hours were spent in travelling to institutions, in meetings and interviews, and in reading briefs.

109 It should, however, be noted that while such programs may be at least as cheap, they should not be implemented with insufficient resources. Many community participation programs have failed because of an inability to transfer money from institutional alternatives to community ones.

During the five-month period, the committee met at least twice a week. Their participation showed that community members are not apathetic when given appropriate alternatives. While the committee members had some concern from the beginning of their investigation, it is safe to say that their commitment increased as they confronted varying aspects of the problem and began to understand the complexities faced by different actors within the system. They were able to look at the whole picture in a way that professionals working within the system are rarely able to do. They were able to bring abuses and inequities into public view precisely because they lacked commitment to the prevailing rules of practice.[110] By looking at the problem from the different viewpoints of inmates, guards, and professionals, it became obvious that efforts to decrease problems experienced by one group often had negative consequences for other groups. Unfortunately, those groups with the least power are the least able to have their concerns addressed.[111] It is the contention of this paper that a community group is in a better position to point out the contradictions between groups and to attempt to redress the balance of power when reforms are being considered.

"The question then is how to harness community energy in such a way that it may be mobilized and released. . . ."[112] The answer in this context may be found by providing links between the three isolated worlds of community, prisons, and researchers. If community groups can utilize the findings of social science research in order to gain access to the political process, then knowledge is more likely to be translated into positive reforms. Academics have, however, usually concentrated their efforts in the areas funded by the state, resulting in stability of the system rather than change. If academics began to look at a change model rather than an order maintenance model, community interest groups would find their insights of greater help.

Hans Schneider commented on some of the points raised in the preceding papers:

Inger Hansen dealt with specific matters, which relate primarily to the

110 This was not entirely true for two members of the committee who were practising lawyers, and their viewpoints were occasionally at variance with other members of the committee. On the other hand, their involvement on the committee gave them a broader view than they would normally acquire in the practice of their profession.

111 One such example involved the movement of prisoners from the detention centre to the court. In order to speed up the court process and accommodate various court actors, the guards at the remand centre were forced to sit in the court holding area for hours while the entire group of defendants appeared. The very real difficulties these staff members were subjected to, were passed on to the inmates through greater control of their movements than would ordinarily be necessary. Thus, a procedure instituted for the convenience of the court had repercussions for both institutional staff and inmates.

112 See F. J. Bregha, *supra*, note 107, p. 77.

federal corrections system. Incidentally, however, Manitoba has responded to the plight of women inmates as positively as possible, inasmuch as we have accepted, without stint, the transfer of female federal inmates to our small institution at Portage la Prairie, so that over time there were, perhaps, only one or two inmates originating from Manitoba who were retained in Kingston. After considerable contention with the federal government, we finally had to exclude inmates sentenced to life imprisonment, because the institution at Portage la Prairie is too confined to keep an inmate there for the mandatory ten or, in the case of inmates sentenced for first degree murder, 25 years, without any kind of conditional release, including parole and temporary absences. We had one female "lifer" whom we wished to employ at the adjacent School for Mental Retardates during the day and bring back into the institution at night, but we could not do it because of federal law.

Now there is an instance where presumably Parliament reflects the will of the nation, inasmuch as the will of the nation, I suppose, if polled,[113] would opt for the return of capital punishment. The resulting compromise, from the corrections perspective, is unduly cruel and harsh.

That is inconsistent with Gail Kellough's argument that advocacy groups should work on the bureaucrats and politicians for progress. The problem is the shaping of public opinion, by such groups as the John Howard and Elizabeth Fry Society, which were the progenitors of our present penitentiary system, now thought to be in such desperate need of improvement. Community participation takes a better informed public.

We should like to develop community participation in the criminal justice system [in the sense of] the acceptance by the local community of responsibility for dealing with offenders, for providing alternatives to jail. Many, perhaps most inmates of our provincial jails should not be there[114] and there are other forms of punishment which would be more appropriate and equally or more effective. It is a matter of making the punishment fit the crime, but it cannot be done without community support. Community groups, such as the John Howard and Elizabeth Fry Society, should direct their attention to these problems rather than see their sole purpose in an advocacy role to influence the established system.

Terry Sawatsky discussed the paradoxes inherent in the "prescribed purposes" of sentencing.[115] The dilemma is the reconciliation of social and individual interests.

It is difficult to reintegrate offenders into the community without commu-

113 See *e.g.*, the Legal Research Institute survey, *supra*, c. 2, questions 80, 81 and 82.

114 We have 900 inmates in our provincial jails, which have a rated capacity of about 800.

115 M. Mandel, *supra*, text to notes 38-42.

nity resources and community support. This is a particular problem with the native population, which at Stony Mountain Penitentiary is some 30 per cent. Often the communities do not want them. Often the opportunities in the city are limited. Many inmates have few alternatives. If we take an aggressive approach to rehabilitation, the probability of success is so low that we run into conflict with the goal of protection of society.

The proverbial Catch-22 facing administrators in all correctional systems, is that it is impossible simultaneously to fulfil all the expectations supported by the survey.[116]

116 The Legal Research Institute survey, *supra*, c. 2, question 83.

8

WORKERS AND MANAGERS

LAW IN A CYNICAL SOCIETY

Dick Martin

[Dick Martin voiced the cynicism that workers, if not always the public at large, display toward labour law, portended by Chief Justice Deschênes.][1]

In the last couple of years a number of well-known union leaders have been fined and imprisoned — all for defying laws banning strikes. Sometimes these laws were there before the strike, at other times legislation was enacted after the strike had commenced. In all cases the workers were demanding a strike because they were so dissatisfied with their pay or working conditions.

How many corporate leaders have been heavily fined or jailed in the last few years for labour law misconduct or for breaking safety and health regulations, environmental laws or, for that matter, any other laws?

I remember Louis Laberge saying after he had served time in jail in Quebec for defying the law and leading the common front, that while in jail he had not met any corporate people, no bank managers, no oil company tycoons; no, he had met only workers.

To be sure there have of late been one or two cases, particularly in Ontario, where companies were convicted of gross violations of the Labour Relations Act[2] and were ordered to pay punitive damages to the union and workers, the most celebrated being the *Radio Shack* case.[3] These instances, however, are few and far between.

There is little doubt that the governments who savagely prosecuted C.U.P.W. and Jean Claude Parrot, C.U.P.E. and Grace Hartman, Lucy Nicholson, Sean O'Flynn, and Ray Arsenault had a fair amount of public

1 *Comm. de Tpt. de la Communauté Urbaine de Montreal v. Syndicat du Tpt. de Montreal et autres,*77 C.L.L.C. 14,098, reversing [1974] Rec de J. 227 (C.A.).

2 R.S.O. 1980, c. 228.

3 *United Steel Wkrs. of Amer. v. Radio Shack,*[1980] 1 Can. L.R.B.R. 99 (O.L.R.B.).

support. These leaders and many of their members, however, are very cynical about the law, which of course includes the government, the police, the courts, and lawyers.

Not too long ago in Winnipeg a young man fell to his death from a scaffold on a construction project. The company had been repeatedly warned about the lack of guard-rails and other safety devices, but they chose to ignore the warnings. They were brought to court, found guilty and fined $1,000 for disobeying the Workplace Safety and Health Act.[4] A life was lost and the penalty was $1,000, but there was no great outcry by the media, the public, or government. It is terrible to lead people on an illegal strike, or even a legal strike which significantly inconveniences the public, it seems, but it is acceptable to have poor working conditions, ignore the law and lose a life. Workers are cynical, outraged and committed to changing this injustice.

Approximately four years ago a manufacturing firm in Brandon was found guilty of violating the Workplace Safety and Health Act after an untrained woman employee had lost five fingers in a shearing machine. The fine was $500.

Approximately a year and a half ago the government of Manitoba refused to prosecute a Winnipeg manufacturing firm for repeated violations of air quality standards, needlessly exposing employees to harmful metal vapours. The union felt so strongly about it that it launched its own court action, but the first question was whether the union had the right to prosecute or not. The union won, on that issue,[5] but the substantive case is still before the courts and to the best of my knowledge the government still refuses to prosecute.

The public perception of the cases of workers and their unions versus companies on safety and health matters is different. Public opinion is either already on our side or increasingly swaying towards workers. The laws and the courts are unjust, outdated and must catch up with public opinion.

Aside from the jailings of C.U.P.E. leaders, the 1980 strike cost C.U.P.E. $150,000 in fines and legal costs. No one was killed or died directly or indirectly because of the strike. Compare that to the $1,000 fine levied against the construction company where the young man fell to his death.

Now we have the Ocean Ranger disaster. It is becoming clear that the oil companies involved in offshore drilling off the coast of Newfoundland have no intention of letting all be known about their operations because, they say, they do not want their competitors to know these details. Meanwhile we have a commission operating with a liberal budget in opulent surroundings to investigate a tragedy, while it appears that the oil companies will obstruct the bringing forward of evidence and that another government (the United States) has little intention of cooperating. This whole operation is the height of

4 1976 (Man.), c. 63 (also C.C.S.M., c. W210).

5 *MacIssac v. Motor Coach Indust. Ltd.*, [1982] 5 W.W.R. 391, 16 Man. R. (2d) 419 (C.A.).

cynicism and is certainly viewed as a pork barrel for the legal profession and the well-connected. I find it rather morbid that so many, already well-to-do, will profit financially at the expense of the public over the bodies of these drowned workers.[6]

In northern Manitoba, throughout the mining towns, the cemeteries hold the bodies of well over 100, if not 200 miners, all killed in these mines, smelters, and mills, and I do not know of one case where a company was convicted of criminal negligence. The odds are that some of these deaths were due to criminal negligence. Those who have worked in that industry know there should have been convictions. We are cynical because little changes. The laws that do exist are not vigorously enforced, prosecutions are uncommon, and the law and the courts frustrate and hinder any prosecutions. When the miners, however, strike over pay, better working conditions, or just from pent-up frustration, the media howl, the Chambers of Commerce wring their hands and the courts allow injunctions. Property and the exercise of the right to pursue profits are the priorities of the law. The right to organize, to work in safe and decent conditions, and to strike are secondary considerations.

Those who are active in the labour movement find the hypocrisy of the leaders of many western capitalist countries almost incomprehensible, as they shake their finger at Poland over the treatment of Solidarity. You would think that Ronald Reagan was the John L. Lewis of Poland, while at home he savagely attacked PATCO and the United States Air Traffic Controllers. I saw on T.V. local union leaders being led from their jail cells to the courts in handcuffs and leg irons. Lech Walesa, it appears, was treated well in comparison. Ronald Reagan and his colleagues impose repressive labour laws in the United States and outlaw unions. I would suggest to you that if the workers in Canada, numbering ten million, the same as in Solidarity in Poland, rose up together, and demanded worker participation in the management of the factories and a major say in government decision-making, the War Measures Act[7] would be declared, the army would be called out, and the repression would be similar to that in Poland. I, too, condemn the Polish military and support Solidarity, but on a stronger and more truthful ground. Unfortunately the public views Poland in isolation and does not draw the analogy to Canada, the United States or Britain.

I believe that the public does have a cynical attitude toward the law, though sometimes it wishes to change it in the wrong direction for the wrong reasons. I believe that there is growing disrespect for many laws and law-makers. The laws are usually obeyed out of fear, but laws should be obeyed by the general public because it respects and agrees with these laws.

For example, this Federation of Labour has forwarded to the government the suggestion that the whole concept of fines should be changed. Fines, we

6 See Royal Commission on the Ocean Ranger Marine Disaster. "Report One: The Loss of the Semisubmersible Drill Rig Ocean Ranger and its Crew" (August 1984).

7 R.S.C. 1970, c. W-2.

believe, should be imposed on individuals, corporations, organizations, institutions, *etc.* on the basis of their gross income. A $100 fine imposed on a person earning $20,000 a year is more punitive than a $100 fine levied against someone earning $100,000 a year or a corporation earning $10,000,000 a year. If the purpose of fines is to deter wrongdoing, then does it not follow that a $500 fine is more suitably imposed on the $100,000 income and the $100 fine on the $20,000 income. The laws of this country are not fair and discriminate against lower income classes. Our jails hold many who are there because they cannot pay the fines. That perhaps explains at least in part why the corporate elite are not in jail.

IDEOLOGY, LAW, PUBLIC OPINION AND WORKERS' HEALTH

Charles E. Reasons

[Charles Reasons and Harry Glasbeek analyzed the symbiotic relationship between policy, law, and public opinion in the creation and reinforcement of an ideology hostile to trade unions and workers.]

DICEY ON LAW AND PUBLIC OPINION

[E]ach kind of opinion entertained by men at a given era is governed by that whole body of beliefs, convictions, sentiments, or assumptions, which, for want of a better name, we call the spirit of an age.[8]

. . . . .

Public opinion itself is, after all, a mere abstraction; it is not a power which has any independent existence; it is simply a general term for the beliefs held by a number of individual human beings. If we are not to become the dupes of abstract conceptions, we must individualise them and fix our attention upon the thoughts and beliefs of men who have lived and worked, and whose ideas are known to us through their conduct, their writings or their biographies.[9]

. . . . .

An author who tried to explain the relation between law and opinion during the nineteenth century undertook to a certain extent the work of an historian, and yet was freed from many of the impediments which often beset historical inquiry. His duty was to draw correct inferences from admitted facts, or at any rate from facts easily to be discovered. They could be ascertained by a careful study of the Statute Book and of legal decisions, and also of the letters and memoirs written by statesmen, teachers, or writers who had affected the legal doctrines of their time.[10]

8 A.V. Dicey, *Law and Public Opinion In England During the Nineteenth Century*, 2nd ed. (1914), p. 465.

9 *Ibid.*, pp. 414-15.

10 *Ibid.*, p. xxiii.

The View From Above

In the above quotations Dicey has provided us with insight as to the significance of a dominant idea system (ideology), what public opinion is and why it is that way (theory), and how to go about researching public opinion (methodology). The significance of the relationship between dominant belief systems and the nature of public opinion, and the way to gauge this, is important for my discussion of Dicey, for he, as a learned lawyer, scholar, and man of letters was himself writing during a specific ideological era from his own perspective. I suggest that his view of history, law, social change and labour is itself a product of his time, position, and ultimately his ideology.[11]

In reading Dicey's work I found a number of modern sociological insights into the relationship between law, public opinion, and public policy. For example, he notes that a law may be *symbolically* progressive but not instrumentally enforced.[12] Thus, he points out that during an era of conservatism in the early nineteenth century, a humanitarian law — the Health and Morals Act of 1802[13] — was passed on behalf of working people.[14] Dicey observes that while the establishment of certain minimal standards of work was benevolent and progressive, "[t]he means provided for [the statute's] enforcement [*e.g.* the inspection of the mills which come under its scope by visitors who owed their appointment to justices of the peace] were ridiculously inadequate. The Act was a moral protest against cruelty but practically produced no effect."[15] This has a modern ring for the student of occupational health and safety laws and their enforcement. More, however, on this later. Suffice it to say that Dicey makes several observations pertinent to law and

---

11 I will define ideology as one's beliefs and perceptions on (1) how the present social economic and political order operates; (2) why this is so, and whether it is good or bad; and (3) what should be done about it. See Charles E. Reasons and Williams D. Perdue, *The Ideology of Social Problems* (1981).

12 See also Gail Kellough, *supra*, c. 7, text to notes 77-84.

13 (41 Geo. 3), c. 73.

14 The law was not entirely altruistic. The Act was carried through by Sir Robert Peel, a manufacturer and a Tory. It appears that there was an epidemic in Manchester resulting in many deaths of apprentices in his cotton mills. The plague was attributed to their scanty diet and to the wretched conditions in which the apprentices lived (they were mostly pauper children who were sent to the north of England by the parochial authorities of the south to work out their time of bondage). The new law was to regulate to a limited extent the employment of these apprentices in cotton and woollen factories, while also containing sanitary and moral rules, *e.g.*, factory rooms should be washed twice a year with quick-lime and water; apprentices should receive two suits of clothes each; have a 12-hour work day; male and female apprentices should have separate apartments and sleep no more than two in one bed; and every Sunday apprentices should receive one hour of instruction and examination in the principles of the Christian religion by a qualified person.

15 A.V. Dicey, *Law and Public Opinion In England During the Nineteenth Century*, 2nd ed. (1914), p. 110. It may be argued that the passage of the Act was to reduce the possibility of worker uprisings and rebellion due to such incidents (involving cruelty). Therefore, such legislation is for the benefit of owners and managers in quelling the workers (a law is passed) without substantially affecting conditions (little enforcement and change). This "have your cake and eat it too" interpretation provides owners and law-makers with an alternative viewpoint which is less generous.

society today. Nonetheless, what were his views of social change, law and labour?

Men of Letters Didn't Have to Worry About the Postage Costs

It may be said that his view of public opinion was elitist.[16] That is, he viewed public opinion as being that of the intellectual and political elite of an era. The assumption that "public opinion" is reflected in such official pronouncements, enactments, and writing suggests that a consensus existed on the desired nature of society at the time. Did the mass of English working people agree with the policies of the nineteenth century? We really do not know by reading Dicey, because his work seldom quotes or notes what the working class thought. The extent to which he addresses the issues of the working class is through an analysis of the growth of collectivism and the decline of individualism. Although he attempts to remain "above the struggle" and a "value-free, detached" scholar without bias, his writing evidences a bemoaning of the decline of laissez-faire individualism and the growth of collectivism.

Creeping Collectivism (Socialism?)

Dicey divides the nineteenth century into three periods:

1. The Period of Old Toryism or Legislature Quiescence (1800-1830).

2. The Period of Benthamism or Individualism (1825-1870).

3. The Period of Collectivism (1865-1900).

The last period is the one most worrisome to Dicey. He identifies collectivism as the favouring of state intervention, even at the sacrifice of individual freedom, for conferring benefit upon the mass of people, and to him it is epitomized by labour laws and legislation intended to regulate trade and business in the interest of the working class.[17]

> The fundamental principle which is accepted by every man who leans toward any form of socialism or collectivism,[18] is faith in the benefit to be derived by the mass of the people from the action or intervention of the State even in matters which might be, and often are, left to the uncontrolled management of the persons concerned.[19]

The indicators of this spreading (creeping?) socialism are, according to Dicey:

(1) extending the idea of state protection, *e.g.*, laws respecting working women and child labour, food and drug Acts, workers' compensation.

16 See also D. Gibson, *supra*, c. 1, text to notes 10-16.

17 *Supra*, note 15, p. 64.

18 In the first edition he cautions against the use of the term "socialism" because of its emotive/political connotations, thus preferring "collectivism". However, he uses the term "socialism" as the equal of "collectivism" in both editions, albeit more often in the second edition.

19 A.V. Dicey, *Law and Public Opinion In England During the Nineteenth Century*, 2nd ed., (1914), p. 259.

(2) restriction of freedom of contract, *e.g.*, landlord-tenant Acts.

(3) preference for collective rather than individual action, *e.g.*, orientation towards unions.

(4) equalization of advantages among unequals, *e.g.*, state schooling, employer liability.

He also suggests that imperialism promoted collectivism because it produced "a sense among Englishmen of their membership in a great imperial State".[20] Apparently his greatest fears are confirmed in his introduction to the second edition written in 1914:[21]

> The main current of legislative opinion from the beginning of the twentieth century has *run vehemently* towards collectivism.[22]

Why such "vehement" change? He states that it is due to the increased recognition of interdependence of private and public interests among "ordinary" English people, the decline of other movements, the acquiescence of the wealthy due to their not seeing the long-term effect of legislation and their benevolence, the advent of parliamentary democracy and extension of suffrage, the spread of collectivism or socialism in foreign countries (*e.g.*, Australia, United States, France), and the existence of industrial discontent or warfare.

Change For Whom, By Whom?

In the second edition he finally acknowledges that workers are struggling to change their situation. Throughout his book one has the feeling that the movement to collectivism is due largely to the benevolence and sensitivity of the politicians, judiciary, and other elites of that time. He seldom suggests that there was massive or even lesser periodic discontent among the masses (public) or particular segments of the population (specific publics). One has the impression that all was rational and relatively tranquil apart from minor, infrequent rumblings from below. Periodically we catch a glimpse of Dicey's view of the working class. For example, in discussing how the Methodist movement produced large scale improvements in the conditions of thousands of minors, labourers and artisans he states:

---

20 *Ibid.*, p. 411. He also points out that the colonial empire and English imperialism were not always viewed as beneficial at p. 452:

> Brougham in 1839 described Wolfe's capture of Quebec as an operation "which crowned our arms with imperishable glory, and loaded our policy with a burden not yet shaken off". He cites also, with the keenest approval, the views of Lord St. Vincent in 1783, that Canada ought to be surrendered, and his opinion that by not then surrendering it, we were retaining "a running sore, the source of endless disquiet and expense" and that "if this fair occasion for giving up Canada is neglected, nothing but difficulty, in either keeping or resigning it, will ever after be known."

21 *Ibid*. The preface is dated 1914, while this printing is 1962. Footnote 1 at liii states that "[a] critic should never forget that the truth of a belief is not necessarily demonstrated by its wide acceptance".

22 *Ibid.*, p. liii (emphasis added). See, *e.g.*, Acts in Dicey, Introduction to the Second Edition, p. xxiii, *ff.* discussed.

> Religious conversion of men, whom ignorance and want of moral guidance had left in a condition of something very like Paganism produced a body of good men and of good citizens, and of persons therefore who in a country like England did as a rule obtain material prosperity.[23]

Furthermore, religion "diverted the ablest men among the wage-earners of England from sympathy with the revolutionary doctrines of 1789".[24]

In discussing reactionary laws, Dicey points out that the Combination Act of 1800[25] was directly aimed at suppressing strikes and trade unions; however, he asserts that it corresponded with the predominant beliefs of the time, although, "*the ideas of the working class were, it may be said, not represented*".[26]

The point is that the dominant beliefs were not those of the working classes and although he notes that there existed countercurrents (oppositional ideologies), he fails to elaborate upon how they emerge from the working class, in what form, *etc*. Given the turbulence of labour strife in the early part of the twentieth century, he cannot ignore the great challenge to the logical, moderate, judicious process of social change he presents as the "hallmark" of English society. After approvingly quoting the president emeritus of Harvard University, Charles W. Elliott,[27] he suggests that the appearance of great disparity between the rich and the workers is conducive to radical ideologies (collectivism). In closing the introduction to the second edition he quotes an "eminent German professor", Herman Levy, who, in his book *Economic Liberation,* characterizes the English people as egalitarian, tolerant, and favouring gradual reform rather than revolution.

> To this consideration may be added the confidence that the increased sympathy assuredly now felt by the best men and women of England within the wants of the poorer classes will facilitate wise legislation, and create or restore the conditions of labour under which the laborer may reasonably be expected to be contented, efficient and happy.[28]

While he also quotes de Tocqueville[29] with approval, Dicey does not accept his definition of democracy as a state of society where there exists a general equality of rights, similarity of conditions, of thoughts, sentiment, and ideas but *no necessary connection with individual freedom or popular government*. Dicey defines democracy as a form of government, *i.e.,* a constitution where "sovereign power is possessed by the numerical majority of the male citizens".[30] This definition of democracy is the way Dicey distinguishes between democracy and collectivism (socialism). After noting

23 *Ibid.*, p. lviii.

24 *Ibid.*, p. lviii.

25 Unlawful Combinations of Workmen Act, 1800 (39 & 40 Geo. 3), c. 106.

26 *Supra,* note 19, p. 100 (emphasis added).

27 *Ibid.*, p. lxviii: "It amounts to warfare, this incessant conflict within the political body between the employed and the employers . . . and in many cases it becomes an actual physical contest."

28 *Ibid.*,p. xciii.

29 *Ibid.*, p. xciv, quoting *Recollections of Alex de Tocqueville* (1893).

30 *Ibid.*, p. 52. Needless to say, women were not a significant factor in "public opinion".

that socialism is a government of experts who know what is best for people, while democracy is a government by the people, he states:

> A nation or a state means, conceal it as you will, a lot of individual selves with unequal talents and in reality unequal conditions, and each of these selves does — or rather must — think not exclusively, but primarily of his own self.[31]

Finally, in discussing the Reformation, he observes that "the revolution to which socialism points cannot be worked out until the lapse of a long period of time".[32] In the concluding remarks of this second edition, Dicey grudgingly admits that collectivism is continuing and growing; therefore, it must be carried out wisely. The change from feudalism to capitalism took several centuries;[33] therefore, one might anticipate that the change from capitalism to socialism will take place over several decades, if not centuries.

ENTER THE WORKING CLASS

If our ideas are moulded by our experiences, class position, training, and social location, then surely a reputable, learned member of the English legal profession is bound to reflect that status in his writings. Some historians call this the "view from above", or history by the accounts of those who were in control of society, *i.e.*, the dominant class. For example, if one looks at English society and the law from "below" in eighteenth century England, the view is rather more disquieting than the "official", elite view.[34] In his massive work, *The Making of the English Working Class*, the English historian E. P. Thompson provides a view of working people entirely omitted from Dicey's work. Using official data, studies, newspaper accounts, and working class documents, among other sources, he presents a lucid and compelling account of how the English working class was created essentially between 1780 and 1832. Thompson documents the day-to-day harshness of labouring conditions, the wretched living conditions and the struggles of working people to change their conditions, the victories and the defeats:

> I am seeking to rescue the poor stocking, the Luddite cropper, the "obsolete" hand-loom weaver, the "utopian" artisan, and even the deluded follower of Joanna Southcott, from the erroneous condescension of posterity. Their hostility to the new industrialism may have been backward looking. Their communitarian ideals may have been fantasies. Their

---

31 *Ibid.*, p. lxxx.

32 *Ibid.*, p. lxxxix.

33 For a discussion of the legal changes this entailed see M. Tigar and M. Levy, *Law and the Rise of Capitalism* (1977).

34 See E.P. Thompson, *Whigs and Hunters: The Origin of the Black Act* (1977). In discussing his point of departure for analyzing the "Black Act" [the Criminal Law Act, 1722 (9 Geo. 1), c. 22, which was repealed by the Criminal Statutes, England, Repeal Act, 1827 (7 & 8 Geo. 4), c. 27], Thompson states at. p. 16:

> Since I started with the experience of humble foresters and followed up, through sketchy contemporary evidence, the lines that connected them to power, there is a sense in which the sources themselves have forced me to see English society in 1723 as they themselves saw it, from "below."

> insurrectionary conspiracies may have been foolhardy. But they lived through these times of acute social disturbances, and we did not. Their aspirations were valid in terms of their own experience; and if they were casualties of history, they remain, condemned in their own lives, as casualties.[35]

While my aim is not to present the other side (underside?) of the picture of nineteenth century England, suffice it to say that Dicey is presenting largely upper class views and interpretations. This brings us to the significance of ideology in both the making of law and its operation.

LAW, IDEOLOGY, AND THE STATE

Part of the dominant (prevailing) ideology of society is a view of law. In the Canadian state, the dominant ideology of law includes the notions of fairness, equality, and justice without favour to any class, group, party, or other special interest. This forms part of the official message of the state and its agents, including the civil service bureaucracy, public corporations, central banks, regulatory commissions, the military, the judiciary, representative assemblies, and subcentral levels of government such as provincial executives, legislatures, and municipal governmental institutions. Thus, the state includes not only elected officials, but also public agencies such as schools, social welfare institutions, *etc*.[36] The Canadian political scientist Leo Panitch points out that the capitalist state must perform the functions of accumulation, social control, and legitimation. For example, tax breaks for industry (accumulation) through proper accounting (social control) help all Canadians (legitimation), or wage controls for employees (social control) help decrease the deficit and increase moneys for stimulating the economy (accumulation), which is good for all Canadians (legitimation).

Marxist students of the state have increasingly addressed the issue of the significance of law and legal ideology in capitalist states,[37] and the role of belief systems in legitimating and reinforcing state policy. Every state has its ideological state apparatus which presents us with an interpretation of the society.[38] Through schools, official pronouncements, political speeches, T.V.,

35 E.P. Thompson, *The Making of the English Working Class* (1968), p. 13. For a discussion of the life and writing of this famous historian, see Bryan D. Palmer, *The Making of E.P. Thompson: Marxism, Humanism, and History* (1981). Some other interesting accounts of workers' struggles against the changes occurring during this period include: Peter Linebough, "Karl Marx, The Theft of Wood and Working Class Composition" (1976), 6 Crime and Social Justice: Issues in Criminology 5; Geoffrey Pearson, "Goths and Vandals — Crime in History" (1978), 2:2 Contemporary Crisis 119; David F. Greenberg, *Crime and Capitalism* (1981); D. Hay *et al.*, *Albion's Fatal Tree* (1975).

36 Leo Panitch, "The Role and Nature of the Canadian State" in *The Canadian State: Political Economy and Political Power,* (1977), pp. 5-8. For a more recent collection concerning the Canadian state see J. Paul Grayson (ed.), *Class, State, Ideology and Change* (1980).

37 My concern here is with law and legal ideology in the capitalist state of Canada. For an excellent discussion of some socialist states see K. Kulcsar, "Ideological Changes and Legal Structure: The Socialist Experience" (1980), Int. Journal of the Sociology of the Law 61-81.

38 For an overview see B. Jessup, "On Recent Marxist Theories of Law, the State, and Juridico-Political Ideology" (1980), 8:4 Int. Journal of the Sociology of Law 339.

radio, books, theatre, *etc.*, we learn about democracy, freedom, and the rule of law.

More and more today, people are questioning social institutions, including the law, and are cynical concerning them. The title of this conference — *Law In a Cynical Society?* — evidences this concern. According to *Webster,* a cynic is one who attributes all actions to selfish motives. The Legal Research Institute survey suggests that most Canadians hold the view that the law is biased in favour of the rich and against the poor and minorities; that you get the justice you can afford; and that most people are out for "number one".[39] While many academics, including Marxist scholars, would view this as a simplistic view of the operation of the state and its institutions, it is nonetheless prevalent. Rather than dismissing the public as naive and in need of education, let us take them seriously and ascertain the accuracy of these views. For example, it is increasingly noted by students of the law, including the Law Reform Commission of Canada, that laws, both in their making and their administration, tend to favour those with power (economic, political, social) and weigh heavily upon those without substantial power.[40] Thus, it appears that we (or, more appropriately, those with a vested interest in the current institutional structures, policies, and operations) have a crisis of legitimation. That is, the professed aims of the law in terms of equality, justice, and humanity for all Canadians are perceived by many for what they often are, a sham and/or a con. Nowhere is this crisis more evident than in the area of labour-management relations.

LABOUR-MANAGEMENT RELATIONS

A great deal is said today about big labour, big government, and big business. We must not forget, however, that in a corporate society, with its orientation toward profit, corporate ownership, growth and concentration, the dominant ideology will look more favourably on corporations and business than on workers and unions.[41] For example, private ownership and individualism are significant aspects of the corporate ideology and since unions are collectively oriented, we are taught that the unions are counter to what made this country great. A study of students in the United States found that as they went from Grade III to Grade XII their views of unions became more negative and their views of private ownership of industry became more positive. Specifically, 48 per cent of those in Grade III were neutral to unions and 17 per cent negative, while by Grade XII 59 per cent were negative and 23 per

39 The Legal Research Institute survey, *supra,* c. 2, questions 41c, 44, 71, 74a, 21.

40 I know that such a general statement may be countered by exceptions, qualifications, *etc.;* however, the bottom line remains, as blues singer Ray Charles states, "Them That's Got Is Them That Gets", or as criminologist Jeffrey Reiman writes *The Rich Get Richer and the Poor Get Prison* (1979). See also M. Debicki, *supra,* c. 7, and M. Mandel, *supra,* c. 7, text to note 38, *ff.*

41 For an elaboration upon the structural imperatives and ideology of corporate society see Charles E. Reasons and William D. Perdue, *The Ideology of Social Problems* (1981).

cent neutral. On the other hand, 66 per cent were neutral and 16 per cent positive toward private ownership of industry in Grade III, while by Grade XII it was 23 per cent neutral and 63 per cent positive.

While more workers are unionized in Canada than in the United States (approximately 35 per cent and 21 per cent, respectively, of non-agricultural paid workers), the general public in Canada appears to have a fairly negative view of unions as self-serving. For example, a study of the portrayal of unions in the major Canadian newspapers found basically anti-labour and anti-union bias.[42] Historically, as Dicey notes, capitalists fought unions and passed legislation against them. The trade union movement, however, was successful in establishing itself, particularly within the industrial sector.[43] Unions have at least been established as legal in certain areas, although not generally accepted ideologically.

As Smucker points out in his analysis of the ideologies of management, unions and collective bargaining are viewed as important to the private enterprise system by many managers, while union leaders are characterized as smug and unconcerned about workers.[44] He also states that:

> The growing emphasis on viewing workers in a more human manner represents a symbolic "flanking" maneuver which in effect, undercuts the legitimacy of unions. Workers come to be viewed as worthy individuals at the very time that unions were viewed as corrupting influences. Up to the point where unions were finally viewed as a permanent fixture in the industrial scene, there was a growing positive orientation toward workers while negative orientations were maintained toward unions.[45]

While the fact of unionization is generally acknowledged, many Canadians view unions as contrary to our basic ideology. The Canadian state, through labour legislation, has attempted to control the effects of unions. For example, it is arguable that the history of Canadian labour law has been as beneficial to management and the state as to labour. More specifically, the requirement of compulsory conciliation with special provision for the mandatory postponement of any strike or lockout during the term of an agreement has helped the accumulation and social control functions of the state.[46]

> What has been particularly notable about Canadian labour legislation, in comparison with the British and even in comparison with the Americans, is the extent to which the rights of unionization and free collective bargaining have been hedged around by, even embedded in a massive legal and penal structure. This places such tremendous statutory restriction on labour and gives such a large role for the law and courts to play, that the legitimation aspect

---

42 See Ray Sentes, *Trade Unions and the Press,* (unpublished Master's Thesis, University of Regina, 1978).

43 Joseph Smucker, *Industrialization in Canada* (1980), pp. 171-216. It should be noted that the majority of Canadian workers are not unionized and many current struggles are going on to unionize them, *e.g.*, secretaries, cab drivers, domestic workers, part-time workers, farm workers, bank workers, *etc.*

44 *Ibid.*, pp. 149-68.

45 *Ibid.*, p. 163.

46 Christopher Huxley, "The State, Collective Bargaining and the Shape of Strikes in Canada" (1979), 4:3 Can. Journal of Sociology 223.

of labour legislation in Canada's case seems at least balanced, if not actually overshadowed, by the coercive aspect.[47]

The problem of legitimation, law, and ideology is particularly evident in the area of workers' health.

THE IDEOLOGY OF WORKERS' HEALTH

The approach one takes towards workers' health is based upon one's assumptions about why there is death, dying, and injury from the workplace. Most of the carnage from the workplace is identified as being an accident. That is, it is an event occurring by chance or unintentionally.[48] When the issue of causation arises, the dominant ideology blames the victim. For example, when I interviewed Dr. Herbert Buchwald, the Managing Director of Alberta's Department of Workers' Health, Safety, & Compensation, he suggested that 70 to 80 per cent of accidents and fatalities in the workplace are caused by "careless workers".

Blaming the Victim[49]

> To say that some of these workers died from accidents due to their own carelessness is about as helpful as saying that some of those who died at the hands of murderers asked for it. It overlooks the fact that where workers are careless, it is not because they love to live dangerously. They have production quotas to meet, quotas they themselves do not set. If quotas were set with an eye to keeping work at a safe pace rather than to keeping the production-to-wages ratio as high as possible, it might be more reasonable to expect workers to take the time to be careful. Beyond this, we should bear in mind that the vast majority of occupational deaths result from disease, not accidents, and disease is generally a function of conditions outside a worker's control, such as the level of coal dust in the air. . . .[50]

By focusing upon the worker as the cause of accidents, we then look for solutions to violence in the workplace by somehow changing the worker, freeing the company or work environment from blame. Attention is turned to certain "kinds of people" theories of the causes of accidents. Accident researchers may try to determine whether certain biological, psychological, or social traits are more evident among accident victims than among non-

47 L. Panitch, "The Role and Nature of the Canadian State" in *The Canadian State: Political Economy and Political Power* (1977), p. 19.

48 Webster's dictionary defines accidental as (1) happening unexpectedly or by chance; (2) happening without intent or through carelessness. The classifying of violence against workers in this manner has a great deal of ideological and legal significance. If something just happens "by chance" then no one is really at fault and thus no victim and offender can be identified with no criminal act (*actus reus*) or criminal mind (*mens rea*). Furthermore, as will be evident in subsequent discussion, when carelessness is ascertained it is generally assigned to the victim (worker).

49 The following discussion of the "blaming the victim" approach is largely taken from the "Dumb Worker: Blaming the Victim" in Reasons, Ross, and Paterson, *Assault on the Worker* (1981), p. 137.

50 See J. Reiman, *The Rich Get Richer and the Poor Get Prison* (1979), p. 68.

accident victims. If certain people are believed to be ''accident prone'', then all we need to do is use pre-employment screening or training to deal with the problem.

If certain ''kinds of environments'' are viewed as causing accidents, then the onus is on the employer to change the environment. For example, if piecework and bonus incentives lead to speed-ups and more accidents, these policies, not the workers, need to be changed. Likewise, if poor equipment design or poor ventilation leads to violence against the worker, studying the characteristics of the worker is futile.

Since, however, management has historically had the power to define ''acceptable'' risks for workers, the degree of violence in the workplace reflects differences in power between management and workers. The conflict between maximization of profits and minimization of violence in the workplace becomes part of the power struggle between workers and management. This ''power/conflict'' explanation suggests the need for a shift of power from owners to workers in order adequately to address the problem.

While all three of the above-mentioned explanations of workplace violence are to be found today, the ''kinds of people'' approach tends to prevail in management and government attempts to ''solve'' the problem. This leads to the initiation of a variety of programs, such as educational and safety training, without changing the structure, nature, or process of work.

The ''blaming the victim'' approach is evident in some traditional crimes of violence. For example, in the violent crime of rape the victim is often viewed as the criminal, or at least as a willing participant in the violence. The same kind of victim-blaming occurs in violence in the workplace. Like the rape myths that ''she was really looking for it'' and that ''anyone who wanted to could avoid being raped'', there are the workplace myths that ''any worker can avoid a violent accident or death'' and ''it's only those who are dumb and/or careless who are hurt''. In rape, the onus is on the woman to prove that she did not ''consent'', and in workplace violence, it is on the victim to prove that the harm was caused by work. Diseases and stress are particularly hard to ''prove'' to the satisfaction of the Workers' Compensation Board, especially as the worker's lifestyle is often used against him or her. For example, smoking habits have been used to disallow for claims for disease. Even in the case of obviously violent ''accidents'', workers may have difficulty obtaining compensation, particularly for permanent disability.

One of the dominant theories used to explain industrial accidents has been ''accident proneness''. The term was coined by Eric Farmer following a study in 1919 which directed students of accident research away from a focus upon the worker environment to a study of individual characteristics. It was thought that a worker's chance of having an accident was due to personal qualities such as ''carelessness'' or ''light-heartedness'' and that, therefore, accidents could be prevented by the use of proper care and thoughtfulness.

"Accident proneness" is a classic example of blaming the victim. It leaves the employer without any culpability and thus without reason to change the working environment. In a devastating critique of the concept, Surry states that "proneness" is a no more useful concept than "fate" — no one stable personality characteristic associated with proneness has been found during the last 50 years of research.[51] She goes on, however, to point out that despite its scientific uselessness as an explanation of accidents, it persists.

> Doctors and psychologists, *particularly those in industry*, seemed to have avidly accepted the concept of accident proneness as an innate stable characteristic, presumably because it gave them something concrete to search for while treating the many accident victims.[52]

This ideology of the "deficient worker" makes little scientific sense but supports the dominant corporate ideology. Management may identify the accident repeater as having a "poor social background", being "socially maladjusted", "emotionally unstable", hyperactive if young or evidencing suppressed aggression if older, "insecure", "frustrated", or as having a number of other "disturbing" qualities. This can be used to not hire workers, fire them, change their jobs, force "treatment" upon them, and other forms of harassment.

A related and particularly dangerous misuse of psychological approaches is to justify, in a circular fashion, administrative actions against individuals who, for whatever reason, have been in repeated accidents. In the present state of our knowledge, we cannot reliably attribute an individual's accident history to his or her psychological characteristics, and hence there are no grounds for basing administrative action upon psychological theory, or for attempting to validate psychological hypotheses on the basis of administratively accumulated accident histories.[53]

The assumption that 90 per cent of accidents are due to unsafe acts was exposed as a myth in Ashford's study, which showed that a third or less of accidental injuries or deaths were caused by unsafe acts, while over half were caused by unsafe and/or illegal conditions.[54] Nonetheless, identifying unsafe acts is often crucial to accident investigations. Unfortunately, this approach ignores the context of work. For example, a worker may be killed by a fall off a highrise construction, the direct cause being the "unsafe act" of not wearing a safety belt. However, safety belts may not be readily available, management may ignore their non-use, a speed-up to complete the project may produce lax standards, *etc*. Nonetheless, an "unsafe act" can be labelled as the most immediate cause. This protects the company and provides an easy

---

51 Jean Surry, Ontario Ministry of Labour, *Industrial Accident Research: A Human Engineering Approach*, March 1971, p. 162.

52 *Ibid.*, p. 163.

53 W. Hadden, E.A. Suchman, and D.A. Klein, *Accident Research: Its Methods and Approaches* (1964).

54 Nicholas A. Ashford, *Crisis In The Workplace: Occupational Disease and Injury* (1976), pp. 114-15.

means of identifying "causes" for accident reports, but does not get to the root of the problem. W. T. Singleton makes the following observation:

> Human errors are an important source of information about equipment design fault. . . . The only real solution is to design in such a way that safety devices and procedures are an inherent and necessary part of machines and tasks, as well as being emphasized in instructions and training schemes — for example, a fuse box so designed that it is physically impossible to open it without switching off the power is obviously safer than one that merely has a note saying "switch off power before opening box".[55]

The Victim's Perspective

We often consult "experts" to tell us why accidents occur, but what do the *workers* think? A survey of injured workers was conducted in one of Mason's studies.[56] In the survey, 618 claimants before the British Columbia Workers' Compensation Board were asked: "Is there anything you feel the Compensation Board should (or should not) be doing in the field of accident prevention?" There were 192 answers to the question and 70 per cent of them concerned more and better safety inspections and safety procedures. Approximately 22 per cent called for more safety instruction, with only one person asking for more Workers' Compensation Board advertising. A major thrust of many Workers' Compensation Boards is safety instruction and advertising, but workers identify the problem as one of establishing and enforcing rules, rather than just education.

In answer to the more specific question "Do you think there is any particular thing that could be done where you work to prevent accidents?", 70 per cent of the responses concerned machinery and equipment, working environment, and production. The workers gave relatively little emphasis to instruction and personal safety equipment, which were emphasized by employers and government.

Those closest to the reality of the workplace — workers — largely reject the "kinds of people" explanation of accidents, and emphasize "kinds of environment" factors such as machinery and "power/conflict" factors, such as policing and enforcement, as the appropriate means to deal with the problem. Those with the most power define the problem and the remedies. Unfortunately, management and government have tended to view health and safety problems as essentially education and training problems. No matter, however, how educated workers are, if hazards exist in the work environment, there will be injuries and deaths. The four workers who fell 36 storeys in Vancouver on 7th January 1981, were killed due to apparent defects in the scaffolding.[57] This is not to say that such programs are totally useless; however, they should not be the major focus of prevention programs.

55 W.T. Singleton, *Introduction to Ergonomics* (1972).

56 Keith Mason, Workers' Compensation Board of British Columbia, *Industrial Accident Survey*, June 1973.

57 "Workers' Fall Blamed on Faulty Scaffolding," *The Calgary Herald*, 3rd March 1981, p. C2.

The New Hype

Another example of the "blaming the victim" approach relates to the use of chemicals in the workplace. In this kind of approach "hypersusceptible" employees are "blamed" for their health problems. This leads to screening out certain employees and essentially finding the problem in the employees' "makeup" rather than in the workplace environment. In a critical analysis of the term "hypersusceptibility", Ashford points out its ideological and political uses.

> The term is abused in precisely the same way as the term accident proneness. By pursuing a policy of detecting the hypersusceptible worker for his own good, an industrial physician may perpetrate a "blame the worker" attitude on the part of management. Unfortunately, to many industrial physicians, "preventative medicine" constitutes identifying the hypersusceptible worker and recommending him for a job transfer — or, in the case of pre-employment examination, for no job at all. The removal of the health hazards, rather than hypersusceptible persons, should be the goal of preventative medicine.[58]

The use of hypersusceptibility may allow the screening out or firing of pregnant or potentially pregnant women, smokers, heavy eaters, diabetics, *etc*. The possibilities are endless for determining which "kinds of people" are more susceptible to hazards in the workplace. This policy provides a convenient "scientific" way for management to save money without changing a hazardous environment.

How is this perspective translated into practice? In the spring of 1980, it was revealed by the Canadian Chemical Workers Union that 43 employees of Johns-Manville Canada had died of asbestos-related diseases during the previous 12 years.[59] Unions urged action to investigate and deal with the crisis. In

58 Nicholas A. Ashford, *Crisis in the Workplace: Occupational Disease and Injury* (1976), p. 118.

59 Both U.S. and Canadian insurance companies stopped selling life policies to asbestos workers in 1918. Subsequent studies in the 1950's and 1960's found excessive death rates for asbestos workers, particularly from lung cancer. Conditions at the Johns-Manville plant, opened in Scarborough, Ontario in 1946, provide insight into the causes of such deaths. Men worked at the plant without respirators in dust so thick they could only see a few yards. In the mid-1960's, Dr. Irving Selikoff, internationally recognized authority on occupational diseases, visited the plant and predicted a high incidence of cancer deaths in the coming decade. Dismissing the claim as alarmist, management made little effort to improve conditions. Subsequently, over 50 workers (10 per cent of the workforce) have been disabled by chronic respiratory diseases, with 27 deaths from lung cancer.

Documents released in product liability suits against the asbestos industry in the United States show that a well organized cover-up of the ill-health effects of asbestos was engineered by representatives of Johns-Manville Corporation, Raybestos-Manhatten Incorporated, and other asbestos companies. The Subcommittee on Crime of the Committee on the Judiciary, U.S. House of Representatives, notes in its report on Corporate Crime:

> South Carolina Circuit Court Judge James Price (who reviewed the material), is quoted as saying "it shows a pattern of denial and disease and attempts at suppression of information" so persuasive that he ordered a new trial for the family of a dead insulation worker whose earlier claim had been dismissed. Judge Price noted that correspondence further reflects a conscious effort by the industry in the 1930s to downplay, or arguably suppress the dissemination of information to employees and the public for fear of promotion of lawsuits. Judge Price also noted compensation disease claims filed by asbestos insulation

the fall of 1980 Johns-Manville announced that it was instituting a ban on smoking in all Johns-Manville facilities that use asbestos fibres. Workers found smoking on company property ran the risk of losing their jobs.[60] Nothing was mentioned about eliminating or reducing the asbestos hazard. While smoking is hazardous to one's health, wherever one works, focusing upon it in addressing the problem of cancer leaves the work environment, and thus management, free from culpability. The need to clean up the environment, to lower levels of dust, and to perform other potentially expensive chores is sidestepped, and once again the victim is blamed on the basis of his or her personal habits. While smoking is carcinogenic, what of its combined effect with asbestos? What about the non-smokers exposed to the same levels? These and many other issues are ignored. Health and safety education becomes merely a ploy to avoid responsibility for establishing an inherently healthy work environment.

Alive: The Ideology of Death

On 5th February 1979, the Alberta Minister of Labour, Neil Crawford, announced the "Alive" campaign to attack problems of health and safety. According to the minister, "[p]ublic information can help reduce industrial accidents in Alberta".[61] The emphasis of the program is to help workers to stay alive by staying alert, through use of mass media advertising, posters and brochures, and has a promotional trailer which travels throughout the province. Like many other provinces, Alberta emphasizes education of the worker as a significant, if not the most significant, aspect of preventing health hazards. This is a particularly insidious form of blaming the victim, since few people are against education and training *per se*. But the point is not whether workers should become aware of hazards and how to protect against them, but whether this should be the major focus of prevention strategies. It is much better to eliminate the hazards rather than try merely to reduce their consequences through abstract calls for education and vigilance.

---

workers against several companies — which quietly settled them — including eleven asbestosis cases settled out of court by Johns-Manville in 1933, all predating the time (1964) when these companies claim they first recognized the hazard to insulators.

In a 1949 survey of a Canadian Johns-Manville plant entitled *Industrial Hygiene — Survey of Men In a Dusty Area,* seven workers were found to have asbestosis. However, the medical director deemed it "inadvisable" to warn the workers of the problem. Labelled the Asbestos Pentagon Papers, the documents, revealing deceit and cover-up, have led to numerous law-suits and compensation claims. But legal action cannot give back lives or good health. We will continue to reap the violence of asbestos for some time, notwithstanding reduced levels of exposure and more public concern. For both workers and non-workers, asbestos will continue to take its toll.

Subcommittee on Crime of the Committee on the Judiciary, House of Representatives, Ninety-Sixth Congress, Second Session, "Corporate Crime" (May 1980), p. 24. Samuel S. Epstein, *The Politics of Cancer* (1978).

60 "Johns-Manville Implements Smoking Ban at All Its Asbestos Plants", *Canadian Occupational Health and Safety News,* 18th August 1980, p. 2.

61 "Minister Introduces Alive Campaign" (1979), 3:2 Alta. Occupational Health & Safety 6.

The ideology of blaming the victim is particularly evident in the "Alive" posters, which have been displayed throughout Alberta. In one poster, "Lloyd's falling down on the job" because of his bad habits. Nothing is said about railings, safety straps, boots, wind, slippery conditions, or a multitude of other hazards Lloyd does not control. In another, Tom made "an ash" of himself and therefore will miss work. It is no wonder that workers generally, and unions specifically, find such accusations repulsive. While machines maim, smart workers do not get hurt. Frank was off guard so he "gave his right arm to work". Again the message is clear: workers cause accidents and only they can prevent them! No mention is made of changing the nature of machines, pace of work, routine or structure of the workplace, *etc.*

The message of these "Alive" posters is that workers are careless, and that one should not be too sympathetic to injured workers, because it is their own fault. The myth of the "dumb worker" is used to explain the increase in workplace violence by assuming that the "unsafe act" equals the "unsafe worker". It is difficult to determine whether such educational programs have any real preventive impact. In one study, 16 of the safety posters distributed by the British Columbia Workers' Compensation Board were evaluated by 1,051 claimants.[62] There was no significant statistical relationship found between seeing a poster and avoiding certain types of accidents. In other words, if Lloyd had seen that type of poster the accident probably would not have been prevented.

Adding Injury to Insult

The ideology of "blaming the victim" is a convenient political weapon of business and government which ignores the reality of health hazards in the workplace. The belief that the large majority of accidents are due to worker carelessness, accident proneness, or unsafe acts is a myth masquerading as a fact. It is not the worker, but the worker's environment, shaped by the policies, practices, and procedures of management, which creates health hazards. Management creates risks, to which workers are subjected and which government attempts to regulate. Since workers have no real power in defining "acceptable risk levels", these are generally taken for granted by management and government, and prevention efforts are aimed at the worker, not the workplace.

The absurdity of blaming the victim is particularly apparent in the case of chemical hazards. Generally, workers are not told what hazards exist, and have no control over the introduction or use of the chemicals, but are expected to "adapt" to their deleterious effects. If they happen to get burned or develop a disease, it is their carelessness, hypersusceptibility, or lifestyle, such as smoking, which is blamed. Likewise, worker stress and its consequences on and off the job are often viewed as due to workers' attitudes, paranoia, temperament, or other personal failings.

62 Keith Mason, Workers' Compensation Board, *A Survey Evaluation of Safety Posters,* June 1973.

The theory of the "big lie" says that if something is repeated often enough it will be taken for a fact. The ideology of the "dumb worker" has indeed permeated health and safety approaches. It is evident not only in educational programs directed at workers, but also in the policing of the workplace. It will take concentrated effort by workers and their allies to counter this prevalent mythology. The "view from above" has dominated health and safety approaches, and is only now being seriously challenged.

Currently across Canada there are continuous struggles by workers and their representatives to counter the "blaming the victim" view from above and argue that workers should be given more power concerning the nature and degree of risks in the workplace. The battle is being fought concerning such issues as the right to know of dangerous hazards, the right to refuse work which is unsafe, the right to participate in defining and policing "acceptable" job hazards, the right to sue negligent employers, *etc*.

This conflict is part of the larger class conflict evident throughout society. The principal victims of unsafe environments are the working class and powerless segments of society.

In a chapter entitled "A Part of the Class Struggle" Gersuny notes that

> refusal to work under what employees perceive as unsafe conditions evokes disciplinary penalties which in turn lead to grievances and cases of arbitration.
>
> Injury awards and compensation rates are frequently assailed as too high or too low, depending upon whether they are cost items or income items. Thus the issues of health hazards epitomize Marshall's description of class conflict over the terms of cooperation.
>
> Resistance to harmful conditions, refusal to work unless hazards are eliminated, the struggle over restitution as well as over legislation and its enforcement — these are basic processes of industrial conflict. In every case the parties to the work contract have divergent interests because the cost incurred by one side varies directly with the other side's "benefit" (for example, in the form of a safe and healthful work environment). So long as insufficient power is brought to bear in order to eliminate hazards, enterprises receive "a subsidy covered in blood, broken bones, broken health, physical pain, mental anguish and the ultimate trauma of death".[63]

A Crime Is a Crime, Is a Crime: Victims Without Crimes

The "view from above" is basically that "accidents" are best dealt with through regulatory laws. When those from below talk about crimes against workers and an "assault on workers", there is much resistance to this "ideological" approach.

Dr. Samuel Epstein describes his book, *The Politics of Cancer,* "as a book on white-collar crime on the one hand and also on the failed democracy. . . ."[64] Henri Lorraine, the president of the Canadian Paperworkers' Union, says that employers have killed workers by refusing to invest profits to

63 Carl Gersuny, *Work Hazards and Industrial Conflict* (1981), p. 16.

64 Quoted in *Canadian Occupational Health and Safety News,* 11th June 1979, p. 3.

improve working conditions.[65] Why do these men call it white-collar crime and killing, when workers die or are injured and disabled at the workplace? We have been taught to think of crime as involving an easily identifiable victim and offender. For example, if our spouse poisons us and we subsequently die, then we have been murdered by our spouse, who is liable to prosecution. If, however, our company causes us to be exposed to toxic substances, and we subsequently die from this exposure, the company is not criminally liable for our deaths and will at the most be cited for violations of health and safety regulations. For example, it has been revealed that asbestos companies continued to expose workers to that substance in spite of the fact that they had had evidence concerning its fatal effects for some 30 years. Such premeditated behaviour undoubtedly led to thousands of deaths and disabilities. Nonetheless, asbestos companies are only liable in civil lawsuits.[66]

Another example is that of Quasar Petroleum Ltd. of Calgary,[67] which was found guilty of violating job-site safety regulations, resulting in the death of three men. The law provided for a maximum fine of $5,000 or imprisonment of up to six months, or both. Quasar was fined $5,000 for killing the three men by not providing respiratory protective equipment and an external gauge on an enclosed tank; thus the men had to go inside the tank without protective equipment and subsequently were overcome by toxic fumes. Furthermore, the company had not trained the workers concerning the hazards of the job and the need for such equipment.[68]

Is this not just an unfortunate "accident"? No, the deaths of these three men could have been avoided if the proper training and equipment had been provided. While the company undoubtedly did not mean to kill these specific three men, it established the conditions for their death by violating the law. By analogy, we could view murder during an armed robbery as an accident. Most armed robbers do not intend to kill the robbery victim but merely want to make some money. Their act of robbery with a dangerous weapon, however, sets the conditions for such violence. Likewise, a company saving money by not purchasing safety equipment may be merely pursuing profit, but its action establishes the conditions for an "accident" or "disaster". Should the company which threatens the workers' safety and health for profit be any less culpable when death occurs than the armed robber who also threatens violence for economic profit?

The violation of safety and health standards and/or the failure to establish adequate standards is usually a conscious choice concerning capital expenses and business profits. In the public sector, it is usually a political decision to

65 "Industry Kills — Union Head", *The Calgary Herald*, 13th November 1979, p. A14.

66 "Asbestos Cover Up", *The Calgary Herald* 13th November 1978, p. A13; Lloyd Tataryn, *Dying for a Living* (1979); See also, Subcommittee on Crime of the Committee on the Judiciary, House of Representatives, Ninety-Sixth Congress, Second Session, "Corporate Crime", (May 1980).

67 *R. v. Quasar Petroleum Ltd.* (1979), 10 Alta. L.R. (2d) 147, 19 A.R. 9 (Dist. Ct.).

68 *Canadian Occupational Health and Safety News* (23rd July 1979), p. 3.

streamline a budget. In both the private and the public sectors, the consequences are the same. The maintenance of unsafe conditions is rational, since the likelihood of detection is low and the penalties are relatively small. No one has ever been imprisoned in Canada for violation of safety and health laws, although prison sentences are available in most provinces. The attitudes among many safety and health personnel reflect a lenient approach toward such law violators. One provincial head of inspection states:

> We are not dealing with criminals when we take people to court. A guy who breaks into your house knows what he is doing and knows the consequences and probably has been through the process before. To be dragged before a judge and be sentenced to twelve months in jail is not pleasant to him, but it is not unexpected, and it isn't demeaning to him; he will stand there with a smile on his face and be defiant. When we are talking about individuals or entities being prosecuted for infractions of Occupational Health and Safety legislation, we are talking about an entirely different animal. We are talking about a person who basically is honest and an upright citizen. We are talking basically of a person who finds this process of being prosecuted and having that process publicized extremely distasteful.[69]

We must look at the consequences of action or inaction. If violating safety and health laws does not cause a death, then the penalty should be less than if it does take a life, just as the penalty for armed robbery is less than that for murder. Unfortunately, current penalties for health and safety violations do not adequately consider this distinction between the law violation and subsequent violence and death.

Does the public view violence from law violation by an organization in the same way? A recent analysis of public survey data by two criminologists found that the public ranks organizational crimes having physical impact much higher in seriousness than those with merely an economic impact, just as the public ranks common crimes with a physical impact as more serious than those with an economic impact. Therefore, "causing the death of an employee by neglecting to repair machinery" is as serious as impulsive homicide or arson which kills someone.[70] Thus, the belief that the public does not view organizational crimes as crimes is wrong, particularly when they entail violence and death.

In their report concerning Criminal Responsibility for Group Action, the Law Reform Commission of Canada distinguishes between "real crimes" and "regulatory offences", when discussing corporate and organizational activity.[71] Real crimes are acts which affront the basic values of society and need to be condemned (in traditional legal language these are *mala in se*, or wrong in themselves). Taking another person's life and seriously harming

---

69 Quoted in G.B. Reschenthaler, Institute for Research on Public Policy, *Occupational Health and Safety in Canada: The Economics and Three Case Studies* (1979), pp. 82-83. See also Grant, *supra*, c. 4, and Mandel, *supra*, c. 7.

70 L.S. Schrager and J.F. Short, Jr., "How Serious A Crime?: Perceptions of Organizational and Common Crime" in G. Geis and E. Stotland (eds.), *White Collar Crime: Theory and Research* (1980), pp. 14-31.

71 Law Reform Commission of Canada, *Criminal Responsibility for Group Actions* (1976).

another person violates our value for life. "Regulatory offences" are deemed necessary for efficiency and convenient for the "public good", but do not violate basic values (these are called *mala prohibita* in legalese, which means that they are made wrong by positive laws). Many traffic regulations are of this nature. On the basis of this distinction, the Law Reform Commission does not recommend criminalizing corporate action. The omission is rationalized because of the purported problems of criminal intent and specific fault. A more appropriate route to follow, however, would be an analysis of the consequences of one's action or inaction.[72] For example, failure adequately to maintain your car may bring a fine; if, however, you run into someone and kill that person due to this failure, criminal proceedings may be pursued. Likewise, a company's failure to maintain safe machinery may bring minimal fines, but if this failure kills a worker the company should be held criminally liable. While this may sound extreme, it is necessary in order to dramatize the magnitude of the problem and to act as a deterrent.

Two Canadian legal experts, Glasbeek and Rowland, have reviewed attempts at stopping the assault on the worker through education, organization, joint workside committees, strong regulatory agencies, and injury tax schemes. They conclude that these are all deficient mechanisms since, for the company, profit ultimately takes priority over life, particularly when the costs of such attempts are weighed against the benefits. The authors then argue for the use of the criminal law, not as a "solution" but to spotlight the problem.

> If the physical onslaught which takes place in the workplace occurred outside the employer-employee environment there is no doubt that society would use the most formidable tool it has to stop such attacks: it would use the criminal process and treat offenders as social pariahs. Prosecution under the criminal law of employers for the harm they do to workers rather than reliance on existing safety and health regulatory schemes would characterize the conduct of such employers as an unjustifiable preference for unregulated profit over the well-being of human beings who are, after all, very important in the governing of such profits. Prosecution of entrepreneurial behaviour which can inflict grievous bodily harm or even death would thus identify the kind of conduct that warrants interference and regulation by government. Expectations that such interference would be more vigorous than it is now would not be misplaced. Indeed, it may become possible to talk openly about what is a "reasonable" profit in view of the need to reduce injury and disease to an "acceptable" rate. . .
>
> The use of the criminal process has another attraction. Because of the assumptions of the liberal state, the ideology of law requires it to claim that it punishes behaviour which has been judged unacceptable by society no matter who the perpetrator of the offensive behaviour is. It will be interesting to see how the administrators of the legal system respond when it is argued that entrepreneurs are offenders against the criminal process in much the same way as robbers of private property and people. It will provide something of an insight if the officers of justice resist the use of criminal prosecution in this context.[73]

The struggle to have some workplace violence designated as "crime" is at once an ideological and a legal struggle. While the impact may be minis-

72 See also M. Mandel, *supra*, c. 7, text to note 38, *ff*.

73 Harry J. Glasbeek and Susan Rowland, "Are Injuring and Killing At Work Crimes?" (1979), 17:3 Osgoode Hall Law Journal 507 at 522-23.

cule in terms of redressing hazards, it has a great deal of ideological significance for those resisting such labelling and those advocating it.[74]

In an ironic juxtaposition, the 11th October 1982 issue of *Maclean's* tells a "crime" story about seven people killed by poisoned Tylenol and a "labour" story about the Bendix Corporation's fight to stop compensation payments to two widows of workers killed at their now closed brake lining plant.[75] The "labour" story goes on to note that the Manville Corporation is reorganizing its corporate structure to avoid some $2 billion in potential lawsuits brought by more than 50,000 asbestos workers or their widows. The significance of ideology is nowhere more evident than in the identification of seven deaths as "crime" and thousands of deaths as "labour".

LAW; REAL AND IDEOLOGICAL CONSTRAINTS ON THE WORKING CLASS

H. J. Glasbeek

INTRODUCTION

Sticks and Stones May Break My Bones, But Words Will Kill Me

Here are some oft-heard assertions about trade unions and business:

1. The presidents of the C.L.C. and the Canadian Union of Postal Workers are trade union bosses.	1. The chairmen of the Royal Bank and Power Corporation are business leaders.
2. Trade unions are militant and irresponsible risk-takers with their members' jobs.	2. Corporations are aggressive, have drive and are bold risk-takers on behalf of their shareholders.
3. Trade unions threaten that they will take militant action against governments.	3. Business indicates to governments that it has lost confidence in them.

74 In 1975 a French magistrate, accompanied by a deputy, arrested and imprisoned the plant manager of a tar refinery where a worker had been killed. A court in Turin, Italy sentenced two owners, two managers, and the company doctor to prison for manslaughter in the deaths of eight workers who died of bladder cancer from toxic substance exposure. These and other incidents of the use of criminal sanctions are reported in C. Gersuny, *Work Hazards and Industrial Conflict* (1981), pp. 1-3. Balmoral Mines Ltd. was charged with eight counts of manslaughter after a cave-in in Val d'Or, Quebec which killed eight miners. The company was found not guilty, and the "accident" was alleged to have been a consequence of fate.

75 L. McQuaig, "A Matter of Compensation" (1982), 95:41 *Maclean's* 55.

4. Trade unions make demands of employers.	4. Employers make offers to employees.
Etc.	*Etc.*

Some Preliminary Assertions About Law

Law responded to the needs of capitalism by developing modern contract law. In the area of labour law this was of immense benefit to both capitalism and capitalists. The legal construct was also seen as a public good in that it supported freedom and individual sovereignty. Law became subject to the pressures of advancing capitalism's need for liberalism. Enfranchisement of non-property owners, including the new industrial working class, led to the granting of political rights to such non-property owners. When, in addition, it became manifest that, for free contracting to be seen to take place, some major interference with the market was necessitated by permitting collective action by workers, a danger arose that workers, with political rights, associated in economic/political groupings, would present a real threat to a body politic which perceived accumulation of capital by capitalists (that is, a minority of the population which owned the means of production), as the optimal goal. Law has played its part in creating and resolving this evolving tension. It has done so by relying on public perception for its initiatives and by tailoring those initiatives to reinforce the public perceptions which permitted them in the first place. In this context, the genesis of popularly held views about union and business activity of the kind sketched out above becomes comprehensible.

Further, the perpetuation of inequality in industrial relations does not depend on the idiosyncrasies of functionaries of the law, such as biased judges, stupid administrators, parasitic lawyers or inhumane arbitrators, but on something fundamental in the construct of law.[76]

PRIVATE CONTRACT AND CAPITALISM'S NEEDS

The essence of labour relations is that capital buys labour, just as it buys raw materials, for productive purposes. In law, this is facilitated by permitting individuals to enter into contracts in which labour power is exchanged for wages. The place of contract is pivotal in a liberal, democratic capitalist state. It is a recognition that all individuals are autonomous beings with a capacity to treat with each other. This sovereignty is to be respected. As a result, a principle was developed by the judiciary to the effect that freely entered-into contracts were to be enforced as they stood. The content of the bargain was not to be questioned by the courts, for this might have suggested that the contracting parties were seen as not capable of deciding for themselves what was good for them; that is, they would be seen not to be sovereign individuals.

Lawyers have obscured this general proposition a little bit because, in a number of cases, they were able to argue that one of the parties had not

76 See also M. Debicki, *supra*, c. 7, note 37, *ff*.

entered into the contract freely. Anything, from physical coercion to ignorance and/or abject ineptitude and helplessness of one of the parties, has been offered as a reason for judicial interference with the bargain. Textbooks and academic journals are replete with articles on the radicalism involved in the unconscionable contract doctrine (as the relief from unhappy contractual obligations has come to be called). The great significance of this preoccupation with these developments is that they are seen as deviations from a basic norm.[77] In this light, note that it has been pointed out that there are far more commentaries and examinations of the doctrine than there are cases where the doctrine was actually used to relieve a party from onerous contractual obligations.[78]

Be that as it may, it is certain that the courts never used the doctrine to relieve wage contractees from bargains which they did not like, no matter what the disparity in economic power between employer and employees had been.[79] Indeed, the contrary was true. So miserable was the position of workers who were blessed with the freedom to bargain for wages in exchange for their labour power that they sought to strengthen their bargaining position by seeking to form monopolies over labour power. They formed unions. The idea was simple: if employers purchasing wage labour could not reduce their costs by having access to a competitive labour market, they would have to pay more for labour than they otherwise would. In this light, trade unions in capitalist society can be seen for what they really are: a reaction to a particular kind of economic situation. Naturally, this collectivism threatened to undermine the doctrine of contract based on the premise of bartering between sovereign individuals. Employers would be coerced into contracts which they would not otherwise have made; employees would not be able to accept bargains which otherwise they might have accepted. Courts reacted savagely. They did everything in their power to stymie trade union organization and activity. Imprisonment, deportation, heavy fines, stigmatization were the order of the day. But workers stubbornly refused to be subjugated. As political rights were won by non-property owners, elected assemblies became more sensitive to these working class struggles and gave grudging recognition to the existence and partial legitimacy of trade unionism. The emphasis is on

77 The argument that the centrality of individual contract-making is reinforced by highlighting the deviant nature of new developments, as in the case of unconscionability, is a major theme of this presentation. The reasoning is that by emphasizing the aberrant nature of collective bargaining, the ideology of individual contract-making is bolstered.

78 A. Leff, "Unconscionability and the Code — The Emperor's New Clause" (1967), 15 *Univ. of Penn. Law Rev.* 405 at 486 & 549 found that at one stage there had been one decided case under a statute encoding the doctrine of unconscionability, but 130 learned discussions.

79 In a remarkably revealing passage, it was noted that slavery would not be tolerated, but anything less oppressive than that would have to be assessed on its facts: see *Davies v. Davies* (1887), 36 Ch.D. 359 at 393, 3 T.L.R. 839 (C.A.) (per Bowen, L.J.); and *Horwood v. Millar's Timber and Trading Co. Ltd.*, [1917] 1 K.B. 305, 33 T.L.R. 86 (C.A.). To illustrate, there is nothing in common law contract law preventing an employer from commanding an employee to work overtime. Minimum standards legislation has been required to stop potential abuse of this power, for *e.g.*, *The Employment Standards Act*, R.S.O. 1980, c. 137, Pt. IV, ss. 17-22.

partial: the basic attitude was that collectivism was a blight on the contract landscape, one that should only be permitted to spread if there was no alternative.[80]

CONTRACT AND LIBERALISM

The concept of contract did not earn its sacrosanct place merely because it obviously helped the dominant class to oppress the working class. Legal institutions and functionaries clasped it to their bosom because it provided legal support for the ideology of the day. The emphasis was on freedom. No longer were people's rights, privileges, duties, and obligations dependent on where and to whom they were born, on whether they owned property, had right of entry to a craft, *etc.*, but rather all individuals were equally free to make the optimal use of their abilities and assets as they saw fit. Their ensuing material conditions were the result of voluntary choices and luck. No conscious, external force hampered the exercise of choice. In this context, it was a moral virtue to enforce bargains just as they were made, because it gave legal force to promises made by a free individual acting in his/her best interest. Assuredly, nothing could be more laudable than giving legal endorsement to such solemnly, voluntarily made promises. Thus, the doctrine of upholding bargains between unequal contracting parties (in the sense of not having equal economic bargaining power) was not just perceived as a way to support the allocation of resources in accordance with the needs of the dominant class in society, but also as a means to progress toward a more moral, freer society.[81] This belief reigns supreme today. Courts and legislatures are fond of referring to the fundamental precepts embedded in private contract-making and their superior qualities

80 The story has been told in many places. Among many texts and articles, see, for a survey of legislative history arising out of judicial activity and social development, Hickling (ed.), *Citrine's Trade Union Law*, 3rd ed. (1967); for an angry denunciation of judicial creativity in defence of pristine contract doctrines, W. Wedderburn, *The Worker and the Law*, 2nd ed. (1971); for an argument about the peculiar development of the partial immunity given to U.K. trade unions, W. Wedderburn, "Industrial Relations and the Courts" (1980), 9 Industrial Law Journal 65. Note that Wedderburn was arguing for a fuller legitimation of trade unionism and collective bargaining in the U.K. to make the U.K. position comparable with other jurisdictions, including Canada. This is not the place to make the argument, but it is to be noted that it is not, legally speaking, accurate to describe North American trade unionism as more than partially legitimated. Moreover, there is a good case to be made that complete legitimation (whatever that means), may not be such an advantage for the working class. That case must be made on another occasion.

81 In jurisprudential terms, there had been an evolution from a status society to a contract society. See Henry Main, *Ancient Law* (1861), c. 5. This has been hailed as a liberating development and, indeed, it is; see O. Kahn-Freund, "A Note on Status and Contract in British Labour Law" (1967), 30 M.L.R. 635. This is not to say, however, that this jurisprudential change worked to the immediate material benefit of the multiplying nineteenth century working class; see H. Ruegg, *Law of Employer and Workman in England* (1905), p. 14; see also H.J. Glasbeek, "The Contract of Employment at Common Law" in Anderson and Gunderson (eds.), *Union-Management Relations in Canada*, (1982), p. 47. [See also, J. Hogarth, *infra*, c. 9.]

over those to be obtained from other kinds of allocative mechanisms. Given the pre-eminence of legal institutions and functionaries in the creation and dissemination of ideology,[82] this adherence to the crucial nature of individual contract-making has a major influence on moulding public opinion which, in turn, reinforces law-makers in their approach.

THE IMBALANCE IN INDIVIDUAL LABOUR CONTRACTING: THE LEGITIMATION OF COLLECTIVE BARGAINING

As it became more and more apparent that private contract-making about terms of employment left a vast army of individuals competing for scarce jobs in very feeble bargaining positions, causing them to accept horrible working conditions, the state developed primitive forms of relief. Factory Acts to alleviate dangers at work, protective statutes concerning child labour, minimum wages, maximum hours, vacation pay, and, most recently, maternity leave, *etc.*, were passed and continue to be passed.[83] Similarly, as trade unions kept on being formed, incremental changes in attitude toward the legitimacy of trade unionism became perceptible, until World War II conditions made it essential to buy off trade unions. Our modern collective bargaining system was spawned.[84] Trade unions were given the legal right to create

---

82 By ideology here I mean the belief system which is so ingrained that it is comprised by beliefs and values which human beings take for granted. There is such certainty about these values that they are seldom debated; see L. Wirth in his introduction to K. Mannheim's (Wirth and Shils (trans.)) *Ideology and Utopia: An Introduction to the Sociology of Knowledge* (1956). Mannheim, at p. 40, wrote:

> There is implicit in the word "ideology" the insight that in certain situations the collective unconscious of certain groups obscures the real condition of society both to itself and to others and thereby stabilizes it.

Thus, although ideas and concepts ought to arise from the objective material conditions in which human beings find themselves, it may well be that illusions are created about the reality of conditions and relations which create, in the Marxian phraseology, a "false consciousness". Such illusions are likely to be perpetuated if their underlying premises are not debated. It may well be that such false consciousness, if it exists, benefits certain groups in society and disadvantages others. Law, as an enunciator of norms and principles, has great influence on both the formation and retention of perceptions. It has such influence for a variety of reasons which include: the apparent independence of the judiciary, a process which permits a large amount of participation to disputants who seek adjudication, the assertion that the adjudicator applies a set of rules derived from unchallengeable principles which coincide with the non-debatable values which make up the existing ideology, the asserted responsiveness and public accountability of legislators, when formulating law, to the consensus represented by that ideology, *etc.*

83 For a useful overview of Canadian legislative history, see Edith Lorentsen and Evelyn Woolner, "Fifty Years of Labour Legislation in Canada" (1950), *Labour Gazette*.

84 For an account of the legal history, see A.W.R. Carrothers, *Collective Bargaining Law in Canada* (1965), Pt. I. It is pertinent to note that collective bargaining did not arise solely out of the state's sense of altruism. In the U.S.A. the precursor of Canadian legislation was, in part, the result of legislators' reaction to working class lobbying and needs. It also found supporters because it was thought that individual capitalists did not know what was good for American capitalism and that they took too much advantage of the depression to bust unions, drive down wages and generally reduce the ability of people to consume. That is, in fact the

monopolies over clusters of previously competitive labour forces. Here then was an apparent departure from pristine contract precepts.

Yet, the predominant ideology was not abandoned. Theorists justify the collective system by pointing out that the basic values promoted by contract law are enhanced by collective bargaining. The scheme provides for the enforceability of promises and obligations after voluntarily-entered-into agreements between the employer and employees have been reached. The major difference between this and the common law contract regime is that the bargaining position of the individuals has been improved by permitting the employees to withhold their services in concert at some specified juncture in the bargaining. In this sense, collective bargaining legislation is not unlike minimum standards' legislation: it ensures that working conditions will not drop below certain levels, but does so not by specifying those levels but rather by creating more bargaining equivalence than would otherwise have existed. This is considered sufficient assistance to otherwise disadvantaged bargainers because of the assumption that collectivism of the kind permitted will create a rough economic equivalence. This, in turn, makes it possible to characterize the agreement-making as voluntary, because the conditions are not prescribed by any outside authority; they are the product of the parties' consensual arrangement. The inherent value of contract-making is thus preserved and, even though something might be lost in theory because employees no longer bargain as individuals, much is gained because the individuals are more truly sovereign when banded together as a bargaining unit.

Now, it is true that the state has had to intervene. It had to guarantee the framework in which appropriate trade unions for appropriate bargaining units can flourish. This required a process of certification and supervision which ensured freedom of choice in the selection of bargaining agents. The theorists see this as a facilitating role, typical of neutral state instruments implementing social policies. That is, the voluntariness of the system is not perceived as being impaired by the state intervention. Moreover, in contrast with individual contract-making, the parties have more direct control over the settlement of disputes arising out of collective agreements. They are permitted to devise their own dispute settlement mechanisms, provided that disputes will be settled ultimately (if necessary) by an arbitration board constituted with the parties' agreement. Unlike common law contract disputants, the parties are thus given much more direct control over their own agreements. Voluntarism and sovereignty are thus furthered. Finally, all of this is achieved in circumstances which allow employees in the bargaining unit to exercise rights analogous to democratic, political rights. They can compare unions and, then, vote for union A over union B, or for no union at all; they can participate, by

labour relations' statute was part of the New Deal program, a mechanism to increase aggregate economic demand. See Forkosch, *A Treatise on Labor Law*, 2nd ed. (1965), pp. 525-27. Similarly, in Canada, although there had been some stirrings in response to unions' demands to have an Act similar to the 1935 American one enacted, it was not until the state found itself in a position which required working class cooperation to fight the war that the state made the necessary adjustments.

debating and voting, in decisions about the work conditions to be fought for and accepted; and, they can participate in the same way in decisions as to whether individual disputes should be taken through the grievance and arbitration process. In sum, the system can be, and has steadfastly been, portrayed as one which provides all the goodness of individual contract-making and which, in addition, gives employees a special status, one analogous to citizenry in society at large. As freedom, including political freedom, is the raison d'être of the legal system's worship of the individual contract model, collective bargaining can be acclaimed for achieving that model's objectives better than a pristine implementation of the model ever did.[85]

---

85 It need not be stressed that theoretical supporters of the collective bargaining regime are far more sophisticated in their reasoning than the above text makes out. Indeed, they go out of their way to assert that they support collective bargaining precisely because it is such a great advance over the individual contract of employment legal regime. It can provide more benefits, gives workers a greater chance to control their own working lives and disenfranchises the unsympathetic, individualism-biased judiciary. All of these developments are seen as evidence of progressive evolution, one warranted because the prior situation was unfair, unacceptable. Indeed, the conventional wisdomeers have gone out of their way to declare the individual contract of employment doctrine obsolete; see *McGavin Toastmaster Ltd. v. Ainscough,* [1976] 1 S.C.R. 718, [1975] 5 W.W.R. 444, 75 C.L.L.C. 14,277, 45 D.L.R. (3d) 687, 4 N.R. 618. For an example of the argument that a new morn' has dawned see H.W. Arthurs, "Developing Industrial Citizenship: A Challenge for Canada's Second Century" (1967), 45 Can. Bar. Rev. 786. But this disassociation from the contract regime does not arise from an abandonment of the values associated with the common law contract model. To the contrary, its genesis is that the common law contract regime can no longer be seen as bringing home the bacon. The values can only be given concrete meaning through new machinery, collective bargaining. In a significant attempt to evaluate labour relations in Canada, the Woods' Commission, after consulting every major theoretician in Canada, as well as major participants in the scheme, defended collective bargaining on this very basis. After noting that free contract-making accorded with all the basic precepts of our society evolved over the centuries, including Magna Carta, the English Bill of Rights of 1689, the United States Bill of Rights, our own (then) declaratory Bill of Rights (1960), the United Nations Declaration of Human Rights, and the preamble to the U.N.'s Charter, and had permitted a remarkable degree of political and economic freedom (unequalled in socialist or authoritarian countries), the Task Force went on to note that there was occasional malfunctioning in capitalism, requiring some intervention. Minimum standards' legislation and collective bargaining were offered as sensible, necessary modifications of the individual contract model which had served us so well because, at least, collective bargaining had similar values embedded in its machinery; Canadian Industrial Relations, The Woods' Commission, The Report of Task Force on Labour Relations, December 1968, paras. 22-37. Finally, to confirm tangentially that the supporters of collective bargaining regime aspire to achieve the very same goals as the proponents of the original free enterprisers who cheered for the common law contract, note that it is the openendedness of collective bargaining which is seen as its prime value. The parties' wishes are to be respected. Voluntariness is to be promoted; there should be no interference with the bargaining process once the initial intervention of sanctioning collective action has taken place. That is, the contents of a collective agreement are not the business of anyone; if workers want to agree to work for peanuts (compare peppercorns of contract law fame) that is their decision. They have been given all the help the ideology of contract permits. It is this approach which forms one of the bastions of opposition to imposition of terms by means of compulsory arbitration or some such mechanism.

COLLECTIVE BARGAINING AS AMPLIFIED INDIVIDUAL CONTRACT; THE RESTRAINING EFFECT OF THIS ON THE POLITICAL/ECONOMIC POWER OF THE WORKING CLASS

From the point of view of containing working class aspirations, a major advantage is obtained, despite the advent of collective bargaining, by retaining the perception that contract, with its moral connotation, is a basic aspect of a liberal, democratic state. Collective action is seen as a privilege which may be taken advantage of in a very limited set of circumstances, namely, when it promotes the values explicit and implicit in the individual contract-making model. Now, individual contract-making is, by definition, about economic subject-matter. Unsurprisingly, despite the grandiose descriptions of collective agreements as constitutions or legislative instruments governing the parties' relations,[86] the substance of collective bargaining is not about political rights (in the social sense) of the participants (which is what those descriptions imply), but about economism. Rights which would be termed political rights in the usual sense of that phrase are given by the legislation creating the system (freedom to associate, politically to control one's union, *etc.*) not by the collective agreements which are negotiated. Canadian collective bargaining legislation ensures that negotiations be so limited:

(i) As an essential prerequisite, it requires that individual employees sell their labour power to a particular employer. While the negotiations about the conditions of employment are now collective, the basic premise that individual labour power is exchanged for remuneration remains intact.

(ii) It requires that the collective agreement be struck on behalf of a bargaining unit of employees, comprising a number of the employees of one common employer. That is, the fundamental assumption is that the array of new rights (both economic and political) is primarily to be used to obtain more of what was theoretically obtainable by employees when bargaining as individuals *vis-á-vis* the same employer: more material gains and more control over the work process (which is often confusingly called the political aspect of collective bargaining).

Some reasons for the apparent enthusiasm the public has for the oppression of working class economic and political aspirations now can be seen to emerge from these fundamental tenets of collective bargaining, tenets which reflect, albeit in a modified form, the essence of the ideology of individual contract-making.

---

86 See *e.g.*, O. Kahn-Freund, "Legal Framework" in Flanders and Clegg (eds.), *The System of Industrial Relations in Britain* (1954), p. 42; G. Adams, *Grievance Arbitration of Discharge Cases* (1979) (see the collective agreement as a rule of law governing continuing relations, breaches of the law, being like breaches of legislation, punishable in the setting of the ongoing relationship); see also S. Kadish, *The Criminal Law and Industrial Discipline as Sanctioning Systems: Some Comparative Observations* (1964).

Right to Refuse to Buy or to Sell Labour Power

A voluntarily made collective agreement, like a voluntarily made contract and for the same reasons, should be binding. Its terms should be inviolate for its duration. Accordingly, regardless of the terms, regardless of changes in conditions, parties must live with the agreement for its prescribed life. Any attempt to force a change in terms should not be tolerated: the law should see this as a punishable breach; public opinion should characterize it as a breach of a solemn promise, made after enormous concessions had already been made to one of the parties, the employees, by permitting them to act collectively. The law does treat such conduct as an offence; public opinion does perceive it as an abuse.

Theoretically, the argument of continuing adherence to the agreement applies to both parties, but in fact it constrains employees far more seriously than it does employers. If for some reason employees want conditions changed in the face of employer resistance during the life of a collective agreement, they can only do so by concerted withdrawal of services.[87] This will be seen and treated as a legal *and* moral misuse of the privilege given by the statutory right to engage in some collective action. If, however, the employer wishes to change conditions in the face of employee resistance during the life of a collective agreement, the hurdles to clear are different. The employer does not have to lock out employees to achieve its aim. (Note that the lockout is the legal equivalent of the strike.) Rather, the employer can always close down its operations. This is the legal equivalent of *individual* employees quitting their employment. This is permitted because (in the world of private contract-making) it is seen as an exercise of freedom that each party to a personal services contract must have, namely, the right to refuse to work with the other. If this freedom were not held sacrosanct, we should still be in the primitive world of slavery and/or status. Note here that this individual contract of employment precept is part and parcel of collective bargaining law because each individual worker must still sell his/her labour power in exchange for remuneration as an individual.[88] Given, then, that the employer, unless it

87 If the dispute can be categorized as arising out of a term of the collective agreement, the employees will be able to use the grievance process to resolve their problem. But this remedial route is not available when new conditions obtain, *e.g.*, escalating cost-of-living, unthought of technical innovation, unexpected availability of independent contractors, *etc*.

88 One of the claims of collective bargaining proponents is that the collective regime has provided the greatest advance over individual contract-making precisely in this area, demonstrating not only its superiority but also its distinctiveness. The reasoning is that arbitrators can, by exercising remedial authority, force the employer to employ a worker whom it sought to dismiss. The remedy of reinstatement is seen as a serious brake on the crude exercise of managerial prerogative. For assertions which typify conventional arguments to the effect that this power to modify discipline indicates how far we have come, see G. Adams, *supra*, note 86. Note further that when the Supreme Court of Canada suggested that arrogation of remedial power was inappropriate in *Port Arthur Shibldg. Co. v. Arthurs*, [1969] S.C.R. 85, 70 D.L.R. (2d) 693, supporters of collective bargaining (many of whom were participating greivance arbitrators) set up howls of protest and successfully lobbied for ameliorating legislation; *see Labour Relations Law, Casebook* Group, 2nd ed. (1974), p. 333, for an account of the politicking. But what is important for the test is that such limited specific

has contracted otherwise,[89] may always close down all or part of its operation, it follows that it can always threaten to close all or part of its operation. In such circumstances (which are rare in good times, but commonplace in bad times — *vide* the concession talks all over North America), a union may very well have to agree to reopen the collective agreement for renegotiation. Because the employer has not breached the law and has, in fact, exercised a fundamental contract right (the right to take its capital wherever it wishes), there is neither legal repression, nor public opprobrium demanding legal repression, of its conduct.[90] By contrast, a union which insisted on retention of the terms negotiated at the last contract-making would assuredly be called irresponsible if this insistence on its legal right led to lay-offs or total loss of jobs for its members.

In the same vein, the equivalence between investor and labour seller prior to entering into an employment relationship remains illusory. While it is true that because of the freedom of contract principle, no one need sell his/her labour power to a particular employer and that, therefore, once a relative monopoly is created over labour (by permitting unionization), employees have some leverage in coming to terms with an employer, it remains palpably true that the employer has more choice in determining whether or not to invest and, if the employer does, how much to invest, than employees have in deciding whether or not to sell their labour power and, if they do, how much of it to sell. A decision not to invest capital unless favourable conditions obtain is not seen as a matter of controversy. Neither would a decision not to seek work unless conditions were right attract attention, unless such a head-strong individual looked for support in making his/her choice not to work by demanding social welfare or unemployment insurance benefits. There's the rub. Workers, as a fact of capitalist relations of production, have to offer themselves for employment. Where collective action is permitted, they must seek to obtain terms and conditions from a party — the employer — who had a right (and, relatively great power) not to invest in the first place. Thus, except in those rare circumstances where there is a shortage of labour and an

---

performance orders in no way affect the might of the employer to close down for business reasons, nor to suspend employment for business reasons. Further, it may well be that the finely graded system of punishments, which has grown up around the remedial power to order specific performance, often has great advantages for the employers' productive needs and constrains the workers' chance of wresting away some control over the relations of production. But that is another debate.

89 For an indication of how seldom trade unions have been able to force protection against severance and redundancy-type terms into collective agreements, even in good times, see Carrothers Commission, Labour Canada, *The Report of the Commission of Inquiry into Redundancies and Lay-offs* (1979).

90 As economic times have become worse, employers have so frequently used their legal right to close part or all of their enterprise so that it has been necessary to pass legislation to make this a little more costly to the employer by providing for compulsory severance payments to dismissed employees in certain circumstances, *e.g.*, Employment Standards Act, R.S.O. 1980, c. 137, s. 40a [en. 1981, c. 22, c. 2(1); am. 1984, c. 31, s. 1]. The very frequency of closures makes the threat to dismiss or to lay-off all the more effective.

employer, to run a profitable enterprise, must seek out employees with a real choice as to whether or not to sell their labour power to a particular employer, workers have to act positively. They must offer themselves for work, organize as best as they can and bargain. They have to initiate the process. Note the paradox: the force of reaction, the trade union, has to adopt the guise of the aggressor. Workers are *seen* to demand, employers are *seen* to offer. Insistence on particular terms by workers, to the point of withholding labour, can thus easily be characterized as an abuse of power. Peculiarly this is the more probable perception where there is a mature enterprise. The employer can no longer easily relocate; its power to make a *free* investment choice is more limited. The workers have been given a monopoly over labour to offset the initial bargaining disadvantage they had. If they now play hardball, as the law permits, they may still be stigmatized. Is social munificence to be repaid by an exercise of naked power against a risk-taking employer who did not have to make the investment which provided work in the first place? This kind of reasoning lies behind much of the talk dominating public discussion. This attitude leads to questions as to whether confrontational collective bargaining should not be replaced by a collaborative system; anxious eyes are cast at Japan. Cries of despair as to why trade union leaders cannot act responsibly are heard rending the firmament of labour relations. The notion of responsibility (that is, not hurting the adversary), in a scheme under which voluntary action which may amount to economic warfare is legitimated, makes no theoretical sense.

Part of the reason for these attitudes can now be seen to flow from the nature of law, its educational force and the particular form it has adopted in labour relations matters. By maintaining the crucial nature and inherently inviolate role of individual contract-making in society, it places collective actions at a serious disadvantage in the political debate. It makes it so easy to make the case that trade union conduct is dangerous, anti-democratic, anti-social and abusive, that theorists and legislators who have created this very situation frequently posture as defenders of trade unionism and *free* collective bargaining. The irony is real.[91] Note further that public opinion is the more likely to be opposed to collective action by workers because, while the law insists that the stereotypic collective bargaining relationship is "one employer — one local of a trade union" (the agent for that employer's work force), unions are portrayed and perceived as huge, centralized bargaining entities. By way of illustration, the might of the Steelworkers' Union is legendary.

91 That Canadians' political and institutional leaders respect free trade unionism, at least in rhetoric, goes without saying. In 1919, Canada, as one of the High Contracting Parties to the *Treaty of Versailles*, endorsed the right of employees to belong to unions (Part XIII) and later ratified the International Labour Organization *ILO Convention* No. 87, which underwrote the same precepts. After the introduction of modern collective bargaining had given these declamations of intent substance in a context where basic values such as freedom, sovereignty and voluntariness were said to be furthered, it became impossible to challenge the rights to associate and to strike in the ideal. For the theorists, it has always been necessary to accept strikes and dislocations as a way to avoid real trouble; see Woods' Commission, *supra*, note 85, p. 9, paras. 392-403.

When Inco has a fierce fight with Local 6500 of that union, there is a tendency to believe that it is the powerful Steelworkers which is battling one lonely employer. All the experts know this to be a farrago. Yet, the public is not so enlightened and no one seems to take the trouble to change its mindset. This misconception makes it more plausible to portray militant (that is, successful) trade unionism as an abuse of the generously granted privilege to use collective power in some circumstances.

An Antinomy: Collective Bargaining, But Not Solidarity

The legal system, for the reasons outlined earlier, has created a scheme which stays as close to the individual contract-making model as is consonant with the grant of some collective bargaining rights. Hence, the "one employer — one unit of employees" context. By definition, this means that the power for such bargaining units to act in solidarity with workers' struggles everywhere is legally denied by the system. When workers in, say for example, the retail industry are engaged in a strike, employees of the retailers' suppliers cannot seek to influence the struggle by coercing their employer, unless there is such a close link between the retailers and the suppliers that they are in fact, if not in law, interrelated enterprises.[92] This will be so even if the retailers' and suppliers' employees belong to the same trade union. Coordinated activity of this kind by workers is thus seen as potentially unacceptable. Whatever the economic merits of the argument (and it might be sensibly argued that, as a matter of economics, for there to be true equivalence between parties, employees must be given some control over market conditions over and above that given by being certified to use collective power *vis-à-vis* one employer), it becomes clear that not only does the law severely inhibit secondary boycott activity (that is, it inhibits exercises in workers' solidarity), but that such activity is yet another factor which helps create the perception that workers exercise undue power in society. The reason for this is that workers engaged in secondary boycott-type conduct will be acting at an ever-greater degree of remoteness from the fundamental mode of bargaining, *viz.*, individual contract-making. To allow a certified bargaining agent of employees working for one employer the use of collective power is enough of a distortion, enough of an attack on fundamental relationships. More than that is intolerable.

Indeed, this kind of reasoning is so persuasive that it convinces workers; it helps to separate workers from workers. Because collective bargaining is seen as a limited struggle, a whole series of particularistic battles, any

92 The ally doctrine, as it is known, leads to much legal argumentation, but for the purposes of this paper, it is sufficient to know that there are serious restrictions on solidarity-type activity. For studies of this subject matter, see D. Beatty, "Secondary Boycotts: A Functional Analysis" (1974), 52 Can. Bar. Rev. 388; J. Manwaring, "Legitimacy in Labour Relations: the Courts, the B.C. Labour Board and Secondary Picketing" (1982), 20:2 Osgoode Hall Law Journal. What is interesting is that the writers disagree about the width of permissible secondary boycott activity, but not about the fact that there are severe constraints.

spill-over effect of other workers' actions is seen, by the workers affected, as well as by the law and the public at large, as an excessive and unwarranted use of labour power. Calls for solidarity, being both illegal and antithetical to the moral ethics teachings of private contract-making, are rare and when made, coolly received. The working class is thus effectively fragmented by labour law, and the ideology it helps create and perpetuate.[93] Gramsci's[94] notion that the triumph of capitalism will be to have workers voluntarily accept the dominant class's sense of right and wrong has been largely realized.

Let me return now to the point made earlier about the perception that unions are stronger than they really are because their total membership, supported by a large central bureaucracy, is believed to be *the* actor in economic bargaining, whereas in fact, local branches of the union, often of minimal size, are the real participants in the legitimated economic struggles. While it is true that large memberships (because of the payment of dues) and efficient central bureaucracies (because of their supply of technical expertise) are of great help in local struggles, the foregoing analysis makes it clear that a local bargaining agent cannot usually call on members of the same union for support in the way of sympathy strikes or similar economic support, even where the same employer, in a separate corporate guise, in a different jurisdiction, employs members of the same union.[95] This is also true when support from members in other unions is sought.

Again, we see the significance of maintaining the ideal of individualistic bargaining precepts and its alleged promotion of liberal values: it has ensured legal restriction of collective action; it has reinforced the notion of the connection between liberal values and individual contract-making; it has made, by implied antithesis, collective action by workers as a class, by region, by union and, even by industry, the enemy of those sacrosanct values. To underscore this, note that if legitimated collective bargaining schemes permitted One Big Union-type organization,[96] it would still permit the following claims to be made on behalf of the system:

(a) the ensuing agreements would be voluntarily reached;

(b) the workers could vote not to have a union, or a union with a different structure or leadership, *etc.*;

---

93 For example, a postal workers' strike will affect workers in a mail order business. Their natural concern may well be turned into antipathy because of their feeling, reinforced by the sermonizing of the law, that the use of collective power is not an inherent right and should not be used to excess.

94 Antonio Gramsci, J. Mathews, (trans.), *Selections from his Political Writings, 1910-1920* (1977).

95 This may also be true even when the legally separate corporate activities are in the same jurisdiction, provided there is nothing which courts or labour relations boards would call an "ally" relationship between them.

96 A notion which is no more tolerated today than when it was savagely repressed in the aftermath of the Winnipeg General Strike.

(c) the workers could decide which dispute to settle by pursuing the grievance process, which to bargain away, *etc*.

That is, the values so beloved and said to be furthered by the existing schemes would still be capable of being enhanced. There would, however, be quite different economic outcomes, as the attempt to create more bargaining power for workers would be far more successful. It is to be remembered that the existing collective bargaining machinery is justified on the basis that it creates more equivalence than does the pristine common law contract model. But apparently, too much bargaining power for workers is not to be granted. Thus, how useful it is to treat deviation from the contract model as a breakthrough of immense proportions, a privilege which must not be abused![97] Not only is the public fooled, but workers *qua* workers are.

A False Antinomy: Politics Separated From Economics to Enfeeble Workers

The utility of treating the fragmented right of workers to exercise collective power as a necessary but limited departure from the ideal of individual contract-making is enhanced by the fact that this approach constrains the subject-matter of bargaining to economic and, to a very small degree in Canada, work process issues. More importantly perhaps, economics is defined as narrowly as it was when that legal instrument for basic capitalistic relations, the modern contract, evolved. Thus, on the face of it, it appears ridiculous for a local of a garment union to insist that the garment manufacturer, with which it bargains, do its best to stop this country from selling Candus to countries which do not sign the nuclear non-proliferation pact. It seems even stranger to think that it might be useful for those same workers to assert that they will not enter into a collective agreement unless their employer agrees to ensure that trade barriers will be erected against clothing made in the Third World. Not only can the employer not affect these matters, but they are also not characterized as economic demands in the narrow sense in which individual contract-making envisages that term. Thus, from both the perspective of the law and that of the contract-model dominated public psyche, such demands are deemed unacceptable. The privilege of collective bargaining was not granted to destroy the most basic dynamic of our free enterprise society, namely that the

97 There is yet another ideological tool at work here. It was noted that one of the assumptions is that the state neutrally intervenes to create equivalent power in workers. It is thus assumed that the certification of a bargaining agent is, in some unspecified sense, a fair process. It is nothing of the kind. Labour relations boards (i) select bargaining agents for bargaining units which suit the production processes of the employer, and (ii) try to ensure that the units are not too big so that, if there should be a strike, the disruptive effect will be minimized (*per* P.C. Weiler, "Insurance Corporation of British Columbia, *et al*," [1974] Can. L.R.B.R. 403 at 407), and not too small, so as to accommodate all the diverse interests of the employees. To permit such fragmentation would face employers with lengthy, protracted and expensive bargaining, making it impossible to carry on "viable and meaningful collective bargaining" (*per* O. Shime, *C.U.P.E. and the Board of Education for the City of Toronto*, [1970] Ont. L.R.B.R. 430 at 436. See H. Glasbeek, "TIP: Another Weapon in the Class War Waged against Workers" (1981), 3:2 Can. Taxation 94.

greatest good for all will be obtained by maximization of individuals' *economic* opportunities which, in legal form, is promoted by contract-making between roughly equal bargaining partners.[98]

Yet, there is something disingenuous about this widely shared view that collective bargaining should only be concerned with economic matters. After all, it is very easy to argue that working conditions are at least as much affected by the government's policies in relation to tariffs, customs, taxation, unemployment insurance, welfare, manpower, health and safety, competition, foreign investment, *etc.*, as they are by bargaining between individual employers and their employees (whether singly or through their representative unions). Why should workers not be able to use their bargaining power to influence policies which vitally affect their existence?

The answer given is that the policies which affect workers' economic conditions are determined in the political arena. Therefore, these policies must be fought over in that arena. Workers can vote; they can lobby; they can form parties, *etc.*, just like everyone else. Workers do all of these things. Frequently, they are publicly led by trade union leaders and/or by trade union umbrella movements, such as the C.L.C., and the like. There are, in fact, institutional leaders who can be politically consulted. But workers cannot exercise their economic power to give those leaders real clout. Those leaders cannot ask workers to withhold their services in order to convince politicians to vote one way rather than another. This would require breaches of the law. Employees working under collective agreements or negotiating for them, would be withholding their labour at times when this is not permitted and/or would be doing so in support of demands which are not economic, not individualistically contract-like. Talk of general strikes, of rotating strikes and of concerted trade union activity in response to government policies perceived as anti-working class has to be muted.[99] Conduct that permits workers to transform the morally sound concept of applying group pressure for the purpose of narrow economic self-defence into an immoral use of artificially created economic power by applying group pressure for the purpose of exercising political muscle, potentially destroying the delicate fabric of a liberal, democratic society is not only illegal, but is an abuse as well. Trade

---

98 By such opportunity-maximizing efforts, demands will be matched by supplies. The demands emanating from individual decision-making will decentralize and diffuse the nature of decision-making. Government will hardly be needed. Individuals, who freely choose what demands to make and what supplies to offer, will have their needs satisfied in this manner. Freedom is enhanced without much reliance on what is popularly termed political action. This is an ideal model; no one believes it can exist in pristine form. But that we should strive towards attainment is a crucial aspect of the ideology underlying the claims of freedom of contract and/or collective bargaining. The most famous proponent of the ideal model is, of course, M. Friedman, *Capitalism and Freedom* (1962).

99 It is therefore no accident that when workers tried to fight the federal government's 1975 wages and prices control program, their one day general strike was termed a Day of Protest. Employers used the law to punish workers and trade unions for the legal offences inevitably committed and for the moral outrage of it all; see H. Glasbeek, *supra*, note 97, p. 108.

union leaders making "political" demands are thus easily characterized as bosses making threats.

Juxtapose this with the position of employers. They, too, are affected by government policies. They, too, can vote, lobby, form parties, *etc*. They do all of these things. In addition, because of the contract paradigm whose hold has not been shaken by the much-lauded novelty of modern collective labour relations, they can withhold investment in order to persuade governments that unless certain policies are adopted, political difficulties can be expected because of the economic crises which will follow investment shortfalls. Failure to invest is not only legal, it is morally praiseworthy. The decision to take a risk must be left to the individual who is, in the world of the individual contract-making model, by definition, in the best position to determine what is in his/her best interests. Given that individuals acting in their own economic interest are enhancing their own liberty and, by decentralizing and diffusing the power of any institution (in particular the state) to make decisions, promoting everyone's liberty, such individualistic economic opportunism is both laudable economic *and* political conduct. When investors refuse to invest they are, therefore, merely business leaders expressing a loss of confidence in government. In this legal and philosophical framework, it is appropriate for a politically sensitive government to take note of their views. Leaving aside whether politicians really want to aid capitalists rather than workers, the pervasive effect of the individual contract model has created a public understanding in which restoration of a climate which will encourage capitalists to invest can easily be seen as a public responsibility.

To emphasize the advantage given to employers/investors by this state of affairs, note that in a liberal, democratic nation, such as Canada, it would be unthinkable that the power and inherent right given to individual decision-makers to determine whether or not to take a risk would only be given to property owners. The equivalent right to the capitalist's absolute discretion to invest is the unemployed worker's right not to offer the sale of his/her labour power unless government policy renews his/her confidence. Somehow the use of this *economic* freedom of the individual worker does not seem as *politically* effective as that of the individual employer. Yet, by maintaining that the narrow economism of individual contract-making is to be the focus when concerted activity by workers is permitted, the relative political and, therefore, economic impotence of workers is perpetuated.

The State as Employer: The Falseness of the Antinomy Revealed; Politics and Economism Permitted to Merge to Enfeeble Workers

As the state is seen in a consensus society merely as the apparatus which implements popular will, the services it renders are seen as an entitlement of all citizens. Inasmuch as the state has to engage workers to render services, the legal construct of contract is used. That is, workers sell their labour power to the state in exchange for remuneration. As it became clear that in this sector, just as in the private one, the individual contract model had to be modified because of the notion that equivalence of bargaining power was a myth, collectivization of workers became legitimized.[100] But, it is instantly clear that every economic demand made of this employer is also a political one, because every decision about the funding of one program affects other state programs and policies. The state has, therefore, severely circumscribed the rights of state employees to use collective power. In some jurisdictions, they are not allowed to strike at all.[101] In others, they may strike after complying with elaborate processes, but they may still only do so if the subject-matter of the dispute is one which permits collective demands to be made. Thus, the state might (as does the federal branch of the state) forbid collective action pertaining to specified subject-matter in addition to any matter that has been dealt with in government legislation.[102] Patently, the state is expressing that certain areas are to be left to political as opposed to economic decision-making.

In this context, whenever state workers withhold their labour, it is easy for the public to be scandalized by such an abuse of power. The public servants (who, it may be reluctantly granted, have the right to better themselves economically by bargaining hard like everybody else) do not have to take these jobs. That is, like capital investors, they can choose whether to take a risk or not. The sale of labour having taken place, the state has granted them more equivalence by permitting some collective bargaining. But to attempt to use this privileged position to alter the priorities of the state is intolerable. It squarely raises the question as to who governs the nation: the elected representatives or their servants who are only in a position to mount a challenge because of the munificence of the state. Once again, there is irony in this apparently inevitable chain of reasoning. I noted earlier that it was considered bizarre to permit workers to make demands of employers which the employers did not have in their power to meet. Now it turns out that where the employer is in a position to meet such demands, the economism of the labour contract model (both individual and collective) still forbids workers from making such demands.

Public opinion to the effect that collective action by state workers (note the significance of the more commonly used term public *servants*) ought to be

---

100 Public servants were slow to seek such organization. In part, they accepted the notions of more ancient times that they had special obligations. In part, they had much greater security of tenure than workers in the private sector which, by giving them more dignity, enhanced their perception of special status and obligations. When workers in the private collective bargaining sector obtained more security and better benefits, and public servants increasingly performed work which was also undertaken in the private sector due to the fact that the state began to transcend its role as a supplier of goods and services not provided by the private sector, the call to equality of treatment became stronger. For a discussion of this history see K. Chatarpaul, *Labour Relations in the Public Service With Some Emphasis on the Ontario Civil Service* (unpublished LL.M. Thesis, Osgoode Hall Law School 1978).

101 See, *e.g.*, Crown Employees Collective Bargaining Act, R.S.O. 1980, c. 108.

102 Public Service Staff Relations Act, 1966-67 (Can.), c. 72, s. 1 [now R.S.C. 1970, c. P-35, s. 1].

severely limited is understandable in a society which believes in a separation between economics and politics, and has had that strenuously reinforced by the legal regimes which apparently spring out of a social consensus laying claim to political liberalism. Another source of support for this public perception is that (perhaps because of the mixed nature of the state as employer and political functionary) until fairly recently, the individual contract model was not the bastion of state employment. Rather, the relationship between the state and public servant was much more paternalistic. A remnant of that period is that public servants have much greater job security than private sector employees. Thus, it becomes easy for the public to be outraged at the idea that a less risk-taking person should claim the same privilege to bargain from strength as those in the private sector. Again, the permeating effect of individual contract-thinking is revealed in this rather prevalent attitude.[103]

All of this shows how easy it is for a government to clobber its employees. It can count on public opinion when it asserts that the overriding national (or provincial) interest requires that the *privilege* to act collectively must be withdrawn from *public servants* because the exercise of economic rights is, in fact, the exercise of political rights. Accordingly, collective economic power (which is, after all, unnatural) can justifiably be removed. Only on this basis can a state, wedded to liberal precepts associated on both an individual and collective level with free contracting, legitimately order people back to work. This happens with increasing frequency in Canada.[104] Only on this basis can a state, wedded to liberal precepts, including the sacrosanct nature of voluntarily-made contracts, attempt to roll back terms of existing agreements, as in the federal government's "6 and 5" program. Only on this basis can such a state remove the right to bargain collectively completely after holding out that people were entitled to rely on it, as in the "6 and 5" program.[105] In respect to this last matter, note that a government which has passed legislation enshrin-

---

103 See *supra*, note 100.

104 Postal workers are often so treated by the federal government (*e.g.* 1978, 1979), as are longshoremen (*e.g.*, St. Lawrence Ports Operation, 1972, 1975, West Coast Port Operations, 1972, 1975, Port of Halifax, 1976), railway workers (1973), grain handlers (1974), air traffic controllers (1976, 1981), postal service workers, (1978, 1980), *etc.* Similarly, in British Columbia, elevator construction industry workers in 1976, hospital workers in 1976, and railway and ferry workers in 1976, were ordered back in this way. In addition, in 1977, the province passed the Essential Services Disputes Act, 1977 (B.C.), c. 83 [see now Essential Service Disputes Act, R.S.B.C. 1979, c. 113], which can suspend all collective action where the government deems the services essential. In Quebec, workers in the construction industry were ordered back to work in 1970, as were public servants in the 1972 common front strike, transit workers in 1975, health services' workers in 1975, 1976, teachers in 1979; in Ontario, transit workers in 1974, 1978, elevator construction industry workers in 1973, teachers in 1976 *etc.* Note that a great number of these workers were not public servants in the narrow sense, but rather rendering services which the state supplied by funding, or had an interest in maintaining, if supplied by private enterprise. This emphasizes the point made in the text about the artificiality of the separation of economics from politics.

105 Public Sector Compensation Restraint Act, 1980-81-82-83 (Can.), c. 122.

ing the freedom to associate[106] is saying that it agrees that its employees may form economic unions, provided that they do not use the economic power for which this right to associate was intended to be used. The letter of the law may have been obeyed; its spirit is being denied. This oppression could not have been as easy to accomplish (and the polls show the public approve) if the split between economic and political had not been so deeply ingrained that the state, as a political guardian, therefore had the mandate to override the economic rights of some individuals when their assertion of those rights interfered with political decision-making.

SUMMATION

Material conditions determine the relations of production. They determine that some persons have capital to invest and others only labour power, and permit investors to appropriate the profit made from labour power as a result of investing capital. Neither law nor public opinion creates the material conditions. They do, however, have an impact on the perpetuation, modification, and abandonment of the relations created by these material conditions. In Canada, law has accommodated the capitalistic nature of the economy by giving pre-eminence to the doctrine of individual contract-making.[107] This echoes the spirit inherent in capitalism, as well as meeting its needs. Values such as individualistic sovereignty, free exchange and the least possible fettering of liberty by the state are associated with the values of a liberal, capitalist society and are perceived as being promoted by the legal system's contract doctrines. This is such a strong, underlying set of values that it is not debated. It is proper for the law to support these values. When political enfranchisement and economic reality led to the acceptance of collective mechanisms, they were created in the shadow of individual contract precepts, although not in the same legal garb. Consequently, it has been defensible to limit the amount of collective power given to workers. It has been feasible to treat the issue of bargaining under collectivism as one relating solely to economics, just as the individual contract regime, by definition, did. This has been aided by the fact that democratic political rights can fairly be said to be available to workers as individual citizens. Workers accepting these overwhelming ideological constructs have thus accepted fragmentation of their interests. Further, the public view that economics are economics and politics are different is reinforced. This prevents the public and workers from seeing the interrelationship of economic and political power which gives capitalists/investors/employers a dominant say in the exercise of democratic

106 Constitution Act, 1982, Pt. I, Charter of Rights and Freedoms, s. 2; Canada Act, 1982 (Eng.), c. 11, s. 52. In addition, the "6 and 5" program, in spirit at least, may well be contrary to the right not to have property taken away without compensation, and to the right to be treated equally before and under the law, and to the right of equal protection of the law and benefit under the law. This is a topic for another debate.

107 And, of course, the inviolate right to own property without which all of this discussion would be moot.

rights. Even where the distinction between employer and political institution is patently non-existent, it is possible to argue that economic and political activity rights must be kept separate. This plays a significant role in persuading the public that state workers' incomes should be severely restrained.

Law not only provides the necessary legal structures and institutions for the capitalist economy; in our context it does better than that — its structures and institutions support the creation of a false consciousness.

THE STATE AS ARBITER IN LABOUR-MANAGEMENT DISPUTES AND THE EVER-WIDENING CONCEPT OF ESSENTIAL SERVICES

Andy Wachtel

[Andy Wachtel's research reflected these negative attitudes towards "big labour" but also showed similar attitudes towards "big business" and "big government". He agreed with Glasbeek that the state has merged economics and politics to intervene not only in strikes by public employees but in all major labour-management disputes.]

PUBLIC OPINION OF ORGANIZED LABOUR

Some years ago, two colleagues and I were engaged in research on public images of law.[108] We focused on areas that touched the everyday lives of our interviewees, including some aspects of labour law — particularly that commonplace of public opinion, the strike/lockout. In all the areas of our inquiry, there was apparent a patterned response, reflecting not a consensus of viewpoint but a notably consistent set of issues which respondents addressed. That is, there is a virtual consensus about what the important points are on which a person is expected to hold opinions and also considerable agreement on the sorts of evidence on which those opinions are properly based.

On the whole, the views we elicited could be construed as cynical — in terms of the questions addressed — but they were hardly cynical in tone. Indeed, the overall impression was very consonant with the stereotypic Canadian quest for "order and good government". Our informants, regard-

108 This paper deals with a fragment of a much too ambitious research project conceived by the late Dr. Pauline Morris. Funded mainly by the Solicitor General, the research unfortunately was not carried out by her but by myself, Brian Burtch, now at the University of British Columbia and Carol Pitcher-LaPrairie, now on the research staff of the Solicitor General.

less of class, presented a series of earnest and well-intentioned notions about the civil individual which my colleagues and I dubbed "the cult of responsibility" — a cult with many priests, not a few prophets, but unfortunately few adherents.

This same righteously judgmental tone was applied to the area of labour-management relations, but here at least the tenor as well as the substance was cynical. We uncovered a singularly widely-held set of images, none of which will surprise public opinion pollsters. It is a set[109] which has been well-documented in the U.S., and the production and perpetuation of these images by the media have been meticulously studied in Great Britain by the Glasglow University Media Group.[110]

In brief, this set of attitudes includes:

(i) that unions were a rational and just response to intolerable conditions faced by earlier generations of workers, but are now too powerful;[111]

(ii) that unions promote featherbedding and retard technological innovation;[112]

(iii) that union leaders run union affairs — and notably, strikes — to advance their personal and political ends;[113]

109 Tables below from the Gallup Polls deal with a single opinion issue, whereas our research emphasized constellations of attitudes, that is, correlated sets which reflect (sometimes ideologically coherent) macro-images. On attempts to use these polls in this fashion, see D. Yankelovich, *New Rules* (1981).

110 Glasgow University Media Group, *Bad News* (1976).

111 Canadian Institute of Public Opinion (19th November 1980). Generally speaking, and thinking of Canada as a whole, do you think that labour unions are a good thing or a bad thing?

	1979	1980
good thing	50%	54%
bad thing	35%	30%
don't know	16%	15%

Do you think that labour unions are becoming too powerful?

too powerful	68%	65%
not powerful enough	7%	7%
about right	19%	19%
don't know	6%	8%

112 *The Gallup Poll, 1972-1977 (1978)*, vol. 1, p. 105 (22nd March 1973). Laws wanted against featherbedding in the U.S.

	yes	no	no opinion
overall sample	55%	32%	13%
families with labour union member	44%	43%	13%

113 Canadian Institute of Public Opinion (19th November 1980). Do you think the views of the labour union leadership are or are not representative of the views of the ordinary labour union member?

	1979	1980
yes, representative	23%	28%
no, not representative	58%	52%
don't know	20%	20%

(iv) in B.C., there is also a strong notion, played up in the media, that union leadership has somehow been seized by English and Scottish demagogues, and industrial strife in the province is an imported "British disease";

(v) that no one wins a strike and the public loses.

This list expresses the modal opinions of our less than representative sample. Of course, there were people who disagreed on each point. It is, however, significant that both yea and nay sayers formed opinions around these rather cynical notions.

COMPARATIVE VIEWS ON MANAGEMENT AND GOVERNMENT

It is important to note that this set of views on unions has its counterpart with regard to management, particularly big business (and predictably, in Canada, multi-national corporations). There too, images of power, greed, and lack of social responsibility are prevalent. One might suppose that notions of mismanagement and adventurism are creeping into this mixture, given public awareness of the issues of "corporate bail-outs" (and refusals by governments to bail out firms, such as the recent DeLorean debacle), and loan restructuring crises in the national and international banking systems. (The inherent biases in the bargaining system between labour and management, analyzed by Glasbeek, in the previous discussion, may modify this lack of confidence in management.)

Attitudes toward the third actor — government — in this tripartite arrangement would hardly seem to require attempts at documentation. Public cynicism about governmental motives and actions is an entrenched feature of almost any state system. Indeed, one could argue that the fickleness of popular support for national leaders is both a mark of and a partial counterweight to underlying cynicism; confidence is very fragile but the capacity for hope has not been entirely undermined. One might predict that, under normal circumstances, disaffection with government would be greater than with either big business or organized labour, because supporters of each of the latter have grave reservations about the former. In any event, polls demonstrate a gradual trend towards increased disillusionment with all three.[114]

---

114 Canadian Institute of Public Opinion (18th August 1982):
Which is the greatest threat to Canada in the years to come?

	big business	big labour	big gov't	don't know
1982	13%	29%	46%	12%
1981	16%	28%	44%	12%
1980	20%	36%	29%	16%
1976	18%	43%	33%	13%

Comparable U.S. Poll *The Gallup Polls 1972-1977 (1978)*, vol. 2, p. 961 (30th January 1977).

1976	23%	26%	38%	13%

Canadian Institute of Public Opinion (2nd October 1982):

GOVERNMENT AS ARBITER AND THE EXTENSION OF THE CONCEPT OF ESSENTIAL SERVICES

Given this general crisis of legitimation, it is curious that a strong countervailing tendency persists, in which people look — however unhappily — to government as the natural arbiter in labour-management disputes. Specifically, a consensus has more or less built up around the notion of government intervention to maintain "essential services". While there might even be enough support for an outright ban on the right to strike by workers in health and public safety, public opinion clearly finds an answer in legislation which prohibits the total withdrawal of such services.[115]

Public sentiment tends to emphasize dispute resolution — and persons who do not like the notion of prohibiting strikes join with those for whom

---

How would you rate the honesty and ethical standards of people in these different fields?

	High	Average	Low	Can't say
Business Execs	18%	61%	18%	3%
M.P.s	14%	46%	39%	1%
Labour Union Leaders	12%	34%	52%	2%

Comparable U.S. Poll *The Gallup Polls 1972-77 (1978)*, vol. 2, p. 1009-16 (26th March 1977):

confidence in

Big business	12%	55%	27%	6%
Congress	12%	63%	19%	6%
Organized Labour	16%	56%	23%	5%

115 Canadian Institute of Public Opinion (21st October 1981):
Do you think that workers should or should not have the right to strike?

	yes	no	no opinion
1981	56%	34%	10%
1978	59%	30%	12%
1977	57%	30%	13%

Canadian Institute of Public Opinion (22nd September 1982):
Do you think strikes by civil service employees — such as office workers, postal workers, customs officials, *etc.* — should or should not be forbidden by law?

	yes	no	no opinion
1982 (national)	62%	33%	5%
(union members households)	53%	43%	4%
1980 (national)	51%	41%	8%
(union member households)	40%	54%	7%

Comparable U.S. Poll *The Gallup Polls 1972-77 (1978)*, vol. 1, p. 562-65 (2nd September 1975):
Do you believe strikes by the following categories of public empllyees should or should not be allowed?

	yes	no	no opinon
police (national)	41%	52%	7%
(union member households)	54%	44%	2%
firefighters (national)	39%	55%	6%
(union member households)	52%	45%	3%
garbageworkers (national)	47%	46%	7%
(union member households)	65%	32%	3%

strikes are anathema, to consider a quite different regime, compulsory arbitration.

> The public for thirty years has favoured compulsory arbitration. One plan which has consistently been backed is for a government-appointed committee to decide an issue and compel both sides to accept terms, if after seven days the union and the employer cannot reach an agreement.[116]

For a number of reasons, state intervention has not gone headlong in this direction.[117] There does, however, appear to be increasing pressure for state intervention (*e.g.*, back-to-work legislation) across an ever increasing front. In fact, it is the growth in the scope of this intervention which is of greatest interest. The argument originally revolved around the issue of whether or not civil servants have a right to strike.[118] Where that is granted, the argument moves to the point of whether the strike must be limited and essential services maintained. But the logic of that point extends beyond the public sector to any labour-management dispute which causes disproportionate public hardship.[119]

Nor is there any logical reason to stop at this point.

> The public interest in the private sector of the economy, intensified by the increasingly powerful collectivities of labour and management, has become of primary concern to our society.[120]

That is, in troubled economic times, people become more acutely aware that the government is concerned not only with a polity but with an economy, in which there is a public stake. Any significant labour-management dispute that threatens our economic well-being provides scope for state intervention. The recent dispute which tied up the port of Vancouver marks a step in this direction. The government justified intervention on the basis that this closure affected prairie grain-growers and Canada's reputation as a trading nation much more than it did the interests of the parties directly involved.

TOWARDS PUBLIC (EXTRA-LEGAL) DISPUTE RESOLUTION

Public approval for ending work stoppages is bolstered not only by perceived self-interest but also by a number of the notions listed above. If strikes/lockouts are no-win situations, it is a kindness to end them. If labour

---

116 *The Gallup Polls 1972-77 (1978)*, vol. 1, p. 565.

117 See, E. Fisher, and H. Starek, *Mediation-Arbitration and Vancouver Police Negotiations: 1945-1975*, (unpublished).

118 See Canadian Institute of Public Opinion (22nd September 1982), p. 8.

119 Canadian Institute of Public Opinion (21st October 1981):
What about strikes in occupations where the public is seriously inconvenienced — such as strikes by employees of the postal service, airlines, railroads, or the telephone service?

	yes	no	no opinion
1981	23%	73%	5%
1978	31%	63%	6%
1977	34%	59%	8%

120 The Pand Commission, Royal Commission of Inquiry into Labour Disputes, Ontario (1968).

leaders are mere adventurers, better to rein them in. If management's capacity for good decision-making, even in the corporation's narrow interests, is suspect, why not take it out of its hands?

One might conjecture that the public interest in "business as usual" means that any major labour dispute is now fairly within the public arena. In order for the notionally "ordinary" process of collective bargaining and dispute to be allowed to progress without the call for state intervention, the private parties to the dispute must be prepared to convince the public that there is no public interest involved. Public relations increasingly supplants labour law:

> Public sector strikes are not won or lost at the negotiating table or on the streets. They are won by the persuasive ability of the union or management with the community.[121]

Again a British Columbia example, the strike in the summer of 1982 of the B.C. Government Employees' Union, may lay claim to be at the cutting edge of this tendency. The union contrived to conduct a strike that teased rather than threatened the public.

LABOUR LAW AND PUBLIC POLICY IN A CYNICAL SOCIETY

John Crispo

[John Crispo, on the contrary, stated that governments were becoming increasingly cautious about ending strikes, because of their cynicism (shared by labour and management) about compulsory arbitration, despite the general public sentiment favouring binding arbitration. (See previous discussion by A. Wachtel.)]

INTRODUCTION

I have been wondering why I was invited to participate in this conference. At first, I thought it must be due to my well-known cynicism, a characteristic acquired in the face of world trends working against the hierarchy of values and institutions I hold dear, embracing what may be termed fundamental western values, liberal democracy, mixed free enterprise or modified capitalism, collective bargaining and trade unionism, none of which are faring well these days.

---

121 L.T. Paterson and J. Liebert, Management Strike Handbook (1974), p. 22.

After listening to the four other speakers, I have concluded that the real reason I was asked to join this panel was to defend the *status quo*, if only for the sake of fairness. Nonetheless, my cynicism precludes an all-out defence, which in any event the present system does not deserve. It does require some major reforms and repairs.

SOME CAUSES OF CYNICISM

My own reasons for cynicism began in the collective bargaining field, spread to the economic domain, and culminated in the world of politics. As for collective bargaining, I have always recognized that the process is as important as the result. Even so, one can only take so much of the ritual dance which is part and parcel of the collective bargaining process before becoming somewhat disenchanted.

On the union side, it is disillusioning, though understandable, to experience labour leaders requesting the imposition of compulsory arbitration, where it will get them off the hook, despite the labour movement's party line against this unwise form of government intervention. It has its humorous side, of course, when the same labour leaders explain that publicly they will have to condemn the government in question for doing what in private they have asked of it.

On the management side, it grates to see the champions of capitalism and free enterprise lining up at the public trough for government bail-outs of one kind or another. Understandable as the motives of these "corporate welfare bums" may be, it hardly suggests that they are true to their professed convictions.

Turning to the political sphere, I can be non-partisan in my scorn. Trudeau's constant contempt for us all is degrading. Whether with respect to wage and price controls, energy prices, or Dome bail-outs, he seems to feel no compunction about telling us one thing one day and doing the opposite the next.

Looking west we have had the spectacle of two provincial Conservative parties successfully outbidding their N.D.P. counterparts in terms of fiscal irresponsibility in order to win elections.

Dick Martin and the other speakers have suggested ample reasons why labour leaders are so cynical about the role of labour law and public policy. I cannot explain the apparent lack of cynicism among the public at large. I suppose that the average citizen has no idea what is happening.

LEGITIMACY IN LABOUR LAW AND PUBLIC POLICY

To begin, I must quarrel with Harry Glasbeek's professed concern about the degree to which labour law and public policy are used to reinforce the existing socio-economic-political order, since this phenomenon prevails in every society. Whether it is Poland or Russia, Britain, Sweden, or Canada, the establishment uses law and public policy in general to strengthen their version of the appropriate order. On balance, I prefer our alternative, if only as the least of the evils and not as the best of all possible worlds.

Having conceded the link between labour law and public policy, and the existing socio-economic-political order, let me now state the three most legitimate roles of labour law and public policy in our kind of society. First, they should facilitate and indeed promote collective bargaining and trade unionism among groups of workers who wish to take advantage of them. In this respect, I would liken our labour relations Acts to our corporation Acts, which are correspondingly designed to facilitate and promote corporate forms of doing business for those who prefer to operate in this manner.

The second purpose of labour law and public policy should be to establish the reciprocal rights and responsibilities of organized labour and management in their dealings with each other and with the public at large.

Third, there is the challenge of protecting the public interests in collective bargaining. The first of these interests should be that of preserving the process itself since it is such an integral part of the hierarchy of values and institutions referred to at the outset.

The second of these public interests pertains to the procedural results of collective bargaining, that is to lost time due to industrial conflict in the form of strikes and lockouts. Here again, I must part company with Glasbeek who seems to believe in the unlimited right to strike and, I presume, to lock out. Since no right can be absolute even in the most free society, I accept the need to place some limits on these rights. One can quarrel about where the limits should lie but surely not about their necessity.

The third public interest relates to the substantive results of collective bargaining and particularly to the purported link between negotiated wage increases and inflation. While collective bargaining can become part of the inflationary process, it is no more likely to do so than any of the many other cost and income settling mechanisms in our economic system.

SHORTCOMINGS IN OUR LABOUR LAW AND PUBLIC POLICY

There are at least three major problems with our labour laws and public policies, which help to explain why so many labour leaders have become cynical. In the first place, the administration of our labour legislation has become so costly as to put justice beyond the reach of many smaller unions and even some smaller employers. To a great extent this is due to excessive legalism and the propensity of lawyers to be more interested in scoring points, setting precedents, and winning cases than in settling problems.

A second set of concerns arises out of the futility of some of our laws. At one end of the spectrum is the fact that it is proving difficult to dissuade employers from discriminating against workers for engaging in union activities. At the other end is the commensurate difficulty of trying to prevent unions from engaging in illegal strikes.

In this general context, I cannot resist following Dick Martin's well-taken point about the double standard with respect to jailings for infractions of our labour laws. Like him, I do not want to see any more jailings of union officials. Too often they seem all too willing to go to jail for the lifetime sinecure it assures them in their union offices as martyrs to the cause. Fines are a much more telling way to punish unions for major infractions of the law.

On the other hand, maybe we should jail responsible management officials when an employer violates critical provisions in the legislation. Even on the employer side, of course, there is the risk that those jailed will form the nucleus of a *cause célèbre*. Absent jailings in such situations, the fines imposed on enterprises must be heavier, since in many instances they constitute little more than licence fees to carry on the offence.

A third and most disturbing cause of concern grows out of the flagrant abuse by government of labour law and public policy, if only on an *ad hoc* basis. On the procedural side, Trudeau ordered an end to a legal C.U.P.W. strike even before it began. Not to be outdone by his political ally, Davis handled a T.T.C. strike in Toronto in roughly the same manner. Even more excessively, David Barrett of the N.D.P. terminated three legal strikes in B.C. in a crass but futile political gesture designed to improve his political image just before an election in that province.

On the substantive side, we now have "6 and 5" and various provincial equivalents of this highly discriminatory form of wage controls aimed at public employees. While wage restraint was called for in much of the public service, this was not the way to achieve it. Instead, governments should have suspended all forms of contract arbitration and simply refused any excessive union demands through the normal course of collective bargaining.

Nothing has produced more cynicism among labour leaders than this unfair effort by government to make public employees and their unions the scapegoat for our inflationary problems. As politically popular as this con and distraction may prove, it is hardly worth the damage it is doing to the possibility of any meaningful labour-management-government cooperation. Moreover, it has little or nothing to do with the desperate need for the beginnings of a solution to our stagflation crisis.

THE NEED FOR BALANCE

What has gone wrong in our industrial relations system is no different than what afflicts our socio-economic-political system in general. In all areas, we have lost sight of the need for balance in the sense of no group having the unrestrained ability to run roughshod over the rest of us.

No group behaves in the public interest unless it is in its own interest to do so. We have created in this country a system under which it is in no group's self-interest to behave in the public interest, as groups are not being called to account for their abuse of society.

The challenge is to begin to reverse this process by introducing or restoring more balance between the contending interest groups in our society. In the field of collective bargaining this requires more deft use of such concepts as accreditation and joint bargaining. It is especially necessary to provide for a review of existing bargaining relationships, where undue imbalance of power on either side appears to have arisen. At least, our labour boards must be empowered to realign existing bargaining units when they no longer provide the locus of an appropriate balance of power between the parties.

It is equally important to apply this same prescription to other areas of cost and income setting. Some mechanism must be developed to contain the self-governing powers of the professional guilds so that they may not use those powers arbitrarily to feather their own nests. It is also vital to ensure that the price and supply management powers of marketing boards be either rolled back or exercised from a consumer as well as a producer point of view. Finally, mention must be made of the disturbing absence of an effective competition policy designed to preclude undue monopolization of any product or service.

If we fail to move in this direction, then we shall become increasingly vulnerable to the emergence of a corporate state in which the only issue becomes the relative amount of power each group is able to extract from the state. The result will be a process that has everything to do with the unbridled pursuit of self-interest and nothing to do with the public interest. It is perhaps this frightening possibility that makes me so cynical.

PART III

THE DYNAMICS

9

WHY DO PEOPLE OBEY, OR DISOBEY, THE LAW?

Are public attitudes about law and legal institutions significant factors in "law abidingness"? Chief Justice Deschênes thought so. If they are, what are the dynamics? How is a general attitude about the legal system translated into specific acts of obedience or disobedience? How do attitudinal factors relate to the other social and psychological mechanisms involved? The papers in this chapter examine aspects of these questions in a wide variety of contexts.

OBEDIENCE AND CYNICISM

Joseph Raz

INTRODUCTION

I have argued elsewhere that there is no general moral obligation to obey the law.[1] That is also one of the themes of Professor Friedenberg's paper.[2] I will not repeat those arguments here, but shall turn to a couple of brief comments on their implications.

The absence of a general obligation to obey the law is a significant fact. The significance of this non-obligation is indirect. It shapes our thinking about the law, and thus indirectly and subtly it shapes our behaviour. But one should be careful not to draw the wrong conclusion. This is not to suggest that we can all start breaking the law whenever we feel like it. There are, in most cases, plenty of reasons to obey the law of a reasonably just society, reasons which do not depend on an obligation to obey the law.

Some may think that instead of an obligation to obey the law there is an obligation either to obey the law or to break it and submit to its penalties. This is saying too much and too little at the same time. It is saying too much, for

1 See e.g., J. Raz, *The Authority of Law*, Pt. IV (1979).

2 See E. Friedenberg, "Law in a Cynical Society?" included *infra*, c. 13.

even though there is no general obligation to obey the law, on many occasions, there are strong reasons to obey, and it is often wrong to disobey, at least in a relatively just society. It is saying too little because where it is not wrong to break the law, it is often not wrong to try to evade the penalties for doing so. Laws imposing penalties have no greater claim to our respect than laws imposing duties.

Clarifying the proper moral attitude to the law is not only of moral importance, but is vital to sociology as well. The difference between the conference organizers, who found their society not to be as cynical as they feared, and Professor Friedenberg, who wishes it to be more cynical than it is, is not factual. They differ in their interpretation of the facts because the one believes in an obligation to obey the law, and the other does not. Furthermore, it is not merely the evaluation of facts that is at stake. The difference is liable to extend to the design of research and to all aspects of its interpretation.

WHY DO PEOPLE ACCEPT AN OBLIGATION TO OBEY?

If there is no general obligation to obey the law, then what are we to make of public opinion surveys which show that so many people are only too happy to express a firm belief in an obligation to obey? Some explanation is called for. It is, after all, much more to be expected that people would deny the duties they have than that they would submit to duties they do not have.

A possible explanation is that many are willing to express a belief which they do not really hold because it is what they think is expected of them. In brief, people may lie when they profess to believe in an obligation to obey the law, but this seems rather unlikely.

There is a more plausible explanation of people's mistaken belief in an obligation to obey. It is based on the assumption that people are predisposed to obey the law for personal reasons of convenience and self-interest, but that the prevailing social and cultural atmosphere induces them to rationalize that attitude and mask it under a sincerely held belief in an obligation to obey.

One possible objection to this explanation denies that people generally have prudential reasons for obeying the law. Is it not plain — the objection runs — that the law limits individual freedom, and that compliance is therefore often against people's interests? The very low rate of crime detection establishes the absence of a prudential reason to obey in the vast majority of those cases. The objection fails for two cumulative reasons.

First, the fact that the law limits our freedom does not show that obedience is against our interest. Consider the following analogy: The fact that our chairperson confines me to 15 minutes does not give me any reason to go on for longer, even though it does restrict my freedom to do so. The law often restricts our freedom, but much less commonly does it deny us our interests.

Sometimes it does, however, so we need to attend to the second reason for the failure of the objection. It underestimates the importance of personal policies in determining behaviour. It may be that in a case-by-case rational assessment of the choices open to us, prudential consideration would lead to widespread disobedience. However, having to make decisions from scratch, with an open mind to all options, probabilities and payoffs, is a highly undesirable situation for most people. We cope by minimizing such choices through the development or adoption of policies which either determine our choices, or, more commonly, reduce the difficulty of decision-making by eliminating certain options. I would surmise that many people avoid shoplifting partly as a result of such a policy which saves them the anxiety of evaluating the possible gains and risks of shoplifting each time they are in a store.

Given that the belief in an obligation to obey is so widespread, it is unlikely that one single explanation could account for it. It is probably the product of a variety of factors, so I should like to suggest a second, complementary explanation.

It turns on the fact that the mistake involved in a belief in a general obligation to obey is more subtle than it may appear. The mistake is in thinking that an obligation to obey is a general obligation binding on all. But I think that often those who believe in the obligation are indeed subject to it and it is, paradoxical though this may sound, their very belief in it which is part of the reason why they are so bound. The thought is really very simple. There are attitudes of identification with an institution or a society which carry moral implications. They are expressed by the recognition of the appropriateness of certain forms of actions, and the inappropriateness of others. Recognition of an obligation to obey is such a case. It expresses, and in part constitutes, an attitude to society which is the reverse of alienation. It is, therefore, a morally significant and morally positive element in the life of those who have it, although it does not follow that those who lack it are in the wrong, or that they offend against morality.

ATTITUDES TO LAW DISTINGUISHED FROM ATTITUDES TO LEGAL TRAPPINGS

The non-existence of an obligation to obey the law and my two explanations of the belief in such an obligation are likely to have implications to people's more specific attitudes to legal institutions.

The courts, the police, and the legal profession are institutions which, to the public at large, bear the trappings of law. It does not follow that in studying public attitudes towards these institutions that we are studying attitudes to the law. Much of the law concerns these institutions only infrequently.

Take welfare legislation, for example. The law concerning the provision of health services, the educational system, health and safety at work and most other public and welfare services affects the life of every individual in our society. The bulk of this law possesses the following three characteristics: (1) It is rarely litigated in courts; (2) For the most part, it affects individuals as beneficiaries only. Their duties are by and large confined to avoiding deceit and paying taxes. Attitudes to such laws cannot be related to recognition of an obligation to obey the law; and (3) People's beliefs about welfare law and their attitudes to it are of great importance in forming people's attitudes to their society and its political institutions. They contribute decisively to one's judgment of the humanity, sensitivity and justice of one's society. Here we have, therefore, social institutions created and sustained through the operation of the law which are not identified in the public mind with the trappings of the law but rather with government and bureaucracy, and which do not, by and large, call for obedience on the part of the individual. And yet these law-created institutions are of decisive importance in assessing attitudes to law.

Take as our second example the law relating to domestic business transactions: an individual's relations with other individuals, or with commercial organizations, for the supply of goods and services, such as gas or domestic help, or the installation of a new window pane, or the purchase of a book. Again, we are in a territory which affects all of us, and where the law is of vital importance. Again, several features stand out: (1) Disputes are rarely settled by litigation. Mostly they are resolved either by direct negotiation between the parties or by negotiation mediated through the intervention of voluntary or public organizations, such as consumer associations or trade associations. Quite often disputes are settled by unilateral action by one party, reluctantly acquiesced in by the other, such as the withholding of pay or the cessation or non-completion of services; (2) Although individuals are subject to duties, they find themselves typically in reciprocal relations in which their obligations are matched by rights, and which were created in the first place through a voluntary undertaking; and (3) People expect such relations to be governed by express agreement, supplemented by prevailing customs and conventions, and the parties' own sense of fairness. A rudimentary knowledge of the law is supplemented by the general expectation, or hope, that the law will lead to a reasonable solution.

I have chosen these two examples because both concern legal areas which affect the daily life of all of us, and because neither is identified in the public mind with the trappings of law. The two examples present marked and important contrasts. For example, welfare law depends for its effectiveness on widespread knowledge of its availability. It is still the case that a very large proportion of welfare benefits remain unclaimed, and this is due, to a considerable extent, to ignorance. Private transactions, on the other hand, are easily conducted by millions of people with no, or only the vaguest, notion of the law. The efficacy of the law in this area largely depends on its success in following conventional ways of doing things.

Such differences are decisive in any exploration of attitudes to the law. But beyond both examples stands a common feature. In both cases the law does not stand out as a distinct separate element. It is, rather, identified with the political system or the bureaucracy in the one case, and with commercial and trade practices in the other. Some may deplore this fragmentation of the public image of the law, and its frequent submersion in attitudes to diverse non-legal institutions. They may feel that the existence of a general obligation to obey the law means that people should focus on the law, as law, above and beyond its contribution to other social institutions. I do not believe in a general obligation to obey, and I therefore find the submersion of the public image of parts of the law in that of other institutions, on the whole, a welcome fact.

I only fear that research which starts from the assumption that there is a distinctive public image to the law as such is liable to end with a survey of attitudes to the trappings of law rather than to the law itself.

ORGANIZED CRIMINALS: SOME OBSERVATIONS REGARDING THEIR ATTITUDES TOWARDS LAW AND ORDER

Joseph L. Albini

INTRODUCTION

The question of why some individuals in society obey the law and others do not is one of the most basic to the study of criminology. It lies at the root of understanding the genesis of those forms of behaviour which are anti-social in nature and those types of individuals whom we label criminals. Indeed, if criminologists could solve this riddle we would be at the brink of solving, or at least controlling, the crime problem.

A number of theories have been offered to explain crime. They have ranged from the biogenetic types, which seek to explain criminal behaviour in terms of influences of physical body structure or chromosomal defects, to psychogenic types, which explore for the cause within the realm of mental dysfunction, low intelligence, and other mental conditions. In our search for causes we have also turned to the environment, both physical and social, arguing that ecology, social class, and other factors cause crime. Social process theories have attempted to describe and explain crime as resulting from a series of changes which individuals undergo as part of their socialization or life-experiences. It seems that for some the associations, attitudes, and definitions learned and developed during this process create a socially adjusted or non-criminal individual, while for others the result is development of a socially acquired need to enter a life of crime. Still other theories explain crime as a result of individual and social-structural forms of conflict which make individuals and groups unequal competitors in the social arena. Inequality is thought to force some individuals into crime careers because these careers are the only, or the more lucrative, means of upward mobility available to them. Each of these theories, although helpful to explain certain aspects of criminal behaviour, fails to answer the ultimate question — why do some people obey the law while others do not?

Perhaps the inability to answer this question stems from an error inherent in the question itself, an error that persists in almost every discussion of crime: the assumption that there is a definite and precise distinction between the criminal and the non-criminal. Admittedly, there are those who commit certain types of crimes to a greater extent than others, but it would be absurd to assume that most individuals have never committed a crime. Indeed one of the classic essays on the topic of crime, that of Emile Durkheim,[3] reminds us that crime is a phenomenon found in all societies and throughout history.

One important factor that has served to create the erroneous distinction between the criminal and non-criminal is the rather arbitrary way in which certain actions and persons have been defined as socially deviant, and others have not. Thus for the past several decades the poor in the slums have been the centre of concentration of both governmental projects and research in two major areas of social deviance — crime and mental illness. Throughout this period, white-collar crime and particularly its most prevalent form — political corruption — were major social realities. Yet it is only recently that white-collar crime has begun to receive the attention it deserves. Is white-collar crime any less serious than the crimes committed in the slums? Of course not. It is a form of crime that, because it rips at the seams of public confidence and honesty, is equally if not more devastating than the crimes of the lower class poor. There is one major difference: white-collar crimes are committed by individuals whom society regards differently from street criminals. Despite the fact that citizens are outraged by the news stories of Watergate and other political or corporate scandals, there is no doubt that the average citizen fears the lower class street criminal far more than the white-collar thief. This distinction is also reflected in the different ways white-collar and street crime are treated by the legal system.

It seems, then, that if we are to examine objectively the question of why certain people obey the law and others do not, we must first admit that "the law" may be applied differently to various individuals and groups. In theory, the law is equal and applies to all, but in reality we know that of those who disobey it, some can and do escape both the criminal process of punishment

3 D. Emile Durkheim, *The Rules of the Sociological Method*, 8th ed. (trans. 1964), pp. 65-66.

and the accompanying labelling process. Above all we must bear in mind that everyone disobeys the law. Hence, the basic question is not why some obey the law and others do not, but rather why do certain individuals disobey certain types of laws?

This question is particularly relevant in the realm of organized crime, since this form of criminality involves many types of activities, and the motivation for violating the law differs radically from one type to another.

In this paper I wish to draw upon the data which I have obtained from two studies concerning organized crime; one conducted in the United States[4] and the other conducted in Great Britain.[5] In both studies I interviewed criminals in the underworld. In both studies my major concern was to analyze the structure and function of syndicated crime. My purpose was not to study directly why these criminals disobeyed the law. However, since my interviews were open-ended, this resulted in my obtaining data concerning the subjects' personal lives, feelings, and attitudes towards a variety of topics, including their attitudes towards the police and the legal system. It is from these data, and the general literature concerning organized crime, that I take the information for the observations that I make in this paper. Although my two studies concentrated upon the analysis of syndicated crime, much of my information came from individuals who were involved in a variety of organized crime enterprises.

CATEGORIES OF ORGANIZED CRIME

In my book *The American Mafia* I identify four categories of organized crime.[6] This distinction will be particularly useful in noting the differences in how and why organized criminals view the law as they do. Let me begin by describing these four categories. I should emphasize, as I did in my book, that these are not mutually exclusive categories. Indeed, criminals can be participating in several or all four types simultaneously. However, since the means as well as the goals of each of these four types of criminal activity differ, the motives of the individuals engaged in each type of activity will also differ.

The first type I refer to as *political-social organized crime*. Here, the ultimate goal of the criminal is not to gain direct financial profit but rather, either to change or maintain the existing social or political structure. In this category we would include such organizations as terrorist groups and labour or other organizations which use sabotage, violence, or other illegal means to achieve their goals. Also included here would be business, government, or special interest groups that employ illegal means to attain their ends.

4 Joseph L. Albini, *The American Mafia: Genesis of a Legend* (1971).

5 Joseph L. Albini, "Mafia as Method: A Comparison between Great Britain and U.S.A. Regarding the Existence and Structure of Types of Organized Crime" (1975), 3 Int. Journal of Criminology and Penology, 295.

6 See *supra*, c. 2, note 2.

In the second category I place those crimes which are committed for direct financial profit, either through the use or potential use of force or intimidation, or through fraud. This category I refer to as *mercenary crime*. It includes auto-theft and burglary rings, mugging teams, and groups which use games of confidence in which fraud and deception are the basic *modus operandi*.

In the third category, *in-group oriented organized crime*, I place those criminals who violate the law because their membership in gangs provides them with a sense of belonging and adventure. In seeking adventure such groups often engage in anti-social behaviour which brings them into conflict with the law. In many cases, as Miller, Geertz and Cutler[7] have noted, the aggression of these gang members is directed not towards outsiders but toward one another. The most recent notorious examples of this type of criminality are the motorcycle gangs and the street-gangs commonly found in the large metropolitan areas.

The fourth category I call *syndicated crime*. This differs from the others in that this form of organized crime provides illegal goods, such as narcotic drugs, and illegal services, such as gambling, to members of society on a continuous basis. In order to provide such services these criminals must develop means of providing "protection" for themselves by bribing police and/or other public officials, or by providing funds or other forms of aid to help elect political candidates who in turn will provide them with immunity from the law. These syndicate criminals, as part of their *modus operandi*, use violence or the threat of it to deal with competing syndicates, as well as to keep order within their own groups. Since they cannot resort to the law, they also employ violence or the threat of it in dealing with clients who fail to honour their debts for goods or services provided.

Having described these four types, let us now consider how and why criminals within these four groups view the legal system itself.

POLITICAL-SOCIAL CRIME

Criminals participating in *political-social* forms of organized crime regard the existing law and the legal system as an illegal form of power. For groups such as guerilla fighters or terrorists, whose aim is to overthrow an existing government, that government represents a legal system which has no basis for existence. They do not recognize the existing government as just or legal. Hence, the laws enacted by such a government are simply not regarded as laws. Yet it is the existing government that has defined the actions of guerilla or terrorist groups as illegal. If the revolutionaries come to power they will acquire the right to legalize their previous activities and make illegal the

7 W. B. Miller, H. Geertz, and H. S. G. Cutler, "Aggression in a Boys' Street Corner Group" (1961), XXIV Psychiatry 286.

actions of the former government. Here we have a case where, in reality, "might makes right". The decision as to what is lawful depends ultimately upon which forces, those in power or those in revolt, will eventually hold the reins of governmental power. The French Revolution is an historical example of how powerless the once-powerful aristocracy was in the hands of those revolutionaries who led them one by one to the guillotine.

Ethically we can argue along with Thorsten Sellin[8] that a social definition of crime is necessary in order to properly evaluate the legal definition in such cases. Yet the reality of power is that legal definitions made by existing governments have, during the time of their existence, the backing of law. When we ask the question then, "Why does the political-social criminal disobey the law?" we face ethical and social ramifications as well as legal ones. This was the issue raised by the late Rev. Martin Luther King, Jr. when he argued that it was immoral to obey an unjust law. If the *political-social* criminal conscientiously and honestly views the existing laws and legal system as unjust, then his or her reason for disobeying the law must be viewed within that context. Until we can develop an accurate scale or other form of measurement for evaluating absolute right or absolute wrong in reference to such issues, this question must remain a debatable one.

MERCENARY CRIME

The motivations that lead individuals to engage in *mercenary organized crime* are so complex that there are more questions regarding this issue than there are answers. To view the mercenary criminal as possessing certain specific characteristics is to produce a stereotype which, like all stereotypes, is very misleading.

In my interviews with criminals in the United States and Great Britain I discovered a number of reasons why these people disobeyed the law. Some individuals stated that they came under the influence of friends who "put them into the life". Usually this meant that a friend had taught them a trade such as "blowing" safes, techniques of "casing" and entering houses for the purpose of burglary, acting as "numbers runners" and a variety of other illegal tasks. In each case they viewed the person who offered this help in positive terms, as apprentices in legitimate trades would admiringly view the persons who taught them. These criminals not only spoke highly of those who taught them their illicit trades, but they also felt that because of this help and training they had bettered themselves. In other words, the general impression they conveyed was that had it not been for these people who taught them a trade, they might have become just ordinary criminals with no skills.

Those who spoke of their criminal activities much as one would speak of life in non-criminal society often showed no signs of guilt. Thus, one criminal

8 J. T. Sellin, *Culture, Conflict and Crime* (1938).

told me in very casual terms how he went about stealing his Christmas gifts for his family. I detected no sense of wrongdoing; he was speaking in the same tone as one would say, "I did my Christmas shopping early this year". This attitude, as Silberman notes[9], is often found among lower-class criminals, as well as by those who buy stolen goods in the lower-class community. There is a generally accepted feeling among such groups that the rich have more than they can use, and there is no reason why the poor should not have some of it.

Some criminals, and I found this more true of criminals in Great Britain than in America, do view themselves as wrongdoers. One Scottish criminal pointedly said, "You can't let people like me be free on the streets. I'll pinch whatever I can get." Others openly defined themselves as criminals, but took recourse to the fact that they were raised in bad neighbourhoods, had negligent parents, or belonged to minority or racial groups whose members were victims of severe discrimination. On one occasion several criminals took me on an excursion to a slum in a Scottish city. They wanted me to see, as they put it, the kinds of conditions that produced potential criminals.

It should be noted that not all criminals disobey all laws. My criminal informants displayed an interesting mixture of attitudes towards right and wrong, both in reference to the law and to other norms, which basically were no different from the attitudes commonly expressed by non-criminals. For example, several of these informants looked down upon rapists, child molesters and muggers who attacked the elderly.

Among the criminals in Great Britain I noted a sense of ethics that permeated their interaction with police. One example gives a perfect illustration of this point. While conducting my study there, I read a newspaper account of a burglary which was stopped by an off-duty police officer. This officer noticed a flash of light in a jewellery store which had been closed for the day. Suspecting a robbery, he knocked on the window and in a loud voice indicated to those inside that he knew what was going on and told them to come out. Soon, one by one, a total of five men came out the door. He then marched them to the police station. We must remember that the officer, as is the custom in Great Britain, did not have a gun. As an American criminologist I was amazed by this account in view of the fact that these five men, in terms of sheer numbers, could have overpowered the officer and escaped. Later I interviewed one of the criminals who had been involved in this burglary. He described the incident in the same terms as those of the newspaper account I had read. I then asked him the crucial question — "Why didn't you and your friends attack the officer and escape?" A look of repulsion came over his face as he replied, "Aw mate, now that wouldn't be fair would it?" What he was describing was an ethical principle that "once you have been caught by the law, the game is over". I do not wish to imply that all the criminals in Great Britain would or do employ this ethic, but it nonetheless seemed to me, from

9 C. E. Silberman, *Criminal Violence, Criminal Justice* (1980), pp. 125-27.

my various interviews, that this mode of behaviour towards police seemed normative among many of them.

We must remember that to the mercenary criminal, for whom crime is an occupation, the law and legal agencies represent an obstacle to his or her work. It is a force that must be reckoned with. This is true of both those who use violence and those who use fraud to accomplish their theft. Some seem to possess anti-legal attitudes before they enter the occupation of crime. Others appear to develop such attitudes as a result of engaging in their work. In either case, the act of being apprehended not only means the possibility of imprisonment and a loss of income while they are incarcerated but also a loss of status among their peers. "If you are really good at what you do, you don't get caught," is a commonly voiced belief among mercenary criminals. As the literature abundantly notes, this is why the successful confidence-game players seem to have such high status in the underworld — because they rarely are caught. Part of the reason for this, as David W. Maurer[10] points out, is the fact that the victim often is either unaware that he or she has been robbed, or is embarrassed or afraid of being involved in something illegal and is reluctant to report the theft to the police. Many con-games are purposefully structured so that the victim is made to believe that he or she will make money by engaging in a "shady deal". Here is a case where it is especially difficult to separate the criminal from the non-criminal in terms of motives for violating the law. Victims of the big con are typically respectable businesspeople who are willing to engage in a dishonest scheme that promises to gain them large sums of money. In such schemes is the victim any less a criminal than the perpetrator of the game?

It seems that for confidence people, the target of attack is not the law but rather the potential victim or mark. Confidence men and women seem to enjoy "taking" suckers. Although they "take" their victims for money, it is the thrill of outwitting the victim that seems to be the most enjoyable part of the game. As Maurer notes, "The confidence games are not always played for money. Sometimes . . . they are played just for fun."[11]

In leaving the topic of *mercenary crime* we should end with an historical reminder of the difficulty of distinguishing between the motives of the criminal and the non-criminal in terms of why they disobey the law. We refer to Gustavus Myers' *History of the Great American Fortunes* in which he notes that such giants and pioneers of American business as Russell Sage and Cornelius Vanderbilt were themselves violators of the law. It seems that Sage and his business partners planned and executed a swindle of their creditors in Milwaukee,[12] and Vanderbilt, in building his fortune, employed such criminal tactics as theft, blackmail, and extortion.[13]

10 D. W. Maurer, *The Big Con* (1962), p. 14.

11 *Ibid*, p. 17.

12 Gustavus Myers, *History of the Great American Fortunes* (1910), vol. III, pp. 14-18.

13 *Ibid*. vol. II, p. 112.

IN-GROUP ORIENTED CRIME

In-group oriented organized crime presents us with a motive for violating the law in which the violation seems to be a by-product of several other motives; laws are violated in the course of activities that gang members define as "fun", or a means of proving their bravery and/or loyalty to the group.

Frequently gang parties, which are often accompanied by the use of alcoholic beverages or drugs, result in the individuals making excessive noise and obscene gestures which bring complaints of disturbing the peace. Sometimes during these activities there is destruction of private and public property. It seems, however, that these crimes are not usually purposefully planned; they are merely the result of the gangs engaging in their own form of entertainment. The exception to this, of course, is the "rumble" or gang fight in which the method is violence and the purpose is to seek revenge, or to settle a dispute regarding territorial boundaries, or other issues.

In-group oriented gangs can and do change both their motives and *modus operandi* to the extent that they take on the characteristics of *mercenary crime*. Thus we note that many motorcycle gangs that were originally formed for in-group types of satisfactions have become mercenary in nature. In a recent interview a member of a motorcycle gang who is knowledgeable about the activity of several such gangs noted how many of these gangs have changed from "fun-having" groups to "profit-making" ones. They have come to use much of their time stealing and selling auto and motorcycle parts, dealing drugs and making money from prostituting women associated with the gang. In these cases, obviously, the motives are not like those of in-group gangs, since here the violation is not a by-product of fun-having activity.

SYNDICATED CRIME

The realm of *syndicated crime* is very interesting in terms of the questions it raises as to why these criminals disobey the law. This stems from the fact that the nature of this form of criminal activity involves a process whereby the criminal serves as a form of broker between legitimate and illegitimate sectors of society. Let us remember that as we defined *syndicated crime* earlier; it is a form of criminality in which the criminal provides illicit goods and services. The irony of this form of crime lies in the fact that it cannot exist without the participation of two types of members of legitimate society — the client or buyer and the political protector.

No criminal syndicate could exist if there were no market or buyers for its goods or services. Hence, the client who wants these goods and services constitutes a vital part of this form of criminality. Who is the client? Typically, members of legitimate society.

Another necessity for the prolonged existence of criminal syndicates is political immunity from the law. By its very nature, *syndicated crime* necessitates a process of continuous contact between the client who wants the goods or services and the criminal who supplies them. If the clients can find the contact, so can the police. Hence, syndicates historically and currently use two major techniques in order to gain political protection — the direct pay-off, and the provision of financial or other assistance to political candidates in return for a promise that if elected the candidate will provide the syndicate with immunity.

Syndicate criminals, like other criminals and people in general, display vast differences in personality and other traits. Unfortunately, the movies and novels, as Dwight C. Smith, Jr.[14] has noted, have created a stereotype which makes them appear identical in character. In reality, we find that they differ not only in personality traits but in attitudes as well.

Some syndicate criminals disobey the law because they have no respect for it. How can they respect a legal system in which they pay the political official in power to allow them to disobey the law?

Others develop an attitude of tolerance. They view the police and the law as a necessary nuisance or hindrance because "That's the way it is and has always been". These types view their work very much like a legitimate business, and the pay-off is simply calculated as a necessary expense.

In other cases, disobeying the law is seen as a functional aspect of the syndicate activity itself. This is particularly true in the loan-shark enterprise, where loans are made at a high rate of interest. Much has been made of the fact that loan-sharkers are very brutal in their handling of their clients. In some cases this is true, but we must remember that the typical client who goes to a loan-shark goes there because he or she is a very bad credit risk. If he or she were not a serious credit risk they certainly could obtain loans from a legitimate source. When the loan-shark's client fails to pay the loan, what actions or recourse does the loan-shark have? They obviously cannot sue the client for breach of contract in a court of law. Their only recourse is to use intimidation or force. However, even here the loan-shark, contrary to the typical newspaper stories about loan-shark cases, does not want to seriously injure or to kill the client. The client's body is viewed and treated as a form of collateral. I am not condoning what loan-sharks do; I am simply trying to illustrate how they view the nature of their work. They feel that because they are engaged in an illegal enterprise this both necessitates and justifies the illegal methods they employ.

Not all syndicate criminals disobey all laws. Some, for example, refuse to deal in narcotics, not because it is illegal to do so but rather because they feel that the results of addiction are too devastating to the people who use the drugs. Those who take this view typically have had problems with their own

14 Dwight C. Smith, Jr., *The Mafia Mystique* (1975).

children being addicts. Yet these same individuals would not hesitate to establish illegal gambling establishments or to run a loan-sharking enterprise.

To suppose that all syndicate criminals are totally against the law would also overlook a very important aspect of the differences in their value systems. This is shown in the ways some socialize their children and the plans they make for their children's future. Many abhor the thought that their sons would want to become a part of a syndicate enterprise. Contrary to the movie image of the "Godfather", syndicate criminals lead a life of stress. Even when they are at the top, life is one in which there is a constant threat either from the law or from other competing syndicate criminals. Some see this life as one they entered because they had few or no alternatives. Hence, they do not want this type of life for their children. They want their children to attend college and enter legitimate professions. In my interviews with police and other sources in my American study I was struck by the fact that the children of many of the syndicate criminals were viewed by these sources as respectable and well-behaved. This attempt at socialization seems to indicate that for many syndicate criminals the process of disobeying the law is not embedded in their value systems; it has simply been adopted as a means to an end.

CONCLUSION

In conclusion, I have tried to show that the reasons for disobeying the law varies among organized criminals in terms of the type or types of organized crime they are engaged in at any given time. Some, such as the *political-social* type, disobey the law because they do not see it as law. Some, such as the *mercenary* types, disobey it because they expect and/or find financial rewards by doing so. Others, like the *in-group* type, violate it not so much purposefully, but as a by-product of their attempt to fulfill gang needs for the show of bravery loyalty, or "for kicks". Finally, in the case of *syndicated crime*, the law is viewed with scepticism because some police and public officials, elected to uphold the law, sell licences to disobey the law for a price. The syndicate criminal wonders what the law really represents if some of society's most upright citizens are also willing to disobey it and become customers.

Let us end this discussion by concluding that if crime is viewed realistically and if we are to discover why people really obey or disobey the law, we must rid ourselves of the labelling process commonly applied only to the criminal. We must study disobedience as an activity found in all areas, classes and categories of society. We must study law in terms of the structure and dynamics of society itself. We must study the legal process from the first step of enactment of the law to the final stages of enforcement. If we begin doing this then perhaps we will reach a point in the future where laws will be passed with a more complete understanding and predictability as to which individuals or groups will obey or disobey them. Only then will we have come to the beginning of an understanding of the complexity of human behaviour as it relates to the law.

Many commentators on contemporary society have drawn attention to a rapidly increasing legalization of life resulting in, among other things, an unprecedented resort to the courts. Law has become, for some, not just a body of norms to be obeyed but an arsenal of useful defensive and offensive weapons. This dramatic growth in the public's reliance on law and legal processes may be an extreme manifestation of law-abidingness. Or it may, on the other hand, stem from factors quite different from those which contribute to legal obedience. Professor John Hogarth examined some aspects of the phenomenon, and deplored its consequences.

STATUS TO CONTRACT: THE LEGALIZATION OF ATTITUDES AND RELATIONSHIPS

John Hogarth

I took the occasion of this conference to try to develop my own thinking about the interrelationship of law and morals. I refer not to the impact of opinion and current contemporary belief on law but the reverse: the impact of law on opinion, belief and morals. My thesis is this: well-meaning attempts to modernize the law by making it consistent with contemporary knowledge, belief and morals run the risk of weakening both moral standards and respect for law and legal institutions insofar as they attempt to deal with primary social relationships: relationships of the family, the profession, the workplace, the school, and so on. Moreover, these relationships themselves have been damaged by the attitudes engendered by these legal changes.

During the past year or so, I have been speaking and writing about what I perceive to be a fundamental cultural shift. A shift has taken place deep within our culture from status-determined relationships to relationships determined by contract.[15] A status relationship is one that comes with one's role or membership in a group. Obligations which are attached to that role are

15 The observation that "the movement of the progressive societies has hitherto been a movement from Status to Contract" was first made by Sir Henry Maine in his 1861 work *Ancient Law* at the conclusion of the fifth chapter; see also G. Feaver, *From Status to Contract* (1969), p. 53,*ff*.

historically and culturally determined. The emphasis is on mutuality, reciprocity and the enduring nature of a common enterprise. Obligations are open-textured, never-ending, and multi-dimensional. Morality, not law, governs. Contractual relationships, on the other hand, are specific, closed and self-contained. The emphasis is not on the group but on the individual within the group, and obligations under the contract exist only to the extent that each individual freely and willingly agrees to undertake them. The only obligations that exist are those which are legally enforceable, and once they are discharged no further action is required.

This shift from status to contract has taken place in stages. Prior to the nineteenth century, obligations were seen as internal, personal matters of conscience, governed by religion and social mores. The notion of debt in law really wasn't translated into contract terms until the Reformation — about 1770. The secularization and externalization of debt law at that time was followed by the so-called Age of Contract.

Such a change was probably necessary for a newly emerging market economy, and for the first century and a half of development after the Reformation, contracts were for the most part limited to commercial transactions. They were freely entered into by willing parties roughly equal in status, and were restricted to the terms of a limited commercial relationship that was not expected to last beyond the terms of the contract.

The period from 1770 to contemporary times was a period of peaceful coexistence between law and morals. While law and morals were never identical or coextensive, morality made the law possible because most human behaviour, particularly in primary social relationships, was still determined by moral standards, cultural determinations and historical roots. In that period the law was instrumental in buttressing, reinforcing, and indeed in sometimes creating, relationships that for the most part were still based on the old status role models. If we refer to the period prior to 1770 as the Age of Morality, one can call the period 1770 to the 1980's the Period of Instrumentality.

I now want to come to what I call the Period of Literalism, in which contract has completely overwhelmed morality, and relations are primarily determined by legal obligations.

First let me elaborate a little on the difference between contractual relationships and those which are built on obligations arising from status. I've mentioned a few already. A contract relationship is specific, closed, and self-contained. A status relationship is open-ended. A contract relationship emphasizes the individual rights and obligations of the individual members. A status relationship emphasizes shared tasks and common enterprises, and depends for its enforcement on human bonding and identification with shared moral values. Contract relationships depend primarily upon enforcement by third parties, such as the police and the courts. Contract relationships are time-limited; status relationships are enduring. Contract relationships concern themselves with procedural fairness; status relationships are more concerned with substance. Contract relationships involve the minimum obligations established by the parties, while status relationships are concerned with the maximum potential. Contract relations are rule-oriented. They tend to be unidimensional and simple. Status relationships tend to be multi-dimensional, polycentric, and complex. Contract relationships are morally neutral. Status relationships are morally charged. Contract relationships are situational. Status relationships are historic. Contract relationships assume a bad person — one who wishes to violate obligations. Status relationships assume a good person — one who will live up to responsibilities. I could go on and on.

What we have seen in the twentieth century, particularly in the post Second World War welfare state era, is the imposition of contract notions into a host of primary relationships to an extent far beyond the scope of contract or quasi-contract in the nineteenth century. We see in labour-management areas, in the family, in the university and the school, and in professional relationships, a vastly increased reliance on formal contracts as the basis of obligations between the parties.

My concern is for the impact this development has had on restructuring and redefining the nature of relationships and the nature of obligations between the parties. Parties are now seeing themselves as the law sees them, and are developing a resulting tendency towards moral neutrality. Minimum standards laid out in a contract become maximum standards of obligation.

We can see, for example, a fundamental transformation of the nature of obligations within universities. Students are no longer there to learn. They are there to pass exams, to receive degrees and to go out and earn a living. The status relationship of professor and student has been replaced by a contract. "What are the rules?" "What do I have to do to get through?" "What's going to be on the examination paper?" These are what concerns the students. Professors are in a similar position. They are no longer there to impart knowledge, to stimulate, and to excite. They are there to pave the students' way to employment by providing a stipulated number of classroom hours, setting fair exams and marking them impartially.

Or take, for example, the workplace generally. The collective agreement has become a self-contained total expression of the obligations that employers and employees have to each other. No responsibility is accepted which is not set out in the collective agreement. A worker can stand back and watch a plant be destroyed if it is not within his or her job description to deal with the situation. The sense of task, of purpose, of common enterprise that used to exist has been undermined by the contract-like notions which have replaced the status obligations that theretofore prevailed, or at least coexisted with contracts.

Let us turn to the most primary of all relationships — the family. The family was traditionally defined in terms of property law. Property law notions are status related, and when applied to family relationships they produced sexist results. They have now been replaced, to a large extent, by contract notions. Marriage contracts are replacing notions of property. This move, like similar shifts in labour law, was well-intentioned, and perhaps even necessary to redress power imbalances in the traditional status relationships. But one of the prices that has been paid is that marriages are now seen as basically commercial unions between people. Marriages have become commercial enterprises.

The law's perception of reality is determined in a large part by the remedies that are offered. Myths and perjury aside, the basic reason why marriages break down is the absence of love. Myths and perjury aside, the remedy open to someone who is not loved is cash. "If you don't love me, pay me", is the message that the modern family law provides.

Furthermore, the sexism involved in the division of matrimonial property upon dissolution of marriage, in some provinces at least, is yielding not only disrespect for law but disrespect for the institution of marriage itself. There is some confusion now because of new legislation, but women appear to be receiving 50 per cent of the total matrimonial property after one year of marriage, having contributed nothing to the marriage economically. That is sexist because it assumes that women are not independent, free people, but rather that their way to achieve success is to marry a wealthy man. And while it was necessary to change the matrimonial property laws in order to correct power imbalances, the risk of those kinds of remedies is that, as I have said, they cause marriage to be regarded as a commercial union.

Such remedies and the attitudes they breed also allow us to avoid dealing with real problems of imbalances between men and women, which could be better solved, it seems to me, by doing such things as ensuring equality in employment, ensuring adequate day care, and so on.

By providing cash alternatives to marriage and substituting an essentially contractual notion for the deservedly disrespected notion of married women as property, we have created a new risk of disrespect and injury to marriage. This, like the examples previously listed, serves as a reminder that there is reason to be sceptical about the effectiveness of law as an instrument for social good.

In response to a question from the audience, John Hogarth extended his thesis to the new *Canadian Charter of Rights and Freedoms:*

> I find it interesting that nowhere do you see a preamble in the Charter that allows us to state as a Canadian society what are the things that hold us all together.[16] . . . [W]e couldn't

16 Except the statement that: "Canada is founded upon principles that recognize the supremacy of God and the rule of law." Constitution Act, 1982, Pt. I, Preamble.

> come to an agreement as to what we stand for . . . but we could agree as to certain kinds of more limited rights and freedoms. . . . It is fundamentally procedural fairness which we are offering people. . . . [S]ince we can't offer people substantive benefits, we'll ensure that whatever happens to them for good or for evil will be done fairly. And so it's a triumph of form or procedure over substance. . . . [T]hat fits the drift toward contract.

Following Professor Hogarth's presentation a member of the audience, Dean John McLaren of the University of Calgary, offered the following observations about the "status to contract" thesis:

> I'd like to press Professor Hogarth a bit on his suggestion that we've moved from an age of morality to an age of contract, because I think that may be an oversimplification.
>
> While I agree with him in part, that we've moved down the road towards contract and a greater series of contractual relationships, it seems to me at the same time that we've also moved further down the road towards status relationships. I say that for two reasons.
>
> In the whole area of consumer transactions, which is theoretically within the ambit of contract, we have moved to what are, in fact, status relationships. When I go out to buy an automobile or insurance, I really don't have any choice in negotiating the terms of that contract with the provider of the automobile or the provider of the insurance. If I want that service, then something is imposed upon me. It's a standard-form contract, created not by a process of bargaining, but by lawyers in the offices of GM and the offices of the insurance company. I am subject to a status regime which is a reflection of the discrepancy in economic power between the auto manufacturer or the insurance company, on one hand, and myself, the little consumer, on the other hand.
>
> It also seems to me that we're dealing with status relationships in the area of social welfare. I don't think that the social welfare recipient can be said to contract with the state as to what he or she gets. It's provided. And the client finds himself or herself in an often very cold, sometimes calculating, status relationship.
>
> That leads me to another point: I'm not so sure that status relationships always betoken moral obligation. I think one thing we may be witnessing is a move down a road towards even status relationships which are bereft of moral feeling, moral obligation, and if we're looking for reasons why people are cynical about law and legal institutions, that may be an explanation.

Adam Podgorecki offered some general observations about the nature of legal systems that provide a useful backdrop against which to examine the papers on the relation between public attitudes and obedience to law.[17] Central to his observations was a distinction between two contrasting models of legal norms: "official law", personified by "homo juris" on the one hand, and "intuitive law", personified by "homo ethicus" on the other.

Homo juris is a person whose behaviour is primarily based on the

17 These observations are extracted and summarized from a longer presentation to the conference by Professor Podgorecki. Other portions from that presentation are included *supra*, c. 3.

dictates of law, rather than of logic, personal satisfaction, social needs, reasonableness, religion, or decency. While the "official law" upon which homo juris relies draws to a considerable extent on those other values and norms, homo juris is concerned only with the letter of the law, and not with its roots or moral legitimacy. Homo juris places much weight on such matters as public respect for law and legal institutions, procedural fairness and the impartiality of those who administer the law.

In Podgorecki's opinion, homo juris shares many of the attributes of the "organization man":

> The organization man is one who fits in smoothly with the impersonal, formalized, compartmentalized, numerically oriented elements of the social structure. The well-rounded organization person makes no attempt to comprehend the total structure, however. This abdication of understanding serves the operational efficiency of the organization, because it enables each person to be "reasonable" within his or her particular domain, without having to foresee consequences beyond that sector. Like a time-bomb, this limited form of "reasonability" both contains and conceals a mortal danger.

Homo ethicus, by contrast, is more concerned with the moral substance of law than with its form. Podgorecki refers to this substance as "intuitive law":

> Homo ethicus — the decent person — personifies the crucial values of his or her society . . .
>
> . . . . .
>
> The decent person is not inclined to seek enlightenment and support from legal norms, since the norms of decency deal with human contingencies in a more comprehensive and appealing way. Thus, legal norms are summoned only on special occasions, when the normal rules of decency are insufficient.
>
> . . . . .
>
> Intuitive law, not being frozen by officially established rules, and recognizing mainly informal ties based on mutually respected attitudes about rights and duties, is pragmatic, easily adaptable, and flexible. Consequently, it is able to cement the social structure in a more cohesive way than official law. Thus, the notion of the decent person plays a decisive role in shaping the tangible spirit of a society.

In Podgorecki's opinion, intuitive law plays a larger role in primitive societies than in modern ones (a view which finds support in the "status to contract" model of social development to which John Hogarth drew attention), and is more significant in oriental and homogeneous systems than in occidental and heterogeneous ones. It nevertheless remains an important feature of modern western societies. In some situations, intuitive law operates without regard to official law:

> One may notice, for example, that within the inner life of every family there are numerous intuitive regulations. . . . "Everybody has the duty to respect Mama's right to one hour's undisturbed sleep after lunch," *etc.* A street-corner community also develops many intuitive regulations for its own use. Although it would be impossible to find these norms in law books or to enforce them through the help of law enforcement officers, these norms remain very firm. . . . The case of the Mafia legal substructure, to which Professor Albini alluded, is a striking example of an exclusive regime of intuitive law.

In other situations, intuitive law supplements and animates official law:

> It might be useful to compare the relationship between positive-official law and intuitive-unofficial law to that between an eloquent dwarf and a dumb giant upon whose shoulders the dwarf sits. The loquacious dwarf is widely recognized and respected so long as he remains on the shoulders of the giant and enjoys his apparent support.

But when the dwarf loses the support of the giant — as in times of revolution — serious social disruption results.

If these observations are valid, those who seek to determine the relationship between public opinion and obedience to law must be careful to distinguish between those forms of law which are merely official in nature, and those which enjoy the "intuitive" support of decent citizens.

Arthur Schafer, who chaired the panel on "Obedience to Law", offered a concluding synthesis of the ideas exposed in his colleagues' presentations, stitched with speculative threads of his own.

OBEDIENCE TO LAW: A SOCIO-POLITICAL CONTEXT

Arthur Schafer

A PRELIMINARY QUESTION: WHAT IS CRIME?

It is widely accepted — both by criminologists and the general public — that our society is faced with a serious "crime problem". So great are the supposed dimensions of this problem that some refer to it as a "crisis".

Professor Albini, in his paper on the attitudes of organized criminals towards "law and order",[18] declares that we would be on our way to solving this crime problem if we could answer the root question of why some individuals in society — the ordinary, law-abiding majority of citizens — obey the law, while others — the criminal classes — do not.

Although Professor Albini's paper focuses primarily on his investigations into the varied motivations of one class of law-breaking individuals —

18 Joseph L. Albini, *supra*.

the "organized criminal" — his discussion reminds us that it can be misleading to assume that we can confidently distinguish between the criminal and the non-criminal. This point is of profound importance. Strenuous efforts of criminologists have been invested in the development of theories to explain crime — ranging from environmental to psychogenic to social-structural — almost all of which have presupposed that criminals and their criminal behaviour can be sharply distinguished from the law-abiding behaviour of the non-criminal majority. This presupposition is highly problematic.

One cannot begin to develop a satisfactory answer to the key question, "Why do people obey/disobey the law?", until one recognizes that the processing of individuals through the mill of the criminal justice system is an intensely political and normative enterprise. An examination of the various processes involved in criminalizing behaviour — selecting only certain kinds of anti-social conduct for criminal sanctions, selectively labelling only some law-breakers as "criminals", and selectively processing only this chosen group through the criminal justice system — raises philosophical and political questions having to do with the distribution of wealth, power and status in society.

Why should there be any special difficulty in attaching the label "criminal" to persons and actions? The answer to this question requires a recognition of the socio-political-economic context in which every system of criminal justice is embedded. It is often the case that significant portions of a society's criminal laws are simply disguised forms of class favouritism, promoting the interests and privileges of some ruling group rather than the universal interests of the society.

The public rationale for legal norms typically invokes ideas of the general good, social progress and the public interest, but the reality is often otherwise. A few examples may be useful to illustrate this socio-economic bias of the criminal justice system. In most discussions of serious crime, the focus is on such crimes as robbery, burglary and violent assaults. The criminal law provides heavy penal sanctions against such actions. By contrast, the business executives and professionals who are responsible for engineering unsafe automobiles are not thought of as "criminals", and their conduct does not usually attract criminal sanctions. Yet, hazardously designed products may well be the cause of death, injury and economic loss that vastly exceeds the harm caused by common assaults, robberies and burglaries. Thus, the public image in Canada of "the criminal" is of a person who is poor, native or belonging to some ethnic or racial minority, young and urban. Diligent armies of sociologists and psychologists undertake careful studies of the residents of inner city slums and ghettos, and native reserves in an effort to locate the causes of crime and the factors that produce criminal behaviour. But corporate boardrooms are not usually viewed as providing equally fruitful evidence on the topic of criminality.

Why are the white-collar perpetrators of such anti-social conduct as environmental pollution, price-fixing and sub-standard housing not usually subjected to close analysis by social scientists when they are investigating the etiology of crime and criminal behaviour? There are several reasons.

First, much seriously anti-social behaviour has not been brought within the ambit of the criminal law. The loss (economic and personal) caused to victims of such "white-collar crime" may greatly exceed that caused by lower class crime, but if the conduct causing the harm has not been made illegal, it will not be recorded in official statistics. Since criminologists (and the media) have recourse to official statistics when they undertake to identify and analyze criminal behaviour, the omission of such "crimes" from official computations has the result of promoting a kind of class "blindness" with respect to crime and criminals.

Second, there is much evidence to suggest that a kind of "double standard" operates within the criminal justice system, creating systemic bias in official approaches to arrest, prosecution and criminal conviction. Thus, even when legislation exists which attaches criminal penalties to such seriously anti-social conduct as the manufacture of hazardous products or the creation of industrial pollution, the teeth of law tend not to bite as often or as deeply against upper-class offenders. This claim needs some explanation.

Victims of certain kinds of crime tend not to report them to the police. When a crime is reported, the police have a wide margin of discretion in selecting from among those who have violated the law which persons (or corporations) will be charged or arrested. And from the class of those arrested, Crown prosecutors and Attorneys General have a wide discretion in selecting which cases to prosecute. When a decision is made to bring a criminal prosecution against an offender, the courts (judges and juries), who tend to share the mores of the privileged strata of society, have considerable discretion in deciding whether or not to convict. And where conviction occurs, the choice between severe sanctions (prison, for example) or mild penalty (nominal fine, let us say) is likely to be similarly influenced.

The conclusion seems inescapable: if the sample of criminals who are fully "processed" — arrested, charged, prosecuted, convicted, sentenced to prison or imprisoned — is unrepresentative and biased against lower class offenders, then it follows that official crime statistics are likely to produce a seriously misleading image of the typical criminal and the typical crime. This, in turn, vitiates efforts to locate the conditions, causes and cures for crime.

Moreover, to the extent that class bias in the legal system is recognized by the general population, it may contribute to disobedience of the law. This possibility will be examined next.

SOCIAL ALIENATION AS A FACTOR PRODUCING DISOBEDIENCE

There is, among many Canadians, a belief that without the general deterrent threat of punishment, social stability — which is generally viewed as a fragile achievement — would disintegrate, and society would relapse into a Hobbesian state of chaos and violent anarchy.

To those who accept this Hobbesian view, it ought to be conceded that there does very likely exist a class of potential criminals whose anti-social propensities are deterred primarily by fear of punishment. It would be foolish to deny that general deterrence plays some (difficult to quantify) role in promoting law-abiding behaviour. But there is evidence to suggest that the great majority of people abstain from *serious* crime (for example, murder, rape, violent assault, bank robbery) because of the socializing influence of such factors as parental training, education, social customs and mores, conscience and so forth. This would seem to accord with Professor Podgorecki's findings that those who exhibit obedient attitudes . . . tend to be well educated, socially integrated and psychologically secure.[19]

Those who adopt the Hobbesian view of society tend to regard human society as a competitive struggle between individuals and groups of individuals, each pursuing private aims and competing desires in a mutually threatening manner. Since the various goals and desires of competing individuals cannot be reconciled, the best society can do is to provide a set of rules, moral and legal, regulating the struggle for self-satisfaction. This view of society as *Gesellschaft* requires an emphasis on legal obligations, such as contracts, enforced by coercive sanctions.

As Professor Hogarth notes, however, in his discussion of the transformation of our society and legal system "from status to contract" and as Professor Podgorecki points out in his contrast of "official law" and "intuitive law", our political culture also contains an alternative model for conceptualizing the role of the individual vis-à-vis his or her fellows in society: society as *Gemeinschaft*. Profesor Hogarth refers to the status of individuals; a political philosopher might refer to this as the conception of society as a series of communities. Political and moral life is viewed as the pursuit of common goals within the setting of such communities as the family, the workplace, or the neighbourhood. Other individuals may threaten one's interests, and some rules — moral and legal — are necessary in order to restrict some kinds of harmful behaviour. But the goals of both morality and legality are viewed primarily as the facilitation of common endeavours rather than as negative restrictions on the pursuit of self-interest.

From the view of society as *Gemeinschaft*, the coercive instrumentality of the law, in its penal role, is viewed as a system of last resort. When community norms are functioning properly, the criminal justice system will

19 A. Podgorecki, *supra*, c. 3.

be required only infrequently, and when required it will signal some sort of breakdown or weakening of the social cement that provides the normal basis for community life. From the view of society as *Gesellschaft,* by contrast, it is entirely normal to invoke the criminal justice system (or the law of contracts) to restrict invasive behaviour, to enforce obligations and to restrict anti-social conflict.

Although both of these perspectives at present coexist in our society, Professor Hogarth is doubtless correct in seeing a shift over time, and an accelerated shift recently, from *Gemeinschaft* to *Gesellschaft* (or, in his terms, from status to contract).

As Fred Hirsch emphasizes in his book, *The Social Limits to Growth,*[20] a competitive market society functions well only so long as it is supported by the social morality inherited from the precapitalist and preindustrial past. The corrosive effects of the culture of the market-place — with its individualistic, egoistic, self-seeking, acquisitive values — have undermined the public-spiritedness necessary to hold the system together. "As individual behaviour has been increasingly directed to individual advantage, habits and instincts based on common attitudes and objectives have lost out."[21] When to this is added the effect of such phenomena as increasing anonymity in large cities, a high degree of labour mobility and intensified economic competition, the cumulative effect is a serious weakening of traditional social values, an increase of criminal behaviour (violation of legal norms when this optimizes self-interest) and an increasing cynicism about individual motivation and about the ability of the criminal justice system to protect individual interests.

Sir Henry Maine's vivid phrase — "from status to contract" — effectively encapsulates the transmutation of social norms in the face of market economy and market culture. And it has meant the progressive withering of internalized moral sanctions. This, in turn, has made it much more difficult for the state to fulfil its role of protecting individual rights to property and personal safety. This phenomenon is of sufficient importance to warrant further elaboration.

The experience of living in a society with a high level of fellow-feeling and altruism can be educative, and can produce a cycle of virtue and public-spiritedness. Conversely, the experience of living in an alienated society with little fellow-feeling and a high level of egotism can produce a cycle of anomic and anti-social behaviour. Public-spiritedness is an important social resource, one which can be enhanced or diminished by the nature of key institutions such as the criminal justice system.

An example may be useful here. Sociologists testing the likelihood that people would return a lost wallet containing money and personal papers found that on the day following the assassination of Senator Robert Kennedy in the

20 Fred Hirsch, *Social Limits to Growth* (1976).

21 *Ibid.*, pp. 117-18.

United States none of the wallets was returned. This deviation from the previous pattern which had prevailed for some months (during which about 45 per cent of "lost" wallets were returned), may be explained by the hypothesis that immediately following the assassination people felt more cynical about social bonds. When people lose faith in the community of attitudes and values which bond them together, their concern for the welfare of others appears rapidly to diminish.[22] A society in which most people feel alienated and powerless and in which the state and its major institutions appear remote, mysterious, and indifferent to ordinary human needs will not likely produce a strong sense of moral commitment and citizenship from its people.

When a significant number of citizens regard legal norms as morally just and as necessary for social life, their internal controls will promote a tendency to comply with legal norms, and the role of penal sanctions in promoting law-abiding behaviour will become secondary. Conversely, when legal norms are widely viewed as foolish or unnecessary or as unjust and oppressive, then compliance can be induced, if at all, only by such means as the deterrent effect of criminal sanctions.

Among those in society who perceive that the enforcement of the law operates to the disadvantage of those with least access to power and other resources, an attitude of cynicism appears to have developed towards the criminal justice system. A system which is thought to victimize the most vulnerable and least advantaged members of society will tend to weaken belief in the legitimacy of authority, and not only among those selected for victimization. Instead of strengthening social integration and cohesion — a principal *desideratum* for any legal system — the presence of structural and procedural bias in the criminal justice system tends to promote cynicism and social alienation.

The criminal justice system is one of the major institutions of a society, and the way in which this institution brings people into relation with one another is a major factor influencing social attitudes, values and behaviour. One may plausibly hypothesize that the greater the extent to which societal institutions are arranged so as to promote fellow-feeling and a sense of shared fate among the different classes and strata of society, the greater will be the strength of social bonds and the sense of social cohesion which binds a community together and which inclines people to consider the welfare of others. When a major institution, such as the criminal justice system, displays class bias and differential treatment based on such divisive factors as race and age and economic status, the sense of shared interdependence is undermined. Shared experiences and fellow-feeling are surely a crucial part of the social cement which enhances the tendency of citizens to obey the law and to provide positive support to those whom they recognize as sharing the same set of basic norms and values. The educational importance of living in a society whose basic institutions and norms elicit respect cannot be overly stressed.

22 Sheleff, "The Bystander: Behaviour, Law, Ethics" (1978), cited by Hornstein, *Ethics* (1980).

The level of fellow-feeling and respect for law prevailing in any society and the willingness to act individually and collectively to protect shared basic values are precious resources that can be seriously eroded by treatment which citizens perceive as discriminatory, unfair or unjust.

It is not realistic to suppose that the biases and injustices of our present system of criminal justice can be easily or painlessly rectified. As the authors of *Struggle for Justice* aptly comment:

> To the extent that equal justice is correlated with equality of status, influence, and economic power, the construction of a just system of criminal justice in an injust society is a contradiction in terms.[23]

This does not, however, entail the conclusion that all reformist efforts are bound to be futile or counter-productive. One may work to reduce, in a piecemeal fashion, the operation of bias and prejudice at the same time as one recognizes that the criminal justice system is merely one aspect of the broader social organization.

June Tapp's study of the socializing impact of jury participation points towards the kind of social reforms which might effectively change public perceptions of the criminal justice system. Participation in the jury process appears to have a significant effect on citizens as a "vehicle to socialize more principled legal reasoning". When the public is given enhanced opportunity to participate in the law-making process, by means such as jury service, the socialization effects can be marked. Citizens who do jury duty are thereby enabled, in however limited a manner, to make and maintain laws. They become thereby "more autonomous, competent, and ethical in their judgments about personal and societal codes of conduct".[24]

It appears reasonable to hypothesize that a society which provided greatly enhanced opportunities for its citizens to participate, directly and indirectly, in the formulation and application of the rules which govern all our lives would be well on the way to diminishing the level of cynicism and alienation which afflict most social institutions, including the criminal justice system. One must recognize, however, that enhanced public participation involves power sharing and decentralization of decision-making and that these objectives are likely to be resisted, in some cases strenuously, by those currently in positions of authority who benefit from the distribution of power under the status quo.

---

23 G. Richard Bacon *et al.*, *Struggle for Justice: A Report on Crime and Punishment in America* (1971).

24 J. L. Tapp, *infra*, c. 10.

10

WHAT INFLUENCES PUBLIC ATTITUDES TOWARDS LAW?

If the public's attitudes about the legal system influence the formulation and administration of laws, it is important to know how those attitudes develop. The news media and the schools are widely thought to play a major role, and religion is seen as an important factor by some. But beyond these institutional educators of attitudes — all of which will be examined in this chapter — are other influences, less formal but perhaps equally significant, such as personal experience with the legal system, and perceived double standards on the part of those who administer the system. These too will be discussed.

MEDIA INFLUENCE ON OPINION AND POLICY

Tom Kent

This is a conference about law and public opinion, and you may wonder why the title for my remarks is not media influence on opinion, period. I've added "and policy" in order to make a point; a point which I think is crucial to understanding the nature of media influence on opinion.

The point is not, of course, that the media have a direct influence on policy. They influence policy, what is done or not done, only to the extent that they are perceived as influencing opinion about what should or should not be done.

My point, however, is that the media influence operates in two main sectors: it operates on public opinion; and it also operates directly on policy-makers. Since this conference assumes a cynical society, perhaps I should say that media influence operates on the vanity of policy-makers. It is a rare politician who is not hooked on the media. What was the TV clip like? Did it make the national news? How was he or she reported in the newspaper, and particularly, with how large a head and on what page? There are even politicians who never learn to be indifferent to what newspaper editorials say about them. Certainly they are much more avid readers of editorials and columns than the public at large.

I have concentrated on politicians because they are most frequently affected by the media. I don't mean to suggest that other people involved in public affairs are different. Businessmen and bureaucrats are less frequently exposed. But when they are, in my observation, most are quite as sensitive to media treatment as the less mature of politicians. I haven't noticed that lawyers or academics are different.

This sensitivity of public people requires emphasis because if it is not recognized, the nature of media influence on opinion will be incomprehensible. The clearest thing about media influence is that the media themselves feel it to be strong. They are justified because they constantly see how much the policy-makers care. In that sense there is a sort of conspiratorial relationship between public people and the media. Though they have different reasons, they share an assumption that public opinion is much influenced by the media. And the assumption, to a degree, makes it so.

I do not mean that it is all done by mirrors. Public people would not take the media seriously, and the media would not be able to take themselves seriously, if almost everyone bought a newspaper solely for the grocery ads, and switched channels when the TV news came on. Undoubtedly media influence on public opinion is a fact. But clearly, in my view, the importance of the influence is magnified by the mirrors of the mutually-regarding relationship between the media and public people.

With that recognized, let me turn to some comments on media influence and the public of a cynical society. The adjective "cynical" isn't one that I myself would choose to delineate a principal characteristic of this society, in comparison with other places and other times, but it fits one aspect of this topic. Nowadays a newspaper that sets out deliberately to propagandize, to express an opinion and win converts to it, faces a public that is harder to convince than was the case 100 or even 50 years ago.

The reasons for this are of two kinds. The more important reason is that the electronic media enable the policy-makers involved in an issue to communicate directly with the public. It is hard for even the elderly among us to remember how great the contrast is between the period previous to the advent of electronic media and current times. The role of opinion-making used to belong to the print media. Before radio, all contact with a politician had to be face-to-face. For most people the opportunity for contact was very limited, even with local politicians. The national politician could be seen only very occasionally, if at all.

On most matters and at most times, the public was dependent on the newspapers not only for information but for a very large part of what it could learn about opinions. The arguments of the politicians reached the public only as filtered through newspaper reports. The statements of opinion that people encountered most frequently were newspaper editorials, either avowed or thinly disguised in the news columns. Fortunately, in those days there were usually two newspapers, or more, even in what we would now consider to be very small communities. Their role in public life was determined by the virtual inevitability that one adhered to the Conservative position and one to the Liberal position. Their editorial battles were at the very centre of opinion-making.

This description applies particularly to political issues. But insofar as there was public opinion on other issues, the influence of print was hardly less dominant. The main difference was that on non-political issues, the daily newspaper shared more of its role with the weekly newspaper and with tracts of various kinds. The only opinion-leaders who could reach the public regularly and on a national scale, by means other than print, were the churches.

That was the past. Today the direct influence of media opinion on public opinion is, by comparison, trifling. The main reason, I repeat, is that the electronic media have created a more direct channel between decision-makers and the public. As yet, of course, it is almost entirely a one-way channel. It doesn't necessarily increase the effectiveness of public opinion, but it does give the public a new access to the expression of opinion, and the clash of opinion, from the people involved in decisions. Therefore, while the role of the press used to be that of both a medium and an active participant in public debate — and more often the second than the first — now the media are primarily conveyors rather than formulators of opinion.

There is a second factor in this change which is less important than the channel-like nature of the electronic media. The fact that they provide direct contact between the public person and the public constitutes a difference in kind from the role of print media in earlier days. But one may hope that the second factor, though less dramatic, will in the long run become even more important. It is, simply, that the public is better informed.

The main reason for that does not lie in the media. Rather, it is the marked increase in the average amount of time devoted to education, the extra years people spend at school and at post-secondary institutions, and the greater extent to which they subsequently obtain further education of some kind. One may groan about the quality of much of the education. Certainly the net improvement in public knowledge and understanding is far less than should have been made possible by the extra years and all the extra resources devoted to education. Nevertheless, the change is considerable. It means that we have a foundation on which we can build increasing benefits from the information explosion.

By the information explosion I mean, of course, the vast increase in the amount of information that is readily available to more and more people. Thanks to the extraordinarily increased speed and ease of communication, information is available almost regardless of time and place. We are barely beginning to understand the implications of this revolution. What is relevant to the present discussion, however, is the simple fact that we are building a society in which vastly more people have vastly more information.

I don't know whether that means a more cynical society, but I'm confident that it means a more sceptical society. Specifically, I think it means a society in which the media will be less and less effective in influencing opinion and expressing opinion. It used to be said that the trouble with newspapers was that if you read anything on a topic you knew well, you would be sure to find that the newspaper had got it wrong. In a more informed society that will be true for more people on more topics. It seems to me that the average reader or viewer is going to be less and less impressed by the opinions of editorialists and columnists and commentators. They are an endangered species.

In saying this, I am disagreeing with the people who fear that the new information technology will result in more manipulation of opinion, in the media telling people what to think. I don't take that bogey seriously. On the contrary, I think that the information revolution will make overtly totalitarian systems more and more difficult to sustain.

However, I have to stress *overtly,* and with that I come to the dark side of the coin. The conclusion I have argued so far is that the direct expression of opinion by the media is having and will have a decreasing influence on public opinion. But that tells us nothing about the influence of the media in their role not as overt propagandists but as gatekeepers. In that more important respect the significance of the information explosion is quite different and the dangers it brings are, I am afraid, greater in Canada than in most western societies.

The primary function of the media is to choose, from a mass of information, hour by hour and day by day, what they will reject and what they will give to their readers, listeners and viewers. From what they choose, decisions must be made about the relative weight to be given to each item and how each will be presented in a way that is accurate and interesting, clear and informative. This is a demanding task. It is not so bad if the audience is a relatively informed one, say that of the *New York Times* or of a number of European papers. To be clear and accurate is not too difficult, even when you are in a hurry, if you know your subject and if you can assume that your readers or listeners have a good deal of background knowledge. Lawyers and professors achieve it regularly. But, as the clients of lawyers and the students of professors know all too well, it is a much rarer talent to be able to combine clarity and accuracy with simplicity. That is the constant requirement if the medium is attempting to serve a broad constituency, such as that of a television network, or of most newspapers in our one-newspaper towns. To do the job at all well in those circumstances requires skills of a very high order.

Generally, it is not well done. It is more poorly done, we should not forget, in totalitarian societies. There the basic fault is that the selection of information is not based on a genuine judgment of what is significant to the reader or listener or viewer, but rather on what is convenient for the regime. For different reasons, it must be said that the work of the media is not generally well done even in relatively free societies. Among those societies, it is particularly badly done in Canada.

In order not to be unfairly harsh, let me quickly enter the main qualification to that judgment. It is my impression — I do not claim exhaustive international study — that in radio the CBC compares favourably with the services of most countries. Certainly there are many Canadian communities where it is by far the best available medium not only for national news but also for regional and local news.

With that exception, however, the predominant character of Canadian media is regrettably clear. They are flung together by too few people, with too little background and experience, with too few resources and too little time. Since I have reason to know how frequently the Canadian media misunderstand or misrepresent criticism of the media, let me make it clear that I am not attacking the journalists as individuals. I am simply saying that there are too few of them. In general, their employers do not give them enough status or enough pay. They have too little opportunity to develop themselves. Too many pass on to other occupations. Those who remain do not have enough incentive or enough time to dig into most of the things they write about. They are neither equipped nor encouraged to develop a full understanding themselves, or to convey it clearly to their readers or viewers.

These are, of course, generalizations. There are considerable differences among units of the Canadian media, print and electronic. Some are very much better, or less bad, than others. While CBC radio is way ahead, it is fair to say of the rest of the electronic media that the quality range is from medium to bad. For daily newspapers the range is wider: it goes down to very bad, and there are many in that category.

These are qualitative judgments, but I emphasize that they are not moral judgments. I am not alleging sinister interests or deliberate perversions of the news. I am speaking simply of the inadequacy of resources for the demanding function of the media. The point was stated very clearly by a Toronto newspaper publisher more than a hundred years ago: ". . . a daily newspaper is good or bad according to the money expended in the preparation of its news."[1] That is not, of course, the whole truth, but it is the first component of the truth. For anyone who has observed the operations of the Canadian media, who has evaluated the resources employed in providing their contents, the marvel is that most are not worse than they are. That they are not is a genuine tribute to the too few people they employ.

However, to recognize that the basic problem is one of resources rather than of motivation is not to make light of the perversion that results. An

1 T. C. Patterson, quoted in Paul Rutherford, *A Victorian Authority* (1982), p. 94.

inadequately staffed newspaper will not tell its readers the truth. The staff, however well motivated, will not get at the truth. They will not have all the information and, in haste and inexperience, they will not make good judgments about the significance of the information they do have.

Apologists for the press, who like to think of themselves either as cynics or as realists, say that the public gets the newspapers — or, in most cases, the newspaper — it deserves. That is silly: there is very little the public can do about it. What the public gets is what the staff of the newspaper is capable of producing. If the staff is small and much of it not very well-informed, what will come out of haste and inexperience will reflect mind-sets rather than investigation; it will be superficial rather than researched; it will be the product, however unintentionally, of prejudice rather than of mature and balanced judgment; it will be confused rather than clear.

I have been describing what we get from almost all of the media most of the time on most subjects. The direct consequence for public opinion relates to the process by which it is formulated. If the media were doing a better job, public opinion would be arrived at on the basis of more and better information, clearer perceptions of issues, more rounded and balanced understanding of causes and effects, of problems and solutions, and of constraints and options.

These are all relatives. I do not want to overemphasize the significance of media weaknesses. On many issues — and particularly on such issues as how to vote in general elections — we rely chiefly on the common sense of the public, assisted by direct viewing of the politicians. I doubt that better information would have more than a marginal influence on the quality of the process by which people make up their minds on some broad issues. The importance of better media lies rather in the difference they might make to opinions on many more specific issues.

Let me take an example from the field of economic policy. It is widely assumed that the "right" exchange rate for the Canadian dollar is parity with the U.S. dollar. That is taken as a sign of health in the Canadian economy and any significant falling from it is seen as a bad thing. The media, by the way they report movements in the exchange rate, constantly reinforce that attitude. There are sound economic reasons for not pursuing parity, however. If journalists were more sophisticated in their understanding of the economics of the exchange rate, public opinion as it is impressed on politicians might well be less inhibiting, and the resulting lower threshold of bravery might permit politicians to adopt wiser economic policies.

I have used an example from my own field. I have no doubt that in the field of law and its administration, and particularly in relation to the penal system, many forceful examples could be given.

So far I have been discussing only direct consequences of media weakness. It is the indirect consequences that have more ideological significance.

A strong newspaper, television or radio service has a staff with enough time, knowledge and detachment for biases to be cancelled out, for the aim of getting at the truth generally to be dominant over personal opinions. The smaller, the more harried, the less knowledgeable the staff, the further from that ideal its output will tend to be; the more the presentation of news will tend to reflect its limited knowledge and experience, and therefore, the biases of the people who do the presenting. If this meant that the treatment of the news reflected the individual biases of staff members, there probably would be a considerable variety even within small units of the media. In practice, however, there are strong magnetic forces that tend to line up the biases in more limited directions.

Most units of the media are businesses. Their business success depends on the extent to which they dominate their communities in readership, viewing or listening. That determines their attractiveness to advertisers. The type of journalism that serves this business incentive varies with community situations. There was a time when in many communities, it meant head-to-head competition between newspapers to be first with the latest that was most exciting or most titillating. Few of those situations survive. In the one-newspaper town readership is to an important degree maximized by not being offensive, by being bland rather than provocative. Even in the most competitive media situations now existing — large communities with many radio stations — the route to maximum income is to establish a place in the market, a special appeal to a segment of the listening public, and within that segment to make no enemies.

In short, and with some qualifications in some situations, the business incentive for journalism is to be bland, to comfort what is established in the community, to challenge no widespread ideas, to see the world as others see it. In our Canadian case, the "others" whose world view is obtainable at lowest cost are American.

I am not suggesting that the whole media staff is consciously instructed along these lines. But the proprietors and their representatives naturally choose for promotion to managerial roles journalists whose cast of mind fits the business requirement. The businessman may not actively intervene to tell the journalists what to put in the paper and what to leave out, but the journalists who make the decisions are largely influenced by what they know to be the business wish.

I do not mean that this is a highly conscious process. The strongly partisan press, deliberately manipulating the news to serve a cause, is almost entirely a thing of the past. Most people in the media today are sincere in saying that their aim is objectivity. However objectivity comes in many colours. The predominant colour of the media might be described as parochial blue. Objectivity on specifics operates within a mind-set that is generally rather narrow, that takes society as it is, that understands little of history or of the world outside North America, that has little feeling for science and a great deal for direct business interests.

Undoubtedly this has some effect on the conditioning of public opinion. This is a fact which must be recognized by any serious analyst. But I do not think that its significance is anywhere near as great as critics of our society and champions of particular causes tend to think. The dominant ideology of the media is essentially conformist and as such it shifts with the tides. It is something of a brake on the formulation of new opinions, but it is not an unmoving obstacle.

There is not much we can do about the basic business orientation or conformist attitude of the Canadian news media. In our kind of society, those characteristics are bound to be what they are. They could be markedly different only in the context of social and economic changes far greater than, in my view, could at present be sensibly accomplished.

This does not mean that we can do nothing. What I am suggesting is that rather than worry about changing the basic attitudes of the media, we should concentrate on trying to increase and improve the resources that go into the media. If that can be done, I think we can then rely on the journalists, gradually at least, to improve the discharge of the media's functions. If the gatekeepers of our information flow have more time, if they are paid at levels that encourage more knowledge and experience, if they can study and investigate and travel more, then I am confident that biases will be eroded, and that the public will be better served with the information on which to formulate opinion.

The resources could be available. Our media are profitable. In general, they produce higher returns than most of the businesses in which Canadians, or indeed foreigners, invest. The business economics of newspapers make it inevitable that most are now local monopolies. As such they can be highly profitable. The electronic media are licensed, and with modern technology there is no reason to license more stations than can generate enough revenue to perform their information function well. The problem, in other words, is not to ensure the existence of a reasonable level of resources, but to ensure that the resources are used within the media, rather than taken out in profits higher than those that suffice in other industries.

In Canada, unavoidably, competition is a less effective spur to performance than it is in larger and denser economies. There is no point in weeping about that. In most trades and professions we have to rely more on the motivation to do a good job, to be well regarded by one's peers. That could be a particularly powerful force in the publicly exposed media if they were run by journalists or media people.

It is here, in my view, that economic policy has gone badly astray. Government has compounded the inevitable limits to competition in any one industry by allowing and even encouraging conglomeration — the growth of firms that embrace many industries. The accountants' criteria become the only one; the motivation of managers to serve the public well in their chosen occupation is often made catastrophically less effective. The media are conspicuous victims of conglomeration. Many countries have been wiser or more fortunate. We ought never to have allowed conglomeration to develop in Canada as it has.

By this stage there is a little, but not much, that we can sensibly do to roll it back. We can stop it going further, and we can take some measures to offset its effects. We can open up the media to a more effective play of public opinion on what they do for the public. We can, by tax measures, create stronger incentives and disincentives that will cause the media, and particularly the conglomerate-owned media, which are the largest part of the problem, to take less profit and put more resources into the provision of information. By those measures we would strengthen the hands of journalists who do their particular job well against the corporate empire builders and their accountants. Those who are interested in an elaboration of these views are referred to the Report of the Royal Commission on Newspapers.[2]

Let me summarize. The media have some influence on public opinion as propagandists, but that role has diminished, and the direction of technological change is to diminish it further. They have a continuing major influence as the gatekeepers of much of the information on which opinion is formed. They do that job badly, not from the perversity of those employed in it but because the resources devoted to a task of great difficulty are generally inadequate. Their inadequacy means that the function is performed not only with less skill than it requires but also with less objectivity. The main route to having the wells of truth flow both more freely and with less contamination is the same: it is to ensure that more resources are put into drilling the wells.

PUBLIC ATTITUDES TOWARDS LAW: THE EFFECTS OF SELECTIVE AND SUPERFICIAL MEDIA REPORTING

John Meisel

There are two essential variables in the universe of this conference: the Law and the Cynical Society. I might say that I have dropped the question mark in the title of the conference; I accept the Cynical Society as given.

These two variables are anything but independent of one another, of course. The law is not absolute, nor is it divorced from its setting. It is a reflection of society: of its economic, national, ethnic, religious, and demo-

2 T. Kent (Chairperson), *Royal Commission on Newspapers* (1981), p. xiii. I would merely emphasize that I mean the report, not most of the newspaper reports of the report.

graphic aspects, to name but a few. I see society here as more or less the independent variable, and law as the dependent variable. Linking them are the opinion leaders, that is, the media, politicians, advertisers, academics, literati, and so on.

The survey underpinning this conference indicates that these opinion leaders sometimes influence attitudes towards the law, but these leaders are not necessarily drawn from the society they influence. It is quite common for Canadians to transfer American experience to their perception of Canadian reality. This is not surprising when we remember how many hours Canadians spend watching television, and how much of it, particularly in peak viewing hours, is American. If it is dangerous to walk in New York at night, people become afraid to walk in Kitchener. Our school children are more familiar with American laws than they are with our own. Thus, the nature and reasons for our own laws are less well known than those of our neighbours.

The way opinion leaders affect the public's attitude is influenced by three major factors: the laws themselves, the law-makers, and the law-breakers. If "the law is an ass", as Bumble said, if law-makers are seen as inept or dishonest, and if law-breakers thrive, then attitudes to the law will be cynical. Ultimately, I believe, legal attitudes themselves will come to reflect this.

I have witnessed a timely example in my present life as a regulator. There exist in this country a number of unauthorized television receiver dishes, and the way in which the public and the media and others react to them is instructive. Basically, what is involved is an act of piracy, by which certain broadcast programs are stolen, usually from American satellites, and then viewed on Canadian sets, or sometimes even distributed by Canadian cable systems. This piracy is widespread, particularly in remote and underserved areas, but not only there. It is engaged in, for the most part, by those who are genuinely starved for a variety of television services. Sometimes it is encouraged by local councils, by people seeking a quick dollar, by some politicians, by vendors of dishes and, I suppose, sometimes by the sheer devilry of doing something illegal. The use of these dishes involves a number of legal infractions: the Radio Act[3] is often violated, the Broadcasting Act[4] is flouted, and breaches of the copyright laws occur.[5] The practice undermines an important element in Canadian life: the effectiveness of regulation, and ultimately the legitimacy of the government itself — not just the federal government but all government.

The argument for doing these things is understandable. Since people living close to the American border have access to all kinds of American programs, why should others be deprived simply because they happen to find

3 R.S.C. 1970, c. R-1.

4 R.S.C. 1970, c. B-11.

5 These comments were made before the revision of federal policy, announced in March 1983, which liberalized the use of dishes.

themselves in more remote areas? There is also an argument to be made on the grounds of freedom of information. Since technology has made a variety of TV signals available, why not make use of it? Why restrict the freedom of the individual? Thus, people simply take the law into their own hands and decide that it's in their interest, and perhaps the public interest, that they should do so.

Now the question arises: what is the role of the media in this process? Very briefly, the media in Canada have given extensive publicity to this practice. While this is neither surprising nor reprehensible, the media have, in their reporting, bestowed a considerable amount of glamour on the offenders. They have also undertaken a sustained sniping at the law itself and at its agents. And they have sometimes actively abetted the illegal conduct. For instance, local newspapers in communities with dishes often list the pirated television schedules. This is no different from advertising the location of a shop for stolen goods.

The media have also, I think, been guilty of what I would call biased reporting in relation to the legal aspects of this whole process. For example, last year the CRTC prosecuted an illegal operator in Newfoundland.[6] The CRTC lost in the first instance, a fact that was widely reported with massive headlines throughout the country. It was a very important case affecting our jurisdiction with respect to cable regulation. On appeal, when CRTC won the case, few newspapers reported the fact at all. By this kind of selective process (which may not have been intentional — it is simply more interesting to see the CRTC slapped down than built up), the newspapers failed to inform the public of the facts.

This kind of activity tends to undermine the law and breed cynicism about it; a cynicism that is sometimes, I think, reinforced by politicians seeking short-term political advantage in espousing what is clearly a popular cause. There is also a certain amount of Ottawa-bashing involved, but that is perhaps of minor importance.

It is useful to compare the way in which the media dealt with the case to which I have just referred with the way they deal with other sorts of illegal behaviour, such as violence during strikes, spy cases, improper behaviour by the police, and infractions of the law by certain minority groups, homosexuals or motorcycle gangs. It becomes obvious that the media, as intervening variables, act very selectively. The results of the various media interpretations, therefore, can be extremely complex, since they deal with different topics in different ways. The items that are stressed and the views that are taken are by no means unrelated to the economic underpinnings of the newspaper or broadcaster in question, or by the economics of the activity itself. Consider, for example, how the treatment of news may affect a newspaper's circulation,

6 *R. v. Shellbird Cable Ltd.* (1982), 67 C.P.R. (2d) 148, 38 Nfld. & P.E.I.R. 224, 108 A.P.R. 224, leave to appeal to S.C.C. refused 68 C.P.R. (2d) 288, 46 N.R. 623, 40 Nfld. & P.E.I.R. 360, 115 A.P.R. 360.

and ultimately its advertising revenue, or how an unpopular program may result in the withdrawing of television ads.

While the media are most cynical with respect to government itself, they are a good deal less so when they look inward at themselves. Self-absorbed they may be, but they are generally most indulgent when it comes to assessing their own performance. As for their treatment of the legal profession, my impression is that the dominant characteristic of the media is not so much cynicism as neglect. They do tend, of course, to sensationalize lurid cases, but on the whole, the media do not lavish much attention on the quality of judges, the selection process leading to their appointment, or the biases inherent in the administration of justice. Other aspects of society make better press.

Many legal issues are, of course, extremely complex and the media are compelled, as Tom Kent has pointed out, to be simple, concrete, and to deal with familiar topics. They tend to play with caricatures more than with fully detailed portraits. The immediate is stressed, the long-term is played down (or, as the media would probably say, down-played). Consequently, both the grandeur and the cobwebs of the law are concealed.

In summary, the media are selective in their treatment of the topics relevant to the universe of this conference. They are also superficial and very powerful. This cannot but help to contribute to an unrealistic perception of the law and the legal process by the public, and hence, again, to a general cynicism with respect to jurisprudence.

LAW IN A CONFUSED SOCIETY: EDUCATION AND LEGAL SOCIALIZATION

T. R. Morrison

EDUCATION AND SOCIALIZATION

Let me begin with the assertion that all real education is political. One underestimated, indeed often overlooked, consequence of education, is that it gradually plants the seeds of dissatisfaction with the way things are. If there is any truth to the adage that ignorance is bliss, then education is the corruption of happiness and contentment. By exposing a mind to the possibility of possibility, to the rudiments of "as if" thinking, and to the world beyond personal and present experience, educators, often unknowingly, create the condition of discontentment. In simple terms, unhappiness is a consequence of many kinds of learning and, as a result, education is politically important.

Politicians cannot afford to have the voters mad at them. An educated and well-informed constituency can be big trouble; a half-educated constituency can be big trouble too. The ignorant and quiescent mind is more easily led than the informed and active one. Public education that transcends mere socialization is thus a source of tension to the less democratically inclined, and this is one reason — albeit a negative one — why we will always need it. Egerton Ryerson, the architect of public education in Canada, apparently had this situation in mind when he warned that any nation expecting to be both ignorant and free expects what never will be.[7]

A half-educated constituency can be big trouble, too, but for very different reasons. Education which accomplishes no more than socialization — conformity to society's norms — can produce a complacent population that accepts institutions of authority unquestioningly. A little learning can indeed be a dangerous thing if it is of this uncritical variety. There is reason for concern that in some respects our public education system does not transcend socialization.

Whatever impact schools have on the development of attitudes toward law is part of the political significance of schooling. Socialization to law within educational settings is but a part of the larger process of political socialization.[8]

Currently, there exists substantial debate on the definition of political socialization: anthropological studies stress the transference of attitudes and values across the generations in a given cultural context; psychological studies often trace attitude formation to the family and childrearing; sociologists concentrate on the learning of appropriate role behaviour in various settings. What all of these definitions have in common is a focus on the process of *induction* into society, and on the role of the school in producing a "model citizen" for society. Political socialization in schools, including legal socialization, is essentially a conservative process which facilitates the maintenance of the status quo by inducing young people to accept the existing system and its legitimacy.[9]

DIRECT LEGAL SOCIALIZATION

In the school, one can distinguish between two different forms of legal socialization: direct and indirect. The direct form of legal socialization consists of transmitting information, and more particularly norms and values, to the young. A number of comments are in order in this context:

7 See Neil G. McDonald and A. Chaiton, *Egerton Ryerson and His Times* (1978).
8 See J. Ackelson, *The Political Imagination of the Adolescent* (1975).
9 See Gintis and Bowles, *Schooling in Capitalist America* (1976).

1. Very little specific legal information, whether about human or civil rights or substantive law, is transmitted to the young as part of the curricula. The exception concerns business or commercial law — an interesting point in itself.

2. The non-commercial legal information that is transmitted focuses mainly on constutitional themes, by far the most abstract and idealistic dimension of law.

3. Noticeably absent from curricula is any attention to legal reasoning or legal culture.

4. When law is mentioned, it is usually as a disembodied concept — something which is to be obeyed and which exists apart from society. The inconsistencies within law, the tensions between law and morality, and the place of law in fostering or forestalling change are rarely, if ever, discussed.

5. Students tend to acquire a particular view of one category of person as a consequence of their legal socialization. This is the law-breaker. Through their historical studies, for example, students acquire a generalized picture of "typical" law-breakers in society: (1) members of union, (2) immigrant groups, (3) political dissidents, or (4) the poor. Moreover, students are often taught to equate "law-breaker" with "bad person".[10] The idea of unjust laws, the possibility of environmental determinants of deviancy, or the relativity of deviancy are concepts that rarely, if ever, penetrate their consciousness through the formal teaching in school.

6. Students acquire a view of school knowledge as being neutral and objectively derived. Facts, concepts, and theories are treated not as notions created by human beings, and hence relative to particular individuals, groups or cultural contexts, but as truths to be understood. Teachers pride themselves on their supposed neutrality in these matters. School officials insist upon it. This aura of objectivity and supposed neutrality which surrounds the school curriculum provides a way in which criticism and dissent can be defined as matters of opinion and expression of bias and, hence, "inappropriate" in a learning setting. This basic objective approach to knowledge, perhaps more than any other factor, explains the willingness of students to accept a disembodied concept of law.[11]

Given this vacuum, it should not be surprising that young people, at least as far as the formal curriculum is concerned, form their attitudes and knowledge of law, as they do of sex, from peer rumour, family attitudes and television. By and large, the contemporary Canadian young person, as a result of his or her schooling, views law as something outside the person, as something to be avoided or obeyed, as something in relation to which he or

10 See K. Osborne, "Labour Studies and Continuing Education" (1980), 14:2 Man. Journal of Educ. 10.

11 See Michael Apple, *Culture and Curriculum* (1980).

she has no rights and no role in shaping, and as something which is representative of a moral code.

INDIRECT LEGAL SOCIALIZATION

School does provide young people with significant indirect exposure to legal notions, however. By participating in school life, they meet a number of concepts and values related to law, at least as pertaining to its role in the regulation of social conduct. This learning through participation in school society has been called the "hidden curriculum". To achieve or succeed in school or, indeed, to survive, one has to learn the norms which govern the organization and develop an awareness of one's role within it. In this process, the student comes to learn about many matters that are also components of law: authority, obligation, the place of rules, concepts of due process, and elemental notions of justice.[12]

What, specifically, do students learn of law through the hidden curriculum?

1. They learn that authority is vested in position rather than person. People in authority are to be obeyed, because they are in positions of authority, not because their actions or decisions justify obedience.

2. They learn that due process is actually due processing. Rules which they had no role in establishing are *consistently* applied to all concerned. This is due processing.

3. They learn that conflict is something to be avoided in a consensual organization like the school.

4. They learn to sublimate their desires for change in the context of their learning. Good educational citizens are those who, for the good of the whole, deny their individuality. In this they acquire a basic notion of the paramountcy of group over individual interests.

5. Above all, students learn compliance and the penalties which accompany failure to comply. This, as Stanley Milgram has observed in his study of *Obedience to Authority,* is the beginning of the agentic role: where the person, within an hierarchical structure, defines himself or herself essentially as an instrument, a means divorced from ends.[13]

The title for this conference is "Law in a Cynical Society?" It could have been called "Cynicism in a Legal Society". Are students cynical in their attitudes toward the law and its associated apparatus? Would that they were! The schools have been remarkably successful in engendering naive compliance and an accepting attitude toward law. This has been accomplished by

12 See T. R. Morrison, "Motivation and The Working World of the School" (1979), 15:1 *History and Social Science Teacher 31*.

13 See S. Milgram, *Obedience to Authority* (1975).

passing on to the young, within a controlled environment, a legal mythology without at the same time providing them with the intellectual tools or experiential base upon which to explore the relationship between that mythology and the reality it supposedly represents. If you are looking for cynicism in relation to the law, you won't find it in the schools.

PROPOSED EDUCATIONAL REFORMS

There are those of us in education who long for ways to engender some cynicism in the young, or at least to awaken an awareness that reality and concepts of it may not always be congruent. We believe that it is possible to reform schools and to develop them as places of learning rather than of mere socialization. Let me propose a number of avenues toward law-focused educational reform, which might lead toward developing a populace which is sensitive to its legal institutions and culture.

The first involves altering the social structure of the school. The work of Lawrence Kohlberg serves as a guide.[14] The basic notion is that if one wants to teach about justice and its associated legal processes, then the young should learn within a context that displays these attributes. Or, at minimum, have some experience in attempting to create these — a learning process itself. The idea is to involve the young in an experiential curriculum — creating justice structures in schools. Most of what is involved in law (the conflict of rights and duty, the place of authority, the regulation of conflict, the development of due process, and so on) would be encountered by the young in such an enterprise. So, it should be underscored, would the current legal mythology and idealism.

The second proposal follows from the first. It involves broadening further the experiential basis from which the student forms his or her basic legal orientation. The basic proposal here is to provide for students experiences with contexts in which the law is at work in our society, beyond what they already have through family, peers, media and school. This involves opening our institutions (the court, the law office, the police station, the prison, the union, the corporation, *etc.*) to the young. It also means accepting the idea that the young should re-enter community and social life. Through practicums, placements or whatever, we have to feed the starving young what they lack the most — experience *while* growing up, with the institutions and settings of our culture.[15]

The third reform, perhaps a generalizeable one, is to demystify the legal mind. It is indeed cynical to urge that people, the young particularly, be deeply involved in and reflectively committed to our legal system when they are denied access to the intellectual processes and rules which govern that

14 See L. Kohlberg, *Moralization and Education* (1981).

15 See J. S. Coleman, *Youth: Transition to Adulthood* (1978).

institution. The young need to be taught such things as legal reasoning and the laws of evidence, even if only to provide a basis from which to criticize them. Currently, there is no one to teach them. In this regard, might I posit the radical suggestion that law schools, as well as training and inducting the novice lawyer into the practice of law, also consider as one of their priorities the training of legal educators? Given the oft-cited surplus of practitioners, perhaps this idea, if implemented, would even open career paths for the graduates of law schools.

My last proposal involves the need to introduce the young to the concept of the "living law"; that is, the idea of law as a cultural and social phenomenon. To do this, ways have to be found to confront the young with the non-formal aspects of law — the roles that power, status, prestige, bargaining and other things play in our legal system. As well, it requires shifting somewhat away from the current consensual bias of the curriculum toward an orientation which at least tolerates, if not fosters, conflict. And it is imperative that the relationship between law and morality be fully explored.

CONCLUSION

Lon Fuller, Carter Professor of Jurisprudence at Harvard University, enunciated eight ways in which to fail to make a law, eight routes to disaster, if you like: (1) The first lies in a failure to achieve rules at all, so that every issue must be decided on an ad hoc basis. The other routes are: (2) a failure to publicize, or at least to make available to the affected party, the rules he or she is expected to observe; (3) the abuse of retroactive legislation, which not only cannot itself guide action, but also undercuts the integrity of rules which are prospective in effect, since it puts them under the threat of retrospective change; (4) a failure to make rules understandable; (5) the enactment of contradictory rules; (6) the creation of rules that require conduct beyond the power of the affected party; (7) the introduction of such frequent changes in the rules that the subject cannot orient his or her actions by them; and, finally; (8) a failure of congruence between the rules as announced and their actual administration. A total failure in any one of these eight directions does not result simply in a bad system of law; it results, in Fuller's opinion, in something which cannot be called a legal system.

Our legal system may be quite far from moving fully in any one of these eight directions. My view, however, is that many people are confused about many aspects of the legal system — so confused that the system can be said to have been partially undermined in several of the ways Fuller identified.

This leads me to my final point. It may be that the real issue is not law in a cynical society but law in a confused society. If Fuller was right in saying that a legal system cannot exist where the population does not know enough about the laws to comply with them, confusion about the legal system constitutes a very serious problem. Removing this confusion is, in part, a task for the schools, but the legal system itself also bears a large responsibility. The law must be not only regulative but instructive as well. One purpose of law should be to teach. While we can deal with confusion and cynicism about the law in schools and other educational settings, this effort will go for naught if law itself is not educative.

ATTITUDES TO LAW OF THE NEW CHRISTIAN RIGHT IN AMERICA

Irving Hexham

INTRODUCTION

A 1970 Gallup Poll showed that 75 per cent of adult Americans believed that religion was losing its influence on American life.[16] By 1980 only 46 per cent of adult Americans still thought that this was true.[17] This significant change in the perception of religious influence on American life can be related to the revival of conservative Protestant Christianity which took place in America during the 1970's. In these years ''born-again'' Christianity came into its own. Having begun as relatively insignificant movements of popular piety in an earlier era, groups of ''born-again'' Christians became a politicized new fundamentalism in the 1970's.

The remarkable growth of conservative Protestantism is documented in numerous works, such as *Religion in America*[18] and *Emerging Trends,*[19] both of which are regular publications of the Princeton Religion Research Centre, established in 1977 by the Gallup Organization. Earlier it was identified and discussed by Dean M. Kelley in his book *Why Conservative Churches are Growing.*[20] The significance of this growth is seen in the fact that when John Warwick Montgomery, a spokesman for evangelical religion, estimated the strength of conservative Protestants in 1968 he was proud to declare that there were 30.5 million Christians in America who could be identified as evangeli-

16 Princeton Religious Research Center, *Emerging Trends*, vol. 3, #1, (January 1982), p. 3.
17 *Ibid.*
18 *Religion in America*, (Princeton Religious Research Centre, Pub.).
19 *Emerging Trends*, (Princeton Religious Research Centre, Pub.).
20 D. M. Kelley, *Why Conservative Churches are Growing*, 1st ed. (1972).

cals or fundamentalists.[21] According to *Time Magazine* this number had grown to 45.5 million by 1977.[22]

The growth of modern evangelical religion and its impact on American consciousness seems to have peaked late in 1977. Early that year *The Humanist* ran a series of articles on "The Resurgence of Fundamentalism," in which it attacked the growing strength of "born-again" Christianity.[23] In a similar critical vein, the *Saturday Review* for 17th September 1977 had as its cover story "The Jesus Mania: Bigotry in the Name of the Lord". But *Time Magazine* took a more positive line: its lead story for 26th December 1977 was "The Evangelicals' New Empire of Faith". Since then conservative Protestantism, which includes both evangelicalism and fundamentalism, has continued to attract widespread attention, both in news items and through sociological research. But while there is as yet no evidence of serious decline, there is also no indication of continued growth. According to the latest Gallup polls, this form of Christianity seems, like a number of other religious groups, to be in a holding pattern.[24]

Anyone attempting to understand conservative Protestantism needs to distinguish carefully between evangelicals and fundamentalists. Evangelicals and fundamentalists share the same basic beliefs, but they differ greatly in their intellectual outlook and lifestyles. Billy Graham and Jimmy Carter are associated with the evangelical stream. To their right, Ronald Reagan and Jerry Falwell are associated with the fundamentalists. Both evangelicals and

---

21 See Robert Campbell, *Spectrum of Protestant Beliefs* (1968), p. 8. Religious issues can be very confusing. The following books are suggested as sources of information about evangelicals and fundamentalists in contemporary America: The best general introduction to American religious history is Sydney E. Ahlstrom's, *A Religious History of the American People* (1972). An excellent historical study of fundamentalism can be found in George M. Marsden's *Fundamentalism and American Culture* (1980). Robert Campbell sets out the differences between various Christian groups in his book *Spectrum of Protestant Beliefs* (1968). This general outline is expanded upon in the context of evangelicals and fundamentalists in the works of Richard Quebedeaux. In particular, Quebedeaux's books *The Worldly Evangelicals (1978)*, and *By What Authority* (1981) are recommended. The political views of traditional fundamentalism are to be found in *Thunder on the Right* by Gary K. Clabaugh (1974), which is helpful in setting the background to the new right. Jerry Falwell's *The Fundamentalist Phenomenon* (1981) provides an insight into contemporary fundamentalism, while Tim La Haye's *Battle for the Mind* (1980) gives the reader a clear insight into the thought world of fundamentalism. Francis S. Schaeffer's *A Christian Manifesto* (1981) is a clear call for political action, especially in the field of law, as is John W. Whitehead's, *The Second American Revolution* (1982). Jeremy Rifkin's, *The Emerging Order* (1979) places these developments in the context of American cultural history in a very useful way. However, Rifkin sees Francis A. Schaeffer on the left wing of evangelism, despite his recent book *A Christian Manifesto* which shows him to be on the right politically. Finally, the Princeton Religion Research Centre of the Gallup Organization provides ongoing statistical data about the development of American religion in its various publications and its regular newsletter *Emerging Trends*.

22 (1977), 110 *Time Magazine* 52.

23 "The Resurgence of Fundamentalism" (1977), 37: 1, 2, 3 The Humanist.

24 *Supra*, note 16, pp. 1-2.

fundamentalists stress the importance of a living faith and a conversion experience, usually described as being "born-again".[25]

Their common religious experience is based upon a conservative understanding of the authority of the Bible in matters of faith and doctrine, and a belief in its inspiration by God. Thus both groups speak about the Bible as the "Word of God". They share a commitment to the historic creeds of the Christian church as understood in the light of the work of the Protestant reformers of the sixteenth century. Thus both groups claim to be the true heirs of Luther and Calvin.

Evangelicals are, however, more likely to take a modern scholarly approach, albeit a guarded one, to the study of the Bible. Fundamentalists reject modern Biblical scholarship, because they believe it is inspired by essentially atheistic attitudes, and presupposes the non-existence of supernatural intervention in our world. For fundamentalists, modern Biblical criticism is built upon false assumptions which are sure to cause the unwary to question their faith, and possibly to lose it altogether.

For fundamentalists, belief in creationism as opposed to evolution is essential. Evangelicals take a more open attitude. Some evangelicals are creationists, others accept a form of theistic evolution, while many are agnostic on the question. In discussing creation versus evolution, most evangelicals would argue that the important point is God's creative activity, not the mode of creation. For them there is no problem if God chose to create by means of evolutionary processes and they willingly accept a form of evolution as a way of understanding God's activity in the world. But to fundamentalists such an easy-going attitude towards what they see as a crucial issue is tantamount to an admission of unbelief.

Politically, evangelicals are divided. Some are ultra-conservatives, others lean to the left. The majority of American evangelicals identify with the conservatively inclined religious magazine *Christianity Today*, while a minority find the radical *Sojourners* more to their taste. Many, like Senator Mark Hatfield, are conservative on some issues and radical on others. American fundamentalists are uniformly conservative, and read magazines like *Moody Monthly*. Their radicalism exists in the degree to which they lean towards libertarian politics rather than more traditional conservatism. Socialism and liberalism are seen by fundamentalists as basic philosophic positions which influence religious as well as political views. Thus for them left-wing political views are inevitably identified with radical theology and lack of faith.

A number of best-selling religious authors represent the views of fundamentalism. Among the best known of these are Jerry Falwell, Tim La Haye and Francis Schaeffer. Of these only Schaeffer has a strong influence on evangelicals. Many evangelicals see him as one of their number, even though Schaeffer himself has adopted the fundamentalist label. All of these, and

25 A term derived from *The New Testament*, St. John: 3:1-21.

many of the spokesmen of the new fundamentalism, are influenced to a greater or lesser degree by the work of Rousas John Rushdooney, whose Chalcedon Foundation was described by *Newsweek* as the "think tank" of the religious right.[26]

BACK TO BASICS: THE INFLUENCE OF R. J. RUSHDOONEY

Evolution, abortion, liberalism, humanism, the need for free "Christian" schools, and a number of other basic issues unite the new Christian right, and are constant themes of their numerous publications. Although there are some variations in their views, most of the writers are popularizers who repeat each other with slightly different illustrations and arguments. Behind them all, however, stands the work of R. J. Rushdooney and the Chalcedon Foundation.

Chalcedon is based in Vallecito, California, where it maintains a library and study centre.[27] It publishes a monthly *Chalcedon Report* and a number of other items, including *The Journal for Christian Reconstruction*. In addition to its own general work of creating a new Christian ethos, Chalcedon has helped establish the Foundation for Christian Economics, and the Foundation for Christian Self-Government. Associated with Chalcedon is economist Gary North, whose newsletter received the endorsement of many of the self-help, economic survival books of the 1970's.

Chalcedon's founder and visionary is the Reverend Rousas John Rushdooney, an American of Armenian descent, and an ordained Presbyterian minister. In the 1970's he came under the influence of the Calvinist philosopher theologian Cornelius van Til, of Westminster Theological Seminary, and as a result he completely rethought his world and life view. This led him to seek a consistent form of Christianity which embraced all aspects of life. For him Calvinism was such a religion. But, to his dismay, American Calvinists have abandoned their heritage and cultural calling under the influence of a seductive secularism which teaches that church and state are separate, in the sense that religion is a Sunday affair,with nothing to say about daily life. He has tried to counter this approach to religion in his many books and articles. Rushdooney's first book *By What Standard?*[28] was a critique of modern religion and theology through an exposition of van Til's thought. He followed this with *Intellectual Schizophrenia: Culture, Crisis and Education,*[29] where he strongly attacked secular education and made a plea for Christian schools. This book was the first important work in the post-war period to argue against modern education and to propose the re-establishment of Christian education in America. He expanded his views on eduction in *The Messianic Character of American Education,*[30] and began writing about law

26 (1981), 97:5 *Newsweek* 60.
27 P.O. Box 158, Vallecito, California 95251, United States.
28 *By What Standard?* (1958).
29 *Intellectual Schizophrenia: Culture, Crisis and Education* (1961).
30 *The Messianic Character of American Education* (1963).

and politics in *This Independent Republic*.[31] Since the publication of these works Rushdooney has been responsible for over twenty other books and numerous articles.

His major work on law is his two volume work *The Institutes of Biblical Law*.[32] A popular exposition of his views on law, politics, and morality is to be found in *Law and Liberty*.[33] In addition to these, he has published a number of *Chalcedon Position Papers* dealing with various aspects of religion, law, politics, and education.

Rushdooney argues that not only can we legislate morality, but we do. The question for him then is not *whether* law and morality interact, but *which* morality will form the basis of law. He believes that secular humanism is the basis of our present law and morality. It is the enemy of Christian thought, and Christians must reject it in all its forms. This implies the abandonment of evolutionary ideas and the espousal of creationism. The Bible is to be our guide in all things, and it provides us with a clear blueprint for the ideal society.

In promoting these views, Rushdooney is remarkably consistent. On the basis of Biblical evidence he ties law and government to property rights, which he relates to family structure. Because of the close relationship between property and family, he argues that what appear to be questions of individual morality, and therefore things which ought not to be legislated, are in fact matters of legal concern because of their effect in supporting or destroying the family as a property-owning unit. In developing these views, Rushdooney takes Mosaic Law very seriously, and is prepared to institute levirate marriage and various other practices found in the Bible but not in western society.

Although writers like Francis Schaeffer, Tim La Haye and Jerry Falwell rarely quote Rushdooney and are not as consistent in their acceptance of the implications of their views, they are clearly influenced by him, and essentially base their thinking about law, politics and society on his works. Anyone wishing to understand the thinking of the new Christian right on law must therefore take Rushdooney seriously and carefully consider his various proposals.

A. M. Watts directed his attention to the other end (the liberal end) of the religious spectrum, and found reason to be concerned about the influence that liberal religious attitudes might have on law. He singled out one factor: misplaced compassion.

> My denomination, the United Church of Canada, is observed by outsiders to be a liberal church, and it often identifies itself as such. I'm also one who belongs in the liberal

31 *This Independent Republic* (1964).

32 *The Institutes of Biblical Law*, vol. 1 (1973); vol. 2 (1979).

33 *Law and Liberty* (1977).

tradition. But I want to comment on something I think is going on within the liberal churches, certainly within my own denomination, that I believe is alarming. It is a tendency which, although not necessarily harmful in the short run, could have a detrimental long-range impact upon attitudes about law. It is to some degree both a reflection of secular liberalism and a contributor to it.

Let me get at it this way. There are many in my denomination who believe that compassion is a hallmark of the Christian, confusing it with the Christian doctrine of forgiveness. When somebody has offended against one of the moral laws, the Christian community displays compassion toward that person in order to ensure that he or she continues to be affirmed as a person of worth, with a full place within the community.

Now how do you express that compassion? How do you affirm the worth of the wrongdoer? Here is where I think members of my denomination often go wrong. They show their compassion for the offender by tending to reduce the seriousness of the offence. They say to the person who acted improperly (as well as to themselves and to the community): "What you did wasn't so bad; it really didn't matter too much." In the name of forgiveness, the importance of the community's moral obligations is being eroded. Misdirected pastoral concerns undermine the normative effectiveness of the moral code. This confusion of pastoral and normative concerns can be seen in a recent United Church publication on human sexuality.[34] And I see a similar confusion in other manifestations of liberalism.

The error, in terms of Christian theology, lies in misunderstanding the meaning of forgiveness. In the classical Christian tradition (and in the Judaic tradition as well, I believe) forgiveness did not reduce the seriousness of the offence. Forgiveness was God's way of affirming you, as an individual, while condemning your behaviour. It implied neither condonation nor minimization of your transgression.

The danger, in terms of public opinion and law, is that attitudes based on misdirected compassion may lead to the dismantling of moral codes and of laws which are in some sense rooted in them.

The media, the schools, and the churches are by no means the only shapers of public attitudes toward law. Alvin Esau, who chaired the conference panel on this topic, drew attention to a number of other influences. As examples, he mentioned socio-economic status, personality characteristics, the loss of a sense of community stemming from what he described as "the moral crisis of legalistic liberalism", and the fact that "legal actors and institutions may not be performing to the degree that makes higher public respect possible".

Aspects of the latter point are picked up in the papers of June Tapp and Alan Borovoy. One's personal experience with the legal system may exert a powerful influence on one's attitude to law and legal institutions. June Tapp describes a study of the attitudinal consequences of jury service during a long, complex, and controversial trial.

34 United Church of Canada, *In God's Image . . . Male and Female: A Study on Human Sexuality* (Division of Mission in Canada, United Church of Canada, 1980).

JURY SERVICE AS LEGAL SOCIALIZATION

June Louin Tapp

INTRODUCTION

As a backdrop, I will briefly describe an incident leading to a trial and then discuss the meaning of socialization.

First, the trial incident. From February to May 1973, members of the American Indian Movement (A.I.M.) occupied the village of Wounded Knee on the Pine Ridge reservation in South Dakota. In staging their protest at Wounded Knee, the site of the 1890 massacre of Indian women and children by U.S. government troops, A.I.M. leaders drew public attention to the treaty obligations ignored by the U.S. government and the impact of these broken treaties on the problems of the American Indian. After 71 days, the government forces (equipped with armoured antipersonnel carriers and M16 rifles) and the Indians (equipped with limited small arms and meagre food supplies) negotiated an end to the occupation. Government indictments from the encounter resulted in over 100 trials in South Dakota. The defence, establishing that fair trials could not be held there, requested a change of venue for Russell Means and Dennis Banks, indicted on charges of conspiring, aiding and abetting. Their trials convened in January 1974 at the U.S. Federal Courthouse in St. Paul, Minnesota. A jury was selected to hear the case brought by the State against these two men and to judge whether they were guilty of violating U.S. law.

One key factor influencing a jury's decision-making, whatever the case, is the history of legal socialization that each juror brings to the jury's deliberations. Socialization is the ongoing process by which people come to adopt the codes of conduct — written or unwritten — of their society. Whether called socialization, internalization, or even conscience development, it is the means by which members of a society acquire its norms (its rules) and learn to abide by or apply them without loss of individuality. Socialization shapes views about which acts and attitudes or behaviours and beliefs violate society's codes and thus are impermissible.

Legal socialization involves the development of a sense of law-consciousness or law-abidingness, and a sense of justice. Through this process people learn standards for making social judgments and for using the legal system to conduct human affairs.

As the Wounded Knee trial will illustrate, socialization is not only a childhood process. It is a lifelong developmental process wherein the individual constantly modifies codes of conduct — guidelines for interaction to use Lon Fuller's phrase — as the society or the individual changes over time. Childhood is a time when many codes of conduct are learned in the context of the home. Adolescence is a time when the individual questions the fairness and legitimacy of the codes, often in the context of the school. Adulthood is a time when long-held beliefs are challenged in a variety of rule settings and new understandings about society and law become possible. This paper will deal with adult socialization.

While home and school are primary contexts for learning social and legal norms from childhood to adolescence, other contexts become more important in adulthood. Among the many interacting contexts within which adult socialization occurs, psychologists have recognized the importance of legal institutions. Since in contemporary society no one escapes the long arm of the law, many legal figures — the judge on the bench, the lawyer in the office, the police officer on the street — educate people about the law and thus function as socializing agents. I have chosen the courtroom as a context in which to discuss adult socialization.

The internalization of rules that socialization involves is greatly assisted by participation in making or maintaining the rules. One place where people can make and maintain law and justice is in the jury box. In this essay I will examine the socializing effect of jury service on adults. Using the Wounded Knee trial, I will describe the effect of a nine-month jury experience on the legal reasoning of jurors.

LEGAL SOCIALIZATION AND COGNITIVE THEORY

Psychologists use a number of theories to describe how humans are socialized. But no one theory — psychoanalytic, cognitive development, social learning, or even ethological — will do. This is the case because socialization is not a one-way, one-time, one-place phenomenon. All formulations are right to some degree. The approach I will use is a socio-cognitive theory of legality based on data gathered for over a decade from more than 6,000 respondents in a variety of age, occupational, status and group settings.

An understanding of the legal socialization process requires describing how people see their legal worlds, how they construct their cognitive and social maps of legality. One advantage of using a socio-cognitive model to examine how people map legality is its identification of underlying reasoning structures. Another is its ready integration of constructs from other orientations, such as social learning and law.

My model of legal reasoning applies to the realm of law the moral typology of Piaget[35] and Kohlberg.[36] It also draws upon social psychological

35 J. Piaget, *Science of Education and the Psychology of the Child* (1970).

36 L. Kohlberg, "Stage and Sequence: The Cognitive-Developmental Approach to Socialization", in D. A. Goslin (ed.), *Handbook of Socialization Theory and Research* (1969), p. 347.

and legal/philosophical (jurisprudential) thought, after the manner of Bandura, and McDonald[37] and Kelman[38] for the former, and Fuller[39] and Rawls[40] for the latter. Such a cognitive theory has been used in legal socialization studies by me and associates since the late 1960's.[41]

In exploring morality, Piaget described children's authorities at the earlier heteronomous, egocentric stage as warranting unilateral respect, and found that such children regard adult rules as obligatory, sacred, and immutable. At the later automonous, sociocentric stage older children see obligations in terms of mutual respect, reciprocity, responsibility, and not mere obedience. Theoretically and methodologically,[42] I have used Kohlberg's terms[43] to characterize levels of legal reasoning, and Piaget's terms to deal with the impact of cultural/social forces.[44] Despite critics,[45] Kohlberg's and Piaget's theories have also proved valuable to other investigators studying legal and political thought.[46]

---

37 A. Bandura and F. J. McDonald, "Influences of Social Reinforcement and the Behaviour of Models in Shaping Children's Moral Judgments" (1963), 67:3 *Journal of Abnormal and Social Psychology* 274.

38 H. C. Kelman, "Compliance, Identification, and Internalization: Three Processes of Attitude Change" (1958), 2:1 *Journal of Conflict Resolution* 51.

39 L. L. Fuller, *The Morality of Law,* 2nd ed. (1969); L. L. Fuller, "Some Presuppositions Shaping the Concept of 'Socialization' " in J. L. Tapp and F. V. Levine (eds.), *Law, Justice, and the Individual in Society* (1977), p. 33.

40 J. Rawls, *A Theory of Justice* (1971).

41 F. J. Levine, *The Legal Reasoning of Youth: Dimensions and Correlates* (unpublished doctoral dissertation, 1979); F. J. Levine and J. L. Tapp, "The Dialectic of Legal Socialization in Community and School" in J. L. Tapp and F. J. Levine (eds.), *Law, Justice, and the Individual in Society* (1977), p. 163; J. L. Tapp, "A Child's Garden of Law and Order" (1970), 4:7 *Psychology Today* 29; J. L. Tapp, "The Psychological Limits of Legality" in J. R. Pennock and J. W. Chapman (eds.), *The Limits of Law: Nomos XV,* (1974); J. L. Tapp, "Psychology and the Law: An Overture" in M. R. Rosenzweig and L. W. Porter (eds.) *Annual Review of Psychology,* vol. 27 (1976), p. 359; J. L. Tapp and L. Kohlberg, "Developing Senses of Law and Legal Justice," in J. L. Tapp and F. J. Levine (eds.), *Law, Justice and the Individual in Society* (1977), p. 89; J. L. Tapp and F. J. Levine, "Persuasion to Virtue: A Preliminary Statement" (1970), 4:4 *Law and Soc. Rev.* 565; J. L. Tapp and F. J. Levine, "Legal Socialization: Strategies for an Ethical Legality" (1974), 27 Stanford Law Rev. 1; Tapp and Levine (eds.), *Law, Justice, and the Individual in Society: Psychological and Legal Issues* (1977); J. L. Tapp, J. R. Vopava, A. S. Kolman and R. M. Richardson, *Rights Consciousness and Child Care: A Report on the Right-to-Care Project* (unpublished, 1981).

42 See *supra,* note 41.

43 See J. L. Tapp and L. Kohlberg, *supra,* note 41. Also note that the first Tapp and Kohlberg version appeared in (1971), 27:2 *Journal of Social Issues* 65.

44 J. Piaget, "Need and Significance of Cross-Cultural Studies in Genetic Psychology," in J. W. Berry and P. R. Dasen (eds.), *Cultural and Cognition: Readings in Cross-Cultural Psychology* (1966), p. 299; see *supra,* note 35; J. Piaget and B. Inhelder, *The Psychology of the Child* (1969).

45 A. Blasi, "Bridging Moral Cognition and Moral Action: A Critical Review of the Literature" (1980), 88:1 *Psychological Bulletin* 1; W. Kurtines and E. B. Greif, "The Development of Moral Thought: Review and Evaluation of Kohlberg's Approach" (1974), 81:8 *Psychological Bulletin* 453.

46 N. Berg and P. Mussen, "The Origins and Development of Concepts of Justice" (1975), 31:3 *Journal of Social Issues* 183; W. Damon, *The Social World of the Child* (1977); J. Fishkin, K. Keniston and C. MacKinnon, "Moral Reasoning and Political Ideology" (1973), 27:1

Social psychology, too, has long employed an interactive, progressive-levels approach to interpret individual, social, or cultural phenomena. In the late nineteenth century, John Dewey's[47] interactional developmental conception of moral stages insured a free yet orderly description. In the mid-twentieth century, Fritz Heider[48] connected judgments of causality, blame, and responsibility to stage-related cognitive processes. At the same time, Herbert Kelman[49] characterized three progressive responses (compliance, identification, and internalization) to social influence.

A socio-cognitive model of legality also draws upon the classic works of lawyer Lon L. Fuller[50] and moral philosopher John Rawls.[51] Each described ethical legal or political development as emerging from an interactive, purposive exchange between natural capacities and social inputs. Fuller described a movement from a "morality of duty" to a "morality of aspiration" in terms of rule compliance and creation. He later delineated three processes of socialization, the third involving the creation of reciprocal expectations that arise from human interactions. Rawls' three progressive natural stages of justice (authority, association, and principle) are triggered by the social nourishment of love and trust, participation and mutuality, shared activity and reciprocity.

Apparently, philosophers and psychologists describe a similar advance from a dependent (heteronomous) and uncritical state to an independent (autonomous), altruistic, reciprocal, and rational stance. Such congruences in psychology and jurisprudence helped me to formulate an interdisciplinary, interactive, and integrative approach to legal socialization.

My socio-cognitive model of legal reasoning has three levels: I — Preconventional; II — Conventional; III — Postconventional. Level I is a law-deferring punishment-oriented stance; II is a law-maintaining, conformity posture; III is a law-creating, principled perspective. Each represents a distinctive way to characterize rules and rights, and roles and responsibilities in relation to the legal system. Together, they comprise a developmental (but not always invariant) sequence where "higher" reflects more accommodative, integrative, and complex reasoning and conflict resolution. Each level of legal

Journal of Personality and Social Psychology 109; J. Gallatin and J. Adelson, "Legal Guarantees of Individual Freedom: A Cross-National Study of the Development of Political Thought" in Tapp and Levine (eds.), *Law, Justice, and the Individual in Society* (1977), p. 106; N. Haan, M. B. Smith and J. Block, "The Moral Reasoning of Young Adults: Political-Social Behavior, Family Background, and Personality Correlates" (1963), 10:3 *Journal of Personality and Social Psychology* 183; F. J. Levine, *The Legal Reasoning of Youth: Dimensions and Correlates* (unpublished doctoral presentation, University of Chicago 1979). G. B. Melton, "Children's Concepts of Their Rights" (1980), 9 *Journal of Clinical Psychology* 186; J. V. Torney, "Socialization of Attitudes Toward the Legal System" in Tapp and Levine (eds.), *Law, Justice, and the Individual in Society* (1977), p. 134.

47 J. Dewey, *On Education: Selected Writings* (1964).

48 F. Heider, *The Psychology of Ihterpersonal Relations* (1958).

49 See *supra*, note 38.

50 See *supra*, note 39.

51 See *supra*, note 40.

reasoning is best viewed as a successive restructuring of ideas about legal matters, with the three progressions displaying increased cognitive complexity in intellectual sophistication, ethical awareness, and critical compliance.

Further, each legal level incorporates certain legal reasoning styles. A level I, Preconventional view of law and legal obligations focuses on external consequences and authority. At the Conventional, law-maintenance level II, people worry about fulfilling role expectations; they obey or disobey for reasons of conformity. The Postconventional level III is the law-creating, principled thinking perspective. Here developmentally advanced (cognitively-complex) persons see the need for social systems, but can also distinguish between the values of a given social order and universal principles. Reciprocity and reversibility are key in the reasoning process.

Each characterization was empirically derived and standardized from the responses of children and adults in six countries to classic jurisprudential problems in an open-ended questionnaire known as the Tapp-Levine Rule-Law Interview (T.L.R.L.I.). The T.L.R.L.I. focuses on five substantive areas: the value and function of rules and laws, the conditions of legal compliance, the changeability and breakability of rules or laws, the dynamics of justice/fairness, and the nature of rights-consciousness. It permits classification of legal reasoning according to three cognitive-developmental levels. The new, basic 16-item version appears in Table 1; a classification of responses in three of the five areas appears in Table 2.

TABLE 1
Tapp-Levine Rule
Law Interview
TLRLI: 1980 Version

1. What is a rule? Why is that a rule?
2. What is a law? Why is that a law?
3. Why do we have laws?
4. Why should we have laws?
5. Can some things be fair and right to do even when there are no laws about them? How can this be?
6. What is a fair law? Why is it fair?
7. What is a right?
8. What kinds of rights should people have? Why?
9. What kinds of rights do people have? Why?
10. What would happen if there were no laws anywhere at all? Why?
11. Why should people follow laws?
12. Why do you follow laws?
13. How and why can laws be changed?

14. Are there times when it might be right to break a law? When, if ever?

15. What does it mean to be right?

16. Can a person be right and break a law? How can this be?

TABLE 2
Classification of Interview Categories by Levels of Legal Reasoning

Subject Question	Level I: Law-Deferring Preconventional Categories	Level II: Law-Maintaining Conventional Categories	Level III: Law-Making Postconventional Categories
1. *Value and Function of Rules and Laws:* What would happen if there were no rules? (What would happen if there were no laws anywhere at all?)	Violence-crime: Laws prevent concrete physical harm like specific bad acts or crimes. They secure physical necessities.	Personal desires not principles: Laws restrain bad, guide weak, and insure personal control over greed. Anarchy-Laws maintain social order. Impossible to imagine: Society cannot exist without rules. Abstract regulation is requisite for society.	Human beings as self-regulatory: Guide behaviour via principles and distinguish law from moral principles.
Function of Rules and Laws: What is a rule? What is a law?	Prohibitive: Functions as proscription or flat command restraining actions that serve no positive social good.	Prescriptive: Functions as shared guide. Generalizes whole system rules as facilitating, "maintaining society", or "preventing anti-social behaviour". Enforcement: Distinguishes between badness of act and consequent punishment.	Beneficial-rational: Functions to achieve rational purpose behind law, usually for maximizing personal and social welfare consequences. Cognizant of the utility of agreed-upon standards.
2. *Conditions of Legal Compliance:* Why should people follow rules?	Avoid negative consequences: Punishment reason for conformity. Simple	Personal conformity: Confuses obedience with socially desirable behav-	Rational-beneficial-utilitarian: Obedience to maintain individual and social

TABLE 2
Classification of Interview Categories by Levels of Legal Reasoning

Subject Question	Level I: Law-Deferring Preconventional Categories	Level II: Law-Maintaining Conventional Categories	Level III: Law-Making Postconventional Categories
Why do you follow rules? (Why should people follow laws?) (Why do you follow laws?)	compliance, not respect for rules. Authority: Obedience to power figures as ultimate guides. Rules derived from them. "Badness" of proscribed activity confused with badness of disobeying authority's rule.	iour in order to be good and maintain what law-makers think is "good" behaviour. Social conformity: Requires compliance to be fair to other obeyers and to avoid chaos.	welfare based on rational, mutual decision-making, and utilitarian considerations. Obedience from weighing consequences. Principled: Obedience guided by principles like sense of justice, independence of society. Conform only with principled rules.
3. *Changeability of Rules and Laws:* Can rules be changed? (How and why can laws be changed?) *Breakability of Rules and Laws:* Are there times when it might be right to break a rule? (Are there times when it might be right to break a law?)	*No:* Laws are fixed, permanent, or quasiphysical things. No: No differentiation between legal and moral. Badness of law-or rule-breaking equated with badness as such. Yes: Simple "yes" but no differentiating moral norm from prudential directives.	*Yes:* Laws not for "good of all" because they permit unkindness or are made by uncharitable persons. Morality of circumstance: Extreme circumstances justify breaking. Recognizes socio-moral function of rules to which law obedience is instrumental.	*Yes:* For reasons of social utility, rational purposes, and to change unprincipled laws. Morality of rule: Justify breaking when law immoral or unjust, when law violates moral principles.

The T.L.R.L.I. had been administered to all age, cultural, and occupational groups, in classrooms, courtrooms, cellrooms, and child care centres.[52]

52 J. Aliotta and J. L. Tapp, *Developmental, Legal, and Social Aspects of Rights-Consciousness* (unpublished, 1976); R. D. Hess and J. L. Tapp, *Authority, Rules, and Aggression: A Cross-National Study of the Socialization of Children into Compliance Systems*, Pt. I (1969); F. J. Levine, *The Legal Reasoning of Youth: Dimensions and Correlates*, (unpublished, 1979); Levine and Tapp, "The Dialectic of Legal Socialization in Community and School" *supra*, note 41; L. Minturn and J. L. Tapp, *Authority, Rules, and Aggression: A Cross-National Study of Children's Judgments of the Justice of Aggressive Confrontations*, Pt. II

Responses on samples totalling nearly 6,000 individuals from four types of populations inside and outside the United States were analyzed: (1) primary age school children from kindergarten to Grade III (5 to 8 years); (2) middle school pre-adolescents from Grades IV, VI and VIII (10 to 14 years); (3) college men and women in diverse university settings (17 to 21 years); and (4) adult groups of graduating law students, school teachers, federal penitentiary inmates, day care parents, and jurors (20 to 60 years). This developmental, cross-cultural, and cross-context data showed a consistent, enduring, and emerging legal consciousness — a sense of justice and sense of law-abidingness — across age, stages, and settings. They also demonstrated several recurrent themes. These themes reveal the origins and operation of a legal belief system. For example:

(1) Across cultures, there are detectable regularities in legal thought (that is, the same stages of development are present in all cultures).

(2) There is a pattern in the development of legal reasoning that progresses through the levels described above.

(3) The movement from I to II to III is related to age and development.

(4) Although this progression is related more closely to age and development than to situational, occupational or cultural factors, there is variation among such groups.

(5) While no one person's answers are 100 per cent at any one level, college and adult groups tended to be postconventional, in contrast to pre-adolescents, who gave more conventional answers, or primary school children (that is, from kindergarten to Grade III) who gave more preconventional answers.

To illustrate, answers to the question, "Are there ever times when it is right to break a rule?" shift from the preconventional to the conventional to the postconventional across the age groups. Primary-school children say "no" vehemently, though they sometimes give a "morality of circumstance" answer, such as: "It is OK to go through a red light if you have to take someone to the hospital to have a baby." But it is not until the middle-school years that there is a real shift into level II; children in pre-adolescence — between 10 and 14 years — are more likely to give "morality of circumstance" answers. There is also some evidence in pre-adolescent responses of the level III, "morality of the rule", answers such as: "It is OK to break the rule if it is a bad or immoral rule." Such responses are much more common among

(1970); Tapp, "A Child's Garden of Law and Order" *supra*, note 41; Tapp, "The Psychological Limits of Legality" *supra*, note 41; J. L. Tapp and A. Keniston, "Wounded Knee-Advocate or Expert: Recipe for a Fair Juror?" in J. L. Tapp (Chair), *What is a Fair Jury? Psychological and Legal Issues* (Symposium presented at the meeting of American Psychological Association, Washington D.C. September 1976); Tapp and Kohlberg, *supra*, note 41; Tapp and Levine, "Persuasion to Virtue: A Preliminary Statement" *supra*, note 41; *Law, Justice, and the Individual in Society*, see *supra*, note 41; Tapp, Vopava, Kolman and Richardson, see *supra*, note 41.

college and adult groups, however. Typical answers to the classical jurisprudential question, "What would happen if there were no rules?" were: level I (Grade II student) — "People would go around killing other people, stealing things and kidnapping people"; level II (Grade IV student) — "A lot of disorganizing in the world"; and level III (College student) — "Humans are self-regulatory, and if people are capable of acting responsibly and morally, nothing would happen."

Taken together, diverse studies by my associates and me over a decade offer support for a progressive, age-related sequence to the growth of ideas on law and justice. But while age is a crucial variable in the legal socialization process, situational variables vitally affect the rate and direction of development. A basic question, then, is the extent to which institutional settings, such as service on a jury, can and do influence the development of socialization.

THE WOUNDED KNEE JURY RESEARCH

In a contemporary society with an Anglo-American type of legal system, jury participation can be a major vehicle for citizen involvement in decision making.[53] Professor Levine and I have identified four ways in which jury service can contribute to the process of legal socialization.[54] Jury duty provides: (1) information about the legal system to jurors whose earlier contacts with law were limited; (2) an opportunity for participation and role-taking; (3) exposure to new, often conflicting, ways of thinking about rule systems; and (4) an occasion to connect ideas of law, justice, and rights from one setting to another. If these four socializing factors — legal information, participation, conflict, and continuity — operate optimally, jurors should progress to a higher level of legal socialization.

The chance to study the jury selection for the Wounded Knee trial provided an excellent opportunity to explore in a real-life setting the hypothesized socializing effect of jury service on legal development.[55] The earlier described trial, a result of incidents between the U.S. government and American Indians in South Dakota, took nine months. The U.S. Federal government lost: that is, A.I.M. leaders Means and Banks were acquitted.

This trial was particularly interesting because of its criminal-political

53 M. R. Kadish and S. H. Kadish, "The Institutionalization of Conflict: Jury Acquittals" in Tapp and Levine (eds), *Law, Justice, and the Individual in Society* (1977), p. 308; H. Kalven, Jr. and H. Zeisel, *The American Jury* (1966); J. Schulman, P. Shaver, R. Colman, B. Emrich and R. Christie, "Recipe for a Jury" (1973), 6:12 *Psychology Today*, pp. 37-44, 77-84.

54 See Tapp and Levine, "Legal Socialization: Strategies for an Ethical Legality" (1974), 27 *Stanford Law Rev*. 1.

55 See J. Aliotta and J. L. Tapp, *supra*, note 52; Tapp and Keniston, *supra*, note 52; J. L. Tapp, M. Gunnar and D. Keating, "Socialization: Three Ages, Three Rule Systems" in D. Perlman and C. Cozby (eds.), *Social Psychology and Social Issues* (1983), p. 42; J. L. Tapp and P. Smolka, *The Jury as a Socialization Experience* (unpublished manuscript, U of Minnesota 1976); C. Zimbrolt, *Will the Real Americans Please Stand Up?* (unpublished manuscript, U. of Minnesota 1974).

nature as well as its socio-historical significance. It was going on at the same time as Watergate. The time coincidence of the Wounded Knee and Watergate trials, and their respective places on a continuum of infamy and conspiracy, speak volumes about the place of the law in a society grown cynical as a result of its experiences with authority in the late 1960's and early 1970's.

The trial began with the selection of the jurors. Of the 93 prospective persons called, 55 were excused: 7 for cause, 48 for hardship. After a 14-day *voir dire* (courtroom questioning), 38 people were candidates for the 12-person jury. The *voir dire* questions ranged from basic demographic items — age, religion, marital status — to attitudes about Indians (''Would you want your son to marry an Indian?'') and beliefs about the law (''Would you require the defendants to prove their innocence?'').

During the questioning, my team of five graduate students observed and rated each potential juror's level of legal reasoning and authoritarianism. the prospective jurors challenged by the government lawyers were predominantly young, single, female, urban residents, with some college education. Basically Democrats, they had some contact with Native Americans, tended to support Indian self-determination, and defined law in process rather than in fixed-rule terms. The defence lawyers tried to remove people middle-aged or older, those from rural areas, white-collar workers, Republicans, those with non-committed attitudes toward Indians, and those with a law-and-order mentality. The 26 challenged jurors included 12 females and 14 males, 19 to 81 years in age (averaging 49.4 years).

The 12 impanelled jurors included 7 females and 5 males from 20 to 53 years of age. They were urban, college educated, and youthful: 9 jurors were 32 or younger (the average being 29.3 years) and 7 had college educations. On attitudes toward Native American self-determination, 7 jurors supported it, (of whom 6 had sympathy for Indian people) while 5 were non-committal. Of the 12 jurors, 7 believed the right to protest to be legitimate.

My associates and I studied three groups. First, those who served as jurors in the Wounded Knee trial. Second, the challenged jurors, those struck by the lawyers. Finally, a randomly-selected group of potential jurors, chosen from the 55 who had been excused.

Both the pre-trial and post-trial attitudes of these three groups were studied. Before the trial, we rated legal levels and authoritarian styles. Courtroom procedures restricted our use of the usual test instruments at that stage, so assessments were based on ratings of potential jurors' answers to questions posed by the judge and lawyers during the *voir dire*. Many questions used in the *voir dire* paralleled ones used in the post-trial study, thus providing reliability and validity checks. For example, the judge's query, ''Do you believe an individual has a right to violate the law to right past wrongs?'' had the same intent as, ''Do good motives justify breaking the law?'', used in the follow-up study.

In the post-trial study, interviews and questionnaires were administered face-to-face to representatives of all three groups in their home settings. The total group interviewed after the trial consisted of 9 impanelled jurors (2 males and 7 females, 19 to 53 years, average 30.6 years), 14 challenged jurors (9 males and 5 females, 27 to 81 years, average 45.9 years), and 23 random jurors (11 males and 12 females, 23 to 68 years, average 43.5 years). The correlation between the courtroom and the out-of-courtroom legal ratings (*i.e.*, T.L.R.L.I. questionnaire scores) was significant: .521 at $p < .025$.[56] On the personality side, the team's legal level ratings correlated significantly ($r = -.54$; $p < .025$) with independent ratings on authoritarianism.[57]

In the courtroom study raters made clinical, global judgments of a prospective juror's personality and level of legal socialization. In the after-trial study, a rule-law interview (the T.L.R.L.I.) was used to assess the legal levels of the impanelled, challenged, random jurors. A forced-choice questionnaire, developed to cover such dimensions as authoritarianism and self-esteem, was used to identify personality correlates of the legal socialization level. A set of open-ended questions was also designed to get impanelled jurors to describe the socializing experiences related to the trial.

According to my theory of cognitive legality, impanelled jurors should have had more opportunity for legal development than the challenged or random jurors. In nine months impanelled jurors, actively exposed to the four socialization factors described above, should have moved to higher levels than the other groups, and beyond their own earlier legal level. Theoretically, jury service, especially at a controversial trial, should promote socialization to a more principled level.

The evidence confirmed this hypothesis. Of the 38 unexcused prospective jurors, the before-trial percentages in levels I, II, and III (Preconventional, Conventional, and Postconventional) were respectively 19 per cent, 67 per cent and 12 per cent for the challenged jurors. For the impanelled jurors, they were 8 per cent, 50 per cent and 42 per cent. The after-trial study revealed that *no one* in any group was at the Preconventional level I. Among the random jurors, 40 per cent were at level II, and 60 per cent at level III after the trial. Among the challenged group, 50 per cent were Conventional (II), 50 per cent were Postconventional (III). However, among the impanelled jurors, 100 per cent scored at the Postconventional level (III) by the end of the trial. Their legal socialization geography had changed! While initially more level III's were among the impanelled jurors, the dramatic shift of the entire group to a Postconventional position suggested important influences at work.

The post-trial assessment revealed some patterns of similarity among the three juror groups. However, differences emerged in response patterns on

56 See J. L. Tapp and P. Smolka, *supra*, note 55.

57 R. Christie, "Probability vs. Precedence: The Social Psychology of Jury Selection" in G. Bermant, C. Nemeth and N. Vidmar (eds.), *Psychology and the Law* (1976).

issues of authority, law function, compliance (law-abidingness), rule-breakability and the meaning of rights.

For example, on the question, "What would you do when told to do something wrong by someone in charge?" 67 per cent of the impanelled jurors appealed to universal moral principles as a basis for disobedience, while only 21 per cent of the challenged group did so. On the question, "What would happen if there were no rules?" *all* challenged and random jurors answered at the Conventional level; only the impanelled gave Postconventional answers, believing that humankind is capable of self-regulation. In answering the question, "Are there times when it is ever right to break a rule?" 67 per cent of the impanelled jurors gave Postconventional answers, stressing fairness and universal morality, compared to 43 per cent of the challenged and 26 per cent of the random jurors.

On the ideal, "Why should you follow rules?", and the real, "Why do you follow rules?" questions, all three juror groups gave more principled (III) answers to the "ideal," but consistently more Preconventional and Conventional (I and II) answers on the "real" one. This pattern paralleled other cross-cultural, cross-contextual, and developmental findings. Among chosen jurors there was also a general trend toward saying that delegation, consensus and participation (all III reasons) should be the basis for changing rules.

The responses to the "rights" questions were particularly interesting. In answering, "What kinds of rights should people have?" the impanelled jurors expressed a rights-consciousness perspective (III) in greater numbers (45 per cent) than the challenged (29 per cent) or random (14 per cent) jurors. In general, challenged and random jurors felt that people's rights should be system-related; that is, linked to the maintenance of the legal system. In contrast, impanelled jurors viewed rights as a basic component of human dignity. One impanelled juror summed it up this way: "When I think of rights in this country, I think of life, liberty, and the pursuit of happiness. No one can take that away. If you didn't have these rights, you wouldn't be a person. You'd be an animal."

The socialization questions were keyed to the four situational factors of legal information, conflict, participation and continuity mentioned previously. The two socialization questions that discriminated well among the juror groups were ones that concerned trial outcome and knowledge of the jury selection process. The effects of information and participation are visible in the 75 per cent acquittal vote of the impanelled jurors, compared to the 23 per cent vote of the challenged jurors and 17 per cent of the random jurors. Sufficiently knowledgeable about the jury process after nine months, all impanelled jurors had some notion why they were selected for the jury. Only 54 per cent of the challenged jurors and 48 per cent of the random jurors could give reasons for their non-selection.

To probe the four socializing dimensions further, the following two questions were asked of the impanelled jurors:

1. How did this jury experience affect you? Your ideas?
2. Do you think you experienced any lasting or permanent change as a result of jury duty?

Overall, impanelled jurors described their experience with more passion and fervour. The impanelled group saw the trial and jury duty as more important than did the challenged or random groups. Many impanelled jurors saw jury service as a socializing and educative experience. Over two thirds of the impanelled jurors felt the jury experience had changed them and their lives. Over two thirds felt their ideas about law compliance, rights and responsibilities, and fair rules and laws had been overhauled too. Over two thirds of the impanelled jurors felt that the jury situation provided information, produced conflict, demanded participation, allowed role-taking and shifted perspectives. All linked their new-found legal values to other rule-guided settings beyond the courtroom, *i.e.*, home, school, and community: the continuity effect. Most reported changes in their attitudes towards minorities, government and the meaning of law and justice.

Specific responses to the questions on the trial's impact illustrate the effect of the four socialization factors. Juror 1 answered the "experience" question thusly: "I always thought I was a reader and a thinker, but the trial made me even more so. Before this jury duty, I probably would have really stumbled around on things like right and wrong, what is fair, what is just and what isn't, questions of rules and laws. But now I have at least given them a little thought." Juror 2 said: "It broadened my scope to take in other people's ideas as well as my own and my family's. I'm more aware of the world. I'm no longer a member of the silent majority. My son calls me a radical. My son is more happy with me; my husband isn't." Juror 3 felt: "It was an awesome responsibility. Trying to understand the rules and laws which probably govern us, and yet not really knowing how deeply they can affect all felt very heavy."

To the "any lasting effect or permanent change" question, Juror 4 answered: "I think a lot about what other people think. I was never really a great one for that before this experience. I thought myself a tolerant person, but in the future I would be even more tolerant than before." Juror 5 reported: "the most change in my ideas about minorities and why people go as far as demonstrations. I never had to think about what it means to be an Indian. Now I understand the meaning of social injustice." Juror 6 felt touched beyond the boundaries of the courtroom: "It broadened my scope. I am now aware of the world. I am no longer a member of the silent majority."

Most impanelled jurors described their jury experience in similar terms. All but one saw it as educative and important socially. Only one regarded the experience as "a waste of time and money". This latter sentiment was frequently expressed by challenged jurors.

The effect of jury service is further illuminated by answers to the question, "Do good motives justify breaking the law?" Almost 88 per cent of the impanelled jurors, compared to 8 per cent of the challenged jurors and 25 per cent of the random jurors, gave principled (level III) answers. Impanelled jurors, typically concerned about the person and the system, reasoned thusly: Juror 7, "It depends on the motives"; Juror 8, "It can be beneficial to the legal system"; Juror 9, "If it is a bad law." The vastly greater percentage of principled responses from the impanelled jurors suggests that they had a distinctly different experience over the nine months, or began at a higher level of legality, or both.

In considering the personality correlates of legal socialization, we found a negative relationship between legal maturity and authoritarianism. Higher socialization-level jurors were less authoritarian. Analyses of other personality dimensions revealed, for example, that impanelled jurors (and level III types generally) scored higher on self-esteem. The correlation between self-esteem and principled legal reasoning suggests that those with high self-esteem scores have a greater sense of justice. They can afford to be more distributive than retributive.

CONCLUSION

The noticeable shift and difference on matters of law and justice between impanelled jurors and the challenged or random jurors indicates that jury service can be an important socializing and educative experience. More advanced, cognitively complex levels and sophisticated legal and ethical positions may result from intellectual-socio-emotional experiences in a jury setting. If this is the case, it is important to maintain the jury process and jury service, not merely for the sake of justice and symbolism, but for the sake of having a vehicle to socialize more principled legal reasoning and law-abidingness in adulthood.

One juror's answer to the question, "What do you think of the jury process?" summarized its importance to and for this adult sample: "I guess I always felt this was a system of justice. It if wasn't for the jury, what would it all be about? What would we all be up to?" Both this answer and the experience from which it was derived suggest that the jury box and the jury service provide an excellent opportunity in adulthood to offset the cynicism that seems increasingly rampant toward both law and society.

[The influence of education, religion, and the media may also be tempered, and perhaps overborne, by another form of "experience": the individual's observation (whether accurate or inaccurate) that those who administer the legal system do so in an inconsistent or hypocritical fashion. Alan Borovoy calls attention to this source of cynicism.]

DOUBLE STANDARDS AND RESPECT FOR THE RULE OF LAW

Alan Borovoy

Ottawa has decided not to prosecute the R.C.M.P. for its admitted illegal mail-opening. I find it difficult to think of a single example in recent history more likely to generate cynicism about that most precious principle, the rule of law, than this decision of the federal government.

It is interesting to examine how the government went about making this decision. They did it in two stages: (1) they set up a royal commission, and (2) they delayed their final decision until an economic recession came to divert the public's attention to other things. I do not suggest that the recession was a deliberate policy, but the federal government certainly took advantage of it. Had they told us four years ago, when all the information about R.C.M.P. wrongdoing became public, that they were not interested in prosecuting members of the R.C.M.P. for these acts, there would have been hell to pay. So they stalled by appointing a royal commission.

The royal commission did perform a useful function. It was important for several reasons. What bothers me is that from the beginning the government of Canada used that commission not as a supplement to but rather as a substitute for normal law enforcement. I would have thought that when evidence of law-breaking became public the government could have done what it would do in the case of alleged civilian law-breaking: investigate and lay charges where appropriate. Where there was some indication that leniency was required, leniency could have been exercised according to the general canons of prosecutorial discretion. If there were a need to ask a royal commission for guidance in the exercise of that prosecutorial discretion, that could have been useful too.

But there was no reason to have a royal commission just to tell us that the R.C.M.P. should obey the law. There was no need for a royal commission to establish that unauthorized mail-opening is unlawful. I grant that some issues examined by the royal commission were more contentious from a legal point of view. Whether certain actions are unlawful or not may require deep legal analysis. But was there any reason to have a royal commission tell us that unauthorized mail-opening is unlawful? Or even that it occurred? The R.C.M.P. admitted that it happened hundreds of times and that it was unlawful.

We are now told that it would be very difficult at this point to dig out the evidence necessary to prosecute particular cases. There are gaps. A number of years have passed and trails have grown cold. I remember a statement made by the Honourable Ron Basford when he was Minister of Justice and was being pilloried about the failure to lay charges with respect to the illegal mail-opening. He said that the government did not have the evidence in case-ready form, and that the McDonald Commission would examine the evidence in the proper way and determine whether there was a basis for laying charges. So the R.C.M.P. and the government did not investigate because the matter was in the hands of the McDonald Commission. However, the McDonald Commission tells us that it did not attempt to investigate individual complaints; apart from a few key cases, it merely investigated patterns. No one investigated the matter on a case-by-case basis. It is now more than four years later. Small wonder that there are gaps in the evidence!

One of my chief concerns about all this is the contrast between the government's reaction to R.C.M.P. wrongdoing, and its approach to illegal conduct by others. In the fall of 1978 there was a strike by the Canadian Union of Postal Workers. Parliament, in its wisdom or lack of it, decided that it should be made unlawful by special legislation. At that point, all eyes were on the Canadian Labour Congress. What was it going to do about what was now an unlawful strike? Dennis McDermot and his colleagues on the executive council of the Canadian Labour Congress decided, despite their bitter opposition to the statute ordering the workers back to work, that it would not endorse an unlawful strike. Dennis McDermot was severely criticized by members of his own constituency. Indeed, a national convention of the Canadian Union of Public Employees demanded his resignation. For what? For having stood up for the rule of law.

What are we going to say to Dennis McDermot now that the government of Canada has failed to stand up for the rule of law? What are we going to say to Dennis McDermot the next time there are elements of his constituency who want to break the law in order to serve what they consider a higher standard of morality? What can we say to the Dennis McDermots of our society in view of this double standard with respect to R.C.M.P. wrongdoing?

11

WHAT INFLUENCES POLICY-MAKERS?

Does public opinion really exert an influence over policy-makers in the formulation and administration of the law? To what extent? How? The contributors to this chapter comment on these key questions from varied perspectives: those of the politician, the bureaucrat, the law reformer and the academic. A note of cynicism crept into the title of the conference panel on this topic: ''What, If Anything, Influences Policy-Makers?'' Although the words ''if anything'' have been removed from the chapter heading, echoes of them remain in some of the papers, particularly in that of Mr. Préfontaine, who sees policy-makers in a democratic country like Canada as very sensitive indeed.

A LAW REFORMER'S PERSPECTIVE

Francis C. Muldoon

INTRODUCTION

The publicity for the ''Cynical Society'' conference posed some interesting questions:

— Can an unpopular law be effective?
— Does public opinion influence law-making?
— Are we more, or less, cynical about legal institutions than in the past? Does it make any difference?
— How do courts and law-makers learn about public opinion?
— What is the impact of the media? Of education? Of religion?

Let me pose an obvious qualification to the conference topic, and then speak an obvious truth about my participation in a discussion about influencing policy-makers.

The conference topic surely has to be qualified to mean law in a cynical *democratic* society. We mean this society: Canada. We must surely mean our own ''free and democratic society'', described in the Canadian Charter of

Rights and Freedoms. Perhaps this conference itself proves the point. A conference such as this would have been made into a government propaganda event, or else would have been simply suppressed as being subversive, if it had been planned in any one of several authoritarian states whose names we can all summon to mind. Accordingly, the obvious qualification is what we are talking about: "What, if anything, influences policy-makers in this 'free and democratic society' of Canada?"

Second, I take the term "policy-makers" to mean those who actually implement policies in or upon the body politic. In that sense the obvious truth about my participation is that I do not do so as a "policy-maker", because I am not one.

It is true enough that the President of the Law Reform Commission of Canada must be constantly thinking of the policy of many of the laws of Canada and helping to perceive, conceive and formulate new or modified policies of law. After all, the Law Reform Commission Act[1] exacts that my colleagues and I

> study and keep under review on a continuing and systematic basis the statutes and other laws comprising the laws of Canada with a view to making recommendations for their improvement, modernization and reform . . . . [and that includes, at least, recommendations for] the removal of anachronisms and anomalies in the law; . . . the elimination of obsolete laws; and the development of new approaches to and new concepts of the law in keeping with and responsive to the changing needs of modern Canadian society and of individual members of that society.

Nevertheless, while my colleagues and I can study diligently, formulate as wisely as we can, and recommend all we want, we cannot implement our recommendations. In our democratic society that is as it should be, since we do not hold office by popular election. Our recommendations, if they are to be implemented at all, must be adopted, ratified and made law by the real policy-makers.

Who, then, are the real policy-makers?

THE COURTS

The law in this allegedly cynical society surely includes the common law (and its Quebec equivalent), which operates outside statutory structures, and which manifests its consistency and continuity by means of the principle of *stare decisis*. The common law, however, as we all know, is not eternally crystallized like the poet's (and the archeologist's) fly in the amber of *stare decisis*. It is developed, shaped and changed by those real policy-makers of the common law: the judges.

Judges are not popularly elected, although they are of course appointed

1 R.S.C. 1970, c. 23 (1st Supp.).

by those who from time to time enjoy the confidence of the majority of our popularly elected assemblies, the House of Commons and the legislative assemblies of the provinces. In part, perhaps, because it lacks a direct democratic mandate, the Canadian judiciary has historically evinced a self-discipline characterized by a diligent effort to declare and transmit the law as it has been received without wrenching departures or surprises to those who govern their conduct according to law. In making that effort, our judiciary is hardly influenced by the social policies and theories of the governments of the day, but dedicates itself first and foremost to that which is called "the rule of law".

Indeed, in making those self-disciplined efforts to impart precision and constancy to our law, the judiciary is frequently criticized by some who see it as being too conservative and too unresponsive to the needs and changing circumstances of a pluralistic and dynamic modern society. But there can be no society without law, because the very notion of society bespeaks the formulation, declaration and enforcement of laws. Judicial self-discipline, then, operates as a baffle to the winds of change — it will not withstand a hurricane, but it does protect from temporary gusts. Judicial self-discipline is a stabilizer of society, permitting us to assess whether or not any particular gust has hurricane force.

What prevents the common law from becoming rigidly crystallized is what has been described as "the inarticulate major premise":[2] the judges' own sense of what is fair and just in the circumstances. It amounts to a sense of equity. The judiciary is particularly well placed to notice the day-to-day practical operation of the law, and to effect corrective "fine-tuning" in its application. It is here that the policy-making role of the judge is brought into operation.

The policy-making of the judiciary can be unexpected; sometimes it is even quite gratifying for law reform commissioners. For example, the Report of the Law Reform Commission of Canada on Evidence proposed an Evidence Code, which was drafted with the intent that it should be enacted into legislation by Parliament. Among the articles of that proposed Evidence Code is that:

> Every rule of law that requires the corroboration of evidence as a basis for a conviction or that requires that the jury be warned of the danger of convicting on the basis of uncorroborated evidence is abrogated.[3]

Neither the Evidence Code nor that particular provision has yet been enacted by Parliament, but it has been cited among the unanimous reasons for judgment of the Supreme Court of Canada in *R. v. Vetrovec; R. v. Gaja*. Dickson J. (as he then was) wrote for the court in that judgment:

> As the study paper of the Law Reform Commission of Canada *"Evidence: 11 Corroboration"*

---

2 See G.W. Paton, *A Text-Book of Jurisprudence*, 3rd ed. (1964), p. 197.

3 Section 88, item (b).

dryly observes an "enormous superstructure . . . has been erected on the original basic proposition that the evidence of some witnesses should be approached with caution."[4]

Of course, many other sources and judicial authorities were gathered and referred to by Dickson J. in formulating that judgment of the Supreme Court of Canada, in addition to the Law Reform Commission's proposals. It is apparent, however, that the Commission's recommendation to abrogate the rule requiring corroboration of the testimony of an accomplice in the trial of an accused person was, itself, sufficiently well supported as to be persuasive to the Supreme Court of Canada. Then, in the *Vetrovec* reasons, we can observe the court actually performing its policy-making role in these words of Dickson J.:

> This Court has in past declared its willingness to depart from its own prior decisions as well as decisions of the Privy Council and the House of Lords (*Reference re Agricultural Products Act*, [1978] 2 S.C.R. 1198; 19 N.R. 361; *A.V.G. Management Science Ltd. v. Barwell Developments Ltd.*, [1979] 2 S.C.R. 43; 24 N.R. 554). The present case is an appropriate occasion to exercise this discretion. The law of corroboration is unduly and unnecessarily complex and technical.
>
> I would hold that there is no special category for "accomplices." An accomplice is to be treated like any other witness testifying at a criminal trial and the judge's conduct, if he chooses to give his opinion, is governed by the general rules.[5]

Since the judiciary cannot repeal, but are obliged to interpret and apply, legislation duly enacted by Parliament, Dickson J. concluded his policy-making dissertation in the *Vetrovec* judgment like this:

> I would point out that my comments have been limited to situations in which corroboration is required as a matter of common law. The *Criminal Code* specifies a number of instances in which corroboration is required, and defines the nature of the corroboration which must be supplied. (See, for example, sections 139 and 195). The statutory requirements would, of course, be controlling in cases coming under any of those sections.[6]

Thus, in the *Vetrovec* judgment, a common law policy was swept aside! The Supreme Court of Canada revised the policy of the common law. Among the scholarly articles, judicial authorities and other sources noticed, the work of the Law Reform Commission of Canada on corroboration in evidence was an acknowleged influence in changing the common law's policy.

The courts sometimes give ample notice of impending change. Recently, the nature and formulation of sexual offences described in the Criminal Code have been debated in Parliament and considered by many others, including the Law Reform Commission and feminist organizations. The question of early complaint on the part of a complainant was addressed again by the Supreme Court of Canada in 1981, in the case of *Timm v. R.*[7] The unanimous judgment of the court was written by Lamer J., who noted:

4 [1983] 1 W.W.R. 193, 27 C.R. (2d) 304, 67 C.C.C. (2d) 1, 136 D.L.R. (3d) 89, 41 N.R. 606 at 613 (S.C.C.).

5 *Ibid.*, p. 624.

6 *Ibid.*, pp. 625-26.

7 *Timm v. R.*, [1981] 2 S.C.R. 315, [1981] 5 W.W.R. 577, 21 C.R. (3d) 209, 28 C.R. (3d) 133, 59 C.C.C. (2d) 396, 124 D.L.R. (3d) 582, 37 N.R. 204, 29 A.R. 509.

> The case law as regards early complaint evidence (see amongst others *R. v. Cook; R. v. Belliveau; R. v. Waddell; R. v. Shonias; R. v. Ball; R. v. Washington*) amply shows that there exists in this area of the law great uncertainty, at least as to some aspects of that evidence. There is disagreement as to the nature of the complaint that may be put to the jury and by whose testimony; also as to the proper function of a judge holding a *voir dire* to determine the admissibility of early complaint evidence. Much of this disagreement and uncertainty is, in my opinion, the result of our considering the admissibility of such evidence as an exception to a general exclusionary rule, whilst what is in fact exceptional is the granting of special probative value to the silence of an alleged victim of a sexual offence. Most scholars and many a judge have in the past explained the historical origins of the rule and attempted, with relative success as far as I am concerned, to rationalize the singling out of that group of victims' complaints as being exceptionally admissible.[8]

Having noted the unsatisfactory state of the common law in this regard, the court, through the words of Lamer J., gave notice of an impending change of policy as follows:

> There are today suggestions (see amongst others the *Eleventh Report* by the *Criminal Law Revision Committee* of England and Wales and comments by Schiff, in vol. 1 of *Evidence in the Litigation Process,* at pp. 574 *et seq.*), that the need for the rule is doubtful and should be reconsidered. We have not been invited by the parties to do so, but I should like to add here that, given the proper opportunity, we should seriously reconsider the soundness of some of the assumptions that are made in order to justify the rule; furthermore, some of those assumptions are even more difficult to accept since the extension of the rule to victims of both sexes and to all sexual offences, including those where consent is not in issue.[9]

Two factors influenced those policy-makers of the Supreme Court of Canada in *Timm v. R*. First, the state of the law, based on previous jurisprudence, evinced "great uncertainty" and "disagreement" or divergence of views about "the nature of the complaint" which may be put to the jury. In less diplomatic words, the earlier judicial decisions had botched it. Second, the rule lacked logic and fairness and was capable, therefore, of thwarting the ends of justice. Testimony which, if believed by the jury, could confirm and support the complainant's credibility, could be kept from the jury. Accordingly, the Supreme Court gave notice that, if and when an appropriate case came before it subsequently, the court would seriously reconsider the law's policy in this regard.

But herein resides a weakness of judicial policy-making. Notice of an intention to reconsider the law's policy is sometimes given by the courts, but, as the *Vetrovec* case illustrates, this is not always the case; some changes of policy come as surprises. Those surprises occur because not even the Supreme Court of Canada can initiate legislation in the manner in which the government, a senator, an M.P. or an M.L.A. can initiate legislation. Courts cannot legislate in the manner in which Parliament, or a provincial legislature, or a municipal council or school board can legislate. They must wait until an appropriate case raising the particular policy issue floats across their horizon before they can make or vary the policy of the common law, or some aspect of the law which has not been specifically provided by legislative expression.

8 *Ibid.*, p. 320.
9 *Ibid.*, p. 321.

Not infrequently, the executive branch of government refers an issue to be determined by the court in order to obtain a policy declaration before embarking on some executive or legislative project. Incidentally, this is *par excellence,* a Canadian way of "smoking out" an interpretation of the law's policies before any real-life litigants enter into the lachrymose labyrinths of litigation.

THE LEGISLATORS

Not infrequently, the legislature pre-empts, ratifies or reverses the policies pronounced by the courts. Thus in an enactment of a section of the Criminal Code with relation to sexual offences and other related matters, Parliament pre-empted the reconsideration of the rule of recent complaint promised by the Supreme Court in the case of *Timm v. R.* Section 246.5 of that enactment provides:

> 246.5 The rules relating to evidence of recent complaint in sexual assault cases are hereby abrogated.[10]

Again, in that same enactment, Parliament confirmed the Supreme Court, but perhaps even went a bit further than the judgment in *R. v. Vetrovec; R. v. Gaja,*[11] by providing in s. 246.4:

> 246.4 Where an accused is charged with an offence under section 150 (incest), 157 (gross indecency), 246.1 (sexual assault), 246.2 (sexual assult with a weapon, threats to a third party or causing bodily harm) or 246.3 (aggravated sexual assault), no corroboration is required for a conviction and the judge shall not instruct the jury that it is unsafe to find the accused guilty in the absence of corroboration.[12]

If that legislative provision were to have been a faithful ratification of the Supreme Court's judgment, it would not have provided that "the judge shall not instruct the jury . . . ", but would rather have stated that "the judge is not required to instruct the jury that it is unsafe to find the accused guilty in the absence of corroboration". In this regard and in regard to many of the other aspects of this enactment, the House of Commons Debates of 4th August 1982 provide a record of intense legislating.

The House of Commons and its Justice and Legal Affairs Committee spent much time during the summer of 1982 in consideration of the then proposed sexual offences legislation. Indeed, the House referred to the committee consideration of the question of soliciting for the purposes of prostitution, and whether such soliciting ought to be retained as an offence in the Criminal Code, or whether Parliament ought to de-criminalize it so that it might, if constitutionally possible, be regulated (or not) by the provinces or municipalities. The members of the Justice and Legal Affairs Committee and the witnesses

---

10 Criminal Code, R.S.C. 1970, c. C-34, s. 246.5 [en. 1980-81-82-83, c. 125, s. 19].

11 *Supra,* note 4.

12 *Ibid.,* s. 246.4 [en. 1980-81-82-83, c. 125, s. 19].

who appeared before the committee, were almost all concerned about the Supreme Court's policy-making interpretation of soliciting, which was pronounced in the case of *Hutt v. R.*[13] The court's judgment in that case interpreted the offence expressed in the Criminal Code's s. 195.1[14] of soliciting any person in public place for the purpose of prostitution. The Supreme Court, in interpreting the legislative policy of that section, held that a private automobile, even when standing or moving on a public street, is not "a public place". It also held that the solicitation referred to in s. 195.1 must be pressing or persistent in order to constitute the offence. Many divergent points of view were expressed to the committee from various organizations and sectors of Canadian society. While some supported the court's interpretation, others, notably the Canadian Association of Chiefs of Police and the Concerned Residents of the West End (C.R.O.W.E.) of Vancouver, urged that the policy enunciated in *Hutt* be reversed by legislation.

Thus within this present year, one can see real examples of how judicial policy-making can be pre-empted, ratified or possibly reversed by legislative policy-makers. In regard to the committee's consideration of legislation on sexual offences, it can be also observed that the religious and social values of much of the electorate seem to influence the elected tribunes of the people in this secular parliamentary democracy of ours. On 27th May 1982, the Vancouver Coalition for a Non-Sexist Criminal Code urged those Members of Parliament to repeal not only the soliciting offence but also the provision directed against those who keep or patronize common bawdy houses. Certainly on that occasion, at least, the conflicting moral, religious and social values of Canadians were brought into such juxtaposition that more than one M.P. allowed that it would be a very courageous legislator indeed who would support the Coalition's brief. This is just a minor example of what everyone knows, or ought to know. Although our parliamentary democracy operates in what is, or was until the Charter's preamble was enacted, a secular state, it is surely illusory to believe that elected legislators would not be influenced by the religious, moral and social tenets of their constituents.

This last observation certainly summons for consideration the question addressed to this panel: What, if anything, influences legislators? Clearly the widely shared beliefs, desires, hopes and aspirations of their constituents influence elected policy-makers. Although Canadian Senators are not oblivious to public opinion, it is elected legislators who are especially close to their constituents.

Sometimes an articulate, forceful pressure-group appearing before a parliamentary committee can constitute a snare and a delusion for elected legislators, simply because such a group, with its own fish to fry, may be at odds with the majority of the electorate. There are times, of course, when a

13 *Hutt v. R.*, [1978] 2 S.C.R. 476, [1978] 2 W.W.R. 247, 1 C.R. (3d) 164, 38 C.C.C. (2d) 418, 82 D.L.R. (2d) 95, 19 N.R. 330.

14 [en. 1972, c. 13, s. 15].

Member of Parliament feels conscience-bound to cleave to good principle, purportedly for the general benefit of the country, and to ignore the possible disfavour of the voters and risk facing the music at the next election. Most of those M.P.'s will take strength from the forthright sentiments expressed long ago in Edmund Burke's great address to the electors of Bristol: in effect, to "dis-elect" him the next time 'round if they disagreed with the policies which he conscientiously espoused. However, lest it come to that, elected legislators usually take every opportunity to return to their ridings not only to listen to their constituents but also to persuade them, insofar as possible, to favour policies for the general benefit of the country as perceived by the member or by the party to which the member adheres. Edmund Burke, about 200 years ago, had clear insights into the nature of the House of Commons, upon which ours is modelled. To some, Burke's views may seem a trifle old fashioned and irrelevant today, but there is nevertheless something of enduring value in these words:

> The House of Commons was supposed originally to be *no part of the standing government of this country*. It was considered as a *control*, issuing *immediately* from the people, and speedily to be resolved into the mass from whence it arose. In this respect it was in the higher part of government what juries are in the lower. The capacity of a magistrate being transitory, and that of a citizen permanent, the latter capacity it was hoped would of course preponderate in all discussions, not only between the people and the standing authority of the Crown, but between the people and the fleeting authority of the House of Commons itself. It was hoped that, being of a middle nature between subject and government, they would feel with a more tender and a nearer interest everything that concerned the people, than the other remoter and more permanent parts of legislature.
>
> Whatever alterations time and the necessary accommodation of business may have introduced, this character can never be sustained, unless the House of Commons shall be made to hear some stamp of the actual disposition of the people at large. It would (among public misfortunes) be an evil more natural and tolerable, that the House of Commons should be infected with every epidemical phrensy of the people, as this would indicate some consanguinity, some sympathy of nature with their constituents, than that they should in all cases be wholly untouched by the opinions and feelings of the people out of doors. By this want of sympathy they would cease to be a House of Commons.[15]

If those ideas are no longer relevant in Canada today, perhaps they still ought to be.

THE BUREAUCRATS

I have discussed the courts and the politicians, but they do not complete the list of policy-makers. The bureaucracy must also be taken into account. The Ottawa bureaucracy seems elephantine to a Manitoban fresh off the prairies, but the provinces also possess elaborate administrative infrastructures. Our modern, well organized public service, overseen by an officers' corps of competent mandarin/managers, with its fiefdoms, duchies and baronies of policy-planning directorates and research components, is an awesome empire.

15 *The Works of Edmund Burke*, vol. 11 (1808), p. 287.

And one must not overlook the flock of administrative tribunals that operate both provincially and federally. Whether they develop policy independently or administer policy crafted for them by ministers and their senior policy advisers, these agencies must be regarded as policy-makers.

What if anything influences the bureaucracy? It is not even pejorative to suggest that conventional wisdom is not far wrong in perceiving that the bureaucracy, as a whole, is much influenced by the requirement of its own survival. We in Canada have accepted the notion of a permanent and secure public service in order to avoid the evil of pork-barreling practised in an earlier time. Nevertheless, we often witness the spectacle of the dismissal of senior manager/mandarins upon a change of government. That is surely an indication that the newly elected "new brooms" believe that the mandarins exert considerable influence on policy-making — that they can and probably will obstruct, impede, divert or dilute the policies of a newly elected government. Such action is seen to be drastic when it occurs. But as between the mandarin and the minister, it may be wondered just which is the more influential policy-maker, after all. Ministers come and go, M.P.'s come and go, but competent mandarin/managers seem to go on forever, especially if given a chance to demonstrate flexibility in serving new masters of a different partisan stripe.

It is not necessarily true that survival skills and policy-making skills are mutually exclusive, but sometimes — perhaps too frequently — justifiable self-confidence in the one role is not matched by justifiable self-confidence in the other. When that occurs, those who should be capable of giving sound advice to the government themselves may be tempted to avoid the responsibility of doing so by retaining external professional advisers. What, if anything, influences external professional advisers is beyond my ken. My perception is that there is a problem here, but I leave it to those who know the bureaucracy better than I do to describe and prescribe. After all, I am still just a stranger in paradise.

IS SOCIETY REALLY CYNICAL?

Having considered who are the policy-makers and what influences them, one is left with the allegedly cynical society. I hope that cynicism does not infest our society, as the conference theme suggests, and I doubt that it does. Cynicism is a dangerously negative quality which displaces the civic virtues. To the extent that a society is cynical, it evinces neither faith nor hope, and precious little charity, either. Having sipped and weathered in our own lifetimes an era characterized by materialism, hedonism and permissiveness far beyond tolerance, Canadians are more aware than before that the party is over in terms of its over-consumption, waste and squandering of resources.

One might venture to say that our society is even now less cynical than it was when the topic for this very conference was planned, back in the mid-seventies. The realization of this conference has taken a long time, and in that time we have witnessed the rise of the Parti Québecois, the Quebec referendum, the patriation of our constitution and its primacy as the supreme law of Canada, including the Canadian Charter of Rights and Freedoms. There have been cynics among us, some of them of high estate, but Canadian society has endured them and still places its confidence in the sincere and the hopeful, the industrious and the innovative. The very notion of society bespeaks law, for there is no society without law. Law in a cynical society would be in a perilous plight, if only because that society itself would be in a perilous plight. We simply cannot afford it, so one hopes that our elected and other policy-makers will, by remaining sensitive to the reasonable aspirations of our people, give them little cause to be cynical.

DID YOU KNOW THAT POLICY-MAKERS ARE VERY SENSITIVE PEOPLE?

D. C. Préfontaine

INTRODUCTION

When I first heard the topic — "What, if anything, influences policy-makers" — I put an unconscious stress on the phrase "if anything", and thought "how cynical". Then I remembered the theme of the conference.

This reaction was caused by my perception that policy-makers are subject to a wide and often bewildering array of influences, representing a multiplicity of viewpoints, concerns, interests and values. This array of influences changes in both composition and intensity according to the issue at stake, but the main point is that policy-makers are exposed to so *many* influences, not — as the panel's theme seems to imply — to so *few*. Hence, my response, "Did you know that policy-makers are very sensitive people?"

Before lauching into my discourse, it is necessary to define a couple of key terms. First, what is a "cynic"? The *Oxford English Dictionary* defines a "cynic" as one "who shows a disposition to disbelieve in the sincerity or goodness of human motives and actions, and is wont to express this by sneers and sarcasms". Further, what is a "policy-maker"? While I am familiar with the less visible "policy-making" roles often attributed to front-line workers in service-oriented systems such as criminal justice, and the supposedly important "agenda-setting" and "issue defining" role of bureaucrats, I am here concerned with the more traditional, formal and highly visible policy-maker: the member of Cabinet and the Member of Parliament.

I will concentrate on the "small p" political dimension of policy-making, because it is the cornerstone of our entire system of democratic government, and because, from my own perspective as a policy adviser to the policy-maker, I think it is widely misunderstood. I would note that I have been engaged in policy-related jobs as a lawyer for the federal government for some ten years now, mostly in the area of social policy and criminal justice. My perceptions as to the major sources of influence on policy are necessarily shaped by that experience.

I would like to discuss briefly five major determinants of policy as they affect policy-makers and their advisers. These are:

— time

— resources

— need to respond to crises

— desire to implement longer term priorities and plans

— personal experience and bias

The first two of these factors have an enormous influence over the ability to make policy. The third and fourth are factors articulated by various actors: "public opinion" in its various elements, political priorities and pressures, bureaucratic plans and processes, personal goals of ministers and M.P.'s. The third factor often conflicts with the fourth. The fifth is the unpredictable variable which humanizes the policy-making process.

TIME

First, time. It is hard to envision, let alone overestimate, the demands made on the time of policy-makers. Cabinet ministers must find time in their schedules for many duties: their constituency responsibilities as elected M.P.'s; their political responsibilities as members of political parties; their responsibilities as members of Cabinet to participate in the work of the various Cabinet committees on which they sit; their duties as departmental ministers to deal with the issues they must themselves steer through Cabinet committees, Treasury Board, full Cabinet and the House of Commons and its committees; and, finally, the incessant demands made on them by routine departmental business. A departmental minister is in brutal competition with his colleagues for the rarest of all commodities, Cabinet time and House time. This constraining influence on policy-makers and policy is, I think, of paramount importance, notwithstanding the fact that you hear almost nothing about it.

RESOURCES

The second factor, resources, is similar in the sense that its rarity, as a commodity, has a constraining influence on policy. The influence of resources in the system's policy direction has shifted drastically in the last decade. While there is much concern about the size of public sector budgets and deficits, it is a fact that the major part of those budgets results from non-discretionary spending for statutory programs introduced two, three or more decades ago. In my opinion, the policy-making process in Ottawa has changed in the past three or four years to reflect the constant pressure to increase resources. Not all that long ago, Cabinet committees made policy decisions "on their merits", as it was called, and the resource implications were considered later, by the Treasury Board. This system was fine in expansionary times. With recent budget restraints, however, the new Policy and Expenditure Management System (P.E.M.S.) — which divides departments into policy section "envelopes", sets a budgetary ceiling for each envelope, and requires each envelope committee of ministers to fund new policy initiatives from within that envelope — has served to combine the policy process with the resource allocation process and, in so doing, to place ministers within each envelope in direct competition with each other for the comparatively scarce resources available. Again, the impact of this factor on policy has not been widely recognized until just recently.

These first two factors — *time* and *resources* — have a large influence on policy-makers, an influence severely *limiting* their scope of action. The third and fourth factors are, by contrast, more positive in nature, in the sense that they reflect pressures to act, rather than brakes or constraints on those pressures.

NEED TO RESPOND TO CRISES

The third factor is the need to respond to crises. The criminal justice system is especially prone to this factor, since the public is often — I'm tempted to say usually — made aware of criminal law and criminal justice issues by the exposure given to sensational negative incidents — murders, hostage-takings, prison riots or escapes. The public, not unnaturally, responds to these incidents, unique though they may be, by exerting pressure on the policy-makers, who, not unnaturally, respond to these pressures. The fact that such responses must necessarily in many cases take the form of policy changes that apply generally throughout the system sometimes gives rise to problems, because the situation being responded to is specific, not general, and because the generally-applicable response may be inappropriate or cause unintended and unforeseen consequences. In addition, the need to devote time to the short-term, atypical, but intense issue further diminishes the time available to deal with less visible, more general and more consequential issues.

This is not to say that crises could or should be ignored. Nor is it to say that crises are always unique and never bring deeper issues to light. Indeed, in this latter sense, the "crisis" factor may actually complement the "longer-term priority" factor, by bringing to public and official attention the existence of a problem, issue, or need that has major implications for the system and for policy as a whole. But, at least in my experience, the attention devoted to crises management serves to *distract* attention from major issues more often than it serves to *focus* attention on such issues.

LONGER TERM PRIORITIES AND PLANS

This leads me to the fourth factor: the desire to implement longer term priorities and plans. I hope it is not simply my bureaucratic bias speaking here, but I am convinced that the interests of Canadian society can only be served if sufficient attention is devoted to this kind of policy perspective, again bearing in mind the need and the reality for policy-makers to devote attention to short-term problems and crises.

A hopeful example of what I mean is the recently launched criminal law review. This review, the need for which was identified by federal and provincial ministers responsible for criminal justice some three years ago, entails a fundamental and comprehensive examination of all aspects of Canadian criminal law. Its need was premised on the perception that criminal law policy over the past 90 years in Canada has emerged as a result of a series of *ad hoc,* incremental, and not necessarily consistent, initiatives launched in response to specific and particular problems. On this basis, and in view of the massive changes that Canadian society has experienced over the past 90 years, it was thought timely to submit the criminal law's basic underlying assumptions to review, in order to equip Canadian society with a tool more clearly focused on the problems it confronts now, and will confront in the future.

In August of 1982, the Minister of Justice released a basic statement of government policy with respect to this review. This document, called *The Criminal Law in Canadian Society,* is the first attempt by government in Canadian history to set down in black and white its conception of the principles that should underlie and guide criminal law policy in the coming decade.

I think this is an instructive example for a number of reasons. One reason is illustrated by some of the press reactions that greeted the release of the document. Much of this press reaction portrayed the review exercise as "bureaucratic" in the extreme, and in the worst sense of that word. It was described as so long-term as to be irrelevant, concerned with marginal issues of interest only to bureaucrats, and designed to distract attention from real problems in need of immediate action. This is illustrative of the point I was attempting to make earlier: the short-term, atypical and nonrepresentative problems confronted by the system from time to time — what I would conceive of as "symptoms" — are mistaken for the disease itself. The fundamental long-term issues embodied by the review have very few immediately identifiable spokesmen or ramifications.

Publication of the document I have referred to was an attempt by the government to involve the broader public in a consideration of some of these basic issues and principles. A serious impediment to any such attempt is the gap that exists between the general public view of the criminal justice system and reality. At the beginning of the criminal law review, we sought information about popular perceptions through a public survey. Instead of asking people what they preferred to have done about crime, or what their general attitudes were, we thought it would be useful to know what perceptions Canadians had about the actual workings of the criminal justice system in practice. Accordingly, in February 1982, we asked the Gallup organization to poll around 2,000 adult Canadians on a series of questions about violent crime in Canada, and on sentencing and release practices in Canada. We asked questions for which we have at least some objective statistical information. The results of this survey indicated that Canadians

> [v]astly over-estimate the proportion of crime which involves violence, they think we are closer in levels of violence to the U.S. than in fact we are, they see the numbers of murders increasing in the past six years, when, in fact, they have not, and they think that people released from prison on parole are more likely than in fact they are to commit crimes of violence soon after release.

To give a bit of detail, only 6 to 8 per cent of all crimes known or reported to police involve violence, whereas the average Canadian thinks that the situation is about seven times as bad as that — that over 50 per cent of all crime involves violence. Two out of three Canadians believe that murders have increased in Canada since the death penalty was abolished in 1976, whereas in fact the murder rate has actually gone down somewhat, whether measured in terms of numbers or of rate. Only one in four Canadians apparently realizes that, in fact, there is only one violent crime in Canada for every five crimes in the United States, after taking into account the differences in population. Around four in five overestimated, or vastly overestimated, the proportion of inmates who commit violent crimes shortly after release on parole, with the average response exaggerating the extent of the problem by a factor of five.

We have to be careful what we conclude from this, because of the well-known limitations of one-shot surveys, the problems with statistics in the criminal justice area, and so on. But I do think it might tell us that we should be wary in responding to perceived public demands for a harsher approach to criminal justice if, as seems to be the case, those demands are partly the result of a distorted and inaccurate picture of the extent of the problem. It also tells us that we in government have a large job to do in better informing Canadians of the very nature of the crime problem. If fear of crime is related to exaggerated perceptions of the extent of crime, which it seems to be, then quality of life should be improved to some degree by merely giving people a more realistic impression of the crime situation. This is especially relevant in the case of elderly people, who are known to have a high rate of fear of crime, and who actually stay at home and otherwise restrict their activities because of that fear, but who are shown in victimization surveys to be among the least victimized segments of the population. Thus does the gap between perception and reality negatively affect the quality of life.

I am not saying here that crime is not a real problem or that policy-makers can content themselves by saying that people's fears are exaggerated. Crime is a real problem. It significantly affects our lives, our economy and our society. What I am saying is that in reforming law, in assessing the weight that should be attached to the various influences that make themselves felt on the policy-making process, we must work from a realistic set of notions about the nature of the problem if we are to arrive at realistic solutions.

PERSONAL EXPERIENCE AND BIAS

Now, let me make a few remarks concerning the impact played by the fifth factor: the personal experience and bias of the policy-maker. What is the extent of its influence? This is the factor that is the most difficult to predict. In my experience, it is the element that makes policy-making exciting. Far from being immune from such influences, policy-makers in Canada are often strongly motivated by such internal factors. A policy-advisor has to be totally aware, and respectful, of these sensitivities if the relationship with the policy-maker he or she serves is to be a success.

I do not believe that policy can or should be founded solely on a "rational-bureaucratic" model of the world. Policy involving the law must be based on a realistic and pragmatic appreciation of the possibilities and limitations inherent in the use of law in a modern, technological, and diverse society such as Canada. Does it make sense? Is it simple? Is it fair and just? When answering these questions the policy-makers must rely, to some extent, on their personal instincts. No law will survive long, or be effectively enforced, in a democratic society if the people who are subject to it do not believe in the sincerity and goodwill of the law-makers, as well as of those who administer and interpret it!

I am reminded of the words of Oliver Wendell Holmes:

> The life of the law has not been logic: it has been experience. The felt necessities of the time, the prevalent moral and political theories, intuitions of public policy, vowed or unconscious, even the prejudices which judges share with their fellow-men, have had a good deal more to do than the syllogism in determining the rules by which men should be governed.[16]

---

16 *The Common Law* (1881), p. 1.

THE VIEW OF AN OPPOSITION M.P.

Pauline Jewett

I want to talk about some of the frustrations of being a Member of Parliament: the fact that you don't have much influence on policy, particularly if you belong to an opposition party; the fact that the political executive operates almost entirely in secret, and we ordinary parliamentarians, and the public, learn about decisions at a point when we can do nothing about them. But I also want to say that some recent developments have made me a little more optimistic on this score.

Before my optimism breaks out, let me give an example of overwhelming secrecy that is certainly not in the best interests of Canadians. I am the external affairs critic for the New Democratic Party. I have become, as, indeed, have great numbers of the Canadian public, very concerned about the fact that Canada is actively participating in the development and testing of the cruise missile: the most destabilizing weapon in the nuclear weapons armoury.

"Destabilizing" is how students of the nuclear weapons armoury describe weapons that are undetectable. Unlike all previous generations of nuclear missiles, including the Soviet SS20, the cruise missile is almost undetectable. And if a missile is undetectable, then it is unverifiable. Such weapons destabilize the arms balance and undermine attempts at arms control. If you don't know how many there are, you are not going to be able to get arms reductions agreements. And, therefore, it is of enormous importance that Canadians know about the framework agreement that the Canadian government has negotiated with Washington to test these and future generations of nuclear missiles. But it was impossible to get any information from Ottawa in time to do anything about it.

The last important defence arrangement with the United States was N.O.R.A.D. in 1958. The Liberals were then in opposition. Mr. Diefenbaker was trying to get it through, as all executives do, without any discussion. The Liberals, who are now in government, then insisted on full information and, indeed, a full parliamentary debate, before this agreement was launched in 1958. So we have degenerated in this country, it seems to me, as regards the opportunity for knowledge, discussion and debate of such major policy issues. And if you don't have that opportunity, how can you influence policy? People will say, of course, that defence is a special case, because national security is involved. All I know is that, like many Canadians, I don't feel very secure with cruise missile testing taking place without my knowledge and consent.

But there is some reason for optimism about the influence that enlightened public opinion can exert on policy-makers. There are two things that have happened in the last couple of years that really are rather exciting.

The first example involved the parliamentary subcommittee on Canada's relations with the Caribbean and Latin America. The subcommittee had 15 members, drawn from all three parties. We met for a year and a half. Our final report is about to be tabled [1982]. Our interim report was tabled in December 1981, after several months' work. People came before us with ideas; we visited the regions, and we held extensive discussions.

The interim report was sharply at variance with previous Canadian policy on the Caribbean, and particularly with Canadian policy on Central and South America. Up to that point, the Canadian policy on Central America was almost completely nonexistent. You know, the minister said: "I'm sorry, but Central America is not a region of interest to Canada." South America was of a bit more interest, because there was more commercial potential, but Central America, he said, several times, was not a region of interest to Canada.

The committee, with only a few exceptions, decided that it is in our deepest interest to know what is happening in El Salvador — the murders, the assassinations, and the actions of the government of that country; it is in our deepest interest to know whether or not the United States is destabilizing Nicaragua, and therefore driving that government into an authoritarian mode; and it is in our deepest interest to know whether or not Honduras will be allowed to live in freedom and independence and peace. Canada is interested because we share the hemisphere with these countries.

The subcommittee discovered that there are important groups of Canadians who are aware of the importance of understanding what is happening in Central America and of trying to assist the forces for progress that exist in those countries. I think particularly of the Interfaith Committee of the churches, the Conference of Catholic Bishops, Project Plowshares and many other groups: the Honduran groups, the Nicaraguan groups, the Salvadoran groups. They just sprouted up. Before I knew it, I was going back to my riding and discovering that the fishermen of British Columbia had collected $150,000 for the Fisheries Institute in Nicaragua. Things like that were happening at a grass roots level, and those developments, combined with the continuing pressure of the subcommittee, showed the government of the day that they could no longer ignore human rights violations in that part of the world. They could no longer ignore the forces for progress in that part of the world. They could no longer ignore American policy in that part of the world. Those of us who have sat and worked on this committee for 16 months feel that we had some influence on the Canadian government in this matter, at least in helping it to get out of the box it had got into when the former Secretary of State for External Affairs said we had no interest or concern in this area.

A second experience that caused me to feel that life as an M.P. is sometimes really worthwhile was watching the progress of the Joint Parliamentary Committee on the Constitution. This was the only parliamentary committee, to my knowledge, that was televised, and it was heartening to hear constituents say that they watched. One new Canadian told me that he had watched, and he said that in the course of the hearings and the briefs and the witnesses, he felt that he had learned something about our history and our legal system, and that he had learned a lot about who is discriminated against, who is disadvantaged and who is persecuted.

Among the discriminated, persecuted and disadvantaged are the 52 per cent of the population known as women. And of course it was chaps, by and large, who were drawing up the constitution. Even in the Department of Justice there was, to my knowledge, only one woman involved. The hearings brought out an incredible series of papers, background documents, by some of the very best academic women in the universities in this country. They constituted a devastating critique of Supreme Court decisions as far as women were concerned. They demonstrated vividly that equal justice under law did not exist for women in Canada — not even in the seventies.

The result of these forceful presentations was a Charter provision which called explicitly for sexual equality. Then, however, the Supreme Court decision came. The Supreme Court decision suggested that the federal government had better get a larger consent for its constitutional amendments from the provinces. So the federal and provincial chaps got together again, and drew up an accord. No women participated. It was called the "Kitchen Accord", and if ever there was a time when a woman ought to have been in the kitchen that was it! They decided to limit the provision for sexual equality (as well as to knock out the guarantee of native rights).

The day after, in the House of Commons, I got up in question period and asked the Prime Minister if he could tell the house what had happened to the sexual equality clause. He said he actually couldn't remember what had happened to it. He just literally couldn't remember. Well! When I flagged it in the House of Commons that the Prime Minister didn't even know what had happened to the clause, the Ad Hoc Committee on Women and the Constitution, which had been so active during the public hearings, got going again. I've never seen a pressure group like it. We got the free-standing sexual equality clause back because of a magnificent combined effort on the part of women academics, women M.P.'s, and powerful women's groups in society like the Ad Hoc Committee on Women and the Constitution and the Women and the Law group. When all these people got going, the premiers just tumbled, one after the other, and the original clause was put back into the Charter. Section 28 reads: "Notwithstanding anything in this Charter, the rights and freedoms referred to in it are guaranteed equally to male and female persons."

Life can be maddening for an opposition Member of Parliament. You wonder sometimes if you have any influence and if you know enough about what's going on to have any influence. At times the frustration fosters cynicism. But there are other times, such as the two personal experiences I have related, when you do feel that the average M.P., and the average member of the Canadian public, can have some influence on the policy-makers.

WHEN LEGISLATORS ACT WITHOUT ADEQUATE PUBLIC CONSULTATION: AN AMERICAN OBJECT LESSON

Nicholas Kittrie

What, if anything, influences policy-makers? Sometimes it takes very little to bring about a major change in legal policy. I will limit myself to one case study: the 1937 federal United States law dealing with marijuana.[17] This law criminalized marijuana by adding it to the list of prohibited narcotics. What influenced the policy-makers to take this step? Let me tell you what happened.

The United States House of Representatives had hearings which lasted a portion of five days. There were 12 witnesses at those hearings. Three of the witnesses represented the hemp seed industry. They were concerned that the legislation would interfere with their business. Four of the witnesses represented the United States Treasury Department, which was proposing the law. The actual hearings took only about two and a half days out of the five. The United States Senate had hearings too; they lasted less than two hours.

Let me tell you what happened at these hearings. Harry Anslinger, the United States Commissioner of Narcotics, testified as follows:

> In Persia, a thousand years before Christ, there was a religious and military order called the Assassins and they derived their name from the drug called hashish which is now known [as] marijuana . . . they were known for their acts of cruelty.[18]

What is most amazing about this statement is not the reliance on Asian evidence, but the completely mistaken historical allusion. The Assassins were not in Persia, they were in Turkey. And they existed 1500 years later than the period he described.

On the question of how dangerous marijuana is, the following interesting exchange took place during the Senate hearings. Senator Davis asked:

> How many cigarettes would you have to smoke before you got this vicious mental attitude toward your neighbor?

Mr. Anslinger replied:

> I believe in some cases one cigarette might develop a homicidal mania, probably to kill his brother, . . . probably some people could smoke five before it takes effect, but the experts agree that the continued use leads to insanity. There are many cases of insanity.[19]

---

17 *Marijuana Tax Act,* 1937.

18 Harry J. Anslinger, *Hearings on H.R. 6385 Before House Committee on Ways and Means,* 75th Congress, 1st Session (1937), p. 18.

19 *Hearings on H.R. 6906 Before Subcommittee of Senate Committee on Finance,* 75th Congress, 1st Session (1937), p. 12.

I submit to you that this was a case of governmental insanity.

The American Medical Association testified against the government. It opposed criminalizing a substance which it thought had some medical use. The testimony of the American Medical Association was rejected out of hand, however, on the grounds that the association had been objecting to all the New Deal legislation and must therefore be regarded as biased with respect to all legislation proposed by the Roosevelt administration.

Somewhere between 8 and 20 million Americans are thought to have some acquaintance with marijuana. About two thirds of them are one-time or occasional experimenters. Some 25 per cent are occasional users, and perhaps 10 per cent are chronic users. The ill-considered law that turned this very significant percentage of the American population into criminals resulted from completely inadequate public and scientific consultations.

How can we avoid repetitions of this kind of law-making? I believe that we should insist that it is the duty of the policy-makers to articulate what has influenced them. Just as judges are required to articulate the reasons for their judgments, it should be the duty of policy-makers to articulate precisely what it is that has influenced them. I think the public is entitled to know what takes place in the minds and in the chambers of policy-makers before they reach their conclusions.

12

POLITICAL RESPONSES

Three prominent politicians, representing Canada's three largest political parties, were asked to address the theme of the conference. They agreed on one thing: that cynicism abounds among the electorate. Their opinions about the causes of the cynicism, and their proposals for reducing it, varied widely, however.

MAKING LAW IN A CYNICAL SOCIETY

Roland Penner

POLITICAL CYNICISM

There is a question mark punctuating the conference title. It appears that after studying the results of Dr. Moore's survey on the public's perceptions of the law and the legal system, the conference organizers had considerable doubt about just how cynical the public really is. Whatever may be the facts concerning public attitudes to law and legal institutions, it is my view — impressionistic, I readily admit — that the public is increasingly cynical about politics, politicians and political institutions, no doubt with considerable justification. Hence it is that there is no question mark forming part of the title of these observations.

Thomas Jefferson's statement that "no man's life, liberty or property are safe when the legislature is in session", expresses, I believe, a sentiment at least as generally accepted today as it appears to have been 200 years ago. "Politics," another wit advises us, "is the gentle art of getting votes from the poor and campaign funds from the rich by promising to protect each from the other." You see, there aren't many good-natured jokes about politics and political institutions. There are, probably, fewer good-natured views.

The Legal Research Institute's Survey, unfortunately, does not provide us with data which quantify public attitudes to law-making and law-makers. I rather wish it had. There is, I know, an opinion recorded in the survey, that governments should do more in the areas of law reform and law enforcement, scoring these almost as high as the need for governments to deal with unemployment. But that's about it. Perhaps we have a measure in the

September 1982 Gallup Poll on political preferences, which showed that 31 per cent of those polled were not committed to any party. Were they, or most of them, simply throwing up their hands and in effect saying they didn't give a damn?

In my view, we are currently experiencing in Canada a degree of political alienation which may have grave consequences, if not for the viability then for the effective functioning of political democracy — a consequence graver by far than any likely to flow from cynicism about legal institutions. Our memories are short (a fact upon which politicians are said to rely) but I hope we are still close enough to the event and its consequences to remember the exploitation of that kind of cynicism preceding the collapse of the Weimar Republic in Germany.

SOURCES OF CYNICISM

What is the source of this dangerous cynicism? As with any other complex social phenomenon, it is unlikely that there is a single source for the political alienation and cynicism about which I speak, but let me mention three probable sources. First, the dismal state of the economy. The path from economic exhaustion to political exhaustion is, no doubt, very short. Second, the reality of the political decision-making process, which is (and in a class society will continue to be) essentially a conflict model rather than a consensus model. Third, and this will become my main point, a style of government to which I refer as the "oval office" style of government.

Let me explore the second and third of these propositions sequentially.

Democracy is a system of government which, no less than any other, "exists to uphold and enforce a certain set of relations between people . . . a system by which power is exerted over individuals and groups within it".[1] In Fuller's words "Our parliamentary democracy is so constituted that much of our legislation is, in fact, the legislation of well organized, articulate and powerful minorities".[2]

This latter fact is perceived by a substantial and growing number of people, who feel that they are not part of the political process, and who feel that their vote makes no real difference. This view seems to be held much more widely with respect to federal than to provincial politics and much more widely in the west than in the east. Western Canadians traditionally feel "hard done by".

In my view, the well organized, articulate and powerful minorities about which Fuller wrote will continue to play a significant role in the formation of public policy and the shaping of legislation. But, as Engels once pointed out

1 C.B. MacPherson, *The Real World of Democracy* (The Massey Lectures Fourth Series).

2 As quoted in Richard Quinney "Crime in a Political Perspective" (1964), 8:4 *Amer. Behavioral Scientist* 19 at 20.

in a letter to Bloch, history is not the result of the exercise of the will of one person, or even of one group of persons; it is, rather, the resultant of the conflict of the wills of all those involved in any way in the various social and economic systems which influence and ultimately shape public policy.

If that resultant is to truly reflect all legitimate interests in society and not just the powerful few, there is a need — I would say an urgent need — to strengthen the voice and influence in the decision-making process of the many who have not had the means (or who perceive that they have not had the means) to become involved in the process. I refer to methods of influence other than through the exercise of the comparatively insignificant right to put an "X" on a piece of paper once every few years. They feel politically alienated because they are politically alienated!

No doubt the democratization of the liberal state has been considerable. The development of parliamentary democracy, the party system, and the universal franchise are all noteworthy, of course. Even more important are the concomitant developments of the freedoms of association, speech and press, all now formally designated as fundamental rights in the Charter. It is MacPherson's view that the "job of the competitive party system is to uphold the competitive market society by keeping the government responsive to the shifting majority interests of those who are running the market."[3] It must be acknowledged, however, that the system allowed the formation and, ultimately, the election of political parties not quite so dedicated to the market society. Moreover, it must also be acknowledged that freedom of association played an important role in the development of the trade union movement, now a powerful third force within the marketplace itself.

But despite all that has marked the democratization of the liberal state, there are still a substantial number who feel that they have no "political purchasing power", and who feel resentful about it!

INNER SANCTUM GOVERNMENT

Feeding this resentment, this political alienation, has been the development of a style of government — really several styles — which I call, compendiously, "the oval office style". Nixon's oval office, where that handful of scoundrels whose names "will live long in infamy" plotted their surprisingly crude but nevertheless dangerous manipulation of the democratic process, represents the worst of the style. But in any of its forms, the oval office style (which may be the political image of the increasing monopolization of financial and industrial power) is a threat to democracy and a barrier to its further development which ought not to be underestimated.

The main feature of the oval office style is the narrowing of the decision-making base. Decision-making is monopolized by fewer and fewer people as

3 See *supra*, note 1, p. 9.

it moves from the forum to Parliament, from Parliament to the Cabinet, from the Cabinet to the inner cabinet, and from the inner cabinet to the inner office, where by now the isolation from the grass roots is virtually complete.

Much criticism has recently been directed against what are perceived to be the negative effects of the "Pitfield style" on the Ottawa mandarins. For example, Christina McCall-Newman recently wrote about "Michael Pitfield and the Politics of Mismanagement".[4] I believe that much of her criticism and that of others is misdirected. The mandarinate is itself a "power elite", removed from the direct influence of either people or Parliament. At most, Pitfield merely hastened the process of confining the exercise of power to fewer and fewer people.

It is not only executive government as such which appears monopolized and remote: Parliament and at least some legislatures are widely perceived as being ineffective and unresponsive. Political alienation grows apace. Responding to a survey conducted by the journal *Parliamentary Government,* on whether Canadians should feel content with the role and function of the House of Commons, John F. Bulloch of the Canadian Federation of Independent Business said as follows:

> Canadians should be, and I contend many are, disturbed with the role and functions of the House of Commons. First, the Executive, then the Bureaucracy, have seized more and more of the power in our system of government. The 282 representatives of the people from across our nation have an ever diminishing role in policy formulation. This lack of meaningful participation in legislative development, coupled with the rigid discipline of the party system, has turned the deliberations of Parliament into an extremely formalized ritual.[5]

Others in the same survey spoke of Parliament as "little more than a voting machine to rubber stamp Cabinet edicts". Another said, "you might as well rely on Lotto Canada to produce a house representative of the Canadian people". You may now see why I don't think there's much justification for a question mark on the topic of making law in a cynical society.

There is, let me acknowledge, considerable and useful debate about the reform of Parliament taking place throughout the country. The report of the Canadian Bar Association Committee on the Reform of Parliament is a good example.[6] But its subject "Parliament as Law-maker" narrows the issue too much, in my view. My primary concern is not so much with Parliament as law-maker as with the concept of the people as law-makers! Parliamentary reform is long overdue — granted! Our own rules and procedures in the Manitoba Legislative Assembly are far from being beyond criticism — granted! Parliament should be more representative of the diversity of regions and regional interests — granted! But if, in the end, steps are not taken to

4 "Michael Pitfield and the Politics of Mismanagement" (1982), 97:10 *Saturday Night* 24.

5 A collection of responses to a set of questions, in "Parliamentary Perceptions" (1982), 3:3 *Parliamentary Govt*. 6.

6 Report of the Canadian Bar Association Committee on the Reform of Parliament, *Parliament as Lawmaker* (1982).

increase, significantly, the direct participation of the people in the decision-making process, parliamentary and electoral reforms will simply not be enough.

POLLS AREN'T THE ANSWER

My concept of how this admittedly difficult job is to be done rejects the questionable practice of initiating government action, including legislative action, in response to the latest message from the pollsters. I'm not opposed to government or oppositions taking comprehensive polls from time to time to sharpen their general perception of public concerns, but as a substitute for the direct interaction between the politicians and the people, polling leaves much to be desired. Single-issue polls on matters about which opinions are held more as articles of faith than as fully thought-out positions ought never to be the basis for government action. (Incidentally, did you ever get the feeling that the only reason we have elections is to find out if the polls were right?)

Paradoxically, I find some support for my argument about polls in the results of a poll: that to which Mr. Préfontaine has made reference.[7] What that poll demonstrated was not merely that the public at large overestimate the amount and degree of crime (that, most of us in the field strongly suspected), but that the overestimation is gross! Let me give only one example: While only 6 to 8 per cent of all crimes known to the police involve violence, the average Canadian thinks that the percentage is over 50! The opinion poll is obviously not the proper instrument by which to involve the general public in law making. It's not the polity of the polls, but the polity of the people, for which I plead.

INVOLVING THE PEOPLE: EXAMPLES

I fully expect that what I have said about involving the people more fully in government and in the law-making process will be dismissed by some as political sentimentality and populist romanticism. Let me, in my own defence, furnish some examples to demonstrate what I consider to be the viability of the concept.

The Canadian Charter of Rights and Freedoms provides an excellent illustration. We should not lose sight of the way in which the Charter took its final shape. I refer particularly to the work of the special Joint Committee of the House and Senate on the Constitution, when the debate on this historic document moved from the oval offices of the nation to the public stage. I quote from an article by Svend Robinson, M.P. for Burnaby, in the summer 1981 issue of the *Canadian Forum*:

---

7 See D.C. Préfontaine, *supra*, c. 11.

> I was privileged to sit as a member of the special Joint Committee on the Constitution, and we heard witness after witness appear before us emphasizing the weaknesses in the *Charter of Rights*[8] as well as other parts of the constitutional resolution. It was an unprecedented and often moving experience as letters, telegrams and briefs were submitted by provincial governments, constitutional authorities, civil liberties groups, women's rights organizations, the Bar, language minorities, ethnic associations, Indian, Inuit, Metis associations, police chiefs, churches, associations concerned with the rights of the handicapped, gays, children; and hundreds of individuals . . . and moved the government was. It had no choice since it could not turn a deaf ear to the powerful submissions made by these many groups and individuals.

There are still significant substantive omissions in the Charter, and it has some obvious blemishes. ''Canadians,'' Frank Scott reminds us, ''never do things by halves which we can do by quarters.'' The prose is inelegant, the process uncertain, the application as yet a matter of speculation. And yet, if it stood as nothing more than a declaration of the values most Canadians in 1981 and 1982 thought significant enough for inclusion as fundamental freedoms and as democratic, legal and equality rights, the Charter would be a political testament of which we could be proud! And, in a very significant way, ''it's our baby''. It's more of a people's than a politician's Charter.

Constitutional discussions of aboriginal rights referred to in s. 37 of the Constitution Act, 1982, require representatives of the aboriginal peoples of Canada to participate in the first ministers' conferences on this issue. To ensure, as far as possible, that this is not mere tokenism, substantial sums of money have been granted to Metis and native organizations to enable them to hire consultants and to hold meetings in their communities and on their reserves, so that no one who wishes to be heard is denied a full opportunity.

With respect to both legislation and programs, the government of Manitoba is consulting extensively with the people of the province. This consultative process is not, let me say, merely a formal exercise in civics, not just an alienation counter-strategy. We genuinely see it as a way of drawing from the experience of those we represent. We genuinely see it as a new approach to politics, required, I believe, to bring us through the crisis of cynicism with our dedication to the democratic process intact. Let me mention a few instances.

With respect to many of our rural and northern programs and policies, we organized a series of community meetings to get feedback. With respect to native land claims, we appointed a land claims commissioner in consultation with the native people, so that, as much as possible, any decision on the fulfilment of treaty obligations will be, in effect, a shared decision. Community meetings were held throughout the province on a new scheme for property assessments. A commission on educational finance conducted public hearings across the province. A commission on social services did the same. An inquiry headed by a judge of the Family Court obtained extensive public input on native adoptions. A judge of the County Court heard representations on lotteries and other forms of commercial gaming. This government organ-

8 As it then was. The committee was responsible for several significant improvements.

ized an economic "summit" of leaders from labour, management and government to discuss pressing economic questions.

We reacted to community concerns about expropriation of residential properties for an industrial park in Winnipeg by holding a public inquiry, and by funding the community group so that its voice could be heard and its views could be expertly presented. We changed the Legal Aid Services Society of Manitoba Act[9] to provide statutory authority for legal aid certificates to issue to groups.[10] At the same time, we provided funds to Legal Aid Manitoba to establish a public interest advocacy centre. Public hearings have been held to solicit views on a multiculturalism policy, and on new daycare legislation. On specific pieces of legislation touching the concerns or sensitivities of particular constituencies, we have adopted the practice of circulating draft policy papers far and wide and inviting submissions.

There is no gimmickry or manipulation here; on the contrary there is considerable political risk in what we are doing. As those with more experience in government than I know, you can take what you think to be a well-conceived program or bill out of the closet and into the streets and the town halls, only to be shot down in flames. The opponents of your measure may come out in force, while your supporters stay home. Machiavelli would never have recommended the process. But, in my view, the risk of inner sanctum decision making is far greater.

If substantial elements of the law-making process are returned to the people by methods like those I have described, the outlook for a better, and somewhat less cynical, society will be good.

A LEGISLATOR'S POINT OF VIEW

Ray Hnatyshyn

The pervasive nature of the current wave of cynicism has grave consequences for our society. It has been said that we can destroy ourselves as effectively by cynicism as by bombs. When cynicism leads further to disrespect for our governments and the laws they pass, and even to disobedience of those laws, the result is anarchy.

I will canvass a few recent legislative and public policy initiatives in this context. The conclusion I will come to is that occasionally cynicism about the law originates with the legislative process.

On 17th April 1982, the Constitution Act 1982, containing the Canadian Charter of Rights and Freedoms, was proclaimed law. For several months

9 1971 (Man.), c. 76 (also C.C.S.M. c. L105).
10 *Ibid.*, s. 3.1 [en. 1982, c. 22, s. 3].

prior to its passage in Parliament, Canadians were inundated with advertising by an agency of the government, the Canada Unity Information Office. We were repeatedly told about the need for this change to our constitution. Taxpayers' money was being spent to convince all Canadians that the Charter was needed, and that the federal government was giving to us certain rights and freedoms. This type of advocacy advertising by government is surely an anathema to law in a democratic society. It is a comment on the legitimacy of the Charter itself that the federal government felt compelled to engage in a multi-million dollar advertising campaign to promote an amendment to our constitution before its adoption by Parliament.

As a parliamentarian who worked on and supported the Charter of Rights and Freedoms, I am worried that the government's actions, or inaction, may put the lie to its words. The government's obligations in the field of human rights and freedoms did not end with the proclamation of the Charter. It has an even greater responsibility now to see that the Charter operates forcefully and creatively. There are countries in the world today that have long lists of human rights in their constitutions; yet, because those nations have no dedication to effectively protecting those rights and freedoms, the lists are meaningless.

What is this government's record on encouraging the Charter's development? I will provide a few examples of situations in which the government has recently sought to limit rights, or at least have the power to limit rights.

At the same time that the constitution resolution case [11] was before the Supreme Court of Canada, the government put into place an order in council, of massive proportions, dealing with emergency planning.[12] The order calls upon ministers of the Crown and civil servants to plan for any and every type of emergency that can be imagined. This document goes far beyond situations of war; it also covers peacetime emergencies such as economic, energy and labour crises. It would involve sweeping derogations of rights and liberties enunciated by the Charter. Civil servants are planning for the establishment of civilian internment camps and for the take-over of financial services and of the means of production, among other things. And there has never been a request to Parliament to debate or consider this issue; it was done by order in council pursuant to the Royal Prerogative.

What is even more disturbing is the fact that the government, which has no legislation in place to authorize these plans (except in cases of war), has said that if it were inconvenient to summon Parliament or if Parliament were dissolved, they would go ahead and act without parliamentary authority. That attitude is shocking, given this country's stated dedication to government

11 *Re Resolution to Amend Constitution*, [1981] 1 S.C.R. 753, (sub nom. *A.G. Man. v. A.G. Can.; A.G. Can. v. A.G. Nfld.; A.G. Que. v. A.G. Can.; A.G. Can. v. A.G. Que.*) [1981] 6 W.W.R. 1, (sub nom. *Ref. re Amendment of Constitution of Can.*) 125 D.L.R. (3d) 1, (sub nom. *Constitutional Amendment Refs. 1981*) 34 Nfld. & P.E.I.R. 1, 95 A.P.R. 1, 11 Man. R. (2d) 1, 39 N.R. 1.

12 Emergency Planning Order, SI/81-76.

under the rule of law. Furthermore, such an attitude adds fuel to the fires of distrust and disrespect for our law-makers.

Another example of the disparity between the government's words and actions is found in the crusade by the Solicitor General to lift the moratorium on the issuance of writs of assistance. These writs provide designated peace officers with an unlimited right of search and seizure in the homes of Canadians. The existing moratorium was put in place after Collier J. made comment in the Federal Court of Canada on a 1976 writ of assistance application.[13] I think it important to repeat what he said in the course of his judgment:

> As can be seen, this writ can be enforced for many years to come. It is not directed to any present particular suspected offence, nor related to the investigation of the activities of any particular person. The powers given are extremely wide and, but for any legal sanctification in the statute, would otherwise be an invasion of privacy and property and civil rights.

The Solicitor General is clearly in conflict with the Charter protections against unreasonable search and seizure. Yet the [then] Minister of Justice, Mr. MacGuigan, also informed the House of Commons that he has this moratorium under review.

The legislation which implemented the government's "6 and 5" inflation reduction program provides another example. It originally contained provisions that would have overridden the Canadian Human Rights Act,[14] and would have gone so far as to ban all collective bargaining in the federal public sector. Through constant pressure in the committee that studied the bill, the government was forced to amend it to make the legislation subject to the Canadian Human Rights Act, and to allow provision for collective bargaining on non-monetary items. It should be appreciated that this bill came less than four months after the Charter's proclamation. Surely this action says something about the government's dedication to the rights and freedoms of Canadians.

What is the average citizen to think of this clear conflict between the words and actions of our government concerning constitutional rights? It is no wonder that cynicism exists in the minds of many Canadians.

There is an immediate need for assistance to be provided to litigants whose cases involve *bona fide* Charter arguments. Because of the inherent bias of the Department of Justice in favour of laws in the federal jurisdiction, as well as the fact that it has a prosecutorial role with regard to many federal statutes, that department is not likely to provide satisfactory assistance. If worthy Charter cases do not receive assistance, individual litigants will be faced with unfair financial burdens, and if these individuals falter under the burden, important Charter issues may be left unresolved. A concept I have suggested, for the purposes of discussion, is that of an independent institute, funded by the federal government, which would assist Canadians in protect-

13 *Re A.G. Can.*, [1976] 1 F.C. 254 at 255 (T.D.).

14 1976-77 (Can.), c. 33.

ing their rights and freedoms in the courts. Perhaps a panel of respected members of the legal community, with others from the community at large, could review applications for assistance. Where an appropriate case existed, the institute could make arrangements for funding or, alternatively, the institute itself could intervene in the case. Our government, if it wants credit for the passage of the Charter, must also take positive steps to assist in its implementation, or the Charter will wither on the vine.

Let me now turn from the Charter to another example of the gulf between rhetoric and reality at the federal level. A recent poll, sponsored by the federal government, asked people about their perceptions of crime in Canada.[15] The results were then compared with "official data" which the government claims is indicative of the "actual" state of affairs in Canada. The bottom line for the government is that Canadians overestimate the amount of crime in Canada. The Minister of Justice, speaking about the extent and nature of crime in Canada, said he wanted to "close the gap" by bringing perceptions more into line with the reality. But even if the "official data" are reliable, the "reality" is shocking enough to justify the "perceptions" of Canadians about the incidence of crime.

Mr. MacGuigan told us that assaults account for less than 4 per cent of all crimes known to police. Yet the fact remains that there were 121,077 assaults in Canada in 1981: an assault every 4.34 minutes. Robbery, says the federal Attorney General, accounts for just over 1 per cent. However, Canadians know that there were 26,292 robberies in 1981, or one every 20 minutes. There were 1,795,542 property crimes in 1981 — one every 18 seconds. And these statistics do not show the whole picture of crime in Canada. Evidence from victimization surveys in the United States indicates that approximately 40 per cent of all crimes against persons, and about 60 per cent of all crimes against property, are never reported to the police, and a similar pattern is indicated for Canada.

When Canadians listen to the federal Attorney General tell them that they overestimate the frequency of crime in Canada, and they then look at the incidence of crime they see around them, they must be forgiven if they view the percentile statistics referred to by the minister with some scepticism, even cynicism.

There is public cynicism, also, because the public knows that the promises made by their politicians often cannot be believed. People go through election campaigns fought over wage and price controls, or cheaper gasoline, and in the aftermath of the campaigns, when inflation persists and gas prices remain high, they are left to shake their heads in disbelief. The political game has become a power play. Getting power and keeping power are the names of the game. That game breeds a cynical public and a cynical political elite.

There are some reasons to be hopeful for an improvement in the future,

15 See D.C. Préfontaine, *supra*, c. 11.

however. Parliament has taken an important initial step in opening up government through the access to information legislation it has passed.[16] Now Canadians enjoy a right of access to much federal government information. Hopefully, this legislation will help to make the term "responsible government" more meaningful. In 1982 an all-party committee of the House of Commons undertook a review of procedure in the House, with a view to making the role of the Member of Parliament more meaningful and effective. As well, the scrutiny of government spending was examined with a view to making government more accountable to Parliament for the taxpayers' money.

The media must do their homework as this process of rejuvenation continues. They must put more priority on fundamental principles, and less on one-day wonders. Journalists have a responsibility to look critically at the government record, and indeed the record of each opposition party.

In the final analysis, accountability of government rests with the electorate. Their cynicism, while aggravated by broken promises and by the gaps between the rhetoric and the deeds of politicians, is nevertheless a product of their own apathy and non-involvement in the political process. The existence of disillusionment challenges us to replace our loss of faith in democratic institutions with involvement in the process. If the political decks have to be cleared, then so be it, but let it be done by an informed and active electorate.

CYNICISM, CRIME PREVENTION AND HELP FOR THE VICTIMS OF CRIME

Robert Kaplan

CYNICISM ABOUT CRIMINAL JUSTICE

I believe there is a good deal of cynicism among Canadians regarding the law and the criminal justice system. I do not believe that this cynicism is deeply rooted, or even that it is particularly widespread. We know, for example, that a vast majority of Canadians believe they have effective and incorruptible police forces. We also know that judges and Crown counsel are respected and admired.[17] Nevertheless, a significant level of cynicism exists about some aspects of the criminal justice system. There is, I think, more cynicism than is warranted but, at the same time, there are a number of reasons for Canadians' doubts about the system.

One reason seems to be the government's failure to accept what many regard as common-sense solutions to problems they perceive in the system. If

16 Access to Information Act, 1980-81-82-83 (Can.), c. 111, Sched. I.

17 See the Legal Research Institute Survey, *supra*, c. 2.

crime is on the increase, why not put more police on the streets? Or give out longer prison sentences? Or impose harsher treatment on the men and women behind bars? Many Canadians seem to feel frustrated by our apparent unwillingness to accept solutions they see as obvious. Unfortunately, hard experience discredits one-track solutions. They never produce the results their proponents urge. Policies for handling crime must be complex. But I sympathize with those who feel bewildered and, perhaps, cynical.

Paradoxically, some cynicism may also be a product of the opposite point of view: that there are no satisfactory solutions. The ''nothing works'' school of thought is prominent in intellectual circles. So much of the criminology literature today is purely critical, in the negative sense. So much research is designed not to improve, but merely to find fault. Those who adopt this approach typically go to great lengths to show that we have serious problems, and then conclude that nothing works to solve those problems. Who would not be cynical?

I believe that the source of much cynicism lies in the views many Canadians hold about two major criminal justice issues: the crime rate, and the plight of the victims of crime. My comments will focus on these two issues, and on improvements my ministry is undertaking in both areas.

THE CRIME RATE AND COMMUNITY CRIME PREVENTION

Just what *do* Canadians think about crime and the criminal justice response? We conducted a rather intriguing survey of Canadian perceptions and attitudes about crime.[18] We found that a majority of Canadians significantly exaggerate the extent of crime in Canada.

Canadians think that crimes of violence account for more than 50 per cent of all crime in this country. The fact is that such crimes constitute only 6 to 7 per cent of all crime. Canadians also believe that the murder rate has increased since the abolition of the death penalty. In fact, the reverse is true. Many people seem to equate the crime rate in Canadian cities with that in their American counterparts, but there is little justification for doing so. My city of Toronto, for example, has one fifth the crime rate, in general, of a similar American city. Canadians also underestimate the severity of punishments meted out to offenders. Indeed, many who believe that the criminal justice system is just not tough enough are not aware of just how tough it is.

Where do these misconceptions come from? Partly from a shortage of reliable data; good criminal justice information has been difficult to come by. At the same time, Canadians are exposed to an extraordinary variety of crime shows, which I think leave a very false impression of Canadian crime. We also have extensive news reporting of the atypical, the aberrant, the frighten-

18 See D.C. Préfontaine, *supra*, c. 11.

ing — the failures of the criminal justice system — and very little about its less lurid successes. While we can well appreciate the reasons — good news is no news — we should also recognize the consequence: a distorted perception of crime and of the criminal justice system in Canada.

The fact that Canadians' perceptions of the crime rate are exaggerated does not mean that we can be satisfied with the existing situation, however. Canada has not reached its present state of development by being satisfied with what is. We are right to be concerned about crime, and we can do something about it.

When I say "do something", I do not mean "more of the same". New approaches must be used: more innovative and cost-effective approaches; approaches which involve communities, individuals, social agencies, and educators; approaches which encourage Canadians to take more control over their futures by taking a share of the responsibility for preventing crime. My ministry is developing such an approach: a community-based crime prevention program.

Some will say that this is what we pay the police to do. This is indeed part of their job, but the police have always needed the active support of informed citizens. Canadians enjoy a very high standard of policing. But there is a better answer to rising crime rates than the traditional solution of more police, more equipment, more courts, more jails — even if money were no object. And money does matter. We can't continue to add to the criminal justice budget at the same rate as in the past. In 1981, in excess of $3 billion was spent by all levels of government in dealing with crime. Some $1.1 billion was spent by my ministry alone. Fiscal restraint must be applied to the criminal justice system, but without impairing its effectiveness.

Communities across Canada vary greatly in the nature of their crime problems. They vary, as well, in the range of community resources which can be brought to bear on crime reduction. It is for this reason that my ministry has worked with various Canadian communities to develop effective crime prevention programs.

[Mr. Kaplan then described several crime prevention programs initiated or supported by his ministry: "Operation Identification", which encourages and assists individuals and businesses to place identifying marks on theft-prone property and to notify potential thieves of the fact by means of appropriate decals on doors and windows; a "Robbery Prevention Kit" to assist small shopkeepers to reduce the risk of robbery; a "Youth Project", aimed at the reduction of juvenile crime by working directly with young people through civilian and police personnel; the "Solicitor General's Award" program, to provide recognition for successful crime prevention efforts; a proposed ''National Crime Prevention Week''; and other related programs. He stressed that all these programs are community-based, being tailored to suit local needs and implemented by resident personnel. Many have been modified over time as experimentation showed the need for improvements.]

The common theme of these new departures in fighting crime is that people themselves take a planned and active role. I see a role for the Solicitor General and the ministry in fighting crime; my ministry will be expanding its existing efforts and incorporating new initiatives into a national strategy for crime prevention. But the success of this strategy will depend upon the informed participation of Canadian communities.

I believe that most Canadians are prepared to respond positively to crime control, but their informed participation requires that the ''misinformation overload'' problem be overcome. To this end, my ministry is producing three documents which will be distributed widely across Canada. The first and most important is ''Community Crime Prevention: A Practical Guide''. This document takes what we have learned and makes it accessible. We are also producing a ''Questions and Answers on Crime Prevention'' booklet, which anticipates and responds to the concerns about, and the obstacles to, crime prevention. My ministry will also publish information about successful projects in crime prevention such as I have described: a ''Community Crime Prevention Newsletter'' will encourage information-sharing and keep crime prevention in sharp focus.

I see an important side benefit to broad community participation in crime prevention programs. I expect that it will reassure Canadians about their criminal justice system. Those who believe that if crime is not as bad here as in Miami, it's only a matter of time until it is, will find through participation a basically healthy, decent and effective set of institutions, federal, provincial, municipal and private, working together to prevent crime.

All of the crime prevention programs in which we are involved can be characterized as police supporting. We still rely on the police to apprehend the offender. I mention this to distinguish the types of crime prevention programs which I am recommending from those to which I am strongly opposed: those which bring the private citizen into direct contact with the offender. Canada does not have a vigilante tradition. We have never needed vigilantes, and we do not need them today.

HELP FOR THE VICTIMS OF CRIME

Let me turn now to what we are doing for victims of crime. I share the anger and frustration of anyone recently victimized by a crime, and I can understand how this anger is fuelled by the perception that we in the criminal justice system are doing more for offenders than for victims. An inevitable tension in every democratic society is that delicate balance between preserving the rights of the accused and those of crime victims. Some Canadians have little patience for protecting the rights of those who appear to be villains. While it is imperative that accused persons be treated fairly, we in the criminal justice system have too often neglected the victims' needs and interests. No doubt this feeds cynicism.

My ministry is developing a victim initiative to improve the quality of justice for those too-long forgotten casualties of crime. This focus on the victims of crime represents a welcome shift in emphasis from an offender-centered system. In the past, when a crime was committed, most of the energies of the criminal justice system were directed to apprehending, sentencing, incarcerating, and rehabilitating the offender. Of course, the victims' interests are indirectly served by correcting an offender. But we have learned that this is often not enough; the impact of criminal victimization often lasts long after the offender has been dealt with. Research has uncovered long-lasting psychic damage of violent victimization. We know too that the victim has sometimes felt bewildered and abused in his or her dealings with the criminal justice system.

We will be using the results of extensive research on victims and victim services to help us expand our programs and services. We will make the criminal justice system more responsive to victims' needs, and we will institute system-wide criminal justice improvements that will emphasize cost-effective delivery of service to victims. These improvements will not only serve to make the criminal justice system more humane, but will also improve public confidence in, and co-operation with, the system.

13

THE ROLE OF CYNICISM

Conference participants differed, not only about the degree of cynicism concerning law they detected among Canadians, but also about its significance. Some saw it as a social evil; others as a beneficial influence. Edgar Friedenberg was among the latter.

LAW IN A CYNICAL SOCIETY?

Edgar Z. Friedenberg

The advance program for this conference posed a number of questions as points of departure for discussion about law and public opinion.[1] All the questions have to do with elucidating the way law and public opinion influence the development of each other. The questions suggest that the law reflects public opinion and will have difficulties if it gets too far out of step with it. That is certainly true: as the now-forgotten turn-of-the-century American humorist Finley Peter Dunne observed in the brogue of his fictional ''Mr. Dooley'': ''No matter whether th'constitution follows th'flag or not, th'Supreme Coort follows th'illiction returns.''

All the questions are interesting and important, and the list is not, I know, intended to be exhaustive. But I was struck at once by something that is not there, and its absence disturbs me. None of the 11 questions suggests that there is any tension or opposition — actual or potential — between public opinion and the law.

Nothing in the list even suggests the existence of what I was brought up to believe was one of the law's two most important functions: half of the dialectic which makes the law the magnificent Hegelian synthesis which at its greatest it can be. The law derives its moral authority, as distinct from its legal authority, from its commitment to protect as well as to control or punish those who come before it and especially those whom public opinion would condemn. It derives its moral authority from the fact that social outcasts whose causes are despised may nevertheless invoke it against their persecutors and claim its protections. Precisely this distinguishes the Western legal tradition from that of Eastern Bloc countries, or of China or Iran, where public opinion and the law become indistinguishable, and the authorities generate either as needed to

1 See *supra*, Preface.

meet what they deem to be the demands of national security. Constitutional safeguards, if they are provided at all in those countries, serve merely to entrap any litigant naive enough to claim their protection.

And Canada? Well, the polar-projection maps seem to be accurate on this. Canada lies between the U.S.A. and the U.S.S.R., much closer to the U.S.A., but not as far from Russia as one might like to think. Read June Callwood's *Portrait of Canada* and Mr. Justice Berger's *Fragile Freedoms,* and consider what has been done to groups like Communists, Oriental persons, Canadians of Japanese descent and Jehovah's Witnesses as evidence of the power and determination of Canadian law to protect unpopular persons and causes from hostile public opinion. I don't think the omission of this issue from the conference agenda was planned, but it wasn't accidental either. The omission doubtless reflects quite accurately the true level of public and judicial concern about civil liberties in Canada.

That unconcern is itself a source of profound concern to me; and when I was invited to participate in this conference, the title raised my hopes. I have come to believe that Canadian society needs cynicism as badly as the British Navy of yore needed lime juice. It's sour, and it isn't enough to keep you going, but without it you could be fatally weakened by scurvy. If the Legal Research Institute of the University of Manitoba felt impelled to convene a conference on "Law In a Cynical Society?", I thought, it must have some reason to believe that our society is cynical.

Almost immediately, my hopes were dashed. The Preliminary Report of the Findings of the Institute's Survey of Perception of the Law and the Legal System,[2] which was pre-circulated to conference participants, came with a covering document that observed: "the preliminary data are fascinating and indicate considerably less cynicism than anticipated". The conclusion that there is not much cynicism about the law to be found among Canadians agrees with my preconceptions. Does the institute feel that this is good news? I fear so. I hope not.

From its earliest days as a nation, Canada has heavily supported the converse side of the legal dialectic: law as the source of social constraint and the guardian of acceptable standards of behaviour. Every nation in the world — Western or Eastern — prizes this view of what law should do, and seeks officially to advance it. This is the conception of law that is always taught in school; but in Canada, it is also widely accepted by adults. It is embodied in s. 91 of the Constitution Act, 1867, which gives the Parliament of Canada power to "make Laws for the Peace, Order, and good Government of Canada" — probably the most familiar phrase in Canadian folklore.

In this view, law becomes not only the instrument of government — good or bad as the case may be — but the very source of peace and order as well. These are not thought of as organic qualities which the community generates

2 See the Legal Research Institute Survey, *supra*, c. 2.

by mutual sensitivity and accommodation, and by shared values and purposes, but as the preserved fruits of surveillance and of systematic though preferably mild coercion. It is rather as if everybody was to be hooked up to a pacemaker to protect them and their fellows from the vagaries of the human heart. Conversely, law is not thought of as the instrument of some fundamental social purpose like establishing justice, promoting the general welfare, or securing the blessings of liberty to ourselves and our posterity. Law is seen, rather, as essentially a mechanism for establishing social control, and as an essential mechanism for maintaining such control. Lawlessness is thought of as synonymous with violence and disorder.

Basically, the desire to ''make Laws for the Peace, Order, and good Government of Canada'' expresses a Hobbesian view of the nature of society, in a document proclaimed nearly two centuries after Hobbes' death. Hobbes was exactly the philosopher the great colonial powers needed. They needed to believe that the autochthones they were about to displace, and usually destroy, had no culture to speak of, and certainly none to respect — no arts, no letters, no society, and that, worst of all, they were marked by continual fear and danger of violent death. Conquest would bring them, among other benefits, the protection of British or Roman law — adapted, to be sure, to the needs of their administrators. In Canada, the Northwest Mounted Police performed this function. They were not, at that time, required to read the native peoples their rights.

Today, we recognize — most of us do, at least — that the white man's law brought disorder and disruption to the native peoples, uprooting them from their homes and their communities, tearing their children from them and committing them to boarding schools in which they were often beaten for speaking their own language, and extinguishing their claims to their homelands (or denying that any such claim could ever have existed, since they themselves had no laws on which it could have been based). My concern here, however, is not with the destructive effects of a foreign legal system on indigenous cultures, but with the effect of this Hobbesian view of law on Canadian society as a whole.

Having convinced themselves that an overdose of law would be a blessing to the natives, the white folks proceeded, in all good faith, to become addicted to it themselves. A little cynicism might have been a useful antidote, but there wasn't much around. Judging from those questionnaire results, Canadians still try to get high on law.

Even though many Canadians, especially in the west, complain bitterly of excessive government regulation, Canadian society seems quite unable to act on the understanding that such regulations often impede the establishment of order, and create difficulties that would not otherwise exist. When Canadians do complain about these difficulties, they tend to treat them as if they were inevitable inconveniences — natural events — and pride themselves on being good-humored about it. They don't seem to realize that they have hired people, usually at great expense, to harass them and make their lives more difficult.

The deprivations are often petty, but the principle isn't. I've lost count of the number of times I've seen on television Vancouver residents lining up to buy liquor in government liquor stores because British Columbia government employees are about to go on strike. There are jokes about running out of beer and a long, dry season — year after year. Nobody ever asks: "Why can't we buy this stuff at a supermarket, or a drug store, or a private liquor store?" There are no more drunks per thousand population in Bellingham (and they tax liquor in Washington State, too) even though private stores sell it. I understand why the system is hard to change against the vested political interests that profit from it; government bureaucracies everywhere are almost indestructible. What I don't understand is why the people don't mind being treated like children.

These are small matters in themselves. What is important is the sad imbalance such petty indications reveal between the major and antithetical functions of the law. Antithetical is the right word; the two functions are not truly opposed. On the contrary, the tension between them is essential to the strength and legitimacy of each: when one is too weak, the other doesn't work well either.

Do law and order really go together like death and taxes? I don't think so. We define as orderly the customary consequences of legal sanctions, ignoring the disorder they cause: the effects of the incarceration of a breadwinner or the foreclosure of a mortgage on the life of a family. We likewise ignore the contributions to order that some unlawful conduct may bring: reuniting families split apart by immigration restrictions; the intimacy and sense of community that come from toking off a shared joint; the function of the much-busted gay baths as a focal point for gay society. Old established slums, held together partly by shared criminality, with organized crime providing a fairly reliable channel of social mobility for able young people unsuited by temperament for academic life, have much more social structure — and lower suicide rates — than suburbs where the adults barely know one another, and the kids have no place to go except to shopping malls. You may call these unlawful behaviours and institutions sinful if you like but you may not call them disorderly.

All systems of law justify themselves by promising order in return for constraint. But western democratic legal systems promise far more. They promise those subject to the law the protection of the law, not merely from their criminal neighbours, but from the community and from the state itself. Unless it affords these protections, the administration of justice falls at once into disrepute, as nothing more than the legitimation of coercive state power, and the ability of the state to maintain order by legal means rapidly weakens, as the courts come to be perceived as impotent and corrupt, as in Poland today, or schizophrenic, as in South Africa.

Canada hardly resembles either of these polities, but it is in some danger, I believe, of surrendering the function of protecting the individual from the officious and often destructive intrusion of the state or of one's neighbours. Surrendering is perhaps too flattering a word here; "refusing to accept the function" might be more accurate. That is precisely what the Supreme Court of Canada did in decisions which established what Professor Tarnopolsky has called the "frozen concepts" theory of interpretation of the old Diefenbaker Canadian Bill of Rights.[3] Section I of the Canadian Bill of Rights asserts "that in Canada there have existed and shall continue to exist without discrimination . . . the following human rights and fundamental freedoms", which are then enumerated. The court concluded that this meant that the Bill of Rights was not intended to change anything, and established no rights that Canadians had not previously enjoyed anyway. More recently, staff members of some provincial Attorneys-General have advanced similar arguments about the Charter of Rights and Freedoms in the new Constitution. You can't blame them for being hopeful; they are in tune with the spirit of the nation. While the new Constitution was slowly making its way through the Parliaments of Canada and the United Kingdom, the federal Cabinet passed an order in council requiring the Solicitor General of Canada to establish, administer and operate civilian internment camps in the event of a serious national emergency, without defining what such an emergency might be.[4] We'll never know just what the Cabinet might have in mind; the freedom of information legislation exempts it from ever having to disclose anything at all.[5]

Even the Canadian Charter of Rights and Freedoms itself is just a little bit pregnant with possibilities for oppression: the override or opting out clause; the cautious and qualified way in which many of the protected rights are expressed; and the queasy acceptance in the very first paragraph of the Charter of "such reasonable limits prescribed by law as can demonstrably be justified in a free and democratic society". All these built-in concessions to the power of the state seem to me fairly good grounds for cynicism.

Why all these concessions to law and order, against the interests of civil liberty? Public opinion, or at least the prevailing image of public opinion, undoubtedly has a lot to do with it. There is a respected position, held primarily by British jurists, that maintains that, whatever social justice or humane regard might require, the law dare not be construed more generously than public opinion is ready to accept. One way the law holds society together is by recognizing and legitimating the malice and irrationality of influential segments of public opinion, and thereby precluding militant representatives of such segments from taking the law into their own hands. The law thus accords the most punitive and vindictive members of society (who are usually called "conservative" — I've never understood why real conservatives don't get upset about this, but they don't) a heckler's veto on law reform and social progress.

3 W. S. Tarnopolsky, *The Canadian Bill of Rights*, 2nd ed. (1975), pp. 128-163.

4 *Emergency Planning Order*, SI/81-76, Sched., Pt. II, Item 6(6).

5 *Privacy Act*, 1980-81-82-83 (Can.), c. 111, Sched. II.

In this rather patronizing view of society, ordinary people, being regarded as less generous-spirited and less well-informed than jurists and legislators, are thought not to be ready to have decent social change encoded in law. For 150 years, Americans weren't thought ready to grant full civil rights to black Americans. In England they were said for years to be unwilling to accept the implications of the Wolfenden Report, and reduce the persecution of homosexuals. And we still hear that public opinion isn't ready for social change: that they aren't ready in England to accord full validity to British Overseas Passports; that they aren't ready in the United States to pass the Equal Rights Amendment; that they aren't ready in Canada to accept the 1977 Report of the Parliamentary Subcommittee on the Penitentiary System in Canada and reduce the level of torment and humiliation in Canadian penitentiaries.

There is something strange about this view of public opinion. I would not be so presumptuous as to argue with any successful politician about what you have to do to stay in office; and certainly not with statespersons of the Liberal Party of Canada, who in this respect are supreme experts. But I rather think they would agree that what they defer to is not massive public opinion, but the sharp, well-funded, well-organized and well-orchestrated demands of special interest groups. These are indeed political realities that cannot be ignored. But they do not represent a social consensus, and they cannot be treated as a source of moral authority.

The comments of Chief Justice Deschênes (as he then was) in his judgment of the Montreal subway workers[6] case suggest a certain nostalgia for a time when this was not yet true, and when a moral consensus existed which the actions of the courts affirmed and dramatized. I don't know whether any such consensus ever did prevail. I do not think Chief Justice Deschênes is dead right about the increasing political awareness of the mass of the population which, in earlier days, simply would not have perceived itself as having the right to make its views felt. And I think it is sad that the Montreal subway workers, having come to feel that they should claim this right, found no means to do so within the legal system except by civil disobedience. But I am troubled by the sentence in the judge's comments which observes that: "The system began to break down when people declared themselves ready to pay the penalty for disobeying injunctions and willing to pay their fines or serve their jail terms." This seems to deplore civil disobedience. I had always thought it to be one of the highest duties of citizenship.

At least since Socrates' time, the Western tradition has held that the law, to be worthy of respect, must itself respect dissent — even unlawful protest if it accepts the penalties prescribed by law. An offence, when one is committed, constitutes an *infraction* of the law. It has nothing to do with disobedience to authority, except in those instances, like contempt of court, where this is essential to the offence as defined. It isn't wrong to disobey the law; it is

6 *Comm. de Tpt. de la Communaté Urbaine de Montréal v. Syndicat du Tpt. de Montréal*, 77 C.L.L.C. 14,098, reversing [1974] Rec. de J. 227 (C.A.).

merely unlawful and punishable to commit acts forbidden by law. Many of these acts are indeed wrongful. Some of them may or may not be so, depending on circumstances. Some of them are noble. The individual perpetrator must decide about the wrongfulness for himself or herself; the courts, however, have the power, within established limits, to decide what to do about the perpetrator.

Nothing could do more to enhance confidence in the legal system, and embellish its moral authority, than an increased commitment to the protection of unpopular and/or dissenting social groups. By doing so, the system would transcend the conflicts that lead many of us at various stages of our lives to perceive the law as our adversary. Would it ever have occurred to the Montreal subway workers that the courts might be useful in defending their right to strike? They would have to be crazy to think that they had any such right under Canadian law, which allows workers to be legislated back to work in the middle of a legal strike by processes that would be unconstitutional — as bills of attainder — under American law. Their respect for law would be enhanced if they had reason to suppose that it might serve as the instrument of their deliverance as well as of their oppression. Law is supposed to do that sometimes.

The moral authority of the law is especially enhanced by decisions which require the state itself to respect the rights of its citizens. On 4th August 1982, according to *The New York Times*:

> A Federal district judge declared today that the United States Government had deliberately concealed evidence, pressured witnesses and engaged in deceitful conduct in a 1956 trial over whether thousands of sheep died from radioactive fallout. . . . Today, Judge A. Sherman Christensen, who ruled in favor of the government 26 years ago, vacated his decision and ordered a new trial on behalf of the ranchers, who since 1953 have been seeking compensation for the loss of more than 4,000 sheep.
>
> In what legal experts characterized as a rare finding, Judge Christensen concluded that the Government, as the defendant in the case, had perpetrated a fraud upon the court. As a result of convoluted actions, the judge said, "the processes of the court were manipulated to the improper and unacceptable advantage of the defendants."

Since there were potentially hundreds of cases alleging personal injury or death resulting from the same incident, and an untold number of similar incidents have occurred, Judge Christensen's ruling stands to cost the government hundreds of millions of dollars. Well, that comes out of the taxpayer's pocket, too; but it will be money well-spent, to assure the American people that justice accepts a responsibility higher than that of defending national security. Could a Canadian court have acted similarly? I don't think so. I know of no mechanism by which the sheep-ranchers could have gathered the evidence to re-open their case a quarter of a century later. Moreover, judicial appointment processes in Canada tend to keep potential mavericks from the bench even more effectively than they do in the United States. As the *Times* duly noted, such legal findings are rare, even in the United States. But it did happen there; and where it can, and the people know it can, the moral authority of the law is secure.

Against this, must be counted the absolute immunity granted to the courts in Canada, Great Britain and the United States against any consequences of possible malpractice. Bitter complaints were made at the recent convention of the Association of Trial Lawyers in Toronto about the imperiousness of judges and their tendency to abuse the character of defendants and witnesses, who have no available redress whatever. The most egregious example of this I know of is the conduct of the judge in the trial of Jeremy Thorpe, a few years ago, for allegedly hiring assassins to kill his former lover. The young man was not killed, but his character was destroyed by the judge's charge to the jury; Mr. Thorpe was acquitted. Even more serious was a recent judgment by the United States Supreme Court holding that although an Indiana judge had had no authority to order the sterilization of an apparently promiscuous young girl brought before him, he nevertheless had absolute immunity against any action for damages for having done so. A little cynicism, it seems, is still in order.

That Indiana judge, in a small community years ago, undoubtedly had reason to believe that he was upholding the moral standards of the community and was filling, by his zeal, an unfortunate hiatus in the law, just as Iranian judges do. Nothing could do more to bring the administration of justice into disrepute. The administrators of justice, including but not restricted to judges, bear heavy moral responsibilities indeed, but these responsibilities are compromised rather than discharged when the administrators use their offices to enforce the moral views of the community as if these had the force of law. The moral obligation of the administrators of justice is owed, not to community standards, but to the principle of justice itself.

This is not to suggest that the law is, or that judges should regard themselves as, above politics. On the contrary, the legal system is both the creature of the state and its central integrating structure. It legitimates the state's activities, many of which would otherwise be common conspiracies. Even its protections of the individual against the state are vouchsafed for political purposes and conceived as, ultimately, in the state's best interests, because they are conducive to innovation and to the peaceful resolution of conflicts. To serve justice well, judges should have a profound interest in and a critical understanding of politics; otherwise they become unwitting servants of existing social interests. Some of the conservatism of judges, I feel sure, stems simply from their belief that their function is apolitical, and that they have no right to consider the political implications of the cases brought before them or, even more fundamentally, of their position in the power structure.

Judges must not base their determinations on personal ideology rather than on law of course, but that hardly means that they should or could be political eunuchs. In a society fraught, or at least badly speckled, with injustice and oppression, even to defend the legal system in principle is to take a political position. The attacks on Berger J. for his public expression of opinion about constitutional protection for native rights, culminating in the report of the Canadian Judicial Council in June 1982,[7] seemed to me atrocious and mean-spirited. They made my cynicism leap like the American dollar. The principle on which they were based is wrong-headed. Teachers and social scientists, like judges, face the problem of protecting their clients and the public from the influence of their biases. Max Weber established 80 years ago that the most honourable and reliable way of providing that protection is by stating your own position clearly and publicly.

Candour, once accepted as such, is most effective in checking cynicism, yet it is sternly proscribed by the Canadian legal system. Members of the public, by and large, don't seem to miss it; they would be embarrassed by it rather than liberated. Secrecy and paternalism, apparently, have not made them very cynical about the way the system operates.

I predict that this situation will change with the passage of time. Faith in the legal system is usually, and for very good reason, positively correlated to social class. It tends to be positively correlated to age, but here the factors involved are more complex. We have usually interpreted this increasing correlation as if it were primarily longitudinal — as if it is natural that as any one individual matures, he or she will usually become less rebellious and better socialized. But that may not be working the same way any longer. For the past 20 years a very large proportion of adolescents and young adults have experienced fairly frequent and fairly serious hassles with the law: drug busts; music festivals broken-up by town councils and police; by-laws forbidding juveniles to patronize arcades with computer games; restrictions against seeing most of the serious movies that are produced. It's pretty well illegal even to be a teenager in Canada. And the adults seem to be getting nastier and smugger about it. The kids, meanwhile, have been growing up — a whole generation now since the 60's — and in a very short time most of the voting population may be a good deal more realistic, and more cynical, about law than has ever been the case before.

I hope the same individuals the Institute surveyed will be retested at intervals to see whether they retain their cynicism as they grow older. I am fairly confident that they will; the prospects for a more cynical Canada may be better than you think.

Not all conference participants shared Dr. Friedenberg's enthusiasm for cynicism. Francis C. Muldoon was so distressed by what he regarded as excessive cynicism by some other participants that he prefaced his own presentation[8] with an outburst of protest:

7 *Globe and Mail*, Toronto, 5th June 1982, p. 1.
8 See *supra*, c. 11.

At times this conference has verged, in my opinion, on an orgy in praise of cynicism. It's rather infectious — it's making me cynical. Cynical about the cynics.

How precious, how clever it is, in the salon, and on the conference and cocktail circuits, to turn a deft phrase, to evince a slightly world-weary wit. The already jaded, the intellectually barren will applaud and praise. Worse still, the impressionable and the susceptible will emulate.

If one waits for the cynic to right wrongs, to effect reforms, to achieve social justice, one will wait till hell freezes over. The cynic is a burnt-out idealist, if that does not defame idealists. In truth the notion of cynicism embodies not one scintilla of idealism, because what cynics do best is sneer.

There's no perfect society. There's no perfect system of law, for the simple reason that *homo sapiens* is not perfect. Therefore, by definition, there will always be imperfect laws, imperfectly applied, and imperfectly formulated for the cynic to sneer at. So long as human society endures, neither the laws nor the state will wither away, and perfection will always elude our species on this planet.

Enter the idealist (in those states, at least, which permit idealists to express themselves). Now cynics are always trying to give us idealists a bad name. They would have you believe that idealists are impractical. But compared with a cynic, the idealist is a veritable paradigm of earnest, hard-working, result-oriented practicality. The idealist is realistic enough to understand that perfection is unattainable, but generous enough to expend the time and energy to keep striving toward that elusive goal. That's how progress is achieved, how civilization flowers, how laws are reformed and adjusted from time to time, approaching closer and closer to the attainment of justice. And what's justice? Well, that's a notion of perfection too, and therefore not perfectly attainable, but well worth striving for.

SOME COMMENTS ON DR. FRIEDENBERG'S CYNICISM

Bryan Schwartz

[Bryan Schwartz, who offered some comments about Dr. Friedenberg's observations, took a more moderate position.]

Dr. Friedenberg speaks of a ''Hegelian dialectic'', and says that Canadians are often insufficiently concerned with the second half of the dialectic, which is protecting people from state depredations. That criticism is valid in some respects. But I think we should explore the question a little further, to find out whether in some cases our deferential attitude towards authority does not in fact well serve the first principle of that dialectic, which is protecting people from each other. Dr. Friedenberg's comparisons are to the United States, and his concrete example is the selling of liquor. Why don't we talk about selling guns? It seems to me that there is a case where American enthusiasm for resisting state encroachments on personal liberties has had gruesome costs in terms of the first half of the dialectic.

One of the very interesting observations in Professor Friedenberg's book *Deference to Authority*[9] is that Canadians are prepared to acknowledge and

9 *Deference to Authority: The Case of Canada* (1980).

vigorously struggle against the harshness of the environment, but they will not openly challenge authority. To some extent I think that is true, but there may be a connection between our attitudes toward nature and authority. It is precisely because the Canadian environment is so threatening that a good deal of government intervention has been necessary to provide both survival and the ordinary amenities of life. It is the party of the moderate right in Canada, the Progressive Conservatives, who are responsible for a great many central state institutions. Our experience that the government may in some cases be a friend rather than a threat may explain to some extent why, in dealing with the threat of disease, Canadians seem much more amenable to a public health system than our American friends.

I have two reservations about Professor Friedenberg's Hobbesian characterization of the Canadian policy. The first is that to characterize Canada as having any clear political stance overlooks one of the saving graces of the Canadian polity: our chronic mushy-mindedness and mealy-mouthedness about ideological principles. Professor Friedenberg has cited the qualifications in the Charter of Rights and Freedoms, and he is quite right. Here we have a document which is taken partly from Thomas Paine, partly from Edmund Burke, and put into a sort of ideological Cuisinart. Our doctrinal ambiguity (which is partly caused by the ethnic diversity in our country — it is very hard to get the English and French speaking communities to agree on common principles), has saved us from some of the worst twentieth century ideological excesses.

A second point about whether we have a Hobbesian society in Canada is that while we are sometimes excessively deferential to authority as order, as Professor Friedenberg has demonstrated, I think we are often respectful to authority not as order, but as an expression of democracy. When determining whether to obey an unjust law, the only issue is not: "Is it good or bad?" Another is: "Does the law have legitimacy as the outcome of a democratic process?" I would maintain that the subjective reasons we have in Canada for our deference to authority can't fairly be characterized as mere deference to the voice of order. Whether our faith is exaggerated or not, we believe in rule by democratically elected representatives of the majority of the people.

Dr. Friedenberg has expressed some cynicism about how the democratic process works in practice. His book, *Deference to Authority*, provides a very thoughtful perspective on Canadian society. It exemplifies cynicism in the best sense: a willingness and ability to portray human affairs as they are, despite what everyone else has said about them. His reversal of the cliché about the Canadian mosaic and the American melting pot is an example of this hard-minded scepticism.

There is also an emotional side to Dr. Friedenberg's cynicism; he speaks of it in terms of a sour beverage. Of course it is necessary to couple a certain emotional response with hard-minded scepticism when criticizing the legal system; otherwise the scepticism will be ineffectual. I would submit, however, that while Canada is neither a just society nor always a humane society — those are ideals too high to approach in reality — we are a decent society. Compared to the rest of the world, that is a rare prize indeed, and one I think we should value at the same time as we try earnestly to improve.

BIBLIOGRAPHY

ABRAMS, M. *Social Surveys and Social Action*. 1951.

ADAMS, G. *Grievance Arbitration of Discharge Cases*. Industrial Relations Centre: Queen's University. 1979.

ADELSON, J. *The Political Imagination of the Adolescent*. 1975.

AHLSTROM, Sydney E. *A Religious History of the American People*. 1972.

ALBERTA BUREAU OF STATISTICS. *Residents' Attitudes Towards the Police*. (Unpublished), 1976.

ALBIG, W. *Public Opinion*. 1939.

ALBINI, Joseph L. *The American Mafia: Genesis of a Legend*. 1971.

———. "Mafia as Method: A Comparison Between Great Britain and U.S.A. Regarding the Existence and Structure of Types of Organized Crime." (1975), 3 *Int. J. of Criminology and Penology* 295.

ALDERSON, J. C. "The Principles and Practice of the British Police." In *The Police We Deserve*. Eds. J. C. Alderson and Philip John Steads. 1973, p. 39.

———. *Policing Freedom*. 1973.

ALIOTTA, J., and J. L. Tapp. *Developmental, Legal, and Social Aspects of Rights-Consciousness*. (Unpublished.) 1981.

ALLEN, C. K. *Law in the Making*. 7th ed. 1974.

ALLOTT, Anthony. *The Limits of Law*. 1980.

AMERICAN BAR ASSOCIATION, Section of Criminal Justice Committee on Economic Offences. *Economic Offences*. Washington D.C.: 1977.

AMERICAN FRIENDS SERVICE COMMITTEE. *Struggle for Justice*. 1971.

ANSLINGER, H. J. *Hearings on H.R. 6385 Before House Committee on Ways and Means*. 75th Congress, 1st Session, 1937.

———. *Hearings on H.R. 6906 Before Subcommittee of Senate Committee on Finance*. 75th Congress, 1st Session, 1937.

APPLE, Michael. *Culture and Curriculum*. 1980.

ARISTOTLE. *Nicomachean Ethics*. Ed. J. L. Ackrill. 1973.

———. *Politics*. Ed. B. Jowett. 1905.

ARNOLD, S. J., and A.D. Gold. "The Use of a Public Opinion Poll on a Change of Venue Application." (1979), 21 *Cr. L.Q.* 445.

ARON, Arthur, and Elaine M. Aron. "Experimental Intervention of High Coherence Groups into Disorderly Social Systems." (Unpublished paper) Annual Convention of the American Psychological Association. 1981.

ARTHURS, H. W. "Developing Industrial Citizenship: A Challenge for Canada's Second Century." (1967), 50 *Can. Bar Rev.* 768.

"Asbestos Cover Up." *Calgary Herald*, 13 Nov. 1978, p. A13.

ASHFORD, N. A. *Crisis in the Workplace: Occupational Disease and Injury*. 1976.

ATKINSON, T. *A Study of Urban Concerns: Final Report*. Ministry of State for Urban Affairs. 1979.

AUERBACH, C., W. Hurst, L. Garris, and S. Mermin. *The Legal Process: An Introduction to Decision-Making by Judicial, Legislative, Executive and Administrative Agencies*. 1961.

AUSTIN, D. M. "Resident Participation: Political Mobilization or Organizational Co-optation." (1972), 32 *Pub. Admin. Rev.* 409.

AUSTIN, J. "The Province of Jurisprudence Determined." In *The Uses of the Study of Jurisprudence*. Ed. Hart. 1954.

AUSTRALIAN BUREAU OF STATISTICS. *Social Indicators No. 3*. 1980.

AUSTRALIAN LAW REFORM COMMISSION. *Sentencing of Federal Offenders*. 1980.

BACON, G. Richard, *et al. Struggle for Justice: A Report on Crime and Punishment in America*. 1971.

BADGER, John. *National Juvenile Justice Project: Special Report*. 1981.

BANDURA, A. and F. J. McDonald. "Influences of Social Reinforcement and the Behaviour of Models in Shaping Children's Moral Judgements." (1963), 67 *Journal of Abnormal and Social Psychology* 274.

BARD, M., and J. Zacker. *The Police and Interpersonal Conflict: Third Party Intervention Approaches*. The Police Foundation. 1976.

BARKSDALE, H. C. *The Use of Survey Research Findings as Legal Evidence*. 1957.

BARKUN, M. *Law Without Sanctions: Order in Primitive Societies and the World Community*. 1968.

BATES, D. *Attitudes Towards the Law: Sample Design Report*. 1980.

BATES, D., and B. Patel. *Urban Concerns Survey: Sample Design Report*. 1979.

BAYLEY, David. "Ironies of American Law Enforcement." *The Public Interest*, Spring 1980, p. 59.

———. "A World Perspective on the Role of the Police in Social Control." Symposium on the Maintenance of Order in Society. 1980.

BEATTIE, J. M. *Attitudes Towards Crime and Punishment in Upper Canada 1830-1850*. 1977.

BEATTY, D. "Secondary Boycotts: A Functional Analysis." (1974), 52 *Can. Bar Rev*. 388.

BEDAU, H. A. "The Death Penalty in the United States: Imposed Law and the Role of Moral Elites." In *The Imposition of Law*. Eds. S. Burman and B. E. Harrell-Bond. 1979, p. 45.

BELL-ROWBOTHAM, R., and C. L. Boydell. "Crime in Canada: Distributional Analysis." In *Deviant Behaviour and Societal Reaction*. Eds. Boydell *et al*. 1972, p. 114.

BENNINGTON, John. "Gosford Green's Residents Association: A Case Study." In *The Sociology of Community Action*. Ed. Peter Leonard. Sociological Review Monograph 21. 1975.

BENSON, Lee. "An Approach to the Scientific Study of Past Public Opinion." In *Communications and Public Opinion*. Ed. R. O. Carlson. 1975, p. 541.

BENTHAM, Jeremy. "Principles of Penal Law." In *The Works of Jeremy Bentham*. Vol. 1. Ed. J. Bowring. 1962, p. 367.

———. "An Introduction to the Principles of Morals and Legislation." In *The Works of Jeremy Bentham*. Vol. 1. Ed. J. Bowring. 1962, p. 1.

BEQUAL, A. *Computer Crime*. 1978.

BERG, N., and P. Musen. "The Origins and Development of Concepts of Justice." (1975), 3:2 *Journal of Social Issues* 183.

BERGERON, G. *Fonctionnement de l'Etat*. 1965.

———. *La Gouverne Politique*. 1977.

BERMAN, Harold J. *Law and Revolution: The Formation of the Western Legal Tradition*. 1983.

BERTRAND, Francine. "Public Opinions About Criminal Justice Issues: Some Cautions About Poll Data." In *Impact #1*. Solicitor General's Department: 1982, p. 11.

BEST, J. J. *Public Opinion: Micro and Macro*. 1973.

BIBBY, R. "Religion." In *Sociology*. Ed. Hagedorn.

BIDERMAN, A. D., *et al. An Inventory of Surveys of the Public on Crime, Justice and Related Topics*. 1972.

BIENVENUE, R. M., and A. H. Latif. "Arrests, Dispositions and Recidivism: A Comparison of the Indians and Whites." (1974), 16 *Can. J. Corr.* 105.

BINNIE, S. *Parole and Ontario Reform Institution Inmates*. 1974.

BIRD. R. N. *Financing Canadian Government: A Quantitative Overview*. 1979.

BING, S. R., and S. Rosenthal. *The Quality of Justice in the Lower Criminal Courts of Metropolitan Boston*. 1970.

BLACK, Donald. *The Behaviour of Law*. 1976.

BLACK, D. J. "Production of Crime Rates." (1970), 35 *Amer. Sociological Rev.* 733.

BLASI, A. "Bridging Moral Cognition and Moral Action: A Critical Review of the Literature." (1980), 88 *Psychological Bulletin* 1.

BLUM, W. H., and Harry Kalven Jr. "The Art of Opinion Research: A Lawyer's Appraisal of an Emerging Science." (1956), 24 *U. of Chicago L. Rev.* 1.

BLUMBERG, A., ed. "Crime and the Social Order." In *Current Perspectives on Criminal Behavior*. 1st ed. 1974.

BOHANNAN, P. *Justice and Judgment Among TIV*. 1957.

BOONE, Richard W. "Reflections on Citizen Participation and the Economic Opportunity Act." (1972), 32 *Pub. Admin. Rev.* 444.

BOROVOY, Alan. "Civil Liberties in the Imminent Hereafter." (1973), 51 *Can. Bar Rev.* 93.

BOSANQUET, B. *The Philosophical Theory of the State*. 1910.

BOTTOMLEY, Keith and C.A. Coleman. *Police Effectiveness and the Public: The Limitations of Official Crime Rates*. (Unpublished.) Institute of Criminology: 1979.

BOX, S., and J. Ford. "The Facts Don't Fit: On the Relationship Between Social Class and Criminal Behaviour." (1971), 19 *The Sociological Rev.* 31.

BOYDELL, C. L., and C. F. Grindstaff. "Public Opinion and the Criminal Law: An Empirical Test of Public Opinion Toward Legal Sanctions." In *Deviant Behavior and Societal Reactions*. Eds. C. L. Boydell, C. F. Grindstaff and P. C. Whitehead. 1972.

BRAITHWAITE, J. *Inequity, Crime and Public Policy*. 1979.

BRANTINGHAM, Paul J., and Patricia L. Brantingham. "A Theoretical Model of Crime Site Selection." In *Crime, Law and Sanctions: Theoretical Perspectives*. Eds. M. D. Krohn and R. L. Akers. 1978.

BREGHA, Francis J. "Community Development in Canada: Problems and Strategies." In *Citizen Participation: Canada*. Ed. James A. Draper. 1971.

BRENNER, M. H. "Effects of the Economy on Criminal Behaviour." In *Economic Crises and Crime*. United Nations Social Defence Research Unit: 1976.

BRICKEY, Stephen L. *Winnipeg Victim/Witness Assistance Program: Planning Phase*. Solicitor General's Department. (Unpublished.) 1982.

BRIGGS, A. "Seventeen Reasonable Men." *New Statesman,* 11 July 1959, p. 52.

BRILLON, Y., C. Louis-Guerin and M.-C. Lamarche. *Les Attitudes du Publique Canadienne envers les Politiques Criminelles: Rapport Final*. (Unpublished.) 1982.

BRITTON, John N. H., and James M. Gilmour. *The Weakest Link: A Technological Perspective on Canadian Industrial Underdevelopment*. Science Council of Canada: 1978.

BROWN, D. "Adolescent Attitudes and Lawful Behaviour." (1974-75), 38 *Pub. Opinion Q*. 98.

BROWN, D. "Canada and the Noose". *Quest Magazine*. (1976).

BROWN, Lorne A. "Unemployment Relief Camps in Saskatchewan 1933-1936." (1970), 23 *Sask. History* 81.

BROWN, William J. "The Future of Policing in Canada." In *The Police Function in Canada*. Eds. W. T. McGrath and M. P. Mitchel. 1981, p. 243.

BULLOCH, John F. "Parliamentary Perceptions." (1982), *Parliamentary Government,* 3:3, p. 6.

BURKE, Edmond. *The Works of Edmond Burke*. Vol. 2. 1808.

BURMAN, S., and B. Harrell-Bond. *The Imposition of Law*. 1979.

BURN, W. L. "The Conservative Tradition and its Reformulations." In *Law and Public Opinion in England in the 20th Century*. Ed. M. Ginsberg. 1959, p. 42.

BUTLER, N. C. "Law and Public Opinion." (1915), 49 *Amer. L. Rev*. 374.

CADRES PROFESSIONNELS INC. *Les Avocats du Quebec*. 1968.

CAHN, M. F., and J. M. Tien. *An Evaluation Report of an Alternative Approach in Police Response: The Wilmington Management of Demand Program*. Public Systems Evaluation: 1981.

CAIN, Maureen. "Towards a Political Sociology of the British Police: A Review of 1979 and 1980." Symposium on the Maintenance of Order in Society. 1980.

———. "Trends in the Sociology of Police Work." [1979] *Int. J. of the Sociology of Law* 143.

CAMPBELL, Robert. *Spectrum of Protestant Beliefs*. 1968.

CANADA DEPARTMENT OF LABOUR. *The Report of the Commission of Inquiry into Redundancies and Lay-offs*. 1979.

CANADA MORTGAGE AND HOUSING CORPORATION. *Public Priorities in Urban Canada: A Survey of Community Concerns*. 1978.

CANADIAN BAR ASSOCIATION. *Model Freedom of Information Act*. 1978.

———. *Parliament as a Lawmaker*. 1981.

———. *Public Legal Education Committee Report*. 1982.

———. *Towards a New Canada*. 1978.

CANADIAN BAR ASSOCIATION COMMITTEE ON THE REFORM OF PARLIAMENT. *Parliament as Lawmaker*. 1982.

CANADIAN CIVIL LIBERTIES ASSOCIATION. *Due Process Safeguards and Canadian Criminal Justice: A One Month Inquiry*. 1971.

CANADIAN CORRECTIONS ASSOCIATION. *Indians and the Law*. 1967.

CANADIAN FACTS CO. LTD. *National Survey of Awareness to the Gun Control Legislation — Highlights Report*. Solicitor General's Department. (Unpublished report.) 1978.

CANADIAN INDUSTRIAL RELATIONS. *The Report of the Task Force on Labour Relations*. The Woods Commission: 1968.

CANADIAN OCCUPATIONAL HEALTH AND SAFETY NEWS. 23 July 1979.

CANTRIL, H., and M. Strunk. *Public Opinion 1935-1946*. 1951.

CAPONE, D. L., and W. W. Nicols, Jr. "Urban Structure and Criminal Mobility." Annual Meeting of the American Society of Criminology. 1975.

CARDOZO. *The Nature of the Judicial Process*. 1921.

CARLSON, R. O. *Communications and Public Opinion*. 1975.

CARRIERE, P., and S. Silverstone. *The Parole Process*. 1976.

CARROTHERS, A. W. R. *Collective Bargaining Law in Canada*. 1965.

CARTER, L., and R. Wilkins. "Some Factors in Sentencing Policy." (1967), 58 *J. Cr. L. Crim. and Police Science*, 503.

CASPER, J. D. "Having Their Day In Court: Defendant Evaluations of the Fairness of Their Treatment." (1979), 13 *L. and Soc. Rev*. 567.

CASS, M., and R. Sackville. *Legal Needs of the Poor*. 1975.

CAWLEY, Donald F. "Managers Can Make A Difference: Future Directions." In *The Future of Policing*. Ed. Alvin W. Cohn. 1978.

CENTRE DE RECHERCHE EN DROIT PUBLIC. *Place du jurist dans la société Quebecoise*. 1976.

CHAMBERLAIN, N. W. *Social Responsibility and Strikes*. 1953.

CHAMBERS, C. D. "Narcotics Addiction and Crime: An Empirical Review." In *Drugs and the Criminal Justice System*. Eds. C. D. Chambers and J. A. Inciardi. 1974.

CHAMBERS, C. D., and J. A. Inciardi. "Forecasts for the Future: Where are We and Where are We Going?" In *Drugs and the Criminal Justice System*. Eds. C. D. Chambers and J. A. Inciardi. 1974.

CHAMBLISS, W., and R. Seidman. *Law, Order and Power*. 2nd ed. 1982.

CHANDLER, D. B. *Capital Punishment in Canada*. 1976.

CHAPPELL, D., R. Gordon, and R. Moore. *Criminal Investigation: A Selective Literature Review and Bibliography*. Minister of Supply and Services Canada: 1982.

CHAPPELL, D., and P. Wilson. *The Police and the Public in Australia and New Zealand*. 1969.

CHATARPAUL, K. "Labour Relations in the Public Service With Some Emphasis on the Ontario Civil Service." LL.M. thesis, Osgoode Hall 1978.

CHOLDIM, H. M., and D. W. Roncek. "Density, Population and Potential and Pathology: A Block-Level Analysis." (1976), 4 *Pub. Data Use* 19.

CHRISTIAN, W. "George Grant and the Twilight of Our Justice." 85 *Queen's Quarterly*, p. 485.

CHRISTIE, N. "Definition of Violent Behaviour." *International Course in Criminology*, 23 (1974).

CHRISTIE, Nils. "Conflicts as Property." (1977), 17 *Br. J. Crim*. 1.

CHRISTIE, R. "Probability vs. Precedence: The Social Psychology of Jury Selection." In *Psychology and the Law*. Eds. G. Bermant, C. Nemeth and N. Vidmar.

CLABAUGH, Gary K. *Thunder on the Right*. 1974.

CLARK, L., and D. Lewis. *Rape: The Price of Coercive Sexuality*. 1977.

CLINARD, M. B. *Cities With Little Crime*. 1978.

CLOWARD, R., and L. Ohlin. *Delinquency and Opportunity*. 1960.

COHEN, G. A. *Karl Marx's Theory of History: A Defense*. 1978.

COHEN, L. E., and M. Felson. "Social Change and Crime Rate Trends: A Routine Activity Approach." (1979), 44 *Amer. Sociological Rev*. 588.

COHN, Edmond. *The Sense of Injustice*. 1949.

COLEMAN, J. S. *Youth: Transition to Adulthood*. 1978.

COLEMAN, T. "The Public, Media and Police Working Together to Solve Crime." (1983), *Canadian Police Chief Newsletter*, 2:4, p. 2.

COMMISSION DES SERVICES JURIDIQUES. *Les mains de la loi*. (1975).

———. *Des avocats de notre bord*. (1978).

CONGALTON, A. A., and J. Najman. *Safety in the Suburbs*. 1974.

CONKLIN, J. E. *The Impact of Crime*. 1975.

CORRIGAN, Paul. "Community Work and Political Struggle." In *The Sociology of Community Action*. Sociological Rev. Monograph. Ed. Peter Leonard. 1975, p. 21.

CORWIN, E. *The "Higher Law" Background of American Constitutional Law*. 1955.

COSGROVE, R. A. *The Rule of Law: Albert Venn Dicey, Victorian Jurist*. 1980.

COURTIS, M. C. "The Police and the Public." In *The Administration of Criminal Justice in Canada*. Eds. C. L. Boydell, P. C. Whitehead and C. F. Grindstaff. 1974.

COURTIS, M. C., and I. Dussuyer. *Attitudes to Crime and the Police in Toronto: A Report on Some Survey Findings*. University of Toronto Centre of Criminology: 1970.

CRANE, Robert, and Tony Burton. "Five Bear Witness and Burden of Nurse's Fate." *Daily News*, 27 Feb. 1980, p. 5.

CRESSEY, D. "The Correlates of Crime." In *Law and the Lawless*. Eds. S. M. Sykes and T. E. Drabek. 1969, p. 192.

CRITCHLEY, J. A. "The Idea of Policing in Britain: Success or Failure." In *The Police We Deserve*. Eds. J. C. Alderson and P. J. Steads. 1969, p. 25.

C.R.O.P. Study. *Omnibus*, 5:3 (1980).

CROSS, R. *Punishment, Prison and the Public*. 1971.

CURRAN, Barbara A., and K. J. Rosich. *Data Manual for the Study of the Legal Needs of the Public*. American Bar Foundation: 1980.

DAMON, W. *The Social World of the Child*. 1977.

DAVIS, K. Culp. *Discretionary Justice: A Preliminaruy Inquiry*. 1969.

DEBICKI, Marek. "Sentencing in a Lower Criminal Court." *Proceedings of the C.P.S.A*. 1976.

DEMERS, D. J. "Discretion, Disparity and the Parole Process." Diss. Department of Sociology, University of Alberta, 1978.

DENNIS, Norman. "Community, Quasi-Community and Anti-Community Action." In *The Sociology of Community Action*. Sociological Rev. Monograph 21. Ed. Peter Leonard. 1975, p. 21.

DEPARTMENT OF THE ATTORNEY-GENERAL OF BRITISH COLUMBIA. *Initial Report on Organized Crime in B.C.* 1974.

DE TOQUEVILLE, Alex. *Recollections of Alex de Toqueville*. Paris, 1893. 1930 ed.

DEVLIN, Patrick. "Judges and Lawmakers." (1976), 39 *Mod. L. Rev.* 1.

———. *Trial by Jury*. 1956.

DEWEY, J. *On Education: Selected Writings*. 1964.

DIAMOND, S. "The Rule of Law Versus the Order of Custom." In *The Sociology of Law*. Eds. C. Reasons and R. Rich. 1978.

DICEY, Albert Venn. *Law and Public Opinion in England During the Nineteenth Century*. 2nd ed. 1914.

———. *Law of the Constitution*. 10th ed. 1965.

———. *Lectures on the Relationship Between Law and Public Opinion in England During the Nineteenth Century*. 1st ed. 1905.

———. *Lectures on the Relationship Between Law and Public Opinion in England During the Nineteenth Century*. 2nd ed. 1930.

DILLBECK, M. C., G. Landrith III, and D. W. Orme-Johnson. "The Transcendental Meditation Program and Crime Rate Change in a Sample of Forty-Eight Cities." *Crime and Justice* IV (1981).

DINITZ, S., and J. P. Conrad. "Thinking About Dangerous Offenders." *Criminal Justice Abstracts*, March, 1978, p. 99.

"Doctor and Police Rated Most Honest." *Winnipeg Free Press*, 29 Sept. 1976, p. 23.

DOMINICK, J. R. "Crime and Law Enforcement on Prime-Time Television." (1973-74), 37 *Pub. Opinion Q.* 241.

DRAPER, James A. *Citizen Participation: Canada*. Social Science Research Council of Canada: 1971.

DURANT, H. "Public Opinion Polls and Foreign Policy." (1955), 6 *Br. J. Sociology* 150.

DURKHEIM, D. Emile. *The Rules of the Sociological Method*. 8th ed. Trans. 1964.

ECK, J. E. *Managing Case Assignments: The Burglary Investigation Decision Model Replication*. Police Executive Research Forum: 1980.

ECKART, B. "Two Hundred Years of Social and Economic Change Have Shaped Our Crime Problem." In *The Centre Magazine* (July-Aug. 1977). Publication of the Centre for the Study of Democratic Institutions.

EHRLICH, E. "Fundamental Principles of the Sociology of Law." In *Civil Justice and the Poor*. Eds. J. E. Carlin, J. Howard and S. L. Messinger. 1967, p. 13.

EHRLICH, Thomas. "Legal Pollution." *New York Times Magazine*, 8 Feb. 1976, p. 17.

ENGLISH. "Keeping in Touch Around the World, Around the Block." *The Financial Post*, 14 June 1980, p. 51.

ENGSTAD, P., and J. L. Evans. *Responsibility, Competence and Police Effectiveness in Crime Control*. Cambridge Research Conference: 1979.

EPSTEIN, Samuel S. *The Politics of Cancer*. 1979.

ERICSON, R. V. *Reproducing Order: A Study of Police Patrolwork*. 1982.

———. *Making Crime*. 1981.

ERICSON, R., and P. M. Baranek. *The Ordering of Justice: A Study of Persons as Dependents in the Criminal Process*. 1982.

ERMANN, D., and R. J. Lundman. *Corporate and Government Deviance*. 1978.

ERSKINE, H. "Fear of Violence and Crime." (1974-75), 38 *Pub. Opinion Q*. 131.

———. "Control of Crime and Violence." (1974-75), 38 *Pub. Opinion Q*. 490.

———. "Politics and Law and Order." (1974-75), 38 *Pub. Opinion Q*. 623.

———. "The Polls." (1974-75), 38 *Pub. Opinion Q*. 131.

EUSDEN, J. "Natural Law and Covenant Theology in New England, 1610-1670." 1, *Natural Law Forum* 1.

EVAN, W. M., ed. *The Sociology of Law*. 1980.

FACER, W. A. P. *Attitudes to Abortion in New Zealand*. 1973.

FAIRCHILD, Erika S. "Interest Groups in the Criminal Justice Process." (1981), 9 *Journal of Criminal Justice*, 181.

FALK-MOORE, S. *Law as Process*. 1978.

FALWELL, Jerry. *The Fundamentalist Phenomenon*. 1981.

FARMER, Michael T., ed. *Differential Police Response Strategies*. The Police Executive Research Forum: 1981.

FARNELL, M. D., and C. D. Shearing. *Private Security: An Examination of Canadian Statistics 1961-71*. 1977.

FARR, Robert. *The Electronic Criminals*. 1975.

FARRAR, J. H. *Law Reform and the Law Commission*. 1974.

FATTAH, E. *The Canadian Public and the Death Penalty: A Study of Social Attitude*. Solicitor General's Department. (Unpublished report.) 1976.

———. "Deterrence: A Review of the Literature." In *Fear of Punishment*. Law Reform Commission of Canada: 1976.

FATTAH, E. A., and A. Normandeau. *Sondage D'Opinion Publique Sur La Justice Criminelle au Quebec Montreal*. Commission d'Enquete sur l'Administration de la Justice en Matiere Criminelle et Penale au Quebec: 1969.

FEAVER, G. *From Status to Contract*. 1969.

"51 Percent Accept Government Interference." Gallup Poll. *Winnipeg Free Press*, 2 Oct. 1976, p. 6.

"56 Percent Think Prison Conditions Liberal." Gallup Poll. *Winnipeg Free Press*, 11 Dec. 1976, p. 8.

FIGGIE, H. E. *America Afraid: The Figgie Report on Fear and Crime, Part 1*. 1980.

FISHKIN, J., W. Keniston and D. McKinnon. "Moral Reasoning and Political Ideology." (1973), 27 *Journal of Personality and Social Psychology* 109.

FITZGERALD, J. *Poverty and the Legal Profession in Victoria*. 1977.

FOGELSON, R. *Big City Police*. 1977.

FORCESE, D. *The Canadian Class Structure*. 1975.

———. "Police Unionism: Employee-Management Relations in Canadian Police Forces." (1980), 4 *Can. Police College J*. 79.

FORKOSCH, Marvin. *A Treatise on Labour Law*. 2nd ed. 1965.

FORSLUND, M. A. "Age, Occupation and Conviction Rates of White and Negro Males: A Case Study." (1969), 6 *Rocky Mountain Social Science J.* 141.

FOSTER, M. "The Christian Doctrine of Creation and the Rise of Modern Nature Science." (1934), 43 *Mind* 446.

———. "Christian Theology and Modern Science of Nature, Part I." (1935), 44 *Mind* 439.

———. "Christian Theology and Modern Science of Nature, Part II." (1936), 45 *Mind* 1.

FOUCAULT, M. *Discipline and Punish.* 1977.

FOX, J., and T. E. Hartnagel. "Changing Social Roles and Female Crimes in Canada: A Time Series Analysis." (1979), 16 *Can. Rev. of Sociology and Anthropology* 96.

FRIEDENBERG, E. *Deference to Authority: The Case of Canada.* 1980.

FRIEDLAND, M. L. "Pressure Groups and the Development of the Criminal Law." In *Reshaping the Criminal Law.* Ed. P. R. Glazebrook. 1978.

———. "Magistrate Court: Functioning and Facilities." (1968), 11 *Cr. L.Q.* 52.

FRIEDMAN, L. M. *Law and Society: An Introduction.* 1977.

FRIEDMAN, L. M., and S. MacAulay. *Law and the Behavioral Sciences.* 2nd ed. 1977.

FRIEDMAN, M. *Capitalism and Freedom.* 1962.

FRIEDMAN, Wolfgang. *Law in a Changing Society.* Pelican: 1964.

FULLER, L. L. "Positivism and Fidelity to Law — A Reply to Professor Hart." (1958), 71 *Harv. L. Rev.* 630.

———. "Some Presuppositions Shaping the Concept of 'Socialization'." In *Law, Justice and the Individual in Society.* Eds. J. L. Tapp and F. J. Levine. 1977.

———. *The Morality of Law.* 2nd ed. 1969.

FULLERTON, K. "Calvinism and Capitalism." (1963), 21 *Harv. Theological Rev.* 163.

GALLATIN, J., and J. Adelson. "Legal Guarantees of Individual Freedom: A Cross-National Study of the Development of Political Thought." In *Law, Justice and the Individual in Society.* Eds. J. L. Tapp and F. J. Levine. 1977.

GALLUP, G. H. *The Gallup Poll: Public Opinion 1935-1971.* (And annual volumes for subsequent years.)

———. *Gallup Report (Canada).* Annual volumes since 1967.

THE GALLUP REPORTS. May 30, 1980.

THE GALLUP REPORTS. November 15, 1980.

GARDNER, J. W. *In Common Cause.* 1972.

GEIS, G., and E. Stotland, eds. *White Collar Crime: Theory and Research.* 1980.

GENDREAU, P., *et al.* "Norms and Recidivism for First Incarcerates: Implications for Programming." (1979), 21 *Can. J. Crim.* 416.

GERSUNY, Carl. *Work Hazards and Industrial Conflict.* 1981.

GHAN, S. L. *Women's Attitudes Toward Oral Contraceptives.* (Unpublished.) 1974.

GIBSON, R. Dale. "Determining Disrepute: Opinion Polls and the Charter of Rights." (1983), 61 *Can. Bar Rev.* 377.

———. "Enforcement of the Canadian Charter of Rights and Freedoms." In *Canadian Charter of Rights and Freedoms: Commentary.* Eds. W. Tarnopolsky and G. Beaudoin. 1982.

GIBSON, Dale, and Lee Gibson. *Substantial Justice*. 1972.

GILMORE, A. *The Ages of American Law*. 1977.

GINSBERG, M., ed. *Law and Opinion in England in the 20th Century*. 1959.

GINTIS, H., and S. Bowles. *Schooling in Capitalist America*. 1976.

GLASBEEK, Harry J. "The Contract of Employment at Common Law." In *Union-Management Relations in Canada*. Eds. Anderson and Gunderson. 1982, p. 47.

———. "TIP: Another Weapon in the Class War Waged Against Workers." (1981), 3 *Can. Taxation* 94.

GLASBEEK, Harry, and Susan Rowland. "Are Injuring and Killing at Work Crimes?" (1979), 17 *Osgoode Hall L.J.* 507.

GLASER, D. *The Effectiveness of a Prison and Parole System*. 1964.

GOETZ, M. L. *Citizen Attitudes Towards the Police in Vancouver*. Vancouver Police Department: 1975.

GOLDFARB CONSULTANTS LTD. *National Attitudes Towards Crime and Gun Control*. Solicitor General's Department. (Unpublished report.) 1977.

GOLDSTEIN, H. "Improving Policing: A Problem-Oriented Approach." (1979), 25 *Crime and Delinquency* 236.

GOOCHMAN, J. "An Economic Theory of the Evaluation of Law." (1978), 7 *J. Legal Studies* 393.

GOODACRE, R. *Operation Knockout*. 1983.

GOULD, L. C. "Crime and the Addict: Beyond Common Sense." In *Drugs and the Criminal Justice System*. Eds. J. A. Inciardi and C. D. Chambers. 1974, p. 74.

GOVERNMENT OF QUEBEC. *La société face au crime (The Prevost Report), Schedule 4, La justice criminelle*. 1969.

GOWER, L. C. B. "Business." In *Law and Opinion in England in the 20th Century*. Ed. M. Ginsberg. 1959, p. 143.

GRABER, Doris A. *Crime News and the Public*. 1980.

GRAMSCI, Antonio. *Selections from His Political Writings, 1910-1920*. Trans. J. Mathews. 1977.

GRAHAM, H. D., and T. R. Gurr, eds. *Violence in America: Historical and Contemporary Perspectives*. 1979.

GRANT, Alan. *The Police: A Policy Paper*. Law Reform Commission of Canada: 1980.

GRANT, G. "In Defence of North America." In *Technology and Empire*. 1969.

———. *English Speaking Justice*. 1978.

———. *Philosophy in the Mass Age*. 1950.

———. *Time as History*. 1969.

GRAYSON, J. P., ed. *Class, State, Ideology and Change*. 1980.

GREEN, E. *Judicial Attitudes Toward Sentencing*. 1961.

———. "Race, Social Status and Criminal Arrest." (1970), 35 *Amer. Sociological Rev*. 35.

GREEN, T. H. *Lectures of the Principles of Political Obligation*. 1967.

GREENBERG, B., O. V. Elliott, L. P. Kraft, and H.S. Proctor. *Felony Investigation Decision Model and an Analysis of Investigative Elements of Information*. 1975.

GREENBERG, B., O. S. Yu, and K. Lang. *Enhancement of the Investigative Function*. Vol. 1. 1973.

———. *Enhancement of the Investigative Function*. Vol. 2. (Unpublished).

GREENBERG, D. F. and D. Humphries. "The Co-optation of Fixed Sentencing Reform." (1980), 26 *Crime and Delinquency* 206.

GREENBERG, D., R. C. Kessler, and C. H. Logan. "A Panel Model of Crime Rates and Arrest Rates." (1979), 44 *Amer. Sociological Rev*. 843.

GREENBERG, D. *Crime and Capitalism* 1981.

GREENBERG, P. W., and J. Petersilia. *The Criminal Investigation Process*. 1975.

GREY, D. L. "Interviewing at the Court." (1967-68), 31 *Pub. Opinion Q*. 285.

GRIFFITH, J. A. G. "The Law of Property (Land)." In *Law and Opinion in England in the 20th Century*. Ed. M. Ginsberg. 1959, p. 116.

GROSS, N., W. S. Mason, and A. W. McEachern. *Explorations in Role Analysis*. 1958.

GROSSMAN, B. *The Prosecutor: An Inquiry into the Exercise of Discretion*. 1969.

GULLIVER, P. "On Mediators." In *Social Anthropology and the Law*. Ed. I. Hamnett. 1977.

———. *Social Control in an African Society: A Study of The Arusha Agricultural Masai of Northern Tanganyika*. 1963.

GUSFIELD, J. "Power, Justice and Sociological Cynicism." (1977), 29 *Stanford L. Rev*. 370.

HAAN, N., M. B. Smith and J. Block. "The Moral Reasoning of Young Adults: Political-Social Behaviour, Family Background, and Personality Correlates." (1968), 10 *Journal of Personality and Social Psychology* 183.

HADDEN, W., E. A. Suchman, and D. A. Klein. *Accident Research: Its Methods and Approaches*. 1964.

HAGAN, J. "Extra-Legal Attributes and Criminal Sentencing: An Assessment of a Sociological Viewpoint." (1974), 83 *L. & Society Rev*. 357.

———. "Parameters of Criminal Prosecution: An Application of Path Analysis to a Problem of Criminal Justice." (1974), 65 *J. Cr. L. & Crim*. 65.

———, et al. "Explaining Official Delinquency: A Spatial Study of Class, Conflict and Control." (1978), 19 *The Sociological Quarterly*, 386.

———, et al. "The Differential Sentencing of White Collar Offenders in Ten Federal District Courts." (1980), 45 *Amer. Sociological Rev*. 802.

HALL, E. L., and A. A. Simkus. "Inequality in the Types of Sentences Received by Native Americans and Whites." (1975), 13 *Criminology* 199.

HANSEN, I. "Notes for Presentation." National Conference on Discretion in the Correctional System. Nov. 1981.

HARDING, J. *A Socio-Demographic Profile of People Prescribed Mood-Modifiers in Saskatchewan*. Alcohol Commission of Saskatchewan: 1978.

———. "The Pharmaceutical Industry as a Public Health Hazard and as an Institution of Social Control." In *Health and Canadian Society*. Eds. D. Coburn, C. D'Arcy, P. New, and G. Torrance. 1981.

HARDING, J., and N. Wolf. *Accounting for Social Environmental Determinants in Developing Alternatives to the Use of Mood-Modifying Drugs*. Conference of the Canadian Addictions Foundation: 1978.

HARRIS, L., et al. *The Public Looks at Crime and Corrections*. 1968.

HARRIS, L., and Assoc. and A. F. Westin. *The Dimensions of Privacy*. 1981.

HART, H. L. A. "Positivism and the Separation of Law and Morals." (1958), 71 *Harv. L. Rev.* 593.

HARTLAND, S. *Primitive Law*. 1924.

HAY, D., et al. *Albion's Fatal Tree*. 1975.

HAYEK, F. *Law, Legislation and Liberty*. 1973.

———. *The Political Order of a Free People*. 1979.

———. "The Results of Human Action, But Not of Human Design." In *Studies in Philosophy: Politics and Economics*. 1967.

HEGEL. *Philosophy of Right*. Ed. H. P. Kainz. 1974.

HEIDER, F. *The Psychology of Interpersonal Relations*. 1958.

"Here's What You Value Most." *Winnipeg Tribune*, 24 Sept. 1977, p. 14.

HESS, R. D., and J. L. Tapp. *Authority, Rules and Aggression: A Cross-National Study of the Socialization of Children into Compliance Systems: Part 1*. 1969.

HEST, J. *Community Policing: An Alternate, Community-Based Policing Model*. R.C.M.P. "E" Division Headquarters: 1982.

HETHERTON, M. *Victoria's Lawyers: A First Report of a Research Project on Lawyers in the Community*. 1978.

———. *Victoria's Lawyers: A Second Report of a Research Project on Lawyers in the Community*. 1981.

HEYWOOD, R. N. "Perspectives of Crime Prevention." (1979), 68 *Canadian Police Chief* 25.

———. "Traditional and Innovative Policing." In *Report of the Proceedings: Workshop on Police Productivity and Performance*. Eds. P. Engstad and M. Lioy. 1980.

HICKLING, ed. *Citrine's Trade Union Law*. 3rd ed. 1967.

HIRSCH, Fred. *Social Limits to Growth*. 1976.

HOBHOUSE, L. T. *The Elements of Social Justice*. 1930.

HOEBEL, E. A. *The Law of Primitive Man*. 1954.

HOGARTH, J. *Sentencing as a Human Process*. 1971.

HOLMES, Oliver Wendell. *Collected Legal Papers*. 1920.

———. *The Common Law, Lecture II*. 1881.

———. *The Holmes-Laski Letters*. 1963.

———. "The Path of the Law." (1897), 10 *Harv. L. Rev.* 457.

HOME OFFICE, SCOTTISH HOME DEPARTMENT. *Homosexual Offences and Prostitution*. Chairman, Sir John Wolfenden. 1957.

HOOD, R. *Sentencing in Magistrates Court*. 1962.

HOOD, R., and R. Sparks. *Key Issues in Criminology*. 1970.

HORWITZ, M. *The Transformation of American Law*. 1978.

HOUSE OF COMMONS STANDING COMMITTEE ON JUSTICE AND LEGAL AFFAIRS, Subcommittee on the Penitentiary System in Canada. *Minutes of Proceedings and Evidence*. 9th March 1977, p. 31.

HOUSE OF COMMONS STANDING COMMITTEE ON JUSTICE AND LEGAL AFFAIRS. *Third Report: The Penitentiary System in Canada*. 1977.

HOWARD, John, and Elizabeth Fry Societies of Manitoba. *Presumed Innocent? A Report on Pre-Trial Detention*. (Unpublished, 1982).

HUNTER, A. A. *Class Tells: On Social Inequality in Canada*. 1981.

HURWITZ, S. J. *State Intervention in Great Britain*. 1912.

HUTCHINSON, Allan C. Rev. of *The Sociology of Law*, ed. William M. Evan. (1981), 97 *L.Q. Rev*. 507.

HUXLEY, Christopher. "The State, Collective Bargaining and the Shape of Strikes in Canada." (1979), 4 *Can. J. Sociology*, 223.

HYLTON, J. H. "The Assessment of Police Job Satisfaction." (1980), 4:3 *Can. Police College J*. 189.

———. *A Directory of Justice Services for Persons of Indian Ancestry in Manitoba, Saskatchewan and Alberta*. 1980.

———, et al. *Public Attitudes Towards the Regina Police Force*. Prairie Justice Research Consortium: 1979.

HYLTON, J. H., and R. Matonovich. *Job Satisfaction in the Regina Police Department*. Regina Police Department: 1979.

IGNATIEFF, M. *A Just Measure of Pain: The Penitentiary in the Industrial Revolution, 1750-1850*. 1978.

INDUSTRIAL RELATIONS CENTRE, QUEEN'S UNIVERSITY. *Labour Relations Law*. 1974.

IRVINE, M. J. *The Native Inmate in Ontario: A Preliminary Survey*. 1978.

IYER, R. *Parapolitics: Toward the City of Men*. 1979.

JACKSON, P. I., and L. Carroll. "Socio-Political Determinants of Policing Expenditures in 90 U.S. Cities." Annual Meeting of the American Sociological Association. 1979.

JACOB, H., and M. J. Rich. "The Effects of the Police on Crime: A Second Look." (1980), 15 *Law & Society Rev*. 109.

———. "The Effects of the Police on Crime: A Rejoinder." (1981), 16 *Law & Society Rev*. 171.

JACOBS, D. "Inequality and Police Strength." (1979), 44 *Amer. Sociological Rev*. 913.

JACOBS, Sydney. "Community Action in a Glasgow Clearance Area." In *The Sociology of Community Action*. Sociological Rev. Monograph 21. Ed. Peter Leonard. 1975.

JAMES, L. *Prisoners' Perception of Parole*. 1971.

JAROS, D., and R. I. Mendelsohn. "The Judicial Role and Sentencing Behaviour." (1967), 11 *Midwestern Journal of Political Science* 471.

JASINSKI, J. "Punitiveness of Criminal Systems." In *Studia Prawnicze (Legal Studies)* 35 (1973).

JAYWARDENE, C. H. S. *The Penalty of Death: The Canadian Experiment*. 1977.

JESSUP, B. "On Recent Marxist Theories of the Law, the State and Juridico Political Ideology." (1980), 8 *Int. J. of the Sociology of Law* 339.

JOBSON, K. B. "Fines." (1970), 16 *McGill L.J*. 663.

"Johns-Mansville Implements Smoking Ban at All Its Asbestos Plants." *Can. Occupational Health and Safey News*, 18 Aug. 1980, p. 2.

JONAS, H. "Judaism, Christianity and the Western Tradition." *Commentary* 62, p. 61.

JONES, J., and D. M. Church. *At the Bar of Public Opinion*. 1939.

JONES, T. E. "The Press as Metropolitan Monitor." (1976-77), 40 *Pub. Opinion Q.* 239.

JONES, W. *The Principles of Psychology*. 1890.

JORDAN, E. *Theory of Legislation: An Essay on the Dynamics of the Public Mind*. 2nd ed. 1974.

KADISH, M. R., and S. H. Kadish. "The Institutionalization of Conflict: Jury Acquittals." In *Law, Justice and the Individual in Society*. Eds. J. L. Tapp and F. J. Levine. 1977.

KADISH, S. "The Criminal Law and Industrial Discipline as Sanctioning Systems: Some Comparative Observations." In *Proceedings of 17th Annual Meeting, National Academy of Arbitrations*. 1964.

KAHN-FREUND, O. "Labour Law." In *Law and Opinion in England in the 20th Century*. Ed. M. Ginsberg. 1959, p. 215.

———. "Legal Framework." In *The System of Industrial Relations in Britain*. Eds. Flanders and Clegg. 1954, p. 42.

———. "A Note on Status and Contract in British Labour Law." (1967), 30 *Mod. L. Rev*. 635.

KALVEN, H., and H. Zeisel. *The American Jury*. 1966.

KAPLAN, A. *The Conduct of Inquiry — Methodology for Behavioral Science*. 1964.

KAPLAN, J., and J. Skolnick. *Criminal Justice: Introductory Cases and Materials*. 3rd ed. 1982.

KARMINSKI, Sir Seymour. "Family Law." In *Law and Opinion in England in the 20th Century*. Ed. M. Ginsberg. 1959, p. 286.

KATZENBACH, N. de B., et al. *The Challenge of Crime in a Free Society*. 1967.

KAUPEN, W. "Public Opinion of the Law in a Democratic Society." In *Knowledge, Opinion and Law*. Ed. A. Podgorecki. 1973, p. 43.

KAWASHIMA, T. "Dispute Resolution in Contemporary Japan." In *Law in Japan*. Ed. A. von Mehren. 1963.

KEGELS, M. L. "Actualities Bibliographiques: Le crime, puis qui'il faut l'appeler par son nom . . . la 'puir du crime.' " (1982), 1 *Deviance et Société*, 209.

KELLEY, D. M. *Why Conservative Churches are Growing*. 1st ed. 1972.

KELLING, G. *The Newark Foot Patrol Experiment*. The Police Foundation: 1981.

KELLING, G., and D. Fogel. "Police Patrol: Some Future Directions." In *The Future of Policing*, Ed. Alvin W. Cohn. 1978, p. 151.

KELLING, G., T. Pate, D. Deikman, and C. E. Brown. *The Kansas City Preventative Patrol Experiment: A Summary Report*. The Police Foundation: 1974.

KELMAN, H. C. "Compliance, identification, and internalization: three processes of attitude change." (1958), 2 *Journal of Conflict Resolution* 51.

KELSEN, H. *General Theory of Law and State*. 1946.

KENNEDY, F. R. "Law and the Courts." In *The Polls and Public Opinion*. Eds. N. C. Meier and H. W. Saunders. 1949.

KENT, T., Chairman. *Royal Commission on Newspapers*. 1981.

KHAN, R. L. "Some Propositions Towards Researchable Conceptualization of Stress." In *Social and Psychological Factors in Stress*. Ed. J. E. McGrath. p. 97.

KIDD, J. Roby. "Adult Education: The Community and the Animateur." In *Citizen Participation: Canada*. Ed. James A. Draper. 1971, p. 156.

KNAPPER, C. K., and A. J. Cropley. *A Quasi-Clinical Strategy for Investigating Attitudes in the Transportation Domain*. 1976.

———. *Property Insurance: A Study of Public Opinion*. 1975.

———. *Social and Interpersonal Factors in Driving*. 1975.

KOENIG, D. J. *British Columbians' Attitudes and Experiences Relevant to the Police, Law and Crime*. 1974.

———. "Police Perceptions of Public Respect and Extra-Legal Use of Force: A Reconsideration of Folk Wisdom and Pluralistic Ignorance." (1975), 1 *Can. J. Sociology* 313.

———. *R.C.M.P. Views of Themselves, Their Jobs and the Public*. 1975.

———. "British Columbia's Social Future." British Columbia Has a Future, Too Conference. 31 Oct. 1978.

KOHLBERG, Lawrence. *Moralization and Education*. 1981.

KOHLBERG, L. "Stage and Sequence: The Cognitive-Developmental Approach to Socialization." In *Handbook of Socialization Theory and Research*. Ed. D. A. Goslin. 1969.

KRUTTSCHNITT, C. "Social Status and Sentences of Female Offenders." (1980-81), 15 *Law and Society Rev*. 247.

KULCSAR, K. "Ideological Changes and Legal Structure: The Socialist Experience." [1980] *Int. J. Sociology of Law* 61.

KURTINES, W., and E. B. Grief. "The Development of Moral Thought: Review and Evaluation of Kohlberg's Approach." (1974), 81 *Psychological Bulletin* 453.

KUTCHINSKI, B. "Law and Education: Some Aspects of Scandinavian Studies into 'The General Sense of Justice.' " (1966), 10 *Studia Sociologica* Fasc. 1-2, p. 21.

———. "Regarding Legal Phenomena in Denmark." In *Scandinavian Studies in Criminology*. 1966.

KUTCHINSKY, Berl. " 'The Legal Consciousness': A Survey of Research on Knowledge and Opinion About Law" in A. Podgorecki, et al. *Knowledge and Opinion About Law*. 1973, p. 101.

LA HAYE, Tim. *Battle for the Mind*. 1980.

LAMBERT J. *Crime, Police and Race Relations*. 1970.

LAMONT, J. M. H. "Public Opinion Polls and Survey Evidence in Obscenity Cases." (1973), 15 *Cr. L.Q.* 135.

LANCOURT, J.E. *Confront or Concede*. 1979.

LAPRADE, W. T. *Public Opinion and Politics in the 18th Century*. 1936.

LAPRAIRIE, C. P. "The Development of Sanctions for Stock Market Manipulators in Ontario." (1979), 21 *Can. J. Crim*. 275.

LARSON, R., ed. *Police Deployment: New Tools for Planners*. 1979.

"Lazer Beam Transmissions are Almost Impossible to Tap." *The Financial Post*, 14 June 1980, p. 58.

LASKIN, B. *The British Tradition in Canadian Law*. 1969.

"Law Credibility Suffers Setback: B.C. Officials." *Winnipeg Tribune*, 24 Dec. 1974, p. 4.

THE LAW REFORM COMMISSION OF CANADA. *Discovery in Criminal Cases*. 1974.

THE LAW REFORM COMMISSION OF CANADA. *The Native Offender and the Law*. 1974.

THE LAW REFORM COMMISSION OF CANADA. *Divorce*. 1975.

THE LAW REFORM COMMISSION OF CANADA. *Criminal Responsibility for Group Actions*. 1976.

THE LAW REFORM COMMISSION OF CANADA. *Fear of Punishment*. 1976.

THE LAW REFORM COMMISSION OF CANADA. *Our Criminal Law*. 1976.

LE DAIN, G. E. "The Role of the Public Inquiry in Our Constitutional System." In *Law and Social Change*. Ed. J. S. Ziegel. 1973.

LEFF, A. "Unconscionability and the Code — the Emperor's New Clause." (1967), 15 *U. Penn. L. Rev*. 405.

LEING, A. *Indians the Law*. The Canadian Corrections Association: 1967.

LEMERT, Edwin M. *Social Action and Legal Change, Revolution Within the Juvenile Court*. 1970.

LEONARD, Peter, ed. *The Sociology of Community Action*. Sociological Rev. Monograph 21. 1975.

LEVINE, F. J. *The Legal Reasoning of Youth: Dimensions and Correlates*. (Unpublished.) 1979.

LEVINE F. J., and J. L. Tapp. "The Dialectic of Legal Socialization in Community and School." In *Law, Justice and the Individual in Society*. Eds. J. L. Tapp and F. J. Levine. 1977.

LEVY, C. *Origins of the Fifth Amendment*. 1968.

LINEBOUGH, Peter. "Karl Marx, The Theft of Wood and Working Class Composition." (1976), 6 *Crime and Social Justice: Issues in Criminology* 5.

LIZOTTE, A. J. "Extra-Legal Factors in Chicago's Criminal Courts: Testing the Conflict Model of Criminal Justice." (1978), 25 *Social Problems* 565.

LLEWELLYN, K. "The Normative, the Legal and the Law Jobs: The problem of Juristic Method." (1940), 49 *Yale L.J.* 1355.

———. "A Realistic Jurisprudence, The Next Step." [1930] *Columbia L. Rev*. 431.

———. *The Bramble Bush*. 1930.

LORENTSEN, Edith, and Evelyn Woolner. "Fifty Years of Labour Legislation in Canada." *Labour Gazette*, Sept. 1950.

LUCAS, J. R. *The Principles of Politics*. 1966.

LUDWIG, David. "The Case Against Skin Mags." *Quest Magazine*, March 1982, p. 26.

MCCALL-NEUMAN, Christina. "Michael Pitfield and the Politics of Mismanagement." *Saturday Night*, 97:10 (1982), p. 24.

MCCALLUM, R. B. "The Liberal Outlook." In *Law and Public Opinion in England in the 20th Century*. Ed. M. Ginsberg. 1959, p. 63.

MCDONALD, Lynne. *The Sociology of Law and Order*. 1979.

MCDONALD, Neil G., and A. Chaiton. *Egerton Ryerson and His Times*. 1978.

MCGLOTHLIN, W. H., and V. C. Tabbush. "Costs, Benefits and Potential for Alternate Approaches to Opium Addiction Control." In *Drugs and the Criminal Justice System*. Eds. J. A. Inciardi and C. D. Chambers. 1974, p. 74.

MCGREGOR, O.R. "Social History and Law Reform." Hamelyn Lecture. 1981.

MCNAUGHTON-SMITH, P. *Permission to be Slightly Free: A Study of the Granting, Refusing and Withdrawing of Parole in Canadian Penitentiaries*. 1976.

MCNEIL. *The History and Character of Calvinism*. 1967.

MACPHERSON, D. G. "The Real World of Democracy." The Massey Lectures, Fourth Series.

MCQUAIG, L. "A Matter of Compensation." *MacLeans*, 95:41 (1982), p. 55.

MADGE, J. H. *The Tools of Social Science*. 1953.

MAINE, H. *Ancient Law*. 1861.

MALINOWSKI, B. *Crime and Custom in Savage Society*. 1926.

MANDEL, M. "Democracy, Class and Canadian Sentencing Law." *Crime and Social Justice*, 21 (1984).

———. "Democracy, Class and the National Parole Board." (Unpublished.) 1984.

———. "Rethinking Parole." (1975), 13 *Osgoode Hall L.J.* 501.

MANITOBA LAW REFORM COMMISSION. *A Review of the Jury System*. 1975.

MANNHEIM, H. "Criminal Law and Penology." In *Law and Opinion in England in the 20th Century*. Ed. M. Ginsberg. 1959, p. 264.

MANNHEIM, Karl. *Ideology and Utopia: An Introduction to the Sociology of Knowledge*. Trans. Wirth and Shils. 1956.

MANNING, P.K. *The Narcs' Game*. 1980.

———. *Police Work: The Social Organization of Policing*. 1977.

MANWARING, J. "Legitimacy in Labour Relations: The Courts, The B.C. Labour Board, and Secondary Picketing." (1982), 20 *Osgoode Hall L.J.* 274.

MARSDEN, George M. *Fundamentalism and American Culture*. 1980.

MARTIN, R. G., Jr., and R. D. Conger. "A Comparison of Delinquency Trends: Japan and the United States." (1980), 18 *Criminology* 53.

MARX, G. "Ironies of Social Control: Authorities as Contributors to Deviance Through Escalation, Non-Enforcement and Covert Facilitation." (1981), 28 *Social Problems*.

———. "The New Police Undercover Work." (1980), 8 *Urban Life* 399.

MARX, Karl. *Capital: A Critique of Political Economy*. 1st ed. 1867.

———. *Capital: A Critique of Political Economy*. Preface. 1959.

MASON, Keith. *Industrial Accident Survey*. Workers' Compensation Board of British Columbia: 1973.

———. *A Survey Evaluation of Safety Posters*. Workers' Compensation Board of British Columbia: 1973.

MAUNHEIM, H. *The Dilemma of Penal Reform*. 1939.

MAURER, D. W. *The Big Con*. 1962.

MAYHEW, L., and A. J. Reiss. "The Social Organization of Legal Contracts." 34 *Amer. Sociological Rev.* 309.

MEAD, Margaret. "Public Opinion Mechanisms Among Primitive Peoples." In *Communications and Public Opinion*. Ed. R. O. Carlson. 1975, p. 529.

MEIER, N. C., and H. W. Saunders. *The Polls and Public Opinion*. 1949.

MELOSSI, D., and M. Pavarini. *The Prison and the Factory: Origins of the Penitentiary System*. Trans. G. Cousin. 1981.

MELTON, G. B. "Children's Concepts of Their Rights." (1980), 9 *Journal of Clinical Psychology* 186.

MERRILLS, J. G. "Law, Morals and the Psychological Nexus." (1969), 19 *U.T.L.J.* 46.

MILESKI, M. "Courtroom Encounters: An Observation Study of a Lower Criminal Court." (1971), 5 *Law & Society Rev*. 473.

MILGRAM, Stanley. *Obedience to Authority: An Experimental View*. 1974.

———. *Obedience to Authority*. 1975.

MILL, John Stuart. *On Liberty*. Oxford University Press: 1933.

MILLER, W. B., H. Geertz, and H. S. G. Cutler. "Aggression in a Boys' Street Corner Group." (1961), XXIV *Psychiatry* 286.

"Minister Introduces Alive Campaign." *Alberta Occupational Health and Safety News*, Apr. 1979, p. 6.

MINISTER OF SUPPLY AND SERVICES, CANADA. *Inquiry Concerning Certain Activities of the Royal Canadian Mounted Police*. Chairman, McDonald. 1980.

———. *Inquiry into the Non-Medical Use of Drugs, Interim Report*. Chairman, LeDain. 1969.

———. *Report 1: Evidence*. 1975.

———. *The Non-Medical Use of Drugs*. Chairman, LeDain. 1973.

———. *Northern Frontier and Northern Homeland*. Chairman, Berger. 1977.

MINISTÈRE DE LA JUSTICE DU QUEBÉC. *Justice*, 2:1 (1980); 3:2 (1981).

MINISTRY OF JUSTICE. *Les justiciables et la justice*. 1982.

MINTURN, L., and J. L. Tapp. *Authority, Rules and Aggression: A Cross-National Study of Children's Judgments of the Justice of Aggressive Confrontations: Part II*. 1970.

MOORE, R. J. *The Attitude of Canadians Toward the Law and the Legal System*. (Unpublished.) 1980.

———. *Perception of the Law and the Legal System: A Preliminary Report of the Findings*. 1981.

———. "The Public's Perception of the Law and the Legal System." (1981), 1 *Windsor Yearbook of Access to Justice* 214.

MOORE, R. J., and D. V. Chalmers. *Traffic Accidents and the Role of Driver Characteristics*. 1982.

MOORE, R. J., C. K. Knapper and A. J. Cropley. *A Quasi-Clinical Strategy for Safety Research*. 1973.

MOORE, R. J., and H. Mullens. *Love, Sexuality, and Growing Old in Special Care Homes and Public Housing in Saskatchewan*. 1976.

MOORE, R. J., and J. Newton. *Attitudes Towards Aging, Hospitalization, Serious Illness and Death among the Life Threatened Elderly*. 1977.

MORRIS, J. W. "Law and Public Opinion." Presidential Address, Holdsworth Club. 1958.

MORRIS, N. *The Future of Imprisonment*. 1974.

MORRISON, T. R. "Motivation and the Working World of the School." *History and Social Science Teacher*, 15:1 (1979), p. 31.

"Most Favour Death Penalty." Gallup Poll. *Winnipeg Free Press*, 19 Apr. 1978, p. 20.

MOTTL, Tahi L. "The Analysis of Counter-Movements." *Social Problems*, 27:5 (1980).

"Murder, Suicide Ratio Switches." *Winnipeg Free Press*, 21 July 1975, p. 29.

MYERS, Gustavus. *History of the Great American Fortunes*. Vol. 3. 1910.

NAGEL, S. *The Legal Process From a Behavioural Perspective*. 1969.

NATIONAL CENTRE FOR STATE COURTS. *The Public Image of Courts*. 1978.

NEATBY, H. *The Politics of Chaos*. 1972.

NELSON, W. *The Americanization of the Common Law*. 1975.

NELSON, W. "The Impact of the Anti-Slavery Movement Upon Styles of Judicial Reasoning in Nineteenth Century America." (1974), 87 *Harv. L. Rev*. 513.

NEWMAN, D. *Introduction to Criminal Justice*. 1975.

NIEDERHOFFER, Arthur. *Behind the Shield: The Police in Urban Society*. 1967.

OFFICE DES PROFESSIONS. *Le public quebecois et les services professionels*. 1980.

OHLIN, Lloyd E. "Organizational Reform In Correctional Agencies." In *Handbook of Criminology*. Ed. Daniel Glaser. 1974.

ORNSTEIN, M., T. Atkinson and H. M. Stevenson. *Political Attitudes and the Quality of Life in Canada*. 1979.

ORTH, J. V. "The British Trade Union Acts of 1824 and 1825: Dicey and the Relation Between Law and Opinion." (1976), 5 *Anglo-Amer. L. Rev*. 131.

———. "On the Relation Between the Rule of Law and Public Opinion." (1982), 80 *Mich. L. Rev*. 753.

OSBORNE, K. "Labour Studies and Continuing Education." *Manitoba Journal of Education*, 14:2 (1980), p. 10.

OZDOWSKI, S. "The Family Law Act 1975 and the Family: A Study in Knowledge and Attitudes." In *Legislation and Society in Australia*. Ed. R. Tomasic. 1979, p. 259.

PACKER, H. *The Limits of the Criminal Sanction*. 1968.

PALMER, Bryan D. *The Making of E. P. Thompson: Marxism, Humanism, and History*. 1981.

PAND COMMISSION. *Royal Commission of Inquiry into Labour Disputes*. 1968.

PANITCH, Leo. "The Role and Nature of the Canadian State." In *The Canadian State: Political Economy and Political Power*. Ed. Leo Panitch. 1977, p. 3.

PATERSON, L. T. and J. Liebert. *Management and Strike Handbook*. 1974.

PATON, G. W. *A Text-Book of Jurisprudence*. 3rd ed. 1964.

PERRY, T. W. *Public Opinion, Propaganda and Politics in 18th Century England: A Study of the Jew Bill of 1753*. 1962.

PETRAZYCKI, L. *O Dopelniajalych Pradach Kulturalnych I Prawach Rozwoyu Handly*. 1936.

PEYREFITTE, A. *Les Chevaux du Lac Lagoda*. 1981.

PHILLIPS, L., and H. L. Votey. "An Economic Analysis of the Effect of Law Enforcement on Criminal Activity." (1972), 63 *J. Cr. L. Crim. & Police Science* 330.

PIAGET, J. "Need and Significance of Cross-Cultural Studies in Genetic Psychology." In *Culture and Cognition: Readings in Cross-Cultural Psychology*. Eds. J. W. Berry and P. R. Dasen. 1966.

———. *Science of Education and the Psychology of the Child*. 1970.

PIAGET, J. and B. Inhelder. *The Psychology of the Child*. 1969.

PLATO. *Crito*. Trans. H. N. Fowler. 1914.

———. *The Republic*. Ed. J. Adam. 2nd ed. 1965.

PODGORECKI, Adam. *Knowledge and Opinion About Law*. 1973.

———. *Law and Society*. 1974.

———. "Public Opinion on Law." In *Knowledge, Opinion and Law*. Ed. A. Podgorecki. 1973, p. 68.

———. *Social Systems Versus Legal Systems — Basic Issues*. (Unpublished manuscript.) n.d.

PODGORECKI, Adam, and M. Los. *Multidimensional Society*. 1979.

POSPISIL, L. *Anthropology of Law*. 1971.

———. *Kupauka Papuans and Their Law*. 1958.

POUND, Roscoe. *Contemporary Juristic Theory*. 1940.

———. *Outlines of Jurisprudence*. 1943.

———. *Philosophy of Law*. 1954

———. *Social Control Through Law*. 1942.

PRIEST, G. "The Common Law and the Selection of Efficient Rules." (1977), 6 *J. Legal Studies* 69.

PRINCETON RELIGIOUS RESEARCH CENTER. *Emerging Trends,* 3:1 (1982).

PRINCETON RELIGIOUS RESEARCH CENTER. *Religion in America*. n.d.

"Public Blinks at Crime." *Winnipeg Free Press,* 5 Aug. 1980, p. 23.

"Public Cynical: M.P." *Winnipeg Tribune,* 20 Apr. 1976, p. 2.

QUEBEDEAUX, Richard. *By What Authority?* 1981.

———. *The Worldly Evangelicals*. 1978.

QUINNEY, Richard. "Crime in a Political Perspective." *Amer. Behavioural Scientist,* 8:4 (1964), 19.

RAWLS, J. *A Theory of Justice*. 1971.

RAZ, J. *The Authority of Law*. Part IV. 1979.

REASONS, Charles E., Ross and Paterson. *Assault on the Worker*. 1981.

REASONS, Charles E., and William D. Perdue. *The Ideology of Social Problems*. 1981.

RECKLESS, Walter, and Simon Dinitz. *The Prevention of Juvenile Delinquency: An Experiment*. 1972.

REIMAN, Jeffrey. *The Rich Get Richer and the Poor Get Prison*. 1979.

RIESSMAN, Frank. "Self-Help Among the Poor: New Styles of Social Action." *Trans-action,* Sept. 1965, p. 32.

RESCHENTHALER, G. B. *Occupational Health and Safety in Canada: The Economics and Three Case Studies*. Institute for Research on Public Policy: 1979.

"The Resurgence of Fundamentalism." *The Humanist*, 37:1, 2, 3. (1977).

RIFKIN, Jeremy. *The Emerging Order*. 1979.

ROGERS, L. *The Pollsters: Public Opinion, Politics and Democratic Leadership* 1949.

ROPER, B.W. "Opinion Polls and the Law of Evidence." (1976), 62 *Virginia L. Rev* 1101.

———. "Public Opinion Surveys." (1965), 51 *Amer. Bar Assn. J.* 44.

———. "Public Opinion Surveys as Evidence: The Pollsters Go To Court." (1953), 66 *Harv. L. Rev*. 498.

ROSE, A. M. *Theory and Method in the Social Sciences*. 1954.

ROSE, Hilary. "Bread and Justice: The National Welfare Rights Organization." In *The Sociology of Community Action*. Sociological Rev. Monograph 21. Ed. Peter Leonard. 1975.

ROSSETT, A., and D. Cressey. *Justice by Consent: Plea Bargains in the American Courthouse*. 1976.

ROSSITER, C. *The Political Thought of the American Revolution*. 1953.

ROSTOW, E. V. *The Ideal in Law*. 1978.

ROYAL CANADIAN MOUNTED POLICE. *Crime Analysis of Maple Ridge/Pitt Meadows, British Columbia, 1981/82*. 1982.

ROYAL CANADIAN MOUNTED POLICE. *Crime Problem Analysis of Selkirk Municipal*. 1981.

ROYAL COMMISSION. *Report on Capital Punishment*. 1980.

RUBIN, P. "Why is the Common Law Efficient?" (1977), 6 *J. Legal Studies* 57.

RUEGG, H. *Law of Employer and Workman in England*. 1905.

RUSHDOONEY, R. J. *By What Standard?* 1958.

———. *The Independent Republic*. 1964.

———. *The Institutes of Biblical Law*. Vols. 1 and 2. 1973, 1979.

———. *Intellectual Schizophrenia: Culture, Crisis and Education*. 1961.

———. *The Messianic Character of American Education*. 1963.

RUSSELL, B. *Power*. 1938.

RUTHERFORD, M. L. *The Influence of the American Bar Association on Public Opinion and Legislation*. 1937.

RUTHERFORD, Paul. *A Victorian Authority*. 1982.

RYAN, M. *Radical Alternatives to Prison and the Penal Lobby*. 1978.

SALTER, L. "The Role of the Public in Scientific Determinations of Policy: The Canadian Inquiry Process." (1981), 31 *U.T.L.J.* 343.

SCHAEFFER, Francis S. *A Christian Manifesto*. 1981.

SCHETTLER, C. *Public Opinion in American Society*. 1960.

SCHIFF, Stanley A. *Evidence in the Litigation Process*. 1st ed. 1978.

SCHMIDT, L., ed. *George Grant in Process*. 1977.

SCHRAGER, L. S. and J. F. Short, Jr. "How Serious a Crime? Perceptions of Organizational and Common Crime." In *White Collar Crime: Theory and Research*. Eds. G. Geis and E. Stotland. 1980, p. 14

SCHULMAN, J., P. Shaver, R. Colman, B. Emrich, and R. Christie. "Recipe for a Jury." *Psychology Today,* 6:12 (1972), p. 37.

SCHWARTZ, R. D. "Book Review." (1956), 65 *Yale L.J.* 572.

SCHWARTZ, R., and J. Miller. "Legal Evolution and Societal Complexity." (1964), 70 *Amer. J. Sociology* 159.

SELLEN, J. T. *Culture, Conflict and Crime.* 1938.

SELZICK, P. *The Sociology of Law.* 1958.

SENTES, Ray. *Trade Unions and the Press.* (Unpublished.) 1978.

SHELEFF. "The Bystander: Behaviour, Law and Ethics." Cited in *Ethics,* by Hornstein. 1980.

SHELEY, J. F., and C. D. Ashkins. "Crime, Crime News and Crime Views." (1981), 45 *Pub. Opinion Q.* 492.

SILBERMAN, C. E. *Criminal Violence, Criminal Justice.* 1980.

SIM, R. Alexander. "The Innocence of Community Development." In *Citizen Participation: Canada.* Ed. James Draper. 1971.

SIMPSON, A. W. B. "The Laws of Ethelbert." In *On the Laws and Customs of England.* Eds. M. S. Arnold *et al.* 1981, p. 3.

SINGER. "Bringing the Constitution to Prison: Substantive Due Process and the Eighth Amendment." 39 *Cincinatti L. Rev.* 650.

SINGH, A. "Attitudes of Canadians Toward Crime and Punishment." (1979), 21 *Can. J. Crim.* 463.

SINGLETON, W. T. *Introduction to Ergonomics.* n.d.

SKOGAN, Wesley G. *Coping With Crime: Individual and Neighbourhood Reactions.* 1981.

SKOLNICK, J. *Justice Without Trial.* 1966.

———. *Justice Without Trial: Law Enforcement in Democratic Society.* 2nd Ed. 1975.

SKORNIA, H. J., and J.W. Kitson, eds. *Problems and Controversies in Television and Radio.* 1968.

SMITH, Dwight C., Jr. *The Mafia Mystique.* 1975.

SMUCKER, Joseph. *Industrialization in Canada.* 1980.

SOLICITOR GENERAL OF CANADA. *Annual Reports.* 1977-78 and following years.

SOLOMON, Peter H. "Policy Process in Canadian Criminal Justice." (1981), 23 *Can. J. Crim.* 5.

———. *Criminal Justice Policy: From Research to Reform.* (Unpublished.) 1982.

SOLZHENITSYN, A. *A World Split Apart.* n.d.

SORENSEN, R. C., and T. C. Sorensen. "The Admissibility and Use of Opinion Research Evidence." (1953), 28 *N.Y.U. L. Rev.* 1213.

"Special Report: Business Communications." *The Financial Post,* 14 June 1980.

STEVENS. *Citrine's Trade Union Law.* Ed. Hickling. 1967.

STINCHCOMBE, L. A., *et al. Crime and Punishment, Changing Attitudes in America.* 1980.

STONE, Julius. *Law and the Social Sciences.* 1966.

———. *Social Dimensions of Law and Justice.* 1966.

STOUFFER, Samuel A. *Communism, Conformity and Civil Liberty: A Cross-Section of the Nation Speaks Its Mind*. 1955.

STRAUSS, L. *Natural Right and History*. 1965.

STREET, T. G. *Handbook on Parole*. 1960.

SUBCOMMITTEE ON CRIME OF THE COMMITTEE OF THE JUDICIARY, HOUSE OF REPRESENTATIVES. *Corporate Crime*. Ninety-sixth Congress, 2d Sess. 1980.

SUDNOW, D. "Normal Crimes: Sociological Features of the Penal Code in a Public Defender Office." (1965), 12 *Social Problems* 255.

SUMMERS, R. "The New Analytical Jurists." (1966), 41 *N.Y.U. L. Rev*. 861.

SURREY, Jean. *Industrial Accident Research: A Human Engineering Approach*. Ontario Ministry of Labour: 1971.

"Survey Finds 81% for Death Penalty." *Winnipeg Free Press*, 4 May 1976, p. 4.

TAPP, June L. "A Child's Garden of Law and Order." *Psychology Today*, 4. (1970).

———. "The Psychological Limits of Legality." In *The Limits of Law: Nomos XV*. 1974.

———. "Psychology and the Law: An Overture." *Annual Review of Psychology*, (1976), p. 27.

TAPP, June L., M. Gunnar and D. Keating. "Socialization: Three Ages, Three Rule Systems." In *Social Psychology and Social Issues*. Eds. D. Perlman and C. Cozby, 1983.

TAPP, June L., and A. Keniston. "Wounded Knee — Advocate or Expert: Recipe for a Fair Juror." In *What is a Fair Jury? Psychological and Legal Issues*. Symposium, American Psychological Association: 1976.

TAPP, June L., and L. Kohlberg. "Developing Senses of Law and Legal Justice." In *Law, Justice and the Individual in Society*. Eds. J. L. Tapp and F. J. Levine. 1977.

TAPP, June L., and F. J. Levine. "Legal Socialization: Strategies for an Ethical Legality." (1974), 27 *Stanford L. Rev*. 1.

———. "Persuasion to Virtue: A Preliminary Statement." (1970), 4 *Law & Society Rev*. 565.

———, Eds. *Law, Justice and the Individual in Society: Psychological and Legal Issues*. 1977.

TAPP, June L., and P. Smolka. *The Jury as a Social Experience*. (Unpublished.) 1979.

TAPP, June L., J. R. Vopava, A. S. Kolman and R. M. Richardson. *Rights Consciousness and Child Care: A Report on the Right-to-Care Project*. (Unpublished.) 1981.

TARNOPOLSKY, Walter S. *The Canadian Bill of Rights*. 2nd ed. 1975.

TATARYN, Lloyd. *Dying for a Living*. 1979.

TEPPERMAN, Lorne. "The Ebb and Flow of Punitiveness in Canadian Society." *Proceedings*. Canadian Society for Legal History: 1977.

"Third Mistrial for Laberge Declared." *Winnipeg Free Press*, 8 June 1978, p. 6.

THOMAS, David. "Chaucer House Tenant's Association: A Case Study." In *The Sociology of Community Action*. Sociological Rev. Monograph 21. Ed. Peter Leonard. 1975.

THOMPSON, E. P. *The Making of the English Working Class*. 1968.

———. *Whigs and Hunters: The Origin of the Black Act*. 1977.

THOMPSON, Fred, and W. T. Stanbury. *The Political Economy of Interest Groups in the Legislative Process in Canada*. Occasional Paper No. 9. Montreal: Institute for Research on Public Policy, 1979.

TIEGER, J. H. "Fining the Indigent." (1971), 71 *Columbia L. Rev*. 1281.

———. "Police Discretion and Discriminatory Enforcement." [1971] *Duke L.J.* 717.

TIGAR, M., and M. Levy. *Law and the Rise of Capitalism*. 1977.

TITMUSS, R. M. *Essays on the Welfare State*. 1958.

TOMASIC, Roman. "Criminal Lawyers and Their Clients." (1981), 14 *Aust. & N.Z. J. Crim*. 147.

———. "From Empiricism to the Quest for Theory: Towards a Synthesis in the Sociology of Law." (1983), 1 *Aust. J. Law and Society* 149.

———. *Law, Lawyers and the Community: Some Observations From a Survey of Community Attitudes and Experiences*. 1976.

———. *Lawyers and the Community*. 1978.

———. "Lawyers and Social Control — a preliminary inquiry." (1983), 3 *Windsor Yearbook of Access to Justice*.

———. "The Quest for an Adequate Theory of Criminal Justice." (1981), 14 *Aust. & N.Z.J. Crim*. 170.

———. "Social Organization Amongst Australian Lawyers." (1983), 19 *Aust. & N.Z.J. Sociology* 447.

———. "Sociology of Legislation." In *Legislation and Society in Australia*. Ed. R. Tomasic. 1980, p. 19.

———. "Typifying Lawyers: A Sociological Study of the Legal Profession in New South Wales." Diss. University of New South Wales 1979.

TOMASIC, Roman, and C. Bullard. *Lawyers and Their Work in New South Wales: A Preliminary Report*. 1978.

———. "Lawyers and Legal Culture in Australia." 7 *Int. J. Sociology of Law* 417.

TORNEY, J. V. "Socialization of Attitudes Towards the Legal System." In *Law, Justice and the Individual in Society*. Eds. J. L. Tapp and F. J. Levine. 1977.

TREBACH, A. S. *The Rationing of Justice: Constitutional Rights and the Criminal Process*. 1969.

TROELTSCH, E. *Protestantism and Progress*. Trans. W. Montgomery. 1912.

TRUDEAU, P. *Federalism and the French Canadians*. 1968.

TURNER, John. "Justice for the Poor: The Courts, The Poor and the Administration of Justice." (1970), 12 *Can. J. Corr*. 1.

ULMER, S. S. "Social Background as an Indicator to the Votes of Supreme Court Justices in Criminal Cases: 1947-56 Terms." (1973), 17 *Amer. J. Political Science* 622.

UNGER, R. *Knowledge and Politics*. 1976.

UNITED CHURCH OF CANADA. *In God's Image . . . Male and Female: A Study on Human Sexuality*. 1980.

UNITED STATES PRESIDENT'S COMMISSION OF LAW ENFORCEMENT AND ADMINISTRATION OF JUSTICE. *The Challenge of Crime in a Free Society*. 1967.

UNIVERSITY OF NEW SOUTH WALES. *Law and Authority in An Age of Protest*. Symposium. 1970.

VAN HOUTTE, J., and P. Vinke. "Attitudes Concerning the Acceptance of Legislation Among Various Social Groups." In *Knowledge, Opinion and Law*. Ed. A. Podgorecki. 1973, p. 13.

VAN JHERING, R. *Law as a Means to an End*. 1924.

VAN LOON, R. J., and M. S. Whittington. *The Canadian Political System*. 1976.

VERDUN-JONES, S., and F. Cousineau. "A Critical Analysis of Plea Bargaining in Canada." In *The Canadian Criminal Justice System*. Eds. Boydell and Connidis. 1982.

VERNER, Coolie. "Community Action and Learning: A Concept Analysis." In *Citizen Participation: Canada*. Ed. James A. Draper. 1971.

VEZINA, Le Batonnier P. "Ouvrez La Cour a l'Electronique." Address to Assembly of Superior Court Judges. Quebec City, 1979.

VORRATH, H. H., and L. K. Brenthro. *Positive Peer Culture*. 1974.

WADE, H. R. W. "Law, Opinion and Administration." (1962), 78 *L.Q. Rev*. 188.

WAITE, P. B. *The Life and Times of Confederation: 1864-1867*. 1962.

WALD, P. M. "Poverty and Criminal Justice." In *Crime and Justice*. Eds. L. Radzinowcz and M. E. Wolfgang. Vol. 2. 1971, p. 582.

WALKER. "Law and Opinion in Britain Since 1900." *Juridical Review*, (1956), 117.

WALLER, I. *Men Released From Prison*. 1974.

WALLER, I., and N. Okihiro. *Burglary: The Victim and the Public*. 1978.

WALLER, J., and J. Chan. "Prison Use: A Canadian and International Comparison." (1974-75), 17 *Cr. L.Q*. 47.

WARD, D. A. "How Fear of Crime has Changed the Daily Living Habits of Most Americans." Wilson Lecture in American Penology, 1982.

"Waves or Tides?" Gallup Poll. *Winnipeg Free Press*, 20 Nov. 1980, p. 14.

WEBER, M. *The Protestant Ethic and the Spirit of Capitalism*. 1958.

WEDDERBURN, W. "Industrial Relations and the Courts." (1980), 9 *Indiana L.J*. 65.

———. *The Worker and the Law*. 2nd ed. 1971.

WEIS, K., and M. E. Milakovich. "Political Misuses of Crime Rates." *Society*, 11:5 (1974), 27.

WESTLEY, W. A. *Violence and the Police: A Sociological Study of Law, Custom and Morality*. 1970.

WHEELER, M. *Lies, Damn Lies and Statistics*. 1976.

WHITE, E. *Tort Law in America: An Intellectual History*. 1980.

WHITEHEAD, John W. *The Second American Revolution*. 1982.

"Why Everybody is Suing Everybody." *U.S. News and World Report*, 4 Dec. 1978.

WIENER. *The Evolution and the Founders of Pragmatism*. 1948.

WILSON, P., and J. W. Brown. *Crime and the Community*. 1973.

WILSON, P., and J. Western. *The Policeman's Position Today and Tomorow*. 1972.

WINCH, P. "The Internality of Social Relations." In *The Idea of Social Science and Its Relation to Philosophy*. Ed. R. F. Holland. 1967.

WIRTH, L. Introduction. In *Ideology and Utopia: The Introduction to the Sociology of Knowledge*. K. Mannheim. Trans L. Wirth and Shils. 1956.

WISNIEWSKI, W. "Tolerancja a Egalitaryzm." [Tolerance versus Egalitarianism]. (1963), 2 *Studia Sociologiczne*.

WOLFE, T. "The Me Decade and the Third Great Awakening." In *Mauve Gloves and Madmen*. Eds. Clutter and Vine.

WOODHOUSE. *Puritanism and Liberty*. 1931.

WOODS COMMISSION. *Canadian Industrial Relations, The Report of the Task Force on Labour Relations*. 1968.

"Workers' Fall Blamed on Faulty Scaffolding." *Calgary Herald*, 3 Mar. 1981, p. C2.

ZANDER, Michael. "Promoting Change in the Legal System." (1979), 42 *Mod. L. Rev*. 489.

ZEISEL, H. "The Uniqueness of Survey Evidence." (1960), 45 *Cornell L.Q*. 322.

ZIMBROLT, C. *Will the Real Americans Please Stand Up?* (Unpublished.) 1974.

ZWEIBACH, B. *Civility and Disobedience*. 1975.

INDEX